ADVANTAGE EDITION

THE EARTH AND ITS PEOPLES

A Global History

SIXTH EDITION

Volume II: Since 1500

Richard W. Bulliet
Columbia University

Pamela Kyle Crossley
Dartmouth College

Daniel R. Headrick
Roosevelt University

Steven W. Hirsch
Tufts University

Lyman L. Johnson
University of North Carolina—Charlotte

David Northrup
Boston College

CENGAGE
Learning·

Australia • Brazil • Mexico • Singapore • United Kingdom • United States

CENGAGE
Learning®

The Earth and Its Peoples: A Global History, Volume II: Since 1500, Sixth Edition, **Advantage Edition**

Richard W. Bulliet, Pamela Kyle Crossley, Daniel R. Headrick, Steven W. Hirsch, Lyman L. Johnson, and David Northrup

Product Director: Suzanne Jeans

Product Manager: Brooke Barbier

Content Developer: Lauren Floyd

Associate Content Developer: Cara Swan

Product Assistant: Katie Coaster

Media Developer: Kate MacLean

Marketing Brand Manager: Melissa Larmon

Manufacturing Planner: Sandee Milewski

Art and Design Direction, Production Management, and Composition: PreMediaGlobal

Cover Image: A relief on Pura Meduwe Karang temple (Singaraja), depicting Dutch artist Nieuwenkamp, riding a bicycle. Bali, Indonesia. Image #4292-40030/SuperStock

Library of Congress Control Number: 2014932005

Student Edition:

ISBN-13: 978-1-285-44570-0

ISBN-10: 1-285-44570-8

Cengage Learning
200 First Stamford Place, 4th Floor
Stamford, CT 06902
USA

Cengage Learning is a leading provider of customized learning solutions with office locations around the globe, including Singapore, the United Kingdom, Australia, Mexico, Brazil, and Japan. Locate your local office at **www.cengage.com/global**.

Cengage Learning products are represented in Canada by Nelson Education, Ltd.

To learn more about Cengage Learning Solutions, visit **www.cengage.com**.

Purchase any of our products at your local college store or at our preferred online store **www.cengagebrain.com**.

Printed in the United States of America
1 2 3 4 5 6 7 18 17 16 15 14

Brief Contents

Contents

Preface

In preparing the sixth edition of this book, we examined the flow of topics from chapter to chapter and decided that certain rearrangements within chapters and in the order of chapters would accommodate the needs of instructors and students better than the template they had followed since the first edition. The first change was reversing the order of the third and fourth chapters to have early Mediterranean and Middle Eastern history directly follow the discussion of the origins of civilization in the Nile Valley and Mesopotamia.

The second change addressed the problem of when and how to discuss the history of pre-Columbian America. The time span to be covered, ranging from roughly 1500 B.C.E. to 1500 C.E., was too long to fit easily into the book's division into eight parts. The new structure we have adopted relocates the long pre-Aztec and pre-Inka narrative from Part III, Growth and Interaction of Cultural Communities, to the end of Part II, The Formation of New Cultural Communities. This change puts the status of the earliest civilizations in the Western Hemisphere on the same footing as the civilizations of early Greece, China, and South and Southeast Asia. It has the added benefit of making the history of East Asia in the Tang and Song periods directly precede the history of the Mongol empire, which allows instructors to have an uninterrupted focus on East Asia. The histories of the Aztecs and Inkas have been shifted to the chapter on tropical history located in Part IV, Interregional Patterns of Culture and Contact. This allows for a discussion of the overall influence of tropical environments and places them in close proximity to our treatment of the coming of Europeans to the New World.

A third structural change has shortened the length of the book from 34 to 33 chapters. To lessen the impression that Europe's domination of the world should always be the primary focus of student attention between the eighteenth and mid-twentieth centuries we have combined the two separate chapters on European imperialism, Chapters 26 and 28 in previous editions, into one. We feel that this change provides a better balance between the saga of European imperialism, accounts of resistance to imperialism, and the rise of independence movements in different parts of the world.

In a related change, we have relocated the chapter dealing with the histories of India, Latin America, and Africa in the first half of the twentieth century from after World War II, the old Chapter 31, to a position between the world wars. The aim of this chapter, titled "Revolutions in Living," is to portray that period not only as a time of political change in parts of the world subjected to European imperialism, but also as one of transformation of daily lives of people in both the industrialized and nonindustrialized worlds. The added focus of the chapter fills a gap between discussion of the Industrial Revolution in the eighteenth and nineteenth centuries and the advent of major technological changes in the post-World War II era.

Finally in this new edition, contributor and East Asian specialist Michael Wert of Marquette University brought a fresh perspective to many of our chapters dealing with East Asia, helping ensure that our coverage is at the forefront of emerging scholarship.

The authors believe that these changes, along with myriad smaller changes detailed below, significantly enhance the overall goal of *The Earth and Its Peoples*, namely, to be a textbook that speaks not only for the past but also to today's student and teacher. Students and instructors alike should take away from this text a broad, and due to the changes, more flowing impression of human societies beginning as sparse and disconnected communities reacting creatively to local circumstances; experiencing ever more intensive stages of contact, interpenetration, and cultural expansion and amalgamation; and arriving at a twenty-first-century world in which people increasingly visualize a single global community.

Process, not progress, is the keynote of this book: a steady process of change over time, at first experienced differently in various regions, but eventually connecting peoples and traditions from all parts of the globe. Students should come away from this book with a sense that the problems and promises of their world are rooted in a past in which people of every sort, in every part of the world, confronted problems of a similar character and coped with them as best they could. We believe that our efforts will help students see where their world has come from and learn thereby something useful for their own lives.

Central Themes and Goals

We subtitled *The Earth and Its Peoples* "A Global History" because the book explores the common challenges and experiences that unite the human past. Although the dispersal of early humans to every livable environment resulted in a myriad of different economic, social, political, and cultural systems, all societies displayed analogous patterns in meeting their needs and exploiting their environments. Our challenge was to select the particular data and episodes that would best illuminate these global patterns of human experience.

To meet this challenge, we adopted two themes for our history: "technology and the environment" and "diversity and dominance." The first theme represents the commonplace material bases of all human societies at all times. It grants no special favor to any cultural group even as it embraces subjects of the broadest topical, chronological, and geographical range. The second theme expresses the reality that every human society has constructed or inherited structures of domination. We examine practices and institutions of many sorts: military, economic, social, political, religious, and cultural, as well as those based on kinship, gender, and literacy. Simultaneously we recognize that alternative ways of life and visions of societal organization continually manifest themselves both within and in dialogue with every structure of domination.

With respect to the first theme, it is vital for students to understand that technology, in the broad sense of experience-based knowledge of the physical world, underlies all human activity. Writing is a technology, but so is oral transmission from generation to generation of lore about medicinal or poisonous plants. The magnetic compass is a navigational technology, but so is Polynesian mariners' hard-won knowledge of winds, currents, and tides that made possible the settlement of the Pacific islands.

All technological development has come about in interaction with environments, both physical and human, and has, in turn, affected those environments. The story of how humanity has changed the face of the globe is an integral part of our first theme. Yet technology and the environment do not explain or underlie all important episodes of human experience. The theme of "diversity and dominance" informs all our discussions of politics, culture, and society. Thus when narrating the histories of empires, we describe a range of human experiences within and beyond the imperial frontiers without assuming that imperial institutions are a more fit topic for discussion than the economic and social organization of pastoral nomads or the lives of peasant women. When religion and culture occupy our narrative, we focus not only on the dominant tradition but also on the diversity of alternative beliefs and practices.

Organization

The *Earth and Its Peoples* uses eight broad chronological divisions to define its conceptual scheme of global historical development.

In **Part One: The Emergence of Human Communities, to 500 B.C.E.**, we examine important patterns of human communal organization primarily in the Eastern Hemisphere. Small, dispersed human communities living by foraging spread to most parts of the world over tens of thousands of years. They responded to enormously diverse environmental conditions, at different times in different ways, discovering how to cultivate plants and utilize the products of domestic animals. On the basis of these new modes of sustenance, population grew, permanent towns appeared, and political and religious authority, based on collection and control of agricultural surpluses, spread over extensive areas.

Part Two: The Formation of New Cultural Communities, 1000 B.C.E.–400 C.E., introduces the concept of a "cultural community," in the sense of a coherent pattern of activities and symbols pertaining to a specific human community. While all human communities develop distinctive cultures, including those discussed in Part One, historical development in this stage of global history prolonged and magnified the impact of some cultures more than others. In the geographically contiguous African-Eurasian landmass, as well as in the Western Hemisphere, the cultures that proved to have the most enduring influence traced their roots to the second and first millennia B.C.E.

Part Three: Growth and Interaction of Cultural Communities, 300 B.C.E.–1200 C.E., deals with early episodes of technological, social, and cultural exchange and interaction on a continental scale both within and beyond the framework of imperial expansion. These are so different from earlier interactions arising from more limited conquests or extensions of political boundaries that they constitute a distinct era in world history, an era that set the world on the path of increasing global interaction and interdependence that it has been following ever since.

In **Part Four: Interregional Patterns of Culture and Contact, 1200–1550**, we look at the world during the three and a half centuries that saw both intensified cultural and commercial contact and increasingly confident self-definition of cultural communities in Europe, Asia, Africa, and the Americas. The Mongol conquest of a vast empire extending from the Pacific Ocean to eastern Europe greatly stimulated trade and interaction. In the West, strengthened European kingdoms began maritime expansion in the Atlantic, forging direct ties with sub-Saharan Africa and entering into conflict with the civilizations of the Western Hemisphere.

Part Five: The Globe Encompassed, 1500–1750, treats a period dominated by the global effects of European expansion and continued economic growth. European ships took over, expanded, and extended the maritime trade of the Indian Ocean, coastal Africa, and the Asian rim of the Pacific Ocean. This maritime commercial enterprise had its counterpart in European colonial empires in the Americas and a new Atlantic trading system. The contrasting capacities and fortunes of traditional land empires and new maritime empires, along with the exchange of domestic plants and animals between the hemispheres, underline the technological and environmental dimensions of this first era of complete global interaction.

In **Part Six: Revolutions Reshape the World, 1750–1870,** the word *revolution* is used in several senses: in the political sense of governmental overthrow, as in France and the Americas; in the metaphorical sense of radical transformative change, as in the Industrial Revolution; and in the broadest sense of a perception of a profound change in circumstances and worldview. Technology and environment lie at the core of these developments. With the rapid ascendancy of the Western belief that science and technology could overcome all challenges—environmental or otherwise—technology became an instrument not only of transformation but also of domination, to the point of threatening the integrity and autonomy of cultural traditions in nonindustrial lands and provoking strong movements of resistance.

Part Seven: Global Diversity and Dominance, 1750–1945, examines the development of a world arena in which people conceived of events on a global scale. Imperialism, international economic connections, and world-encompassing ideological tendencies, such as nationalism and socialism, present the picture of a globe becoming increasingly involved with European political and ideological concerns. Two world wars arising from European rivalries provide a climax to these developments, and European exhaustion affords other parts of the world new opportunities for independence and self-expression.

For **Part Eight: Perils and Promises of a Global Community, 1945 to the Present,** we divide the period since World War II into three time periods: 1945–1975, 1975–2000, and 2000 to the present. The challenges of the Cold War and postcolonial nation building dominate much of the period and unleash global economic, technological, and political forces that become increasingly important in all aspects of human life. With the end of the Cold War, however, new forces come to the fore. Technology is a key topic in Part Eight because of its integral role in both the growth and the problems of a global community. However, its many benefits in improving the quality of life become clouded by negative impacts on the environment.

Features and New Pedagogical AIDS   As with previous editions, the sixth edition offers a number of valuable features and pedagogical aids designed to pique student interest in specific world history topics and help them process and retain key information. Historical essays for each of the eight parts called Issues in World History are specifically designed to alert students to broad and recurring conceptual issues that are of great interest to contemporary historians; this feature has proved to be an instructor and student favorite. The Environment and Technology feature, which has been a valuable resource in all prior editions of *The Earth and Its Peoples*, serves to illuminate the major theme of the text by demonstrating the shared material bases of all human societies across time. Finally, Diversity and Dominance, also core to the theme of the text, is the primary source feature that brings a myriad of real historical voices to life in a common struggle for power and autonomy.

Changes in this Edition   Here are a few highlights:

- Chapter 16 reflects new research on South Asian and Polynesian maritime cultures.

- Chapter 17 includes expanded coverage of early capitalism, including a discussion of stock markets and speculative bubbles like the Tulip, South Sea, and Mississippi Company frenzies.

- Chapter 19 includes a new feature, "Hurricanes and the Caribbean Plantation Economy."

- Chapter 20 has expanded to include the history of Russia, hence a new opening that features a Russian popular hero and the change of title to "Territorial Empires Between Europe and China."

- Chapter 21 has a new discussion of Korean history and the Imjin War.

- Chapters 22–23 have been reversed in sequence to provide better continuity to discussions of revolutions in Europe and parallel changes in the Americas.

- Chapter 22 includes a new discussion of proto-industrialization as well as augmented discussions of the spread of industrialization to continental Europe and North America and the early career of Karl Marx. The section "Protest and Reform" has been broadly revised to include machine breaking in the textile sector and rural resistance to mechanization in the Captain Swing riots.
- Chapter 25 has a new feature: "Industrializing Sugar Agriculture in Cuba."
- Chapter 26 combines accounts of European imperialism that were previously contained in this chapter and in Chapter 28.
- Chapter 27 features a revised discussion of early Japanese industrialization as well as an expanded treatment of Marx and Marxism and a new discussion of Mikhail Bakunin and anarchism.
- Chapter 29 combines in a new chapter a discussion of technology and lifestyle changes that occurred between 1900 and 1945 with accounts of political movements in India, Latin America, and Africa that were previously located in Chapter 31. Highlights include an Environment and Technology feature, "New Materials."
- Chapter 31 includes an updated discussion about the Cold War confrontation between West and East plus a revised discussion of apartheid and South Africa's struggle for independence.
- Chapter 33 updates world affairs through the first half of 2013 and incorporates new statistical information on maps.

Formats   To accommodate different academic calendars and approaches to the course, *The Earth and Its Peoples* is available in three formats. There is a one-volume version containing all 33 chapters, along with a two-volume edition: Volume I: To 1550 (Chapters 1–16) and Volume II: Since 1500 (Chapters 16–33). Volume II includes an Introduction that surveys the main developments set out in Volume I and provides a groundwork for students studying only the period since 1500.

Ancillaries

A wide array of supplements accompany this text to assist students with different learning needs and to help instructors master today's various classroom challenges.

Instructor Resources   Aplia™ [ISBN: 9781285767949] is an online interactive learning solution that improves comprehension and outcomes by increasing student effort and engagement. Founded by a professor to enhance his own courses, Aplia provides automatically graded assignments with detailed, immediate explanations on every question. The interactive assignments have been developed to address the major concepts covered in *The Earth and Its Peoples* and are designed to promote critical thinking and engage students more fully in learning. Question types include questions built around animated maps, primary sources such as newspaper extracts, or imagined scenarios, like engaging in a conversation with a historical figure or finding a diary and being asked to fill in some blanks; more in-depth primary source question sets address a major topic with a number of related primary sources and questions that promote deeper analysis of historical evidence. Many of the questions incorporate images, video clips, or audio clips. Students get immediate feedback on their work (not only what they got right or wrong, but why), and they can choose to see another set of related questions if they want more practice. A searchable eBook is available inside the course as well so that students can easily reference it as they work. Map-reading and writing tutorials are also available to get students off to a good start.

Aplia's simple-to-use course management interface allows instructors to post announcements, upload course materials, host student discussions, e-mail students, and manage the gradebook; a knowledgeable and friendly support team offers assistance and personalized support in customizing assignments to the instructor's course schedule. To learn more and view a demo for this book, visit www.aplia.com.

MindTap Reader for *The Earth and Its Peoples* is an eBook specifically designed to address the ways students assimilate content and media assets. MindTap Reader combines thoughtful navigation ergonomics, advanced student annotation, note-taking, and search tools, and embedded media assets such as video and MP3 chapter summaries, primary source documents with critical thinking questions, and interactive (zoomable) maps. Students can use the eBook as their primary text or as a multimedia companion to their printed book. The MindTap Reader eBook is available within the MindTap and Aplia online offerings found at www.cengagebrain.com.

Online PowerLecture with Cognero® This PowerLecture is an all-in-one online multimedia resource for class preparation, presentation, and testing. Accessible through Cengage.com/login with your faculty account, you will find the following available for download.

The **Test Bank**, offered in Cognero® format, contains multiple-choice and essay questions for each chapter. Cognero® is a flexible, online system that allows you to author, edit, and manage test bank content for *The Earth and Its People*, sixth edition. Create multiple test versions instantly and deliver through your LMS from your classroom, or wherever you may be, with no special installs or downloads required.

The **Instructor's Manual** contains for each chapter: an outline and summary; critical thinking questions; in-class activities; lecture launching suggestions; a list of key terms with definitions; and suggested readings and Web resources.

The *Microsoft® PowerPoint® presentations* are ready-to-use, visual outlines of each chapter. These presentations are easily customized for your lectures. These PowerPoint Lecture Tools include presentations of only lecture or only images, as well as combined lecture and image presentations.

History CourseMate Cengage Learning's History CourseMate brings course concepts to life with interactive learning, study tools, and exam preparation tools that support the printed textbook. Use Engagement Tracker to monitor student engagement in the course and watch student comprehension soar as your class works with the printed textbook and the textbook-specific website. An interactive eBook allows students to take notes, highlight, search, and interact with embedded media (such as quizzes, flashcards, primary sources, and videos). Learn more at **www.cengage.com/coursemate**.

CourseReader CourseReader is an online collection of primary and secondary sources that lets you create a customized electronic reader in minutes. With an easy-to-use interface and assessment tool, you can choose exactly what your students will be assigned—simply search or browse Cengage Learning's extensive document database to preview and select your customized collection of readings. In addition to print sources of all types (letters, diary entries, speeches, newspaper accounts, etc.), their collection includes a growing number of images and video and audio clips.

Each primary source document includes a descriptive headnote that puts the reading into context and is further supported by both critical thinking and multiple-choice questions designed to reinforce key points. For more information visit **www.cengage.com/coursereader**.

Cengagebrain.com Save your students time and money. Direct them to **www.cengagebrain.com** for choice in formats and savings and a better chance to succeed in your class. Cengagebrain.com, Cengage Learning's online store, is a single destination for more than 10,000 new textbooks, eTextbooks, eChapters, study tools, and audio supplements. Students have the freedom to purchase a-la-carte exactly what they need when they need it. Students can save 50% on the electronic textbook, and can pay as little as $1.99 for an individual eChapter.

Reader Program Cengage Learning publishes a number of readers, some containing exclusively primary sources, others a combination of primary and secondary sources, and some designed to guide students through the process of historical inquiry. Visit Cengage.com/history for a complete list of readers.

Custom Options Nobody knows your students like you, so why not give them a text that is tailor-fit to their needs? Cengage Learning offers custom solutions for your course—whether it's making a small modification to The Earth and Its Peoples to match your syllabus or combining multiple sources to create something truly unique. You can pick and choose chapters, include your own material, and add additional map exercises along with the Rand McNally Atlas to create a text that fits the way you teach. Ensure that your students get the most out of their textbook dollar by giving them exactly what they need. Contact your Cengage Learning representative to explore custom solutions for your course.

Student Resources *Writing for College History,* first edition [ISBN: 9780618306039] Prepared by Robert M. Frakes, Clarion University. This brief handbook for survey courses in American history, Western Civilization/European history, and world civilization guides students through the various types of writing assignments they encounter in a history class. Providing examples of student writing and candid assessments of student work, this text focuses on the rules and conventions of writing for the college history course.

The History Handbook, second edition [ISBN: 9780495906766] Prepared by Carol Berkin of Baruch College, City University of New York and Betty Anderson of Boston University. This book teaches students both basic and history-specific study skills such as how to read primary sources, research historical topics, and correctly cite sources. Substantially less expensive than comparable skill-building texts, *The History Handbook* also offers tips for Internet research and evaluating online sources.

Doing History: Research and Writing in the Digital Age, second edition [ISBN: 9781133587880] Prepared by Michael J. Galgano, J. Chris Arndt, and Raymond M. Hyser of James Madison University. Whether you're starting down the path as a history major, or simply looking for a straightforward and systematic guide to writing a successful paper, you'll find this text to be an indispensible handbook to historical research. This text's "soup to nuts" approach to researching and writing about history addresses every step of the process, from locating your sources and gathering information, to writing clearly and making proper use of various citation styles to avoid plagiarism. You'll also learn how to make the most of every tool available to you—especially the technology that helps you conduct the process efficiently and effectively.

The Modern Researcher, sixth edition [ISBN: 9780495318705] Prepared by Jacques Barzun and Henry F. Graff of Columbia University. This classic introduction to the techniques of research and the art of expression is used widely in history courses, but is also appropriate for writing and research methods courses in other departments. Barzun and Graff thoroughly cover every aspect of research, from the selection of a topic through the gathering, analysis, writing, revision, and publication of findings, presenting the process not as a set of rules but through actual cases that put the subtleties of research in a useful context. Part One covers the principles and methods of research; Part Two covers writing, speaking, and getting one's work published.

Rand McNally Historical Atlas of the World, second edition [ISBN: 9780618841912] This valuable resource features over 70 maps that portray the rich panoply of the world's history from preliterate times to the present. They show how cultures and civilization were linked and how they interacted. The maps make it clear that history is not static. Rather, it is about change and movement across time. The maps show change by presenting the dynamics of expansion, cooperation, and conflict. This atlas includes maps that display the world from the beginning of civilization; the political development of all major areas of the world; expanded coverage of Africa, Latin America, and the Middle East; the current Islamic World; and the world population change in 1900 and 2000.

ACKNOWLEDGMENTS

In preparing the sixth edition, we benefited from the critical readings of many colleagues. Our sincere thanks go in particular to contributor Michael Wert of Marquette University who lent his fresh perspective to our coverage of East Asia. We thank Beatrice Manz of the History Department at Tufts University who provided guidance on the new Pastoral Nomads section in Part I. We are also indebted to the following instructors who lent their insight over various editions: Hedrick Alixopuilos, Santa Rosa Junior College; Hayden Bellenoit, U.S. Naval Academy; Dusty Bender, Central Baptist College; Cory Crawford, Ohio University; Adrian De Gifis, Loyola University New Orleans; Peter de Rosa, Bridgewater State University; Aaron Gulyas, Mott Community College; Darlene Hall, Lake Erie College; Vic Jagos, Scottsdale Community College; Adrien Ivan, Vernon College; Andrew Muldoon, Metropolitan State College of Denver; Percy Murray, Shaw University; Dave Price, Santa Fe College; Anthony Steinhoff, University of Tennessee-Chattanooga; Anara Tabyshalieva, Marshal University; Susan Autry, Central Piedmont Community College; Christopher Cameron, University of North Carolina at Charlotte; Anna Collins, Arkansas Tech University; William Connell, Christopher Newport University; Gregory Crider, Winthrop University; Shawn Dry, Oakland Community College; Nancy Fitch, California State University, Fullerton; Christine Haynes, University of North Carolina at Charlotte; Mark Herman, Edison College; Ellen J. Jenkins, Arkansas Tech University; Frank Karpiel, The Citadel; Ken Koons,

Virginia Military Institute; David Longfellow, Baylor University; Heather Lucas, Georgia Perimeter College; Jeff Pardue, Gainesville State College; Craig Patton, Alabama A & M University; Amanda Pipkin, University of North Carolina at Charlotte; Linda Scherr, Mercer County Community College; Robert Sherwood, Georgia Military College; Brett Shufelt, Copiah-Lincoln Community College; Peter Thorsheim, University of North Carolina at Charlotte; Kristen Walton, Salisbury University; Christopher Ward, Clayton State University; William Wood, Point Loma Nazarene University.

When textbook authors set out on a project, they are inclined to believe that 90 percent of the effort will be theirs and 10 percent that of various editors and production specialists employed by their publisher. How very naïve. This book would never have seen the light of day had it not been for the unstinting labors of the great team of professionals who turned the authors' words into beautifully presented print. Our debt to the staff of Cengage Learning remains undiminished in the sixth edition. Brooke Barbier, product manager, has offered us firm but sympathetic guidance throughout the revision process. Tonya Lobato, senior content developer, offered astute and sympathetic assistance as the authors worked to incorporate many new ideas and subjects into the text. Carol Newman, senior content project manager, moved the work through the production stages to meet a challenging schedule. Abbey Stebing did an outstanding job of photo research.

We thank also the many students whose questions and concerns, expressed directly or through their instructors, shaped much of this revision. We continue to welcome all readers' suggestions, queries, and criticisms. Please contact us at our respective institutions.

ABOUT THE AUTHORS

RICHARD W. BULLIET   Professor of Middle Eastern History at Columbia University, Richard W. Bulliet received his Ph.D. from Harvard University. He has written scholarly works on a number of topics: the social and economic history of medieval Iran (The Patricians of Nishapur and Cotton, Climate, and Camels in Early Islamic Iran), the history of human-animal relations (The Camel and the Wheel and Hunters, Herders, and Hamburgers), the process of conversion to Islam (Conversion to Islam in the Medieval Period), and the overall course of Islamic social history (Islam: The View from the Edge and The Case for Islamo-Christian Civilization). He is the editor of the Columbia History of the Twentieth Century. He has published four novels, coedited The Encyclopedia of the Modern Middle East, and hosted an educational television series on the Middle East. He was awarded a fellowship by the John Simon Guggenheim Memorial Foundation and was named a Carnegie Corporation Scholar.

PAMELA KYLE CROSSLEY   Pamela Kyle Crossley received her Ph.D. in Modern Chinese History from Yale University. She is currently the Robert and Barbara Black Professor of History at Dartmouth College. Her books include The Wobbling Pivot: An Interpretive History of China Since 1800; What Is Global History?; A Translucent Mirror: History and Identity in Qing Imperial Ideology; The Manchus; Orphan Warriors: Three Manchu Generations and the End of the Qing World; and (with Lynn Hollen Lees and John W. Servos) Global Society: The World Since 1900.

DANIEL R. HEADRICK   Daniel R. Headrick received his Ph.D. in History from Princeton University. Professor of History and Social Science, Emeritus, at Roosevelt University in Chicago, he is the author of several books on the history of technology, imperialism, and international relations, including The Tools of Empire: Technology and European Imperialism in the Nineteenth Century; The Tentacles of Progress: Technology Transfer in the Age of Imperialism; The Invisible Weapon: Telecommunications and International Politics; Technology: A World History; Power Over Peoples: Technology, Environments and Western Imperialism, 1400 to the Present; and When Information Came of Age: Technologies of Knowledge in the Age of Reason and Revolution, 1700–1850. His articles have appeared in the Journal of World History and the Journal of Modern History, and he has been awarded fellowships by the National Endowment for the Humanities, the John Simon Guggenheim Memorial Foundation, and the Alfred P. Sloan Foundation.

STEVEN W. HIRSCH   Steven W. Hirsch holds a Ph.D. in Classics from Stanford University and is currently Associate Professor of Classics and History at Tufts University. He has received grants from the National Endowment for the Humanities and the Massachusetts Foundation for Humanities and Public Policy. His research and publications include The Friendship of the Barbarians: Xenophon and the Persian Empire, as well as articles and reviews in the Classical Journal, the American Journal of Philology, and the Journal of Interdisciplinary History. He is currently completing a comparative study of ancient Greco-Roman and Chinese civilizations.

LYMAN L. JOHNSON   Professor Emeritus of History at the University of North Carolina at Charlotte, Lyman L. Johnson earned his Ph.D. in Latin American History from the University of Connecticut. A two-time Senior Fulbright-Hays Lecturer, he also has received fellowships from the Tinker Foundation, the Social Science Research Council, the National Endowment for the Humanities, and the American Philosophical Society. His recent books include Workshop of Revolution: Plebeian Buenos Aires and the Atlantic World, 1776-1810; Death, Dismemberment, and Memory; The Faces of Honor (with Sonya Lipsett-Rivera); Aftershocks: Earthquakes and Popular Politics in Latin America (with Jürgen Buchenau); Essays on the Price History of Eighteenth-Century Latin America (with Enrique Tandeter); and Colonial Latin America (with Mark A. Burkholder). He also has published in journals, including the Hispanic American Historical Review, the Journal of Latin American Studies, the International Review of Social History, Social History, and Desarrollo Económico. He has served as president of the Conference on Latin American History.

DAVID NORTHRUP   David Northrup earned his Ph.D. in African and European History from the University of California, Los Angeles. He has published scholarly works on African, Atlantic, and world history. His most recent books are How English Became the Global Language, the third edition of Africa's Discovery of Europe, 1450–1850, and the Diary of Antera Duke, an Eighteenth-Century African Slave Trader. He taught at a rural secondary school on Nigeria, Tuskegee Institute in Alabama, Boston College, and Venice International University and is a past president of the World History Association.

NOTE ON SPELLING AND USAGE

Where necessary for clarity, dates are followed by the letters C.E. or B.C.E. The abbreviation C.E. stands for "Common Era" and is equivalent to A.D. (anno Domini, Latin for "in the year of the Lord"). The abbreviation B.C.E. stands for "before the Common Era" and means the same as B.C. ("before Christ"). In keeping with our goal of approaching world history without special concentration on one culture or another, we chose these neutral abbreviations as appropriate to our enterprise. Because many readers will be more familiar with English than with metric measurements, however, units of measure are generally given in the English system, with metric equivalents following in parentheses.

In general, Chinese has been Romanized according to the pinyin method. Exceptions include proper names well established in English (e.g., Canton, Chiang Kaishek) and a few English words borrowed from Chinese (e.g., kowtow). Spellings of Arabic, Ottoman Turkish, Persian, Mongolian, Manchu, Japanese, and Korean names and terms avoid special diacritical marks for letters that are pronounced only slightly differently in English. An apostrophe is used to indicate when two Chinese syllables are pronounced separately (e.g., Chang'an).

For words transliterated from languages that use the Arabic script—Arabic, Ottoman Turkish, Persian, Urdu—the apostrophe indicating separately pronounced syllables may represent either of two special consonants, the hamza or the ain. Because most English-speakers do not hear the distinction between these two, they have not been distinguished in transliteration and are not indicated when they occur at the beginning or end of a word. As with Chinese, some words and commonly used place-names from these languages are given familiar English spellings (e.g., Quran instead of Qur'an, Cairo instead of al-Qahira). Arabic romanization has normally been used for terms relating to Islam, even where the context justifies slightly different Turkish or Persian forms, again for ease of comprehension.

Before 1492 the inhabitants of the Western Hemisphere had no single name for themselves. They had neither a racial consciousness nor a racial identity. Identity was derived from kin groups, language, cultural practices, and political structures. There was no sense that physical similarities created a shared identity. America's original inhabitants had racial consciousness and racial identity imposed on them by conquest and the occupation of their lands by Europeans after 1492. All of the collective terms for these first American peoples are tainted by this history. Indians, Native Americans, Amerindians, First Peoples, and Indigenous Peoples are among the terms in common usage. In this book the names of individual cultures and states are used wherever possible. Amerindian and other terms that suggest transcultural identity and experience are used most commonly for the period after 1492.

There is an ongoing debate about how best to render Amerindian words in English. It has been common for authors writing in English to follow Mexican usage for Nahuatl and Yucatec Maya words and place-names. In this style, for example, the capital of the Aztec state is spelled Tenochtitlán, and the important late Maya city-state is spelled Chichén Itzá. Although these forms are still common even in the specialist literature, we have chosen to follow the scholarship that sees these accents as unnecessary. The exceptions are modern place-names, such as Mérida and Yucatán, which are accented. A similar problem exists for the spelling of Quechua and Aymara words from the Andean region of South America. Although there is significant disagreement among scholars, we follow the emerging consensus and use the spellings khipu (not quipu), Tiwanaku (not Tiahuanaco), and Wari (not Huari). In this edition we have introduced the now common spelling Inka (not Inca) but keep Cuzco for the capital city (not Cusco), since this spelling facilitates locating this still-important city on maps.

16

THE MARITIME REVOLUTION, TO 1550

I n 1511 young Ferdinand Magellan sailed from Europe around the southern
tip of Africa and eastward across the Indian Ocean as a member of the first
Portuguese expedition to explore the East Indies (maritime Southeast Asia).
Eight years later, this time in the service of Spain, he led an expedition that
sought to reach the East Indies by sailing westward. By the middle of 1521
Magellan's expedition had achieved its goal by sailing across the Atlantic, round-
ing the southern tip of South America, and crossing the Pacific Ocean—but at a
high price.

Of the five ships that had set out from Spain in 1519, only three made the long
passage across the vast Pacific. Dozens of sailors died from starvation and disease
during the voyage. In the Philippines, Magellan, having survived numerous mutinies
during the voyage, died in battle on April 27, 1521, while aiding a local ruler who
had promised to become a Christian.

To consolidate their dwindling resources, the expedition's survivors
burned the least seaworthy of their remaining three ships and consolidated men
and supplies. In the end only the *Victoria* made it home across the Indian
Ocean and back to Europe. Nevertheless, the *Victoria*'s return to Spain on
September 8, 1522, was a crowning example of Europeans' determination to
make themselves masters of the oceans. A century of daring and dangerous
voyages backed by the Portuguese crown had opened new routes through the
South Atlantic to Africa, Brazil, and the rich trade of the Indian Ocean. Rival
voyages sponsored by Spain since 1492 opened new contacts with the American
continents. A maritime revolution was under way that would change the course
of history.

This new maritime era marked the end of a long period when Asia had initiated
most overland and maritime expansion. Asia had been the source of the most useful
technologies and the most influential systems of belief. It was also home to the most
powerful states and the richest trading networks. The success of Iberian voyages of
exploration in the following century would redirect the world's center of power,
wealth, and innovation to the West.

This maritime revolution broadened and deepened contacts, alliances, and conflicts across ancient cultural boundaries. Some of these contacts ended tragically for individuals like Magellan. Some proved disastrous for entire populations: Amerindians, for instance, suffered conquest, colonization, and a rapid decline in numbers. And sometimes the results were mixed: Asians and Africans found both risks and opportunities in their new relations with Europe.

GLOBAL MARITIME EXPANSION BEFORE 1450

Since ancient times travel across the world's seas and oceans had been one of the great challenges to technological ingenuity. Ships had to be sturdy enough to survive heavy winds and seas, and pilots had to learn how to cross featureless expanses of water to reach their destinations. In time ships, sails, and navigational techniques perfected in the more protected seas were adapted to open oceans.

However complex the solutions and dangerous the voyages, the rewards of sea travel made them worthwhile. Ships could move goods and people more profitably than any form of overland travel then possible. Crossing unknown waters, finding new lands, developing new markets, and establishing new settlements attracted adventurers from every continent. By 1450 daring mariners had discovered and settled most of the islands of the Pacific, the Atlantic, and the Indian Ocean, but no one had yet crossed the Pacific in either direction. Even the smaller Atlantic remained a barrier to contact between the Americas, Europe, and Africa. The inhabitants of Australia were also nearly cut off from contact with the rest of humanity. All this was about to change.

The Indian Ocean   The archipelagos and coastal regions of Southeast Asia were connected in networks of trade and cultural exchange from an early date. While the region was divided politically, culturally, and religiously, the languages of Malaysia, Indonesia, and the Philippines—as well as coastal regions of Thailand, southern Vietnam, Cambodia, and Hainan, China—all originated from a common Austronesian linguistic root. Scholars often use the term *Malayo Indonesians* or *Malay* to describe the early peoples of this maritime realm.

The region's sailors were highly skilled navigators as well as innovative shipbuilders and sail makers who, in addition to their own achievements, influenced later Chinese and Arab maritime advances. Around 350 they discovered two direct sea routes between Sri Lanka and the South China Sea through the Straits of Malacca and Sunda, thus opening a profitable link to China's silk markets. They were also the first to use the seasonal monsoon winds of the Indian Ocean to extend their voyages for thousands of miles, ultimately reaching East Africa and settling in Madagascar.

By the first century C.E. the mariners and merchants of India and Southeast Asia were trading across the region for spices, gold, and aromatic woods, even sending spices as far west as Rome through Mediterranean intermediaries (see Chapter 7). Their success attracted African, Arab, and Chinese mariners and merchants into the region, creating a large, integrated, and highly profitable market in the centuries that followed. By 1000 the dhows (dow) of Arabs and Africans, as well as Malay *jongs* and Chinese junks, came together in the region's harbors for commerce.

The rise of medieval Islam (see Chapter 10) gave Indian Ocean trade an important boost. The great Muslim cities of the Middle East provided a demand for valuable commodities, and networks of Muslim traders were active across the region. These traders shared a common language, ethic, and law and actively spread their religion to distant trading cities. By 1400 there were Muslim trading communities all around the Indian Ocean. Chinese merchant communities were present as well.

Indian Ocean traders largely operated outside the control of the empires and states they served, but in East Asia imperial China's rulers were growing more and more interested in these wealthy ports of trade. In 1368 the Ming dynasty overthrew Mongol rule and began to reestablish China's predominance and prestige abroad. Having restored Chinese power and influence in East Asia, the Ming moved to establish direct contacts with the peoples around the Indian Ocean, sending out seven imperial fleets between 1405 and 1433 (see Chapter 13). The enormous size of these expeditions, far larger than needed for exploration or promoting trade, indicates that the Ming sought to inspire awe of their power and achievements. While curiosity about this prosperous region may have been a motive, the fact that the ports visited by the fleets were major commercial centers suggests that expanding China's trade was also an objective.

The scale of the Ming expeditions to the Indian Ocean Basin reflects imperial China's resources and importance. The first consisted of sixty-two specially built "treasure ships," large Chinese junks each about 300 feet long by 150 feet wide (90 by 45 meters). There were also at least a hundred smaller vessels. Each treasure ship had nine masts, twelve sails, many decks, and a carrying capacity of 3,000 tons (six times the capacity of Columbus's entire fleet). One expedition carried over 27,000 crew and passengers, including infantry and cavalry troops. The ships were armed with small cannon, but in most Chinese sea battles arrows from highly accurate crossbows dominated the fighting.

Admiral **Zheng He** (jung huh) (1371–1435) commanded the expeditions. A Chinese Muslim with ancestral connections to the Persian Gulf, Zheng was a fitting emissary to the increasingly Muslim-dominated Indian Ocean Basin. The expeditions carried other Arabic-speaking Chinese as interpreters. One of them recorded local customs and beliefs in a journal, observing new flora and fauna and noting exotic animals such as the black panther of Malaya and the tapir of Sumatra. In India he described the division of the coastal population into five classes, which correspond to the four Hindu varna and a separate Muslim class. He also recorded that traders in the rich Indian trading port of Calicut (KAL-ih-kut) could perform error-free calculations by counting on their fingers and toes rather than using the

Dugald Stermer

Chinese Junk *This modern drawing shows how much larger one of Zheng He's ships was than one of Vasco da Gama's vessels. Watertight interior bulkheads made junks the most seaworthy large ships of the fifteenth century. Sails made of pleated bamboo matting hung from the junk's masts, and a stern rudder provided steering. European ships of exploration, though smaller, were faster and more maneuverable.*

Chinese abacus. After his return, the interpreter went on tour in China, telling of these exotic places and "how far the majestic virtue of [China's] imperial dynasty extended."[1]

The Chinese "treasure ships" carried rich silks and other valuable goods intended as gifts for distant rulers. In return those rulers sent back gifts of equal or greater value to the Chinese emperor. Although the main purpose of these exchanges was diplomatic, they also stimulated trade between China and its southern neighbors. Interest in new contacts was not limited to the Chinese.

At least three trading cities on the Swahili (swah-HEE-lee) Coast of East Africa sent delegations to China between 1415 and 1416. The delegates from one of them, Malindi, presented the emperor of China with a giraffe, creating quite a stir among normally reserved imperial officials. These African delegations may have encouraged more contacts because the next three of Zheng's voyages reached the African coast. Unfortunately, no documents record how Africans and Chinese reacted to each other during these historic meetings between 1417 and 1433, but it appears that China's lavish gifts stimulated the Swahili market for silk and porcelain.

---

[1]Ma Huan, *Ying-yai Sheng-lan: "The Overall Survey of the Ocean's Shores,"* ed. Feng Ch'eng-Chün, trans. J. V. G. Mills (Cambridge, England: Cambridge University Press, 1970), 180.

Had the Ming court wished to promote trade for the profit of its merchants, Chinese fleets might have come to play a dominant role in Indian Ocean trade. But some high Chinese officials opposed increased contact with peoples whom they regarded as barbarians incapable of making contributions to China. Such opposition caused a suspension in the voyages from 1424 to 1431. The final Chinese expedition sailed between 1432 and 1433.

While later Ming emperors would focus their attention on internal matters, long-established Chinese merchant communities continued as major participants in Indian Ocean trade, contributing to the rapid growth of prosperous commercial entrepôts (ON-truh-pohs) (places where goods are stored or deposited and from which they are distributed) throughout the region. As the sultan of one of the most prosperous trade centers, Melaka (in modern Malaysia), described the era in 1468, "We have learned that to master the blue oceans people must engage in commerce and trade. All the lands within the seas are united in one body. Life has never been so affluent in preceding generations as it is today."[2]

The Pacific Ocean

Around 3000 B.C.E. seafaring peoples from Southeast Asia reached the island of New Guinea. Sustained contact between these Austronesian-speaking migrants and the island's original population accelerated agricultural development and led to population expansion and the settlement of nearby islands. The descendants these peoples eventually forged a new cultural identity, called Lapita by archaeologists, as they colonized the island chains of Melanesia (mel-uh-NEE-zhuh). Lapita settlers reached Tonga, Fiji, and Samoa around 1000 B.C.E.

By 500 B.C.E. a linguistically and culturally distinct Polynesian culture emerged from this Lapita origin. While the dates for Polynesian colonization of the remote islands of the Pacific are still debated, their mastery of long-distance maritime exploration in an era when European sailors still stayed close to shore is undeniable. Pushing east from Tonga, Samoa, and Fiji, Polynesians colonized the Marquesas (mar-KAY-suhs) and the Cook and Society archipelagos by approximately 300 B.C.E. Before 500 C.E. Polynesian colonies were established on the Hawaiian Islands 2,200 miles (3,541 kilometers) away, and Polynesian colonists settled Easter Island, 2,300 miles (3,702 kilometers) to the southeast, by 800 C.E. Finally, they established permanent colonies in New Zealand around 1000 C.E. Polynesian voyagers also made periodic contact with the mainland of South America after 1000 C.E., passing on the domesticated Asian chicken and returning with the sweet potato, an American domesticate that soon became a staple throughout the Pacific region.

Both DNA evidence and linguistic evidence make clear that the Polynesian settlement of the islands of the eastern Pacific was planned and not the result of accident. Following voyages of reconnaissance, Polynesian mariners carried colonizing expeditions in fleets of large double-hulled canoes that relied on scores of paddlers

---

[2]Quotation in Craig A. Lockard, "'The Sea Common to All': Maritime Frontiers, Port Cities, and Chinese Traders in the Southeast Asian Age of Commerce, ca. 1400–1750," *Journal of World History* 21, no. 2 (2010): 228.

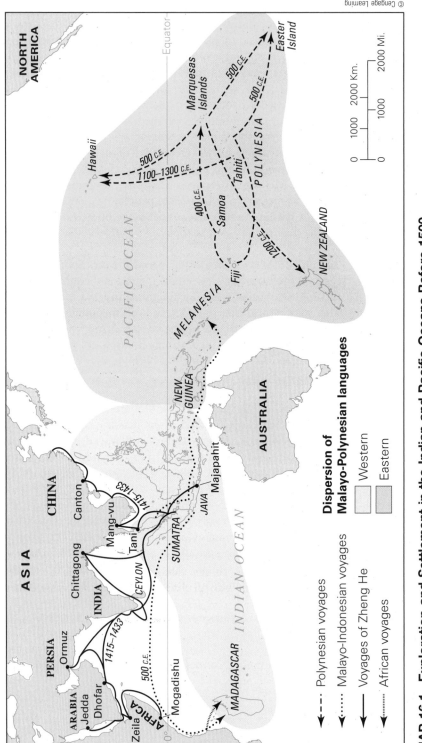

MAP 16.1 Exploration and Settlement in the Indian and Pacific Oceans Before 1500

Over many centuries, mariners originating in Southeast Asia gradually colonized the islands of the Pacific and Indian Oceans. The Chinese voyages led by Zheng He in the fifteenth century were lavish official expeditions.

as well as sails. Their largest canoes reached 120 feet (37 meters) in length and carried crews of fifty. A wide platform connected the two hulls of these crafts and permitted the transportation of animals and plants crucial to the success of distant and isolated settlements. Long-range expeditions took pigs, dogs, and chickens with them as well as domesticated plants such as taro, bananas, yams, and breadfruit. Their success depended upon reliably navigating across thousands of miles of ocean using careful observation of the currents and stars as the crews searched for ·evidence of land.

The most hierarchical social structures and political systems developed in the Hawaiian and Tongan archipelagos, where powerful hereditary chiefs controlled the lives of commoners and managed resources. Here, as well as in New Zealand, competition among chiefs led to chronic warfare.

While all Polynesian societies descended from the same originating culture and all began with the same tools and the same farming and fishing technologies, significant differences in the geography and climate led inexorably to the development of unique social, political, and economic systems. Most Polynesian communities depended on farming and fishing, but the intensity of these practices depended on local conditions. In Hawaii, for example, low-lying native forests were converted to farmland using controlled burns, and fishponds were built to increase fish yields. As a result, the Polynesian communities of this archipelago thrived into the era of European expansion. However, on Easter Island, among the most isolated of the Polynesian colonies, population growth led to total deforestation, soil erosion, intense resource competition, and, ultimately, to a brutal cycle of warfare that drastically reduced the population.

The Atlantic Ocean   The Vikings were the greatest mariners of the Atlantic in the early Middle Ages. These northern European raiders used their small, open ships to attack Europe's coastal settlements for several centuries. Like the Polynesians, the Vikings used their knowledge of the heavens and the seas rather than maps and other navigational devices to find their way over long distances.

The Vikings first settled Iceland in 770 and established a colony on Greenland in 982. By accident one group sighted North America in 986. Fifteen years later Leif Ericsson established a short-lived Viking settlement on the island of Newfoundland, which he called Vinland. When a colder climate returned after 1200, the northern settlements in Greenland went into decline and the Vikings abandoned Vinland.

Some southern Europeans applied maritime skills acquired in the Mediterranean and along the North Atlantic coast to explore to the south. Genoese and Portuguese expeditions pushed into the Atlantic in the fourteenth century, eventually exploring and settling the islands of Madeira (muh-DEER-uh), the Azores (A-zorz), and the Canaries.

There is some evidence of African voyages of exploration in this period. The celebrated Syrian geographer al-Umari (1301–1349) relates that when Mansa Kankan Musa (MAHN-suh KAHN-kahn MOO-suh), the ruler of the West African empire of Mali, passed through Egypt on his lavish pilgrimage to

Mecca in 1324, he told of voyages into the Atlantic undertaken by his predecessor, Mansa Muhammad. According to this source, Muhammad had sent out four hundred vessels with men and supplies, telling them, "Do not return until you have reached the other side of the ocean or if you have exhausted your food or water." After a long time one canoe returned, reporting that the others were lost in a "violent current in the middle of the sea." Muhammad himself then set out at the head of a second, even larger, expedition, from which no one returned.

In the Americas, early Amerindian voyagers from the Caribbean coast of South America colonized the West Indies. By the year 1000 Amerindians known as the **Arawak** (AR-uh-wahk) (also called Taino) had followed the small islands of the Lesser Antilles (Barbados, Martinique, and Guadeloupe) to the Greater Antilles (Cuba, Hispaniola, Jamaica, and Puerto Rico) as well as to the Bahamas. The Carib followed the same route in later centuries, and by the late fifteenth century they had overrun most Arawak settlements in the Lesser Antilles and were raiding parts of the Greater Antilles. Both Arawak and Carib peoples also made contact with the North American mainland.

The transfer of maize cultivation to South America after its domestication in Mesoamerica is suggestive of an early chain of contacts among Amerindian peoples, including the use of small boats along the Pacific coast. In the centuries after 100 there were significant ongoing maritime contacts between Pacific coast populations in South America and Mesoamerica. Mariners carried pottery, copper, gold and silver alloy jewelry, and textiles from the coast of Ecuador north in two-masted, balsa wood rafts that measured up to 36 feet (11 meters) in length. Rafts of this size could carry more than 20 metric tons of cargo and ten or more crew members. Travel north was facilitated by the favorable winds and currents of the Pacific, but these craft had the capacity to make the return trip carrying cargos of sacred spondylus shells as well. One important result of these contacts was the introduction of metallurgy to Mesoamerica after 500.

EUROPEAN EXPANSION, 1400–1550

While the pace and intensity of maritime contacts increased in many parts of the world before 1450, the epic sea voyages sponsored by the Iberian kingdoms of Portugal and Spain are of special interest because they began a maritime revolution that profoundly altered the course of world history. The Portuguese and Spanish expeditions ended the isolation of the Americas and increased the volume of global interaction.

Iberian overseas expansion was the product of two related phenomena. First, Iberian rulers had strong economic, religious, and political motives to expand their influence. And second, improvements in maritime and military technologies gave Iberians the means to master treacherous and unfamiliar ocean environments, seize control of existing maritime trade routes, and conquer new lands.

Motives for Exploration

The ambitions and adventurous personalities of the rulers of Portugal and Spain led them to sponsor voyages of exploration in the fifteenth century, but these voyages built upon four trends evident in Latin Europe since about the year 1000: (1) the revival of urban life and trade, (2) the unique alliance between merchants and rulers in Europe, (3) a struggle with Islamic powers for dominance of the Mediterranean that mixed religious motives with the desire for trade, and (4) growing intellectual curiosity about the outside world.

By 1450 the city-states of northern Italy had well-established trade links to northern Europe, the Indian Ocean, and the Black Sea, and their merchant princes had also sponsored an intellectual and artistic Renaissance. The Italian trading states of Venice and Genoa also maintained profitable commercial ties in the Mediterranean that depended on alliances with Muslims and gave their merchants privileged access to lucrative trade from the East. Even after the expansion of the Ottoman Empire disrupted their trade to the East, these cities did not take the lead in exploring the Atlantic. However, many individual Italians played leading roles in the Atlantic explorations.

In contrast, the history and geography of the Iberian kingdoms led them in a different direction. Muslim invaders from North Africa had conquered most of Iberia in the eighth century. Centuries of warfare between Christians and Muslims followed, and by 1250 the Iberian kingdoms of Portugal, Castile, and Aragon had reconquered all of Iberia except the southern Muslim kingdom of Granada (see Chapter 14). The dynastic marriage of Isabel of Castile and Ferdinand of Aragon in 1469 facilitated the conquest of Granada in 1492 and began the creation of Spain, sixteenth-century Europe's most powerful state.

Christian militancy continued to be an important motive for both Portugal and Spain in their overseas ventures. But the Iberian rulers and their adventurous subjects also sought material returns. With only a modest share of the Mediterranean trade, they were much more willing than the Italians to seek new routes to the rich trade of Africa and Asia via the Atlantic. Both kingdoms participated in the shipbuilding and the gunpowder revolutions that were under way in Atlantic Europe, and both were especially open to new geographical knowledge.

Portuguese Voyages

Portugal's decision to invest significant resources in new exploration rested on a well-established Atlantic fishing industry and a history of anti-Muslim warfare. When the Muslim government of Morocco in northwestern Africa showed weakness in the fifteenth century, the Portuguese attacked, conquering the city of Ceuta (say-OO-tuh) in 1415. The capture of this rich North African city gave the Portuguese better intelligence of the caravans bringing gold and slaves to Ceuta from African states south of the Sahara. Militarily unable to push inland and gain direct access to the gold trade, the Portuguese sought contact with the gold producers by sailing down the African coast.

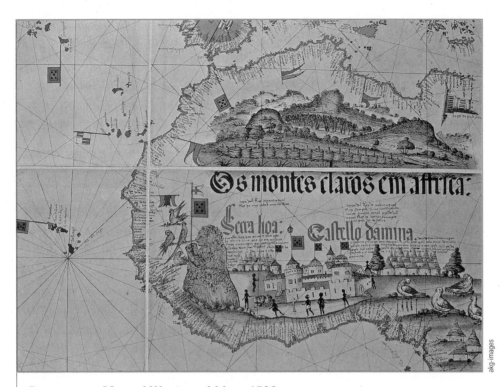

Portuguese Map of Western Africa, 1502 *This map shows in great detail a section of African coastline that Portuguese explorers charted and named in the fifteenth century. The cartographer illustrated the African interior, which was almost completely unknown to Europeans, with drawings of birds and views of coastal sights: Sierra Leone (Serra lioa), named for a mountain shaped like a lion, and the Portuguese Castle of the Mine (Castello damina) on the Gold Coast.*

Prince Henry (1394–1460), third son of the king of Portugal, had led the attack on Ceuta. Because he devoted the rest of his life to promoting exploration, he is known as **Henry the Navigator**. His official biographer emphasized Henry's mixed motives for exploration—converting Africans to Christianity, making contact with Christian rulers in Africa, and launching joint crusades with them against the Ottomans. Prince Henry also wished to discover new places and hoped that such new contacts would be profitable. Early explorations focused on Africa, but reaching India became the eventual goal of Portuguese explorers. While called "the Navigator," Henry himself never ventured far from home. Instead, he founded a center of research at Sagres (SAH-gresh) to study navigation that built on the pioneering efforts of Italian merchants and fourteenth-century Jewish cartographers. This center collected geographical information from sailors and travelers and sponsored new expeditions to explore the Atlantic. Henry's ships established permanent contact with the islands of Madeira in 1418 and the Azores in 1439.

Henry's staff also improved navigational instruments that had been first developed elsewhere. These instruments included the magnetic compass, first developed in China, and the astrolabe, an instrument of Arab or Greek invention that enabled mariners to determine their location at sea by measuring the position of the sun or the stars in the night sky. Even with such instruments, however, voyages still depended on the skill and experience of navigators.

Portuguese mariners also developed vessels appropriate for voyages of long-distance exploration. Neither the galleys in use in the Mediterranean, powered by large numbers of oarsmen, nor the three-masted ships of northern Europe with their square sails proved adequate for the Atlantic. The large crews of the galleys could not carry enough supplies for long voyages and the square-rigged northern vessels had trouble sailing at an angle to the wind. Instead, the voyages of exploration made use of a new vessel, the **caravel** (KAR-uh-vel), that was much smaller than either the largest European ships or the Chinese junks Zheng used to explore the Indian Ocean. Their size permitted them to enter shallow coastal waters and explore upriver, but they were strong enough to weather ocean storms. They could be equipped with triangular lateen sails that could take the wind on either side for enhanced maneuverability or fitted with square Atlantic sails for greater speed in a following wind. The addition of small cannon made them good fighting ships as well. The caravels' economy, speed, agility, and power justified a contemporary's claim that they were "the best ships that sailed the seas."[3]

Pioneering captains had to overcome the common fear that South Atlantic waters were boiling hot or contained ocean currents that would prevent any ship entering them from ever returning home. It took Prince Henry fourteen years—from 1420 to 1434—to coax an expedition to venture beyond southern Morocco. It would ultimately take the Portuguese four decades to cover the 1,500 miles (2,400 kilometers) from Lisbon to Sierra Leone (see-ER-uh lee-OWN); it then took only three additional decades to explore the remaining 4,000 miles (6,400 kilometers) to the southern tip of the African continent. With experience, navigators learned how to return home speedily by sailing northwest into the Atlantic to the latitude of the Azores, where they picked up prevailing westerly winds. The knowledge that ocean winds tend to form large circular patterns helped later explorers discover many other ocean routes.

During the 1440s Portuguese raids on the northwest coast of Africa and the Canary Islands began to return with slaves, finding a profitable market in an Iberia still recovering from the population losses of the Black Plague. The total number of Africans captured or purchased on voyages exceeded eighty thousand by the end of the century and rose steadily thereafter. However, the gold trade quickly became more important once the Portuguese contacted the trading networks that flourished in West Africa and reached across the Sahara. By 1457 enough African gold was coming back to Portugal for the kingdom to issue a new gold coin called the

---

[3]Alvise da Cadamosto in *The Voyages of Cadamosto and Other Documents*, ed. and trans. G. R. Crone (London: Hakluyt Society, 1937), 2.

cruzado (crusader), another reminder of how deeply the Portuguese entwined religious and secular motives.

While the Portuguese crown continued to sponsor voyages, the growing participation of private commercial interests accelerated the pace of exploration. In 1469 a prominent Lisbon merchant named Fernão Gomes purchased from the Crown the privilege of exploring 350 miles (550 kilometers) of African coast in return for a trade monopoly. He discovered the uninhabited island of São Tomé (sow toh-MAY) located on the equator and converted it to a major producer of sugar dependent on slaves imported from the African mainland. In the next century the island would serve as a model for the sugar plantations of Brazil and the Caribbean. Gomes also explored the **Gold Coast**, which became the headquarters of Portugal's West African trade.

The desire to find a passage around Africa to the rich spice trade of the Indian Ocean spurred the final thrust down the African coast. In 1488 **Bartolomeu Dias** became the first Portuguese explorer to round the southern tip of Africa and enter the Indian Ocean. In 1497–1498 **Vasco da Gama** sailed around Africa and reached India. Then, in 1500, ships on the way to India under the command of Pedro Alvares Cabral (kah-BRAHL) sailed too far west and reached the South American mainland. This discovery established Portugal's claim to Brazil, which would become one of the Western Hemisphere's richest colonies. The gamble that Prince Henry had begun eight decades earlier was about to pay off handsomely.

Spanish Voyages   In contrast to the persistence and planning behind Portugal's century-long exploration of the South Atlantic, haste and blind luck lay behind Spain's early discoveries. Throughout most of the fifteenth century, the Spanish kingdoms were preoccupied with internal affairs: completion of the reconquest of southern Iberia from the Muslims; consolidation of the territories of Isabel and Ferdinand; and the conversion or expulsion of religious minorities. The Portuguese had already found a new route to the Indian Ocean by the time the Spanish monarchs were ready to turn to overseas exploration.

The leader of the Spanish overseas mission was **Christopher Columbus** (1451–1506), a Genoese mariner. His four voyages between 1492 and 1504 established the existence of a vast new world across the Atlantic, whose existence few in "old world" Eurasia and Africa had ever suspected. But Columbus refused to accept that he had found unknown new continents and peoples, insisting that he had succeeded in finding a shorter route to the Indian Ocean.

As a young man Columbus gained considerable experience of the South Atlantic while participating in Portuguese explorations along the African coast, but he had become convinced there was a shorter way to reach the riches of the East than the route around Africa. By his reckoning (based on a serious misreading of a ninth-century Arab authority), the Canaries were a mere 2,400 nautical miles (4,450 kilometers) from Japan. The actual distance was five times as far.

Columbus proposed to reach Asia by sailing west, but Portuguese authorities twice rejected his plan. Columbus first proposed his expedition to Castile's able ruler Queen Isabel in 1486, but he was rejected. In 1492 his persistence was finally rewarded when the queen and her husband, King Ferdinand of Aragon, agreed to fund a modest expedition.

Columbus recorded in his log that he and his crew of ninety men "departed Friday the third day of August of the year 1492" toward "the regions of India." Their mission, the royal contract stated, was "to discover and acquire certain islands and mainland in the Ocean Sea." He carried letters of introduction from the Spanish sovereigns to Eastern rulers, including one to the "Grand Khan" (meaning the Chinese emperor), and brought along an Arabic interpreter to facilitate communication with the peoples of eastern Asia. The expedition traveled in three small ships, the *Santa María*, the *Niña*, and the *Pinta*. The *Niña* and the *Pinta* were caravels.

Unfavorable headwinds had impeded other attempts to explore the Atlantic west of the Azores, but Columbus chose a southern route because he had learned in his service with the Portuguese of west-blowing winds in the latitudes of the Canaries. In October 1492 the expedition reached the islands of the Caribbean. Columbus insisted on calling the inhabitants "Indians" because he believed that the islands were part of the East Indies. His second voyage to the Caribbean in 1493 did nothing to change his mind. Even when, two months after Vasco da Gama reached India in 1498, Columbus first sighted the mainland of South America on his third voyage, he stubbornly insisted it was part of Asia. But by then other Europeans were convinced that he had discovered islands and continents previously unknown to the Old World. Amerigo Vespucci's explorations, first on behalf of Spain and then for Portugal, led mapmakers to name the new continents "America" after him, rather than "Columbia" after Columbus.

To prevent disputes arising from their efforts to exploit their new discoveries and spread Christianity, Spain and Portugal agreed to split the world between them. The Treaty of Tordesillas (tor-duh-SEE-yuhs), negotiated by the pope in 1494, drew an imaginary line down the middle of the North Atlantic Ocean. The treaty allocated lands east of the line in Africa and southern Asia to Portugal; lands to the west in the Americas were reserved for Spain. Cabral's discovery of Brazil, however, gave Portugal a valid claim to the part of South America located east of the line.

Where would Spain's and Portugal's spheres of influence divide in the East? Given Europeans' ignorance of the earth's true size in 1494, it was not clear whether the Moluccas (muh-LOO-kuhz), whose valuable spices had been a goal of the Iberian voyages, were on Portugal's or Spain's side of the Tordesillas line. The size of the Pacific Ocean would determine the boundary. In the end, the Moluccas turned out to lie well within Portugal's sphere, as Spain formally acknowledged in 1529.

In 1519 **Ferdinand Magellan** (ca. 1480–1521) began his expedition to complete Columbus's interrupted westward voyage by sailing around the Americas and across the Pacific. Despite his death during this voyage on behalf of the king of Spain, Magellan was considered the first person to encircle the globe because a decade earlier he had sailed from Europe to the East Indies as part of an expedition sponsored by his native Portugal. His two voyages took him across the Tordesillas

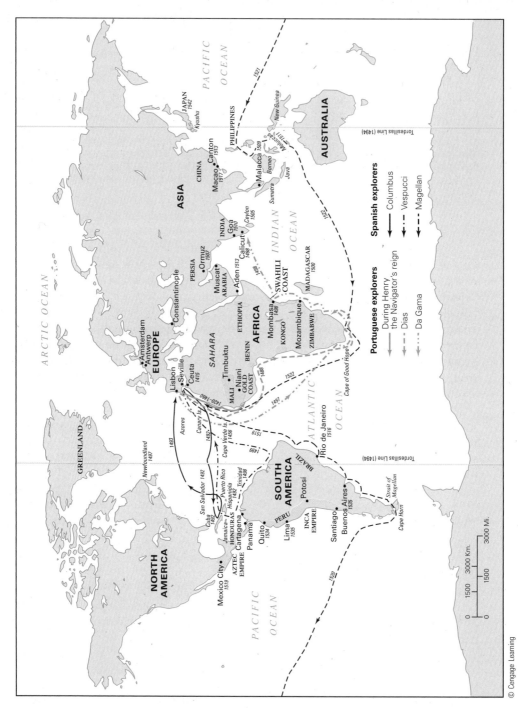

MAP 16.2 European Exploration, 1420–1542

Portuguese and Spanish explorers showed the possibility and practicality of intercontinental maritime trade. Before 1540 European trade with Africa and Asia was much more important than that with the Americas, but after the Spanish conquest of the Aztec and Inca Empires transatlantic trade began to increase. Notice the Tordesillas line, which in theory separated the Spanish and Portuguese spheres of activity.

line, through the separate spheres claimed by Portugal and Spain, and established the basis for Spanish colonization of the Philippines after 1564.

Although Columbus failed to find a new route to the East, the consequences of his voyages for European expansion were momentous. Those who followed in his wake laid the basis for Spain's large colonial empire in the Americas and for the empires of other European nations. In turn, these empires promoted the growth of a major new trading network whose importance rivaled and eventually surpassed the Indian Ocean network. Both the eastward and the westward voyages of exploration marked a tremendous expansion of Europe's role in world history.

ENCOUNTERS WITH EUROPE, 1450–1550

European actions alone did not determine the global consequences of these new contacts. The ways in which Africans, Asians, and Amerindians perceived these visitors and interacted with them influenced developments as well. Everywhere indigenous peoples evaluated the Europeans as potential allies or enemies, and everywhere Europeans attempted to insert themselves into existing commercial and geopolitical arrangements. In general, Europeans made slow progress in establishing colonies and asserting political influence in Africa and Asia, even while profiting from new commercial ties. In the Americas, however, Spain, Portugal, and later other European powers moved rapidly to create colonial empires. In this case the long isolation of the Amerindians from the rest of the world made them more vulnerable to the diseases that these outsiders introduced, limiting their potential for resistance and facilitating European settlement.

Western Africa   Many along the West African coast were eager for trade with the Portuguese, since it offered new markets for exports and access to imports cheaper than those transported overland from the Mediterranean. This was evident along the Gold Coast of West Africa, first visited by the Portuguese in 1471. Miners in the hinterland had long sold their gold to traders, who took it to trading cities along the southern edge of the Sahara, where it was sold to traders who had crossed the desert from North Africa. Recognizing that they might get more favorable terms from the new visitors from the sea, coastal Africans were ready to negotiate with the royal representative of Portugal who arrived in 1482 to seek permission to erect a trading fort.

This Portuguese noble and his officers (likely including the young Christopher Columbus, who had entered Portuguese service in 1476) were eager to make a proper impression. They dressed in their best clothes, erected and decorated a reception platform, celebrated a Catholic Mass, and signaled the start of negotiations with trumpets, tambourines, and drums. The African king, Caramansa, staged his entrance with equal ceremony, arriving with a large retinue of attendants and musicians. Through an African interpreter, the two leaders exchanged flowery speeches pledging goodwill and mutual benefit. Caramansa then gave permission for a small trading fort, assured, he said, by the appearance of the Portuguese that they were honorable persons, unlike the "few, foul, and vile" Portuguese visitors of the previous decade.

Neither side made a show of force, but the Africans' upper hand was evident in Caramansa's warning that he and his people would move away, depriving their fort of food and trade, if the Portuguese acted aggressively. Trade at the post of Saint George of the Mine (later called Elmina) enriched both sides. The Portuguese crown had soon purchased gold equal to one-tenth of the world's production at the time. In return, Africans received large quantities of goods that Portuguese ships brought from Asia, Europe, and other parts of Africa.

After a century of aggressive expansion, the kingdom of Benin in the Niger Delta was near the peak of its power when it first encountered the Portuguese. Its oba (king) presided over an elaborate bureaucracy from a spacious palace in his large capital city, also known as Benin. In response to a Portuguese visit in 1486, the oba sent an ambassador to Portugal to learn more about these strangers. He then established a royal monopoly on trade with the Portuguese, selling pepper and ivory tusks (for export to Portugal) as well as stone beads, textiles, and prisoners of war (for resale as slaves at Elmina). In return, Portuguese merchants provided Benin with copper and brass, fine textiles, glass beads, and a horse for the king's royal procession. In the early sixteenth century, as the demand for slaves for the Portuguese sugar plantations on the nearby island of São Tomé grew, the oba first raised the price of slaves and then imposed restrictions that limited their sale.

Early contacts generally involved a mix of commercial, military, and religious exchanges. Some African rulers appreciated the advantage of European firearms over spears and arrows in conflicts with their enemies and actively sought them in trade. Because African religions were generally not exclusive, coastal rulers were also willing to test the value of the Christian practices promoted by the Portuguese. The rulers of Benin and Kongo, the two largest coastal kingdoms, accepted both Portuguese missionaries and soldiers as allies in battle to test the efficacy of the Christian religion and European weaponry.

However, Portuguese efforts to persuade the king and nobles of Benin to accept the Catholic faith ultimately failed. Early kings showed some interest, but after 1538 rulers declined to receive more missionaries. They also closed the market in male slaves for the rest of the sixteenth century. We do not know why Benin chose to limit its contacts with the Portuguese, but the result makes clear that these rulers had the power to control their contacts with Europeans.

Farther south, on the lower Congo River, relations between the kingdom of Kongo and the Portuguese began similarly but had a very different outcome. Like the oba of Benin, the manikongo (mah-NEE-KONG-goh) (king of Kongo) sent delegates to Portugal, established a royal monopoly on trade with the Portuguese, and expressed interest in Christian teachings. Deeply impressed with the new religion, the royal family made Catholicism the kingdom's official faith. But Kongo, lacking ivory and pepper, had less to trade than Benin. To acquire the goods brought by Portugal and to pay the costs of the missionaries, it had to sell more and more slaves.

Soon the manikongo began to lose his royal monopoly over the slave trade. In 1526 the Christian manikongo, Afonso I (r. 1506–ca. 1540), wrote to his royal "brother," the king of Portugal, begging for his help in stopping the trade because unauthorized Kongolese were kidnapping and selling people, even members of good families (see Diversity and Dominance: Kongo's Christian King). Alfonso's appeals for help received no reply from Portugal, whose interests were now concentrated in the Indian Ocean. Soon the effects of rebellion and the relocation of the slave trade from his kingdom to the south weakened the manikongo's authority.

Eastern Africa   Different still were the reactions of the Muslim rulers of the coastal trading states of eastern Africa. As Vasco da Gama's fleet sailed up the coast in 1498, most rulers gave the Portuguese a cool reception, suspicious of the intentions of visitors who painted Crusaders' crosses on their sails. But the ruler of one of the ports, Malindi, seeing the Portuguese as potential allies who could help him expand the city's trading position, provided da Gama with a pilot to guide him to India. The initial suspicions of the other rulers were proven correct seven years later when a Portuguese war fleet bombarded and looted most of the coastal cities of eastern Africa in the name of Christianity and commerce, while sparing Malindi.

Christian Ethiopia was another eastern African state that saw potential benefit in an alliance with the Portuguese. In the fourteenth and early fifteenth centuries, Ethiopia faced increasing conflict with Muslim states along the Red Sea. Emboldened by the rise of the Ottoman Turks, who had conquered Egypt in 1517 and launched a major fleet in the Indian Ocean to counter the Portuguese, the talented warlord of the Muslim state of Adal launched a furious assault on Ethiopia. Adal's decisive victory in 1529 reduced the Christian kingdom to a precarious state. At that point Ethiopia's contacts with the Portuguese became crucial.

For decades, delegations from Portugal and Ethiopia had explored a possible alliance based on their mutual adherence to Christianity. A key figure was Queen Helena of Ethiopia, who acted as regent for her young sons after her husband's death in 1478. In 1509 Helena sent a letter to "our very dear and well-beloved brother," the king of Portugal, along with a gift of two tiny crucifixes said to be made of wood from the cross on which Christ had died in Jerusalem. In her letter she proposed an alliance between her army and Portugal's fleet against the Turks; however, Helena's death in 1522 occurred before the alliance could be arranged. Ethiopia's situation then grew more desperate.

Finally, in 1539, when another woman ruler was holding what was left of the empire together, a small Portuguese force commanded by Vasco da Gama's son Christopher arrived to aid Ethiopia. With Portuguese help the Ethiopians renewed their struggle. While Muslim forces captured and tortured to death Christopher da Gama, their attack failed when their own leader was mortally wounded in battle.

Kongo's Christian King

The new overseas voyages brought conquest to some and opportunities for fruitful borrowings and exchanges to others. The decision of the ruler of the kingdom of Kongo to adopt Christianity in 1491 added cultural diversity to Kongolese society and in some ways strengthened the hand of the king. From then on Kongolese rulers sought to introduce Christian beliefs and rituals while at the same time Africanizing Christianity to make it more intelligible to their subjects. In addition, the kings of Kongo sought a variety of more secular aid from Portugal, including schools and medicine. But trade with the Portuguese introduced new social and political tensions, especially in the case of the export trade in slaves for the Portuguese sugar plantations on the island of São Tomé to the north.

Two letters sent to King João (zhwao) III of Portugal in 1526 illustrate how King Afonso of Kongo saw his kingdom's new relationship with Portugal and the problems that resulted from it. (Afonso adopted that name when baptized as a young prince.) After the death of his father in 1506, Afonso successfully claimed the throne and ruled until 1542. His son Henrique became the first Catholic bishop of the Kongo in 1521.

These letters were written in Portuguese and penned by the king's secretary, João Teixera (tay-SHER-uh), a Kongo Christian who, like Afonso, had been educated by Portuguese missionaries.

6 July 1526
To the very powerful and excellent prince Dom João, our brother:

On the 20th of June just past, we received word that a trading ship from your highness had just come to our port of Sonyo. We were greatly pleased by that arrival for it had been many days since a ship had come to our kingdom, for by it we would get news of your highness, which many times we had desired to know, ... and likewise as there was a great and dire need for wine and flour for the holy sacrament; and of this we had had no great hope for we have the same need frequently. And that, sir, arises from the great negligence of your highness's officials toward us and toward shipping us those things....

Sir, your highness should know how our kingdom is being lost in so many ways that we will need to provide the needed cure, since this is caused by the excessive license given by your agents and officials to the men and merchants who come to this kingdom to set up shops with goods and many things which have been prohibited by us, and which they spread throughout our kingdoms and domains in such abundance that many of our vassals, whose submission we could once rely on, now act independently so as to get the things in greater abundance than we ourselves; whom we had formerly held content and submissive and under our vassalage and jurisdiction, so it is doing a great harm not only to the service of God, but also to the security and peace of our kingdoms and state.

And we cannot reckon how great the damage is, since every day the mentioned merchants are taking our people, sons of the land and the sons of our noblemen and vassals and our relatives, because the thieves and men of bad conscience grab them so as to have the things and wares of this kingdom that they crave; they grab them and bring them to be sold. In such a manner, sir, has been the corruption and deprivation that our land is becoming completely depopulated, and your highness should not deem this good nor in your service. And to avoid this we need from these kingdoms [of yours] no more than priests and a few people to teach in schools, and no other goods except wine and flour for the holy sacrament, which is why we beg of your highness to help and assist us in this matter. Order your agents to send here neither merchants nor wares, because it is our will that in these kingdoms there should not be any dealing in slaves nor outlet for them, for the reasons stated above. Again we beg your highness's agreement, since otherwise we cannot cure such manifest harm. May Our Lord in His mercy have your highness always under His protection and may you always do the things of His holy service. I kiss your hands many times.

From our city of Kongo....

The King, Dom Afonso

18 October 1526

Very high and very powerful prince King of Portugal, our brother,

Sir, your highness has been so good as to promise us that anything we need we should ask for in our letters, and that everything will be provided. And so that there may be peace and health of our kingdoms, by God's will, in our lifetime. And as there are among us old folks and people who have lived for many days, many and different diseases happen so often that we are pushed to the ultimate extremes. And the same happens to our children, relatives, and people, because this country lacks physicians and surgeons who might know the proper cures for such diseases, as well as pharmacies and drugs to make them better. And for this reason many of those who had been already confirmed and instructed in the things of the holy faith of Our Lord Jesus Christ perish and die. And the rest of the people for the most part cure themselves with herbs and sticks and other ancient methods, so that they live putting

all their faith in these herbs and ceremonies, and die believing that they are saved; and this serves God poorly.

And to avoid such a great error, I think, and inconvenience, since it is from God and from your highness that all the good and the drugs and medicines have come to us for our salvation, we ask your merciful highness to send us two physicians and two pharmacists and one surgeon, so that they may come with their pharmacies and necessary things to be in our kingdoms, for we have extreme need of each and every one of them. We will be very good and merciful to them, since sent by your highness, their work and coming should be for good. We ask your highness as a great favor to do this for us, because besides being good in itself it is in the service of God as we have said above.

Moreover, sir, in our kingdoms there is another great inconvenience which is of little service to God, and this is that many of our people, out of great desire for the wares and things of your kingdoms, which are brought here by your people, and in order to satisfy their disordered appetite, seize many of our people, freed and exempt men. And many times noblemen and the sons of noblemen, and our relatives are stolen, and they take them to be sold to the white men who are in our kingdoms and take them hidden or by night, so that they are not recognized. And as soon as they are taken by the white men, they are immediately ironed and branded with fire. And when they are carried off to be embarked, if they are caught by our guards, the whites allege that they have bought them and cannot say from whom, so that it is our duty to do justice and to restore to the free their freedom. And so they went away offended.

And to avoid such a great evil we passed a law so that every white man living in our kingdoms and wanting to purchase slaves by whatever means should first inform three of our noblemen and officials of our court on whom we rely in this matter, namely Dom Pedro Manipunzo and Dom Manuel Manissaba, our head bailiff, and Gonçalo Pires, our chief supplier, who should investigate if the said slaves are captives or free men, and, if cleared with them, there will be no further doubt nor embargo and they can be taken and embarked. And if they reach the opposite conclusion, they will lose the aforementioned slaves. Whatever favor and license we give them [the white men] for the sake of your highness in this case is because we know that it is in your service too that these slaves are taken from our kingdom; otherwise we should not consent to this for the reasons stated above that we make known completely to your highness so that no one could say the contrary, as they said in many other cases to your highness, so that the care and remembrance that we and this kingdom have should not be withdrawn....

We kiss your hands of your highness many times.

From our city of Kongo, the 18th day of October,

The King, Dom Afonso

Questions for Analysis

1. What sorts of things does King Afonso desire from the Portuguese?
2. What is he willing and unwilling to do in return?
3. What problem with his own people has the slave trade created, and what has King Afonso done about it?
4. Does King Afonso see himself as an equal to King João or his subordinate? Do you agree with that analysis?

Source: From António Brásio, ed., *Monumenta Missionaria Africana: Africa Ocidental (1471–1531)* (Lisbon: Agência Geral do Ultramar, 1952), I: 468, 470–471, 488–491. Translated by David Northrup.

Portuguese aid helped the Ethiopian kingdom save itself from extinction, but a permanent alliance faltered because Ethiopian rulers refused to transfer their Christian affiliation from the patriarch of Alexandria to the Latin patriarch of Rome (the pope) as the Portuguese insisted.

As these examples illustrate, African encounters with the Portuguese before 1550 varied considerably, as much because of the strategies and leadership of particular African states as because of Portuguese policies. Africans and Portuguese might become royal brothers, bitter opponents, or partners in a mutually profitable trade, but Europeans remained a minor presence in most of Africa in 1550. By then the Portuguese had become far more interested in the Indian Ocean trade.

Indian Ocean States   Vasco da Gama did not make a great impression on the citizens of Calicut when he arrived on the Malabar Coast of India in May 1498. Da Gama's four small ships were far less imposing than the Chinese fleets that had called at Calicut sixty-five years earlier and no larger than many of the dhows that filled the harbor of this rich and important trading city. The samorin (ruler) of Calicut and his Muslim officials showed only mild interest in the Portuguese as new trading partners, since the gifts

Portuguese in India *In the sixteenth century Portuguese men moved to the Indian Ocean Basin to work as administrators and traders. This Indo-Portuguese drawing from about 1540 shows a Portuguese man speaking to an Indian woman, perhaps making a proposal of marriage.*

brought by da Gama had provoked derisive laughter. The twelve pieces of fairly ordinary striped cloth, four scarlet hoods, six hats, and six wash basins he presented had seemed inferior goods to those accustomed to the luxuries of the Indian Ocean trade. When da Gama tried to defend his gifts as those of an explorer, not a rich merchant, the samorin cut him short, asking whether he had come to discover men or stones: "If he had come to discover men, as he said, why had he brought nothing?"

Coastal rulers soon discovered that the Portuguese had no intention of remaining poor competitors in the rich trade of the Indian Ocean. Upon da Gama's return to Portugal in 1499, the jubilant King Manuel styled himself "Lord of the Conquest, Navigation, and Commerce of Ethiopia, Arabia, Persia, and India," thus setting forth the ambitious scope of his plans. Previously the Indian Ocean had been an open sea, used by merchants (and pirates) of all the surrounding coasts. Now the Portuguese crown intended to make it a Portuguese sea, the private property of Portugal alone.

The ability of little Portugal to assert control over the Indian Ocean stemmed from the superiority of its ships and weapons over those of the regional powers, especially the lightly armed merchant dhows. In 1505 a Portuguese fleet of eighty-one ships and some seven thousand men bombarded Swahili Coast cities. Indian ports were the next targets. Goa, on the west coast of India, fell to a well-armed fleet in 1510, becoming the base from which the Portuguese menaced the trading cities of Gujarat (goo-juh-RAHT) to the north and Calicut and other Malabar Coast cities to the south. The Portuguese also took the port of Hormuz, controlling entry to the Persian Gulf, in 1515, but Aden, at the entrance to the Red Sea, successfully resisted. The addition of the Gujarati port of Diu in 1535 consolidated Portuguese dominance of the western Indian Ocean.

Meanwhile, Portuguese explorers had reconnoitered the Bay of Bengal and the waters farther east. The city of Malacca (muh-LAH-kuh) on the strait between the Malay Peninsula and Sumatra became the focus of their attention. During the fifteenth century Malacca had become the main entrepôt for the trade from China, Japan, India, the Southeast Asian mainland, and the Moluccas. Among the city's more than 100,000 residents an early Portuguese visitor counted eighty-four different languages, including those of merchants from as far west as Cairo, Ethiopia, and the Swahili Coast of East Africa. Many non-Muslim residents of the city supported letting the Portuguese join its cosmopolitan trading community, perhaps hoping to offset the growing power of Muslim traders. In 1511, however, the Portuguese seized this strategic trading center outright with a force of a thousand fighting men, including three hundred recruited in southern India.

Force was not always necessary. On the China coast, local officials and merchants interested in profitable new trade with the Portuguese persuaded the imperial government to allow the Portuguese to establish a trading post at Macao (muh-COW) in 1557. Operating from Macao, Portuguese ships came to nearly monopolize trade between China and Japan.

In the Indian Ocean, the Portuguese used their control of major port cities to enforce an even larger trading monopoly. As their power grew, they required all spices, as well as goods carried between major ports like Goa and Macao, to be carried in Portuguese ships. In addition, the Portuguese tried to control and tax other Indian Ocean trade by requiring all merchant ships entering and leaving one of their ports to carry a Portuguese passport and pay customs duties. Portuguese patrols seized vessels that attempted to avoid these monopolies, confiscated their cargoes, and either killed the captain and crew or sentenced them to forced labor.

Reactions to this power grab varied. Like the emperors of China, the Mughal (MOO-gahl) emperors of India largely ignored Portugal's maritime intrusions, seeing their interests as maintaining control over their vast land possessions. The Ottomans responded more aggressively, supporting Egypt against the Christian intruders with a large fleet and fifteen thousand men between 1501 and 1509. Then, having absorbed Egypt into their empire, the Ottomans sent another large expedition against the Portuguese in 1538. Both expeditions failed because Ottoman galleys were no match for the faster, better-armed Portuguese vessels in the open ocean. However, the Ottomans continued to exercise control over the Red Sea and Persian Gulf.

The smaller trading states of the region were less capable of challenging Portuguese domination head-on, since rivalries among them impeded the formation of a common front. Some chose to cooperate with the Portuguese to maintain their prosperity and security. Others engaged in evasion and resistance. Two examples illustrate the range of responses among Indian Ocean peoples.

The merchants of Calicut put up some of the most sustained resistance. In retaliation, the Portuguese embargoed all trade with Aden, Calicut's principal trading partner, and centered their trade on the port of Cochin, which had once been a dependency of Calicut. Some Calicut merchants became adept at evading Portuguese naval patrols, but the price of resistance was the shrinking of Calicut's commercial importance as Cochin gradually became the major pepper-exporting port on the Malabar Coast.

The traders and rulers of the state of Gujarat farther north had less success in keeping the Portuguese at bay. At first they resisted Portuguese attempts at monopoly and in 1509 joined Egypt's failed effort to sweep the Portuguese from the Arabian Sea. But in 1535, finding his state at a military disadvantage due to Mughal attacks, the ruler of Gujarat made the fateful decision to allow the Portuguese to build a fort at Diu in return for their support. Once established, the Portuguese gradually extended their control, so that by midcentury they were licensing and taxing all Gujarati ships. Even after the Mughals (who were Muslims) took control of Gujarat in 1572, the Mughal emperor Akbar permitted the Portuguese to continue their maritime monopoly in return for allowing one ship a year to carry pilgrims to Mecca without paying the Portuguese any fee.

The Portuguese never gained complete control of the Indian Ocean trade, but their naval supremacy allowed them to dominate key ports and trade routes during the sixteenth century. The resulting profits from spices and other luxury goods had a dramatic effect. The Portuguese were now able to break the pepper monopoly long held by Venice and Genoa, who both depended on Egyptian middlemen, by selling at much lower prices. They were also able to fund a more aggressive colonization of Brazil.

In both Asia and Africa the consequences flowing from these events were startling. Asian and East African traders were now at the mercy of Portuguese warships, but their individual responses affected their fates. Some were devastated. Others prospered by meeting Portuguese demands or evading their patrols. Because the Portuguese sought to control trade routes, not occupy large territories, Portugal had little impact on the Asian and African mainlands, in sharp contrast to what was occurring in the Americas.

The Americas   In contrast to the trading empires the Portuguese created in Africa and Asia, the Spanish established a vast territorial empire in the Americas. This outcome had little to do with differences between the two kingdoms, even though Spain had a much larger population and greater resources. The Spanish and Portuguese monarchies had similar motives for expansion and used identical ships and weapons. Rather, the isolation of the Amerindian peoples made their responses to outside contacts different from those of African and Indian Ocean peoples. Isolation slowed the development of metallurgy and other militarily useful technologies in the Americas and also made these large populations more susceptible to new diseases introduced by Europeans. It was the spread of deadly new diseases, especially smallpox, among Amerindians after 1518 that weakened their ability to resist and facilitated Spanish and Portuguese occupation.

The first Amerindians to encounter Columbus were the Arawak of Hispaniola (modern Haiti and the Dominican Republic) in the Greater Antilles and the Bahamas to the north. They cultivated maize (corn), cassava (a tuber), sweet potatoes, and hot peppers, as well as cotton and tobacco. Although the islands did not have large gold deposits, and, unlike West Africans, the Arawak had not previously traded gold over long distances, the natives were skilled at working gold. While the Arawak at first extended a cautious welcome to the Spanish, they soon learned to tell exaggerated stories about gold deposits in other places to persuade them to move on.

When Columbus made his second trip to Hispaniola in 1493, he brought several hundred settlers who hoped to make their fortune, as well as missionaries who were eager to persuade the Amerindians to accept Christianity. The bad behavior of the settlers, including forced labor and sexual assaults on native women, provoked the Arawak to rebel in 1495. In this and later conflicts, steel swords, horses, and body armor led to Spanish victories and the slaughter of thousands. Thousands more were forced to labor for the Spanish. Meanwhile, cattle, pigs, and goats introduced by the settlers devoured the Arawak's food crops, causing deaths from famine and disease. A governor appointed by the Spanish crown in 1502 institutionalized these demands by dividing the surviving Arawak on Hispaniola among his allies as laborers.

The actions of the Spanish in the Antilles imitated Spanish actions and motives during the wars against the Muslims in Spain in previous centuries: they sought to serve God by defeating nonbelievers and placing them under Christian control—and to become rich in the process. Individual **conquistadors** (kon-KEY-stuh-dor) (conquerors) extended that pattern around the Caribbean as gold and indigenous labor became scarce on Hispaniola. New expeditions searched for gold and Amerindian laborers across the Caribbean region, capturing thousands of Amerindians and relocating them to Hispaniola as slaves. The island of Borinquen (Puerto Rico) was conquered in 1508 and Cuba between 1510 and 1511.

Following two failed expeditions to Mexico, Governor Velázquez of Cuba appointed an ambitious and ruthless nobleman, **Hernán Cortés** (kor-TEZ) (1485–1547), to undertake a new effort. Cortés left Cuba in 1519 with six hundred fighting men, including many who had sailed with the earlier expeditions, and most of the island's stock of weapons and horses. After demonstrating his military skills in a series of battles with the Maya, Cortés learned of the rich Aztec Empire in central Mexico.

The Aztecs (also called Mexica) had conquered their vast empire only during the previous century and a half, and many subject peoples were ready to embrace the Spanish as allies. They resented the tribute payments, forced labor, and large-scale human sacrifices demanded by the Aztecs. The Aztecs also had powerful native enemies, including the Tlaxcalans (thlash-KAH-lans), who became crucial allies of Cortés. Like the peoples of Africa and Asia when confronted by Europeans, Amerindian peoples, like the Tlaxcalans of Mexico, calculated as best they could the potential benefit or threat represented by these strange visitors. Individual Amerindians also made these calculations. Malintzin (mah-LEENT-zeen) (also called Malinche), a native woman given to Cortés shortly after his arrival in the Maya region, became his translator, key source of intelligence, and mistress. As peoples and as individuals, native allies were crucial to the Spanish campaign.

While the emperor **Moctezuma II** (mock-teh-ZOO-ma) (r. 1502–1520) hesitated to use force and attempted diplomacy instead, Cortés pushed toward the

The Execution of Inka Ruler Atahuallpa *Felipe Guaman Poma de Ayala, a native Andean from the area of Huamanga in Peru, drew this representation of the execution. While Pizarro sentenced Atahuallpa to death by strangulation, not beheading, Guaman Poma's illustration forcefully made the point that Spain had imposed an arbitrary and violent government on the Andean people.*

The Execution of the Inca King Atahualpa (woodcut), Poma de Ayala, Felipe Huaman (1526-1613)/Private Collection/The Bridgeman Art Library

Aztec capital of Tenochtitlan (teh-noch-TIT-lan). Spanish forces used firearms, cavalry tactics, and steel swords to great advantage in battles along their route. In the end Moctezuma agreed to welcome the Spaniards. As they approached his island capital, the emperor went out in a great procession, dressed in his finery, to welcome Cortés.

Despite Cortés's initial pledge that he came in friendship, Moctezuma was quickly imprisoned. The Spanish looted his treasury, interfered with the city's religious rituals, and eventually massacred hundreds during a festival. These actions provoked a mass rebellion directed against both the Spanish and Moctezuma. During the Spaniards' desperate escape, the Aztecs killed half the Spanish force and four thousand of Cortés's native allies. In the confusion Moctezuma also lost his life, either killed by the Spanish or in the Aztec attack.

The survivors, strengthened by Spanish reinforcements and aided by the Tlaxcalans, renewed their attack and captured Tenochtitlan in 1521. Their victory was aided by a smallpox epidemic that killed more of the city's defenders than did the fighting. One source remembered that the disease "spread over the people as a great destruction." Many Amerindians as well as Europeans blamed the devastating spread of this disease on supernatural forces. Cortés and other Spanish leaders then led expeditions to the north and south accompanied by the Tlaxcalans and other indigenous allies. Everywhere epidemic disease, especially smallpox, helped crush indigenous resistance.

Spanish settlers in Panama had heard tales of rich and powerful civilizations to the south even before the conquest of the Aztecs. During the previous century the Inka had built a vast empire along the Pacific coast of South America (see Chapter 15). As the empire expanded through conquest, the Inka enforced new labor demands and taxes and even exiled rebellious populations from their lands.

About 1525 the Inka ruler Huayna Capac (WHY-nah KAH-pak) died in Quito, where he had led a successful military campaign. Two of his sons then fought for the throne. In the end **Atahuallpa** (ah-tuh-WAHL-puh) (r. 1531–1533), the candidate of the northern army, defeated Huascar, the candidate of the royal court at Cuzco. As a result, the Inka military was decimated and the empire's political leadership weakened by the violence; at this critical time **Francisco Pizarro** (pih-ZAHR-oh) (ca. 1478–1541) and his force of 180 men, 37 horses, and two cannon entered the region.

Pizarro had come to the Americas in 1502 at the age of twenty-five to seek his fortune and had participated in the conquest of Hispaniola and in Balboa's expedition across the Isthmus of Panama to the Pacific. In the 1520s he gambled his fortune to finance the exploration of the Pacific south of the equator, where he learned of the riches of the Inka. With a license from the king of Spain, he set out from Panama in 1531 to conquer them.

Having seen signs of the civil war after landing, Pizarro arranged to meet the Inka emperor, Atahuallpa, near the Andean city of Cajamarca (kah-hah-MAHR-kah) in November 1532. With supreme boldness and brutality, Pizarro's small band of armed men attacked Atahuallpa and his followers as they entered an enclosed courtyard. Though surrounded by an Inka army of at least forty thousand, the Spaniards were able to use their cannon to create confusion while their swords brought down thousands of the emperor's lightly armed retainers and servants. Pizarro now replicated in Peru Cortés's strategy by capturing the Inka ruler.

Atahuallpa, seeking to guard his authority, quickly ordered the execution of his imprisoned brother Huascar. He also attempted to purchase his freedom. Having noted the glee with which the Spaniards seized gold and silver, Atahuallpa offered a ransom he thought would satisfy even the greediest among them: rooms filled to shoulder height with gold and silver. The Inka paid the ransom of 13,400 pounds (6,000 kilograms) of gold and 26,000 pounds (12,000 kilograms) of silver, but the Spaniards still executed Atahuallpa. With the unity of the Inka Empire already battered by the civil war and the death of the ruler, the Spanish occupied Cuzco, the capital city.

Nevertheless, Manco Inka, whom the Spanish had placed on the throne following the execution of his brother Atahuallpa, led a massive native rebellion in 1536. Although defeated by the Spanish, Manco Inka and his followers retreated to the interior and created a much-reduced independent kingdom that survived until 1572. The victorious Spaniards, now determined to settle their own rivalries, initiated a bloody civil war fueled by greed and jealousy. Before peace was established, this struggle took the lives of Francisco Pizarro and most of the other prominent conquistadors. Incited by the fabulous wealth of the Aztecs and Inka, conquistadors now extended their exploration and conquest of South and North America, dreaming of new treasures to loot.

Conclusion

The voyages of exploration undertaken by the Malays, Chinese, and Polynesians pursued diverse objectives. Malay voyagers were crucial participants in the development of the rich and varied commerce of Southeast Asia and initiated connections between these markets and Arabia and Africa. The great voyages of the Chinese in the early fifteenth century were motivated by an interest in trade, curiosity, and the desire to project imperial power. For the Polynesians, exploration opened the opportunity to both project power and demonstrate expertise while at the same time settling satellite populations that would relieve population pressures. The Vikings, Africans, and Amerindians all undertook long-distance explorations as well, although with fewer lasting consequences.

The projection of European influence between 1450 and 1550 was in some ways similar to that of other cultural regions in that it expanded commercial linkages, increased cross-cultural contacts, and served the ambitions of political leaders. But the result of their voyages proved to be a major turning point in world history. During those years European explorers opened new long-distance trade routes across the world's three major oceans, for the first time establishing regular contact among all the continents. As a result, a new balance of power arose in parts of Atlantic Africa, the Indian Ocean, and the Americas.

The rapid expansion of European empires and the projection of European military power around the world would have seemed unlikely in 1492. No European power matched the military and economic strength of China, and few could rival the Ottomans. Spain lacked strong national institutions, and Portugal had a small population; both had limited economic resources. Because of these limitations, the monarchs of Spain and Portugal allowed their subjects greater initiative as they engaged distant cultures.

The pace and character of European expansion in Africa and Asia were different than in the Americas. In Africa local rulers were generally able to limit European military power to coastal outposts and to control European trade. Only in the Kongo were the Portuguese able to project their power inland. In the Indian Ocean there were mature markets and specialized production for distant consumers when Europeans arrived. Here Portuguese (and later Dutch and British) naval power allowed Europeans to harvest large profits and influence regional commercial patterns, but most native populations continued to enjoy effective autonomy for centuries.

In the Americas, however, the terrible effects of epidemic disease and the destructiveness of the conquest led to the rapid creation of European settlements and the subordination of the surviving indigenous population. The Spanish and Portuguese found few long-distance markets and little large-scale production of goods that they could export profitably to Europe. The Americas would eventually produce great amounts of wealth, but this production of gold, silver, and sugar resulted from the introduction of new technologies, the imposition of oppressive new forms of labor, such as slavery, and the development of new roads and ports.

Important Events to 1500

400–1300	Polynesian settlement of Pacific islands
770–1200	Viking voyages
Early 1300s	Mali voyages
1300s	Settlement of Madeira, Azores, Canaries
1405–1433	Voyages of Zheng He
1418–1460	Voyages of Henry the Navigator
1440s	First slaves from West Africa sent to Europe
1482	Portuguese at Gold Coast and Kongo
1486	Portuguese at Benin
1488	Bartolomeu Dias reaches Indian Ocean
1492	Columbus reaches Caribbean
1492–1500	Spanish conquer Hispaniola
1493	Columbus returns to Caribbean (second voyage)
1497–1498	Vasco da Gama reaches India
1498	Columbus reaches mainland of South America (third voyage)
1500	Cabral reaches Brazil
1505	Portuguese bombard Swahili Coast cities

1510	Portuguese take Goa
1511	Portuguese take Malacca
1513	Ponce de León explores Florida
1515	Portuguese take Hormuz
1519–1521	Cortés conquers Aztec Empire
1519–1522	Magellan expedition
1531–1533	Pizarro conquers Inca Empire
1535	Portuguese take Diu
1536	Rebellion of Maco Inca in Peru
1538	Portuguese defeat Ottoman fleet
1539	Portuguese aid Ethiopia

ISSUES IN WORLD HISTORY

Climate and Population to 1500

During the millennia before 1500, human populations expanded in three momentous surges. The first occurred after 50,000 B.C.E. when humans emigrated from their African homeland to all of the inhabitable continents. After that, the global population remained steady for several millennia. During the second expansion, between about 5000 and 500 B.C.E., population rose from about 5 million to 100 million as agricultural societies spread around the world (see Figure 1). Again population growth then slowed for several centuries before a third surge took world population to over 350 million by 1200 C.E. (Figure 2 shows population in China and Europe).

For a long time historians tended to attribute these population surges to cultural and technological advances. Indeed, a great many changes in culture and technology are associated with adaptation to different climates and food supplies in the first surge and with the domestication of plants and animals in the second. However, historians have not found a cultural or technological change to explain the third surge, nor can they explain why creativity would have stagnated for long periods between the surges. Something else must have been at work.

Recently historians have begun to pay more attention to the impact of long-term variations in global climate. By examining ice cores drilled out of glaciers, scientists have been able to compile records of thousands of years of climate change. The comparative width of tree rings from ancient forests has provided additional data on periods of favorable and unfavorable growth. Such evidence shows that cycles of population growth

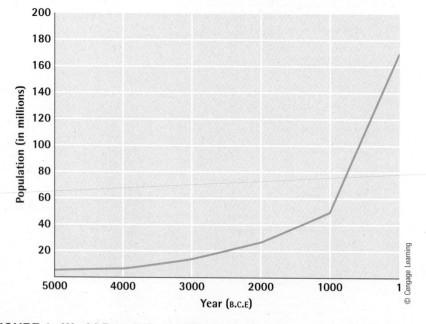

FIGURE 1 World Population, 5000–1 B.C.E.

and stagnation followed changes in global climate.

Historians now believe that global temperatures were above normal for extended periods from the late 1100s to the late 1200s C.E. In the temperate lands where most of the world's people lived, above-normal temperatures meant a longer growing season, more bountiful harvests, and thus a more adequate and reliable food supply. The ways in which societies responded to the medieval warm period are as important as the climate change, but it is unlikely that human agency alone would have produced the medieval surge. One notable response was that of the Vikings, who increased the size and range of their settlements in the North Atlantic, although their raids also caused death and destruction.

Some of the complexities involved in the interaction of human agency, climate, and other natural factors are also evident in the demographic changes that followed the medieval warm period. During the 1200s the Mongol invasions caused death and disruption of agriculture across Eurasia. China's population, which had been over 100 million in 1200, declined by a third or more by 1300. The Mongol invasions did not cause harm west of Russia, but climate changes in the 1300s resulted in population losses in Europe. Unusually heavy rains caused crop failures and a prolonged famine in northern Europe from 1315 to 1319.

The freer movement of merchants within the Mongol Empire also facilitated the spread of disease across Eurasia, culminating in the great pandemic known as the Black Death in Europe. The demographic recovery under way in China was reversed. The even larger population losses in Europe may have been affected by the decrease in global temperatures to their lowest point in many millennia between 1350 and 1375. After 1400 improving economic conditions enabled population to recover more rapidly in Europe than in China, where the conditions of rural life remained harsh.

Because many other historical circumstances interact with changing weather patterns, historians have a long way to go in deciphering the role of climate in history. Nevertheless, it is a factor that can no longer be ignored.

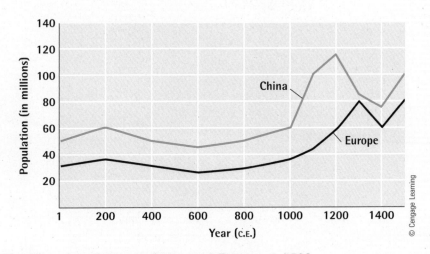

FIGURE 2 Population in China and Europe, 1–1500 C.E.

PART FIVE

THE GLOBE ENCOMPASSED, 1500–1750

The decades between 1500 and 1750 witnessed a tremendous expansion of commercial, cultural, and biological exchanges around the world. New long-distance sea routes linked Europe with sub-Saharan Africa and the already established maritime networks of the Indian Ocean and East Asia. Spanish and Portuguese voyages ended the isolation of the Americas and created new webs of exchange in the Atlantic and Pacific. Overland expansion of Muslim, Russian, and Chinese empires also increased global interaction.

These expanding contacts had major demographic and cultural consequences. Domesticated animals and crops from the Old World transformed agriculture in the Americas, while Amerindian foods such as the potato became staples of the Old World diet. European diseases, meanwhile, devastated the Amerindian population, facilitating the establishment of large Spanish, Portuguese, French, and British empires. Europeans introduced enslaved Africans to relieve the labor shortage. Europe itself underwent significant change. The Protestant Reformation broke the hegemony of the Catholic Church and led to a long period of warfare. Nevertheless, Europe's population increased, its cities grew richer, and its economies gained strength. New colonial empires created by European powers in Africa, Asia, and the Americas contributed significantly to this mounting prosperity. While Spain, France, and England continued to dominate the continent, they faced stiff competition in distant markets from the Dutch, who had achieved independence and who introduced innovative economic institutions.

In Asia and Africa, unlike the Americas, the most important changes owed more to internal forces than to European actions. The Portuguese seized control of some important trading ports and networks in the Indian Ocean and pioneered new contacts with China and Japan. In time, the Dutch, French, and English expanded these profitable connections, but in 1750 Europeans were still primarily a maritime force. Asians and Africans generally retained control of their lands and participated freely in overseas trade.

The Islamic world saw the dramatic expansion of the Ottoman Empire in the Middle East and the establishment of the Safavid Empire in Iran and the Mughal Empire in South Asia. In northern Eurasia, Russia and China acquired vast new territories and populations, while a new national government in Japan promoted economic development and resisted foreign influence.

17

TRANSFORMATIONS IN EUROPE, 1500–1750

I n the late sixteenth century Dutch cities grew rich from long-distance trade routes that linked them to traditional markets of the Baltic and Mediterranean and to the newly opened markets of South Asia, Africa, and the Americas. Prosperity allowed the households of merchants, ship owners, and even artisans to consume luxuries with an extravagance previously limited to the nobility. They built substantial houses, wore rich clothing, and developed a taste for the exotic goods of distant lands.

By the 1570s tulips had been introduced from the Ottoman lands and were avidly collected by Dutch enthusiasts. Scarce and expensive, owning tulips became a sign of sophistication and wealth. The collectors and botanists who originally purchased tulips were joined by thousands of eager consumers who recognized potential profit in a rare commodity. As prices began to surge upward in the 1620s and then accelerated in the 1630s, a speculative market developed and ownership of tulip bulbs became a form of investment. Confident that prices would continue upward, individuals and partnerships paid extravagant amounts for bulbs. Between December 1636 and February 1637, for example, one of the most popular tulip varieties increased 12 times in value, becoming a speculative "bubble." At the peak of this frenzy the rarest bulbs sold for three times the annual income of a skilled carpenter. Then, in February 1637, the tulip market crashed as panicked investors rushed to unload their bulbs. If some had been made rich in this extraordinary trade, many of those who entered the market at the height of Tulipmania and paid peak prices were financially ruined.

While speculative bubbles roiled European economies throughout the early modern period, Europe was also growing richer and more powerful. The voyages of exploration and conquests of distant lands in the fifteenth and sixteenth centuries (see Chapter 16) had initiated a dramatic commercial expansion. Greater opportunities and accumulating wealth contributed to the growth of manufacturing and to the introduction of commercial and financial innovations such as stock markets, commercial insurance, and expanded property right protections. This was also an era of dramatic social and cultural change, as cities grew in power relative to the countryside and wealthy merchants, investors, and manufacturers grew in power relative to Europe's hereditary nobility.

During this period Europe also developed powerful and efficient armies and governments that large states elsewhere in the world feared, envied, and sometimes imitated. The balance of power was shifting slowly in Europe's favor. At the beginning of this era, the Ottomans threatened Europe, but by 1750, as the remaining chapters of Part V detail, Europeans had brought much of the world under their control. No single nation was responsible for this success. The Dutch eclipsed the pioneering Portuguese and Spanish; then the English and French bested the Dutch.

This was also a period of dynamic cultural change. At the beginning of this era a single Christian tradition dominated western Europe. By its end secular political institutions and economic interests had grown stronger, while Catholic and new Protestant churches were weakened by religious wars. Equally influential was the challenge to Christianity's long domination of European intellectual life posed by the Scientific Revolution and the first stages of the Enlightenment.

The years from 1500 to 1750 were not simply an age of progress for Europe. For many, the ferocious competition of European armies, merchants, and ideas was a wrenching experience. The growth of powerful states extracted a terrible price in death and destruction, and the Reformation brought widespread religious persecution and religious warfare as well as greater individual choice in religion. Women's fortunes remained closely tied to their social class, and few gained equality with men. The expanding economy benefited members of the emerging merchant elite and their political allies, but in an era of rising prices Europe's urban and rural poor struggled to survive.

CULTURE AND IDEAS

During the Reformation, theological controversies broke the religious unity of the Latin Church and contributed to long and violent wars. While the influence of classical ideas from Greco-Roman antiquity increased among better-educated Europeans, some bold thinkers challenged the authority of the ancients. They introduced new ideas about the motion of the planets and the natural world, encouraging others to challenge traditional social and political systems. Once in place, these new ideas would influence revolutionary political and social movements in the period after 1750. The transformative impact of these challenges to long-standing religious and intellectual beliefs was multiplied by the technology of the printing press and expanded European literacy.

Early Reformation   In 1500 the **papacy**, the central government of Latin Christianity, held an unrivaled position as Europe's preeminent religious and intellectual authority, although lax clerical standards and corruption were endemic. Recovered from a period when competing popes supported by rival secular rulers disputed control of the church, popes now exercised greater power, which was funded by larger donations and by income from the church's enormous real estate holdings. The construction of fifty-four new churches and other buildings in Rome demonstrated the church's power and showcased the artistic **Renaissance** then under way. The church leadership intended the size and splendor of the magnificent new Saint Peter's Basilica in Rome to glorify God, display the skill of Renaissance artists and builders, and enhance the standing of the papacy, but the vast expense of its construction and rich decoration also caused scandal.

The skillful overseer of the design and financing of the Saint Peter's Basilica was Pope Leo X (r. 1513–1521), a member of the wealthy Medici (MED-ih-chee) family of Florence, famous for its patronage of the arts. Pope Leo's artistic taste was superb and his personal life free from scandal, but he was more a man of action than a spiritual leader. During his papacy the church aggressively raised funds through the sale of **indulgences**—a forgiveness of the punishment due for past sins.

A young professor of sacred scripture, Martin Luther (1483–1546), saw this practice and other excesses as intolerably corrupt. As the result of a powerful religious experience, Luther had forsaken money and marriage for a monastic life of prayer, self-denial, and study. In his religious quest, he found personal consolation in a passage in Saint Paul's Epistle stating that salvation resulted from religious faith, not from "doing certain things." That passage led Luther to object to the way preachers emphasized giving money to the church more than they emphasized faith. He wrote to Pope Leo to complain of this abuse and challenged the preachers to a debate on the theology of indulgences.

This theological dispute was also a contest between two strong-willed men. Largely ignoring the theological objections, Pope Leo regarded Luther's letter as a challenge to papal power and moved to silence him. During a debate in 1519, a papal representative led Luther into open disagreement with church doctrines, for which the papacy condemned him. Blocked in his effort to reform the church from within, Luther burned the papal bull (document) of condemnation, rejected the pope's authority, and began the movement known as the **Protestant Reformation**.

Accusing those whom he called "Romanists" (Roman Catholics) of relying on "good works," Luther insisted that the only way to salvation was through faith in Jesus Christ. He further declared that Christian belief should be based on the word of God in the Bible and on Christian tradition, not on the authority of the pope. Luther's use of the printing press to spread his ideas won him the support of powerful Germans, who responded to his nationalist portrayal of an Italian pope seeking to beautify Rome with German funds.

Luther's denunciation of the ostentation and corruption of the church led others to call for a return to what they saw as authentic Christian practices and beliefs. John Calvin (1509–1564), a well-educated Frenchman who left the study of law for theology after experiencing a religious conversion, became an influential Protestant leader. Although Calvin agreed with Luther's emphasis on faith over works, he denied that human faith alone could merit salvation. Salvation, Calvin believed, was a gift God gave to those He "predestined." Calvin also went farther than Luther in curtailing the power of the clerical hierarchy and in simplifying religious rituals. Calvinist congregations elected their own governing committees and created regional and national synods (councils) to regulate doctrinal issues. Calvinists also displayed simplicity in dress, life, and worship, avoiding ostentatious living and stripping churches of statues, most musical instruments, stained-glass windows, incense, and vestments.

The Reformers appealed to genuine religious sentiments, but their successes and failures were also due to local political and economic conditions. It was no coincidence that German-born Luther had his greatest success among German speakers and linguistically related Scandinavians. Nor was it surprising that peasants and urban laborers sometimes defied their masters by adopting a different faith. Protestants were no more inclined than Roman Catholics to question male dominance in the church and the family, but most Protestants rejected the medieval tradition of celibate priests and nuns and advocated Christian marriage for all adults.

The Counter-Reformation and the Politics of Religion   Shaken by the intensity of the Protestant attack, the Catholic Church initiated a campaign of internal reforms. A church council meeting in Trent in northern Italy between 1545 and 1563 sought to distinguish Catholic doctrines from Protestant "errors" and reaffirmed the supremacy of the pope. It also reaffirmed traditional teaching, including salvation through both faith and good works, the importance of oral confession and penance, and the authority of ecclesiastical authorities in interpreting Scriptures. Bishops allied with the pope dominated the council and limited efforts to reform practices that Luther had condemned as corrupt. Seeking to address unpopular practices condemned by Protestants, the council called for bishops to reside in their dioceses and for dioceses to maintain a theological seminary to train priests.

The creation in 1540 of a new religious order, the Society of Jesus, or "Jesuits," by the Spanish nobleman Ignatius of Loyola (1491–1556) was among the most important events of the **Catholic Reformation** (also called the Counter-Reformation). Well-educated Jesuits helped stem the Protestant tide by their teaching and preaching, and they gained converts through missions in Asia, Africa, and the Americas (see Chapters 18 and Chapters 21).

Given the complexity and intensity stirred by the Protestant Reformation, it is not surprising that both sides persecuted and sometimes executed those of differing views. Bitter "wars of religion" would continue in parts of western Europe until 1648. The rulers of Spain and France were the chief defenders of the Catholic tradition against these Protestant challenges.

Charles V, Holy Roman Emperor and King of Spain, and his son, King Philip II, were the key political and military architects of the Counter-Reformation. To confront the Protestant threat in northern Europe, Charles V dialed back his campaign against the Ottoman Empire and North African Muslim states in the Mediterranean and sent large armies to central Europe and the low countries. As a result, Spain's enormous windfall of Western Hemisphere bullion went to subsidize this new military commitment rather than to develop its economy. Philip II continued his father's policies to their disastrous ends, the destruction of the Spanish Armada in 1588 and the recognition of effective Dutch independence in 1609.

In France the Calvinist opponents of the Valois dynasty gained the military advantage in the French Wars of Religion (1562–1598), but, in the interest of national unity, their leader Prince Henry of Navarre ultimately accepted the Catholic faith when he ruled as Henry IV of France. In pursuit of their objective of a union of church and state, Henry IV, his son King Louis XIII, and his grandson King Louis XIV supported the Catholic Church. Ultimately, Louis XIV revoked the Edict of Nantes (nahnt) by which his grandfather had granted religious freedom to his Protestant supporters in 1598.

In England King Henry VIII had initially been a strong defender of the papacy against Lutheran criticism. But when Henry failed to obtain a papal annulment of his marriage to Catherine of Aragon, who had not furnished him with a male heir, he challenged the papacy's authority over the English church. First the English archbishop of Canterbury annulled Henry's marriage in 1533 and then Parliament made the king head of an autonomous Church of England.

Like many Protestant rulers, Henry used this controversy to strengthen his authority and fatten his pocketbook by closing monasteries and convents and seizing their lands. He gave some land to his powerful allies and used profits from selling other land to pay for his new navy. While the king's power had grown at the expense of the Catholic Church, religious belief and practice were changing also. The new Anglican Church distanced itself from Catholic ritual and theology, but English Puritans (Calvinists who wanted to "purify" the church of all Catholic practices and beliefs) sought more. In 1603 they petitioned the first Stuart king, James I, to eliminate bishops.

Local Religion, Traditional Culture, and Witch-Hunts
Both in the Protestant north and the Catholic south the institutions that enforced religious orthodoxy were weakest in villages and small towns. In these settings, local religion commonly blended the rituals and beliefs of the established churches with local folk customs, pre-Christian beliefs, ancient curing practices, love magic, and the casting of spells. The vigor of these local religious traditions ebbed and flowed in response to the strength of national and regional religious institutions as well as to the experience of economic dislocations, famine, and epidemic. The widespread **witch-hunts** that Protestants and Catholics undertook in early modern Europe were linked to this widespread belief in white and black magic. Yet, these beliefs and fears would not have had such deadly consequences if many educated and powerful city dwellers did not believe in the Devil's power to affect society broadly.

Prevailing European ideas about the natural world blended two distinct traditions. One was an enduring belief in magic and spirits passed down orally from pre-Christian times. The second was the biblical teachings of the Christian and Jewish Scriptures, heard by all in church and read by growing numbers in vernacular translations. In the minds of most Europeans, Christian teachings about miracles, saints, and devils coincided easily with beliefs about magic, sorcery, and witchcraft rooted in the distant past.

It was widely assumed that some men and women possessed special powers derived from occult knowledge or, in some cases, from a compact with the Devil. In its benign version, practitioners could heal the sick, cause love to flourish, or guarantee good fortune. They could also solve disputes with masters or employers or punish enemies. The malevolent version was practiced by witches and warlocks who could cause infertility, illness, or death of loved ones and neighbors, cause crops or businesses to fail, or even provoke epidemics or droughts, sometimes in association with the Devil. While some theologians and jurists questioned the intellectual and religious underpinnings of these assumptions before the mid-sixteenth century, many European civil and ecclesiastical courts would continue to arrest and punish witches until the last decades of the seventeenth century.

Art Resource, NY

Death to Witches *This woodcut from 1574 depicts three women convicted of witchcraft being burned alive in Baden, Switzerland. The scene on the left illustrates the purported witchcraft practiced by the three condemned women.*

The attribution of human triumphs and tragedies to supernatural causes persisted among Europeans long after the end of the witch hysteria. When an earthquake destroyed much of Lisbon, Portugal's capital city, in November 1755, for example, both educated and uneducated people saw the event as a punishment sent by God. A Jesuit stated that it was "scandalous to pretend that the earthquake was just a natural event." An English Protestant leader agreed, comparing Lisbon's fate with that of Sodom, the city that God destroyed because of the sinfulness of its citizens, according to the Hebrew Bible.

The extraordinary fear of witches that swept across Europe in the late sixteenth and seventeenth centuries was powerful testimony to the endurance of these beliefs among commoners and the governing class alike. The initial wave of mass witch-hunts began in Protestant regions of Germany in the last decades of the sixteenth century. They continued, and in some areas accelerated, during the Catholic Counter-Reformation. Before this hysteria ended, secular and church authorities had tried approximately 100,000 people and executed 60,000—some three-fourths of them women—for practicing witchcraft. The scale of these trials and executions reflected the participation of rulers and judicial authorities in this process. In German city-states like Würzburg and Bamberg, for example, local princes condoned and promoted the trials, thus contributing to hundreds of deaths, including scores of children, in the 1620s and 1630s.

Trial records make it clear that both the accusers and the accused believed that it was possible for angry, jealous, and evil individuals to use black magic in concert with the Devil to cause injury to others. Many, in fact, appear to have willingly admitted to having occult powers and even to consorting with the Devil, but some educated contemporaries wondered if these individuals were mentally unbalanced or simply very old. Clearly the common use of judicial torture by religious and secular authorities explains most of the confessions of accused witches.

The trials and executions transcended national and religious boundaries, but there were significant differences in regional and national practice, even in nations with similar religious traditions. While England's population was roughly five times larger than Scotland's, roughly three times as many witches were executed by the Scots, 120 in the two-year period 1661–1662 alone. The relatively strong Catholic states of France and Spain also had low numbers of executions relative to the German states. In Spain the Inquisition limited arrests of suspected witches based on testimony as early as 1526. The judges of the Parlement of Paris mandated appeals of convictions for witchcraft and began to overturn many before the wave of executions crested in northern Europe in the 1620s. Similarly, the more egalitarian and less centralized government of Holland also limited trials and executions. The death toll was highest in German states like Wurzburg and Bamberg, which executed 900 and 600, respectively, between 1626 and 1631. Sweden hosted one of the last mass campaigns of extirpation, executing 71 convicted witches on a single day in 1675. Even in Orthodox Russia, far from the center of this hysteria, 99 were accused of witchcraft and 10 were burned at the stake between 1622 and 1700.

While no single reason can explain the rise in witchcraft accusations and executions in early modern Europe, these events coincided with rising social tensions, growing rural poverty, and environmental strains. They also coincided with the violence of the wars in the Reformation period. While far from being a bizarre aberration, witch-hunts also reflected the tension between popular beliefs and practices and the ambitions of aggressive new religious and political institutions. The Reformation's focus on the Devil—the enemy of God—as the source of evil and the Catholic Counter-Reformation's effort to enforce orthodoxy both helped to propel the brutal persecutions of this period. In the eighteenth century the era of witchcraft persecutions effectively came to an end. The underlying beliefs were no longer credible among judges and rulers, while central governments were stronger and less willing to allow popular passions to sway the local administration of justice.

The Scientific Revolution   Europe's intellectual environment proved to be as tumultuous and unstable as its religious institutions and political organization in the early modern period. At the beginning of the period the writings of classic antiquity and the Bible were the most trusted guides to the natural world. The greatest authority on physics was Aristotle, a Greek philosopher who taught that the surface of the earth was composed of the two heavy elements, earth and water. The atmosphere was made up of two lighter elements, air and fire, which floated above the ground. Higher still were the sun, moon, planets, and stars, which, according to Aristotelian physics, were so light and pure that they floated in crystalline spheres. This division between the ponderous, heavy earth and airy, celestial bodies accorded perfectly with the commonsense perception that all heavenly bodies revolved around the earth.

Beginning in the sixteenth century, however, European understandings of the natural world were transformed by a new form of scientific inquiry that emphasized experimentation, careful observation, and mathematical calculations. While this period is often called the **Scientific Revolution**, many of the most influential intellectuals were committed Christians (both Catholic and Protestant) who sought to use science to reinforce religious beliefs. Nevertheless, as this movement gained momentum, and as the convincing results of the experimental method accumulated, European intellectual life became more secular and independent.

Nicholas Copernicus (1473–1543), a Polish monk and mathematician, helped initiate the new era when he proposed that the sun, not the earth, as taught by both religious and classical authorities, was the center of the universe (see Chapter 14). To escape anticipated controversies with church authorities, Copernicus delayed the publication of his heliocentric (sun-centered) theory until the end of his life. Once disseminated, his research began a revolution in the way human beings understood the structure of the heavens.

Other astronomers, including the Danish Tycho Brahe (1546–1601) and his German assistant Johannes Kepler (1571–1630), strengthened and improved on Copernicus's model, showing that planets actually move in elliptical, not circular, orbits. The most brilliant of the Copernicans was the Italian Galileo Galilei (gal-uh-LAY-oh gal-uh-LAY-ee) (1564–1642). In 1609 Galileo built a telescope through which he could look more closely at the heavens, thus confirming the speculations of other astronomers.

At first, those supporting the heliocentric universe faced formidable resistance because they directly challenged the intellectual synthesis of classical and biblical authorities. Many intellectual and religious leaders sought to suppress the new ideas. Most Protestant leaders, following the lead of Martin Luther, condemned the heliocentric universe as contrary to the Bible. Catholic authorities did not react immediately, but, when they did act, they proved more effective in suppressing the new scientific discoveries.

Copernicus died before his book was deemed heretical by Catholic authorities in 1616 and placed on the index of prohibited books. Yet his discoveries helped lead to a more accurate calendar issued in 1582 by Pope Gregory XIII and still used today. Galileo's empirical demonstration of the heliocentric theory led ultimately to a confrontation with the Inquisition. Galileo argued that the Bible was an inspired text, but, when science had established a demonstrable fact, the Bible should be interpreted to coincide with the evidence, since it could not be God's intention to mislead. Despite the controversial nature of his opinions, he continued to publish, pressing for a reliance on physical evidence and accurate measurement. Ordered before the Inquisition in 1633, Galileo was forced to recite and then sign a formal renunciation of his research. An apparent victory for tradition, this action put the Catholic Church in untenable opposition to a key early achievement of the new science.

Tycho Brahe at Work *Between 1576 and 1597, on the island of Ven between Denmark and Sweden, Tycho built the best observatory in Europe and set a new standard for accurate celestial observations before the invention of the telescope. This contemporary hand-colored engraving shows the Danish astronomer at work.*

Despite opposition from religious and secular authorities, printed books spread the new scientific ideas across Europe. Among the most influential intellectuals was the French philosopher and mathematician René Descartes (1595–1650), who furthered the development of physics and calculus when he demonstrated the usefulness of algebra to geometry. After hearing of Galileo's condemnation by the Inquisition in 1633, however, Descartes decided to delay publishing a potentially controversial work on optics and astronomy. In England, another intellectual, Robert Boyle (1627–1691), advocated tirelessly for the usefulness of the experimental method. One of the founders of modern chemistry, he developed an effective vacuum pump and demonstrated that air was necessary for the transmission of sound. He was also among the first to publish the details of experiments, including his failures. Boyle along with others became an enthusiastic missionary of mechanical science and played a key role in the 1662 founding of the Royal Society to promote science. Its motto is "Nullius in Verba" or "nothing in words," a demand that science should be based on experiments alone.

Another Englishman, the mathematician Isaac Newton (1642–1727), began his work in optics and mathematics, building on the work of Boyle and Descartes. He later carried Galileo's demonstration that the heavens and earth share a common physics to its logical conclusion by formulating mathematical laws that governed all physical objects. His Law of Gravity and his role in developing the calculus made him the most famous and influential man of his era, serving as president of the Royal Society from 1703 until his death.

As late as 1700 most religious and intellectual leaders viewed the new science with suspicion or hostility because it challenged long-established ways of thought. Yet most of the principal pioneers of the Scientific Revolution, including the Catholics Galileo and Descartes as well as the Protestant Boyle, were convinced that scientific discoveries and revealed religion could be reconciled. However, by showing that the Aristotelians and biblical writers held ideas about the natural world that were unsupportable in the face of scientific discovery, these pioneers opened the door to others who used reason and logic to challenge a broader range of unquestioned traditions and superstitions. The world of ideas was forever changed.

The Early Enlightenment

Advances in scientific thought inspired some to question the reasonableness of everything from agricultural methods to laws, religion, and social hierarchies. They believed that they could apply the scientific method to analyze economics, politics, and social organization and devise the best policies. This enthusiasm for an open and critical examination of human society energized a movement known as the **Enlightenment**. Like the Scientific Revolution, this movement was the work of a few "enlightened" individuals, who often faced bitter opposition from the political and religious establishments. Leading Enlightenment thinkers became accustomed to having their books burned or banned, and many spent long periods in exile to escape persecution.

Influences besides the Scientific Revolution affected the Enlightenment. The religious warfare and intolerance associated with the struggle between Catholicism and Protestantism undermined the moral authority of religion for many, and the efforts of church authorities to impugn the breakthroughs of science also pushed European intellectuals in a secular direction. The popular bigotry manifested in the brutal treatment of suspected witches also shocked many thoughtful people. The leading French thinker François-Marie d'Arouet, better known by his pen name Voltaire (1694–1778), declared: "No opinion is worth burning your neighbor for."

Although many circumstances shaped "enlightened" thinking, new scientific methods and discoveries provided the clearest model for changing European society. Accused of defamation by a powerful aristocrat, Voltaire fled to England, where he met many leading scientists as well as intellectual lights like Alexander Pope and Jonathan Swift. When he returned to France, he became a leading advocate for Newtonian physics in opposition to his countryman Descartes. In his publications he linked the prestige of the newly ascendant scientific method with his generation's mounting political and social concerns in these terms: "It would be very peculiar that all nature, all the planets, should obey eternal laws" but a human being, "in contempt of these laws, could act as he pleased solely according to his caprice." The English poet Alexander Pope (1688–1774) made a similar point in verse: "Nature and Nature's laws lay hidden in night; / God said, 'Let Newton be' and all was light."

The Enlightenment was more a frame of mind than a coherent movement. Individuals who embraced it drew inspiration from different sources and promoted different agendas. Its proponents were clearer about what they disliked than about what changes were necessary. Some thought an "enlightened" society could function with the mechanical orderliness of planets spinning in their orbits. Nearly all were optimistic that—at least in the long run—their discoveries would improve human beliefs and institutions. This faith in progress would help foster political and social revolutions after 1750, as Chapter 23 recounts.

While the Catholic Church and many Protestant clergymen opposed the Enlightenment, European monarchs selectively endorsed new ideas. Monarchs, ambitious to increase their power, found anticlerical intellectuals useful allies against church power and wealth. More predictably, monarchs and their reforming advisers discovered in the Enlightenment's demand for more rational and predictable policies justification for the expansion of royal authority and modern tax systems. Europe in 1750 was a place where political and religious divisions, growing literacy, and the printing press made it possible for these controversial and exciting new ideas to thrive despite opposition from ancient and powerful institutions.

Social and Economic Life

There were large and important differences in the social structures of the major European nations, but there were many shared characteristics as well. European society was dominated by a small number of noble families who enjoyed privileged access to high offices in the church, government, and military and, in most cases, exemption from taxation. Below them was a much larger class of prosperous commoners that included many clergy, bureaucrats, professionals, and military officers as well as merchants, some artisans, and rural landowners. The vast majority of men and women were very poor. Laborers, journeymen, apprentices, and rural laborers struggled to earn their daily bread and often faced unemployment and privation. The poorest members of society lived truly desperate lives, surviving only through guile, begging, or crime. Women remained subordinated to men.

Some social mobility did occur, however, particularly in the middle. The principal engine of social change was an economy stimulated by long-distance trade and by access to the gold and silver of the Americas. Because cities enjoyed the benefits of this expansion disproportionally, they were the principal arenas of new opportunity and social mobility.

The Bourgeoisie   Europe's cities grew in response to expanding trade and rising commercial profits. In 1500 Paris was the only northern European city with over 100,000 inhabitants. By 1700 both Paris and London had populations over 500,000, and eleven other European cities contained over 100,000 people.

Urban wealth came from manufacturing and finance, but especially from trade, both within Europe and overseas. The French called the urban class that dominated

The Fishwife, 1572 *Women were essential partners in most Dutch family businesses. This scene by the Dutch artist Adriaen van Ostade shows a woman preparing fish for retail sale.*

these activities the **bourgeoisie** (boor-zwah-ZEE) (burghers, town dwellers). Members of the bourgeoisie devoted long hours to their businesses and poured much of their profits back into them or into new ventures. Even so, most had enough money to live comfortably in large houses, and some had servants. In the seventeenth and eighteenth centuries wealthier consumers could buy exotic luxuries imported from the far corners of the earth—Caribbean and Brazilian sugar and rum, Mexican chocolate, Virginia tobacco, North American furs, East Indian cotton textiles and spices, and Chinese tea.

The Netherlands provides one of the best examples of this new bourgeois reality. The Dutch Republic was the most egalitarian European country in the early modern period. While it retained a nobility, wealthy commoners dominated its economy and politics. Manufacturers and craftsmen turned out a great variety of goods in their factories and workshops. The highly successful textile industry concentrated on the profitable weaving, finishing, and printing of cloth, leaving spinning to low-paid workers elsewhere. Along with fine woolens and linens, the Dutch also made cheaper textiles for mass markets. Factories in Holland refined

West Indian sugar, brewed beer made from Baltic grain, cut Virginia tobacco, and made imitations of Chinese ceramics (see Environment and Technology: East Asian Porcelain in Chapter 21). Free from the censorship and religious persecution imposed by political and religious authorities elsewhere, Holland's intellectuals were active in the Scientific Revolution and early Enlightenment, and its printers published books in many languages, including manuals with the latest advances in machinery, metallurgy, agriculture, and other technical areas. For a small nation that lacked timber and other natural resources, this was a remarkable achievement.

With a population of 200,000 in 1700, Amsterdam was Holland's largest city and Europe's major port. The Dutch developed huge commercial fleets that dominated sea trade in Europe and overseas. Around 1600 they introduced new ship designs, including the *fluit*, or "flyboat," a large-capacity cargo ship that was inexpensive to build and required only a small crew. As their trade with distant markets developed they introduced another successful type of merchant ship, the heavily armed "East Indiaman," that helped the Dutch establish their supremacy in the Indian Ocean. By one estimate, the Dutch conducted more than half of all the oceangoing commercial shipping in the world in the seventeenth century (for details see Chapters 20 and Chapters 21). Dutch mapmaking supported these distant commercial connections (see Environment and Technology: Mapping the World).

Amsterdam also served as Europe's financial center. Seventeenth-century Dutch banks had such a reputation for security that wealthy individuals and governments from all over western Europe entrusted them with their money. The banks in turn invested these funds in real estate, loaned money to factory owners and governments, and provided capital for commercial operations overseas.

Individuals seeking higher returns than those provided by banks could purchase shares in a **joint-stock company**, a sixteenth-century forerunner of the modern corporation. Individuals bought and sold shares in specialized financial markets called **stock exchanges**, an Italian innovation transferred to the cities of northwestern Europe in the sixteenth century. The lively Amsterdam Exchange, begun as an outdoor market around 1530, moved into impressive new quarters in 1611. It remained Europe's greatest stock market in the seventeenth and eighteenth centuries.

The Dutch government played a direct role in this process by pioneering the creation of monopoly commercial enterprises like the Dutch East and West India Companies, which were granted monopolies for trade with the East and West Indies. France and England soon chartered monopoly trading companies of their own. These companies then sold shares to individuals to raise large sums for overseas enterprises while spreading the risks (and profits) among many investors (see Chapter 19). In this same era insurance companies were developed to insure long-distance voyages against loss; by 1700, purchasing insurance had become standard commercial practice.

Governments also sought to promote trade by investing in infrastructure. The Dutch built numerous canals to speed transport, lower costs, and drain the lowlands for agriculture. Other governments financed canals as well, including systems of locks to raise barges up over hills. One of the most important was the 150-mile (240-kilometer) Canal du Midi built by the French government between 1661 and 1682 to link the Atlantic and the Mediterranean.

After 1650 the Dutch faced growing competition from the English, who were developing their own close association between business and government. With government support, the English merchant fleet doubled between 1660 and 1700, and foreign trade rose by 50 percent. As a result, state revenue from customs duties tripled. In a series of wars (1652–1678) the English government used its new naval might to break Dutch dominance in overseas trade and to extend England's colonial empire.

Some successful members of the bourgeoisie in England and France chose to use their wealth to raise their social status. By retiring from their businesses and buying country estates, they could become members of the **gentry**. They loaned money to impoverished peasants and to members of the nobility and in time increased their land ownership. Some sought aristocratic husbands for their daughters. The old nobility found such alliances attractive because of the large dowries that the bourgeoisie provided. Even in colonial settings, a small number of affluent and ambitious families purchased titles of nobility. While this kind of social mobility satisfied the desire for elevated status in hierarchical societies, it also removed the capital of the most successful bourgeoisie families from commerce and production.

Peasants and Laborers

Serfdom, which bound men and women to land owned by a local lord, had begun to decline after the great plague of the mid-fourteenth century. As population recovered in western Europe, the competition for work exerted a downward pressure on wages, reducing the usefulness of serfdom and other forms of forced labor to landowners. While there had been a brief expansion of slavery in southern Europe with the introduction of African slaves around 1500, Europeans shipped nearly all African slaves to the Americas after 1600. In eastern Europe, on the other hand, forced labor endured. Large-scale landowners in Russia and elsewhere who produced grains for growing urban markets continued to rely on the bound labor of serfs to ensure their profits.

There is much truth in the argument that western Europe continued to depend on unfree labor but kept it at a distance in its colonies rather than at home (see Chapters 18 and Chapters 19). In any event, legal freedom did little to make a peasant's life safer and more secure. The efficiency of European agriculture had improved little since 1300. As a result, bad years brought famine; good ones provided only small surpluses. Indeed, the material conditions experienced by the poor in western Europe may have worsened between 1500 and 1750 as the result of warfare, environmental degradation, and economic contractions. Europeans also felt the adverse effects of a century of relatively cool climate that began in the 1590s. During this **Little Ice Age** average temperatures fell only a few degrees, but the effects were startling (see Issues in World History: Climate and Population to 1500).

By 1700 high-yielding new crops from the Americas were helping the rural poor avoid starvation. Once grown only as famine foods, potatoes and maize (corn) became staples for the rural poor in the eighteenth century. Potatoes sustained life in northeastern and central Europe and in Ireland, while poor peasants in Italy subsisted on maize. The irony is that all of these lands were major exporters of wheat, but the laborers who planted and harvested this crop could not afford to eat it.

Other rural residents made their living as miners, lumber-jacks, and charcoal makers. The expanding iron industry in England provided work for all three, but the high consumption of wood fuel caused serious **deforestation**. One early-seventeenth-century observer lamented: "Within man's memory, it was held impossible to have any want of wood in England. But ... at present, through the great consuming of wood ... and the neglect of planting of woods, there is a great scarcity of wood throughout the whole kingdom."[1] Eventually, the high price of wood and charcoal encouraged smelters to use coal as an alternative fuel. England's coal mining increased twelvefold, from 210,000 tons in 1550 to 2,500,000 tons in 1700 and nearly 5 million tons by 1750.

France was more heavily forested than England, but increasing deforestation prompted Jean Baptiste Colbert, France's minister of finance, to predict that "France will perish for lack of wood." In Sweden and Russia, where wood fueled the furnaces of iron foundries, deforestation became an economic threat in the late eighteenth century as iron production rose.

Even in the prosperous Dutch towns, half of the population lived in acute poverty. Authorities estimated that permanent city residents who were too poor to tax, the "deserving poor," made up 10 to 20 percent of the population. That calculation did not include the large numbers of "unworthy poor"—recent migrants from impoverished rural areas, peddlers traveling from place to place, and beggars (many with horrible deformities and sores) who tried to survive on charity. The pervasive poverty of rural and urban Europe shocked those who were not hardened to it. In about 1580 the mayor of the French city of Bordeaux (bor-DOH) asked a group of visiting Amerindian chiefs what impressed them most about European cities. The chiefs are said to have expressed astonishment at the disparity between the fat, well-fed people and the poor, half-starved men and women in rags. Why, the visitors wondered, did the poor not grab the rich by the throat or set fire to their homes?[2]

In fact, misery provoked many rebellions in early modern Europe. For example, in 1525 peasant rebels in the Alps attacked both nobles and the clergy as representatives of the privileged and landowning classes. They had no love for merchants either, whom they denounced for lending at interest and charging high prices. Rebellions multiplied as rural conditions worsened. In southwestern France alone some 450 uprisings occurred between 1590 and 1715, many of them set off by food shortages and tax increases. A rebellion in southern France in 1670 began when a mob of townswomen attacked the tax collector. It quickly spread to the country, where peasant leaders cried, "Death to the people's oppressors!" Authorities dealt severely with such revolts and executed or maimed their leaders.

Women and the Family   Women's social and economic status was closely tied to that of their husbands. In some nations a woman could inherit a throne (see Table 17.1 on page 454 for examples)—in the absence of a male heir. These rare exceptions do not negate the rule that women everywhere ranked below men, but one should also not forget that class and wealth

---

[1]Quoted by Carlo M. Cipolla, "Introduction," *The Fontana Economic History of Europe*, vol. 2, *The Sixteenth and Seventeenth Centuries* (Glasgow: Collins/Fontana Books, 1976), 11–12.

[2]Michel de Montaigne, *Essais* (1588), ch. 31, "Des Cannibales."

ENVIRONMENT + TECHNOLOGY

Mapping the World

In 1602 in China the Jesuit missionary Matteo Ricci printed an elaborate map of the world. Working from maps produced in Europe and incorporating the latest knowledge gathered by European maritime explorers, Ricci introduced two changes to make the map more appealing to his Chinese hosts. He labeled it in Chinese characters, and he split his map down the middle of the Atlantic so that China lay in the center. This version pleased the Chinese elite, who considered China the "Middle Kingdom" surrounded by lesser states. A copy of Ricci's map in six large panels adorned the emperor's Beijing palace.

The stunningly beautiful maps and globes of sixteenth-century Europe were the most complete, detailed, and useful representations of the earth that any society had ever produced. The best map-maker of the century was Gerhard Kremer, who is remembered as Mercator (the merchant) because his maps were so useful to European ocean traders. By incorporating the latest discoveries and scientific measurements, Mercator could depict the outlines of the major continents in painstaking detail, even if their interiors were still largely unknown to outsiders.

To represent the spherical globe on a flat map, Mercator drew the lines of longitude as parallel lines. Because such lines actually meet at the poles, Mercator's projection greatly exaggerated the size of every landmass and body of water distant from the equator. However, Mercator's rendering offered a very practical advantage: sailors could plot their course by drawing a straight line between their point of departure and their destination. Because of this useful feature, the Mercator projection of the world remained in common use until quite recently. To some extent, its popularity came from the exaggerated size this projection gave to Europe. Like the Chinese, Europeans liked to think of themselves as at the center of things. Europeans also understood their true geographical position better than people in any other part of the world.

defined a woman's position in life more than her sex. The wife or daughter of a rich man, for example, though often closely confined, had a materially better life than any poor man. Sometimes a single woman might secure a position of responsibility, as in the case of women from good families who headed convents in Catholic countries. But while unmarried women were routinely controlled by fathers and married women controlled by husbands, some widows independently controlled substantial properties and other assets.

In contrast to the arranged marriages that prevailed in much of the rest of the world, young men and women in early modern Europe often chose their own spouses, but privileged families were much more likely to arrange marriages than poor ones. Royal and noble families carefully plotted the suitability of their children's marriages in furthering family interests. Bourgeois parents were less likely to force their children into arranged marriages, but the fact that nearly all found spouses within their own social class strongly suggests that the bourgeoisie promoted marriages that advanced their social aspirations or furthered their business interests.

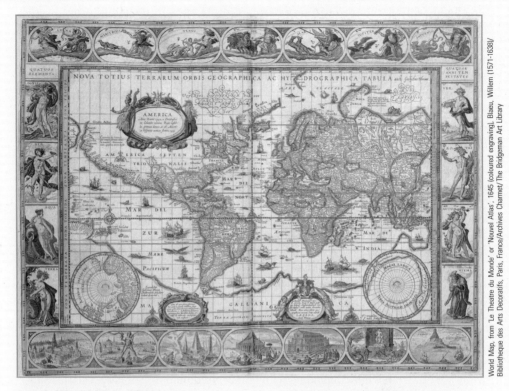

Dutch World Map, 1641 *It is easy to see why the Chinese would not have liked to see their empire at the far right edge of this widely printed map. Besides the distortions caused by the Mercator projection, geographical ignorance exaggerates the size of North America and Antarctica.*

Europeans also married later than people in other cultural regions. Sons often put off marriage until they could live on their own. Many young women also had to work—helping their parents, as domestic servants, or in some other capacity—to save money for the dowry expected by potential husbands. A dowry was the money and household goods—the amount varied by social class—that enabled a young couple to begin marriage independent of their parents. As a result, the typical groom in western and central Europe could not hope to marry before his late twenties, and his bride would be a few years younger—in contrast to the rest of the world, where people usually married in their teens.

Besides enabling young people to be independent of their parents, the late age of marriage in early modern Europe also held down the birthrate and thus limited family size. Even so, about one-tenth of urban births were to unmarried women, often servants. Many mothers, unable to provide for these infants, left them on the doorsteps of churches, convents, or rich households to be raised as "orphans." Many neglected children perished; and many young women newly arrived in Europe's fast-growing cities from the countryside were forced into brothels or begging by their poverty.

POLITICAL INNOVATIONS

The monarchs of early modern Europe occupied the apex of the social order, were arbitrators of the intellectual and religious conflicts of their day, and exercised important influence on the economies of their realms. Many European monarchs introduced reforms that achieved a higher degree of political centralization and order in this era, but their ambitions and rivalries could also provoke destructive and costly conflicts. In some cases, civil and international conflicts forced monarchs to find common ground with potential enemies or introduce political innovations that strengthened their nations. During this period, political leadership in Europe passed from Spain to the Netherlands and then to England and France.

State   There was a great deal of political diversity in early modern
Development   Europe. City-states and principalities abounded, either inde-
                     pendently or bound together in federations, of which the
Holy Roman Empire of the German heartland was the most notable example.
There were also a small number of republics. At the same time a number of strong
monarchies emerged and developed national identities.

Dynastic ambitions and historical circumstances combined to favor and then block the creation of an integrated European empire in the early sixteenth century. Electors of the Holy Roman Empire chose Charles V (r. 1519–1556) to be emperor in 1519. Like his predecessors for three generations, Charles belonged to the powerful **Habsburg** (HABZ-berg) family of Austria. Three years earlier he had inherited the kingdoms of Castile and Aragon, becoming the first monarch of Spain as Charles I. With these vast resources, Charles sought to turn back the advance of Islam on Europe's Mediterranean flank while contending with France for dominance of Italy. Charles and his allies did stop the Ottomans at the gates of Vienna in 1529, but the Ottoman Empire as well as North African Muslim states continued to attack his territories in Italy and Spain, supported at times by the Christian king Francis I of France, who was more interested in defeating Charles's ambitions than in defending Christian Europe.

With the beginning of the Reformation, Charles redirected his attention and his resources northward in support of the Counter-Reformation. Charles's defense of Catholic doctrine in the imperial Diet (assembly) was opposed by German princes swayed by Luther's appeals to German nationalism. These disputes led to open warfare in 1546 (the German Wars of Religion). Even though Charles could rely on the great wealth transferred to Spain from the conquests of Mexico and Peru (see Chapter 18), these costly and destructive religious wars drained his treasury and forced him to accept a stalemate in the Mediterranean with the Ottomans.

In the end the ambitions of Charles V were overwhelmed by the scale of his challenges, despite his enormous resources. In the Peace of Augsburg (1555) he recognized the right of German princes to choose whether Catholicism or Lutheranism would prevail in their particular states. He also accepted that Protestant princes would keep any church lands they had seized. This triumph of religious diversity ended Charles's political ambitions and put off German political unification for three centuries. In poor health and exhausted by his efforts, Charles decided to abdicate both the Holy Roman and Spanish thrones and retire to a monastery in 1556.

Charles V's son, Philip II, inherited his father's European territories in the low countries and Italy. Defending these legacies would drain his resources for decades.

He also inherited the throne of Spain with its rich American empire. In 1580 Philip inherited the throne of Portugal as well, adding Brazil and Portuguese colonies in Africa and Asia to his Spanish possessions. Ruler of sixteenth-century Europe's mightiest state, Philip II aggressively pursued the geopolitical policies that had thwarted his father. For a time, an accelerating flow of silver and gold from American colonies filled his treasury, but Philip's ambitions outstripped the flow of treasure, and he followed his father's practice of borrowing against future bullion shipments.

In the end, Philip's wars against the Ottomans, northern European Protestants, and rebellious Dutch subjects squandered the great wealth flowing through Iberian ports from the colonial empire, leading to four bankruptcies during his reign. Philip's ambitious military campaigns also increased his dependence on the Spanish nobility, which directed his military forces. While Spain's aristocracy made up only 3 percent of the population, it controlled 97 percent of the land in 1600 and was exempt from normal taxation. The nation's commoners, on the other hand, faced high sales taxes on manufacturing and commerce. In the end, Philip's commitments consumed the great wealth of his empire, leaving Spain unprepared to maintain its early domination of the Atlantic when faced by sustained challenges from the Dutch, English, and French.

American bullion shipments dramatically increased the money supply in Europe. In Spain the effects of the resulting inflation (rising prices) made the nation's products uncompetitive, so that goods manufactured in France, Italy, or other European countries were cheaper than goods made in Spain. In this distorted market, Spanish guilds and merchants lost ground while the pace of technological innovation and commercial expansion grew across northern Europe. By 1700 most goods imported into Spain's colonies were of foreign origin. A Spanish saying captured the problem: American silver was like rain on the roof—it poured down and washed away.

Philip's effort to seal Spain off from the Protestant Reformation and the intellectual tumult of the Scientific Revolution also imposed economic costs. He ordered the borders closed to all foreign publications not licensed by the Catholic Church and commanded all Spanish students to leave foreign universities and return home. Spain had longsuffered from the negative intellectual and economic effects of the expulsions of Jews and Muslims in the period of Ferdinand and Isabel, and now Philip's commitment to the Counter-Reformation further isolated the nation's intellectuals from the debates and innovations of the era.

Despite Spain's problems, its rulers, like those of France and England, enjoyed some success promoting national political unification and religious unity. The most successful rulers reduced the autonomy of the church and the nobility by making them part of a unified national structure with the monarch at its head. The imposition of royal power over religious institutions in the sixteenth century was stormy, but the eventual outcome was clear. Bringing the nobles and other powerful interests into a centralized political system took longer and led to more diverse outcomes.

The Monarchies of England and France   Over the course of the seventeenth century, the monarchs of England and France faced intense conflict with powerful rivals. Religion was never absent as an issue in these struggles, but the very different constitutional outcomes they produced in these two countries were of more significance in the long run.

To evade any check on his power, King Charles I of England (see Table 17.1) ruled for eleven years without summoning Parliament, his kingdom's representative

TABLE 17.1 | RULERS IN EARLY MODERN WESTERN EUROPE

Spain	France	England/Great Britain
Habsburg Dynasty	**Valois Dynasty**	**Tudor Dynasty**
Charles I (1516–1556)	Francis I (1515–1547)	Henry VIII (1509–1547)
(Holy Roman Emperor	Henry II (1547–1559)	Edward VI (1547–1553)
Charles V)	Francis II (1559–1560)	Mary I (1553–1558)
Philip II (1556–1598)	Charles IX (1560–1574)	Elizabeth I (1558–1603)
	Henry III (1574–1589)	
	Bourbon Dynasty	**Stuart Dynasty**
Philip III (1598–1621)	Henry IV (1589–1610)[a]	James I (1603–1625)
Philip IV (1621–1665)	Louis XIII (1610–1643)	Charles I (1625–1649)[a,b]
Charles II (1665–1700)	Louis XIV (1643–1715)	(Puritan Republic,
		1649–1660)
		Charles II (1660–1685)
		James II (1685–1688)[b]
		William III (1689–1702)
		and Mary II
Bourbon Dynasty		(1689–1694)
Philip V (1700–1746)		Anne (1702–1714)
	Hanoverian Dynasty	
	Louis XV (1715–1774)	George I (1714–1727)
Ferdinand VI (1746–1759)		George II (1727–1760)

[a]Died a violent death.
[b]Was overthrown.

© Cengage Learning

body. Lacking Parliament's consent to new taxes, he raised funds by coercing "loans" from wealthy subjects and applying existing tax laws more broadly. In 1640 a rebellion in Scotland forced him to summon Parliament to approve new taxes to pay for an army. Noblemen and churchmen sat in the House of Lords while representatives from towns and counties sat in the House of Commons. Before it would authorize new taxes, Parliament insisted on strict guarantees that the king would never again ignore the body's traditional rights. King Charles refused and attempted to arrest his critics in the House of Commons in 1642, plunging the kingdom into the **English Civil War**.

Militarily defeated in 1648, Charles refused to compromise. A year later a "Rump" Parliament purged of his supporters ordered his execution. Parliament then replaced the monarchy with a republic led by the Puritan general Oliver Cromwell, who ruled until his death in 1658. Cromwell expanded England's presence overseas and imposed firm control over Ireland and Scotland, but he was also unwilling to share power with Parliament. With his death, Parliament restored the Stuart line in the person of the executed king's son, Charles II (r. 1660–1685). James II, his brother, then inherited the throne, but he provoked new conflict by again refusing to respect Parliament's rights and by baptizing his heir as a Roman Catholic. The leaders of Parliament forced him into exile in the bloodless Glorious Revolution of 1688. The Bill of Rights of 1689 formalized this new constitutional order by requiring the king to call Parliament frequently to consent to changes in laws or to raise an army in peacetime. Another law reaffirmed the official status of the Church of England but extended religious toleration to dissenting Puritans.

In France the Estates General, like the English Parliament, represented the traditional rights of the clergy, the nobility, and the towns (that is, the bourgeoisie). The Estates General was able to assert its rights during the sixteenth-century French Wars of Religion, when the monarchy was weak. Thereafter France's Bourbon monarchs generally ruled without calling it into session. They put off financial crises by more efficient tax collection and by selling appointments to high government offices, but by 1700 French debt levels challenged traditional fiscal practice. While some historians have used the term *absolutism* to describe the power of French monarchs in this era, even the most powerful, Louis XIV, carefully negotiated his policies with both the nobility and city authorities. While the king's power grew, long-established ways of governing like the sale of offices and reliance on patronage networks and personal relationships continued to frame decision making.

Louis XIV moved his court to a gigantic new palace at **Versailles** (vuhr-SIGH) in 1682. Capable of housing ten thousand people and surrounded by elaborately landscaped grounds and parks, the palace became an effective symbol of growing royal grandeur and power. The relocation of the court to this splendid palace created an arena where the high nobility and ecclesiastical hierarchy more intensely interacted with the monarch in a dense cycle of rituals and ceremonies that emphasized royal power.

Most contemporary European rulers admired and imitated the centralized powers and apparent absolutist authority of the French monarch. The checks and balances of the English model were more admired in later times and gained a favorable press with the beginnings of the Enlightenment. In his influential *Second Treatise of Civil Government* (1690), for example, the English political philosopher John Locke (1632–1704) disputed monarchial claims to absolute authority by divine right, arguing that rulers derived their authority from the consent of the governed and were subject to the law. If monarchs overstepped the law, Locke asserted, citizens had the right and the duty to rebel. The consequences of this idea are considered in Chapter 23.

Warfare and Diplomacy   In addition to the civil wars that afflicted the Holy Roman Empire, France, and England, European states fought numerous international conflicts provoked in part by efforts to protect or extend colonial empires. As a result, the major European nations were nearly always at war somewhere (see the Chronology at the beginning of the chapter). As the geographic scope of warfare and the size of armies and navies grew, monarchs expended ever-larger sums of money and caused widespread devastation and death. The worst of the international conflicts, the Thirty Years' War (1618–1648), caused long-lasting depopulation and economic decline in much of the Holy Roman Empire.

These wars led to dramatic improvements in the skill and weaponry of European armed forces, making them among the most powerful in the world. The numbers of men in arms increased steadily throughout the early modern period. French forces, for example, grew from 88 regiments of infantry and 72 of cavalry in 1691 to 238 regiments of infantry and 94 of cavalry in 1714. Even smaller European states built up impressive armies. Sweden, for example, with under a million people, had one of the finest and best-armed military forces in the seventeenth century, and Prussia, though it had fewer than 2 million inhabitants in 1700, boasted a large, well-disciplined army that made it one of Europe's major powers.

Larger armies required more effective command structures. But although some progress was made, the officer corps of the major powers was largely drawn from the nobility, and patronage, not skill, guided promotion and advancement. Training and battlefield control were marginally improved through more frequent drilling for professional troops and the introduction of new signaling techniques, but battlefields remained chaotic. Fortifications were expanded and improved in Europe and in colonial possessions, and even Spain, facing a deep fiscal crisis, borrowed to fortify Havana and Cartagena in the Americas. Paying for larger and better-armed fleets proved similarly expensive, but in the face of an intensifying competition for colonial wealth that stretched from the East Indies to the Caribbean and South Atlantic, no great power could afford to cut back.

Safe from the threat of direct invasion, only England among major European powers did not maintain a standing army. Its power depended on its navy. England's rise as a sea power had begun under King Henry VIII, who spent heavily on ships and promoted a domestic iron industry to supply cannon. The Royal Navy also copied innovative ship designs from the Dutch in the second half of the seventeenth century. The crushing defeat of the Spanish Armada in 1588 by Henry's daughter, Elizabeth I, demonstrated the usefulness of these decisions and accelerated Spain's decline under Philip II. By the early eighteenth century, the Royal Navy had surpassed the rival French fleet in numbers. Now more secure, England merged with Scotland to become Great Britain. It then annexed Ireland and built a North American empire.

As nations built up their strength, they also acted to preserve a **balance of power**. Although France was Europe's most powerful state, coalitions of the other great powers frustrated Louis XIV's efforts to expand its borders. In a series of costly eighteenth-century wars beginning with the War of the Spanish Succession (1701–1714), the combination of Britain's naval strength and the land armies of Austria and Prussia blocked French expansionist efforts and prevented the Bourbons from uniting the thrones of France and Spain.

Paying the Piper   European nations struggled to pay these heavy military costs while at the same time funding expanded bureaucracies, infrastructure improvements, and the growing extravagance of monarchs, but the obstacles were formidable. Governments collected taxes indirectly using **tax farmers**, private individuals who paid a flat rate to the government, typically less than 50 percent of the estimated tax obligation, for the right to collect the tax. This

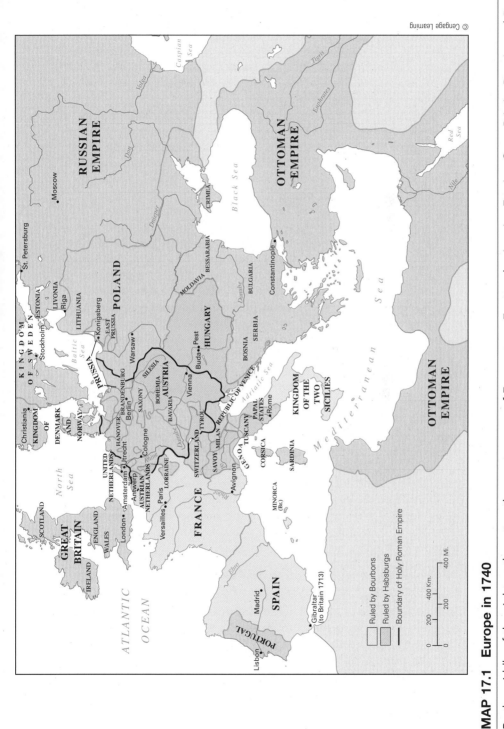

MAP 17.1 Europe in 1740

By the middle of the eighteenth century the great powers of Europe were France, the Austrian Empire, Great Britain, Prussia, and Russia. Spain, the Holy Roman Empire, and the Ottoman Empire were far weaker in 1740 than they had been two centuries earlier.

system allowed governments to avoid creating expensive new bureaucracies, but it also guaranteed corruption and limited revenue growth. The tax exemptions enjoyed by the nobility and clergy were among the greatest obstacles to increasing revenues, since these sectors controlled most of Europe's wealth. In the case of France and Spain, this situation led to the imposition of regressive new taxes on peasants and on commerce. Desperate governments were therefore attracted to dangerous short-term fiscal expedients that included currency debasement and cynical defaults on debts like Philip II's four bankruptcies.

It was inevitable that the success of early capitalism's innovations—joint-stock companies and stock markets—would draw the attention of governments thwarted by the tax intransigence of the elite to look to these highly speculative and largely unregulated novelties to solve fiscal problems. The results were spectacularly visible in two nearly simultaneous speculative bubbles associated with the French Mississippi Company and the English South Sea Company.

After debasing the value of the nation's silver and gold coinage, the French government granted a license to create a bank to a fugitive Scottish nobleman, John Law, in 1716. The bank was allowed to issue paper money based on the promise to exchange these bills at face value for silver or gold coin. To everyone's surprise, the notes issued by Law's bank not only maintained their value but were preferred to coin for many transactions. As a result, the value of shares in the bank increased dramatically. Then in 1717 the French government allowed Law to create a monopoly company to develop French colonial territories along the Mississippi, a region erroneously believed to have rich mines. The value of the initial share offering soared and was supplemented by issues of additional shares that also quickly increased in value. In the midst of the bubble, prices for shares rose 10 or 20 percent in the course of a few hours. Stories of once-poor servants buying mansions and marrying their children into noble families abounded.

As the frenzy for shares mounted, the French government used Law's bank to print more paper money. After all, it was much easier to print money than collect taxes. The bank's apparent success fed a speculative bubble in Mississippi Company shares as well, even though the company never earned a profit. Then, in 1720, fears that the bank no longer had the resources to exchange coin for its paper bills put pressure on the entire edifice. Even though Law got the government to first discount gold and silver coin against the paper currency and then to restrict individual possession of coin, a nervous French public hoarded coins and avoided paper currency. This situation led to the panicked selling of shares in both the bank and the Mississippi Company. As huge amounts of paper wealth disappeared in a matter of days, Law was forced to run for his life, leaving the French government to face once again its structural fiscal crisis.

In the English example, in 1711 the English lord treasurer created the South Sea Company and granted it exclusive rights to trade with the Spanish colonies in the Americas. While the company issued stock that traded freely in the nation's nascent stock market, it was primarily a scheme to reduce the government's huge wartime debt. Holders of these debts were forced by statute to accept shares in the company to replace government debt obligations. Once in possession of the government bonds, the company borrowed new funds based on the supposed security of government debt. To individual investors, the South Sea Company seemed a profitable investment because it enjoyed both large annual interest payments from the government and a monopoly right to trade slaves to the Spanish colonies. In 1719, with news of the fast-rising share values of the French Mississippi Company on everyone's lips, the British government used the company to transform another £30,000,000 in debt into shares. When South Sea shares issued at £300 rose to £325, the company issued more stock, even though the company had almost no income from its commercial ventures.

In January 1720 share prices reached £1,050 before the inevitable crash dropped prices to £128 and thousands of investors found themselves ruined. Among the investors was the scientist Isaac Newton, who said, "I can calculate the motions of the heavenly bodies but not the madness of people." While financial markets would eventually recover from these crashes and grow stronger still, the governments of France and Britain would now be forced to pay their bills by imposing taxes on reluctant citizens (see Chapter 23).

The rise of the Netherlands as an economic power stemmed from very different policies. The Spanish crown had acquired these resource-poor but commercially successful provinces as part of Charles V's inheritance. The decision of his son, King Philip II, to impose Spain's ruinous sales tax and to enforce Catholic orthodoxy drove the Dutch to revolt in 1566 and again in 1572. If successful, those measures would have discouraged business and driven away the Calvinists, Jews, and others who were essential to Dutch prosperity. The Dutch fought with skill and ingenuity, raising and training an army and a navy that were among the most effective in Europe. Unable to bear the military costs any longer, Spain accepted a truce that recognized autonomy in the northern Netherlands in 1609. Finally, in 1648, the independence of the seven United Provinces of the Free Netherlands (their full name) became final.

Rather than being ruined by the long war, the Netherlands emerged as the world's greatest trading nation. This economic success owed much to a decentralized government. During the long struggle against Spain, the provinces united around the prince of Orange, their sovereign, who served as commander-in-chief of the armed forces. But in economic matters each province was free to pursue its own interests. The maritime province of Holland grew rich by favoring commercial interests.

After 1650 the Dutch faced growing competition from the English, who were developing their own close association of business and government. In a series of wars (1652–1678) England used its naval might to break Dutch dominance in overseas trade and extend its own colonial empire. With government support, the English merchant fleet doubled between 1660 and 1700, and foreign trade rose by 50 percent. As a result, state revenue from customs duties tripled. During the eighteenth century Britain's trading position strengthened still more.

The debts run up by the Anglo-Dutch Wars helped persuade the English monarchy to greatly enlarge the government's role in managing the economy. Instead of continuing to use tax farmers, the government increased revenues by taxing the formerly exempt landed estates of the aristocrats and by collecting taxes directly. To secure cash quickly for warfare and other emergencies and to reduce the burden of debts from earlier wars, England imitated the Dutch by creating a central bank that could issue long-term loans at low rates.

The French government also developed its national economy, especially under the royal adviser Jean Baptiste Colbert. He streamlined tax collection, promoted French manufacturing and shipping by imposing taxes on foreign goods, and improved transportation within France itself. Yet the power of the wealthy aristocrats kept the French government from following England's lead in taxing wealthy landowners, collecting taxes directly, and securing low-cost loans. Nor did France succeed in managing its debt as efficiently as England. (The role of governments in promoting overseas trade is also discussed in Chapter 19.)

CONCLUSION

Early modern Europe witnessed the weakening of the Catholic Church and the Protestant Reformation. Rejecting the authority of the pope and criticizing the institution of indulgences, Luther insisted on the moral primacy of faith over deeds; Calvin went further, holding that salvation was predestined by God. The pioneers of the Scientific Revolution such as Copernicus and Newton showed that they could explain the workings of the physical universe in natural terms. These scientists did not see any conflict between science and religion, but they paved the way for more secular thinkers of the Enlightenment, who believed that human reason was capable of—and responsible for—discovering the laws that govern social behavior.

Thanks to foreign and domestic trade, European cities in this period experienced rapid growth and the rise of a wealthy commercial class. It was also an era of growing speculative risk and market bubbles like Tulipmania and the Mississippi Company and South Sea bubbles. The Netherlands in particular prospered from expanded manufacturing and trade: with the formation of joint-stock companies and a powerful stock market, Amsterdam became Europe's major port and financial center. For peasants and laborers, however, life did not improve much, although serfdom was all but ended in western Europe. Rural poverty, coupled with the exemption from taxation enjoyed by wealthy landowners, sparked numerous armed rebellions. Women were dependent on their families' and husbands' wealth or lack of it and were barred from attending schools or joining guilds and professions.

Differing policies in the areas of religion, foreign relations, and economics explain the different histories of Europe's early modern states. Charles V, unable to reconcile the diverse interests of his Catholic and Protestant territories and their powerful local rulers, failed to create a unified Holy Roman Empire. Henry VIII, having failed to win an annulment of his marriage to Catherine of Aragon, severed all ties with the pope and led Parliament to accept him as head of the Church of England. Power struggles in England in the seventeenth century led to a stronger Parliament, while in contemporary France a stronger monarchy emerged, symbolized by Louis XIV's construction of the palace at Versailles. Spain was Europe's mightiest state in the sixteenth century, but its failure to suppress the Netherlands Revolt and the costs of other wars led to bankruptcy and decline. In the seventeenth century the United Netherlands became the dominant commercial power on the continent.

The growth of English naval power led to the defeat of the Dutch in the Anglo-Dutch Wars and of France in the early eighteenth century when it attempted to expand its own empire through a union with Spain. Unlike Spain and France, which maintained aristocrats' traditional exemption from taxation, England began to tax their estates, and this policy—together with the establishment of direct taxation and the creation of a central bank from which it could secure low-cost loans—gave England a stronger financial foundation than its rivals enjoyed.

IMPORTANT EVENTS 1500–1750

1519	Protestant Reformation begins
1526–1571	Ottoman wars
1540s	Scientific Revolution begins
1545	Catholic Reformation begins
1546–1555	German Wars of Religion
1562–1598	French Wars of Religion
1566–1648	Netherlands Revolt
1590s	Dutch develop flyboats; Little Ice Age begins
1609	Galileo's astronomical telescope
1618–1648	Thirty Years War
1642–1648	English Civil War
1652–1678	Anglo-Dutch Wars
1667–1697	Wars of Louis XIV
1682	Canal du Midi completed
1683–1697	Ottoman wars
1700s	The Enlightenment begins
1700–1721	Great Northern War
1701–1714	War of the Spanish Succession
1755	Lisbon Earthquake

18

THE DIVERSITY OF AMERICAN COLONIAL SOCIETIES, 1530–1770

Shulush Homa—an eighteenth-century Choctaw leader called "Red Shoes" by the English—faced a dilemma. For years he had befriended the French who had moved into the lower Mississippi Valley, protecting their outlying settlements from other indigenous groups and producing a steady flow of deerskins for trade. In return he received guns and gifts as well as honors previously given only to chiefs. Though born a commoner, he had parlayed his skillful politicking with the French—and the shrewd distribution of the gifts he received—to enhance his position in Choctaw society. Then his fortunes turned. In the course of yet another war between England and France, the English cut off French shipping. Faced with followers unhappy over his sudden inability to supply French guns, Red Shoes forged a dangerous new arrangement with the English that led his former allies, the French, to put a price on his head. His murder in 1747 launched a civil war among the Choctaw. By the end of this conflict both the French colonial population and the Choctaw people had suffered greatly.

The story of Red Shoes reveals a number of themes from the period of European colonization of the Americas. First, although the wars, epidemics, and territorial loss associated with European settlement threatened Amerindians, many adapted the new technologies and new political possibilities to their own purposes and thrived—at least for a time. In the end, though, the best that they could achieve was a holding action. The people of the Old World were coming to dominate the people of the New World.

Second, after centuries of isolation, the political and economic demands of European empires forced the Americas onto the global stage. The influx of Europeans and Africans resulted in a vast biological and cultural transformation, as new plants, animals, diseases, peoples, and technologies fundamentally altered the natural environment. This was not a one-way transfer, however. The technologies and resources of the New World also contributed to profound changes in the Old. Among them, American staple crops helped fuel a population spurt in Europe, Asia, and Africa while American riches altered European economic, social, and political relations.

Third, the story of Red Shoes and the Choctaw illustrates the complexity of colonial society, in which Amerindians, Europeans, and Africans all contributed to the creation of new cultures. Although similar processes took place throughout the

Americas, the particulars varied from place to place, creating a diverse range of cultures. The society that arose in each colony reflected the colony's mix of native peoples, its connections to the slave trade, and the characteristics of the European society establishing the colony. As the colonies matured, new concepts of identity developed, and those living in the Americas began to see themselves as distinct.

THE COLUMBIAN EXCHANGE

The term **Columbian Exchange** refers to the transfer of peoples, animals, plants, and diseases between the New and Old Worlds. The European invasion and settlement of the Western Hemisphere opened a long era of biological and technological transfers that altered American environments. Within a century of the first European settlement, the domesticated livestock and major agricultural crops of the Old World (the known world before Columbus's voyage) had spread over much of the Americas, and the New World's useful staple crops had enriched the agricultures of Europe, Asia, and Africa. Old World diseases that entered the Americas with European immigrants and African slaves devastated indigenous populations. These dramatic population changes weakened native peoples' capacity for resistance and accelerated the transfer of plants, animals, and related technologies. As a result, the colonies of Spain, Portugal, England, and France became vast arenas of cultural and social experimentation.

Demographic Changes   Because of their long isolation from other continents (see Chapter 15), the peoples of the New World lacked immunity to diseases introduced from the Old World. As a result, death rates among Amerindian peoples during the epidemics of the early colonial period were very high. The lack of reliable estimates of the Amerindian population at the moment of contact has frustrated efforts to measure the deadly impact of these diseases, but scholars agree that Old World diseases had a terrible effect on native peoples. According to one estimate, the population of central Mexico fell from more than 13 million to approximately 700,000 in the century that followed 1521. In this same period the populations of the Maya and Inka regions declined by nearly 75 percent or more. Brazil's native population fell by more than 50 percent within a century of the arrival of the Portuguese.

Smallpox, which arrived in the Caribbean in 1518, was the most deadly of the early epidemics. In Mexico and Central America, 50 percent or more of the Amerindian population died during the first wave of smallpox epidemics. The disease then spread to South America with equally devastating effects. Measles arrived in the New World in the 1530s and was followed by diphtheria, typhus, influenza, and pulmonary plague. Mortality was often greatest when two or more diseases struck at the same time. Between 1520 and 1521 influenza and other ailments attacked the Cakchiquel of Guatemala. Their chronicle recalls:

> Great was the stench of the dead. After our fathers and grandfathers succumbed, half the people fled to the fields. The dogs and vultures devoured the bodies.... So it was that we became orphans, oh my sons! ... We were born to die![1]

---

[1]Quoted in Alfred W. Crosby, Jr., *The Columbian Exchange: Biological and Cultural Consequences of 1492* (Westport, CT: Greenwood, 1972), 58.

By the mid-seventeenth century malaria and yellow fever were also present in tropical regions of the Americas. The deadliest form of malaria arrived with the African slave trade, ravaging the already reduced native populations and afflicting Europeans as well.

The development of English and French colonies in North America in the seventeenth century led to similar patterns of contagion and mortality. In 1616 and 1617 epidemics nearly exterminated New England's indigenous groups. Epidemics also followed French fur traders as far as Hudson Bay and the Great Lakes. Although there is very little evidence that Europeans consciously used disease as a tool of empire, the deadly results of contact clearly undermined the ability of native peoples to resist settlement.

Transfer of Plants and Animals   Even as epidemics swept through the indigenous population, the New and the Old Worlds were participating in a vast exchange of plants and animals that radically altered diet and lifestyles in both regions. Settlers brought all the staples of southern European agriculture—such as wheat, olives, grapes, and garden vegetables—to the Americas soon after contact. Colonization also introduced African and Asian crops such as rice, bananas, coconuts, breadfruit, and sugar. While natives remained loyal to their traditional staples, they added many foods like citrus fruits, melons, figs, and sugar as well as onions, radishes, and salad greens to their cuisines.

In return the Americas offered the Old World an abundance of useful plants. Maize, potatoes, and manioc revolutionized agriculture and diet in parts of Europe, Africa, and Asia. Many experts assert that the growth of world population after 1700 resulted from the spread of these useful crops, which provided more calories per acre than did most Old World staples. Beans, squash, tomatoes, sweet potatoes, peanuts, chilies, and chocolate also gained widespread acceptance in the Old World. In addition, the New World provided the Old with plants that provided dyes, medicine, varieties of cotton, and tobacco.

The introduction of European livestock had a dramatic impact on New World environments and cultures. Faced with few natural predators, cattle, pigs, horses, and sheep, as well as pests like rats and rabbits, multiplied rapidly in the Americas. On the vast plains of southern Brazil, Uruguay, and Argentina, for example, herds of wild cattle and horses exceeded 50 million by 1700.

Where Old World livestock spread most rapidly, environmental changes were dramatic. Many priests and colonial officials noted the destructive impact of marauding livestock on Amerindian agriculturists. The first viceroy of Mexico, Antonio de Mendoza, wrote to the Spanish king: "May your Lordship realize that if cattle are allowed, the Indians will be destroyed." Sheep, which grazed grasses close to the ground, were also an environmental threat.

Yet the viceroy's stark choice misrepresented the complex response of indigenous peoples to these new animals. For example, wild cattle on the plains of South America, northern Mexico, and Texas also provided indigenous peoples with abundant supplies of meat and hides. In the present-day southwestern United States, the Navajo became sheepherders and expert weavers. Even in the centers of European settlement, Amerindians turned European animals to their own advantage by becoming muleteers, cowboys, and sheepherders.

No animal had a more striking effect on the cultures of native peoples than the horse, which increased the efficiency of hunters and the military capacity of warriors on the plains. The horse permitted the Apache, Sioux, Blackfoot, Comanche, Assiniboine, and others to more efficiently hunt the vast herds of buffalo in North America. The horse also revolutionized the cultures of the Mapuche and Pampas peoples in South America.

SPANISH AMERICA AND BRAZIL

The frontiers of conquest and settlement expanded rapidly. Within one hundred years of Columbus's first voyage to the Western Hemisphere, the Spanish Empire in America included most of the islands of the Caribbean and a vast area that stretched from northern Mexico to the plains of the Rio de la Plata region (a region that includes the modern nations of Argentina, Uruguay, and Paraguay). Portuguese settlement developed more slowly, but before the end of the sixteenth century, Portugal had occupied most of the Brazilian coast.

Early settlers from Spain and Portugal sought to create colonial societies based on the institutions and customs of their homelands. They viewed society as a vertical hierarchy of estates (classes of society), as uniformly Catholic, and as an arrangement of patriarchal extended-family networks. They quickly moved to establish the religious, social, and administrative institutions that were familiar to them.

Despite the imposition of foreign institutions and loss of life caused by epidemics, indigenous peoples exercised a powerful influence on the development of colonial societies. Aztec and Inka elite families sought to protect their traditional privileges and rights through marriage or less formal alliances with Spanish settlers. They also used colonial courts to defend their claims to land. In Spanish and Portuguese colonies, indigenous military allies and laborers proved crucial to the development of European settlements. Nearly everywhere, Amerindian religious beliefs and practices survived beneath the surface of an imposed Christianity. Amerindian languages, cuisines, medical practices, and agricultural techniques also survived the conquest and influenced the development of Latin American culture.

The African slave trade added a third cultural stream to colonial Latin American society. At first, African slaves were concentrated in plantation regions of Brazil and the Caribbean (see Chapter 19), but by the end of the colonial era, Africans and their descendants were living throughout Spanish and Portuguese America, introducing elements of their agricultural practices, music, religious beliefs, cuisine, and social customs to colonial societies.

State and Church   The Spanish crown moved quickly to curb the independent power of the conquistadors and to establish royal authority over both defeated native populations and European settlers, but geography and technology thwarted this ambition. European officials could not control the distant colonies too closely because it took a ship more than two hundred days to make a roundtrip voyage from Spain to Veracruz, Mexico. Additional months of travel were required to reach Lima, Peru.

As a result, the highest-ranking Spanish officials in the colonies, the viceroys of New Spain and Peru, enjoyed broad power, but they also faced obstacles to their authority in the vast territories they sought to control. Created in 1535, the Viceroyalty of New Spain, with its capital in Mexico City, included Mexico, the southwest of what is now the United States, Central America, and the islands of the

Caribbean. Created five years later, the Viceroyalty of Peru, with its capital in Lima, governed all of Spanish South America.

Until the seventeenth century, most colonial officials were born in Spain, but fiscal mismanagement eventually forced the Crown to sell appointments. As a result, local-born members of the colonial elite gained many offices.

In the sixteenth century Portugal concentrated its resources and energies on Asia and Africa. Because early settlers found neither mineral wealth nor rich native empires in Brazil, the Portuguese king was slow to create expensive mechanisms of colonial government in the New World, but mismanagement forced the king to appoint a governor-general in 1549 and make Salvador Brazil's capital. In 1720 the king named the first viceroy of Brazil.

The government institutions of the Spanish and Portuguese colonies had a more uniform character and were much more extensive and costly than those later established in North America by France and Great Britain. The enormous wealth produced in Spanish America by silver and gold mines and in Brazil by sugar plantations and, after 1690, gold mines financed these large and intrusive colonial bureaucracies. These institutions made the colonies more responsive to the initiatives of Spanish and Portuguese monarchs, but they also thwarted local economic initiative and political experimentation. More importantly, the heavy tax burden imposed by these two European states drained capital from the colonies, slowing investment and retarding economic growth.

In both Spanish America and Brazil, the Catholic Church became the primary agent for the introduction and transmission of Christian belief as well as European language and culture. The church undertook the conversion of Amerindians, ministered to the spiritual needs of European settlers, and promoted intellectual life through the introduction of the printing press and the founding of schools and universities.

Spain and Portugal justified their American conquests by assuming an obligation to convert native populations to Christianity. This effort to convert America's native peoples expanded Christianity on a scale similar to its earlier expansion in Europe at the time of Constantine in the fourth century. In New Spain alone hundreds of thousands of conversions and baptisms were achieved within a few years of the conquest. However, the small numbers of missionaries limited the quality of indoctrination. One Dominican claimed to the king that the rival Franciscans "have taken and occupied three fourths of the country, though they do not have enough friars for it. . . . In most places they are content to say a mass once a year; consider what sort of indoctrination they give them!"[2]

The Catholic clergy sought to achieve their evangelical ends by first converting members of the Amerindian elites, in the hope that they could persuade others to follow their example. To pursue this objective, Franciscan missionaries in Mexico created a seminary to train members of the indigenous elite to become priests, but they curtailed these idealistic efforts when church authorities discovered that many converts were secretly observing old beliefs and rituals. The trial and punishment of two converted Aztec nobles for heresy in the 1530s and the torture of hundreds of Maya in the 1560s repelled the church hierarchy and led it to end the violent

---

[2]Fray Andés de Moguer, 1554, quoted in James Lockhart and Enrique Otte, eds., *Letters and People of the Spanish Indies Sixteenth Century* (Cambridge, U.K. Cambridge University Press: 1976), 216.

Saint Martín de Porres (1579–1639)

Martín de Porres was the illegitimate son of a Spanish nobleman and a black servant. He entered the Dominican Order in Lima, Peru, where he was known for his generosity, his religious visions, and his ability to heal the sick. In this painting the artist celebrates Martín de Porres's spirituality while representing him doing the type of work presumed to be suitable for a person of mixed descent.

Private Collection

repression of native religious practice and limit the recruitment of an Amerindian clergy. In Peru a native millenarian movement sought to roll back the Christian evangelical effort in 1564, leading after 1609 to a focused effort by the Catholic Church to eradicate surviving indigenous belief and ritual.

Despite its failures, the Catholic clergy did provide native peoples with some protections against the abuse and exploitation of Spanish settlers. The priest **Bartolomé de Las Casas** (1474–1566) was the most influential defender of the Amerindians in the early colonial period. He arrived in Hispaniola in 1502 as a settler and initially lived from the forced labor of Amerindians. Deeply moved by the deaths of so many Amerindians and by the misdeeds of the Spanish, Las Casas entered the Dominican Order and later became the first bishop of Chiapas, in southern Mexico. For the remainder of his long life Las Casas served as the most important advocate for native peoples. His most important achievement was the enactment of the New Laws of 1542—reform legislation that outlawed the enslavement of Amerindians and limited other forms of forced labor.

European clergy had arrived in the Americas with the intention of transmitting Catholic Christian belief and ritual without alteration. The linguistic diversity of Amerindian populations and their geographic dispersal over a vast landscape defeated this ambition. The resulting slow progress and limited success of evangelization led to the appearance of a unique Amerindian Christianity that blended European Christian beliefs with important elements of traditional native cosmology and ritual. The Catholic clergy and most European settlers viewed this evolving mixture as the work of the Devil or as evidence of Amerindian inferiority. Instead, it was one component of the process of cultural borrowing and innovation that contributed to a distinct and original Latin American culture.

After 1600 the terrible loss of Amerindian population caused by epidemics and growing signs of resistance to conversion led the Catholic Church to redirect most of its resources from native regions in the countryside to growing colonial cities and towns with large European populations. One important outcome of this altered mission was the founding of universities and secondary schools and the stimulation of urban intellectual life. Over time, the church became the richest institution in the Spanish colonies, controlling ranches, plantations, and vineyards as well as serving as the society's banker.

Colonial Economies

The silver mines of Peru and Mexico and the sugar plantations of Brazil dominated the economic development of colonial Latin America. The mineral wealth of the New World fueled the early development of European capitalism and funded Europe's greatly expanded trade with Asia. Profits produced in these economic centers also promoted the growth of colonial cities, concentrated scarce investment capital and labor resources, and stimulated the development of livestock raising and agriculture in neighboring rural areas. Once established, this colonial dependence on mineral and agricultural exports left an enduring social and economic legacy in Latin America.

The Spanish and later the Portuguese produced gold worth millions of pesos, but silver mines in the Spanish colonies generated the most wealth and therefore exercised the greatest economic influence. The first important silver strikes occurred in Mexico in the 1530s and 1540s. In 1545 the Spanish discovered the single richest silver deposit in the Americas at **Potosí** (poh-toh-SEE) in Alto Peru (what is now Bolivia). The silver of Alto Peru and Peru dominated the Spanish colonial economy until 1680, when it was surpassed by Mexican silver production. At first, miners extracted silver ore by smelting, a process during which crushed ore, packed with charcoal, was fired in a furnace. But this wasteful use of forest resources led to deforestation near the mining centers. Faced with rising fuel costs, Mexican miners developed an efficient method of chemical extraction that relied on mixing mercury with the silver ore. Silver yields and profits increased with the use of mercury amalgamation, but this process, too, had severe environmental costs, since mercury is a poison that contaminated the environment and sickened the Amerindian workforce.

From the time of Columbus, indigenous populations had been compelled to provide labor for European settlers in the Americas. Until the 1540s in Spanish colonies, Spanish authorities divided Amerindians among settlers, who forced them to provide labor or goods. This form of forced labor was called **encomienda** (in-co-mee-EN-dah). As epidemics and mistreatment led to the decline in Amerindian population, reforms such as the New Laws sought to eliminate the encomienda. The discovery of silver, however, led to new forms of compulsory labor. In the mining region of Mexico, where epidemics had reduced Amerindian populations, silver miners came to rely on wage laborers. Peru's Amerindian population survived in larger numbers, allowing the Spanish to impose a form of labor called the mita (MEE-tah). Under this system, one-seventh of adult male Amerindians were compelled to work for two to four months each year in mines, farms, or textile factories.

As the Amerindian population declined with new epidemics, villages were forced to shorten the period between mita obligations. Instead of serving every seven years, many men returned to mines after only a year or two. Unwilling to accept mita service and the other tax burdens imposed on Amerindian villages, thousands abandoned traditional agriculture and moved permanently to Spanish mines and farms as laborers. The long-term result of these individual decisions weakened Amerindian village life and promoted the assimilation of Amerindians into Spanish-speaking Catholic colonial society.

Before the settlement of Brazil, the Portuguese had already developed sugar plantations using African slave labor on the Atlantic islands of Madeira, the Azores, the Cape Verdes, and São Tomé. Because of the success of these early experiences, they were able to quickly transfer this profitable form of agriculture to Brazil. After 1540 sugar production expanded rapidly, and by the seventeenth century it dominated the Brazilian economy.

At first the Portuguese sugar planters enslaved Amerindians captured in war or seized from their villages. As a result of the epidemics that raged across Brazil in the sixteenth and seventeenth centuries thousands of Amerindian slaves died, creating a labor shortage. Slave raiders then pushed into the interior, even attacking Amerindian populations in neighboring Spanish colonies.

Amerindian slaves remained an important source of labor and slave raiding a significant business in frontier regions into the eighteenth century. But sugar planters eventually came to rely more on African slaves. African slaves at first cost much more than Amerindian slaves, but planters found them more productive and more resistant to disease. As profits from the plantations increased, imports of African slaves rose from an average of two thousand per year in the late sixteenth century to approximately seven thousand per year a century later, outstripping the immigration of free Portuguese settlers. Between 1650 and 1750, for example, nearly five African slaves arrived in Brazil for every immigrant from Europe.

Within Spanish America, the mining centers of Mexico and Peru eventually exercised global economic influence. American silver increased the European money supply, promoting commercial expansion and, later, industrialization. Large amounts of silver also flowed to Asia. Both Europe and the Iberian colonies of Latin America ran chronic trade deficits with Asia. As a result, massive amounts of Peruvian and Mexican silver flowed to Asia via Middle Eastern middlemen or across the Pacific to the Spanish colony of the Philippines, where it paid for Asian spices, silks, and pottery.

The rich mines of Peru, Bolivia, and Mexico stimulated urban population growth as well as commercial links with distant agricultural and textile producers. The population of the city of Potosí, high in the Andes, reached 120,000 inhabitants by 1625. This rich mining town became the center of a vast regional market that depended on Chilean wheat, Argentine livestock, and Ecuadorian textiles.

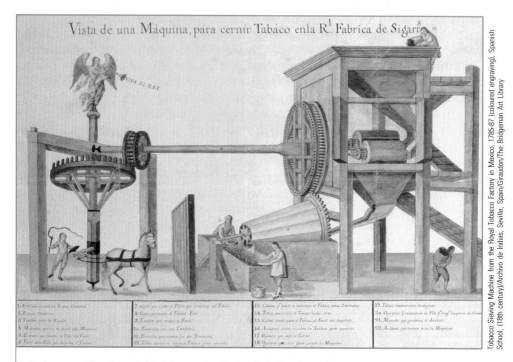

Vista de una Máquina, para cernír Tabáco enla R¹ Fabrica de Sigar⁵

VIVA EL REY

Tobacco Factory Machinery in Colonial Mexico City *The tobacco factory in eighteenth-century Mexico City used a horse-driven mechanical shredder to produce snuff and cigarette tobacco.*

The sugar plantations of Brazil played a similar role in integrating the economy of the south Atlantic region. Brazil exchanged sugar, tobacco, and reexported slaves for yerba (Paraguayan tea), hides, livestock, and silver produced in neighboring Spanish colonies. Portugal's increasing openness to British trade also allowed Brazil to become a conduit for an illegal trade between Spanish colonies and Europe. At the end of the seventeenth century, the discovery of gold in Brazil promoted further regional and international economic integration.

Society in Colonial Latin America
With the exception of some early viceroys, few members of Spain's nobility came to the New World. *Hidalgos* (ee-DAHL-goes)—lesser nobles—were well represented, as were Spanish merchants, artisans, miners, priests, and lawyers. Small numbers of criminals, beggars, and prostitutes also found their way to the colonies. This flow of immigrants from Spain was never large, and Spanish settlers were always a tiny minority in a colonial society numerically dominated by Amerindians and rapidly growing populations of Africans, **creoles** (whites born in America to European parents), and people of mixed ancestry (see Diversity and Dominance: Race and Ethnicity in the Spanish Colonies: Negotiating Hierarchy).

The most powerful conquistadors and early settlers sought to create a hereditary social and political class comparable to the European nobility. But their systematic abuse of Amerindian communities and the catastrophic effects of the epidemics of the sixteenth century undermined their control of colonial society. With the passage of time colonial officials, the clergy, and the richest merchants came to dominate the social hierarchy. Europeans controlled the highest levels of the church and government as well as commerce, while wealthy American-born creoles exercised a similar role in colonial agriculture and mining. Although tensions between Spaniards and creoles were inevitable, most elite families included both groups.

Before the Europeans arrived in the Americas, the native peoples were members of a large number of distinct cultural and linguistic groups. The effects of conquest and epidemics undermined this rich social and cultural complexity, and the relocation of Amerindian peoples to promote conversion or provide labor further eroded ethnic boundaries among native peoples. Application of the racial label *Indian* by colonial administrators and settlers helped organize the tribute and labor demands imposed on native peoples, but it also registered the cultural costs of colonial rule.

Amerindian elites struggled to survive in the new political and economic environments created by military defeat and European settlement. Some sought to protect their positions by forging marriage or less formal relations with colonists. As a result, some indigenous and settler families were tied together by kinship in the decades after conquest, but these links weakened with the passage of time. Indigenous leaders also established political alliances with members of the colonial administrative classes. Hereditary native elites gained some security by becoming essential intermediaries between the indigenous masses and colonial administrators, collecting Spanish taxes and organizing the labor of their dependents for colonial enterprises.

Indigenous commoners suffered the heaviest burdens. Tribute payments, forced labor obligations, and the loss of traditional land rights were common. European domination dramatically changed the indigenous world by breaking the connections between peoples and places and transforming religious life, marriage practices, diet, and material culture. The survivors of these terrible shocks learned to adapt to the new colonial environment by embracing some elements of the dominant colonial culture or entering the market economies of the cities. They also learned new forms of resistance, like using colonial courts to protect community lands or to resist the abuses of corrupt officials.

Thousands of blacks, many born in Iberia or long resident there, participated in the conquest and settlement of Spanish America. Most of these were slaves; more than four hundred slaves participated in the conquests of Peru and Chile alone. In the fluid social environment of the conquest era, many were able to gain their freedom. Juan Valiente escaped from his master in Mexico and then participated in Francisco Pizarro's conquest of the Inka Empire. He later became one of the most prominent early settlers of Chile.

With the opening of a direct slave trade with Africa (for details, see Chapter 19), the cultural character of the black population of colonial Latin America was altered dramatically. While Afro-Iberians spoke Spanish or Portuguese and were Catholic, African slaves arrived in the colonies with different languages, religious beliefs, and cultural practices. European settlers viewed these differences as signs of inferiority that served as a justification for prejudice and discrimination.

A large percentage of slaves imported in the sixteenth century came from West Central Africa, where they had been exposed to elements of Iberian culture, including religion, language, and technology. The legacy of these shared African cultural

Race and Ethnicity in the Spanish Colonies: Negotiating Hierarchy

Many European visitors to colonial Latin America were interested in the mixing of Europeans, Amerindians, and Africans in the colonies. Many also commented on the treatment of slaves. The passages that follow allow us to examine these issues in two Spanish colonial societies.

Two young Spanish naval officers and scientists, Jorge Juan and Antonio de Ulloa, arrived in the colonies in 1735 as members of a scientific expedition. They later wrote the first selection after visiting the major cities of the Pacific coast of South America and traveling across some of the most difficult terrain in the hemisphere. In addition to their scientific chores, they described architecture, local customs, and the social order. In this section they describe the ethnic mix in Quito, now the capital of Ecuador.

The second selection was published in Lima under the pseudonym Concolorcorvo around 1776. We now know that the author was Alonso Carrío de la Vandera. Born in Spain, he traveled to the colonies as a young man. He served in many minor bureaucratic positions, one of which was the inspection of the postal route between Buenos Aires and Lima. Carrío used his experiences during this long and often uncomfortable trip as the basis of an insightful, and sometimes highly critical, examination of colonial society. The selection that follows describes Córdoba, Argentina.

Juan and Ulloa, as well as Carrío, were perplexed by colonial efforts to create and enforce a racial taxonomy that stipulated and named every possible mixture of European, Amerindian, and African. They were also critical of the vanity and social presumptions of the dominant white population. We are fortunate to have these contemporary descriptions of the diversity of colonial society, but it is important to remember that these authors were clearly rooted in their time and culture and were confident of European superiority. Although they noted many of the abuses suffered by the non-white population, their descriptions of these groups often reveal racial bias and the presumption of inferiority.

Quito

This city is very populous, and has, among its inhabitants, some families of high rank and distinction; though their number is but small considering its extent, the poorer class bearing here too great a proportion. The former are the descendants either of the original conquerors, or of presidents, auditors, or other persons of character [high rank], who at different times came over from Spain invested with some lucrative post, and have still preserved their luster, both of wealth and descent, by intermarriages, without intermixing with meaner families though famous for their riches. The commonalty may be divided into four classes; Spaniards or Whites, Mestizos, Indians or Natives, and Negroes, with their progeny.

The name of Spaniard here has a different meaning from that of Chapitone [sic] or European, as properly signifying a person descended from a Spaniard without a mixture of blood. Many Mestizos, from the advantage of a fresh complexion, appear to be Spaniards more than those who are so in reality; and from only this fortuitous advantage are accounted as such. The Whites, according to this construction of the word, may be considered as one sixth part of the inhabitants.

The Mestizos are the descendants of Spaniards and Indians.... Some are, however, equally tawny with the Indians themselves, though they are distinguished from them by their beards: while others, on the contrary, have so fine a complexion that they might pass for Whites, were it not for some signs which betray them, when viewed attentively. These marks... make it very difficult to conceal the fallacy of their complexion. The Mestizos may be reckoned a third part of the inhabitants.

The next class is the Indians, who form about another third; and the others, who are about one sixth, are the Castes [mixed]. These four classes...amount to between 50 and 60,000 persons, of all ages, sexes, and ranks. If among these classes the Spaniards, as is natural to think, are the most eminent for riches, rank, and power, it must at the same time be owned, however melancholy the truth may appear, they are in proportion the most poor, miserable and distressed; for they refuse to apply themselves to any mechanic business, considering it as a disgrace to that quality they so highly value themselves upon, which consists in not being black, brown, or of a copper color. The Mestizos, whose pride is regulated by prudence, readily apply themselves to arts and trades, but chose those of the greatest repute, as painting, sculpture, and the like, leaving the meaner sort to the Indians.

Córdoba

In my computation, there must be within the city and its limited common lands around 500 to 600 [property-owning] residents, but in the principal houses there are a very large number of slaves, most of them [native born blacks] of all conceivable classes, because in this city and in all of Tucumán there is no leniency about granting freedom to any of them.

As I was passing through Córdoba, they were selling 2,000 Negroes, all Creoles from Temporalidades [property confiscated from the Jesuit order in 1767].... Among this multitude of Negroes were many musicians and many of other crafts; they proceeded with the sale by families. I was assured that the nuns of Santa Teresa alone had a group of 300 slaves of both sexes, to whom they give their just ration of meat and dress in the coarse cloth which they make, while these good nuns content themselves with what is left from other ministrations. The number attached to other religious establishments is much smaller, but there is a private home which has 30 or 40, the majority of whom are engaged in various gainful activities. The result is a large number of excellent washerwomen whose accomplishments are valued so highly that they never mend their outer skirts in order that the whiteness of their undergarments may be seen. They do the laundry in the river, in water up to the waist, saying vaingloriously that she who is not soaked cannot wash well. They make ponchos [hand-woven capes], rugs, sashes, and sundries, and especially decorated leather cases which the men sell for 8 reales each, because the hides have no outlet due to the great distance to the port; the same thing happens on the banks of the Tercero and Cuarto rivers, where they are sold at 2 reales and frequently for less.

The principal men of the city wear very expensive clothes, but this is not true of the women, who are an exception in both Americas and even in the entire world, because they dress decorously in clothing of little cost. They are very tenacious in preserving the customs of their ancestors. They do not permit slaves, or even freedmen who have a mixture of Negro blood, to wear any cloth other than that made in this country, which is quite coarse. I was told recently that a certain bedecked mulatto [woman] who appeared in Córdoba was sent word by the ladies of the city that she should dress according to her station, but since she paid no attention to this reproach, they endured her negligence until one of the ladies, summoning her to her home under some other pretext, had the servants undress her, whip her, burn her finery before her eyes, and dress her in the clothes befitting her class; despite the fact that the [victim] was not lacking in persons to defend her, she disappeared lest the tragedy be repeated.

Questions for Analysis

1. What do the authors of these selections seem to think about the white elites of the colonies? Are there similarities in the ways that Juan and Ulloa and Carrío describe the mixed population of Quito and the slave population of Córdoba?

2. How do these depictions of mestizos and other mixtures compare with the image of the family represented in the painting of castas?

3. What does the humiliation of the mixed-race woman in Córdoba tell us about ideas of race and class in this Spanish colony?

Sources: Jorge Juan and Antonio de Ulloa, *A Voyage to South America*, The John Adams translation (abridged), Introduction by Irving A. Leonard (New York: Alfred A. Knopf, 1964), 135–137, copyright © 1964 by Alfred A. Knopf, a division of Random House, Inc.; Concolorcorvo, *El Lazarillo, A Guide for Inexperienced Travelers Between Buenos Aires and Lima, 1773*, translated by Walter D. Kline (Bloomington: Indiana University Press, 1965), 78–80.

elements became enduring components of the colonial cultures of Latin America. But significant differences were present as well, and in regions with large slave majorities, especially the sugar-producing regions of Brazil, these cultural and linguistic barriers often divided slaves and made resistance more difficult. Over time, elements from many African traditions blended and mixed with European (and in some cases Amerindian) language and beliefs to forge distinct local cultures.

Slave resistance took many forms, including sabotage, malingering, running away, and rebellion. Although many slave rebellions occurred, colonial authorities were always able to reestablish control. Groups of runaway slaves, however, were sometimes able to defend themselves for years. In both Spanish America and Brazil, communities of runaways (called quilombos [key-LOM-bos] in Brazil and palenques [pah-LEN-kays] in Spanish colonies) were common. The largest quilombo was Palmares in Brazil.

Slaves served as skilled artisans, musicians, servants, artists, cowboys, and even soldiers. However, the vast majority worked in agriculture. Conditions for slaves were worst on the sugar plantations of Brazil and the Caribbean, where harsh discipline, brutal punishments, and backbreaking labor were common. Because planters preferred to buy male slaves, there was nearly always a gender imbalance on plantations, proving a significant obstacle to the traditional marriage and family patterns of both Africa and Europe.

Brazil attracted smaller numbers of European immigrants than did Spanish America, and its native populations were smaller and less urbanized. It also came to depend on the African slave as a source of labor earlier than any other American colony. By the early seventeenth century, Africans and their American-born descendants were by far the largest racial group in Brazil. As a result, Brazilian colonial society (unlike Spanish Mexico and Peru) was more influenced by African culture than by Amerindian culture.

Both Spanish and Portuguese law provided for manumission, the granting of freedom to individual slaves, and colonial courts sometimes intervened to protect slaves from the worst physical abuse or to protect married couples from forced separation. The majority of those gaining their liberty had saved money and purchased their own freedom. This meant that manumission was more about the capacity of individual slaves and slave families to earn income and save than about the generosity of slave owners. Among the minority of slaves to be freed without compensation, household servants were the most likely beneficiaries. Slave women received the majority of manumissions, and because children born subsequently were considered free, the free black population grew rapidly.

Within a century of settlement, groups of mixed descent were in the majority in many regions. There were few marriages between Amerindian women and European men, but less formal relationships were common. Few European fathers recognized their mixed offspring, who were called **mestizos** (mess-TEE-zoh). Nevertheless, this rapidly expanding group came to occupy a middle position in colonial society, dominating urban artisan trades and small-scale agriculture and ranching. Many members of the elite in frontier regions were mestizos, some proudly asserting their descent from Amerindian noble families. The African slave trade also led to the appearance of new American ethnicities. Individuals of mixed European and African descent—called **mulattos**—came to occupy an intermediate position in the tropics similar to the social position of mestizos in Mesoamerica and the Andean region. In Spanish Mexico and Peru and in Brazil, mixtures of Amerindians and Africans were also common. These mixed-descent groups were called castas (CAZ-tahs) in Spanish America.

ENGLISH AND FRENCH COLONIES IN NORTH AMERICA

The North American empires of England and France had many characteristics in common with the colonial empires of Spain and Portugal. The governments of England and France hoped to find easily extracted forms of wealth like gold and silver or great indigenous empires like those of the Aztecs and Inka. Like the Spanish and Portuguese, English and French settlers responded to native peoples with a mixture of diplomacy and violence. All four colonial empires also imported large numbers of African slaves to spur the economic development of their colonies.

Important differences, however, distinguished North American colonial development from the Latin American model. The English and French colonies were developed nearly a century after Cortés's conquest of Mexico and the initial Portuguese settlement of Brazil. The intervening period had witnessed significant economic and demographic growth in Europe. By the time England and France secured a foothold in the Americas, increased trade had led to greater integration of world cultural regions. Distracted by ventures elsewhere and by increasing military confrontation in Europe, neither England nor France imitated the large and expensive colonial bureaucracies established by Spain and Portugal. As a result, private companies and individual proprietors played a much larger role in the development of English and French colonies. This period had also witnessed the Protestant Reformation, an event that helped frame the character of English and French settlement in the Americas.

Early English Experiments   England's effort to gain a foothold in the Americas in the late sixteenth century failed, but its effort to establish colonies in the seventeenth century proved more successful. The English relied on private capital to finance settlement and continued to hope that the colonies would become sources of high-value products such as silver, citrus, and wine. English experience in colonizing Ireland after 1566 also influenced these efforts. In Ireland land had been confiscated, cleared of its native population, and offered for sale to English investors. The city of London, English guilds, and wealthy private investors all purchased Irish "plantations" and then recruited "settlers." By 1650 investors had sent nearly 150,000 English and Scottish immigrants to Ireland. Indeed, Ireland attracted six times as many colonists in the early seventeenth century as did New England.

The South   In 1606 London investors organized as the Virginia Company took up the challenge of colonizing Virginia. A year later 144 settlers disembarked at Jamestown, an island 30 miles (48 kilometers) up the James River in the Chesapeake Bay region. Additional settlers arrived in 1609. The investors and settlers hoped for immediate profits, but the location was a swampy and unhealthy place where nearly 80 percent of the settlers died in the first fifteen years from disease or Amerindian attacks. There was no mineral wealth, no passage to Asia, and no docile and exploitable native population.

In 1624 the English crown dissolved the Virginia Company because of its mismanagement. Freed from the company's commitment to the original location, colonists pushed deeper into the interior and developed a sustainable economy based on furs, timber, and, increasingly, tobacco. The profits from tobacco soon attracted additional immigrants. Along the shoreline of Chesapeake Bay and the rivers that fed it, settlers spread out, developing plantations and farms. Colonial Virginia's dispersed population contrasted with the greater urbanization of Spanish and Portuguese America, where large and powerful cities and networks of secondary towns flourished. No city of any significant size developed in colonial Virginia.

From the beginning, colonists in Latin America had relied on forced labor of Amerindians to develop the region's resources. The African slave trade compelled the migration of millions of additional forced laborers to the colonies of Spain and Portugal. The English settlement of the Chesapeake Bay region added a new system of forced labor to the American landscape: indentured servitude. **Indentured servants** were racially and religiously indistinguishable from free settlers and eventually accounted for approximately 80 percent of all English immigrants to Virginia and the neighboring colony of Maryland. A young man or woman unable to pay for transportation to the New World accepted an indenture (contract) that bound him or her to a term ranging from four to seven years of labor in return for passage and, at the end of the contract, a small parcel of land, some tools, and clothes.

During the seventeenth century approximately fifteen hundred indentured servants, mostly male, arrived each year (see Chapter 19 for details on the indentured labor system). Planters were more likely to purchase the cheaper limited contracts of indentured servants rather than African slaves during the initial period of high mortality rates. As life expectancy improved, planters began to purchase more slaves because they believed they would earn greater profits from slaves owned for life than from indentured servants bound for short periods of time. As a result, Virginia's slave population grew rapidly from 950 in 1660 to 120,000 by 1756.

By the 1660s Virginia was administered by a Crown-appointed governor and by representatives of towns meeting together as the **House of Burgesses**. When elected representatives began to meet alone as a deliberative body, they initiated a form of democratic representation that distinguished the English colonies of North America from the colonies of other European powers. Ironically, this expansion in colonial liberties and political rights occurred along with the dramatic increase in the colony's slave population. The intertwined evolution of American freedom and American slavery gave England's southern colonies a unique and conflicted political character that endured after independence.

English settlement of the Carolinas initially relied on profits from the fur trade. English fur traders pushed into the interior to compete with French trading networks based in New Orleans and Mobile. Native peoples eventually provided over 100,000 deerskins annually to this profitable commerce, but at a high environmental and cultural cost. As Amerindian peoples hunted more intensely, they disrupted the natural balance of animals and plants in southern forests. The profits of the fur trade altered Amerindian culture as well, leading villages to place less emphasis on subsistence hunting, fishing, and traditional agriculture. Amerindian life was profoundly altered by deepening dependencies on European products, including firearms, metal tools, textiles, and alcohol.

While being increasingly tied to the commerce and culture of the Carolina colony, indigenous peoples were simultaneously weakened by epidemics, alcoholism, and a rising tide of ethnic conflicts generated by competition for hunting grounds. Conflicts among indigenous peoples—who now had firearms—became more deadly, and many captured Amerindians were sold as slaves to local colonists, who used them as agricultural workers or exported them to the sugar plantations of the Caribbean. Dissatisfied with the terms of trade imposed by fur traders and angered by this slave trade, Amerindians launched attacks on English settlements in the early 1700s. Their defeat by colonial military forces inevitably led to new seizures of Amerindian land by European settlers.

The northern part of the Carolinas, settled from Virginia, followed that colony's mixed economy of tobacco and forest products. Slavery expanded slowly in this region. Charleston and the interior of South Carolina followed a different path. Settled first by planters from Barbados in 1670, this colony developed an economy based on plantations and slavery in imitation of the colonies of the Caribbean and Brazil. In 1729 North and South Carolina became separate colonies.

Despite an unhealthy climate, the prosperous rice and indigo plantations near Charleston attracted both free immigrants and increasing numbers of African slaves. African slaves had been present from the founding of Charleston and were instrumental in introducing irrigated rice agriculture along the coastal lowlands. They were also crucial to developing plantations of indigo (a plant that produced a blue dye) at higher elevations away from the coast. Many slaves were given significant responsibilities. As one planter sending two slaves and their families to a frontier region put it: "[They] are likely young people, well acquainted with Rice & every kind of plantation business, and in short [are] capable of the management of a plantation themselves."[3]

As profits from rice and indigo rose, the importation of African slaves created a black majority in South Carolina. African languages, as well as African religious

---

[3]Crosby, *The Columbian Exchange*, 58.

beliefs and diet, strongly influenced this unique colonial culture. Gullah, a dialect with African and English roots, evolved as the common idiom of the Carolina coast. Africans played a major role in South Carolina's largest slave uprising, the Stono Rebellion of 1739. Twenty slaves, many of them African Catholics seeking to flee south to Spanish Florida, seized firearms and other weapons and then recruited about a hundred slaves from nearby plantations. Although the colonial militia defeated the rebels and executed many of them, the rebellion shocked slave owners throughout England's southern colonies and led to greater repression.

Colonial South Carolina was the most hierarchical society in British North America. Planters controlled the economy and political life. The richest families maintained impressive households in Charleston, the largest city in the southern colonies, as well as on their plantations in the countryside. Small farmers, cattlemen, artisans, merchants, and fur traders held an intermediate but clearly subordinate social position. Native peoples continued to participate in colonial society but lost ground from the effects of epidemic disease and warfare. As in colonial Latin America, a large mixed population blurred racial and cultural boundaries. On the frontier, the children of white men and Amerindian women held an important place in the fur trade. In the plantation regions and Charleston, the offspring of white men and black women often held preferred positions within the slave workforce or worked as free craftsmen.

New England   The colonization of New England by two separate groups of Protestant dissenters, Pilgrims and Puritans, put the settlement of this region on a different course. The **Pilgrims**, who came first, wished to break completely with the Church of England, which they believed was still essentially Catholic. As a result, in 1620 approximately one hundred settlers—men, women, and children—established the colony of Plymouth on the coast of present-day Massachusetts. Although nearly half of the settlers died during the first winter, the colony survived until 1691, when the larger Massachusetts Bay Colony of the Puritans absorbed Plymouth.

The **Puritans** wished to "purify" the Church of England, not break with it. They wanted to abolish its hierarchy of bishops and priests, free it from governmental interference, and limit membership to people who shared their beliefs. Subjected to increased discrimination in England for their efforts to transform the church, large numbers of Puritans began emigrating from England in 1630.

The Puritan leaders of the Massachusetts Bay Company—the joint-stock company that had received a royal charter to finance the Massachusetts Bay Colony—carried the company charter with them from England to Massachusetts. By bringing the charter, which spelled out company rights and obligations as well as the direction of company government, they limited Crown efforts to control them. By 1643 more than twenty thousand Puritans had settled in the Bay Colony.

Immigration to Massachusetts differed from immigration to the Chesapeake and to South Carolina. Most newcomers to Massachusetts arrived with their families. Whereas 84 percent of Virginia's white population in 1625 was male, Massachusetts had a normal gender balance in its population almost from the beginning. It was also the healthiest of England's colonies. The result was a rapid natural increase in population. The population of Massachusetts quickly became more "American" than the population of southern or Caribbean colonies, whose survival depended on a steady flow of

English immigrants and slaves to counter high mortality rates. Massachusetts also was more homogeneous and less hierarchical than the southern colonies.

Political institutions evolved from the terms of the company charter. Settlers elected a governor and a council of magistrates drawn from the board of directors of the Massachusetts Bay Company. By 1650, disagreements between this council and elected representatives of the towns led to the creation of a lower legislative house that selected its own speaker and developed procedures and rules similar to those of the House of Commons in England. The result was much greater autonomy and greater local political involvement than in the colonies of Latin America.

Economically, Massachusetts differed dramatically from the southern colonies. Agriculture met basic needs, but poor soils and harsh climate offered no opportunity to develop cash crops like tobacco or rice. To pay for imported tools, textiles, and other essentials, the colonists needed to discover some profit-making niche in the growing Atlantic market. Fur, timber, and fish provided the initial economic foundation, but New England's economic well-being soon depended on providing commercial and shipping services in a dynamic and far-flung commercial arena that included the southern colonies, the Caribbean islands, Africa, and Europe.

In Spanish and Portuguese America, heavily capitalized monopolies (companies or individuals given exclusive economic privileges) dominated international trade. In New England, by contrast, individual merchants survived by discovering smaller but more sustainable profits in diversified trade across the Atlantic. The colony's commercial success rested on market intelligence, flexibility, and streamlined organization. Urban population growth suggests the success of this development strategy. With sixteen thousand inhabitants in 1740, Boston, the capital of Massachusetts Bay Colony, was the largest city in British North America.

Lacking a profitable agricultural export like tobacco, New England did not develop the extreme social stratification of the southern plantation colonies. Slaves and indentured servants were present, but in very small numbers. While New England was ruled by the richest colonists and shared the racial attitudes of the southern colonies, it also was the colonial society with fewest differences in wealth and status and with the most uniformly British and Protestant population in the Americas.

The Middle Atlantic Region   Much of the future success of English-speaking America was rooted in the rapid economic development and remarkable cultural diversity that appeared in the Middle Atlantic colonies. In 1624 the Dutch West India Company established the colony of New Netherland and located its capital on Manhattan Island. Although poorly managed and underfinanced from the start, the colony commanded the potentially profitable and strategically important Hudson River. Dutch merchants established trading relationships with the **Iroquois Confederacy**—an alliance among the Mohawk, Oneida, Onondaga, Cayuga, and Seneca peoples—and with other native peoples that gave them access to the rich fur trade of Canada. When confronted by an English military expedition in 1664, the Dutch surrendered without a fight. James, duke of York and later King James II of England, became proprietor of the colony, which was renamed New York.

Tumultuous politics and corrupt public administration characterized colonial New York, but the development of New York City as a commercial and shipping center guaranteed the colony's success. Located at the mouth of the Hudson River, the city played an essential role in connecting the region's grain farmers to the booming markets of the Caribbean and southern Europe. By the early eighteenth century, this colony had a diverse population that included English, Dutch, German, and Swedish settlers as well as a large slave community.

Pennsylvania began as a proprietary colony and as a refuge for Quakers, a persecuted religious minority. The prominent Quaker William Penn secured an enormous grant of territory (nearly the size of England) in 1682 because the English king Charles II was indebted to his father. As proprietor (owner) of the land, Penn had sole right to establish a government, subject only to the requirement that he provide for an assembly of freemen.

Even though Penn quickly lost control of the colony's political life, the colony enjoyed remarkable success. By 1700 Pennsylvania had a population of more than 21,000, and Philadelphia, its capital, soon overtook Boston to become the largest city in the British colonies. Healthy climate, excellent land, relatively peaceful relations with native peoples (prompted by Penn's emphasis on negotiation rather than warfare), and access through Philadelphia to exterior markets led to rapid economic and demographic growth.

While both Pennsylvania and South Carolina were grain-exporting colonies, they were very different societies. South Carolina's rice plantations depended on the labor of large numbers of slaves. In Pennsylvania free workers produced the bulk of the colony's grain crops on family farms. As a result, Pennsylvania's economic expansion in the late seventeenth century occurred without reproducing South Carolina's hierarchical and repressive social order. By the early eighteenth century, however, a rich merchant elite was in place and the prosperous city of Philadelphia had a large population of black slaves and freedmen; the fast-growing economy continued to offer opportunities in skilled crafts, trade, and agriculture to free immigrants.

French America   Patterns of French colonial settlement more closely resembled those of Spain and Portugal than of England. The French were committed to missionary activity among Amerindian peoples and emphasized the extraction of natural resources—in this case furs rather than minerals. Between 1534 and 1542 the navigator and promoter Jacques Cartier explored the region of Newfoundland and the Gulf of St. Lawrence in three voyages. A contemporary of Cortés and Pizarro, Cartier hoped to find mineral wealth, but the stones he brought back to France turned out to be quartz and iron pyrite, "fool's gold."

The French waited more than fifty years before establishing settlements in North America. Coming to Canada after spending years in the West Indies, Samuel de Champlain founded the colony of **New France** at Quebec (kwuh-BEC), on the banks of the St. Lawrence River, in 1608. This location provided ready access to Amerindian trade routes, but it also compelled French settlers to take sides in the region's ongoing warfare. Champlain allied New France with the Huron and Algonquin peoples, traditional enemies of the powerful Iroquois Confederacy. Although French firearms and armor at first tipped the balance of power to France's native allies, the Iroquois Confederacy proved to be a resourceful and persistent enemy.

The European market for fur, especially beaver, fueled French settlement. Young Frenchmen were sent to live among native peoples to master their languages and customs. These **coureurs de bois** (koo-RUHR day BWA), or runners of the woods, often began families with indigenous women. Their mixed children, called

Canadian Fur Traders *The fur trade provided the economic foundation of early Canadian settlement. Fur traders were cultural intermediaries. They brought European technologies and products like firearms and machine-made textiles to native peoples and native technologies and products like canoes and furs to European settlers. This canoe with sixteen paddlers was adapted from the native craft by fur traders to transport large cargoes.*

métis (may-TEES), helped direct the fur trade. Amerindians actively participated in the trade because they came to depend on the goods they received in exchange for furs—firearms, metal tools, textiles, and alcohol. This change in the material culture of native peoples led to overhunting, which rapidly transformed the environment and led to the depletion of beaver and deer populations. It also increased competition among native peoples for hunting grounds, thus promoting warfare.

The proliferation of firearms made indigenous warfare more deadly. The Iroquois Confederacy responded to the increased military strength of France's Algonquin allies by forging commercial and military links with Dutch and later English settlements along the Hudson River. Now well armed, the Iroquois Confederacy nearly eradicated the Huron in 1649 and inflicted a series of humiliating defeats on the French. At the high point of their power in the early 1680s, Iroquois hunters and military forces gained control of much of the Great Lakes region and the Ohio River Valley. A large French military expedition and a relentless attack focused on Iroquois villages and agriculture finally checked Iroquois power in 1701.

In French Canada, the Jesuits led the effort to convert native peoples to Christianity as they had in Brazil and Paraguay. Missionaries mastered native languages, created boarding schools for young boys and girls, and set up model agricultural communities for converted Amerindians. The Jesuits' greatest successes coincided with a destructive wave of epidemics and renewed warfare among native peoples in the 1630s. Eventually, they established churches throughout Huron and Algonquin territories. Nevertheless, native culture persisted. In 1688 a French nun who had devoted her life to instructing Amerindian girls expressed her frustration with the resilience of indigenous culture:

> We have observed that of a hundred that have passed through our hands we have scarcely civilized one.... When we are least expecting it, they clamber over our wall and go off to run with their kinsmen in the woods, finding more to please them there than in all the amenities of our French house.[4]

Even though the fur trade flourished, population growth was slow. Founded at about the same time as French Canada, Virginia had twenty times more European residents by 1627. Canada's small settler population and the fur trade's dependence on the voluntary participation of Amerindians allowed indigenous peoples to retain greater independence and more control over their traditional lands than was possible in the colonies of Spain, Portugal, or England. Unlike these colonial regimes, which sought to transform ancient ways of life or force the transfer of native lands, the French were compelled to treat indigenous peoples as allies and trading partners.

Despite Canada's small population and limited resources, the French aggressively expanded to the west and south. They founded Louisiana in 1699, but by 1708 there were fewer than three hundred soldiers, settlers, and slaves in this vast territory. Like Canada, Louisiana depended on the fur trade and on alliances with Amerindian peoples who in turn became dependent on European goods. In 1753 a French official reported a Choctaw leader as saying, "[The French] were the first ... who made [us] subject to the different needs that [we] can no longer now do without."[5]

France's North American colonies were threatened by wars between France and England and by the population growth and increasing prosperity of neighboring English colonies. The "French and Indian War" that began in 1754 led to the wider conflict called the Seven Years' War, 1756–1763, that determined the fate of French Canada. England committed a larger military force to the struggle and, despite early defeats, took the French capital of Quebec in 1759. The peace agreement forced France to yield Canada to the English and cede Louisiana to Spain. Amerindian populations soon recognized the difference between the English and the French. One Canadian indigenous leader commented to a British officer after the French surrender: "We learn that our lands are to be given away not only to trade thereon but also ... in full title to various [English] individuals.... We have always been a free nation, and now we will become slaves, which would be very difficult to accept after having enjoyed our liberty so long."[6] With the loss of Canada the French concentrated their efforts on their sugar-producing colonies in the Caribbean (see Chapter 19).

---

[4]Quoted in R. Douglas Francis, Richard Jones, and Donald B. Smith, *Origins: Canadian History to Confederation* (Toronto: Holt, Rinehart, and Winston of Canada, 1992), 52.

[5]Quoted in Daniel H. Usner, Jr., *Indians, Settlers and Slaves in a Frontier Exchange Economy: The Lower Mississippi Valley Before 1783*, Institute of Early American History and Culture Series (Chapel Hill: University of North Carolina Press, 1992), 96.

[6]Quoted in Cornelius J. Jaenen, "French and Native Peoples in New France," in *Interpreting Canada's Past*, ed. J. M. Bumsted, vol. 1, 2nd ed. (Toronto: Oxford University Press, 1993), 73.

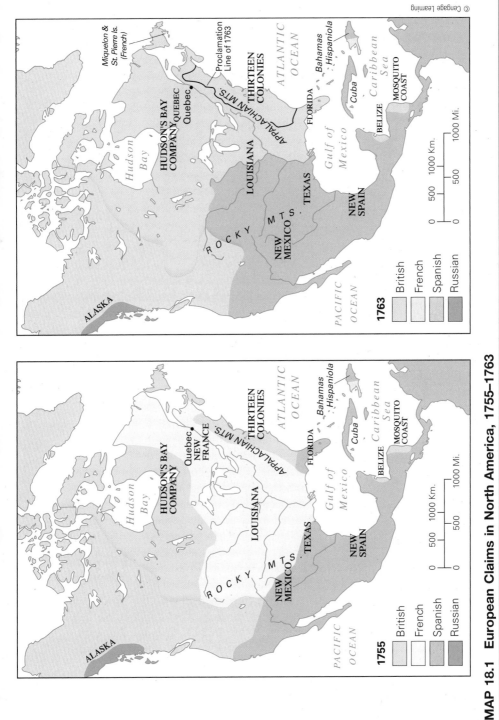

MAP 18.1 European Claims in North America, 1755–1763

The results of the French and Indian War dramatically altered the map of North America. France's losses precipitated conflicts between Amerindian peoples and the rapidly expanding population of the British colonies.

COLONIAL EXPANSION AND CONFLICT

Beginning in the last decades of the seventeenth century, nearly all the European colonies in the Americas experienced economic expansion and population growth. In the next century, the imperial powers responded by strengthening administrative and economic control of their colonies. They also sought to force colonial populations to pay a larger share of the costs of administration and defense. These efforts at reform and restructuring coincided with a series of imperial wars fought along Atlantic trade routes and in the Americas. France's loss of its North American colonies in 1763 was one of the most important results of these struggles. Equally significant, colonial populations throughout the Americas became more aware of separate national identities and more aggressive in asserting local interests against the will of distant monarchs.

Imperial Reform in Spanish America and Brazil   Spain's Habsburg dynasty ended when Charles II died without an heir in 1700 (see Table 17.1 on page 454). After thirteen years of conflict involving the major European powers, Philip of Bourbon, grandson of Louis XIV of France, gained the Spanish throne. Under Philip V and his heirs, Spain reorganized its administration and tax collection and liberalized colonial trade policies. Spain also created new commercial monopolies and strengthened its navy to protect colonial trade.

For most of the Spanish Empire, the eighteenth century was a period of remarkable economic expansion associated with population growth. Amerindian populations began to recover from the early epidemics; the flow of Spanish immigrants increased; and the slave trade to plantation colonies was expanded. Mining production increased, with silver production rising steadily into the 1780s. Agricultural exports also expanded, especially exports of tobacco, dyes, hides, chocolate, cotton, and sugar.

The Spanish and Portuguese kings also sought to reduce the power of the Catholic Church while at the same time transferring some church wealth to their treasuries. These efforts led to a succession of confrontations between colonial officials and the church hierarchy. To the kings of Portugal and Spain, the Jesuits symbolized the independent power of the church. In 1759 the Portuguese king expelled this powerful order from his territories, and the Spanish king imitated this decision in 1767. In practice these actions forced many colonial-born Jesuits from their native lands and closed the schools that had educated many members of the colonial elite.

Bourbon political and fiscal reforms also contributed to a growing sense of colonial grievance by limiting creoles' access to colonial offices and by imposing new taxes and monopolies that transferred more colonial wealth to Spain. Consumer and producer resentment in the colonies led to a series of violent confrontations with Spanish administrators. Many colonials, including members of the elite, resented what they saw as the unilateral overturning of the arrangements and understandings that had governed these societies for centuries. However, the Spanish effort to recruit local elites as military officers to improve imperial defense offered some colonial residents a compensatory opportunity for higher social status and greater responsibility.

In addition to tax rebellions and urban riots, colonial reforms also provoked Amerindian uprisings. In 1780 the Peruvian Amerindian leader José Gabriel Condorcanqui began the largest rebellion. He assumed the name of his Inka ancestor

Tupac Amaru (TOO-pack a-MAH-roo), whom the Spanish executed in 1572. Although a hereditary Quechua leader, **Tupac Amaru II** received his education from the Jesuits and had close ties to the local bishop and other powerful colonial authorities. He was also actively involved in colonial trade. Tupac Amaru II did not clearly state whether he sought only to end local injustices or overthrow Spanish rule, but he clearly sought to redress the grievances of Amerindian communities who suffered from forced labor and from high taxes. As his rebellion spread, he attracted creoles, mestizos, and slaves as well as Amerindians to his cause. After his capture in 1781, the Spanish brutally executed Tupac Amaru II along with his wife and fifteen other family members and allies. By the time Spanish authority was firmly reestablished, more than 100,000 lives had been lost and enormous amounts of property destroyed.

Brazil also experienced a similar period of expansion and reform after 1700. Portugal created new administrative positions and gave monopoly companies exclusive rights to little-developed regions. As in Spanish America, a more intrusive colonial government that imposed new taxes led to rebellions and plots, including open warfare in 1707 between local-born "sons of the soil" and "outsiders" in São Paulo. The most aggressive period of reform occurred during the ministry of the marquis of Pombal (1750–1777). The discovery in Brazil of gold in the 1690s and diamonds after 1720 financed the reforms. Brazil's exports of minerals as well as coffee and cotton deepened dependence on the slave trade, and nearly 2 million African slaves were imported in the eighteenth century.

Reform and Reorganization in British America	England's efforts to reform and reorganize its North American colonies began earlier than the Bourbon initiative in Spanish America. After the period of Cromwell's Puritan Republic (see Chapter 17), the restored Stuart king, Charles II, undertook an ambitious campaign to establish greater control

over the colonies. Between 1651 and 1673 a series of Navigation Acts sought to severely limit colonial trading and colonial production that competed directly with English manufacturers. England also attempted to increase royal control over colonial political life by replacing colonial charters and proprietorships. Because the king viewed the New England colonies as centers of smuggling, he temporarily suspended their elected assemblies while appointing colonial governors and granting them new fiscal and legislative powers.

James II's overthrow in the Glorious Revolution of 1688 ended this confrontation, but not before colonists were provoked to resist and, in some cases, rebel. Colonials overthrew the governors of New York and Massachusetts and removed the Catholic proprietor of Maryland. William and Mary restored relative peace, but these conflicts alerted colonials to the potential aggression of the English government. Colonial politics would remain confrontational until the American Revolution.

During the eighteenth century the English colonies experienced renewed economic growth and attracted a new wave of European immigration, but social divisions were increasingly evident. The colonial population in 1770 was more urban, more clearly divided by class and race, and more vulnerable to economic downturns. Crises were provoked when imperial wars with France and Spain disrupted trade in the Atlantic, increased tax burdens, forced military mobilizations, and

Sir Henry Chamberlain, Views and Costumes of the City and Neighborhoods of Rio de Janeiro, London, 1822

Market in Rio de Janeiro *In many of the cities of colonial Latin America, female slaves and black free women dominated retail markets. In this scene from late colonial Brazil, Afro-Brazilian women sell a variety of foods and crafts.*

provoked frontier conflicts with Amerindians. On the eve of the American Revolution, England defeated France and weakened Spain, but the cost was great. The administrative, military, and tax policies imposed to gain this empire-wide victory had also alienated much of the North American colonial population.

Conclusion

The New World colonial empires of Spain, Portugal, France, and England had many characteristics in common. All subjugated Amerindian peoples and introduced large numbers of enslaved Africans. Within all four empires European settlement and the introduction of Old World animals and plants also transformed the natural environment. Europeans introduced Old World diseases, such as smallpox, that had a devastating effect on the native populations. Settlers in all four colonial empires applied the technologies of the Old World to the resources of the New, producing mineral and agricultural wealth and exploiting the commercial possibilities of the emerging Atlantic market in ways that accelerated the integration of Europe, Asia, and America.

Each of the New World empires also reflected the distinctive cultural and institutional heritages of its colonizing power. Mineral wealth allowed Spain to develop the most centralized empire, with political and economic power concentrated in great cities like Mexico City and Lima. Portugal and France pursued objectives similar to Spain's, but neither Brazil's agricultural economy, based on sugar, nor France's Canadian fur trade produced the financial resources and levels of centralized control achieved by Spain. Nevertheless, unlike Britain, all three of these Catholic powers were able to impose and enforce significant levels of religious and cultural uniformity in their colonies.

Greater cultural and religious diversity characterized British North America. Immigrants came to the colonies from the British Isles, including all of Britain's religious traditions, as well as from Germany, Sweden, the Netherlands, and France. British colonial government varied somewhat from colony to colony and was much more responsive to local interests. Thus colonists in British North America were better able than those in the areas controlled by Spain, Portugal, and France to respond to changing economic and political circumstances and to influence government policies. Most importantly, the British colonies attracted many more European immigrants than did the other New World colonies. Between 1580 and 1760 French colonies received 60,000 European immigrants, Brazil 523,000, and the Spanish colonies 678,000. Within a shorter period—between 1600 and 1760—the British settlements welcomed 746,000. Population in British North America—free and slave combined—had reached an extraordinary 2.5 million by 1775.

IMPORTANT EVENTS 1500–1770

1518	Smallpox arrives in Caribbean
1534–1542	Jacques Cartier's voyages to explore Newfoundland of St. Lawrence
1535	Creation of Vice royalty of New Spain
1540s	Creation of Viceroyalty of Peru
After 1540	Sugar begins to dominate the Brazilian economy
1607	Jamestown founded
1608	Quebec founded
1620	Plymouth founded
1630s	Quilombo of Palmares founded
1664	English take New York from Dutch
1699	Louisiana founded
1700	Last Habsburg ruler of Spain dies
1713	First Bourbon ruler of Spain crowned
1750–1777	Reforms of marquis de Pombal
1754–1763	French and Indian War
1760	English take Canada
1770s and 1780s	Amerindian revolts in Andean region

19

The Atlantic System and Africa, 1550–1800

By the eighteenth century, Caribbean colonies had become the largest producers of sugar in the world. Slaves represented about 90 percent of the islands' population and provided nearly all the labor for harvesting and processing sugar cane. The profitable expansion of sugar agriculture in the seventeenth century opened a new era in the African slave trade. As larger and faster ships carried growing numbers of slaves from Africa, the human cost escalated, as the following example demonstrates.

In 1694 the English ship *Hannibal* called at the West African port of Whydah (WEE-duh) to purchase slaves. The king of Whydah invited the ship's captain and officers to his residence, where they negotiated an agreement on the prices for slaves. In all, the *Hannibal* purchased 692 slaves, of whom about a third were women and girls. The ship's doctor then carefully inspected the naked captives to be sure they were of sound body, young, and free of disease. After their purchase, the slaves were branded with an H (for *Hannibal*) to establish ownership. Once they were loaded on the ship, the crew put shackles on the men to prevent their escape.

To keep the slaves healthy, the captain had the crew feed them twice a day on boiled corn meal and beans brought from Europe and flavored with hot peppers and palm oil purchased in Africa. Each slave received a pint (half a liter) of water with every meal. In addition, the slaves were made to "jump and dance for an hour or two to our bagpipe, harp, and fiddle" every evening to keep them fit. Despite the incentives and precautions for keeping the cargo alive, deaths were common among the hundreds of people crammed into every corner of a slave ship. The *Hannibal*'s experience was worse than most; it lost 320 slaves and 14 crew members to smallpox and dysentery during the seven-week voyage to Barbados.

As the *Hannibal*'s experience suggests, the Atlantic slave trade took a devastating toll in African lives and was far from a sure-fire money maker for European investors, who in this case lost more than £3,000 on the voyage. Nevertheless, the slave trade and plantation slavery were crucial pieces of a booming new **Atlantic system** that moved goods and wealth, as well as peoples and cultures, around the Atlantic.

PLANTATIONS IN THE WEST INDIES

The West Indies was the first place in the Americas reached by Columbus, and it was also the first region in the Americas where native populations collapsed from epidemics. It took a long time to repopulate these islands and forge economic links with other parts of the Atlantic. But after 1650 sugar plantations, African slaves, and European capital made these islands a major center of the Atlantic economy.

Colonization Before 1650   Spanish settlers introduced sugar-cane cultivation into the West Indies shortly after 1500, but these colonies soon fell into neglect as attention shifted to colonizing the Western Hemisphere mainland. After 1600 the West Indies revived as a focus of colonization, this time by northern Europeans interested in growing tobacco and other crops. In the 1620s and 1630s, English and French colonists settled many islands of the Antilles. With greater government support, the English colonies prospered first, largely by producing tobacco.

Tobacco, a New World leaf long used by Amerindians for recreation and medicine, was finding a new market among seventeenth-century Europeans. Despite the opposition of individuals like King James I of England, who condemned tobacco smoke as "dangerous to the eye, hateful to the nose, harmful to the brain, and dangerous to the lungs," the habit spread. By 1614 seven thousand shops in and around London sold tobacco.

The first tobacco colonies suffered from diseases, hurricanes, and attacks by native Caribs and the Spanish (see Environment and Technology: Hurricanes and the Caribbean Plantation Economy). They also suffered from shortages of supplies from Europe and shortages of labor sufficient to clear land and plant tobacco. The governments of France and England controlled costs by allowing private investors organized as **chartered companies** to develop the colonies in exchange for monopoly control and annual fees. These companies provided passage to the colonies for poor Europeans who were obligated to work three or four years as indentured servants. As a result the French and English populations grew rapidly in the 1630s and 1640s. By the middle of the century, however, these Caribbean colonies were in crisis due to stiff competition from Virginia tobacco, also cultivated by indentured servants (see Chapter 18). As the English, French, and Dutch colonies of the Caribbean switched from tobacco to sugar cane and from European indentured laborers to the labor of African slaves, profits reached new heights.

The Portuguese first developed sugar plantations that relied on African slaves on islands along the African coast. They later introduced this complex in Brazil (see Chapter 18). By 1600 Brazil was the Atlantic world's greatest sugar producer. The Dutch were early participants in the Brazilian sugar business as investors, merchants, and processors.

Dramatic events in Europe overturned this prosperous alliance in the sugar business. Beginning in the 1560s, Dutch Protestants began a rebellion against their Spanish overlords. Then in 1580 the Spanish king Philip II inherited the throne of Portugal (see Chapter 17). As a result, Philip barred the rebellious Dutch from the rich sugar business of Brazil. Decades before formal independence in 1648, however, the Dutch were militarily and economically strong enough to extend their war against the king of Spain to the coast of Brazil. In 1621 the Dutch government chartered the **Dutch West India Company**, and in 1624 this commercial enterprise led an attack on Brazil's key sugar port, Salvador. The Dutch were soon forced to retreat in the face of local resistance. Then in 1628 a company fleet captured a Spanish treasure convoy in the Caribbean and used some of the windfall to finance an assault on Pernambuco, one of Brazil's valuable sugar-producing areas. Once established, the Dutch improved the efficiency of the Brazilian sugar industry and also profited from supplying African slaves and European goods to the region.

Once free of Spanish rule in 1640, the reestablished Portuguese crown turned its attention to reasserting its control in Brazil and by 1654 had driven the last of the Dutch from the colony. Some of the expelled planters transferred their capital and knowledge of sugar production to Dutch Caribbean colonies as well as to the English and French islands, modernizing the industry and dramatically expanding exports.

Like its assault on Brazil, the Dutch West India Company's entry into the African slave trade combined economic and political motives. It seized the important West African trading station of Elmina from the Portuguese in 1638 and took their port of Luanda (loo-AHN-duh) on the Angolan coast in 1641. From these coasts the Dutch shipped slaves to Brazil and the West Indies. Although the Portuguese were able to drive the Dutch out of Angola after a few years, Elmina remained the Dutch West India Company's headquarters in West Africa.

Sugar and Slaves   The infusion of Dutch expertise and money revived the French colonies of Guadeloupe and Martinique, but the English colony of Barbados best illustrates the dramatic transformation that sugar brought to the seventeenth-century Caribbean. In 1640 Barbados's economy depended largely on tobacco, mostly grown by European settlers, both free and indentured. By the 1680s sugar had become the principal crop and enslaved Africans were three times as numerous as Europeans. Exporting up to 15,000 tons of sugar a year, Barbados had become the wealthiest and most populous of England's American colonies. By 1700 Barbados and other West Indian colonies had collectively surpassed Brazil as the world's principal source of sugar.

This transformation was accomplished at a high environmental cost. Originally covered in tropical forest, Barbados was virtually deforested in a matter of decades. Forests were cut to provide fuel for the refineries and to make more land available for sugar. This deforestation led to soil erosion, silted rivers, and fields exhausted of nutrients. As colonists turned to sugar production, similar patterns appeared elsewhere in the Caribbean as well.

The expansion of sugar plantations in the West Indies required a sharp increase in the volume of the slave trade from Africa (see Figure 19.1). During the first half of the seventeenth century about ten thousand slaves a year had arrived from Africa. Most were destined for Brazil and the mainland Spanish colonies. In the second half of the century the trade averaged twenty thousand slaves annually, and more than half landed in the English, French, and Dutch West Indies. As sugar production surged between 1640 and 1807, more than 4 million slaves were imported into the Caribbean region, ten times the slave imports of British North America.

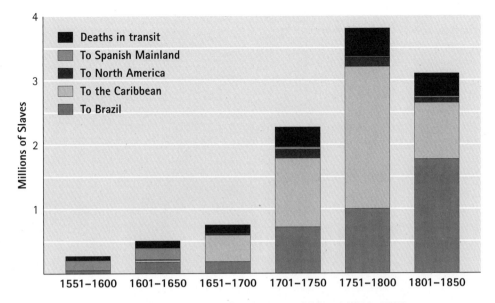

FIGURE 19.1 Transatlantic Slave Trade from Africa, 1551–1850

Source: Data from David Eltis, "The Volume and Structure of the Transatlantic Slave Trade: A Reassessment," *William and Mary* Quarterly, 3rd Series, 58 (2001), tables II and III.

Cash-short tobacco planters in the seventeenth century preferred indentured Europeans to African slaves because they cost half as much. Poor European men and women were willing to work for little in order to get to the Americas, where they could acquire their own land cheaply at the end of their term of service. However, as the cultivation of sugar spread after 1750, speculators drove land prices in the West Indies so high that former indentured servants could no longer afford to buy land. As a result, poor Europeans chose to indenture themselves in Britain's North American colonies, where cheap land was still available (see Chapter 18). Rather than raise wages to attract European laborers, Caribbean sugar planters switched to slaves.

Rising sugar prices allowed West Indian sugar planters to afford the higher cost of African slaves. The fact that slaves lived seven years on average after their arrival, while the typical indentured labor contract was for only three or four years, also made slaves a better investment. Dutch and other traders responded to rising labor demands by increasing the flow of slaves to meet the needs of the expanding plantations (see Figure 19.1), but slave prices rose throughout the eighteenth century. These high labor costs were one more factor favoring more-efficient large plantations over smaller operations.

PLANTATION LIFE IN THE EIGHTEENTH CENTURY

To find more land for sugar plantations, France and England expanded their Caribbean holdings by attacking older Spanish colonies. In 1655 the English seized Jamaica from the Spanish. They also took Havana, Cuba, in 1762 and held the

British Library Board

Plantation Scene, Antigua, British West Indies *The sugar made at the mill in the background was sealed in barrels and loaded on carts that oxen and horses drew to the beach. By means of a succession of vessels the barrels were taken to the ship that hauled the cargo to Europe. The importance of African labor is evident from the fact that only one white person appears in the painting.*

city for a year. By the time the occupation ended, English merchants had imported large numbers of slaves and Cuba had begun to switch from tobacco to sugar production. The French had seized the western half of the Spanish island of Hispaniola in the 1670s. During the eighteenth century this new French colony of Saint Domingue (san doh-MANGH) (present-day Haiti) became the greatest producer of sugar in the Atlantic world, while Jamaica surpassed Barbados as England's most important sugar colony. The technological, environmental, and social transformation of these island colonies illustrates the power of the new Atlantic system.

Technology and Environment   Sugar production had both an agricultural and an industrial character. On both small farms and large plantations, growing and harvesting sugar cane required only simple tools like spades, hoes, and machetes. Once the cane was cut, however, a more complex and expensive process was needed to produce sugar. Slaves rushed the cane to mills, where it was crushed and the juice extracted. Lead-lined wooden troughs carried cane juice to a series of large copper kettles where excess water was boiled off, leaving thick syrup. Placed in conical clay molds, the syrup turned to crystallized sugar as it dried. While small refiners used crushing mills powered by animals or even by laborers, large plantations used larger and more efficient mills that relied on wind or water power. The economies of scale generated by larger mills meant that over time the more-efficient, large-scale producers had lower costs and greater profits.

To make the operation more efficient and profitable, investors sought to utilize the costly crushing and refining machinery intensively. As a result, West Indian plantations expanded from an average of around 100 acres (40 hectares) in the seventeenth century to at least twice that size in the eighteenth century. Some plantations were even larger. In 1774 Jamaica's 680 sugar plantations averaged 441 acres (178 hectares), with the largest over 2,000 acres (800 hectares). By this date Jamaica was so specialized in sugar production that this agricultural colony had to import most of its food. Saint Domingue had a comparable number of plantations of smaller average size but generally higher productivity. This French colony was also more diverse in its economy. Although sugar production was paramount, some planters raised provisions for local consumption as well as crops such as coffee and cacao for export.

Sugar agriculture had a mixed environmental record. Some practices were not destructive. Planters powered their mills by water, wind, or animals and fueled their boilers by burning crushed cane. They fertilized their fields using manure from their livestock. Yet high profits led planters to exploit nature ruthlessly in other ways. Everywhere in the Caribbean, forests were cleared to plant sugar or other export crops. Repeated cultivation of a single crop was also damaging because it removed more nutrients from the soil than animal fertilizer and fallow periods could restore. Instead of rotating sugar with other crops to restore the nutrients naturally, planters found it more profitable to clear new lands when yields declined in the old fields. When land was finally exhausted, planters often moved on to new islands. Many of the English who settled Jamaica had been planters on Barbados. Similarly, the pioneer planters on Saint Domingue came from older French sugar colonies where production had begun to decline. As a result of these destructive practices, Jamaican sugar production began to fall behind Saint Domingue, which still had virgin land in the second half of the eighteenth century.

In addition to soil exhaustion and deforestation, the introduction of nonnative animals and cultivated plants transformed the Caribbean region. The Spanish brought cattle, pigs, and horses, which multiplied rapidly. They also introduced new plants. Bananas and plantains from the Canary Islands were a valuable addition to the food supply, and sugar and rice formed the basis of plantation agriculture, along with native tobacco. Other food crops arrived with the slaves from Africa, including okra, black-eyed peas, yams, grains such as millet and sorghum, and mangoes. Many of these new animals and plants were useful additions to the islands, but they crowded out indigenous species. The most tragic and dramatic transformation of the West Indies was demographic. Chapter 16 detailed how disease and abuse nearly eliminated the indigenous peoples of the large islands within fifty years of Columbus's first voyage. Far earlier and more completely than in any mainland colony, the West Indies were repeopled from across the Atlantic—first with thousands of free Europeans and then with millions of captive Africans.

Slaves' Lives   During the eighteenth century West Indian plantation colonies were the world's most polarized societies. On most islands 90 percent or more of the inhabitants were slaves. Power resided in the

ENVIRONMENT + TECHNOLOGY

Hurricanes and the Caribbean Plantation Economy

The European plantation colonies of the Caribbean produced prodigious amounts of wealth, but they were vulnerable to hurricanes and other natural disasters. By the middle of the eighteenth century this prosperous region was dominated by large sugar plantations and dependent on the labor of its fast-growing slave population. Between 1768 and 1786 alone the number of slaves in Jamaica increased from 168,900 to 255,700.

While Europe's growing demand for sugar created the potential for enormous profits in Caribbean plantation colonies,

Courtesy of the John Carter Brown Library at Brown University

Caribbean Hurricane *View of town of Léogane in French sugar colony of Saint Domingue (Haiti) during 1791 hurricane. Shipwreck with rescued passengers in foreground.*

hands of a **plantocracy**, a small number of very rich men who owned most of the slaves and most of the land. Between the slaves and the masters was a small middle group of estate managers, government officials, artisans, and small farmers, nearly all white. While some free blacks owned property or entered commerce, it is, nevertheless, only a slight simplification to describe eighteenth-century Caribbean society as being made up of a large, abject class of slaves and a small, powerful class of masters.

European planters and investors repeatedly faced the disastrous consequences of natural disasters, especially earthquakes and hurricanes. The 1692 earthquake that flattened Port Royal, Jamaica, was among the most destructive, but the Spanish colony of Puerto Rico also experienced powerful earthquakes in 1670 and 1787. Similarly, the French colony of Saint Domingue suffered four earthquakes in less than a century, with the 1751 quake causing the greatest loss of life and property destruction.

While earthquakes could be devastating, these geological events were typically separated by decades if not much longer time periods. The Caribbean hurricane season of the late summer and fall, however, routinely threatened this region annually. Hurricanes can also affect the Atlantic coast of North America, but they are much more frequent and generally more destructive in the Caribbean.

The prosperous British sugar colony of Jamaica, for example, experienced five hurricanes in a seven-year period in the late eighteenth century. One survivor of the October 1780 hurricane reported to readers in London that "every [sugar] cane, every plantain tree, every fruit-tree, every building [is] entirely blown down." This same storm ravaged Barbados, causing £1,000,000 sterling in damage. Slaves housed in the least substantial buildings in both colonies faced the greatest risks. More than two thousand slaves died in Barbados, and more than five hundred more died in Jamaica in the same 1780 hurricane.

By the end of the eighteenth century the accumulated effects of hurricanes had played an important role in shaping the society and economy of the Caribbean. In an era without insurance for crops, homes, or refineries, planters attempted to reduce risk by bending every effort to harvest, process, and ship sugar before the hurricane season began, but this difficult schedule required ideal weather conditions, rapid refining, and the availability of shipping. Since these conditions were seldom present, nearly every planter was forced to absorb the disastrous costs of hurricane damage sooner or later. Following a hurricane, the poorest, most vulnerable planters were often compelled to sell land and slaves purchased with borrowed money at depreciated prices. Generally, the richest planters with the largest slaveholdings had the best chance to recover, since they could rebuild quickly and could absorb the steep short-term losses. But even the wealthiest planters were often forced to borrow at high interest rates for repairs, making them more vulnerable to ruin during the next hurricane season.

Source: This discussion relies in part on Matthew Mulcahy, "Weathering the Storms: Hurricanes and Risk in the British Greater Caribbean," *Business History Review* 78 (2004): 635–663.

The profitability of a Caribbean plantation depended on extracting as much work as possible from the slaves, and plantations achieved exceptional productivity through the threat and use of force. Slaves worked long hours in difficult conditions throughout the year, but, when the cane harvest and milling were in full swing, workdays might stretch to eighteen hours or more. As Table 19.1 shows, on a typical Jamaican plantation about 80 percent of the slaves were actively engaged in productive tasks; the only exceptions were infants, the seriously ill, and the very old.

TABLE 19.1 | SLAVE OCCUPATIONS ON A JAMAICAN SUGAR PLANTATION, 1788

Occupations and Conditions	Men	Women	Boys and Girls	Total
Field laborers	62	78		140
Tradesmen	29			29
Field drivers	4			4
Field cooks		4		4
Mule-, cattle-, and stablemen	12			12
Watchmen	18			18
Nurse		1		1
Midwife		1		1
Domestics and gardeners		5	3	8
Grass-gang			20	20
Total employed	125	89	23	237
Infants			23	23
Invalids (18 with yaws)				32
Absent on roads				5
Superannuated [elderly]				7
Overall total				304

Source: Adapted from "Edward Long to William Pitt," in Michael Craton, James Walvin, and David Wright, eds., *Slavery, Abolition, and Emancipation* (London: Longman, 1976), 103. © Michael Craton, James Walvin, and David Wright, reprinted by permission of Pearson Education Limited.

Table 19.1 also illustrates how planters organized slaves by age, sex, and ability. Only 2 or 3 percent of the slaves were house servants. About 70 percent of the able-bodied slaves worked in the fields, generally in one of three labor gangs. A "great gang," made up of the strongest slaves in the prime of life, did the heaviest work, such as breaking up the soil at the beginning of the planting season. A second gang of youths, elders, and less fit slaves did somewhat lighter work. A "grass gang," composed of children under the supervision of an elderly slave, was responsible for weeding and other simple work, such as collecting grass for the animals. Slaves too old for any field labor tended the toddlers. Women sometimes formed the majority of the field laborers, even in the great gang of some plantations. Owners seeking maximum profits even forced nursing mothers to take their babies with them to the fields.

Because the slave trade imported twice as many males as females, men outnumbered women on Caribbean plantations. As Table 19.1 shows, a little over half of adult males did nongang work. Some tended livestock, and others were skilled craftsmen, such as blacksmiths and carpenters. The most important artisan slave was the head boiler, who oversaw the delicate process of reducing the cane sap to crystallized sugar and molasses.

Planters often rewarded skilled slaves with better-quality food and clothing or with time off, but most field slaves were compelled to work without respite by fear of the lash. Slave gangs were led by a privileged male slave, appropriately called the **driver**, whose job was to ensure that the gang completed its work. Since production quotas were high, slaves toiled in the fields from sunup to sunset, except for meal breaks. Those who fell behind due to fatigue or illness soon felt the sting of the whip. Planters punished openly rebellious slaves who refused to work, disobeyed orders, or tried to escape with floggings, confinement in irons, or mutilation. While slaves usually did not work in the fields on Sunday, they could not rest, but had to use this time to farm their own provisioning grounds to supplement meager rations, maintain their dwellings, and do other chores, such as washing and mending their rough clothes.

Except for occasional holidays—including the Christmas-week revels in the British West Indies—there was little time for recreation and relaxation. Slaves might sing in the fields, but singing was simply a way to distract themselves from fatigue and the monotony of the work. There was certainly no time for schooling, nor were masters willing to educate slaves beyond the basic skills useful to the plantation.

Time for family life was also inadequate. Although the large proportion of young slaves in plantation colonies ought to have led to a high rate of natural increase, despite the sex imbalance that resulted from the slave trade, the opposite occurred. Poor nutrition and overwork led to lower fertility rates, but high mortality rates for infant slaves also limited population growth. The continuation of heavy fieldwork during the pregnancies of slave women made it difficult to carry a baby to term. Similarly, work demands limited a slave mother's ability to ensure her child's survival. As a result of these conditions, along with disease and accidents from dangerous mill equipment, deaths heavily outnumbered births on West Indian plantations (see Table 19.2). Life expectancy for slaves in nineteenth-century Brazil, for example, was only 23 years of age for males and 25.5 years for females. The figures were probably similar for the eighteenth-century Caribbean. A callous opinion, common among slave owners in

| TABLE 19.2 | BIRTH AND DEATH ON A JAMAICAN SUGAR PLANTATION, 1779–1785 |

| Year | Born | | | Died | | |
	Males	Females	Purchased	Males	Females	Proportion of Deaths
1779	5	2	6	7	5	1 in 26
1780	4	3	—	3	2	1 in 62
1781	2	3	—	4	2	1 in 52
1782	1	3	9	4	5	1 in 35
1783	3	3	—	8	10	1 in 17
1784	2	1	12	9	10	1 in 17
1785	2	3	—	0	3	1 in 99
Total	19	18	27	35	37	
	Born 37			Died 72		

Source: From "Edward Long to William Pitt," in Michael Craton, James Walvin, and David Wright, eds., *Slavery, Abolition, and Emancipation* (London: Longman, 1976), 105. © Michael Craton, James Walvin, and David Wright, reprinted by permission of Pearson Education Limited.

the Caribbean and in parts of Brazil, held that it was cheaper to import a youthful new slave from Africa than to raise one to the same age on a plantation.

The harsh conditions of plantation life played a major role in shortening slaves' lives, but the greatest killer was disease. Dysentery caused by contaminated food and water was common. Slaves newly arrived from Africa went through the period of adjustment to a new environment known as **seasoning**, during which one-third, on average, died of unfamiliar diseases. Slaves also suffered from diseases brought with them, including malaria. On the plantation profiled in Table 19.1, for example, more than half of the slaves incapacitated by illness had yaws, a painful and debilitating skin disease common in Africa. As a consequence, only slave populations in the healthier temperate zones of North America experienced natural increase.

The combination of high mortality and low fertility among the slaves of the Caribbean plantation colonies led inexorably to an ever-larger African slave trade. Plantation owners had to continually purchase new slaves to replace those who died and to expand sugar production. As a result, the majority of slaves on most West Indian plantations were African-born, and African religious beliefs, patterns of speech, styles of dress and adornment, and music were prominent parts of West Indian life.

Alfredo Dagli Orti/The Art Archive at Art Resource

The Brutal Foundation of Plantation Prosperity *In Caribbean slave societies the punishment of slaves was often conducted in public places in order to intimidate other slaves. In this early nineteenth-century illustration, the slave in the foreground is whipped by two other slaves supervised by the owner. In the background a female slave is suspended by her wrists from a tree branch after being whipped.*

Given the harsh conditions of their lives, it is not surprising that slaves in the West Indies often sought to gain their freedom. Individual slaves often ran away, and sometimes large groups of plantation slaves rose in rebellion against their bondage and abuse. On Jamaica alone there were sixteen rebellions between 1655 and 1813. For example, a slave named Tacky, who had been a chief on the Gold Coast of Africa, led a large rebellion in Jamaica in 1760. After his followers broke into a fort and armed themselves, slaves from nearby plantations joined the rebellion. This force attacked several plantations, setting them on fire and killing the planter families. Tacky ultimately died in the fighting, and three of his lieutenants stoically endured cruel deaths by torture by colonial authorities who sought to deter others from rebellion.

Because European planters believed that slaves with the strongest African heritage led rebellions, they tried to curtail African cultural traditions. They required slaves to learn the colonial language and discouraged the use of African languages by deliberately mixing slaves from different parts of Africa. In French and Portuguese colonies, slaves were encouraged to adopt Catholic religious practices, though African deities, beliefs, and practices survived, serving as the foundation for modern African-derived religions like Brazilian candomblé. In the British West Indies, where only Quaker slave owners encouraged Christianity among their slaves before 1800, African herbal medicine remained strong, as did African beliefs concerning nature spirits and witchcraft.

Free Whites and Free Blacks The lives of free men and women were very different from the lives of slaves. In the French colony of Saint Domingue, which had nearly half of all slaves in the Caribbean in the eighteenth century, there were three categories of free people. At the top were wealthy owners of large sugar plantations (the *grands blancs* [grawn blawnk], or "great whites"), mostly French nationals, who dominated the economy and society of the island. Second came less-well-off Europeans (*petits blancs* [pay-TEE blawnk], or "little whites"). Most served as colonial officials, retail merchants, or small-scale agriculturalists. Nearly all members of both groups owned slaves. Third came the free blacks. There were almost as many free blacks as free whites in Saint Domingue. While they ranked below whites socially, many free blacks owned property, and a surprising number also owned slaves.

The plantation elite was even more powerful in British colonies. Whereas sugar constituted about half of Saint Domingue's exports, in Jamaica the figure was over 80 percent. Such concentration on sugar crowded out small cultivators, white or black, and confined most landholding to a few larger owners. At midcentury three-quarters of the farmland in Jamaica belonged to individuals who owned 1,000 acres (400 hectares) or more.

One source estimated that a planter had to invest nearly £20,000 in 1774 (about £2,000,000 or $3,200,000 in 2012) to acquire a medium-size Jamaican plantation of 600 acres (240 hectares). A third of this money went for land on which to grow sugar and food crops, pasture animals, and cut timber and firewood. A quarter of the expense was for the mill and refinery. The largest expense was the purchase of 200 slaves at £40 (about £4,116 or $6,586 in 2012) each. In comparison, the wage of an English rural laborer at this time was about £10 (about £1,029 or $1,646 in 2012) a year (one-fourth the price of a slave), and the annual incomes of the ten wealthiest noble families in Britain in 1760 averaged only £20,000 each.

Reputedly the richest Englishmen of this time, West Indian planters often translated their wealth into political power and social prestige. The richest planters put their plantations under the direction of managers and lived in Britain. Between 1730 and 1775 seventy of these absentee planters secured election to the British Parliament, where they formed an influential voting bloc. Planters who continued to reside in the West Indies exercised political power through the control of colonial assemblies.

In most European plantation colonies it was possible to grant freedom to an individual slave or group of slaves. **Manumission** (the legal grant of freedom by an owner) was more common in Brazil and the Spanish and French colonies than in English colonies. Among English colonies, manumissions were more common in the Caribbean than in North American colonies like South Carolina. While some plantation owners in the Caribbean freed slave women with whom they had had sexual relationships or freed the children of their mistresses, the largest group of freed slaves across the Americas purchased their freedom from masters. Manumissions led to the development of a large free black population in many colonies. Since the legal condition of children followed that of the mother, slave families often struggled to free women in childbearing years first so that their children would be born free. By the late eighteenth century free blacks made up a large portion of the black populations of Brazil and the French colonies.

As in Brazil and Spanish colonies (see Chapter 18), escaped slaves constituted another part of the free black population. Communities of runaways, called **maroons**, were numerous in Jamaica and Hispaniola as well as in the Guianas (guy-AHN-uhs). Jamaican maroons, after withstanding several attacks by the colony's militia, signed a treaty in 1738 that recognized their independence in return for their cooperation in stopping new runaways and suppressing slave revolts. Unable to win decisive victories, colonial authorities in Spanish, Dutch, and Portuguese colonies signed similar treaties with runaway leaders as well.

CREATING THE ATLANTIC ECONOMY

At once archaic in their cruel system of slavery and oddly modern in their specialization in a single product for export and efforts to improve refining machinery, the West Indian plantation colonies were the bittersweet fruits of a new Atlantic trading system. Changes in the character of Atlantic commerce illustrate the rise of this new system. In the sixteenth century Spanish treasure fleets laden with silver and gold bullion had dominated Atlantic trade. In the late seventeenth and eighteenth centuries the Atlantic trade was dominated by sugar ships returning to Europe from the West Indies and Brazil and by slave ships transporting an average of 250 African captives each to the Americas.

In addition to the plantation system, new economic institutions, new partnerships between private investors and governments in Europe, and new working relationships between European and African merchants created the Atlantic economy. This new trading system is a prime example of how European capitalist relationships were reshaping the world.

Capitalism and Mercantilism   Many of the Spanish and Portuguese voyages of exploration in the fifteenth and sixteenth centuries were government ventures, and both Spain and Portugal tried to restrict the overseas trade of their colonies using royal monopolies (see Chapters 16 and 18). Monopoly control, however, proved both expensive and inefficient. The success of the Atlantic economy in the seventeenth and eighteenth centuries depended much more on private enterprise, which made trade more efficient and profitable and spread risk among a large number of participants. European private investors were attracted to colonial trade by the rich profits generated by New World agriculture and mining, but their success depended on new institutions and the continuation of government protection to reduce the possibility of catastrophic loss.

The growth of the Atlantic economy played an important role in the development of modern **capitalism**. The essence of this economic system was the expansion of credit and the development of large financial institutions—banks, stock exchanges, and chartered trading companies—that enabled merchants and investors to conduct business at great distances from their homes while reducing risks and increasing profits (see Chapter 17). Originally developed for business dealings within Europe, the capitalist system expanded overseas in the seventeenth century, when slow economic growth in Europe led many investors to seek profits in the production and export of colonial products and in satisfying the colonial demand for European products. Among the Western Hemisphere's exports after 1650, sugar yielded a far higher and more reliable profit than any other cash crop. These profits and the trade they lubricated proved crucial to linking Europe, Africa, and the Americas in the fast-growing Atlantic commercial region.

Europe reaped a far larger share of the wealth produced in this commercial expansion than American or African participants because it had developed institutions that facilitated investment and reduced commercial risks. Chief among these innovations were private banks, joint-stock companies, speculative markets in commodities and shares, and commercial insurance. It took more than a century for these novelties to take root across the continent, but the earliest adopters, especially the English and Dutch, led the commercial expansion and enjoyed most of the benefits. Spain, Portugal, and France changed more slowly, leaving intrusive state controls of commerce in place until the eighteenth century.

European empires sought to monopolize the profits produced in their colonies by controlling trade and accumulating capital in the form of gold and silver, a system called **mercantilism**. Mercantilist policies strongly discouraged trade with foreign merchants, especially in the colonies, because any balance of trade deficit would be paid in gold or silver. These commercial policies were enforced by customs authorities, navies, and coast guards when necessary to secure exclusive relations. The practical result of these policies was to make European goods imported into American colonies more expensive and the products of colonial planters and other exporters cheaper when purchased by European merchants.

Chartered companies were an important part of mercantilist capitalism. In 1602 the Netherlands gave the Dutch East India Company a monopoly over trade in the Indian Ocean. Private investors who bought shares in the company were amply rewarded when the Dutch East India Company captured control of long-distance trade in the Indian Ocean from the Portuguese (see Chapter 20). As we

have seen, the Dutch West India Company, chartered in 1621, sought similar benefits in the Atlantic trade by seizing sugar-producing areas in Brazil and African slav-
ing ports from the Portuguese.

These successes inspired other governments to set up their own chartered companies. In 1672 a royal charter placed all English trade with West Africa in the
hands of the **Royal African Company** (RAC), which established its headquarters
at Cape Coast Castle, just east of Elmina on the Gold Coast. The French government also chartered companies and promoted overseas trade and colonization.
Jean Baptiste Colbert (kohl-BEAR), King Louis XIV's minister of finance from
1661 to 1683, chartered the French East India and French West India Companies
to expel Dutch and English traders from French colonies.

French and English governments also used military force to gain trade advantages in the Americas. For example, restrictions on Dutch access to French and
English colonies provoked a series of wars with the Netherlands between 1652
and 1678 (see Chapter 17). The larger English and French navies ultimately
defeated the Dutch and drove the Dutch West India Company into bankruptcy.
Military and diplomatic pressure also forced Spain after 1713 to grant England
and later France monopoly rights to supply slaves to its colonies.

With Dutch competition in the Atlantic reduced, the French and English limited
the privileges of their chartered companies. Such new mercantilist policies fostered
competition among a nation's own citizens, while using high tariffs and restrictions
to exclude foreigners. In the 1660s England passed a series of Navigation Acts that
confined trade with its colonies to English ships and cargoes; it later opened trade
in Africa to any English subject, claiming that competition would cut the cost of
slaves to West Indian planters. The French called their mercantilist legislation, codi-
fied in 1698, the *Exclusif* (ek-skloo-SEEF), highlighting its exclusionary intentions.
Other mercantilist laws sought to protect national manufacturing and agricultural
interests from the competition of colonies, imposing prohibitively high taxes on
their manufactured goods and products like refined sugar.

As a result of these mercantilist measures, the Atlantic became Britain, France,
and Portugal's most important overseas trading area. The value of imports from
West Indian colonies alone accounted for over one-fifth the value of total British
imports, while French West Indian colonies played an even larger role in France's
overseas trade. Only the Dutch, closed out of much of the American trade,
depended more heavily on Asian trade (see Chapter 20). Profits from the Atlantic
economy, in turn, promoted further economic expansion and increased the revenues
of European governments.

The Atlantic Circuit   At the heart of this trading system was a clockwise network
of sea routes known as the **Atlantic Circuit**. The first leg,
from Europe to Africa, carried European manufactures—
notably metals, hardware, and guns—as well as great quantities of cotton textiles
brought from India. While some of these goods were exchanged for West African
gold, ivory, timber, and other products, most goods went to purchase slaves, who
were transported across the Atlantic to the plantation colonies in what was known
as the **Middle Passage**. On the third leg, plantation goods from the colonies
returned to Europe. Each leg carried goods from where they were abundant and

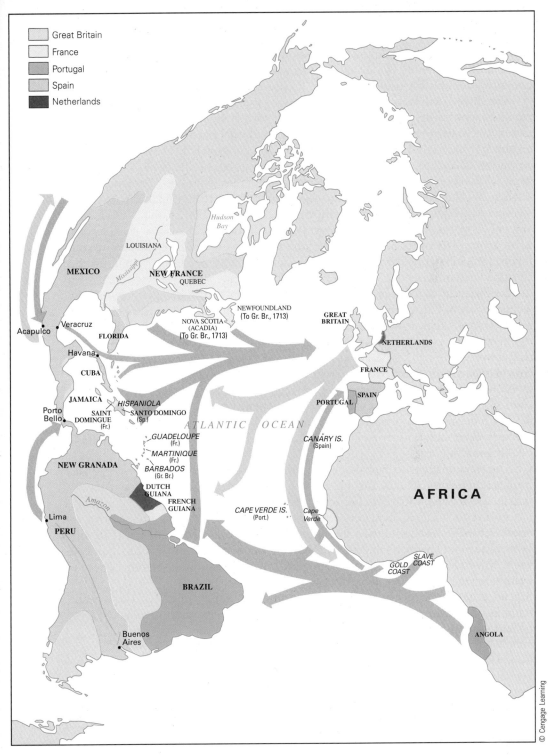

Legend:
- Great Britain
- France
- Portugal
- Spain
- Netherlands

Hudson Bay

LOUISIANA

MEXICO

NEW FRANCE
QUEBEC

Mississippi

NEWFOUNDLAND
(To Gr. Br., 1713)

NOVA SCOTIA
(ACADIA)
(To Gr. Br., 1713)

GREAT
BRITAIN

Acapulco
Veracruz
FLORIDA

Havana

CUBA

NETHERLANDS

FRANCE

JAMAICA
HISPANIOLA

Porto
Bello
SAINT
DOMINGUE
(Fr.)

SANTO DOMINGO
(Sp.)

PORTUGAL   SPAIN

ATLANTIC OCEAN

GUADELOUPE
(Fr.)

MARTINIQUE
(Fr.)

BARBADOS
(Gr. Br.)

DUTCH
GUIANA
FRENCH
GUIANA

CANARY IS.
(Spain)

NEW GRANADA

Amazon

AFRICA

Lima

PERU

CAPE VERDE IS.
(Port.)

Cape
Verde

SLAVE
COAST
GOLD
COAST

BRAZIL

Buenos
Aires

ANGOLA

© Cengage Learning

MAP 19.1 The Atlantic Economy

By 1700 the volume of maritime exchanges among the Atlantic continents had begun to rival the trade of the Indian Ocean Basin. Notice the trade in consumer products, slave labor, precious metals, and other goods. Silver trade to East Asia laid the basis for a Pacific Ocean economy.

relatively cheap to where they were scarce and therefore valuable. Thus, in theory, each leg of the Atlantic Circuit could earn profits. In practice, shipwrecks, deaths, piracy, and other risks could turn profit into loss.

The three-sided Atlantic Circuit is only one of many commercial routes that serviced Atlantic trade. Ships making the long voyage from Europe to the Indian Ocean and Asia typically exchanged African gold and American silver for cotton textiles and spices. Merchants then sold these Asian goods in Africa and the Americas as well as in Europe. Many commercial routes were more direct, carrying manufactured goods from Europe or foodstuffs and lumber from New England to the Caribbean. Some Rhode Island and Massachusetts merchants participated in a "Triangular Trade" that carried rum to West Africa, slaves to the West Indies, and molasses and rum back to New England. There was also a considerable two-way trade between Brazil and Angola that exchanged Brazilian tobacco and liquor for slaves. Brazilian tobacco also found its way north as a staple of the Canadian fur trade.

European investment capital, manufactured goods, and shipping dominated the Atlantic system. Europe was also the principal market for American plantation products, products that helped transform European material culture. Before the seventeenth century, sugar was scarce and expensive in Europe and was mostly consumed by the rich. As colonial production increased, prices fell and consumption of sugar in England rose to about 4 pounds (nearly 2 kilograms) per person in 1700. Europeans of modest means spooned sugar into popular new beverages imported from overseas—tea, coffee, and chocolate—to overcome the beverages' natural bitterness. Consumption increased to about 18 pounds (8 kilograms) by the early nineteenth century (well below the American average of about 152 pounds [69 kilograms] a year today).

The flow of sugar to Europe depended on the flow of slaves from Africa. The rising volume of the Middle Passage is one measure of the expansion of the Atlantic system. During the 150 years following the arrival of Europeans in the Americas, the slave trade brought some 800,000 Africans across the Atlantic. Volume rose to nearly 7.5 million slaves during the boom in sugar production between 1650 and 1800. The West Indies, including Cuba, imported nearly 50 percent of this total, while Brazil received nearly a third and North America another 5 percent. The rest went to Spain's mainland colonies (see Figure 19.1).

Seventeenth-century mercantilist policies placed much of the Atlantic slave trade in the hands of chartered companies. During their existence the Dutch West India Company and the English Royal African Company each carried about 100,000 slaves across the Atlantic. In the eighteenth century private English traders from Liverpool and Bristol controlled about 40 percent of the slave trade. The French, operating out of Nantes and Bordeaux, handled about 20 percent and the Dutch only 6 percent. The Portuguese supplying Brazil and other places had nearly 30 percent of the Atlantic slave trade, in contrast to the 3 percent carried in North American ships.

While the volume and duration of the slave trade indicate that it was profitable, the relative value of European goods and African slaves as well as slave prices in American ports determined the profit of individual voyages. Slave traders also had to deliver as many healthy slaves as possible for sale in the plantation colonies, but

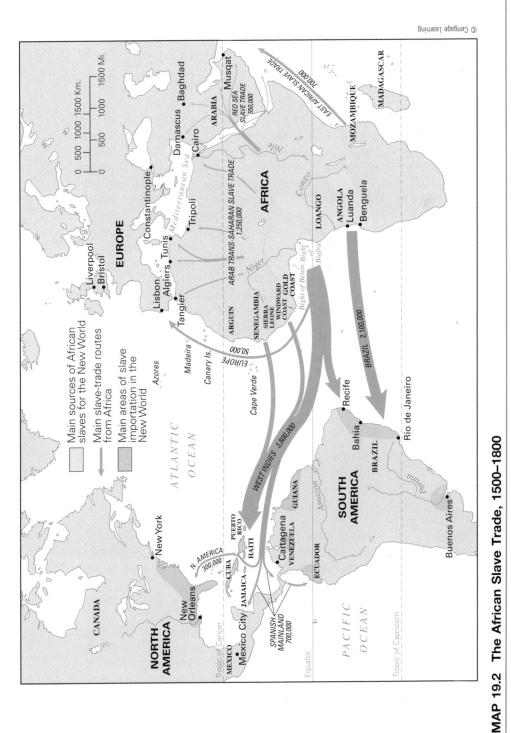

© Cengage Learning

MAP 19.2 The African Slave Trade, 1500–1800

After 1500 a vast new trade in slaves from sub-Saharan Africa to the Americas joined the ongoing slave trade to the Islamic states of North Africa, the Middle East, and India. The West Indies were the major destination of the Atlantic slave trade, followed by Brazil.

the terrible conditions on slave ships and a long and treacherous voyage lasting from six to ten weeks led to high mortalities. Some ships arrived with all of their slaves alive, but large, even catastrophic, losses of life were common (see Figure 19.1). On average, however, slave traders succeeded in lowering mortality during the Middle Passage from about 23 percent on voyages before 1700 to half that in the last half of the eighteenth century.

Failed escapes and mutinies contributed to mortality. When opportunities presented themselves (nearness to land, illness among the crew), some enslaved Africans tried to overpower their captors and escape. As result, male slaves were routinely shackled together to prevent escapes while they were still in sight of land or when mutiny was feared while at sea. As an additional precaution, slave traders also commonly confined male slaves below deck during most of the voyage, except at mealtimes, when the crew brought them up in small groups under close supervision. In any event, "mutinies" were rarely successful and defeated mutineers were treated with brutality.

Mistreatment also contributed to the high mortality of the Middle Passage. Although it was in the interests of the captain and crew to deliver their slave cargo in good condition, slavers used whippings, beatings, and even executions to maintain order. Some slaves developed deep psychological depression, known to contemporaries as "fixed melancholy," and refused to eat. Crews attempted to force-feed these slaves, but some successfully willed themselves to death. The dangers and brutalities of the slave trade were so notorious that many ordinary seamen shunned such work. As a consequence, cruel and brutal officers and crews abounded on slave ships.

Although examples of unspeakable cruelties are common in the records, most deaths in the Middle Passage were the result of disease. Dysentery spread by contaminated food and water caused many deaths. Others died of contagious diseases such as smallpox carried on board by infected slaves or crew members. These maladies spread quickly in the crowded and unsanitary confines of the ships, claiming the lives of slaves already physically weakened and mentally traumatized by their ordeals. Crew members were exposed to the same epidemics. It is a measure of the callousness of the age, as well as the cheapness of European labor, that over the course of a round-trip voyage from Europe the proportion of crew deaths could be as high as the slave deaths.

AFRICA, THE ATLANTIC, AND ISLAM

The Atlantic system took a terrible toll in African lives both during the Middle Passage and under the harsh conditions of plantation slavery. Many other Africans died while being marched to African ports for sale. The overall effects on Africa of these losses and of other aspects of the slave trade have been the subject of considerable historical debate. It is clear that the trade's impact depended on the intensity and terms of different African regions' involvement.

Any assessment of the Atlantic system's effects in Africa must also take into consideration the fact that some Africans profited from the trade by capturing and selling slaves. They chained the slaves or bound them together using forked sticks fastened at the neck for the march to the coast. Once there, captives were bartered to the European slavers for trade goods. The effects on the enslaver were different from the effects on the enslaved. Finally, a broader understanding of the Atlantic system's effects in sub-Saharan Africa comes from comparisons with the effects of Islamic contacts.

The Gold Coast and the Slave Coast   As Chapter 16 showed, early European visitors to Africa's Atlantic coast were interested more in trading than in colonizing the continent. As the Africa trade mushroomed after 1650, this pattern continued. African kings and merchants sold slaves and other goods at many coastal sites, but the growing slave trade did not lead to substantial European colonization.

The transition to slave trading was not sudden. Even as slaves were becoming Atlantic Africa's most valuable export, goods such as gold, ivory, and timber remained important. For example, during its eight decades of operation from 1672 to 1752, the Royal African Company made 40 percent of its profits from gold, ivory, and forest products. In some parts of West Africa, such nonslave exports remained predominant even at the peak of the Atlantic trade.

African merchants were very discriminating about merchandise they took in exchange for slaves or other goods. A ship that arrived with goods of low quality or not suited to local tastes found it hard to purchase a cargo at a profitable price. European guidebooks to the African trade carefully noted the color and shape of beads, the pattern of textiles, the type of guns, and the sort of metals that were in demand on each section of the coast. Although African preferences for merchandise varied, textiles, hardware, and guns were in high demand. Of the goods the English Royal African Company traded in West Africa in the 1680s, over 60 percent were Indian and European textiles and 30 percent were hardware and weaponry. In the eighteenth century, tobacco and rum from the Americas became welcome imports.

Both Europeans and Africans sought to drive the best bargain for themselves and sometimes engaged in deceitful practices. The strength of the African bargaining position, however, may be inferred from the fact that as the demand for slaves rose, so too did their price in Africa. In the course of the eighteenth century the value of goods needed to purchase a slave on the Gold Coast doubled and in some places tripled or quadrupled.

African governments on the Gold and Slave Coasts forced Europeans to observe African trading customs and prevented them from taking control of African territory. Rivalry among European nations, each of which established its own trading "castles" along the Gold Coast, also reduced bargaining strength because Africans could shop for better deals among these competitors. In 1700 the head of the Dutch East India Company in West Africa, Willem Bosman (VIL-uhm boos-MAHN), bemoaned the fact that, to stay competitive against other European traders, his company had to include large quantities of muskets and gunpowder in the goods it exchanged, thereby adding to Africans' military power.

Bosman also related that his agents had to both pay the local king a substantial customs duty when buying slaves at Whydah and then pay a premium price for the slaves. By African standards, Whydah was a rather small kingdom controlling only the port and its immediate hinterland. In 1727, Dahomey (dah-HOH-mee), strengthened militarily by firearms acquired in the slave trade, annexed Whydah.

Two other regional powers, the kingdoms of Oyo (aw-YOH) and Asante (uh-SHAN-tee), also participated in the Atlantic trade, but neither kingdom was as dependent on it as Dahomey. Overseas trade formed a relatively modest part of the economies of these large and populous states, which maintained extensive overland trade with their northern neighbors and with states across the Sahara. Like the great medieval empires of the western Sudan, Oyo and Asante grew more powerful from external trade but were not dependent on it. In 1730, the Oyo kingdom over-ran Dahomey, forcing it to pay an annual tribute to keep its independence.

How did African kings and merchants obtain slaves for sale? Bosman dismissed misconceptions prevailing in Europe in his day. "Not a few in our country," he wrote to a friend in 1700, "fondly imagine that parents here sell their children, men their wives, and one brother the other. But those who think so, do deceive themselves; for this never happens on any other account but that of necessity, or some great crime; but most of the slaves that are offered to us are prisoners of war, which are sold by the victors as their booty."[1] His statement confirms other accounts claiming that prisoners of war were the most common source of slaves, but it is harder to prove that capturing slaves for export was a main cause of wars. "Here and there," conclude two respected historians of Africa, "there are indications that captives taken in the later and more peripheral stages of these wars were exported overseas, but it would seem that the main impetus of conquest was only incidentally concerned with the slave-trade."[2]

An early-nineteenth-century king of Asante had a similar view: "I cannot make war to catch slaves in the bush, like a thief. My ancestors never did so. But if I fight a king, and kill him when he is insolent, then certainly I must have his gold, and his slaves, and his people are mine too. Do not the white kings act like this?"[3] English rulers had indeed sentenced seventeenth-century Scottish and Irish prisoners to forced labor in the West Indies. One may imagine that neither African nor European prisoners shared their kings' view that such actions were legitimate.

The Bight of Biafra and Angola In the eighteenth century the slave trade expanded eastward to the Bight (bite) of Biafra. In contrast to the Gold and Slave Coasts, where strong kingdoms predominated, the densely populated interior of the Bight of Biafra contained no large states. Even so, powerful merchant princes of the coastal ports made European traders give them rich presents.

Using a network of markets and inland routes, regional merchants supplied European slave traders at the coast with debtors, victims of kidnapping, and convicted criminals. As the volume of the Atlantic trade along the Bight of Biafra expanded in the late eighteenth century, some inland markets evolved into giant fairs with different sections specializing in slaves and imported goods. In the 1780s an English ship's doctor reported that African merchants collected slaves at fairs in the interior and that groups of twelve hundred to fifteen hundred enslaved men and women were then sent to the coast from a single fair.[4]

The local context of the Atlantic trade was different south of the Congo estuary at Angola, the greatest source of slaves for the Atlantic trade. This was also the one

---

[1]Willem Bosman, A New and Accurate Description of Guinea, etc. (London, 1705), quoted in David Northrup, ed., The Atlantic Slave Trade (Lexington, MA: D. C. Heath, 1994), 72.

[2]Roland Oliver and Anthony Atmore, The African Middle Ages, 1400–1800 (Cambridge, England: Cambridge University Press, 1981), 100.

[3]King Osei Bonsu, quoted in Northrup, ed., The Atlantic Slave Trade, 93.

[4]Alexander Falconbridge, Account of the Slave Trade on the Coast of Africa (London: J. Phillips, 1788), 12.

place along Africa's Atlantic coast where a single European nation, Portugal, controlled a significant amount of territory. Except for a brief period when the Dutch exercised control in the seventeenth century, Portuguese residents of the main ports of Luanda and Benguela (ben-GWAY-luh) served as middlemen between the caravans that arrived from the interior and the ships that crossed from Brazil. From these coastal cities Afro-Portuguese traders guided large caravans of trade goods inland to exchange for slaves at special markets.

Many of the slaves sold at these markets were prisoners of war captured by expanding African states. By the late eighteenth century prisoners captured in wars fought as far away as 600 to 800 miles (1,000 to 1,300 kilometers) were carried to the ports for transportation. Many were victims of wars of expansion fought by the giant federation of Lunda kingdoms. As elsewhere in Africa, prisoners sold as slaves seem to have been a byproduct of African wars, rather than the objective of the warring parties.

Research has identified a link between severe eighteenth-century droughts and the development of the Angolan slave trade. The environmental crisis in the hinterland drove famished refugees to better-watered areas.[5] Powerful African leaders gained control of these refugees in return for supplying them with food and water. These leaders valued refugee children, who would quickly assimilate, and adult women, who were valued as food producers and for reproduction. They often sold adult male refugees as slaves because they were more likely than women and children to escape or to challenge the ruler's authority. They used the textiles, weapons, and alcohol they received in return for slaves as gifts to attract new followers and to cement the loyalty of their established allies. The most successful became heads of powerful new states, stabilizing areas devastated by war and drought and repopulating them with the refugees and prisoners.

Although the organization of Atlantic trade varied from African region to region, it expanded and prospered because both European merchants and African elites benefited. African rulers and merchants exported slaves and other products to obtain foreign goods that made them wealthier and more powerful, and most of the exported slaves were prisoners taken in wars associated with African state growth. But strong African states or powerful merchant communities also proved better able to defend African territory and limit European economic advantages. The Africans who gained from this trade were the rich and powerful few. Many more Africans were losers in the exchanges.

Africa's European and Islamic Contacts The ways in which sub-Saharan Africans established new contacts with Europe paralleled their much older pattern of relations with the Islamic world. But there were striking similarities and differences in Africans' political, commercial, and cultural interactions with these two external influences between 1500 and 1800.

During the three and a half centuries of contact up to 1800, Africans ceded very little territory to Europeans. Local African rulers kept close tabs on the European trading posts they permitted along the Gold and Slave Coasts and collected

---

[5] Joseph C. Miller, "The Significance of Drought, Disease, and Famine in the Agriculturally Marginal Zones of West-Central Africa," *Journal of African History* 23 (1982): 17–61.

lucrative rents and fees. Aside from some uninhabited islands off the Atlantic coast, Europeans established colonial beachheads in only two places, the Portuguese colony of Angola and the Dutch East India Company's Cape Colony at the southern tip of the continent. The Dutch colony was tied to Indian Ocean trade, not to the Atlantic trade, and, unlike Angola, did not export slaves. Most the Cape Colony's 25,750 slaves in 1793 were from Madagascar, South Asia, and the East Indies, not Africa.

North Africa had become a part of the Islamic world in the first century of Islamic expansion. Sub-Saharan Africans gradually learned of Muslim beliefs and practices from traders who crossed the Sahara from North Africa or who sailed from the Middle East to the Swahili trading cities of East Africa. In the sixteenth century the new Islamic Ottoman Empire annexed all of North Africa except Morocco, while Ethiopia lost extensive territory to other Muslim conquerors.

Until 1590 the Sahara remained an effective buttress against invasion from powerful northern states. The **Songhai** (song-GAH-ee) Empire of West Africa challenged the status quo when it pushed its frontier into the Sahara from the south. Ruled by an indigenous Muslim dynasty, Songhai drew its wealth from the trans-Saharan trade. This expansion led the kingdom of Morocco to challenge Songhai by sending a military expedition of four thousand men south across the desert. Although half the invading force perished, the survivors, armed with firearms, defeated Songhai's army of forty thousand in 1591. While Morocco was never able to annex the western Sudan, its forces extracted a massive tribute in slaves and goods from the local population and imposed tolls on trade for the next two centuries.

With Morocco's destruction of Songhai, the **Hausa** trading cities in the central Sudan attracted most of the caravans bringing textiles, hardware, and weapons across the Sahara. The goods the Hausa imported and distributed through their trading networks were similar to those that coastal African traders commanded from the Atlantic trade, except for the absence of alcohol, prohibited to Muslims. The goods they sent back in return also resembled the major African exports into the Atlantic: gold, textiles and leather goods, and slaves.

Few statistics of the slave trade to the Islamic north exist, but the size of the trade seems to have been substantial, if smaller than the transatlantic trade at its peak. Between 1600 and 1800 slave traders sent about 850,000 slaves to Muslim North Africa. A nearly equal number of slaves from sub-Saharan Africa entered the Islamic Middle East and India by way of the Red Sea and the Indian Ocean.

In contrast to the plantation slavery of the Americas, most African slaves in the Islamic world served as soldiers and servants. In the late seventeenth and eighteenth centuries Morocco's rulers employed an army of 150,000 African slaves, trusting their loyalty more than that of recruits from their own lands. Moroccans also used slaves on sugar plantations, as servants, and as artisans. Unlike in the Americas, the majority of African slaves in the Islamic world were women who served wealthy households as concubines, servants, and entertainers. The trans-Saharan slave trade also included a much higher proportion of children than the Atlantic trade.

The central Sudanese kingdom of **Bornu** illustrates several aspects of trans-Saharan contacts. Ruled by the same dynasty since the ninth century, this Muslim state had grown and expanded in the sixteenth century as the result of guns

Entrance of Heinrich Barth's (1821–65) Caravan into Timbuktu in 1853, from "Travels and Discoveries in North and Central Africa" by Barth, engraved by Eberhard Emminger (1808–85) published 1857 (colour engraving), Bernatz, Johann Martin (1802–1878) (after)/Bibliotheque Nationale, Paris, France/Archives Charmet/The Bridgeman Art Library

Traders Approaching Timbuktu *As they had done for centuries, traders brought their wares to this ancient desert-edge city. Timbuktu's mosques tower above the ordinary dwellings of the fabled city.*

imported from the Ottoman Empire. Bornu retained many captives from its wars or sold them as slaves to the north in return for the firearms and horses that underpinned the kingdom's military power. One Bornu king, Mai Ali, conspicuously displayed his kingdom's new power and wealth while on four pilgrimages to Mecca between 1642 and 1667. On the last, an enormous entourage of slaves—said to number fifteen thousand—accompanied him.

Like Christians of this period, Muslims saw no moral impediment to owning or trading in slaves. Indeed, Islam considered enslaving "pagans" to be a meritorious act because it brought them into the faith. Although Islam forbade the enslavement of Muslims, Muslim rulers in Bornu, Hausaland, and elsewhere were not strict observers of that rule.

Sub-Saharan Africans had much longer exposure to Islamic cultural influences than to European cultural influences. Scholars and merchants learned to use the Arabic language to communicate with visiting North Africans and to read the Quran. Islamic beliefs and practices as well as Islamic legal and administrative systems were influential in African trading cities on the southern edge of the Sahara and on the Swahili coast. In some places Islam had extended its influence among rural people, but in 1750 it was still very much an urban religion.

European cultural influence in Africa was more limited. Some coastal Africans had shown an interest in Western Christianity after contacts with the Portuguese, but in the 1700s only Angola had a significant number of Christians. Coastal African traders found it useful to learn European languages, but African languages continued to dominate inland trade routes. A few African merchants sent their sons to Europe to learn European ways. One of these young men, Philip Quaque (KWAH-kay), who was educated in England, was ordained as a priest in the Church of England and became the official chaplain of the Cape Coast Castle from 1766 until his death in 1816.

Overall, how different and similar were the material effects of Islam and Europe in sub-Saharan Africa by 1800? While Muslims and Europeans obtained slaves from sub-Saharan Africa, the European trade was larger. The Atlantic trade carried about 8 million Africans to the Americas between 1550 and 1800. During this period the Islamic trade to North Africa and the Middle East transported per- haps 2 million African captives. What were the effects on Africa's population? Scholars generally agree on three points: (1) even at the peak of the trade in the 1700s, sub-Saharan Africa's overall population remained very large; (2) localities that contributed heavily to the slave trade, such as lands near the Slave Coast, suf- fered acute losses; (3) the ability of a population to recover from losses was related to the proportion of fertile women who were shipped away. The fact that Africans sold fewer women than men into the larger Atlantic trade somewhat reduced the long-term demographic effects of this larger trade.

The slave trade had a mixed impact on sub-Saharan economies. Africans were very particular about what they received in exchange for slaves, and their imports reflected their tastes and needs. The limited volume of manufactured imports could not overwhelm established African weavers, metalworkers, and other producers, and some imported products like textiles and metal bars actually stimulated the local production of tools and clothing. However, while African as well as European states benefited by taxing this trade, most of the economic benefits went to European nations and to their American colonies.

Profits from transporting and selling slaves mostly went to European merchants and ship owners. European manufacturers, like the producers of textiles and metal goods, profited as well. But Europe's American colonies were the major benefici- aries of the African slave trade. With Amerindian population diminished by epi- demics and European immigration inadequate to develop American resources, it was the forced labor of African slaves that made possible the enormous wealth pro- duced in a vast region that spread from the Chesapeake to the Río de la Plata. This wealth accelerated the rapid expansion of Western capitalism in the seventeenth and eighteenth centuries, a period that witnessed the political and economic decline of the Ottoman Empire, the dominant state of the Middle East, and other Muslim kingdoms (see Chapter 20).

CONCLUSION

European merchants and investors played a central role in the creation of the Atlantic system. European merchants had expanded trade in the century before Columbus, trading over longer distances and using new credit mechanisms to facilitate transactions. They had engaged the markets of Asia through Muslim middlemen and initiated the first tentative contacts with African markets. By the seventeenth century a more confident and adventurous European investor class was ready to promote colonial production and long-distance trade in a much more aggressive way. The development of banks, stock exchanges, maritime insurance, and chartered companies supported these new ambitions.

The new Atlantic trading system had great importance in world history. In the first phase of their expansion Europeans conquered and colonized the Americas and captured major Indian Ocean trade routes. The development of the Atlantic system showed their ability to move beyond capturing the benefits of existing systems to create a major new trading network. Beginning in the seventeenth century, the English, Dutch, and French created new colonies in the Caribbean to compete with earlier colonies created by the Spanish and Portuguese (see Chapter 18). While these colonies remained fragile for decades, settlers found ways to profitably produce goods sought by European consumers. Tobacco was the first, but sugar soon supplanted it.

The establishment of plantation societies was not just a matter of replacing native vegetation with alien plants and native peoples with Europeans and Africans. More fundamentally, it made these once-isolated islands part of a dynamic trading system controlled from Europe. The West Indies was not the only place affected. Brazil, large parts of Spanish Central and South America, and the southern region of British North America developed similar linkages, producing sugar, cacao, cotton, coffee, and indigo and using slave labor.

Despite the central importance of their shared dependence on export markets and African slaves, there were important differences among Europe's American tropical colonies. Only the English experimented with indentured labor on a large scale. But like the colonies of the Portuguese, Dutch, and French, they soon depended on African slave labor. Joint-stock companies and individual investors were crucial to the English colonies. The French entered the process late, but the French state and French monopoly companies quickly developed a massive flow of slaves while securing a profitable home market for the sugar of Saint Domingue and other colonies. After the Dutch attacked but failed to hold Portugal's sugar-producing colony of Brazil and the slave-exporting colony of Angola, they became influential in the transfer of sugar technology and the expansion of the slave trade. While Spain had introduced sugar to the Caribbean and imported African slaves in the early sixteenth century, its most important Caribbean colony, Cuba, joined the sugar revolution late, becoming the major destination for the slave trade and the major producer of sugar by 1820.

While Africa played an essential role in the Atlantic system, importing trade goods and exporting slaves to the Americas, the Atlantic system dominated Europe's American colonies much more comprehensively. Africans remained in control of their continent and interacted culturally and politically more with the Islamic world than with the Atlantic.

Sub-Saharan Africa had long-established trade connections with the Islamic world that included the sale of slaves. These trade relationships facilitated the spread of Islam to sub-Saharan Africa and the creation of Islamic states like Mali and Songhai (see Chapter 15). The volume of the Atlantic trade was much larger than the Islamic slave trade, but the Islamic trade persisted after European reformers ended the Atlantic trade (see Chapter 25). Between 1550 and 1800 four slaves crossed the Atlantic to European colonies for every slave carried across the Sahara. While more males were carried across the Atlantic, the Islamic trade took more women and children, and few slaves in the Islamic region were subjected to the brutal labor conditions of the West Indian plantations.

IMPORTANT EVENTS 1500–1800

ca. 1500	Spanish settlers introduce sugar-cane cultivation to West Indies
1500–1700	Gold trade predominates in Africa
1530	Amsterdam Exchange opens
1591	Morocco conquers Songhai
1620s and 1630s	English and French colonies in Caribbean
1621	Dutch West India Company chartered
1638	Dutch take Elmina
1640s	Dutch bring sugar plantation system from Brazil
1654	Dutch expelled from Brazil
1655	English take Jamaica
1660s	English Navigation Acts
1670s	French occupy western half of Hispaniola (modern Haiti)
1672	Royal African Company chartered
1698	French Exclusif
1700	West Indies surpass Brazil in sugar production
1700–1830	Slave trade predominates in Africa
1713	English receive slave trade monopoly from Spanish Empire
1760	Tacky's rebellion in Jamaica

20

BETWEEN EUROPE AND CHINA, 1500–1750

I n 1667, Stenka Razin, the leader of a robber band camped on a tributary of the Don River in southern Russia, pillaged a rich convoy of government and merchant barges on the Volga River and sailed southward toward the trading city of Astrakhan. The city's governor was unable to stop their progress, and they established a new camp by the Caspian Sea at the mouth of the Ural River. From there Razin raided across the sea and down into Iran, defeating both Iranian and Russian armies. In 1670, his forces swollen to 20,000, Razin moved up the Volga, threatening to take Moscow and overthrow the tsar. There a tsarist army finally stopped him, and he was executed in the following year.

Razin's followers were Cossacks, people of various ethnic origins who made their way to southern Russia, many of them escaping serfdom in the north, to live as social equals in societies with minimal government and the power to maintain their independence. Modern Russian culture has glorified Razin in music and poetry as a defender of the poor and foe of noble privilege. A famous folksong portrays him sacrificing his bride for the sake of leading his warriors.

> So that peace may reign forever
> In this band so free and brave
> Volga, Volga, Mother Volga
> Make this lovely girl a grave.

A less lurid historical understanding of his revolt focuses on the unsettled state of the lands north of the Caspian Sea that had once been the center of the Mongol Golden Horde (see Chapter 13). Muslim Tartars, Buddhist Kalmyks from western Mongolia, and Orthodox Christian Ukrainians and Russians mingled in the sparsely populated frontier between the tsars, the Ottoman sultans, and the Iranian shahs.

But this zone was also becoming a trading nexus. The old Silk Road traversing Central and Inner Asia from East to West had faded, but a new axis was in the process of opening, one that linked the Ottoman, Safavid, and Mughal Empires to the south with a growing Russian Empire to the north. Few Russian merchants traveled beyond the tsarist frontiers, but Indian and Armenian traders abounded. Twenty-seven Indians resided on the outskirts of Moscow in 1684, along with various Armenian, Iranian, and Bukharan merchants. Ten times that number lived in Astrakhan, which Ivan IV, "The Terrible," had added to his domains in 1556 and defended against Ottoman attack in 1569.

Russia imported cotton and silk textiles from Iran and India and exported furs, leather goods, walrus tusks, and some woolens. In their business organization, the Indian family firms closely resembled the Italian merchant enterprises of the Renaissance era.

Thus a pattern was set that would last into the twentieth century: while western Europe maintained rigid religious boundaries with very few Muslims living under Christian monarchs, Russia more closely resembled the Muslim empires to its south in tolerating the ethnic and religious diversity that had been a hallmark of Mongol rule. This pattern of various religious groups living together extended into the maritime states of the period as well.

THE OTTOMAN EMPIRE, TO 1750

The most durable of the post-Mongol Muslim realms was the **Ottoman Empire**, founded around 1300. By extending Islamic conquests into eastern Europe starting in the late fourteenth century, and by taking Syria and Egypt from the Mamluk rulers in the early sixteenth, the Ottomans seemed to re-create the might of the medieval Islamic caliphate. However, the empire more closely resembled the new centralized monarchies of Europe (see Chapter 17) than any medieval model.

Enduring until 1922, the Ottoman Empire survived several periods of wrenching change, some caused by economic and political problems and others by military innovations. These periods of change reveal the problems faced by the land-based empires situated between Europe and China.

Expansion and Frontiers   The Ottoman Empire grew from a tiny state in northwestern Anatolia because of three factors: (1) the shrewdness of its founder, Osman (from which the name *Ottoman* comes), and his descendants, (2) control of a strategic link between Europe and Asia on the Dardanelles strait, and (3) the creation of an army that took advantage of the traditional skills of the Turkish cavalryman and the new military possibilities presented by gunpowder.

Ottoman armies attacked Christian enemies in Greece and the Balkans before conquering neighboring Muslim principalities. In 1389 a strong Serbian kingdom was defeated at the Battle of Kosovo (KO-so-vo), and by 1402 the sultans ruled much of southeastern Europe and Anatolia. In 1453, Sultan Mehmed II, "the Conqueror," laid siege to Constantinople. His forces used enormous cannon to crush the city's walls, dragged warships over a high hill from the Bosporus strait to the city's inner harbor to get around its sea defenses, and finally overcame the city's land walls with direct infantry assaults. The fall of Constantinople—henceforward commonly known as Istanbul—brought to an end over eleven hundred years of Byzantine rule and made the Ottomans seem invincible.

Selim (seh-LEEM) I, "the Grim," conquered Egypt and Syria in 1516 and 1517, making the Red Sea the Ottomans' southern frontier. His son, **Suleiman** (SOO-lay-man) **the Magnificent** (r. 1520–1566), presided over the greatest Ottoman assault on Christian Europe. Seemingly unstoppable, he conquered Belgrade in 1521, expelled the Knights of the Hospital of St. John from the island of Rhodes the following year, and laid siege to Vienna in 1529. Vienna was saved by the need to retreat before the onset of winter more than by military action. Later Ottoman historians looked back on the reign of Suleiman as the period when the imperial system worked to perfection, and they spoke of it as the golden age of Ottoman greatness.

While Ottoman armies pressed deeper and deeper into eastern Europe, the sultans also sought to control the Mediterranean. Between 1453 and 1502, the Ottomans fought the opening rounds of a two-century war with Venice, the most powerful of Italy's commercial city-states. The initial fighting left Venice in control of its lucrative islands like Crete and Cyprus for another century. But it also left Venice a reduced military power compelled to pay tribute to the Ottomans.

In the early sixteenth century, merchants from southern India and Sumatra sent emissaries to Istanbul requesting naval support against the Portuguese. The Ottomans responded vigorously to Portuguese threats close to their territories, such as at Aden at the southern entrance to the Red Sea, and seemed to have a coherent policy for defending Muslim lands bordering the Indian Ocean. By century's end, however, they had pulled back from major maritime commitments outside the Mediterranean Sea. Since eastern luxury products still flowed to Ottoman markets and Portuguese power was territorially limited to fortified coastal points, such as Hormuz at the entrance to the Persian Gulf, Goa in western India, and Malacca in Malaya, it seemed wiser to concentrate the state's resources on defending territory in Europe.

mozcann/iStockphoto.com

Aya Sofya Mosque in Istanbul *Originally a Byzantine cathedral, Aya Sofya (in Greek, Hagia Sophia) was transformed into a mosque after 1453, and four minarets were added. It then became a model for subsequent Ottoman mosques. To the right behind it is the Bosporus strait dividing Europe and Asia, to the left the Golden Horn inlet separating the old city of Istanbul from the newer parts. The gate to the Ottoman sultan's palace is to the right of the mosque. The pointed tower to the left of the dome is part of the palace.*

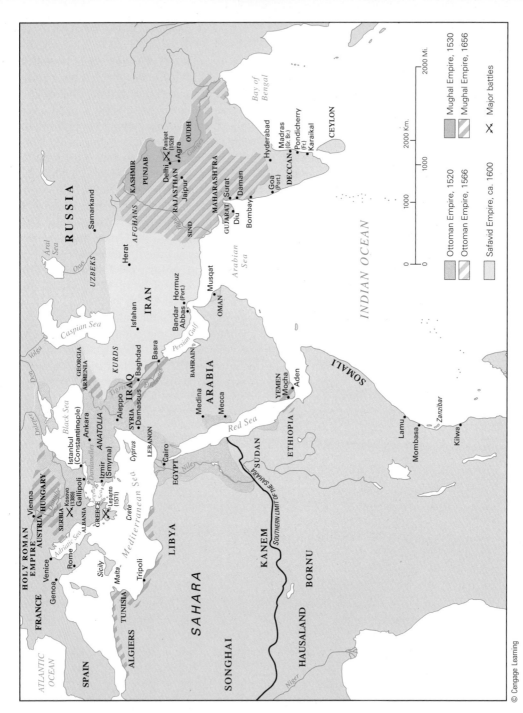

MAP 20.1 Muslim Empires in the Sixteenth and Seventeenth Centuries

Iran, a Shi'ite state flanked by Sunni Ottomans on the west and Sunni Mughals on the east, had the least exposure to European influences. Ottoman expansion across the southern Mediterranean Sea intensified European fears of Islam. The areas of strongest Mughal control dictated that Islam's spread into Southeast Asia would be heavily influenced by merchants and religious figures from Gujarat instead of from eastern India.

Central Institutions

By the 1520s, the Ottoman Empire was the most powerful and best-organized state in either Europe or the Islamic world. Its military was balanced between cavalry archers, primarily Turks, and military slaves known as **Janissaries** (JAN-nih-say-rees).

Slave soldiery had a long history in Islamic lands, but the conquest of Christian territories in the Balkans in the late fourteenth century gave the Ottomans access to a new military resource. Originating as Christian prisoners of war converted to Islam, these "new troops," called *yeni cheri* in Turkish and *Janissaries* in English, gave the Ottomans unusual military flexibility. Since horseback riding and bowmanship were not part of their cultural backgrounds, they readily accepted the idea of fighting on foot and learning to use guns, which at that time were still too heavy and awkward for a horseman to load and fire. The Janissaries lived in barracks and trained all year round.

The recruitment of Janissaries from prisoners changed early in the fifteenth century. A new system, called the *devshirme*, imposed a levy of male children on Christian villages in the Balkans and occasionally elsewhere. Selected children were placed with Turkish families for language learning and then sent to Istanbul for an education that included instruction in Islam, military training, and, for the top 10 percent, skills that could be used in government administration. Senior military commanders and heads of government departments up to the rank of grand vizier were commonly drawn from among the chosen few who received special training.

The cavalrymen were supported by land grants and administered most rural areas in Anatolia and the Balkans. They maintained order, collected taxes, and reported for each summer's campaign with their horses, retainers, and supplies, all paid for from the taxes they collected. When not campaigning, they stayed at home.

The Ottoman galley-equipped navy was manned by Greek, Turkish, Algerian, and Tunisian sailors, usually under the command of an admiral from one of the North African ports. The balance of the Ottoman land forces brought success to Ottoman arms in recurrent wars with the Safavids of Iran, who were slower to adopt firearms, and in the inexorable conquest of the Balkans. Expansion by sea was less dramatic. A major expedition against Malta in the western Mediterranean failed in 1565. Combined Christian forces also achieved a massive naval victory at the Battle of Lepanto, off Greece, in 1571. But the Ottomans' resources were so extensive that in a year's time they had replaced all of the galleys sunk in that battle.

The Ottoman Empire became cosmopolitan in character. The sophisticated court language, Osmanli (os-MAHN-lih) (the Turkish form of *Ottoman*), shared basic grammar and vocabulary with Turkish, but Arabic and Persian elements made it distinct from the Turkish spoken by Anatolia's nomads and villagers. Everyone who served in the military or the bureaucracy and conversed in Osmanli was considered to belong to the *askeri* (AS-keh-ree), or "military," class. Members of this class were exempt from taxes and owed their positions to the sultan.

The Ottomans saw the sultan as providing justice for his "flock of sheep" (*raya* [RAH-yah]) and military forces to protect that flock. In return, the raya paid the

Islamic Law and Ottoman Rule

Ebu's-Su'ud was the Mufti of Istanbul from 1545 to 1574, serving under the sultans Suleiman the Magnificent (1520–1566) and his son Selim II (1566–1574). Originally one of many city-based religious scholars giving opinions on matters of law, the mufti of Istanbul by Ebu's-Su'ud's time had become the top religious official in the empire and the personal adviser to the sultan on religious and legal matters. The position would later acquire the title Shaikh al-Islam.

Historians debate the degree of independence these muftis had. Since the ruler, as a Muslim, was subject to the Shari'a, the mufti could theoretically veto his policies. On important matters, however, the mufti more often seemed to come up with the answer that best suited the sultan who appointed him. This bias is not apparent in more mundane areas of the law.

The collection of Ebu's-Su'ud's fatwas, or legal opinions, from which the examples below are drawn shows the range of matters that came to his attention. They are also an excellent source for understanding the problems of his time, the relationship between Islamic law and imperial governance, and the means by which the state asserted its dominance over the common people. Some opinions respond directly to questions posed by the sultan. Others are hypothetical, using the names Zeyd, 'Amr, and Hind the way police today use John Doe and Jane Doe. While qadis, or Islamic judges, made findings of fact in specific cases on trial, muftis issued only opinions on matters of law. A qadi as well as a plaintiff or defendant might ask a question of a mufti. Later jurists consulted collections of fatwas for precedents, but the fatwas had no permanent binding power.

On the plan of Selim II to attack the Venetians in Crete in 1570

A land was previously in the realm of Islam. After a while, the abject infidels overran it, destroyed the colleges and mosques, and left them vacant. They filled the pulpits and the galleries with the tokens of infidelity and error, intending to insult the religion of Islam with all kinds of vile deeds, and by spreading their ugly acts to all corners of the earth.

His Excellency the Sultan, the Refuge of Religion, has, as zeal for Islam requires, determined to take the aforementioned land from the possession of the shameful infidels and to annex it to the realm of Islam.

When peace was previously concluded with the other lands in the possession of the said infidels, the aforenamed land was included. An explanation is sought as to whether, in accordance with the pure shari'a, this is an impediment to the Sultan's determining to break the treaty.

Answer: There is no possibility that it could ever be an impediment. For the Sultan of the People of Islam (may God glorify his victories) to make peace with the infidels is legal only when there is a benefit to all Muslims. When there is no benefit, peace is never legal. When a benefit has been seen, and it is then observed to be more beneficial to break it, then to break it becomes absolutely obligatory and binding.

His Excellency [Muhammad] the Apostle of God (may God bless him and give him peace) made a ten-year truce with the Meccan infidels in the sixth year of the Hegira. His Excellency 'Ali (may God ennoble his face) wrote a document that was corroborated and confirmed. Then, in the following year, it was considered more beneficial to break it and, in the eighth year of the Hegira, [the Prophet] attacked [the Meccans], and conquered Mecca the Mighty.

On war against the Shi'ite Muslim Safavids of Iran

Is it licit according to the shari'a to fight the followers of the Safavids? Is the person who kills them a holy warrior, and the person who dies at their hands a martyr?

Answer: Yes, it is a great holy war and a glorious martyrdom.

Assuming that it is licit to fight them, is this simply because of their rebellion and enmity against the [Ottoman] Sultan of the People of Islam, because they drew the sword against the troops of Islam, or what?

Answer: They are both rebels and, from many points of view, infidels.

Can the children of Safavid subjects captured in the Nakhichevan campaign be enslaved?

Answer: No.

The followers of the Safavids are killed by order of the Sultan. If it turns out that some of the prisoners, young and old, are [Christian] Armenian[s], are they set free?

Answer: Yes. So long as the Armenians have not joined the Safavid troops in attacking and fighting against the troops of Islam, it is illegal to take them prisoner.

On the Holy Land

Are all the Arab realms Holy Land, or does it have specific boundaries, and what is the difference between the Holy Land and other lands?

Answer: Syria is certainly called the Holy Land. Jerusalem, Aleppo and its surroundings, and Damascus belong to it.

On land-grants

What lands are private property, and what lands are held by feudal tenure [i.e., assignment in exchange for military service]?

Answer: Plots of land within towns are private property. Their owners may sell them, donate them or convert them to trust. When [the owner] dies, [the land] passes to all the heirs. Lands held by feudal tenure are cultivated lands around villages, whose occupants bear the burden of their services and pay a portion of their [produce in tax]. They cannot sell the land, donate it or convert it to trust. When they die, if they have sons, these have the use [of the land]. Otherwise, the cavalryman gives [it to someone else] by *tapu* [title deed].

On the consumption of coffee

Zeyd drinks coffee to aid concentration or digestion. Is this licit?

Answer: How can anyone consume this reprehensible [substance], which dissolute men drink when engaged in games and debauchery?

The Sultan, the Refuge of Religion, has on many occasions banned coffee-houses. However, a group of ruffians take no notice, but keep coffee-houses for a living. In order to draw the crowds, they take on unbearded apprentices, and have ready instruments of entertainment and play, such as chess and backgammon. The city's rakes, rogues and vagabond boys gather there to consume opium and hashish. On top of this, they drink coffee and, when they are high, engage in games and false sciences, and neglect the prescribed prayers. In law, what should happen to a judge who is able to prevent the said coffee-sellers and drinkers, but does not do so?

Answer: Those who perpetrate these ugly deeds should be prevented and deterred by severe chastisement and long imprisonment. Judges who neglect to deter them should be dismissed.

On matters of theft

How are thieves to be "carefully examined"?

Answer: His Excellency 'Ali (may God ennoble his face) appointed Imam Shuraih as judge. It so happened that, at that time, several people took a Muslim's son to another district. The boy disappeared and, when the people came back, the missing boy's father brought them before Judge Shuraih. [When he brought] a claim [against them on account of the loss of his son], they denied it, saying: "No harm came to him from us." Judge Shuraih thought deeply and was perplexed.

When the man told his tale to His Excellency 'Ali, [the latter] summoned Judge Shuraih and questioned him. When Shuraih said; "Nothing came to light by the shari'a," ['Ali] summoned all the people who had taken the man's son, separated them from one another, and questioned them separately. For each of their stopping places, he asked: "What was the boy wearing in that place? What did you eat? And where did he disappear?" In short, he made each of them give a detailed account, and when their words contradicted each other, each of their statements was written down separately. Then he brought them all together, and when the contradictions became apparent, they were no longer able to deny [their guilt] and confessed to what had happened.

This kind of ingenuity is a requirement of the case. [This fatwa appears to justify investigation of crimes by the state instead of by the qadi. Judging from court records, which contain very few criminal cases, it seems likely that in practice, many criminal cases were dealt with outside the jurisdiction of the qadi's court.]

Zeyd takes 'Amr's donkey without his knowledge and sells it. Is he a thief?
Answer: His hand is not cut off.
Zeyd mounts 'Amr's horse as a courier and loses it. Is compensation necessary?
Answer: Yes.
In which case: What if Zeyd has a Sultanic decree [authorizing him] to take horses for courier service?
Answer: Compensation is required in any case. He was not commanded to lose [the horse]. Even if he were commanded, it is the person who loses it who is liable.

On homicides

Zeyd enters Hind's house and tries to have intercourse forcibly. Since Hind can repel him by no other means, she strikes and wounds him with an axe. If Zeyd dies of the wound, is Hind liable for anything?
Answer: She has performed an act of Holy War [jihad].

Questions for Analysis

1. What do these fatwas indicate with regard to the balance between practical legal reasoning and religious dictates?
2. How much was the Ottoman government constrained by the Shari'a?
3. What can be learned about day-to-day life from materials of this sort?

Source: Excerpts from Colin Imper, Ebu's-Su'ud: The Islamic Legal Tradition. Copyright © 1997 Colin Imber, originating publisher Edinburgh University Press. All rights reserved. Used with permission of Stanford University Press: www.sup.org, and Edinburgh University Press, www.euppublishing.com.

taxes that supported both the sultan and the military. In reality, the sultan's government remained comparatively isolated from the lives of most subjects. As Islam gradually became the majority religion in some Balkan regions, Islamic law (the Shari'a [sha-REE-ah]) conditioned urban institutions and social life (see Diversity and Dominance: Islamic Law and Ottoman Rule). Local customs prevailed among non-Muslims and in many rural areas, and non-Muslims looked to their own religious leaders for guidance in family and spiritual matters.

Crisis of the Military State, 1585–1650   As military technology evolved, cannon and lighter-weight firearms played an ever-larger role on the battlefield. Accordingly, the size of the Janissary corps—and its cost to the government—grew steadily, and the role of the Turkish cavalry diminished. To pay the Janissaries, the sultan started reducing the number of landholding cavalrymen. Revenues previously spent on their living expenses and military equipment went directly into the imperial treasury. Inflation caused by a flood of cheap silver from the New World bankrupted many of the remaining landholders, who were restricted by law to collecting a fixed amount of taxes. Their land was returned to the state. Displaced cavalrymen, armed and unhappy, became a restive element in rural Anatolia.

This complicated situation, exacerbated after 1600 by the climatic deterioration known as the Little Ice Age (see p. 559), resulted in revolts that devastated Anatolia between 1590 and 1610. Former landholding cavalrymen, short-term soldiers released at the end of the campaign season, peasants overburdened by emergency

Topkapi Palace Museum

Ottoman Glassmakers on Parade *Celebrations of the circumcisions of the sultan's sons featured parades organized by the craft guilds of Istanbul. This float features glassmaking, a common craft in Islamic realms. The most elaborate glasswork included oil lamps for mosques and colored glass for the small stained-glass windows below mosque domes.*

taxes, and even impoverished students of religion formed bands of marauders. Anatolia experienced the worst of the rebellions and suffered greatly from emigration and the loss of agricultural production. But an increase in banditry, made worse by the government's inability to stem the spread of muskets among the general public, beset other parts of the empire as well.

In the meantime, the Janissaries took advantage of their growing influence to gain relief from prohibitions on their marrying and engaging in business. Janissaries who involved themselves in commerce lessened the burden on the state budget, and married Janissaries who enrolled sons or relatives in the corps made it possible in the seventeenth century for the government to save state funds by abolishing forced recruitment. These savings, however, were more than offset by the increase in the total number of Janissaries and in their steady deterioration as a military force, which necessitated the hiring of more and more supplemental troops.

Economic Change and Growing Weakness   A very different Ottoman Empire emerged from this crisis. Sultans once had led armies. Now they mostly resided in palaces and had little experience of the real world. The affairs of government were overseen more and more by the chief administrators—the grand viziers.

Involvement in business and transmission of corps membership by heredity did not prevent the Janissaries from becoming a powerful faction in urban politics. Tax farming created other new pressures. Tax farmers paid specific taxes, such as customs duties, in advance in return for the privilege of collecting a greater amount from the actual taxpayers.

Rural administration, already disrupted by the rebellions, suffered from the transition to tax farms. The former military landholders had kept order on their lands in order to maintain their incomes. Tax farmers were less likely to live on the land. The imperial government therefore faced greater administrative burdens and came to rely heavily on powerful provincial governors or on wealthy men who purchased lifelong tax collection rights and behaved more or less like private landowners.

Military power slowly ebbed. The ill-trained Janissaries sometimes resorted to hiring substitutes to go on campaign, and the sultans relied on partially trained seasonal recruits and on armies raised by the governors of frontier provinces. A second mighty siege of Vienna failed in 1683, and by the middle of the eighteenth century it was obvious to the Austrians and Russians that the Ottoman Empire was weakening. On the eastern front, however, Ottoman exhaustion after many wars was matched by the demise in 1722 of their perennial adversary, the Safavid state of Iran.

The Ottoman Empire lacked both the wealth and the inclination to match western European economic advances, but it remained much more prosperous than the Russian Empire. While overland trade from the East dwindled as political disorder in Safavid Iran cut deeply into Iranian silk production, new products also came into vogue. Farmers in Greece, Macedonia, Bulgaria, and Anatolia grew mild-flavored, low-nicotine tobacco; and coffee, a Yemeni product, rose from obscurity in the fifteenth century to become the rage first in the Ottoman Empire and then in Europe.

By 1770, Muslim merchants trading in the Yemeni port of Mocha (MOH-kuh) (literally "the coffee place") were charged 15 percent in duties and fees, while European traders, benefiting from long-standing trade agreements with the Ottoman Empire, paid little more than 3 percent.

Such trade agreements, called capitulations, from Latin *capitula*, or "chapter," were first granted as favors by powerful sultans, but they eventually led to European domination of Ottoman seaborne trade. Nevertheless, the Europeans did not control strategic ports in the Mediterranean comparable to Malacca in the Indian Ocean and Hormuz on the Persian Gulf, so their economic power stopped short of colonial settlement or direct control in Ottoman territories.

A few astute Ottoman statesmen observed the growing disarray of the empire and advised the sultans to re-establish the land-grant and devshirme systems of Suleiman's reign. Most people, however, could not perceive the downward course of imperial power, much less the reasons behind it. Far from seeing Europe as the enemy that would eventually dismantle the empire, the Istanbul elite experimented with European clothing and furniture styles and purchased printed books from the empire's first (and short-lived) press. Ottoman historians named the period between 1718 and 1730 when European fashions were in favor the "**Tulip Period**" because of the craze for high-priced tulip bulbs that swept Ottoman ruling circles. The craze echoed a Dutch tulip mania that had begun in the mid-sixteenth century, when the flower was introduced into Holland from Istanbul. The mania peaked in 1636 with particularly rare bulbs going for 2,500 florins apiece—the value of twenty-two oxen.

In 1730, however, gala soirees at which guests watched turtles with candles on their backs wander in the dark through massive tulip beds gave way to a conservative Janissary revolt with strong religious overtones. Sultan Ahmed III abdicated, and the leader of the revolt, Patrona Halil (pa-TROH-nuh ha-LEEL), an Albanian former seaman and stoker of the public baths, swaggered around the capital for several months dictating government policies before he was seized and executed.

The Patrona Halil rebellion confirmed the perceptions of a few that the Ottoman Empire was facing severe difficulties. Yet decay at the center spelled benefit elsewhere. In the provinces, ambitious and competent governors, wealthy landholders, urban notables, and nomad chieftains took advantage of the central government's weakness. By the middle of the eighteenth century groups of mamluks had regained a dominant position in Egypt. Though Selim I had defeated the mamluk sultanate in the early sixteenth century, the practice of buying slaves in the Caucasus and training them as soldiers reappeared by the end of the century in several Arab cities. In Baghdad, Janissary commanders and Georgian mamluks competed for power, with the latter emerging triumphant by the mid-eighteenth century.

In Aleppo and Damascus, however, the Janissaries came out on top. Meanwhile, in central Arabia, a puritanical Sunni movement inspired by Muhammad ibn Abd al-Wahhab began a remarkable rise beyond the reach of Ottoman power. Although no region declared full independence, the sultan's power was slipping away to the advantage of a broad array of lower officials and upstart chieftains in all parts of the empire while the Ottoman economy was reorienting itself toward Europe.

THE SAFAVID EMPIRE, 1502–1722

The **Safavid Empire** of Iran resembled its long-time Ottoman foe in many ways: it initially relied militarily on cavalry paid through land grants, and its population spoke several languages and included many non-Muslims. It also had distinct qualities that to this day set Iran off from its neighbors: it derived part of its legitimacy from the pre-Islamic dynasties of ancient Iran, and it adopted the Shi'ite form of Islam.

Safavid Society and Religion   The ultimate victor in a complicated struggle for power among Turkish chieftains east of the Ottoman lands was Ismail (IS-ma-eel), a boy of Kurdish, Iranian, and Greek ancestry. In 1502, at age sixteen, Ismail proclaimed himself Shah of Iran and declared that from that time forward his realm would be devoted to **Shi'ite** Islam, which revered the family of Muhammad's cousin and son-in-law Ali. Although Ismail's reasons for compelling Iran's conversion to Shi'ism are unknown, the effect of this radical act was to create a deep chasm between Iran and its Sunni Muslim neighbors. For the first time since its incorporation into the Islamic caliphate in the seventh century, Iran became a truly separate country.

The imposition of Shi'ite belief confirmed differences between Iran and its neighbors that had been long in the making. Persian, written in the Arabic script from the tenth century onward, had emerged as the second language of Islam. Iranian scholars and writers normally read Arabic as well as Persian and sprinkled their writings with Arabic phrases, but their Arab counterparts were much less inclined to learn Persian. After the Mongols destroyed Baghdad, the capital of the Islamic caliphate, in 1258, Iran developed largely on its own, having more extensive contacts with India—where Muslim rulers favored the Persian language—than with the Arabs.

In the post-Mongol period, artistic styles in Iran, Afghanistan, and Central Asia also went their own way. Painted and molded tiles and tile mosaics, often in vivid turquoise blue, became the standard exterior decoration of mosques in Iran but never were used in Syria and Egypt. Persian poets raised verse to peaks of perfection that had no counterpart in Arabic poetry, generally considered to be in a state of decline.

To be sure, Islam itself provided a tradition of belief, learning, and law that crossed ethnic and linguistic borders, but Shah Ismail's imposition of Shi'ism set Iran significantly apart. Shi'ite doctrine says that all temporal rulers, regardless of title, are temporary stand-ins for the **Hidden Imam**, the twelfth descendant of Ali, who disappeared as a child in the ninth century. Some Shi'ite scholars taught the faithful to calmly accept the world as it was and wait quietly for the Hidden Imam's return. Others maintained that they themselves should play a stronger role in political affairs because they were best qualified to know the Hidden Imam's wishes. These two positions, which still play a role in Iranian Shi'ism, enhanced the self-image of religious scholars as independent of imperial authority and stood in the way of their becoming subordinate government functionaries, as happened in the Ottoman Empire.

Shi'ism also affected popular psychology. Annual commemoration of the martyrdom of Imam Husayn (d. 680), Ali's son and third Imam, regularized an emotional outpouring with no parallel in Sunni lands. Day after day for two weeks, preachers recited the woeful tale to crowds of weeping believers, and elaborate street processions, often organized by craft guilds, paraded chanting and self-flagellating men past crowds of reverent onlookers. Of course, Shi'ites elsewhere observed rites of mourning for Imam Husayn, but the impact of these rites was especially great in Iran, where 90 percent of the population was Shi'ite. Over time, the subjects of the Safavid shahs came to feel more than ever a people apart.

A Tale of Two Cities: Isfahan and Istanbul   Outwardly, Ottoman Istanbul looked quite different from Isfahan (is-fah-HAHN), which became Iran's capital in 1598 by decree of **Shah Abbas I** (r. 1587–1629). Built on seven hills beside the narrow Golden Horn inlet, Istanbul boasted a skyline punctuated by the gray stone domes and thin, pointed minarets of the great imperial mosques. The mosques surrounding the royal plaza in Isfahan, in contrast, had unobtrusive minarets and brightly tiled domes. High walls surrounded the sultan's palace in Istanbul. Shah Abbas in Isfahan focused his capital on the giant royal plaza, which was large enough for his army to play polo, and he used an airy palace overlooking the plaza to receive dignitaries and review his troops.

Istanbul's harbor teemed with sailing ships and smaller craft, many of them belonging to a colony of European merchants perched on a hilltop on the other side of the Golden Horn. Isfahan, far from the sea, was only occasionally visited by Europeans. Trade was mostly in the hands of Jews, Hindus and Jains from India, and especially a colony of Armenian Christians brought in by Shah Abbas.

Beneath these superficial differences, the two capitals had much in common. Wheeled vehicles were scarce in hilly Istanbul and nonexistent in Isfahan. Both cities were built for walking and lacked the open spaces common in contemporary European cities. Streets were narrow and irregular. Houses crowded against each other in dead-end lanes. Residents enjoyed their privacy in interior courtyards. Artisans and merchants organized themselves into guilds that had strong social and religious bonds. The shops of each guild adjoined one another in the markets.

Women seldom appeared in public, even in Istanbul's mazelike covered market or in Isfahan's long, serpentine bazaar. At home, the women's quarters—called *anderun* (an-deh-ROON), or "interior," in Iran and *harem*, or "forbidden area,"

Istanbul Family on the Way to a Bath House *Public baths, an important feature of Islamic cities, set different hours for men and women. Young boys, such as the lad in the turban shown here, went with their mothers and sisters. Notice that the children wear the same styles as the adults.*

in Istanbul—were separate from the public rooms where the men of the family received visitors. In both areas, low cushions, charcoal braziers for warmth, carpets, and small tables constituted most of the furnishings.

The private side of family life has left few traces, but women's society—consisting of wives, children, female servants, and sometimes one or more eunuchs—was not entirely cut off from the outside world. Ottoman court records reveal that women, using male agents, were very active in the urban real estate market. Often they were selling inherited shares of their father's estate, but some both bought and sold real estate on a regular basis and even established religious endowments for pious purposes.

The fact that Islamic law, unlike European codes, permitted a wife to retain her property after marriage gave some women a stake in the general economy and a degree of independence from their spouses. Women also appeared in other types of court cases, where they often testified for themselves, for Islamic courts did not recognize the role of attorney. Although comparable Safavid court records do not survive, historians assume that a parallel situation prevailed in Iran.

European travelers commented on the veiling of women outside the home, but the norm for both sexes was complete coverage of arms, legs, and hair. Miniature paintings indicate that ordinary female garb consisted of a long, ample dress with a scarf or shawl pulled tight over the forehead to conceal the hair. Lightweight baggy trousers were worn under the dress. This mode of dress differed little from that of men. Poor men wore light trousers, a long shirt, a jacket, and a hat or turban. Wealthier men wore over their trousers ankle-length caftans, often closely fitted around the chest.

Public life was a male domain. Poetry and art, both more elegantly developed in Isfahan than in Istanbul, were as likely to extol the charms of beardless boys as pretty women. Despite religious disapproval of homosexuality, attachments to adolescent boys were neither unusual nor hidden. Women who appeared in public—aside from non-Muslims, the aged, and the very poor—were usually slaves. Miniature paintings frequently depict female dancers, musicians, and even acrobats in attitudes and costumes that range from decorous to decidedly erotic.

Despite social similarities, the overall flavors of Isfahan and Istanbul were not the same. Isfahan had its prosperous Armenian quarter across the river from the city's center, but it was not as cosmopolitan as Istanbul. Shah Abbas located his capital toward the center of his domain away from any unstable frontier. Istanbul, in contrast, was a great seaport and a crossroads located on the straits separating the sultan's European and Asian possessions.

People of all sorts lived or spent time in Istanbul: Venetians, Genoese, Arabs, Turks, Greeks, Armenians, Albanians, Serbs, Jews, Bulgarians, and more. In this respect, Istanbul conveyed the cosmopolitan character of major seaports from Venice to Canton (Guangzhou), though its prosperity rested on the vast reach of the sultan's territories rather than on the voyages of Muslim merchants.

Economic Crisis and Political Collapse   The Safavid Empire's foreign trade rested on the silk fabrics of northern Iran. However, the products that eventually became most powerfully associated with Iran were deep-pile carpets made by knotting colored yarns around stretched warp threads. Different cities produced distinctive carpet designs. Women and girls did much of the actual knotting work.

Overall, Iran's manufacturing sector was neither large nor notably productive. Most of the shah's subjects, whether Iranians, Turks, Kurds, or Arabs, lived by subsistence farming or herding. Neither area of activity recorded significant technological advances during the Safavid period.

The Safavids, like the Ottomans, had difficulty finding the money to pay troops armed with firearms. By the end of the sixteenth century, it was evident that a more systematic adoption of cannon and firearms in the Safavid Empire would be needed to hold off the Ottomans and the Uzbeks (UHZ-bek) (Turkish rulers who had succeeded the Timurids on Iran's Central Asian frontier. Like the Ottoman cavalry a century earlier, warriors from nomadic groups were not inclined to trade their bows for firearms. Shah Abbas responded by establishing a slave corps of year-round soldiers and arming them with guns. The Christian converts to Islam who initially provided the manpower for the new corps were mostly captives taken in raids on Georgia in the Caucasus (CAW-kuh-suhs).

In the late sixteenth century, the inflation caused by cheap silver spread into Iran; then overland trade through Safavid territory declined because of mismanagement of the silk monopoly after Shah Abbas's death in 1629. As a result, the later shahs could not afford to pay their army and bureaucracy. Trying to unseat the nomads from their lands to regain control of taxes was more difficult and more disruptive militarily than the piecemeal dismantlement of the land-grant system in the Ottoman Empire. The nomads remained cohesive military forces, and pressure from the center simply caused them to withdraw to their mountain pastures. By 1722, the government had become so weak and commanded so little support from the nomadic groups that an army of marauding Afghans was able to capture Isfahan and effectively end Safavid rule.

THE MUGHAL EMPIRE, 1526–1739

What distinguished the Indian empire of the Mughal (MOH-guhl) sultans from the empires of the Ottomans and Safavids was the fact that India was a land of Hindus ruled by a Muslim minority. Repeated military campaigns from the early eleventh century onward had established Muslim dominion, but five centuries later the Mughals still had to contend with the Hindus' long-standing resentment. Thus, the challenge facing the Mughals was not just conquering and organizing a large territorial state but also finding a formula for Hindu-Muslim coexistence.

Political Foundations   Babur (BAH-bur) (1483–1530), the founder of the **Mughal Empire**, was a Muslim descendant of both Timur and Chinggis Khan (*Mughal* is Persian for "Mongol"). Invading from Central Asia, Babur defeated the last Muslim sultan of Delhi (DEL-ee) in 1526. Babur's grandson **Akbar** (r. 1556–1605), a brilliant but mercurial man, established the central administration of the expanding state. Under him and his three successors—the last of whom died in 1707—all but the southern tip of India fell under Mughal rule, administered first from Agra and then from Delhi.

Akbar granted land revenues to military officers and government officials in return for their service. Grants were called *mansabs* (MAN-sab) and their holders *mansabdars* (man-sab-DAHR). As in the other Islamic empires, revenue grants were not considered hereditary, and the central government kept careful track of them.

With a population of 100 million, a thriving trading economy based on cotton cloth, and a generally efficient administration, India under Akbar was probably the most prosperous empire of the sixteenth century. He and his successors faced few external threats and experienced generally peaceful conditions in their northern Indian heartland.

European trade boomed at the port of Surat in the northwest, but merchants from Multan, today on the Indus River in Pakistan, did more business with Iran and Russia. Lacking a regular navy, the rulers saw the Europeans—after Akbar's time, primarily Dutch and English, the Portuguese having lost most of their Indian ports—less as enemies than as shipmasters whose support could be procured as needed in return for trading privileges.

Hindus and Muslims   The Mughal state inherited traditions of religious tolerance from both the Islamic caliphate and the Mongols. Seventy percent of the *mansabdars* appointed under Akbar were Muslim soldiers born outside India, but 15 percent were Hindus. Most of the Hindu appointees were warriors from the north called **Rajputs** (RAHJ-put), one of whom rose to be a powerful revenue minister.

Akbar differed from his Ottoman and Safavid counterparts—Suleiman the Magnificent and Shah Abbas the Great—in his striving for social harmony and not just for territory and revenue. His marriage to a Rajput princess encouraged reconciliation and even intermarriage between Muslims and Hindus. The birth of a son in 1569 ensured that future rulers would have both Muslim and Hindu ancestry.

Akbar ruled that in legal disputes between two Hindus, decisions would be made according to village custom or Hindu law as interpreted by local Hindu scholars, while Shari'a law was for Muslims. Akbar made himself the legal court of last resort.

Akbar also made himself the center of a new "Divine Faith" incorporating Muslim, Hindu, Zoroastrian, Sikh (sick), and Christian beliefs. He liked Sufi ideas, which permeated the religious rituals he instituted at court. To promote serious consideration of his religious doctrines, he personally oversaw, from an elevated catwalk, debates among scholars of all religions assembled in his octagonal audience chamber. When courtiers uttered the Muslim exclamation "Allahu Akbar"—"God is great"—they also understood it in its second grammatical meaning: "God is Akbar."

Akbar's religious views did not survive him, but the court culture he fostered, reflecting a mixture of Muslim and Hindu traditions, flourished until his zealous great-grandson Aurangzeb (ow-rang-ZEB) (r. 1658–1707) reinstituted many restrictions on Hindus. Mughal and Rajput miniature paintings reveled in realistic portraits of political figures and depictions of scantily clad women, even though they brought frowns to the faces of pious Muslims, who deplored the representation of human beings. Most of the leading painters were Hindus. In addition to the florid style of Persian verse favored at court, a new taste developed for poetry and prose in the popular language of the Delhi region. The modern descendant of this language is called *Urdu* in Pakistan and *Hindi* in India.

Central Decay and Regional Challenges Mughal power did not long survive Aurangzeb's death in 1707. Aurangzeb's additions to Mughal territory in southern India were not all well integrated into the imperial structure, and strong regional powers arose to challenge Mughal military supremacy. A climax came in 1739 when Nadir Shah, a warlord who had seized power in Iran after the fall of the Safavids, invaded the Mughal capital and carried off to Iran the "peacock throne," the priceless jewel-encrusted symbol of Mughal grandeur. Another throne was found for the later Mughals to sit on; but their empire, which survived in name to 1858, was finished.

In 1723, Nizam al-Mulk (nee-ZAHM al-MULK), the sultan's powerful vizier, gave up on the central government and established his own nearly independent state at Hyderabad in the eastern Deccan. Other officials bearing the title *nawab* (nah-WAHB) became similarly independent in Bengal and Oudh (OW-ad) in the northeast, as did the militant Hindu Marathas in the center. In the northwest, simultaneous Iranian and Mughal weakness allowed the Afghans to establish an independent kingdom.

Some of the new regional powers were prosperous and benefited from the removal of the sultan's heavy hand. Linguistic and religious communities, freed from Aurangzeb's religious intolerance, similarly enjoyed greater opportunity for political expression. However, this disintegration of central power favored the intrusion of European adventurers.

In 1741 Joseph François Dupleix (doo-PLAY) took over the presidency of the French stronghold of Pondicherry (pon-dih-CHER-ree) and began a new phase of European involvement in India. He captured the English trading center of Madras and used his small contingent of European and European-trained Indian troops to become a power broker in southern India. Though offered the title *nawab,* Dupleix preferred to operate behind the scenes, using Indian princes as puppets. His career ended in 1754 when he was called home. Deeply involved in European wars, the French government declined further adventures in India. Dupleix's departure opened the way for the British, whose exploits in India are described in Chapter 26.

THE RUSSIAN EMPIRE, 1500–1725

Though it was Christian rather than Muslim, the Russian Empire encountered problems and opportunities not unlike the large territorial empires discussed above. Before 1500, the Russian principalities had been dominated by steppe nomads (see Chapter 13). During the next three centuries, however, the rulers of **Muscovy** (MUSS-koe-vee), the principality based on Moscow, forged an empire that stretched from eastern Europe across northern Asia and into North America. Moscow lay in the forest zone north of the treeless steppe (grasslands) favored by Mongol horse nomads (also known as Tatars or, in western European languages, Tartars). The princes of Muscovy led the movement against the Golden Horde and ruthlessly annexed the territories of the neighboring Russian state of Novgorod in 1478. Prince Ivan IV (r. 1533–1584), known as "the Terrible" (meaning the fearsome), pushed Muscovy's conquests south and east at the expense of the Tatar Khanates of Kazan and Astrakhan.

Since 1547 the Russian ruler used the title **tsar** (zahr) (from the Roman imperial title *caesar*), the term Russians had earlier used for the rulers of the Mongol Empire. The

Russian church called Moscow the "third Rome," successor to the Roman Empire's second capital, Constantinople, which had fallen to the Ottoman Turks in 1453.

Yet Russian claims to greatness were exaggerated: in 1600 the empire was poor, backward, and landlocked. Only one seaport—Arkhangelsk near the Arctic circle—connected to the world's oceans. The Crimean Tatars to the south were powerful enough to sack Moscow in 1571, just as Stenka Razin's Cossacks from a nearby region threatened to do a century later. Beyond them, the Ottoman Empire controlled access to the Black Sea, while trade with India had to go through Iran. The kingdoms of Sweden and Poland-Lithuania to the west similarly blocked Russian access to the Baltic Sea.

The Drive Across Northern Asia   The one route open to expansion, **Siberia**, turned out to be Russia's version of the New World, an immense region of little-known peoples and untapped resources. The Russians and their trading partners particularly prized the soft, dense fur that sables and other forest animals grew to survive the long northern winters. The Strogonovs, a wealthy Russian trading family, led the early Russian exploration of Siberia. The small bands of foragers and reindeer herders already living there could not resist the armed adventurers the Strogonovs hired. Using rifles, their troops destroyed the only political power in the region, the Khanate of Sibir, in 1582. Moving through the dense forests by river, Russian fur trappers reached the Pacific Ocean during the seventeenth century and soon crossed over into Alaska. Russian political control followed more slowly into what was more a frontier zone with widely scattered forts than a province under full control. Beginning in the early seventeenth century the tsars also used Siberia as a penal colony for criminals and political prisoners. In the 1640s Russian settlers began to grow grain in the Amur River Valley east of Mongolia, where they came into contact with Chinese authorities (see Chapter 21).

Russian Society and Politics to 1725   As the empire expanded, it incorporated people with different languages, religious beliefs, and ethnic identities. Orthodox missionaries strove to Christianize the peoples of Siberia, but among the relatively more populous steppe peoples, Islam prevailed as the dominant religion. Differences in how people outside of cities made their living were equally fundamental. Russians tended to live as farmers and hunters, while the peoples newly incorporated into the empire were either herders and caravan workers or hunters and fishers living along the Siberian rivers.

Diversity arose even among Russian speakers of Orthodox faith. The name *Cossack*, referring to bands of people living on the steppe between Moscovy and the Caspian and Black Seas, probably comes from a Turkic word for a warrior or mercenary soldier. Actually, Cossacks had diverse origins and beliefs, but they all belonged to close-knit bands, fought superbly from the saddle, and terrified both villagers and legal authorities. Cossack allegiances with rulers were temporary; loyalty to the chiefs of their bands was paramount. Cossacks provided most of the soldiers and settlers employed by the Strogonovs, and they founded every major town in Russian Siberia. They also manned the Russian camps on the Amur River. West of the Urals the Cossacks defended Russia against Swedish and Ottoman incursions, but they also preserved their political autonomy (see beginning of this chapter).

The early seventeenth century was a "Time of Troubles" marking the end of the old line of Muscovite rulers. During this era, which coincided with the beginning of the Little Ice Age and a similar period of internal disorder in the Ottoman Empire, Swedish and Polish forces briefly occupied Moscow on separate occasions. Eventually the Russian aristocracy—the boyars (BOY-ar)—allowed one of their own, Mikhail Romanov (ROH-man-off or roh-MAN-off) (r. 1613–1645), to inaugurate a dynasty that would soon consolidate its own authority while successfully competing with neighboring powers. The Romanovs often represented conflicts between Slavic Russians and Turkic steppe peoples as being between Christians and "infidels" or between the civilized and the "barbaric." Despite this rhetoric, there were many similarities between their empire and those of their Muslim neighbors to the south.

As centralized tsarist power rose, the freedom of the peasants who tilled the land in European Russia fell. The Moscovy rulers and early tsars, like the sultans and shahs, rewarded the loyal nobles who dominated the military with grants of land that obliged the local peasants to work for the lords. Law and custom permitted peasants to change masters during a two-week period each year, which encouraged lords to treat their peasants well; but the rising commercialization of agriculture also raised the value of these labor obligations.

Long periods of warfare in the late sixteenth and early seventeenth centuries disrupted peasant life and caused many to flee to the Cossacks or into Siberia. Some who couldn't flee sold themselves into slavery to keep from starving. When peace returned, landlords sought to recover the runaways and bind them more tightly to their land. A law change in 1649 finally transformed the peasants into **serfs** by eliminating the period when they could change masters and ordering runaways to return to their masters.

Like slavery, serfdom was hereditary. In theory the serf was tied to a piece of land, not owned by a master. In practice, strict laws narrowed the difference between serf and slave. In the Russian census of 1795, serfs made up over half the population: landowners made up only 2 percent.

Peter the Great   The greatest of the Romanovs, Tsar **Peter the Great** (r. 1689–1725), came to the throne a century or so later than the eminent Muslim potentates Suleiman the Magnificent, the Safavid Shah Abbas, and the Mughal sultan Akbar. Whereas Suleiman fought wars with Europeans, and Abbas and Akbar knew them as merchant adventurers, Peter was aware that Europe's wealth and military power had increased enormously during the intervening period. Some Ottoman officials shared this awareness, as evidenced by the vogue for European styles during the "Tulip Period" that coincided with Peter's reign. But no Muslim notable could safely sojourn in Christian Europe long enough to master the new techniques of ruling and acquiring power.

When Peter ascended the throne, there were already hundreds of foreign merchants in Moscow, as there were in Istanbul. Military officers from western Europe, who were paralleled by European converts to Islam in the Ottoman Empire, had already introduced new weapons and techniques, and Italian builders were already influencing church and palace architecture.

Peter the Great *This portrait from his time as a student in Holland in 1697 shows Peter as ruggedly masculine and practical, quite unlike most royal portraits of the day that posed rulers in foppish elegance and haughty majesty. Peter was a popular military leader as well as an autocratic ruler.*

UniversalImagesGroup/Getty Images

Peter accelerated these tendencies in unprecedented fashion. While his half-sister Sophia governed as regent for him and her sickly brother Ivan, he lived on an estate near the foreigners' quarter outside Moscow, where he busied himself gaining practical skills in blacksmithing, carpentry, shipbuilding, and the arts of war. When Princess Sophia tried to take complete control of the government in 1689, Peter rallied enough support to send her to a monastery, secure the abdication of Ivan, and take charge of Russia. He was still in his teens.

To secure a port on the Black Sea, he constructed a small but formidable navy. Describing his wars with the Ottoman Empire as a new crusade to liberate Constantinople from the Muslim sultans, Peter fancied himself the legal protector of Orthodox Christians living under Ottoman rule. His forces seized the port of Azov in 1696 but lost it again in 1713, thus calling a halt to southward expansion.

In the winter of 1697–1698, after his Black Sea campaign, Peter traveled in disguise across Europe to discover how western European societies were becoming so powerful and wealthy. He paid special attention to ships and weapons, even working for a time as a ship's carpenter in the Netherlands. Upon his return to Russia, Peter resolved to expand and reform his vast but backward empire.

In the long and costly Great Northern War (1700–1721), Peter's modernized armies broke Swedish control of the Baltic Sea, making possible more direct contacts between Russia and Europe. This victory forced the European powers to recognize Russia as a major power for the first time, just as the Ottoman Empire was then being viewed as past its prime.

On land captured from Sweden at the eastern end of the Baltic, Peter built St. Petersburg, his window on the West. In 1712 the city became Russia's capital. To demonstrate Russia's new sophistication, Peter ordered architects to build St. Petersburg's houses and public buildings in the baroque style then fashionable in France.

Peter also pushed the Russian elite to imitate European fashions. He personally shaved off his noblemen's long beards to conform to Western styles. To end the traditional seclusion of upper-class Russian women, Peter required officials, military officers, and merchants to bring their wives to the social gatherings he organized in the capital. He also directed the nobles to educate their children.

A decree of 1716 proclaimed that the tsar "is not obliged to answer to anyone in the world for his doings, but possesses power and authority over his kingdom and land, to rule them at his will and pleasure as a Christian ruler." Under this expansive definition of his role, Peter sharply reduced the traditional roles of the boyars in government and the army, brought the Russian Orthodox Church more firmly under state control, built factories and foundries to provide supplies for the military, increased taxes, and imposed more forced labor on the serfs. Peter was an absolutist ruler of the sort then common in western Europe, but he is equally comparable to the most authoritarian rulers in the contemporary Muslim empires.

THE MARITIME WORLDS OF ISLAM, 1500–1750

As land powers, the Mughal, Safavid, Ottoman, and Russian Empires faced similar problems in the seventeenth and eighteenth centuries. Complex changes in military technology and in the world economy, along with the increasing difficulty of basing an extensive land empire on military forces paid through land grants, affected them all adversely.

The new pressures faced by land powers were less important to seafaring countries intent on turning trade networks into maritime empires. Improvements in ship design, navigation accuracy, and the use of cannon gave an ever-increasing edge to European powers competing with local seafaring peoples. Moreover, the development of joint-stock companies, in which many merchants pooled their capital, provided a flexible and efficient financial instrument for exploiting new possibilities. The English East India Company was founded in 1600, the Dutch East India Company in 1602.

Although the Ottomans, Safavids, and Mughals did not effectively contest the growth of Portuguese and then Dutch, English, and French maritime power, the majority of non-European shipbuilders, captains, sailors, and traders were Muslim. The sizable groups of Armenian, Jewish, and Hindu traders remained almost as aloof from the Europeans as the Muslims did. The presence in every port of Muslims following the same legal traditions and practicing their faith in similar ways cemented the Muslims' trading network, and conversion to Islam encouraged the growth of coastal Muslim communities.

Although European missionaries, particularly the Jesuits, tried to extend Christianity into Asia and Africa (see Chapters 16 and 21), most Europeans, the Portuguese excepted, did not treat local converts or the offspring of mixed marriages as full members of their communities. Islam was generally more welcoming. As a consequence, Islam spread extensively into East Africa and Southeast Asia during precisely the same time as rapid European commercial expansion.

Muslims in Southeast Asia   Historians disagree about the chronology and manner of Islam's spread in Southeast Asia. Arab traders appeared in southern China as early as the eighth century, so Muslims probably reached the East Indies (the island portions of Southeast Asia) at a similarly early date. Nevertheless, the continuing dominance of Indian cultural influences in the area indicates that early Muslim visitors had little impact on local beliefs. Clearer indications of the formation of Muslim communities date from roughly the fourteenth century, with the strongest overseas linkage being to the port of Cambay in India rather than to the Arab world. Islam first took root in port cities and in some royal courts and spread inland only slowly, possibly transmitted by itinerant Sufis.

Although appeals to the Ottoman sultan for support against the Europeans ultimately proved futile, Islam strengthened resistance to Portuguese, Spanish, and Dutch intruders. When the Spaniards conquered the Philippines during the decades following the establishment of their first fort in 1565, they encountered Muslims on the southern island of Mindanao (min-duh-NOW) and the nearby Sulu archipelago. They called them "Moros," the Spanish term for their old enemies, the Muslims of North Africa. In the ensuing Moro wars, the Spaniards portrayed the Moros as greedy pirates who raided non-Muslim territories for slaves. In fact, they were political, religious, and commercial competitors whose perseverance enabled them to establish the Sulu Empire based in the southern Philippines, one of the strongest states in Southeast Asia from 1768 to 1848.

Other local kingdoms that looked on Islam as a force to counter the aggressive Christianity of the Europeans included the actively proselytizing Brunei (BROO-neye) Sultanate in northern Borneo and the **Acheh** (AH-cheh) **Sultanate** in northern Sumatra. At its peak in the early seventeenth century, Acheh succeeded Malacca as the main center of Islamic expansion in Southeast Asia, prospering by trading pepper for cotton cloth from Gujarat in India. Acheh declined after the Dutch seized Malacca from Portugal in 1641.

How well Islam was understood in these Muslim kingdoms is open to question. In Acheh, for example, a series of women ruled between 1641 and 1699. This practice ended when local Muslim scholars obtained a ruling from scholars in Mecca and Medina that Islam did not approve of female rulers. After this ruling, scholarly understandings of Islam gained greater prominence in the East Indies.

Historians have looked at merchants, Sufi preachers, or both as the first propagators of Islam in Southeast Asia. The scholarly vision of Islam, however, took root in the sixteenth century by way of pilgrims returning from years of study in Mecca and Medina. Islam promoted the dissemination of writing in the region. Some of the returning pilgrims wrote in Arabic, others in Malay or Javanese. As Islam continued to spread, *adat* ("custom"), a form of Islam rooted in pre-Muslim religious and social practices, retained its preeminence in rural areas over practices centered on the Shari'a, the religious law. But the royal courts in the port cities began to heed the views of the pilgrim teachers.

Muslims in Coastal Africa   Muslim rulers also governed the East African ports that the Portuguese began to visit in the fifteenth century. People living in the millet and rice lands of the Swahili Coast—from the Arabic *sawahil* (suh-WAH-hil) meaning "coasts"—had little contact with those in the dry hinterlands. Throughout this period, the East African lakes region and the highlands of Kenya witnessed unprecedented migration and relocation of peoples because of drought conditions that persisted from the late sixteenth through most of the seventeenth century.

Cooperation among the trading ports of Kilwa, Mombasa, and Malindi was hindered by the thick bush country that separated the cultivated tracts of coastal land and by the fact that the ports competed with one another in the export of ivory, ambergris (AM-ber-grees) (a whale byproduct used in perfumes), and forest products such as beeswax, copal tree resin, and wood. Kilwa also exported gold. In the eighteenth century slave trading, primarily to Arabian ports but also to India, increased in importance. Because Europeans—the only peoples who kept consistent records of slave-trading activities—played a minor role in this slave trade, few records have survived to indicate its extent. Perhaps the best estimate is that 2.1 million slaves were exported between 1500 and 1890, a little over 12.5 percent of the total traffic in African slaves during that period (see Chapter 19).

Initially, the Portuguese favored the port of Malindi, which caused the decline of Kilwa and Mombasa. Repeatedly plagued by local rebellion, Portuguese power suffered severe blows when the Arabs of **Oman** in southeastern Arabia captured their south Arabian stronghold at Musqat (1650) and then went on to seize Mombasa (1698), which had become the Portuguese capital in East Africa. The Portuguese briefly retook Mombasa but lost control permanently in 1729. From then on, the Portuguese had to content themselves with Mozambique in East Africa and a few remaining ports in India (Goa) and farther east (Macao and Timor).

The Omanis created a maritime empire of their own, one that worked in greater cooperation with the African populations. The Bantu language of the coast, broadened by the absorption of Arabic, Persian, and Portuguese loanwords, developed into **Swahili** (swah-HEE-lee), which was spoken throughout the region. Arabs and other Muslims who settled in the region intermarried with local families, giving rise to a mixed population that played an important role in developing a distinctive Swahili culture.

In Northwest Africa the seizure by Portugal and Spain of coastal strongholds in Morocco provoked a militant response. The Sa'adi family, which claimed descent from the Prophet Muhammad, led a resistance to Portuguese aggression that climaxed in victory at the battle of al-Qasr al-Kabir (Ksar el Kebir) in 1578. The triumphant Moroccan sultan, Ahmad al-Mansur, restored his country's strength and independence. By the early seventeenth century naval expeditions from the port of Salé, referred to in British records as "the Sally Rovers," raided European shipping as far as Britain itself.

Corsairs, or sea raiders, working out of Algerian, Tunisian, and Libyan ports brought the same sort of warfare to the Mediterranean. European governments called these Muslim raiders pirates and slave-takers, and they leveled the same charges against other Muslim mariners in the Persian Gulf and the Sulu Sea. But there was little distinction between the actions of the Muslims and of their European adversaries.

European Powers in Southern Seas   Through their well-organized Dutch East India Company, the Dutch played a major role in driving the Portuguese from their possessions in the East Indies. Just as the Portuguese had tried to dominate the trade in spices, so the Dutch concentrated at first on the spice-producing islands of Southeast Asia. The Portuguese had seized Malacca, a strategic town on the narrow strait at the end of the Malay Peninsula, from a local Malay ruler in 1511 (see Chapter 16). The Dutch took it away from them in 1641, leaving Portugal little foothold in the East Indies except the islands of Ambon (am-BOHN) and Timor.

Although the United Netherlands was one of the least autocratic countries of Europe, the governors-general appointed by the Dutch East India Company deployed almost unlimited powers in their efforts to maintain their trade monopoly. They could even order the execution of their own employees for "smuggling"—that is, trading on their own. Under strong governors-general, the Dutch fought a series of wars against Acheh and other local kingdoms on Sumatra and Java. In 1628 and 1629 their new capital at **Batavia**, now the city of Jakarta on Java, was besieged by a fleet of fifty ships belonging to the sultan of Mataram (MAH-tah-ram), a Javanese kingdom. The Dutch held out with difficulty and eventually prevailed when the sultan was unable to get effective help from the English.

In the course of the eighteenth century, the Dutch gradually turned from being middlemen between Southeast Asian producers and European buyers to producing crops in areas they controlled, notably in Java. Javanese teak forests yielded high-quality lumber, and coffee, transplanted from Yemen, grew well in the western hilly regions. In this new phase of colonial export production, Batavia developed from being the headquarters town of a far-flung enterprise to being the administrative capital of a conquered land.

CONCLUSION

The complex changes in military technology and economic organization that were under way in smaller European countries in the seventeenth and eighteenth centuries affected the Ottoman, Safavid, and Mughal Empires adversely. Only Russia, by virtue of a single ruler who was able to learn western European techniques at first hand, found success in adopting some of the changes. By western European standards, however, Russia was still a poor and backward country when Peter's reign ended in 1725 while the Muslims ruled rich lands that were ripe for European exploitation.

Improvements in ship design, navigation accuracy, and the use of cannon gave an ever-increasing edge to European powers competing with local seafaring peoples. In contrast to the age-old Eurasian belief that imperial wealth came from controlling broad expanses of land, western European rulers promoted joint-stock companies and luxuriated in the prosperity gained from their ever-increasing control of Indian Ocean commerce. Eighteenth-century European observers marveled no less at the riches and industry of these eastern lands than at the fundamental weakness of their political and military systems. Yet they persistently underestimated the importance of Islam as a focus of local allegiance and political opposition.

IMPORTANT EVENTS 1500–1750	
1502–1524	Shah Ismail establishes Safavid rule in Iran
1511	Portuguese seize Malacca from local Malay ruler
1514	Selim I defeats Safavid Shah at Chaldiran; conquers Egypt and Syria (1516–1517)

1514	Defeat by Ottomans at Chaldiran limits Safavid growth
1520–1566	Reign of Suleiman the Magnificent; peak of Ottoman Empire
1526	Babur defeats last sultan of Delhi at Panipat
1529	First Ottoman siege of Vienna
1533–1584	Rule of Prince Ivan IV
1556–1605	Akbar rules in Agra; peak of Mughal Empire
1565	Spanish establish their first fort in the Philippines
1571	Ottoman naval defeat at Lepanto
1582	Russians conquer Khanate of Sibir
1587–1629	Reign of Shah Abbas the Great; peak of Safavid Empire
1600	English East India company founded
1602	Dutch East India Company founded
1606	Dutch reach Australia
1610	End of Anatolian revolts
1613–1645	Rule of Mikhail, the first Romanov tsar
1622	Iranians oust Portuguese from Hormuz after 108 years
1641	Dutch seize Malacca from Portuguese
1650	Omani Arabs capture Musqat from Portuguese
1658–1707	Aurangzeb imposes conservative Islamic regime
1689–1725	Rule of Peter the Great
1698	Omani Arabs seize Mombasa from Portuguese
1712	St. Petersburg becomes Russia's capital
1718–1730	Tulip Period
1722	Afghan invaders topple last Safavid Shah
1736–1747	Nadir Shah temporarily reunites Iran; invades India (1739)
1739	Iranians under Nadir Shah sack Delhi
1741	Expansion of French Power in India

21

EAST ASIA IN GLOBAL PERSPECTIVE

In the sixteenth century Ming China became a driving force in the first truly global economy, one that joined together Asia, Europe, the Americas, and, to a lesser extent, Africa. To meet China's skyrocketing demand for silver, European traders imported American silver and in return shipped silk, spices, tea, and other precious goods back to Europe. Christian missionaries joined European merchants as intellectual middlemen in this global interaction.

At century's end, however, from 1592 to 1598, the Imjin War, a conflict surpassed in violence only by the wars of the nineteenth and twentieth centuries, embroiled Korea, Japan, and China. After attempting to conquer China, the Japanese finally returned to their islands, leaving the weakened Ming to face other foes. Korea, the devastated battleground, did not recover for centuries.

In the seventeenth century, **Manchu** armies from Manchuria on China's northeast frontier succeeded where Japan had failed. The Ming emperor had slashed the government payroll to pay the army defending Beijing (**bay-JING**) against the Manchu. Among those losing his job was an apprentice ironworker named Li Zicheng (**lee ZUH-cheng**). By 1630 Li Zicheng had found work as a soldier, but he and his fellow soldiers mutinied when the government failed to provide needed supplies. A natural leader, Li soon headed several thousand Chinese rebels, and in 1635 he and other rebel leaders gained control over much of north-central China.

Wedged between the Manchu armies to the north and the rebels south of Beijing, the Ming government tottered. Li Zicheng's forces moved on Beijing, promising an end to Ming abuses and a restoration of peace and prosperity. In April 1644 Li's forces took the city without a fight. The last Ming emperor hanged himself in the palace garden, bringing to an end the dynasty that had ruled China since 1368.

Li's victory was short-lived, however. Preferring the Manchus to an uneducated warlord, the Ming general Wu Sangui and his new northern allies retook Beijing in June. Li's forces scattered, and a year later he was dead, either a suicide or beaten to death by peasants whose food he tried to steal.[1] Now the new masters of China, the Manchus installed their young sovereign as emperor, declared the beginning of a new dynasty called "Qing" (**ching**), and over the next two decades hunted down the last of the Ming loyalists and heirs to the throne.

---

[1]Adapted from Jonathan D. Spence, *The Search for Modern China* (New York: W. W. Norton, 1990), 21–25.

These centuries may be referred to as the early modern period, a time of greater cultural, commercial, and military connectivity within East Asia. Maritime networks replaced the land-based Silk Road trade. This led to increased presence of Europeans. Some people in China, Korea, and Japan welcomed the European presence, but rulers in Korea and Japan eventually sought to curb foreign influence. Japan and Korea would eventually experience relative peace during the early modern period, while China suffered from large-scale warfare, rebellions, and natural disasters at the beginning and end of the early modern period. Each country, however, at its peak generated commercial and cultural developments that rivaled achievements in Europe.

EAST ASIA AND EUROPE

In the sixteenth century, European merchant adventurers traveling from Southeast Asia helped build thriving trade networks in East Asia. Because of changes in the Ming fiscal system that required taxes to be paid in cash, China had an urgent demand for silver. Prior to 1500, Japan had supplied much of the foreign silver China needed, as much as 30 percent of the world's total output. This was replaced by American silver, however, mostly from the mines at Potosí in Bolivia (see Chapter 18). European ships transported the bullion with their masters also acting as middlemen in Asian trade routes, sometimes operating as privateers and even pirates.

Trading Companies and Missionaries   For European merchants, the China trade was second in importance only to the spice trade of Southeast Asia. China's vast population and manufacturing skills drew a steady stream of would-be merchants from western Europe; however, enthusiasm for the trade developed only slowly at the Ming court.

In late 1513 a Portuguese ship reached China but was not permitted to trade. A formal Portuguese embassy in 1517 got bogged down in Chinese protocol and procrastination, and China expelled the Portuguese in 1522. Finally, in 1557, the Portuguese gained permission to trade from a base in Macao (**muh-KOW**) on the southern coast. Spain's China trade was conducted from Manila in the Philippines, where silver-laden galleons arrived from South America. For a time, the Spanish and the Dutch both maintained trading outposts on the island of Taiwan (then called Formosa), but in 1662 they were forced to concede control to the Qing, who for the first time incorporated Taiwan into China.

By then, the Dutch East India Company (VOC for Vereenigde Oost-Indische Compagnie) (see Chapter 19) had displaced the Portuguese as the paramount European traders in the Indian Ocean. The Portuguese had tried to dominate the trade in spices by seizing Malacca, a strategic town on the narrow strait at the end of the Malay Peninsula, from a local Malay ruler in 1511. The Dutch took it away from them in 1641, leaving Portugal little foothold in the East Indies except the Islands of Ambon (**am-BOHN**) and Timor.

The governors-general appointed by the VOC deployed almost unlimited authority in their efforts to maintain their trade monopoly. They could even order the execution of their own employees for "smuggling"—that is, trading on their own. Under strong governors-general, the Dutch fought a series of wars against

Martyn Vickery/Alamy

Great Pagoda at Kew Gardens *A testament to Europeans' fascination with Chinese culture is the towering Pagoda at the Royal Botanic Gardens in London. Completed in 1762, it was designed by Sir William Chambers as the principal ornament in the pleasure grounds of the White House at Kew, residence of Augusta, the mother of King George III.*

local rulers in Southeast Asia, such as the sultan of a Javanese kingdom called Mataram (**MAH-tah-ram**). Suppressing local rulers, however, was not enough to control the spice trade once other Europeans countries adopted Dutch methods, learned where goods could be acquired, and started to send ships into eastern waters.

In East Asia as well, the VOC established itself as the main European trader. VOC representatives courted official favor in China by acknowledging the moral superiority of the emperor. This meant performing the ritual kowtow (in which the visitor knocked his head on the floor while crawling toward the throne) to the Ming emperor.

Along with trade came missionaries. Catholic missionaries accompanied the Portuguese and Spanish merchants to China. While the Franciscans and Dominicans pursued the conversion efforts at the bottom of society, a strategy pioneered in Japan, the Jesuits (members of the Catholic religious order the Society of Jesus) focused on China's intellectual and political elite.

The outstanding Jesuit of late Ming China, Matteo Ricci (**mah-TAY-oh REE-chee**) (1552–1610), became expert in the Chinese language and an accomplished scholar of the Confucian classics. Under Ricci's leadership, the Jesuits adapted Catholicism to Chinese cultural traditions while introducing the Chinese to the latest science and technology from Europe. After 1601 Ricci resided in Beijing on an imperial stipend as a Western scholar. Later Jesuits headed the office of astronomy that issued the official calendar.

Jesuits helped create maps in the European style as practical guides to newly conquered regions and as symbols of Qing dominance. One Chinese emperor, Kangxi, considered introducing the European calendar, but protests from the Confucian elite caused him to drop the plan. When he fell ill with malaria in the 1690s, Jesuit medical treatment (in this case, South American quinine) aided his recovery. Kangxi also ordered the creation of illustrated books in Manchu detailing European anatomical and pharmaceutical knowledge.

To gain converts, the Jesuits made important compromises in their religious teaching. Most importantly, they tolerated Confucian ancestor worship. This excited controversy between the Jesuits and their Catholic rivals in China, the Franciscans and Dominicans, and also between the Jesuits and the pope. In 1690 the disagreement reached a high pitch. Kangxi wrote to Rome supporting the Jesuit position and after further dispute ordered the expulsion of all missionaries who refused to sign a certificate accepting his position. The Jesuit presence in China declined in the eighteenth century, and later Chinese emperors persecuted Christians rather than naming them to high office.

Chinese Influences on Europe

The exchange of information between Chinese and Europeans was never one-way. While the Jesuits brought forward new knowledge of anatomy, for example, the Chinese demonstrated an early form of inoculation, called "variolation," that had helped curtail smallpox after the conquest of Beijing. The technique inspired Europeans to develop other vaccines.

Similarly, Jesuit writings about China excited admiration in Europe. The wealthy and the aspiring middle classes demanded Chinese things, or at least "chinoiserie," that is, things that looked Chinese. Silk, porcelain, and tea were avidly sought, along with cloisonné jewelry, jade, lacquered and jeweled room dividers, painted fans, and carved ivory (which originated in Africa and was finished in China). Wallpaper began as an adaptation of the Chinese practice of covering walls with enormous loose-hanging watercolors or calligraphy scrolls. By the mid-1700s special workshops throughout China were producing wallpaper and other items according to the specifications of European merchants. The items were exported to Europe via Canton.

Chinese political philosophy impressed Europeans, too. In the late 1770s poems supposedly written by Emperor Qianlong were translated into French and disseminated in intellectual circles. In these poems the Chinese emperors rule as benevolent despots campaigning against superstition and ignorance, curbing aristocratic excesses, and patronizing science and the arts. This image of a practical, secular, compassionate ruler impressed the French thinker Voltaire, who proclaimed that Chinese emperors were model philosopher-kings and advocated such rulership as a protection against the growth of aristocratic privilege.

Japan and the Europeans   European contacts with Japan also presented that country with new opportunities and problems. Within thirty years of the arrival of the first Portuguese in 1543, warlords known as *daimyo* (DIE-mee-oh) were fighting with Western-style firearms, copied and improved upon by Japanese armorers.

The Japanese welcomed but closely regulated traders from Portugal, Spain, the Netherlands, and England. Aside from a brief boom in porcelain exports in the seventeenth century, few Japanese goods went to Europe, and not much from Europe found a market in Japan. The Japanese sold the Dutch copper and silver, which the Dutch exchanged in China for silks that they then resold in Japan. The Japanese, of course, had their own trade with China.

Portuguese and Spanish merchant ships also brought Catholic missionaries. One of the first, Francis Xavier, a co-founder of the Jesuit Order, went to India in the mid-sixteenth century looking for converts and later traveled throughout Southeast and East Asia. He spent two years in Japan, where he died in 1552, hoping to gain entry to China.

Japanese responses to Xavier and other Jesuits were mixed. Many ordinary Japanese found the new faith deeply meaningful, but the Japanese elite more often opposed it as disruptive and foreign. By 1580 more than 100,000 Japanese had become Christians, and one daimyo gave Jesuit missionaries the port city of Nagasaki (NAH-guh-SAHK-kee). In 1613 Date Masamune (DAH-tay mah-suh-MOO-nay), the fierce and independent daimyo of northern Honshu (HOHN-shoo), sent his own embassy to the Vatican, by way of the Philippines (where there were significant communities of Japanese merchants and pirates) and Mexico City. Some daimyo converts ordered their subjects to become Christians as well.

By the early seventeenth century there were some 300,000 Japanese Christians and even some Japanese priests. However, suspicions about the intentions of the Europeans turned the shogunal regime against Christianity. A decree issued in 1614 banned Christianity and charged its adherents with seeking to overthrow true doctrine, change the government, and seize the country. Some missionaries left Japan; others worked underground. In 1617 the government began persecutions in earnest, and the beheadings, crucifixions, and forced recantations over the next several decades destroyed almost the entire Christian community. Small groups of Christians practiced their religion in secret, but missionary efforts were generally far less successful than in China, at least until the modern era.

To keep Christianity from resurfacing, a series of decrees issued between 1633 and 1639 sharply curtailed trade with Europe. Europeans who entered the country illegally faced the death penalty, and Japanese subjects were required to produce certificates from Buddhist temples attesting to their religious orthodoxy and loyalty to the regime.

The exclusion of Europe was not total, however. A few Dutch were permitted to reside on a small artificial island in Nagasaki's harbor, and a few Japanese were licensed to supply their needs. What these intermediaries learned about European weapons technology, shipbuilding, mathematics and astronomy, anatomy and medicine, and geography was termed "Dutch studies."

Japanese restrictions on the number of Chinese ships that could trade in Japan were harder to enforce. Regional lords in northern and southern Japan not only pursued overseas trade and piracy but also claimed dominion over islands between Japan and Korea and southward toward Taiwan, including present-day Okinawa. Despite such evasions, the new shogunate achieved substantial success in exercising its authority, keeping most daimyo from forming their own relations with European interests.

THE IMJIN WAR AND JAPANESE UNIFICATION

The Imjin War, the largest pre-twentieth-century conflict in East Asian history, had no European involvement. Named in Korean for the year of the water dragon (Imjin), it also has many Chinese names, including "the Korean campaign." In Japan today, it is called "Hideyoshi's invasions." Seven years long (1592–1598), the war had lasting effects in Korea, facilitated the demise of the Ming dynasty in China, and produced bad feelings between Japan and Korea that have lasted down to the present.

Japan changed in three different dimensions between 1500 and 1800: internal and external military conflicts, political growth and strengthening, and expanded commercial and cultural contacts. Along with its relatively homogeneous population and natural boundaries, Japan's smaller size made political unification more achievable than in the great empire of China.

The Ashikaga Shogunate had weakened after the Onin War (see Chapter 13), opening opportunities for daimyo across Japan to fight for land and influence. Warfare among the different daimyo was common, and in the late 1500s it culminated in a prolonged civil war. Each daimyo had a castle town, a small bureaucracy, and a band of warriors, their *samurai*. Daimyo pledged a loose allegiance to the Japanese emperor and to the shogun residing in the capital city of Kyoto (**KYOH-toh**), but neither figure wielded significant political power. Three warlords, often referred to as the "three unifiers," gradually consolidated control over parts of Japan, ending in full unification in the early seventeenth century. First, Oda Nobunaga succeeded in unifying the central part of Japan, including the influential area around Kyoto. When he was betrayed by one of his generals, the second of the unifiers, Hideyoshi Toyotomi, avenged his death, taking control of Nobunaga's forces.

Although born a lowly peasant, Hideyoshi (**HEE-day-YOH-shee**) rose through the warrior ranks and eventually unified the country. Even as he was consolidating his control over Japan, he planned to invade Korea in order to conquer China. In addition, he dispatched retainers to meet officials as far away as the Spanish governor in the Philippines and the Portuguese viceroy in Goa (western India), demanding that they submit to him and send tribute. In 1592, buoyed with his progress in unifying Japan, the supremely confident Hideyoshi sent a 160,000-man invasion force to the Asian mainland. Various reasons are given for his decision to invade: to impress domestic rivals, to keep major daimyo busy fighting outside of Japan so they could not rebel, to push out Christian daimyo (who provided a sizable portion of the forces sent to Korea), to dominate East Asian trade networks. His sights were set on China, however.

Several centuries of peace and court factionalism had left the Koreans ill prepared to handle the battle-tested samurai-led armies. But although the Koreans failed to implement large-scale musket manufacturing or training, a policy that changed after the war began, they did possess cannon. After initial disastrous defeats, what eventually saved them was assistance from the Ming Chinese and their own advanced naval strategy.

While daimyo armies sent to Korea were skilled at land-based fighting, the Japanese navy was unprepared for serious combat. To intercept a portion of the Japanese fleet, Korean admiral Yi Sunshin successfully deployed "turtle ships," highly maneuverable vessels with large cannon and completely covered decks. All told, Yi won some twenty-three consecutive naval battles. On land, the Koreans called upon China for help. Regarding Korea as one of its client states, China obliged. At first the Ming sent only a few thousand troops to Korea, but Hideyoshi's military successes and the fear that his armies might actually reach China convinced the emperor to send more soldiers, eventually totaling some 100,000.

After 1593, the Chinese negotiated a peace with the Japanese, but after a short time Hideyoshi decided that the terms of the peace were inadequate. His forces invaded again in 1597, employing brutal punitive measures as they advanced through the Korean peninsula. However, many daimyo were losing interest in Hideyoshi's dream of defeating China and hoped instead to secure a few provinces in southern Korea for Japan. In poor health, Hideyoshi too grew tired of the war. On his deathbed he gave an order to withdraw all troops from Korea, an order that was followed after his passing in 1598. It still took many years, however, for Japan to conclude peace with Korea. Formal relations did not resume until 1617.

The invasion devastated Korea. In the turmoil after the Japanese withdrawal, the Korean ruling class of nobles laid claim to so much taxpaying land that royal revenues may have fallen by two-thirds. Roughly 80 percent of the arable land was devastated, and nearly 20 percent of the population lost, either killed in the fighting or taken as slaves to Japan. Confucian scholars and artisans were included in that number. The occasionally used phrase "pottery wars" refers to the fact that Korean pottery technology, in particular, was so advanced that transplanted Korean specialists transformed Japanese ceramics production in the postwar period.

China also suffered dire consequences. Fighting in Korea depleted the Ming coffers at a time when the empire was also battling peoples to the north. When the emperor established a new tax to recover revenue, protests erupted in the provinces. The battles in Manchuria weakened the Chinese garrisons there, permitting Manchu opposition to consolidate. Manchu forces invaded Korea in the 1620s and eventually compelled Korea to become a tributary state. By 1644 the Manchus would be in possession of Beijing, China's capital.

Tokugawa Japan and Choson Korea to 1800

Japanese Reunification and Economic Growth

Despite wartime losses, Japan flourished in the postwar era. After Hideyoshi's demise, the last of the three unifiers, Tokugawa Ieyasu (**TOH-koo-GAH-wah ee-ay-YAH-soo**) (1543–1616), asserted his domination over other daimyo and in 1603 established a new military regime known as the **Tokugawa Shogunate**. The shoguns also created a new administrative capital at

Edo (**EH-doh**) (now Tokyo). Trade along the well-maintained road between Edo and the imperial capital of Kyoto promoted the development of the Japanese economy and the formation of other trading centers.

Although the Tokugawa Shogunate gave Japan more political unity than the islands had seen in centuries, the regionally based daimyo retained a great deal of power and autonomy. Ieyasu and his successors struggled for political centralization, but economic integration proved to be a more important feature of Tokugawa Japan. Because the shoguns required the daimyo to visit Edo frequently, good roads and maritime transport linked the city to the castle towns on three of Japan's four main islands. Commercial traffic developed along these routes. Lords received their incomes locally in rice, and they paid their followers in rice. Recipients converted much of this rice into cash, a practice that led to the development of rice exchanges at Edo and at Osaka (**OH-sah-kah**), where merchants speculated in rice prices. By the late seventeenth century Edo was one of the largest cities in the world, with nearly a million inhabitants.

The domestic peace of the Tokugawa era forced the warrior class to adapt to the growing bureaucratic needs of the state. As the samurai became better educated and more attuned to the tastes of the civil elite, they became important customers for merchants dealing in silks, *sake* (**SAH-kay**) (rice wine), fans, porcelain, lacquer ware, books, and moneylending. The state attempted—unsuccessfully—to curb the independence of the merchants when the economic well-being of the samurai was threatened by low rice prices or high interest rates.

The 1600s and 1700s were centuries of high achievement in artisanship. Japanese skills in steel making, pottery, and lacquer ware were joined by excellence in the production of porcelain (see Environment and Technology: East Asian Porcelain), thanks in no small part to Korean experts brought back to Japan after the invasion of 1592. In the early 1600s manufacturers and merchants amassed enormous family fortunes. Several of the most important industrial and financial enterprises of the twentieth century—for instance, the Mitsui (**MIT-sue-ee**) companies—had their origins in sake breweries of the early Tokugawa period and then branched out into manufacturing, finance, and transport.

Wealthy merchants weakened the Tokugawa policy of controlling commerce by cultivating close alliances with their regional daimyo and, when possible, with the shogun himself. By the end of the 1700s the merchant families of Tokugawa Japan held the key to future modernization and the development of heavy industry.

Japanese Elite Decline and Social Crisis   During the 1700s population growth put a great strain on the well-developed lands of central Japan. In more remote provinces, where the lords promoted new settlements and agricultural expansion, the rate of economic growth was significantly greater.

Also troubling the Tokugawa government in the 1700s was the shogunate's inability to stabilize rice prices and halt the economic decline of the samurai. The Tokugawa government realized that the rice brokers could manipulate prices and interest rates to enrich themselves at the expense of the samurai, who had to convert their rice allotments into cash. Early Tokugawa laws designed to regulate interest and prices were later supplemented by laws requiring moneylenders to forgive

ENVIRONMENT + TECHNOLOGY

East Asian Porcelain

By the 1400s artisans in China, Korea, and Japan were all producing high-quality pottery with lustrous surface glazes. The best-quality pottery, intended for the homes of the wealthy and powerful, was made of pure white clay and covered with a hard translucent glaze. Artisans often added intricate decorations in cobalt blue and other colors. Cheaper pottery found a huge market in East Asia.

Such pottery was also exported to Southeast Asia, the Indian Ocean, and the Middle East. Little found its way to Europe before 1600, but imports soared once the Dutch established trading bases in East Asia. Europeans called the high-quality ware "china" or "porcelain." Blue and white designs were especially popular.

One of the great centers of Chinese production was at the large artisan factory at Jingdezhen (**JING-deh-JUHN**). No sooner had the Dutch tapped into this source than the civil wars and Manchu conquests disrupted production in the middle 1600s. Desperate for a substitute source, the Dutch turned to porcelain from Japanese producers at Arita and Imari, near Nagasaki. Despite Japan's restriction of European trade, the Dutch East India Company transported some 190,000 pieces of Japanese ceramic ware to the Netherlands between 1653 and 1682.

In addition to a wide range of Asian designs, Chinese and Japanese artisans made all sorts of porcelain for the European market. These included purely decorative pottery birds, vases, and pots as well as utilitarian vessels and dishes intended for table use. The serving dish illustrated here came from dinnerware sets the Japanese made especially for the Dutch East India Company. The VOC logo is the acronym of the company's name in Dutch. It is surrounded by Asian design motifs.

After peace returned in China, the VOC imported tens of thousands of Chinese porcelain pieces a year. The Chinese artisans sometimes produced imitations of Japanese designs that had become popular

samurai debts. But these laws were not always enforced. By the early 1700s many lords and samurai were dependent on the willingness of merchants to provide credit.

The legitimacy of the Tokugawa shoguns rested on their ability to reward and protect the interests of the lords and samurai who had supported their rise to power. Moreover, the Tokugawa government, like the governments of China, Korea, and Vietnam, accepted the Confucian idea that agriculture should be the basis of state wealth and that merchants, who were considered morally weak, should occupy lowly positions in society. Tokugawa decentralization, however, not only failed to hinder but actually stimulated the growth of commercial activities.

From the founding of the Tokugawa Shogunate in 1603 until 1800, the economy grew faster than the population. Household amenities and cultural resources that in China appeared only in the cities were common in the Japanese countryside. Despite official disapproval, merchants enjoyed relative freedom and influence in

in Europe. Meanwhile, the Dutch were experimenting with making their own imitations of East Asian porcelain, right down to the Asian motifs and colors that had become so fashionable in Europe.

Photograph courtesy Peabody Essex Museum, #83830

Japanese Export Porcelain *Part of a larger set made for the Dutch East India Company.*

eighteenth-century Japan. They produced a vivid culture of their own, fostering the development of *kabuki* theater, colorful woodblock prints and silk-screened fabrics, and restaurants.

The "Forty-Seven Ronin" (**ROH-neen**) incident of 1701–1703 exemplified the ideological and social crisis of Japan's transformation from a military to a civil society. A senior minister provoked a young daimyo into drawing his sword at the shogun's court. For this offense the young lord was sentenced to commit *seppuku* (**SEP-poo-koo**), the ritual suicide of the samurai. His own followers then became *ronin*, "masterless samurai," obliged by the traditional code of the warrior to avenge their deceased master. They broke into the house of the senior minister and killed him and others in his household. Then they withdrew to a temple in Edo and notified the shogun of what they had done out of loyalty to their lord and to avenge his death.

A legal debate ensued. To deny the righteousness of the ronin would be to deny samurai values. But to approve their actions would create social chaos, undermine

Woodblock Print of the "Forty-Seven Ronin" Story *The saga of the forty-seven ronin and the avenging of their fallen leader has fascinated the Japanese public since the event occurred in 1702. This watercolor from the Tokugawa period shows the leaders of the group pausing on the snowy banks of the Sumida River in Edo (Tokyo) before storming their enemy's residence.*

Archives Charmet/The Bridgeman Art Library

laws against murder, and deny the shogunal government the right to try cases of samurai violence. The shogun ruled that the ronin had to die but would be permitted to die honorably by committing seppuku. Traditional samurai values had to surrender to the supremacy of law. The purity of purpose of the ronin is still celebrated in Japan, but since then Japanese writers, historians, and teachers have recognized that the self-sacrifice of the ronin for the sake of upholding civil law was necessary.

Choson Korea   Recovery after the Imjin War was hindered by Manchu invasions that lasted until the late 1630s. Even after the Korean king submitted to the new Qing dynasty, factionalism broke out among the officials that turned violent, an on-again, off-again problem throughout the Choson dynasty (1392–1910). Despite these challenges, the Choson dynasty proved to be the longest-lasting state in East Asian history (see Chapter 13). The dominant influence on Korean culture had long been China, to which Korean rulers generally paid tribute. Thus, although the Korean and Japanese languages are closely related, and although Korea had developed its own system of writing in 1443 and made extensive use of printing with movable type from the fifteenth century on, most printing continued to use Chinese characters.

In many ways the Choson dynasty was also a model Confucian state. The government was staffed by men who passed the civil examination system, modeled on the Chinese institution of the same name. But there was one important difference. In theory, if not in practice, anyone could sit for the civil examinations in China, but by the sixteenth century in Choson Korea, one had to be born into the *yangban* (YAHNG-bahn) class to take an examination and work in any position of real influence in government. The yangban, literally "two orders," were a hereditary status group who dominated the civil and military examinations, filling nearly all of the official positions in the national and local governments. Only occasionally was social mobility possible for commoners who tested into the military yangban group, a status typically disdained by the civil yangban. This played a role in stifling recovery from the devastation of war.

The growing influence of Confucianism throughout the Choson dynasty affected attitudes toward women, as it did throughout East Asia. In the previous Koryo period, and early Choson, women were listed in family genealogies alongside their brothers, even after marriage. By the latter part of the Choson dynasty, however, when a woman married, she was removed from her natal family's register. As in China, Confucian teachings discouraged widows from remarrying. Like China and Japan however, Korean women negotiated Confucian dogma toward women. Women dominated shaman positions, influencing royalty, while some women even became philosophers.

Unlike the majority of commoners, the yangban did not have to pay a household tax, nor did they have to serve in the military (unless they were military yangban). During the Choson period they also owned most of the slaves, which at one point made up nearly 30 percent of the population. In addition to privately owned slaves, local governments also maintained slaves for a variety of clerical and labor jobs. Even Buddhist temples owned slaves. The slave population dropped to about 10 percent in the eighteenth century, when runaway slaves increased and the poor economy meant that most yangban simply hired poor commoners to work in agriculture.

From Ming to Qing

The internal and external forces at work in China were different from those in Japan and operated on a much larger scale, but they led in similar directions. By 1800 China had a greatly enhanced empire, an expanding economy, and growing doubts about the importance of European trade and Christianity.

Ming Economic Growth, 1500–1644   The economic and cultural achievements of the early **Ming Empire** (see Chapter 13) continued during the 1500s. But this productive period was followed by many decades of political weakness, warfare, and rural woes until a new dynasty, the Qing from Manchuria, guided China back to peace and prosperity.

European accounts from the early sixteenth century express astonishment at the power, exquisite manufactures, and vast population of Ming China, where cities had long been culturally and commercially vibrant. Many large landowners and absentee landlords lived in town, as did officials, artists, and rich merchants who had purchased ranks or prepared their sons for the examinations. The elite classes had created a brilliant culture in which novels, operas, poetry, porcelain, and painting were all closely interwoven. Catering to these urban elites were many small businesses that prospered through printing, tailoring, running restaurants, or selling paper, ink, ink-stones, and writing brushes. The imperial government operated factories for the production of ceramics and silks, and enormous government complexes at Jingdezhen and elsewhere invented assembly-line techniques and produced large quantities of high-quality ceramics for sale in China and abroad.

Despite these achievements, serious problems developed that left the Ming Empire economically and politically exhausted. There is evidence that the climate changes known as the Little Ice Age in seventeenth-century Europe affected the climate in China as well (see Issues in World History: The Little Ice Age). Annual temperatures dropped, reached a low point around 1645, and remained low until the early 1700s. The resulting agricultural distress and famine fueled large uprisings that hastened the end of the Ming Empire. The devastation caused by these uprisings and the spread of epidemic disease resulted in steep declines in local populations.

The rapid urban growth and business speculation that were part of the burgeoning trading economy also produced problems. Some provinces suffered from price inflation caused by the flood of silver from America. In contrast to the growing involvement of European governments in promoting economic growth, the Ming government pursued some policies that hindered growth. Ming governments persisted, despite earlier failed experiments, in issuing new paper money and copper coinage, even after silver had won the approval of the markets. Corruption compounded government problems. Disorder and inefficiency came to plague the imperial factories, touching off strikes in the late sixteenth and seventeenth centuries. During a labor protest at Jingdezhen in 1601, workers threw themselves into the kilns to protest working conditions.

Yet the urban and industrial sectors of later Ming society fared much better than the agricultural sector. Despite knowledge of new African and American crops gained from European traders, farmers were slow to change their ways. Neither the rice-growing regions in southern China nor the wheat-growing regions in northern China experienced a meaningful increase in productivity under the later Ming. After 1500 economic depression in the countryside, combined with recurring epidemics in central and southern China, kept rural population growth in check.

Ming Collapse and the Rise of the Qing   Environmental, economic, and administrative problems aside, the primary reasons for the fall of the Ming Empire were internal rebellion and threats on the borders. Powerful Mongol federations in the north and west had long exerted pressure on the frontiers. In the late 1500s large numbers of Mongols were unified by their devotion to the Dalai Lama (**DAH-lie LAH-mah**), or universal teacher of Tibetan Buddhism. Building on this spiritual unity, a brilliant leader named Galdan restored Mongolia as a regional military power around 1600. At the same time, the Manchus, an agricultural people who controlled the region north of Korea, grew stronger in the northeast (see chapter opening).

Pirates based in southwest Japan, Okinawa, and Taiwan, many of them Japanese, frequently looted the southeast coast. Ming military resources, concentrated against

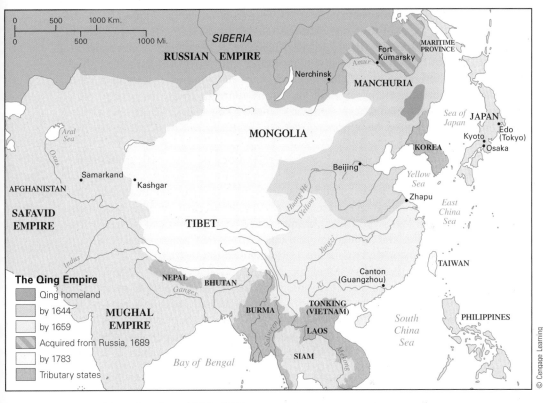

MAP 21.1   The Qing Empire, 1644–1783

The Qing Empire began in Manchuria and captured north China in 1644. Between 1644 and 1783 the Qing conquered all the former Ming territories and added Taiwan, the lower Amur River basin, Inner Mongolia, eastern Turkestan, and Tibet. The resulting state was more than twice the size of the Ming Empire.

the Mongols and the Manchus in the north, could not be deployed to defend the coasts. As a result, many southern Chinese migrated to Southeast Asia to profit from the sea-trading networks of the Indian Ocean.

The Imjin War had prompted the Ming to seek the assistance of Manchu troops that then became enemies after the war. With the rebel leader Li Zicheng in possession of Beijing (see the beginning of this chapter) and the emperor dead by his own hand, a Ming general joined forces with the Manchu leaders in the summer of 1644. Instead of restoring the Ming, however, the Manchus claimed China for their own and began a forty-year conquest of the rest of the Ming territories, as well as Taiwan and parts of Mongolia and Central Asia.

A Manchu family headed the new **Qing Empire**, and Manchu generals commanded the military forces. But Manchus made up a very small portion of the population. Most Qing officials, soldiers, merchants, and farmers were ethnic Chinese. Like other successful invaders of China, the Qing soon adopted Chinese institutions and policies.

Emperor Kangxi   The seventeenth and eighteenth centuries—particularly the reigns of the **Kangxi** (KAHNG-shee) (r. 1662–1722) and Qianlong (chee-YEN-loong) (r. 1736–1796) emperors—saw renewed economic, military, and cultural achievement in China. Roads and waterworks were repaired, transit taxes lowered, rents and interest rates cut, and incentives established for resettling areas devastated by peasant rebellions. Foreign trade was encouraged. Vietnam, Burma, and Nepal sent embassies to the Qing tribute court and carried the latest Chinese fashions back home. Overland routes from Korea to Central Asia revived.

The Manchu aristocrats who led the conquest of Beijing and north China dominated the first Qing emperor and served as regents for his young son, who was declared emperor in 1662. This child-emperor, Kangxi, sparred politically with the regents until 1669, when at age sixteen he executed the chief regent and thereby gained real control of the government. An intellectual prodigy who had mastered classical Chinese, Manchu, and Mongolian and memorized the Chinese classics, Kangxi guided imperial expansion and maintained stability until his death in 1722.

In the north, the Qing rulers feared an alliance between Galdan's Mongol state and the expanding Russian presence along the **Amur** (AH-moor) **River**. In the 1680s Qing forces attacked the wooden forts built by hardy Russian scouts on the river's northern bank. Neither empire sent large forces into the Amur territories, so the contest was partly a struggle for the goodwill of the local peoples. The Qing emperor emphasized the importance of treading lightly in the struggle:

> Upon reaching the lands of the Evenks and the Dagurs you will send to announce that you have come to hunt deer. Meanwhile, keep a careful record of the distance and go, while hunting, along the northern bank of the Amur until you come by the shortest route to the town of Russian settlement at Albazin. Thoroughly reconnoiter its location and situation. I don't think the Russians will take a chance on attacking you. If they offer you food, accept it and show your gratitude. If they do attack you, don't fight back. In that case, lead your people and withdraw into our own territories.[2]

Qing forces twice attacked Albazin. The Qing were worried about Russian alliances with other frontier peoples, while Russia wished to protect its access to the furs, timber, and metals concentrated in Siberia and Manchuria. The Qing and Russians were also rivals for control of northern Asia's Pacific coast. Seeing little benefit in continued conflict, in 1689 the two empires negotiated the Treaty of Nerchinsk, using Jesuit missionaries as interpreters. The treaty fixed the border along the Amur River and regulated trade across it. Although this was a thinly settled area, the treaty proved important, and the frontier it demarcated has long endured.

The next step was to settle the Mongolian frontier. Kangxi personally led troops in the great campaigns that defeated Galdan, and by 1691 he had brought Inner Mongolia under Qing control.

Tea and Diplomacy   Like the Ming before them, the Qing were reluctant to grant too much access to Europeans. To maintain control over trade, facilitate tax collection, and suppress piracy, the Qing

---

[2]Adapted from G. V. Melikhov, "Manzhou Penetration into the Basin of the Upper Amur in the 1680s," in *Manzhou Rule in China*, ed. S. L. Tikhvinshii (Moscow: Progress Publishers, 1983).

permitted only one market point for each foreign sector. Thus Europeans could trade only at Canton.

This system worked well enough until the late 1700s, when Britain became worried about its massive trade deficit with China. From bases in India and Singapore, British traders moved eastward and by the early 1700s dominated European trading in Canton, displacing the Dutch. The directors of the East India Company (EIC) anticipated limitless profits from China's gigantic markets and advanced technologies.

One item of interest was tea. In medieval and early modern times, tea from China had spread overland to Russia, Central Asia, and the Middle East to become a prized import. Consumers knew it by its northern Chinese name, *cha*—as did the Portuguese. Other western Europeans acquired tea from the sea routes and with it the name used in the Fujian province of coastal China and Taiwan: *te*. In much of Europe, tea competed with chocolate and coffee as a fashionable drink by the mid-1600s.

Emperor Kangxi *In a portrait from about 1690, the young Manchu ruler is portrayed as a refined scholar in the Confucian tradition. He was a scholar and had great intellectual curiosity, but this portrait would not suggest that he was also capable of leading troops in battle.*

Wu Chingteng/Xinhua/Photoshot/Newscom

British tea importers accumulated great fortunes. However, the Qing Empire took payment in silver and rarely bought anything from Britain. With domestic revenues declining in the later 1700s, the Qing government needed the silver and was disinclined to loosen import restrictions. To make matters worse, the East India Company (EIC) had managed its worldwide holdings badly. As it teetered on bankruptcy, its attempts to manipulate Parliament became increasingly intrusive. In 1792 the British government dispatched Lord George Macartney, a well-connected peer with practical experience in Russia and India, to China. Staffed by scientists, artists, and translators as well as guards and diplomats, the **Macartney mission** showed Britain's great interest in the Qing Empire as well as the EIC's desire to revise the trade system.

To fit Chinese traditions, Macartney portrayed himself as a "tribute emissary" come to salute the Qianlong emperor's eightieth birthday. However, he refused to perform the kowtow, though he did agree to bow on one knee as he would to King George III. The Qianlong emperor received Macartney courteously in September 1793 but refused to alter the Canton trading system, open new ports of trade, or allow the British to establish a permanent mission in Beijing. The emperor sent a letter to King George explaining that China had no need to increase its foreign trade, had no use for Britain's ingenious devices and manufacturers, and set no value on closer diplomatic ties.

Dutch, French, and Russian missions to achieve what Macartney could not do also failed. European frustration mounted while admiration for China faded. The Qing court would not communicate with foreign envoys or observe the simplest rules of the European diplomatic system. In Macartney's view, China was like a venerable old warship, well maintained and splendid to look at, but obsolete and no longer up to the task.

Population Growth and Environmental Stress

The Chinese who escorted Macartney and his entourage in 1792–1793 took them through China's prosperous cities and productive farmland. They did not see, however, the economic and environmental decline that had set in during the last decades of the 1700s.

Population growth—a tripling in size since 1500—had intensified demand for food and for more intensive agriculture. With an estimated 350 million people in the late 1700s, China had twice the population of all of Europe. Despite efficient farming and the gradual adoption of New World crops like corn and sweet potatoes, population pressure touched off social and environmental problems. Increased demand for building materials and firewood shrank woodlands. Deforestation, in turn, accelerated wind and water erosion and increased flooding. Dams and dikes were not maintained, and silted-up river channels were not dredged. By the end of the eighteenth century parts of the thousand-year-old Grand Canal linking the rivers of north and south China were nearly unusable, and the towns that bordered it were starved for commerce.

Some interior districts responded to this misery by increasing their output of export goods like tea, cotton, and silk. Some peasants sought seasonal jobs in better-off agricultural areas or worked in low-status jobs as barge pullers, charcoal burners, or night soil (human waste) carriers. Begging, prostitution, and theft increased in the cities. Rebellions broke out in flood-ravaged central and southwestern China. Indigenous peoples concentrated in the less fertile lands in the south and in the northern and western borderlands of the empire often joined in revolts.

The Qing government was not up to controlling its vast empire. It was twice the size of the Ming geographically, but it employed about the same number of officials. The government's dependence on working alliances with local elites had led to widespread corruption and shrinking government revenues. The Qing's spectacular rise had ended, and decline had set in.

CONCLUSION

It would be a mistake to think of early modern East Asia as three strictly defined countries filled with people who invariably acted on behalf of their homelands in trade or warfare. During the Imjin War, some Japanese grew tired of fighting in Korea, decided to join the Ming military, and were promoted to high posts by the Chinese. Similarly, some Chinese troops remained in Korea, married local women, and became part of local Korean communities.

Trade and warfare also presented opportunities for groups of people who did not identify with any one country. For example, the Ming-Qing transition and growth in sea trade spurred an increase in piracy during the seventeenth century. The Zheng family dominated piracy in East Asia, defeated the Dutch bases in Taiwan, and eventually worked for the Ming regime to battle the Manchu. The most prominent Zheng pirate-merchant was the half Japanese, half Chinese, Zheng Chenggong. An enemy of the Qing, he continued to expand the Zheng enterprise and was well-known even among Europeans in Asia, who called him Koxinga, the European pronunciation for the name given to him by the Ming loyalists. Even early modern Japanese knew of his exploits through puppet plays. The Zheng also pursued state-building activities, such as establishing an office to collect taxes and regulating trade in the South China Sea.

China is one example of the flourishing of empires in Eurasia between 1500 and 1800. Already a vast empire under the Ming, China doubled in size under the Qing, mostly through westward expansion into less densely populated areas. Like the Russian, Ottoman, and Mughal Empires, it had the strengths and problems of administrative control and tax collection that characterized a large land-based state. The expansion of China incorporated not just new lands but also new peoples. Chinese society had long been diverse, and its geographical, occupational, linguistic, and religious differences grew as the Qing expanded. China had also long used Confucian models, imperial customs, and a common system of writing to transcend such differences and to assimilate elites.

Japan was different. Though it was nominally headed by an emperor, real power lay with the successive shoguns. However, Japan lacked a centralizing, common political philosophy like China's Confucianism, which became a common denominator for a wide variety of elites from different cultures, ethnicities, and regions. Tokugawa Japan was similar in size and population to France, the most powerful state of western Europe, but its political system was much more decentralized. As the chapter has shown, Japan's efforts to add colonies on the East Asian mainland failed.

By the late eighteenth century, the weaknesses in China and Japan were becoming more evident to Europeans and would ultimately make these countries vulnerable to Western penetration. China had once led the world in military innovation, including the first uses of gunpowder, but Chinese armies continued to depend on superior numbers and tactics for their success rather than on new technology. Infantrymen armed with guns served alongside others armed with bows and arrows, swords, and spears. The military forces of Japan underwent more innovative changes than those of China and Korea, in part through Western contacts, and in the course of its sixteenth-century wars of unification, Japan produced its own gunpowder revolution. Thereafter, however, it lacked the means to stay abreast of the world's most advanced military technology.

Finally, neither China nor Japan developed navies commensurate with their size and coastlines. Korea had a small but effective navy during the Imjin War, but it could not match China's or Russia's in strength or size. China's defenses against pirates and other sea invaders were left to the small war junks of its maritime provinces, and Japan's naval capacity was similarly decentralized. In 1792, when Russian ships exploring the North Pacific turned toward the Japanese coast, the local daimyo used his own forces to chase them away. All Japanese daimyo understood that they would be on their own if and when foreign incursions increased. As later chapters show, these foreign incursions became reality in the nineteenth century.

IMPORTANT EVENTS 1500–1800	
1517	Portuguese embassy to China
1543	First Portuguese contacts
1592	Japanese invasion of Korea
1601	Matteo Ricci allowed to reside in Beijing
1603	Tokugawa Shogunate formed
1633–1639	Edicts close down trade with Europe
1644	Qing conquest of Beijing
1662–1722	Rule of Emperor Kangxi
1689	Treaty of Nerchinsk with Russia
1691	Qing control of Inner Mongolia
1702	Trial of the Forty-Seven Ronin
1736–1795	Rule of Emperor Qianlong
1762–1796	Rule of Catherine the Great
1792	Russian ships first spotted off the coast of Japan

ISSUES IN WORLD HISTORY

The Little Ice Age

A giant volcanic eruption in the Peruvian Andes in 1600 affected the weather in many parts of the world for several years. When volcanic ash from the eruption of Mount Huanyaputina (hoo-AHN-yah-poo-TEE-nuh) shot into the upper atmosphere and spread around the world, it screened out sunlight. As a result, the summer of 1601 was the coldest in two hundred years in the Northern Hemisphere.

Archaeologist Brian Fagan has pointed out that Mount Huanyaputina's chilling effects were a spectacular event in a much longer pattern of climate change that has been called the Little Ice Age.[1] Although global climate had been cooling since the late 1200s, in the northern temperate regions the 1590s had been exceptionally cold. Temperatures remained cooler than normal throughout the seventeenth century.

The most detailed information on the Little Ice Age comes from Europe. Glaciers in the Alps grew much larger. Trade became difficult when rivers and canals that had once been navigable in winter froze solid from bank to bank. In the coldest years, the growing season in some places was as much as two months shorter than normal. Unexpectedly late frosts withered the tender shoots of newly planted crops in spring. Wheat and barley ripened more slowly during cooler summers and were often damaged by early fall frosts.

People could survive a smaller-than-average harvest in one year by drawing on food reserves, but when cold weather damaged crops in two or more successive years, the consequences were devastating. Deaths due to malnutrition and cold increased sharply when summer temperatures in northern Europe registered 2.7°F (1.5°C) lower than average in 1674 and 1675 and again in 1694 and 1695. The cold spell of 1694 and 1695 caused a famine in Finland that carried off a quarter to a third of the population.

At the time people had no idea what was causing the unusual cold of the Little Ice Age. Advances in climate history make it clear that the cause was not a single terrestrial event such as the eruption of Mount Huanyaputina. Nor was the Little Ice Age the product of human actions, unlike some climate changes such as today's global warming.

Ultimately, the earth's weather is governed by the sun. In the seventeenth century astronomers in Europe reported seeing fewer sunspots, dark spots on the sun's surface that are indicative of solar activity and thus the sun's warming power. Diminished activity in the sun was primarily responsible for the Little Ice Age.

If the sun was the root cause, the effects of global cooling should not have been confined to northern Europe. Although contemporary accounts are much scarcer in other parts of the world, there is evidence of climate changes around the world in this period. Observations of sunspots in China, Korea, and Japan drop to zero between 1639 and 1700. China experienced unusually cool weather in the seventeenth century, but the warfare and disruption accompanying the fall of the Ming and the rise of the Qing probably were much more to blame for the famines and rural distress of that period. The Ottoman Empire also experienced rural unrest during the coldest years.

By itself, a relatively slight decrease in average annual temperature would not have a significant effect on human life outside the northern temperate areas. However, evidence suggests that there was also a significant rise in humidity in this period in other parts of the world. Ice cores drilled into ancient glaciers in the Arctic and Antarctic show increased snowfall. Information compiled by historian James L. A. Webb, Jr., shows that lands south of the Sahara received more rainfall between 1550 and 1750 than they had during the previous era.[2] Increased rainfall would have been favorable for pastoral people, whose herds found new pasture in what had once been desert, and for the farmers farther south whose crops got more rain.

In the eighteenth century the sun's activity began to return to normal. Rising temperatures led to milder winters and better harvests in northern Eurasia. Falling rainfall allowed the Sahara to advance again southward, forcing the agricultural frontier to retreat.

[1]Brian Fagan, *The Littlest Ice Age: How Climate Made History, 1300–1850* (New York: Basic Books, 2000).

[2]James L. A. Webb, Jr., *Desert Frontier: Ecological Change Along the Western Sahel, 1600–1850* (Madison: University of Wisconsin Press, 1995).

PART SIX

REVOLUTIONS RESHAPE THE WORLD, 1750–1870

Between 1750 and 1870, nearly every part of the world experienced dramatic political, economic, and social change. The beginnings of industrialization and the American, French, and Haitian revolutions, as well as the revolutions for independence in Latin America, transformed political and economic life. European nations expanded into Africa, Asia, and the Middle East, while Russia and the United States acquired vast new territories.

The Industrial Revolution introduced new technologies and patterns of work that made these societies wealthier and militarily more powerful. Western intellectual life became more secular. The Atlantic slave trade and later slavery itself were abolished, and the first efforts to improve the status of women were initiated.

The Industrial Revolution also led to a new wave of imperialism. France conquered Algeria, and Great Britain expanded its colonial rule in India and established colonies in Australia and New Zealand. European political and economic influence also expanded in Africa and Asia. The Ottoman Empire and the Qing Empire met this challenge by implementing reform programs that preserved traditional structures while adopting elements of Western technology and organization. Though lagging behind western Europe in transforming its economy and political institutions, Russia attempted modernization efforts, including the abolition of serfdom.

The economic, political, and social revolutions that began in the mid-eighteenth century shook the foundations of European culture and led to the expansion of Western power around the globe. Some of the nations of Asia, Africa, and Latin America reformed and strengthened their own institutions and economies, while others pushed for more radical change. After 1870 Western imperialism became more aggressive, and few parts of the world were able to resist it.

22

THE EARLY INDUSTRIAL REVOLUTION, 1760–1851

Manchester was just a small town in northern England in the early eighteenth century. A hundred years later, it had turned into the fastest-growing city in history. To contemporaries, it was both a marvel and a horror. Prosperous cotton mills were interspersed with workers' housing, built as cheaply as possible. The economist Nassau Senior described these workers' quarters:

> But when I went through their habitations ... my only wonder was that tolerable health could be maintained by the inmates of such houses. These towns ... have been erected by small speculators with an utter disregard to everything except immediate profit.... In one place we saw a whole street following the course of a ditch, in order to have deeper cellars (cellars for people, not for lumber) without the expense of excavation. Not a house in this street escaped cholera.... the streets are unpaved, with a dunghill or a pond in the middle; the houses built back to back, without ventilation or drainage, and whole families occupy each a corner of a cellar or of a garret.[1]

Not everyone deplored the living conditions in the new industrial city. Friedrich Engels, both a factory owner and critic of capitalism, recounted a meeting with a well-to-do citizen:

> One day I walked with one of these middle-class gentlemen into Manchester. I spoke to him about the disgraceful unhealthy slums and drew his attention to the disgusting condition of that part of the town in which the factory workers lived. I declared that I had never seen so badly built a town in my life. He listened patiently and at the corner of the street at which we parted company, he remarked: "And yet there is a great deal of money made here. Good morning, Sir!"[2]

Manchester's rise as a large, industrial city was a result of what historians call the **Industrial Revolution**, the most profound transformation in human life since the beginnings of agriculture. This revolution involved dramatic innovations in

---

[1] Nassau W. Senior, *Letters on the Factory Act, as it affects the cotton manufacture, addressed to the Right Honourable, the President of the Board of Trade*, 2d ed. (London: Fellows, 1844), 20.

[2] Friedrich Engels, *Condition of the Working Class in England*, trans. and ed. by W. O. Henderson and W. H. Chaloner (Oxford: Blackwell, 1958), 312.

manufacturing, mining, transportation, and communications and equally rapid changes in society and commerce, as new relationships between social groups created an environment that was conducive to technical innovation and economic growth. These changes allowed the industrializing countries—first Britain, then western Europe and the United States—to unleash massive increases in production and productivity, exploit the world's natural resources as never before, and transform the environment and human life in unprecedented ways.

Industrialization widened the gap between rich and poor. The people who owned and controlled industrial innovations amassed wealth and power over nature as well as over other people. While some lived in spectacular luxury, workers, including large numbers of children, worked long hours in dangerous factories and lived crowded together in unsanitary tenements. At the same time, the middle class of industrializing nations grew rapidly, exercising increased influence in politics and culture.

The effect of the Industrial Revolution around the world was also very uneven. The first countries to industrialize grew rich and powerful, facilitating a second great wave of European imperialism in the nineteenth century. In Egypt and India, the economic and military power of Europe stifled the tentative beginnings of industrialization. The disparity in wealth and power between the industrial and the developing countries that exists today has its origins in the early nineteenth century.

CAUSES OF THE INDUSTRIAL REVOLUTION

What caused the Industrial Revolution, and why did it develop so rapidly in England in the eighteenth century? These are two of the great questions of history. The basic preconditions of this momentous event seem to have been population growth that increased demand for goods, an agricultural revolution, the expansion of trade, and an openness to experimentation and innovation.

Population Growth Population growth helped fuel the Industrial Revolution by increasing the demand for goods and by lowering labor costs. Between 1650 and 1850 Europe's population grew from 100 million to 266 million. Simultaneously, Europe became more urban, with the number of city dwellers more than doubling in this same period. This pattern was clearest in England and Wales, where population increased from about 6 million in 1700 to 9 million in 1800 and 18 million by 1850—increases never before experienced in European history. As the pace of manufacturing mounted in the eighteenth century, rural laborers and their families moved to cities in hope of higher earnings and better lives.

The growth of population resulted from more widespread resistance to disease and from more abundant and reliable food supplies, thanks to the new crops that originated in the Americas (see Chapter 18). Gradual improvements in income allowed Europeans to marry at earlier ages and have more children. As a result, roughly 40 percent of the population of Britain was under fifteen years of age in the nineteenth century. This high proportion of youths explains the vitality of the British people in that period as well as the widespread use of child labor. People also migrated at an unprecedented rate—not only from the countryside to the cities, but also from Ireland to England and, more generally, from Europe to the Americas. Thanks to immigration, the population of the United States rose from 4 million in 1791 to 9.6 million in 1820 and 31.5 million in 1860—faster than in any other part of the world at the time.

The Agricultural Revolution   A revolution in farming provided an increased food supply to fast-growing urban populations and at the same time forced many peasants off the land. This **agricultural revolution** had begun long before the eighteenth century. One important aspect was the introduction of new crops like the potato, introduced from South America in the sixteenth century. In the cool and humid regions of Europe, potatoes yielded two or three times more calories per acre than did the wheat, rye, and oats they replaced. Maize (American corn) was also grown across Europe from northern Iberia to the Balkans, adding substantially to the food supply.

Prosperous landowners with secure titles to their land could afford to bear the risk of trying new methods and new crops. In Great Britain rich landowners "enclosed" the land—that is, consolidated their holdings—and got Parliament to give them title to the commons that in the past had been open to all. Once in control of the land, they could drain and improve the soil, breed better livestock, and introduce crop rotation. This "enclosure movement" further impoverished the rural poor by turning tenants and sharecroppers into landless farm laborers. Many of the displaced rural poor moved to the cities to seek work; others became vagrants; still others emigrated to Canada, Australia, and the United States.

Trade and Inventiveness   The Industrial Revolution was preceded by a long period of commercial expansion based on growing population and on a much deeper engagement with colonial possessions and with other foreign markets. The innovations of the industrial age came about in part as manufacturers sought to meet increased domestic and foreign demand for textiles and other products through improved efficiency and productivity.

Traditionally, European textiles were produced by skilled artisans organized in guilds using centuries-old technologies. In this system increasing production meant training more artisans, an expensive process that took years. Beginning in the seventeenth century, merchant investors began to relocate some basic textile production away from guild-dominated cities to benefit from lower-cost rural labor, especially during the period between harvesting and planting. Called proto-industrialization, merchant investors delivered raw materials and supplied simple machinery, like looms and spinning wheels, to the homes of farm families and to rural jobbers who organized groups of laborers. In this system the complex tasks associated with artisan production were subdivided into simple procedures that allowed rural workers to quickly gain competence and become productive. Unlike urban artisans, who typically earned daily wages, these proto-industrial workers were only paid for what they produced thus reducing labor costs. Skilled manufacturers then transformed the spun wool and rough cloth produced by rural laborers into finished goods for domestic and foreign consumers. While proto-industrialization increased cloth production and lowered labor costs, there were chronic problems with quality control and inefficiencies that resulted from the dispersal of production.

In the eighteenth century a dramatic expansion of European commerce with markets in the Americas, Africa, and Asia reinforced the economic effects of the fast-growing European population. Nearly all the European powers profited from plantation colonies in the Americas. As Europeans of even modest means consumed ever-growing quantities of sugar to sweeten their tea, coffee, cocoa, pastries, and candies, the demand for manufactures like porcelain cups and dinnerware increased as well. At the same time planters in the Caribbean imported a steeply rising volume of cotton textiles to clothe themselves and their slaves. Initially, these cotton textiles were imported from Asia, but increasing demand led to the creation of domestic cotton textile industries, the first truly modern mechanized industry.

European governments played a key role in this economic expansion. Governments across Europe sponsored improvements in road networks, but maintenance was often inadequate. In Britain local governments' neglect of the roads that served long-distance traffic led to the formation of private "turnpike trusts" that built numerous toll roads. As the volume of commerce increased, canal-building booms occurred in Britain, France, and the low countries in the late eighteenth century. Governments also directly invested in skills and new technologies by creating royal manufacturers that produced fine china, silks, and carpets. Authorities in England, France, Prussia, and Spain, among other European nations, recruited skilled artisans from rival nations, subsidized periodicals that disseminated new technologies, and expanded their navies to better protect foreign trade.

Beginning in the seventeenth century, educated people throughout Europe and the Americas were increasingly fascinated by technology and innovation (see Chapter 17). Across Europe inexpensive periodicals informed the general public of new technologies and scientific discoveries. But it was the *Encyclopédie*, published in France over a period of more than twenty years, that most influenced the dissemination of useful technologies by providing detailed diagrams of everything from printing and textile machinery to canal locks and foundry equipment. During the eighteenth century the French, Spanish, and British governments also sought to promote economic growth by sending expeditions around the world to collect plants that could profitably be grown domestically or in their colonies. They also offered prizes for scientific discoveries, like determining the longitude of a ship at sea and the accurate measurement of the earth's circumference. It was an era when innovators and scientists were celebrities.

Britain and Continental Europe   Industrialization did not take place everywhere at once. Great Britain took the lead in introducing new technologies and maintained its place as Europe's major industrial power to the end of the nineteenth century. It is useful to divide the British experience into two phases. In the eighteenth century inventors developed machines that multiplied the productive capacities of individual workers, especially in the textile industry. While production increased dramatically, British industry continued to rely on traditional sources of energy, particularly wind, water, and animal power. Then early in the nineteenth century the development of efficient steam engines allowed British entrepreneurs to apply this potent source of energy to industrial machinery.

The technologies associated with both stages of this revolution spread rapidly to continental Europe and the United States. British engineers and skilled machinists were the most active agents in the dissemination of the new technologies. European and American investors quickly recognized the advantages of the new technologies and provided high salaries and other inducements to skilled British workers willing to immigrate and introduce the newest technologies. Belgium had the earliest successes in imitating the British industrial model, becoming the continent's most industrialized economy by 1840. While slower to embrace the new technologies, Germany after 1850 became the continent's major producer of coal, iron, and steel. The United States was well established as a major industrial power by 1860, having quickly adopted textile and metallurgical technologies developed first in Great Britain.

Historians disagree about why Britain played such an important role in the introduction of industrial technologies in the eighteenth and nineteenth centuries. It is clear that Britain enjoyed a rising standard of living, thanks to good harvests and a booming overseas trade, and that this prosperity increased consumption and stimulated innovation in manufacturing. Britain was already the world's leading exporter of tools, guns, hardware, clocks, and other manufactured goods, and it had a strong craft tradition that trained a large number of skilled mechanics. At the same time, its mining and metal industries employed engineers with a tradition of experimentation and innovation. British commercial culture was also among Europe's most modern, having long enjoyed the benefits of strong banks, joint-stock companies, a stock market, and commercial insurance. In addition, its patent system offered inventors the hope of rich rewards by protecting their intellectual property rights. Growing public awareness of early innovators who became wealthy and respected for their inventions stimulated others to experiment.

At the dawn of the industrial age, Britain had one of the most fluid societies in Europe. The court was less ostentatious, its aristocracy was less powerful, and the lines separating the social classes were not as sharply drawn as elsewhere in Europe, with the exception of the Netherlands. Compared to France or Spain, the two most important continental powers, British political power was not as centralized or intrusive. There were fewer bureaucrats and officials and fewer obstacles to commerce and manufacturing than in most continental nations. As commoners grew wealthy in trade and manufacturing, society became less hierarchical and more fluid.

At a time when transportation by land was very costly, Great Britain had good water transportation thanks to its long coastline, navigable rivers, and growing network of canals. It also had a unified internal market with none of the duties and tolls that goods had to pay every few miles in France or Spain. This advantage facilitated a growing trade between regions. More important still, Britain had abundant supplies of coal and iron ore, two key ingredients in the Industrial Revolution.

In contrast to Britain, the economies of continental Europe were hampered by high transportation costs, misguided government regulations, and rigid social structures. As a result, attempts to import British techniques and organize factory production elsewhere often foundered for lack of markets or management skills. Nevertheless, British textile machinery was introduced in France and Spain before the French Revolution (see Chapter 23). From then until the end of the Napoleonic wars in 1815, Europe's economies were distorted by the effects of mass military mobilizations and warfare. Although war created opportunities for suppliers of weapons and uniforms, the interruption of trade between Britain and continental Europe slowed the diffusion of new technologies, and the insecurity of countries at war discouraged businessmen from investing in factories and machinery.

Once revolutions had swept away most of the restrictions of Europe's old regimes, both private investors and European governments acted to import new technologies and adapt them to local conditions. Acutely aware of Britain's head start and the need to stimulate their own industries, continental governments sponsored efforts to imitate or steal British industrial secrets. They recruited British engineers and artisans, created technical schools, and eliminated internal tariff barriers, tolls, and other hindrances to trade. By the 1820s there were several thousand Britons working on the continent, setting up machines, training workers in the new methods, and even starting their own businesses. European governments also encouraged the formation of joint-stock companies and banks to channel private savings into industrial investments. By 1830 the political climate in western Europe had become as favorable to business as Britain's had been a half century earlier. First Belgium and then, after 1850, Germany and France enjoyed industrial booms based on iron, cotton, steam engines, and railroads. Key to the success of Belgium and Germany was the existence of abundant coal and iron-ore deposits. Without abundant coal, France retained a more traditional manufacturing economy until the introduction of electricity late in the nineteenth century.

THE TECHNOLOGICAL REVOLUTION

Five innovations spurred industrialization: (1) mass production through the division of labor, (2) new machines and mechanization, (3) a great increase in the manufacture of iron, (4) the steam engine, and (5) the electric telegraph. While the full realization of these innovations occurred first in Great Britain and then spread to the United States and continental Europe in the nineteenth century, China had achieved the first three during the Song dynasty (960–1279). But China did not develop the steam engine or electricity, innovations that dramatically multiplied human productivity. The transformation of Western economies through industrialization depended on the full integration of these new forms of energy with the process of mechanical innovation.

Mass Production: Pottery   The pottery industry offers a good example of **mass production**, the making of many identical items by breaking the process into simple repetitive tasks. Before the mid-eighteenth century, only the wealthy could afford imported Chinese porcelain. Middle-class people used pewter tableware, and the poor ate from wooden or earthenware bowls. Royal manufacturers produced exquisite handmade products for the courts and aristocracy, but their products were much too expensive for mass consumption. As more and more Europeans acquired a taste for tea, cocoa, and coffee, they wanted porcelain that would not spoil the flavor of hot beverages. This demand created opportunities for inventive entrepreneurs.

Adam Smith and the Division of Labor

*Adam Smith (1723–1790), a Scottish phi-
losopher, is famous for his book* An Inquiry
into the Nature *and Causes of the Wealth of*
Nations, *first published in 1776. It was the
first work to explain the economy of a
nation as a system. Smith criticized the
notion, common in the eighteenth century,
that a nation's wealth was synonymous
with the amount of gold and silver in the
government's coffers. Instead, he defined
wealth as the amount of goods and services
produced by a nation's people. By this definition, labor and its products are an essential element in a nation's prosperity.*

*In the passage that follows, Smith con-
trasts two methods of making pins. In one
a team of workers divided up the job of
making pins and produced a great many
every day; in the other pin workers
"wrought separately and independently"
and produced very few pins per day. It is
clear that the division of labor produced
more pins per worker per day. But who
benefited? Left unsaid is that a pin factory
had to be owned and operated by a manufacturer who hired workers and assigned a
task to each one.*

*The illustration shows a pin-maker's
workshop in late-eighteenth-century France.
Each worker is performing a specific task
on a few pins at once, and all the energy
comes from human muscles. These are
the characteristics of a proto-industrial
workshop.*

To take an example, therefore, from a
very trifling manufacture—but one in
which the division of labour has been very
often taken notice of—the trade of the pin-
maker: a workman not educated to this

business (which the division of labour has
rendered a distinct trade), nor acquainted
with the use of machinery employed in it (to
the invention of which the same division of
labour has probably given occasion), could
scarce, perhaps, with his utmost industry,
make one pin in a day, and certainly could
not make twenty. But in the way in which
this business is now carried on, not only the
whole work is a peculiar trade, but it is
divided into a number of branches, of
which the greater part are likewise peculiar
trades. One man draws out the wire,
another straights it, a third cuts it, a fourth
points it, a fifth grinds it at the top for
receiving the head; to make the head
requires two or three distinct operations,
to put it on, is a peculiar business, to whiten
the pins is another; it is even a trade by itself
to put them into the paper; and the important business of making a pin is, in this
manner, divided into about eighteen distinct operations, which, in some manufac-
tories, are all performed by distinct hands,
though in others the same man will sometimes perform two or three of them. I have
seen a small manufactory of this kind
where ten men only were employed, and
where some of them, consequently, performed two or three distinct operations.
But though they were very poor, and therefore but indifferently accommodated with
the necessary machinery, they could, when
they exerted themselves, make among them
about twelve pounds of pins in a day.

There are in a pound upwards of four
thousand pins of a middling size. Those ten
persons, therefore, could make among them
upwards of forty-eight thousand pins in a

Britain had many small pottery workshops where craftsmen made a few plates
and cups at a time. Much of this activity took place in a part of the Midlands
that possessed good clay, coal for firing, and lead for glazing. In 1759, **Josiah
Wedgwood**, the son of a potter, started his own pottery business. Today the name
Wedgwood is associated with expensive, highly decorated china. But Wedgwood's

day. Each person, therefore, making a tenth part of forty-eight thousand pins, might be considered as making four thousand eight hundred pins a day. But if they had all wrought separately and independently, and without any of them having been educated to this peculiar business, they certainly could not each of them have made twenty, perhaps not one pin in a day; that is, certainly, not the two hundred and fortieth, perhaps not the four thousand eight hundredth part of what they are at present capable of performing, in consequence of a proper division and combination of their different operations.

Questions for Analysis

1. Why does dividing the job of pin-making into ten or more operations result in the production of more pins per worker? How much more productive are these workers than if each one made complete pins from start to finish?

2. How closely does the picture of a pin-maker's workshop illustrate Smith's verbal description?

3. What disadvantage would there be to working in a pin factory where the job was divided as in Smith's example, compared to making entire pins from start to finish?

4. What other examples can you think of, from Adam Smith's day or from more recent times, of the advantages of the division of labor?

Source: Adam Smith, *An Inquiry into the Nature and Causes of the Wealth of Nations*, ed. Edward Gibbon Wakefield (London: Charles Knight and Co., 1843), 7–9.

A Pin-Maker's Workshop *The man in the middle (Fig. 2) is pulling wire off a spindle (G) and through a series of posts. This ensures that the wire will be perfectly straight. The worker seated on the lower right (Fig. 3) takes the long pieces of straightened wire and cuts them into shorter lengths. The man in the lower left-hand corner (Fig. 5) sharpens twelve to fifteen wires at a time by holding them against a grindstone turned by the worker in Fig. 6. The men in Figs. 4 and 7 put the finishing touches on the points. Other operations—such as forming the wire to the proper thickness, cleaning and coating it with tin, and attaching the heads—are depicted in other engravings in the same encyclopedia.*

The Pin Factory, plate 2 from Volume IV of the Encyclopedia of Denis Diderot (1713–84) and Jean le Rond d'Alembert (1717–83), 1751–52 (engraving), French School, (18th century) / Private Collection/The Bridgeman Art Library

most important contribution lay in producing ordinary porcelain cheaply by means of the **division of labor** (see Diversity and Dominance: Adam Smith and the Division of Labor).

Wedgwood subdivided the work into simple repetitive tasks, such as unloading the clay, mixing it, pressing flat pieces, dipping the pieces in glaze, putting handles on cups, packing kilns, and carrying things from one part of his plant to another. To prevent interruptions, he instituted strict discipline among his workers. He substituted molds for the potter's wheel whenever possible, a change that not only saved labor but also created uniform plates and bowls that could be stacked. The end result was that while workers became more productive, they had fewer skills and were paid less.

Wedgwood's interest in applying technology to manufacturing was sparked by his membership in the Lunar Society, a group of businessmen, scientists, and craftsmen that met each month when the moon was full to discuss the practical application of knowledge. In 1782, the naturalist Erasmus Darwin encouraged him to purchase a steam engine from Boulton and Watt, a firm founded by two other members of the society. The engine that Wedgwood bought to mix clay and grind flint was one of the first to be installed in a factory. The division of labor and new steam-driven machinery allowed Wedgwood to lower the cost of his products while improving their quality, and to offer his wares for sale at lower prices.

Mechanization: The Cotton Industry

The cotton industry, the largest industry in this period, illustrates the role of **mechanization**, the use of machines to do work previously done by hand. Cotton had long been grown in China, India, and the Middle East, where it was spun and woven by hand. The cloth was so much cooler, softer, and cleaner than wool that wealthy Europeans developed a liking for the costly import. When the powerful English woolen industry persuaded Parliament to forbid the import of cotton cloth, that prohibition stimulated attempts to import cotton fiber and make the cloth domestically. Here was an opportunity for enterprising inventors to reduce costs with laborsaving machinery.

Beginning in the 1760s a series of inventions revolutionized the spinning of cotton thread. The first was the jenny, invented in 1764, which mechanically drew out the cotton fibers and twisted them into thread. The jenny was simple, cheap to build, and easy for one person to operate. Early models permitted a single worker to spin six or seven threads at once, later ones up to eighty. The thread, however, was soft and irregular and could be used only in combination with linen, a strong yarn derived from the flax plant.

In 1769, **Richard Arkwright** invented another spinning machine, the water frame, which produced thread strong enough to be used without linen. Arkwright was both a gifted inventor and a successful businessman. His machine was larger and more complex than the jenny and required a source of power such as a water wheel, hence the name "water frame." To obtain the necessary energy, he installed dozens of machines in a building next to a fast-flowing river. The resemblance to a flour mill gave such enterprises the name *cotton mill*. Within a few decades of the introduction of the jenny and water frame, these technologies were imported and adapted to local conditions elsewhere. The skilled mechanics who built British machines served as vectors for this dissemination as they moved to France, Belgium, and the United States to seek higher wages.

In 1785, British inventor Samuel Crompton patented a machine that combined the best features of the jenny and the water frame. This device, called a mule, produced a strong thread that was thin enough to be used to make a high-quality cotton cloth called muslin. The mule could make a finer, more even thread than could any human being, and at a lower cost. At last British industry could undersell high-quality handmade cotton cloth from India. With these innovations in place, British cotton output increased tenfold between 1770 and 1790, despite the fact that these large-scale producers still depended on waterpower.

The boom in thread production and the soaring demand for cloth encouraged inventors to mechanize the rest of textile manufacturing. Power looms were perfected after 1815. Other inventions of the period included carding machines, chlorine bleach, and cylindrical presses to print designs on fabric. By the 1830s large textile mills powered by steam engines were performing all the steps necessary to turn raw cotton into printed cloth.

Mechanization offered two advantages: increased productivity for the manufacturer and lower prices for the consumer. Whereas in India it took five hundred hours to spin a pound of cotton, the mule of 1790 could do so in three person-hours, and the self-acting mule—an improved version introduced in 1830—required only eighty minutes. Cotton mills needed very few skilled workers, and managers often hired children to tend the spinning machines. The same was true of power looms, which gradually replaced handloom weaving: the number of power looms rose from 2,400 in 1813 to 500,000 by 1850. Meanwhile, the price of cloth fell by 90 percent between 1782 and 1812 and kept on dropping.

The industrialization of Britain made cotton America's most valuable crop (see Chapter 25). In the 1790s most of Britain's cotton came from India. But in 1793 the American Eli Whitney patented his cotton gin, a simple device that separated the bolls or seedpods from the fiber and made cotton growing economical. This invention permitted the spread of cotton farming into Georgia, then into Alabama, Mississippi, and Louisiana, and finally as far west as Texas. By the late 1850s the southern states were producing a million tons of cotton a year, five-sixths of the world's total.

With the help of British craftsmen who introduced jennies, mules, and power looms, Americans developed their own cotton industry in the 1820s. Immigrants from Great Britain played a key role in this process, as did the willingness of American investors to ignore the patent rights of British inventors. By 1840, the United States had twelve hundred cotton mills that served the booming domestic market, two-thirds of them in New England.

While the resistance of long-established artisan guilds to the introduction of new technologies slowed technological innovation in the wool textile industry in Britain and elsewhere, machinery adapted from cotton production quickly transformed the spinning of woolen thread by the 1830s. Steam-driven looms soon followed. In Belgium in 1810, only 5 of 144 woolen factories were mechanized, but they produced more than 50 percent of total production.

The Iron Industry   Iron making also was transformed during the Industrial Revolution. Throughout Eurasia and Africa, iron had long been used for tools, weapons, and household items. During the Song period, Chinese forges had produced cast iron in large quantities. Although production declined after the Song, iron continued to be common and inexpensive in China. Wherever iron was produced, however, deforestation eventually drove up the cost of charcoal (used for smelting) and restricted output. Furthermore, iron had to be repeatedly heated and hammered to drive out impurities, a difficult and costly process. Because of limited wood supplies and the high cost of skilled labor, iron was a rare and valuable metal outside China before the eighteenth century.

A first breakthrough occurred in 1709 when Abraham Darby discovered that coke (coal from which the impurities have been cooked out) could be used in place of charcoal. The resulting metal was of lower quality than charcoal-smelted iron but much cheaper to produce, for coal was plentiful. In 1784, British inventor Henry Cort found a way to remove some of the impurities in coke-iron by puddling—stirring the molten iron with long rods. Cort's process made it possible to turn coal into coke to produce wrought iron (a soft and malleable form of iron) very cheaply. By 1790 four-fifths of Britain's iron was made with coke, while other countries still used charcoal. Coke-iron allowed a great expansion in the size of individual blast furnaces. As a result, Britain's iron production rose fast, from 17,000 tons in 1740 to 3 million tons in 1844, as much as in the rest of the world put together. As in Britain, the existence of large supplies of coal and iron ore largely explains the fast pace of industrialization of Belgium and Germany after 1820.

In turn, there seemed no limit to the novel applications for this cheap and useful material. In 1779, Abraham Darby III (grandson of the first Abraham Darby) built a bridge of iron across the Severn River. In 1851 Londoners marveled at the **Crystal Palace**, a huge exhibition hall made entirely of iron and glass. The Great Exhibition showcased British industry and power but included exhibits from the colonies and from other nations.

The availability of cheap iron made the mass production of objects such as guns, hardware, and tools appealing. However, fitting together the parts of these products required a great deal of labor. To reduce labor costs, manufacturers, like the Americans Eli Whitney (firearms) and Eli Terry (clocks), contributed to the development of standardized interchangeable parts. By the mid-nineteenth century, interchangeable-parts manufacturing had been widely adopted, including the manufacture of farm equipment and sewing machines. By the 1850s Europeans had begun to call this the "American system of manufactures."

The Steam Engine   In the history of the world, there had been a number of periods of great technological inventiveness and economic growth. But in all previous cases, the dynamism eventually faltered. The Industrial Revolution, in contrast, has only accelerated. One reason has been increased interactions between scientists, technicians, and businesspeople. Another has been access to a source of cheap energy, namely fossil fuels. The first machine to transform fossil fuel into mechanical energy was the **steam engine**, a device that set the Industrial Revolution apart from all previous periods of growth and innovation.

Before the eighteenth century, deep mines filled with water faster than pumps powered by horses could lift it out. Then, between 1702 and 1712, Thomas Newcomen developed the first practical steam engine, a crude but effective device that could clear water from mines much faster than earlier pumps. The Newcomen engine's voracious appetite for fuel mattered little in coal mines, where fuel was cheap, but it made the engine too costly for other uses. In 1764 another Briton, **James Watt**, a maker of scientific instruments at Glasgow University in Scotland, was asked to repair the university's model Newcomen engine. Watt realized that the engine wasted fuel because the cylinder had to be alternately heated and cooled. He developed a separate condenser—a vessel into which the steam was allowed to escape, leaving the cylinder always hot and the condenser always cold. Watt patented his idea in 1769 and enlisted the help of the iron manufacturer Matthew Boulton to turn his invention into a commercial product. Their first engines were sold to pump water out of copper and tin mines, where fuel was too costly for Newcomen engines. In 1781, Watt invented the sun-and-planet gear, which turned the back-and-forth action of the piston into rotary motion. This allowed steam engines to power machinery in flour and cotton mills, pottery manufactures, and other industries as well. Because there seemed almost no limit to the amount of coal in the ground, steam-generated energy appeared to be an inexhaustible source of power, and steam engines could be used where animal, wind, and water power were lacking. By the 1820s steam engines were powering textile machinery in Belgium and the United States as well as in Great Britain. In places where coal supplies were limited, like France, the application of steam power to manufacturing developed slowly.

Science & Society Picture Library/Contributo/Getty Images

Transatlantic Steamship Race *In 1838, two ships equipped with steam engines, the* Sirius *and the* Great Western, *steamed from England to New York. Although the* Sirius *left a few days earlier, the* Great Western—*shown here arriving in New York harbor*—*almost caught up with it, arriving just four hours after the* Sirius. *This race inaugurated regular transatlantic steamship service.*

Inspired by the success of Watt's engine, several inventors put steam engines on boats. The first commercially successful steamboat was Robert Fulton's *North River*, which sailed the Hudson River between New York City and Albany, New York, in 1807. Soon steamboats were launched on the Ohio and the Mississippi, gateways to the Midwest. By 1830, some three hundred steamboats plied the Mississippi and its tributaries. The United States was fast becoming a nation that moved by water.

Oceangoing steam-powered ships were much more difficult to build than river boats, for the first steam engines used so much coal that no ship could carry more than a few days' supply. The *Savannah*, which crossed the Atlantic in 1819, was a sailing ship with an auxiliary steam engine that was used for only ninety hours of its twenty-nine-day trip. Engineers soon developed more efficient engines, and in 1838 two steamers, the *Great Western* and the *Sirius*, crossed the Atlantic on steam power alone.

Railroads

After Watt's patent expired in 1800, inventors experimented with lighter, more powerful high-pressure engines—an idea Watt had rejected as too dangerous. In 1804, Richard Trevithick built an engine that consumed only one-third the coal used by Watt's design and then created several steam-powered vehicles able to travel on roads or rails.

By the 1820s England had many railways on which horses pulled heavy wagons. In 1829, the owners of the Liverpool and Manchester Railway organized a contest between steam-powered locomotives and horse-drawn wagons. George Stephenson and his son Robert won the contest with their locomotive *Rocket*, which pulled a 20-ton train at up to 30 miles (48 kilometers) per hour. After that triumph, a railroad-building mania swept Britain. In the late 1830s, as passenger traffic soared, entrepreneurs built lines between the major cities and even to small towns. Railroads were far cheaper, faster, and more comfortable than stagecoaches, and millions of people got in the habit of traveling. By 1850 Great Britain had 6,087 miles (9,797 kilometers) of railroad line.

The introduction of railroads had their most transformative effects in the United States. By the 1840s, 6,000 miles (10,000 kilometers) of track radiated from Boston, New York, Philadelphia, and Baltimore. In the 1850s, 21,000 miles (34,000 kilometers) of additional track were laid, much of it westward across the Appalachians to Memphis, St. Louis, and Chicago. After 1856 the trip from New York to Chicago, which had once taken three weeks by boat and on horseback, could be made in forty-eight hours. This rapid expansion of railroads opened up the Midwest, dispersing the waves of immigrants, turning the vast prairie into farms to feed the industrial cities of the eastern United States, and creating a vast internal market for manufactures.

Railways also accelerated the industrialization of Europe. Belgium, independent since 1830, quickly copied the British railways. In France and Prussia, construction was delayed until the mid-1840s. When it began, however, it not only satisfied the long-standing need for transportation in those countries but also stimulated the iron, machinery, and construction industries. By 1850 Germany had built 3,639 miles (5,856 kilometers) of railroad line and France 1,811 miles (2,915 kilometers).

The *De Witt Clinton* Locomotive, 1835–1840 *The De Witt Clinton was the first steam locomotive built in the United States. The high smokestack let the hot cinders cool so they would not set fire to nearby trees, an important consideration at a time when eastern North America was still covered with forest. The three passenger cars are clearly horse carriages fitted with railroad wheels.*

Communication over Wires After the Italian scientist Alessandro Volta invented the battery in 1800, making it possible to produce an electric current, many inventors tried to apply electricity to communication. The first practical **electric telegraph** systems were developed almost simultaneously in England and America. In 1837, in England, Charles Wheatstone and William Cooke introduced a five-wire telegraph, while the American Samuel Morse introduced a code of dots and dashes that could be transmitted with a single wire. Morse convinced the Congress to provide $30,000 (nearly $800,000 in 2012) to "wire" America in 1842 and built a telegraph line connecting Baltimore and Washington D.C. a year later.

The railroad companies allowed telegraph companies to string wires along the tracks in exchange for the right to send telegrams from station to station announcing the departure and arrival of trains. Such messages made railroads much safer as well as more efficient. By the late 1840s telegraph wires crisscrossed the eastern United States and western Europe. In 1851, the first submarine telegraph cable was laid across the English Channel from England to France (cutting the transmission of news from up to four days to minutes); it was the beginning of a network that eventually connected the entire globe. No longer were communications limited to the speed of a sailing ship, a galloping horse, or a fast-moving train. Together railroads and telegraphs had an enormous economic impact. While railroads could move bulk goods more rapidly and at lower cost than other forms of land transportation, telegraphs dramatically transformed market intelligence by making it possible for producers to keep track of distant consumer needs and prices, thus making markets more efficient and profits more dependable.

The Impact of the Early Industrial Revolution

The Industrial Revolution led to profound changes in society, politics, and the economy. At first, the changes were local. Some people became wealthy and built mansions, while others lived in slums with polluted water and air. By the mid-nineteenth century, the worst local effects were being alleviated and cities had become cleaner and healthier. Industrial nations then faced more complex problems: business cycles, labor conflicts, and the degradation of entire regions by mining and industrial pollution. At the global level, industrialization empowered the nations of western Europe and North America to impose themselves on less developed nations.

The New Industrial Cities   The most dramatic environmental changes brought about by industrialization occurred in the towns. Towns had never before grown so fast. London, one of the largest cities in Europe in 1700 with 500,000 inhabitants, grew to 1,117,000 by 1800 and to 2,685,000 by 1850; it was then the largest city the world had ever known. Manchester, a small town of 20,000 in 1758, reached 303,000 a century later, a fifteenfold increase. New York City, already 100,000 strong in 1815, reached 600,000 (including Brooklyn) in 1850. In some areas, towns merged and formed megalopolises, such as Greater London, the English Midlands, central Belgium, and the Ruhr district of Germany.

A great deal of money went into the building of fine homes, churches, museums, and theaters in wealthy neighborhoods. Much of the beauty of London dates from the time of the Industrial Revolution. Yet, by all accounts, industrial cities grew much too fast, and much of the growth occurred in the poorest neighborhoods. As poor migrants streamed in from the countryside, developers built the cheap, shoddy row houses for them to rent that Nassau Senior described.

Sudden population growth caused serious urban environmental problems. Town dwellers recently arrived from the country brought country ways with them. People threw their sewage and trash out the windows to be washed down the gutters in the streets. The poor kept pigs and chickens; the rich kept horses; and pedestrians stepped into the street at their own risk. Air pollution from burning coal, a problem since the sixteenth century, got steadily worse. People drank water drawn from wells and rivers contaminated by sewage and industrial runoff. The River Irwell, which ran through Manchester, was, in the words of one visitor, "considerably less a river than a flood of liquid manure."[3] "Every day that I live," wrote an American visitor to Manchester, "I thank Heaven that I am not a poor man with a family in England."[4] At the same time, railroads invaded the towns, bringing noise

---

[3] Quoted in Lewis Mumford, *The City in History* (New York: Harcourt Brace, 1961), 460.

[4] Quoted in F. Roy Willis, *Western Civilization: An Urban Perspective*, vol. II (Lexington, MA: D.C. Heath, 1973), 675.

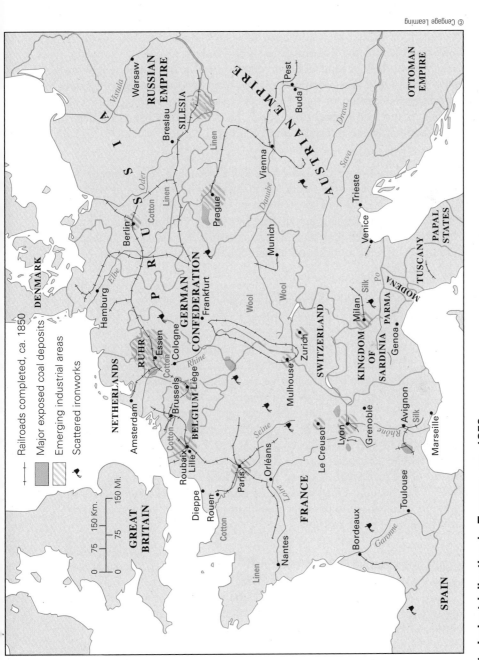

© Cengage Learning

MAP 22.1 Industrialization in Europe, ca. 1850

In 1850, industrialization was in its early stages on the European continent. The first industrial regions were comparatively close to England and possessed rich coal deposits: Belgium and the Ruhr district of Germany. Politics determined the location of railroads. Notice the star-shaped French network of rail lines emanating from Paris and the lines linking the different parts of the German Confederation.

and smoke into densely populated neighborhoods. On the outskirts of cities, rail-road yards, sidings, and repair shops covered acres of land, surrounded by miles of warehouses and workers' housing.

Under these conditions, diseases proliferated. To the long list of preindustrial diseases, industrialization added new ailments. Rickets, a bone disease caused by lack of sunshine, became endemic in dark and smoky industrial cities. Steamships brought cholera from India, causing great epidemics that struck poor neighbor-hoods especially hard. Observers documented the horrors of slum life in vivid detail. Their shocking reports led to municipal reforms, such as garbage removal, water and sewage systems, and parks and schools. These measures began to allevi-ate the ills of urban life after the mid-nineteenth century.

Rural Environments

Long before the Industrial Revolution began, practically no wilderness areas were left in Britain and very few in western Europe. Almost every piece of land was covered with fields, forests, or pastures shaped by human activity, or by towns; yet humans continued to alter the environment. As they had been doing for centuries, people cut timber to build ships and houses, to heat homes, and to manufacture bricks, iron, glass, beer, bread, and many other items.

North Americans transformed their environment on a vast scale. The Canadian and American governments seized land from the Indians and made it available at low cost to farmers and logging companies. Settlers viewed forests not as a valuable resource but as a hindrance to development. In their haste to "open up the wilder-ness," pioneers felled trees and burned them, built houses and abandoned them, and moved on. The cultivation of cotton in the South was especially harmful. Plan-ters cut down forests, grew cotton for a few years until the soil was depleted, and then moved west, abandoning the land to scrub pines (see Chapter 25).

In industrializing Europe, raw materials once grown on the land—such as wood, hay, and wool—were replaced by materials found underground, like iron ore and coal, or obtained overseas, like cotton. Across Europe the expansion of coal and iron mining had dramatic effects on the environment. As the population increased and land grew scarcer, the cost of growing feed for horses rose, creating incentives to find new, less land-hungry means of transportation. Likewise, as iron became cheaper and wood more expensive, ships and many other objects formerly made of wood began to be made of iron.

Working Conditions

Industrialization offered new opportunities to the enterpris-ing. Carpenters, metalworkers, and machinists were in great demand. Some workers became engineers or went into busi-ness for themselves. The boldest Britons moved to the European continent, the Americas, or India, using their skills to establish new industries.

The successful, however, were a minority. Most industrial jobs were unskilled, repetitive, and boring. Factory work did not vary with the seasons or the time of day but began and ended by the clock. Gas lighting expanded the working day past sunset. Workdays were long, there were few breaks, and foremen watched con-stantly. Workers who performed one simple task over and over had little sense of

Section of a Parisian building, illustration from 'Le Magasin Pittoresque', engraved by John Quartley (fl.1835–67) 1847 (engraving) (b/w photo), Girardet, Karl (1813–71) (after) / Bibliotheque des Arts Decoratifs, Paris, France / Archives Charmet / The Bridgeman Art Library

Paris Apartment at Night *This cutaway drawing in a French magazine shows the vertical segregation by social class that prevailed in the 1840s. The lower level is occupied by the concierge and her family. The first floor belongs to a wealthy family throwing a party for high-society friends. Middle-class people living on the next floor seem annoyed by the noise coming from below. Above them, a thief has entered an artist's studio. A poor seamstress and her child live in the garret under the roof. When elevators were introduced in the late nineteenth century, people of different income levels were more likely segregated by neighborhoods instead of by floors.*

achievement or connection to the final product. Industrial accidents were common and could ruin a family. Unlike the artisans they replaced, factory workers had no control over their tools, jobs, or working hours.

Industrial work had a major impact on women and family life. Women who could not afford servants had always worked, but mostly within the family: spinning and weaving, sewing hats and clothes, preparing food, washing, and doing a myriad other household chores. In rural areas, women also did farm work, especially caring for gardens and small animals.

In the early years of industrialization, even where factory work was available, it was never the main occupation of working women. Most young women who sought paid employment became domestic servants in spite of the low pay, drudgery, and risk of sexual abuse by male employers. Women with small children tried hard to find work they could do at home, such as laundry, sewing, embroidery, millinery, or taking in lodgers. Those who worked in factories were concentrated in textile mills, because textile work required less strength than metalworking, construction, or hauling. On average, women earned one-third to one-half as much as men. The economist Andrew Ure wrote in 1835: "It is in fact the constant aim and tendency of every improvement in machinery to supersede human labour altogether or to diminish its cost, by substituting the industry of women and children for that of men."[5] Young unmarried women worked to support themselves or to save for marriage. Married women took factory jobs when their husbands were unable to support the family. Mothers of infants faced a hard choice: whether to leave their babies with wet nurses at great expense or bring them to the factory and keep them drugged. Husbands and wives increasingly worked in different places.

As in preindustrial societies, parents thought children should contribute to their upkeep as soon as they were able to. The first generation of industrial workers brought children as young as five or six with them to the factories and mines, since there were no public schools or day-care centers. Employers preferred child workers because they were cheaper and more docile than adults and because they were better able to tie broken threads or crawl under machines to sweep the dust. In Arkwright's cotton mills, for example, two-thirds of the workers were children. Mine operators used children to pull coal carts along the low passageways from the coal face to the mine shaft. Nearly all these children worked fourteen to sixteen hours a day and were beaten if they made mistakes or fell asleep. Some manufacturers tried to provide more humane environments. When Francis Cabot Lowell built a cotton mill in Massachusetts, he hired the unmarried daughters of New England farmers, promising them decent wages and housing in dormitories under careful moral supervision. Other manufacturers eager to combine profits with morality followed his example. But soon these early social experiments were overwhelmed by the profit motive, and manufacturers, especially in highly competitive industries, imposed longer hours, harsher working conditions, and lower wages. When young women in New England factories went on strike, the mill owners replaced them with impoverished Irish immigrants willing to accept lower pay and worse conditions.

The cotton boom enriched planters, merchants, and manufacturers and also reinforced and expanded the institution of slavery in the Americas. In the 1790s, there were 700,000 slaves of African descent in the United States. As the "Cotton Kingdom" expanded, the number of slaves increased, reaching 3.2 million by 1850,

---

[5] Quoted in Joan W. Scott, "The Mechanization of Women's Work," *Scientific American* 247, no. 3 (September 1982): 171.

"Love Conquers Fear" *This is a sentimental Victorian drawing of children in a textile mill. Child labor was common in the first half of the nineteenth century, and workers were exposed to dangerous machines and moving belts, as well as to dust and dirt.*

From William Playfair, The Commercial and Political Atlas, 1801. Visual Connection Archive

60 percent located in the cotton region. While cotton profits soared, the lives of slaves grew more oppressive. Thousands of slave families were broken up by the internal slave trade that moved slaves from tobacco regions to the cotton frontier. At the same time, slave states also limited or outlawed manumissions, closing the door on slave families' hopes for freedom. Similarly, European demand for sugar prolonged plantation slavery in the West Indies and spread it to the coffee-growing regions of southern Brazil. Slavery was not, as white American southerners maintained, a "peculiar institution," a consequence of biological differences or biblical injunctions, but an integral part of both commercial capitalism and the Industrial Revolution.

Changes in Society

In his novel *Sybil, or, The Two Nations*, the British politician Benjamin Disraeli (**diz-RAY-lee**) (1804–1881) spoke of "two nations between whom there is no intercourse and no sympathy, who are as ignorant of each other's habits, thoughts, and feelings as if they were dwellers in different zones, or inhabitants of different planets ... the rich and the poor."[6]

In Britain the worst-off were those who clung to an obsolete skill or craft. The high wages and low productivity of handloom weavers in the 1790s induced inventors to develop power looms. As a result, by 1811 handloom weavers' wages had fallen by a third; by 1832, by two-thirds. Even by working longer hours, they could not escape destitution. The standard of living of factory workers did not decline steadily like those of handloom weavers but fluctuated wildly.

During the war years of 1792 to 1815, the price of food, on which the poor spent most of their income, rose faster than wages, causing widespread hardship. Then, in the 1820s real wages and public health began to improve. Prices for food, housing, and clothing fell and wages rose. Even the poor could afford comfortable, washable cotton clothes and underwear. But hard times returned in the "hungry forties." In 1847–1848 the potato crop failed in Ireland. One-quarter of the Irish population died in the resulting famine, and another quarter emigrated to England and North America. As these desperate men and women entered the workforce, wages fell.

The real beneficiaries of the early Industrial Revolution were the middle class. In Britain landowning gentry and merchants had long shared wealth and influence. In the late eighteenth century a new group arose: entrepreneurs whose money came from manufacturing. Most, like Arkwright and Wedgwood, were the sons of middling shopkeepers, craftsmen, or farmers. Their enterprises were usually self-financed, for little capital was needed to start a cotton-spinning or machine-building business. A generation later, in the nineteenth century, some newly rich industrialists bought their way into high society. The same happened in western Europe and the United States after 1815.

Before the Industrial Revolution, wives of merchants had often participated in the family business, and widows occasionally managed sizable businesses on their own. With industrialization came a "cult of domesticity" to justify removing middle-class women from contact with the business world. Instead, they became responsible for the home, the servants, the education of children, and the family's social life (see Chapter 27). Not all women accepted the change; in response Mary Wollstonecraft (1759–1797) wrote the first feminist manifesto, *Vindication of the Rights of Woman*, in 1792.

Middle-class people who attributed their success to their own efforts and virtues believed that if some people could succeed through hard work, thrift, and temperance, then those who did not succeed had no one but themselves to blame. Many workers, however, were newly arrived from rural districts and earned too little to save for the long stretches of unemployment they experienced. The moral position of the middle class mingled condemnation with concern, coupled with feelings of helplessness in the face of terrible social problems, such as drunkenness, prostitution, and child abandonment.

New Economic and Political Ideas

The profound changes unleashed by the Industrial Revolution triggered political ferment and ideological conflict. So many wars and revolutions took place during those years that we cannot neatly separate out the consequences of industrialization from the rest (see Chapter 23). But it is clear that by undermining social traditions and causing a growing gap between rich and poor, the Industrial Revolution strengthened the ideas of laissez faire (**LAY-say fair**) and socialism and sparked workers' protests.

Laissez Faire and Its Critics   The most celebrated exponent of **laissez faire** ("let them do") was Adam Smith (1723–1790), a Scottish economist. In *The Wealth of Nations* (1776) Smith argued that if individuals were allowed to seek personal gain, the effect, as though guided by an "invisible hand," would be to increase the general welfare. The government should refrain from interfering in business, except to protect private property; it should even allow duty-free trade with foreign countries. By advocating free-market capitalism, Smith was challenging the prevailing economic doctrine, **mercantilism**, which argued that governments should regulate trade in order to maximize their hoard of precious metals (Chapter 19).

Persuaded by Adam Smith's arguments, governments after 1815 dismantled many of their regulations, but no major power opened its economy to foreign competitors. Nonetheless, it was obvious that industrialization was causing widespread misery. Two other British thinkers, Thomas Malthus (1766–1834) and David Ricardo (1772–1832), attempted to explain the poverty they saw without challenging the basic premises of laissez faire. The cause of the workers' plight, they said, was the population boom, which outstripped the food supply and led to falling wages. The workers' poverty, they claimed, was as much a result of "natural law" as was the wealth of successful businessmen. For them the only way for the working class to avoid mass famine was to delay marriage and practice self-restraint and sexual abstinence.

Businesspeople in Britain eagerly adopted laissez-faire ideas that justified their activities and kept the government at bay. But not everyone accepted the grim conclusions of the "dismal science," as economics was then known. The British philosopher Jeremy Bentham (1748–1832) believed that it was possible to maximize "the greatest happiness of the greatest number," if only Parliament would study the social problems of the day and pass appropriate legislation. The German economist Friedrich List (1789–1846) rejected laissez faire and free trade as a British trick "to make the rest of the world, like the Hindus, its serfs in all industrial and commercial relations." To protect their "infant industries" from British competition, he argued, the German states had to erect high tariff barriers against imports from Britain. On the European continent, List's ideas helped lead to the formation of the Zollverein (**TSOLL-feh-rine**), a customs union of most of the German states, in 1834.

French social thinkers, moved by sincere concern for the poor, offered a radically new vision of a just civilization. Espousing a philosophy called **positivism**, the count of Saint-Simon (1760–1825) and his disciple Auguste Comte (**COMB-tuh**) (1798–1857) argued that the scientific method could solve social as well as technical problems. They recommended that the poor, guided by scientists and artists, form workers' communities under the protection of benevolent business leaders. These ideas attracted the enthusiastic support of bankers and entrepreneurs, for whom positivism provided a rationale for investing in railroads, canals, and other symbols of modernity. Positivism was most influential in Latin America, where the political elites of Brazil and Mexico pursued a top-down program of economic development reinforced by harsh police controls and the manipulation of political institutions. Its chief tenets are emblazed on the Brazilian flag: Order and Progress.

As numerous protest organizations formed across Europe in the wake of the Industrial Revolution, a minority sought to overthrow the new industrial order. Groups calling themselves communists were the most prominent of these radical groups. Two German-born intellectuals, Karl Marx (1818–1883) and his long-time collaborator and benefactor Friedrich Engels (1820–1895), played key roles in formulating this movement's criticism of industrial capitalism. They argued that the concentration of wealth and power associated with industrialization had led to the unbearable oppression of industrial workers (what they called the **proletariat**) and justified revolution. While the monumental work *Das Kapital* (Capital) was Marx's major intellectual achievement, it was *The Communist Manifesto*, published in 1848 with Engels, that proved most influential in spreading his radical critique of capitalism and urging the mobilization of the working class. This short, powerful book argued that history was dominated by class struggle and that proletarians would inevitably come together to overthrow the bourgeoisie, the modern class that controlled industry. The book's final words were "Proletarians of all countries unite!"

Protests and Reforms   Workers benefited little from the ideas of these middle-class philosophers. Instead, they resisted harsh working conditions in their own ways. Periodically, they rioted or went on strike, especially when food prices were high or when downturns in the business cycle left many unemployed. In some places, craftsmen broke into factories and destroyed the machines that threatened their livelihoods. Such acts of resistance did little to change the nature of industrial work.

From the beginnings of the Industrial Revolution workers resisted the introduction of new technologies. They believed that mechanized production would diminish the value of their skills and force them into poverty. As early as 1767, disgruntled textile workers mobilized to destroy one of the first innovations, James Hargreaves' spinning jenny. Subsequent innovations in both the cotton and woolen industries were also attacked by angry crowds of workers. In 1779, for example, workers destroyed nearly every machine driven by waterpower in Blackburn, England. Then in 1811 angry workers in the lace and stocking industries began a campaign of systematic machine breaking. Calling themselves Luddites, they attacked more than one hundred businesses and destroyed nearly every machine in the district. Machine breaking in France was even more violent. As French entrepreneurs began introducing British industrial technologies in textiles and metallurgy in the late 1770s, workers organized protests against these "foreign" innovations, attacking British craftsmen and destroying the new machines. In the early stages of the French Revolution (see Chapter 23), popular revolutionary sentiment reinforced the resistance of workers to new machinery and undermined the ability of the government to protect factories. The result was that French artisans retained traditional control of production and France fell decades behind Britain in industrializing.

Mechanization was also resisted in rural areas. The effects of enclosure (described earlier in this chapter) and rural population growth combined to force many rural families in Great Britain into poverty. Thousands of tenants and small farmers lost their land, becoming seasonal labors or migrating to industrial cities. This impoverished class of rural workers rose up when wealthy farmers began to introduce reapers and other machines. Often called the "Captain Swing" riots, rural laborers organized against mechanization, setting fires, threatening landlords, demanding higher wages, and breaking machines. This popular movement culminated after 1830 when widespread rural riots forced the British government to mobilize troops and militia in defense of property. In the end, thousands of protestors were arrested and either imprisoned in Britain or transported to Australia as convict laborers.

These violent efforts to block innovation and protect long-established customs in manufacturing and agriculture were superseded by laboring class organizations focused on workplace reform, higher wages, and expanded political rights. Gradually, workers organized to demand universal male suffrage and shorter workdays. In 1834, Robert Owen founded the Grand National Consolidated Trade Union to lobby for an eight-hour workday; it quickly gained half a million members but collapsed a few months later in the face of government prosecution. A new movement called Chartism arose soon thereafter, led by William Lovett and Fergus O'Connor, that appealed to miners and industrial workers. It demanded universal male suffrage, the secret ballot, salaries for members of Parliament, and annual elections. Chartism collapsed in 1848, but it left a legacy of labor organizing (see Chapter 23). By 1850 the beginnings of the modern union movement were in place in Europe's most industrialized nations.

Eventually, mass movements persuaded the British Parliament to investigate conditions in factories and mines and initiate some reforms. The Factory Act of 1833 prohibited the employment of children younger than nine in textile mills. It also limited the working hours of children between the ages of nine and thirteen to eight hours a day and of fourteen- to eighteen-year-olds to twelve hours. The Mines Act of 1842 prohibited the employment of women and boys under age ten underground. Belgium and other European nations were slower to introduce workplace reforms. The British learned to seek reform through accommodation. On the European continent, in contrast, the revolutions of 1848 revealed widespread discontent with repressive governments but failed to soften the hardships of industrialization (see Chapter 27).

THE LIMITS OF INDUSTRIALIZATION OUTSIDE THE WEST

Egypt   The spread of the Industrial Revolution in the early nineteenth century transformed the relations of western Europe and North America with the rest of the world. Egypt, strongly influenced by European ideas since the French invasion of 1798, began to industrialize in the early nineteenth century. The driving force was its ruler, **Muhammad Ali** (1769–1849), a man who was to play a major role in the history of the Middle East and East Africa (see Chapters 24 and 26). Muhammad Ali wanted to build up the Egyptian economy and military in order to become less dependent on the Ottoman sultan, his nominal overlord. To do so, he imported advisers and technicians from Europe and built cotton mills, foundries, shipyards, weapons factories, and other industrial enterprises. To pay for all this, he made the peasants grow wheat and cotton, which the government bought at a low price and exported at a profit. He also imposed high tariffs on imported goods to force the pace of industrialization.

Muhammad Ali's efforts fell afoul of the British, who did not want a powerful country threatening to interrupt the flow of travelers and mail across Egypt, the shortest route between Europe and India. When Egypt went to war against the Ottoman Empire in 1839, Britain intervened and forced Muhammad Ali to eliminate all import duties in the name of free trade. Unprotected, Egypt's fledgling industries could not compete with the flood of cheap British products. Thereafter, Egypt exported raw cotton, imported manufactured goods, and became an economic dependency of Britain.

India

Until the late eighteenth century, India had been the world's largest producer and exporter of cotton textiles, handmade by skilled spinners and weavers. The British East India Company took over large parts of India just as the Industrial Revolution was beginning in Britain. It then allowed cheap British factory-made yarn and cloth to flood the Indian market duty-free, putting spinners and handloom weavers out of work. Unlike Britain, India had no factories to which displaced handicraft workers could turn for work and most of them became landless peasants, eking out a precarious living.

Like other tropical regions, India became an exporter of raw materials and an importer of British industrial goods. To hasten the process, British entrepreneurs and colonial officials introduced railroads into the subcontinent. The construction of India's railroad network began in the mid-1850s, along with coal mining to fuel the locomotives and the installation of telegraph lines to connect the major cities.

Some Indian entrepreneurs saw opportunities in the atmosphere of change that the British created. In 1854, the Bombay merchant Cowasjee Nanabhoy Davar imported an engineer, four skilled workers, and several textile machines from Britain and started India's first textile mill. This was the beginning of India's mechanized cotton industry. Despite many gifted entrepreneurs, however, India's industrialization proceeded at a snail's pace, for the government was in British hands and the British did nothing to encourage Indian industry.

China

In the eighteenth century, the Chinese economy benefited from a long period of relative political stability and from population growth and commercial expansion. During the Qing dynasty, specialized market towns devoted to cotton textiles, silk, and staples developed in east-central China. At the same time, China developed markets in land and labor as well as rudimentary banking and credit mechanisms that facilitated long-distance trade. There were few direct threats to either Chinese borders or Chinese trade. This situation changed as European powers, first the Portuguese and Dutch and then the British and French, established highly militarized commercial presences in Asia. Nevertheless, even as European power grew, China continued to play a major role in the major markets of Asia, maintaining a favorable balance of trade with Europe that was financed by silver from European colonies.

China, however, remained an agrarian empire much less dependent on foreign trade than the major European powers, especially Great Britain. As a result, the Chinese government focused its attention and resources on the production and distribution of food, an effective guarantee of social peace, rather than on trade. While Britain and its European rivals viewed foreign trade as crucial to national well-being and as inherently competitive, the Chinese government saw foreign trade as narrowly supplemental to the domestic economy.

With inexpensive and abundant labor, the absence of a true national market, and limited engagement in foreign markets, the Chinese government did not see a clear need to subsidize or promote technology transfers as new machine technologies rapidly transformed the European economy in the first half of the nineteenth century. This situation began to rapidly change when Great Britain, its military transformed by the Industrial Revolution, pressed to reverse the steep trade imbalance long enjoyed by China. Compelled now to recognize the economic and military transformations wrought by industrial innovation in Europe, China faced a succession of internal and foreign threats to stability before its own reforms could begin to take hold.

In January 1840, a shipyard in Britain launched a radically new ship. The *Nemesis* had an iron hull, a flat bottom that allowed it to navigate in shallow waters, and a steam engine to power it upriver and against the wind. In November it arrived off the coast of China, heavily armed. Though ships from Europe had been sailing to China for three hundred years, the *Nemesis* was the first steam-powered iron gunboat in Asian waters. It was soon joined by other steam-powered warships that collectively established European control of Chinese rivers, bombarding forts and cities and transporting troops and supplies far more quickly than Chinese soldiers could move on foot. With this new weapon, Britain, a small island nation half a world away, was able to defeat the largest and most populated country in the world (see Chapter 24). The cases of Egypt, India, and China show how the demands of Western nations and the military advantage they gained from industrialization led them to interfere in the internal affairs of nonindustrial societies. As we shall see in Chapter 27, this was the start of a new age of Western dominance.

CONCLUSION

The Industrial Revolution was the most momentous transformation in history since the beginning of agriculture. The steam engine and other new machines greatly lowered the cost and increased the production of goods like cotton and iron, as well as increased the speed of transportation and communication.

The process caused social upheavals and environmental problems, however. Many entrepreneurs and businesspeople became very wealthy, while industrial workers—many of them children—worked under appalling conditions and lived in overcrowded tenements in badly polluted cities. Economists and philosophers proposed many theories and offered many solutions to the radical problems of industrial societies.

Industrialization had political consequences on a global scale. A small number of industrializing nations—first Great Britain, then those of western Europe and

North America—grew more powerful. Other parts of the world were left behind to become political or economic dependencies of these powerful nations.

Eventually the industrial nations learned to alleviate their social problems, but the disparity between the rich and poor nations persisted for two centuries or more, and the environmental effects of industrialization have changed from local to global.

IMPORTANT EVENTS 1750–1854

1702–1712	Thomas Newcomen builds first steam engine
1776	Adam Smith's *Wealth of Nations*
1776–1783	American Revolution
1779	First iron bridge
1789–1799	French Revolution
1792	Mary Wollstonecraft's *A Vindication of the Rights of Woman*
1793	Eli Whitney's cotton gin
1804–1815	Napoleonic Wars
1820s	Construction of Erie Canal
1820s	U.S. cotton industry begins
1829	*Rocket*, first prize-winning locomotive
1833	Factory Act in Britain
1834	German Zollverein; Robert Owen's Grand National Consolidated Trade Union
1837	Wheatstone and Cooke's telegraph
1838	First ships steam across the Atlantic
1840	*Nemesis* sails to China
1843	Samuel Morse's Baltimore-to-Washington telegraph
1846	Repeal of British Corn Laws
1847–1848	Irish famine
1848	Collapse of Chartist movement; revolutions in Europe
1851	Crystal Palace opens in London
1854	First cotton mill in India

23

REVOLUTIONARY CHANGES IN THE ATLANTIC WORLD, 1750–1850

In August 1791, slaves and free blacks began an insurrection in the plantation district of northern Saint Domingue (san doe-MANG) (present-day Haiti). During the following decade and a half, Haitian revolutionaries abolished slavery; defeated military forces from Britain and France; and achieved independence.

News and rumors about revolutionary events in France had helped move the island's slave community to rebel. These same events had divided the island's white population into royalists (supporters of France's King Louis XVI) and republicans (who sought an end to monarchy). The large free mixed-race population had secured some political rights from the French Assembly but was forced into rebellion by the violent resistance of the slave-owning elite to these reforms.

A black freedman, François Dominique Toussaint, led the insurrection. Taking the name Toussaint L'Ouverture (too-SAN loo-ver-CHORE), he became one of the most remarkable representatives of the revolutionary era. He organized the rebels militarily, negotiated with the island's competing factions and with representatives of Britain and France, and wrote his nation's first constitution. Commonly portrayed as a fiend by slave owners, Toussaint became a towering symbol of resistance to oppression to slaves everywhere.

The Haitian slave rebellion was an important event in the political and cultural transformation of the Western world. Profound changes to the economy, politics, and intellectual life occurred as well. The Industrial Revolution (see Chapter 22) increased manufacturing productivity and led to greater global interdependence, new patterns of consumerism, and altered social structures. At the same time, intellectuals questioned the traditional place of monarchy and religion in Western society. Enriched by the economic dynamism of this period, merchants, professionals, and manufacturers provided an audience for the new intellectual currents as they pressed for a larger political role.

This revolutionary era turned the Western world "upside down." The *ancien régime* (ahn-see-EN ray-ZHEEM), the French term for Europe's old order, rested on medieval principles: politics dominated by powerful monarchs, intellectual and cultural life dominated by religion, and economics dominated by hereditary agricultural elites. In the West's new order, commoners entered political life; science took the place of religion in intellectual life; and economies opened to competition.

This radical transformation did not take place without false starts or setbacks. Imperial powers resisted the loss of colonies; monarchs and nobles struggled to retain their ancient privileges; and church authorities fought against the claims of science. While the liberal and nationalist ideals of the eighteenth-century revolutionary movements were sometimes thwarted in Europe and the Americas, belief in national self-determination and universal suffrage and a passion for social justice continued to animate reformers into the twentieth century.

PRELUDE TO REVOLUTION: THE EIGHTEENTH-CENTURY CRISIS

The cost of wars fought among Europe's major powers over colonies and trade helped precipitate the revolutionary era that began in 1775 with the American Revolution. Britain, France, and Spain were the central actors in these global struggles, but other imperial powers participated as well. While these nations had previously fought unpopular and costly wars and paid for them with new taxes, changes in Western intellectual and political environments now produced a much more critical response. Any effort to extend monarchical power or impose new taxes now raised questions about the rights of individuals and the legitimacy of political institutions.

Colonial Wars and Fiscal Crises   In the seventeenth century competition among European powers became global in character. The newly independent Netherlands attacked the trade routes that linked Spain and Portugal to their American and Asian colonies, even seizing parts of Portugal's colonial empire in Brazil and Angola. Europe's other emerging sea power, Great Britain, also attacked Spanish fleets and seaports in the Americas. These rivalries made the defense of trade routes and distant colonies more expensive and difficult.

The eighteenth century further tested the ability of European powers to pay for their imperial ambitions. As Dutch power ebbed, Britain and France began a long struggle for political preeminence in western Europe and for territory and trade outlets in the Americas and Asia as the older empires of Spain and Portugal struggled to hang on. Nearly all of Europe's great powers participated in the War of the Spanish Succession (1701–1714). A few decades later war between Britain and Spain over smuggling broadened into a generalized European conflict, the War of Austrian Succession (1740–1748). Less than two decades later a frontier conflict between French and British forces and their Amerindian allies then led to a wider struggle, the Seven Years' War (1756–1763). With peace Britain emerged with undisputed control of North America east of the Mississippi River while France had been forced to surrender Canada and its holdings in India.

The enormous cost of these conflicts distinguished them from earlier wars. Traditional taxes collected in traditional ways no longer covered the obligations of governments. While Britain's total budget before the Seven Years' War had averaged only £8 million, in 1763 its war debt had reached £137 million and interest payments alone exceeded £5 million. Even as European economies expanded, fiscal crises overtook one European government after another. In an intellectual environment transformed by the Enlightenment, the need for new revenues provoked debate and confrontation within a vastly expanded and more critical public.

**The
Enlightenment
and the Old
Order**

The complex and diverse intellectual movement called the **Enlightenment** applied the methods and questions of the Scientific Revolution of the seventeenth century to the study of human society as well as to the natural world (see Chapter 17). Some European intellectuals sought to systematize knowledge and organize reference materials. For example, the Swedish botanist Carolus Linnaeus (kar-ROLL-uhs lin-NEE-uhs) sought to categorize all living organisms, and Samuel Johnson published a comprehensive English dictionary. In France Denis Diderot (duh-nee DEE-duh-roe) worked with other thinkers to create a compendium of human knowledge, the thirty-five-volume *Encyclopédie*.

Other thinkers pursued lines of inquiry that more directly challenged long-established religious and political institutions. Some argued that if scientists could understand the laws of nature, then surely similar forms of disciplined investigation might reveal laws of human nature. The most radical wondered whether society and government could be better regulated and more productive if guided by science rather than by hereditary rulers and the church. These new perspectives and the intellectual optimism that fed them helped guide the revolutionary movements of the late eighteenth century.

The English political philosopher John Locke (1632–1704) argued in 1690 that governments were created to protect life, liberty, and property and that the people had a right to rebel when a monarch violated these natural rights. Locke's closely reasoned theory began with the assumption that individual rights were the foundation of civil government. In *The Social Contract*, published in 1762, the French-Swiss intellectual Jean-Jacques Rousseau (zhan-zhock roo-SOE) (1712–1778) asserted that the will of the people was sacred and that the legitimacy of monarchs depended on the consent of the people. Although both men believed that government rested on the will of the people, Locke emphasized the importance of individual rights secured institutionally while Rousseau, much more distrustful of society and government, envisioned the people acting collectively as a result of their shared historical experience.

All Enlightenment thinkers were not radicals like Rousseau. There was never a uniform program for political and social reform, and the era's intellectuals often disagreed about principles and objectives. While the Enlightenment is commonly associated with hostility toward religion and monarchy, few intellectuals openly expressed republican or atheist sentiments. Even Voltaire, one of the Enlightenment's most critical intellects and great celebrities, believed that Europe's monarchs were likely agents of political and economic reform.

Indeed, sympathetic members of the nobility and reforming European monarchs such as Charles III of Spain (r. 1759–1788), Catherine the Great of Russia (r. 1762–1796), and Frederick the Great of Prussia (r. 1740–1786) actively sponsored and promoted the dissemination of new ideas, providing patronage for many intellectuals. They recognized that elements of the Enlightenment buttressed their own efforts to expand royal authority at the expense of religious institutions, the nobility, and regional autonomy. Goals such as the development of national bureaucracies staffed by civil servants selected on merit, the creation of national legal systems, and the modernization of tax systems united many of Europe's monarchs and intellectuals. Monarchs also understood that the era's passion for science and technology held the potential of fattening national treasuries and improving economic performance.

Though willing to embrace reform proposals when they served royal interests, Europe's monarchs moved quickly to suppress or ban radical ideas that promoted republicanism or directly attacked religion. However, too many channels of communication were open to permit a thoroughgoing suppression of ideas. In fact, censorship tended to enhance intellectual reputations, and persecuted intellectuals generally found patronage in the courts of foreign rivals.

Many of the major intellectuals of the Enlightenment corresponded with each other as well as with political leaders. This communication led to numerous first-hand contacts among the intellectuals of different nations and helped create a more coherent assault on what they saw as ignorance—beliefs and values associated with the ancien régime. Rousseau met the Scottish philosopher David Hume in Paris. Later, when Rousseau feared arrest, Hume helped him seek refuge in Britain. Similarly, Voltaire sought patronage and protection in England and later in Prussia when facing threats in France.

Women were instrumental in the dissemination of these new ideas. In England large numbers of educated middle-class women purchased and discussed books and pamphlets. Some, like Mary Wollstonecraft, were important contributors to intellectual life as writers and commentators, raising by example and in argument the issue of the rights of women. In Paris wealthy women made their homes centers of debate, intellectual speculation, and free inquiry. Their salons brought together philosophers, social critics, artists, members of the aristocracy, and the commercial elite.

The intellectual ferment of the era deeply influenced the expanding middle class in Europe and the Western Hemisphere. Members of this class were eager consumers of books and inexpensive newspapers and journals, which were widely available. This broadening of the intellectual audience overwhelmed traditional institutions of censorship. New public venues like the thousands of coffeehouses and teashops of cities and market towns also became locations to discuss scientific discoveries, new technologies, and controversial works on human nature and politics, expanding the Enlightenment's influence beyond the literate minority.

Many European intellectuals were interested in the Americas. Some continued to dismiss the region as barbaric and inferior, but others used idealized accounts of the New World to support their critiques of European society. Many looked to Britain's North American colonies for confirmation of their belief that human nature unconstrained by the corrupted practices of Europe's old order would quickly produce material abundance and social justice. More than any other American, the writer and inventor **Benjamin Franklin** came to symbolize the vast potential of America to Europe's intellectuals.

Born in Boston in 1706, the young Franklin trained as a printer. In Philadelphia he succeeded in business and became famous for his *Poor Richard's Almanac*. At forty-two he retired to pursue writing, science, and public affairs. Franklin was instrumental in the creation of the Philadelphia Free Library, the American Philosophical Society, and the University of Pennsylvania. His contributions were both practical and theoretical. The inventor of bifocal glasses, the lightning rod, and an efficient wood-burning stove, he also contributed to scientific knowledge with publications like his 1751 paper, *Experiments and Observations on Electricity*, which won him acclaim from European intellectuals.

Franklin was also an important political figure. He served in many capacities in the colonies and was selected as a delegate to the Continental Congress that issued the Declaration of Independence in 1776. He later became ambassador to Paris, where his achievements, witty conversation, and careful self-promotion made him the symbol of the era. His life seemed to confirm the Enlightenment's most radical objective, the freeing of human potential from the effects of inherited privilege.

As Franklin demonstrates, the Western Hemisphere shared in Europe's intellectual ferment. As the Enlightenment penetrated the New World, intellectuals actively debated the legitimacy of colonialism itself. European efforts to reform colonial policies by unilaterally altering colonial institutions and overturning long-established political practices further radicalized colonial intellectuals. Among peoples compelled to accept the dependence and inferiority explicit in colonial rule, the idea that government authority rested on the consent of the governed proved explosive.

Many intellectuals resisted the Enlightenment, seeing it as a dangerous assault on the authority of the church and monarchy. This Counter Enlightenment was most influential in France and other Catholic nations. Its adherents emphasized the importance of faith to human happiness and social well-being. They also emphasized duty and obligation to the community of believers in opposition to the concern for individual rights and individual fulfillment common in the works of the Enlightenment. Most importantly for the politics of the era, they rejected their enemies' enthusiasm for change and utopianism, reminding their readers of human fallibility and the importance of history and tradition. While the central ideas of the Enlightenment gained strength across the nineteenth century, the Counter Enlightenment provided ideological support for the era's conservatism and later popular antidemocratic movements.

Folk Cultures and Popular Protest
While intellectuals and the reforming royal courts of Europe debated the rational and secular enthusiasms of the Enlightenment, most people in Western society remained loyal to competing cultural values grounded in the preindustrial past. Regional folk cultures were rooted in the memory of shared experience and nourished by religious practices that encouraged emotional release. These cultural traditions included coherent expressions of the rights and obligations that connected people with their rulers. Authorities who violated these understandings were likely to face violent opposition.

In the eighteenth century, European monarchs sought to increase their authority and to centralize power by reforming tax collection, judicial practice, and public administration. Although monarchs viewed these changes as reforms, common people often saw them as violations of sacred customs and responded with bread riots, tax protests, and attacks on royal officials. These violent actions sought to preserve custom and precedent rather than overturn traditional authority. In Spain and the Spanish colonies, protesting mobs often expressed love for their monarch while at the same time assaulting his officials and preventing the implementation of reforms, shouting "Long Live the King! Death to Bad Government!"

Enlightenment-era reformers sought to bring order and discipline to the citizenry by banning or altering numerous popular traditions—such as harvest festivals, religious holidays, and country fairs—that enlivened the drudgery of

The Art Archive

Beer Street (1751) *William Hogarth's engraving shows an idealized London street scene where beer drinking is associated with manly strength, good humor, and prosperity. The self-satisfied corpulent figure in the left foreground reads a copy of the king's speech to Parliament. We can imagine him offering a running commentary to his drinking companions as he reads.*

everyday life. These events were popular celebrations of sexuality and individuality as well as opportunities for masked and costumed celebrants to mock the greed, pretension, and foolishness of government officials, the wealthy, and the clergy. Hard drinking, gambling, and blood sports like cockfighting and bearbaiting were popular in preindustrial mass culture, but reformers viewed them as corrupt and decadent. As reforming governments undertook to substitute civic rituals, patriotic anniversaries, and institutions of self-improvement for older customs, they often provoked protests and riots.

The efforts of ordinary men and women to resist the growth of government power and the imposition of new cultural forms provide an important political undercurrent to much of the revolutionary agitation and conflict between 1750 and 1850.

Spontaneous popular uprisings and protests punctuated nearly every effort at reform in the eighteenth century. But popular protest gained revolutionary potential only when it coincided with ideological division and conflict within the governing class.

THE AMERICAN REVOLUTION, 1775–1800

In British North America, clumsy efforts to increase colonial taxes to cover rising defense expenditures and to diminish the power of elected colonial legislatures outraged a populace accustomed to local autonomy. Once begun, the American Revolution ushered in a century-long process of political and cultural transformation in Europe and the Americas. By the end of this revolutionary century, constitutions had limited or overturned the authority of monarchs, and religion had lost its dominance of Western intellectual life. At the same time revolutionary changes in manufacturing and commerce replaced the long-established social order determined by birth with a new social ideal emphasizing competition and social mobility.

Frontiers and Taxes   After defeating the French in 1763, the British government faced two related problems in its North American colonies. As settlers pushed west into Amerindian lands, Britain feared the likelihood of renewed conflict and rising military expenses. Already burdened with heavy debts, Britain tried to limit settler pressure on Amerindian lands and get colonists to shoulder more of the costs of colonial defense and administration.

In the Great Lakes region the British tried to contain costs by reducing fur prices and by refusing to continue the French practice of giving gifts and paying rent for frontier forts to Amerindian peoples. But lower fur prices forced native peoples to hunt more aggressively, putting pressure on the environment and endangering some species. The situation got worse as settlers and white trappers pushed across the Appalachians to compete directly with native hunters. The predictable result was renewed violence along the frontier led by Pontiac, an Ottawa chief. His broad alliance of native peoples forged in 1763 drove the British military from some western outposts but was unable to take Fort Detroit. Failure led to disaffection among the Amerindian allies and finally to a peace treaty in 1766.

With the outbreak of this conflict the British government reacted by publishing the Proclamation of 1763. This policy established a western limit for settlement, thus undermining the claims of thousands of established farmers without effectively protecting Amerindian land. No one was satisfied. In 1774, Britain tried again to slow the movement of settlers onto Amerindian lands by annexing western territories to the province of Quebec. Like the 1763 proclamation, this action provoked bitter resentment in the colonies.

In comparison with the French, Spanish, and Portuguese colonies of the Americas, the settlers of the British colonies enjoyed substantial political autonomy, exercising effective local control through elected legislatures and courts. Even as slavery expanded in the southern colonies, free settlers prospered. One measure of this mounting, broadly distributed wealth was the rising tide of imported British consumer goods. While enriching metropolitan producers and merchants, colonial consumption of British cloth, porcelains, tea, and other imports also played a key role in forging a unified colonial culture that transcended regional economic, social, and even religious differences.

When the British government sought to assert greater political control and force the colonies to pay a much larger share of the costs of defense and governance in the wake of the French and Indian War, colonial settlers would use consumer boycotts to great effect. While frontier policies imposed following Pontiac's rebellion led to colonial hostility and suspicion, they did not lead to a breach. British fiscal reforms and new taxes, however, sparked a series of political confrontations that led to political mobilizations and popular protests across the colonies and, ultimately, to rebellion. For example, British regulations imposed in 1764 threatened New England's profitable trade with Spanish and French Caribbean sugar colonies and more effectively policed colonial smuggling. More disruptive still was Britain's outlawing of colonial issues of paper money, a custom made necessary by the colonies' chronic balance-of-payments deficits. Each of these measures met with the protests of colonial legislatures and popular assemblies.

The Stamp Act of 1765—a tax on all legal documents, newspapers, pamphlets, and nearly all printed material—caused especially deep resentment. Propertied colonists, including holders of high office and members of the colonial elite, assumed leading roles in protests and used fiery political language, identifying Britain's rulers as "parricides" and "tyrants" and suggesting that a dependence on British imports threatened traditional liberties. Women from prominent colonial families played a crucial role in organizing boycotts of British goods. For them and for poorer women as well, producing and wearing homespun textiles was increasingly seen as a patriotic obligation. Organizations such as the Sons of Liberty were more confrontational, holding public meetings, intimidating royal officials, and organizing committees to enforce the boycotts. Although this combination of protest and boycott forced the repeal of the Stamp Act, Britain imposed new taxes and duties in 1767. Parliament also sent British troops to quell colonial riots. While the boycotts against the Stamp Act were mostly confined to cities, these new taxes ignited protests across the colonies. Legislatures, town governments, and *ad hoc* committees mobilized the colonists to boycott British goods. One indignant woman expressed her anger to a British officer:

> [T]he most ignorant peasant knows ... that no man has the right to take their money without their consent. The supposition is ridiculous and absurd, as none but highwaymen and robbers attempt it. Can you, my friend, reconcile it with your own good sense, that a body of men in Great Britain, who have little intercourse with America ... shall invest themselves with a power to command our lives and properties [?][1]

British authorities reacted to boycotts and attacks on royal officials by threatening colonial liberties. They dissolved the colonial legislature of Massachusetts and sent two regiments of soldiers to re-establish control of Boston's streets. Popular support for a complete break with Britain grew after March 5, 1770, when British soldiers fired at an angry Boston crowd, killing five civilians. The "Boston Massacre" exposed the naked force on which colonial rule rested and radicalized public opinion throughout the colonies.

Parliament attempted to calm colonial opinion by repealing some taxes and duties, but it stumbled into another crisis when it granted the East India Company

---

[1] Quoted in Ray Raphael, *A People's History of the American Revolution* (New York: Perennial, 2001), 141.

a monopoly to import tea to the colonies. This decision raised again the constitutional issue of Parliament's right to tax the colonies. It also provided the perfect target for colonial dissidents seeking to organize protest on a broad scale. Since tea was consumed by nearly everyone, its boycott would potentially unite nearly every class and region. In the heated language of protest, buying and drinking tea was acquiescing to British tyranny. The crisis came to a head when protesters dumped tea worth £10,000 (about £1.3 million or $1.9 million in 2012) into Boston harbor. As news of this act spread, tea was surrendered or, in some cases, seized and burned in innumerable towns and villages across the colonies. Britain responded by appointing a military man, Thomas Gage, as governor of Massachusetts and by closing the port of Boston. British troops now enforced public order in Boston, and public administration was in the hands of a general. This militarization of colonial government undermined Britain's constitutional authority and made rebellion inevitable.

The Course of Revolution, 1775–1783   In 1775 representatives from the colonies met in Philadelphia to discuss the situation. Most of the representatives elected to this Continental Congress had been active in the boycotts and protests of the previous decade, and they again used nonimportation as a political weapon. But events were moving quickly toward armed confrontation and revolution. Patriot militias had already fought British troops at Lexington and Concord, Massachusetts, and few thought compromise possible. The Congress now assumed the powers of government, created a currency, and organized an army led by **George Washington** (1732–1799), a Virginia planter who had served in the French and Indian War.

The angry rhetoric of thousands of street-corner speakers and the inflammatory pamphlet *Common Sense*, written by Thomas Paine, a recent immigrant from England, propelled popular support for independence. On July 4, 1776, Congress approved the Declaration of Independence, the document that proved to be the most enduring statement of the revolutionary era's ideology:

> *We hold these truths to be self evident: That all men are created equal; that they are endowed by their creator with certain unalienable rights; that among these are life, liberty and the pursuit of happiness; that, to secure these rights, governments are instituted among men, deriving their just powers from the consent of the governed.*

The Declaration's affirmation of popular sovereignty and individual rights would influence the language of revolution and popular protest around the world.

Great Britain reacted by sending additional military forces to pacify the colonies. By 1778 Britain had 50,000 British troops and 30,000 German mercenaries in the colonies. Despite the existence of a large loyalist community, the British army found it difficult to control the countryside. Although British forces won most of the battles, Washington slowly built a competent Continental army as well as civilian support networks that provided supplies and financial resources.

The British government also tried to find a political compromise that would satisfy colonial grievances. Half-hearted efforts to resolve the conflict over taxes failed, and an offer to roll back the clock and re-establish the administrative arrangements of 1763 made little headway. Overconfidence in its military and poor leadership kept the British from finding a political solution before revolutionary institutions were in place and the armies engaged. By allowing confrontation to occur, the British government lost the opportunity to mobilize and give direction to the large numbers of loyalists and pacifists in the colonies.

Along the Canadian border, both sides solicited Amerindians as allies and feared them as potential enemies. For over a hundred years, members of the powerful Iroquois Confederacy—Mohawk, Oneida, Onondaga, Cayuga, Seneca, and (after 1722) Tuscarora—had protected their traditional lands with a combination of diplomacy and warfare. Just as the American Revolution forced settler families to join the rebels or remain loyal, it divided the Iroquois, who fought on both sides.

The Mohawk proved to be valuable British allies. Their loyalist leader **Joseph Brant** (Thayendanegea [ta-YEHN-dah-NEY-geh-ah]) organized Britain's most potent fighting force along the Canadian border. His raids along the northern frontier earned him the title "Monster" Brant, but he was actually a man who moved easily between European and Amerindian cultures. Educated by missionaries, he was fluent in English and helped translate Protestant religious tracts into Mohawk. He was friendly with many loyalist families and British officials and had traveled to London for an audience with George III (r. 1760–1820).

The defeat in late 1777 of Britain's general John Burgoyne by General Horatio Gates at Saratoga, New York, put the future of the Mohawk at risk. American forces followed this victory with destructive attacks on Iroquois villages that reduced their political and military power. After Britain's defeat, Brant and the Mohawk joined the loyalist exodus to Canada.

The British defeat at Saratoga also convinced France to enter the war as an ally of the United States in 1778. French military help proved crucial, supplying American forces and forcing the British to defend their colonies in the Caribbean. The French contribution was most clear in the final battle, fought at Yorktown, Virginia, in 1781. With the American army supported by French soldiers and a French fleet, General Charles Cornwallis surrendered to Washington as the British military band played "The World Turned Upside-Down."

This victory effectively ended the war, and the Continental Congress sent representatives to the peace conference with instructions to work in tandem with the French. Believing that France was more concerned with containing British power than with guaranteeing a strong United States, America's peace delegation chose to negotiate directly with Britain and gained a generous settlement. The Treaty of Paris (1783) granted unconditional independence and established generous boundaries for the former colonies. In return the United States promised to repay prewar debts due to British merchants and to allow loyalists to recover property confiscated by patriot forces. In the end, loyalists were badly treated, and thousands left for Canada.

The Construction of Republican Institutions, to 1800

Even before the Declaration of Independence, many colonies had created new governments and summoned constitutional conventions to draft formal charters. Europeans were fascinated by the drafting of written constitutions and by their ratification by popular vote. Many early state constitutions were translated and published in Europe. Remembering colonial conflicts with royal governors, state constitutions placed severe limits on executive authority and granted broad powers to legislatures. Many also included bills of rights to provide further protection against tyranny.

It proved more difficult to frame a national constitution. The Second Continental Congress sent the Articles of Confederation—the first constitution of the United States—to the states for approval in 1777, but it was not accepted until 1781. It created a one-house legislature in which each state had a single vote. While a simple majority of the thirteen states was sufficient to pass minor legislation, nine votes were necessary for declaring war, imposing taxes, and coining or borrowing money. A committee, not a president, exercised executive power. Given the intended weakness of this government, it is remarkable that it defeated Great Britain.

Many of the most powerful political figures in the United States recognized that the Confederation was unable to enforce unpopular requirements of the peace treaty such as the recognition of loyalist property claims, the payment of prewar debts, and even the payment of military salaries and pensions due veterans. As a result, in September 1786 Virginia invited the other states to discuss the government's failure to deal with trade issues. This assembly called for a new convention to meet in Philadelphia. A rebellion led by Revolutionary War veterans in western Massachusetts gave the assembling delegates a sense of urgency.

The **Constitutional Convention**, which met in May 1787, achieved a nonviolent second American Revolution. The delegates pushed aside the announced purpose of the convention—"to render the constitution of the federal government adequate to the exigencies of the union"—and secretly undertook to write a new constitution with George Washington serving as presiding officer.

Debate focused on representation, electoral procedures, executive powers, and the relationship between the federal government and the states. The final compromise distributed political power among executive, legislative, and judicial branches and divided authority between the federal government and the states. The chief executive—the president—was to be elected indirectly by "electors" selected by ballot in the states.

Although this constitution created the most democratic government of the era, only a minority of the adult population had full political rights. While some northern states were hostile to slavery, southern leaders protected the institution. Slaves were denied participation in the political process, but slave states were permitted to count three-fifths of the slave population to allocate the number of congressional representatives, thus multiplying the political power of the slave-owning class. Southern delegates also gained a twenty-year continuation of the slave trade to 1808 and a fugitive slave clause that required all states to return runaway slaves to masters.

During the war, women had led prewar boycotts and organized relief and charitable organizations. Some had also served in the military as nurses, and a smaller number had joined the ranks disguised as men. Nevertheless, women were denied political rights in the new republic. Only New Jersey granted the vote to women and African Americans who met property requirements, and in 1807 state lawmakers eliminated this right.

THE FRENCH REVOLUTION, 1789–1815

The French Revolution undermined traditional monarchy and hereditary aristocracy as well as the power of the Catholic Church but, unlike the American Revolution, did not create enduring representative institutions. The colonial revolution in North America, however, did not confront so directly the entrenched privileges of an established church, monarchy, and aristocracy. Among its achievements, the French Revolution expanded mass participation in political life and radicalized the democratic tradition inherited from the English and American experiences. The political passions unleashed by revolutionary events in France also ultimately led to rule by popular demagogues and the dictatorship of Napoleon.

French Society and Fiscal Crisis   French society was divided in three estates. The clergy, called the First Estate, numbered about 130,000 in a nation of 28 million. The Catholic clergy was organized hierarchically, and priests from noble families held almost all top positions in the church. The church owned about 10 percent of the nation's land and extracted substantial amounts of wealth from the economy in the form of tithes and ecclesiastical fees, but it paid few taxes.

The 300,000 members of the nobility, the Second Estate, controlled about 30 percent of the land and retained ancient rights on much of the rest. Nobles held most high administrative, judicial, military, and church positions. Though barred from some types of commercial activity, nobles were important participants

Parisian Stocking Mender *The poor lived very difficult lives. This woman uses a discarded wine barrel as a shop where she mends socks.*

Private Collection

in wholesale trade, banking, manufacturing, and mining. Like the clergy, this estate was hierarchical: important differences in wealth, power, and outlook separated the higher from the lower nobility. In the eighteenth century many wealthy commoners who purchased administrative and judicial offices claimed noble status.

The Third Estate included everyone else, from wealthy financiers to beggars. The number of propertied and successful commoners grew rapidly in the eighteenth century. Commerce, finance, and manufacturing accounted for much of the wealth of the Third Estate. Wealthy commoners also owned nearly a third of the nation's land. This literate and socially ambitious group supported an expanding publishing industry, subsidized the fine arts, and purchased many of the extravagant new homes built in Paris and other cities.

Artisans, shopkeepers, and small landowners owned property and lived decently when crops were good and prices stable, but by 1780 poor harvests had increased their cost of living and led to a decline in consumer demand for their products. They were rich enough to fear the loss of their property and status and well educated enough to be aware of the growing criticism of the king, but they lacked the means to influence policy.

Poverty was common. Among peasants, who accounted for 80 percent of the French population, family poverty and vulnerability forced young children to seek seasonal work and led many to crime and beggary. In Paris and other French cities the vile living conditions and unhealthy diet of the urban poor were startling to visitors from other European nations. City streets swarmed with beggars and prostitutes. The problem of child abandonment suggests the wretchedness of the French poor: on the eve of the French Revolution French parents gave up at least 40,000 children per year. Their belief that these children would be adopted was no more than a convenient fiction; in reality the majority died of neglect.

Unable to afford decent housing, obtain steady employment, or protect their children, the poor periodically erupted in violent protest and rage. In the countryside the decisions of the nobility or clergy to increase taxes and other burdens often led to violence. In towns and cities any increase in the price of bread could spark a riot, since bread prices determined the quality of life of the poor. These explosive episodes, however, were not revolutionary in character; rioters sought immediate relief rather than structural change. That was to change when the Crown tried to solve its fiscal crisis.

The cost of the War of the Austrian Succession (1740–1748) began the crisis. When Louis XV (r. 1715–1774) tried to impose new taxes on the nobility and other privileged groups, widespread protests erupted. New debt from the Seven Years' War deepened the crisis and compelled the king to impose emergency fiscal measures, but the Parlement of Paris, an appeal court, resisted these measures. Frustrated by these actions, French authorities exiled members of the Parlement and pushed through a series of unpopular fiscal measures.

When the twenty-two-year-old Louis XVI assumed the throne in 1774, he faced a desperate fiscal situation compounded by the growing opposition of French courts to new taxes. In 1774 his chief financial adviser warned that the government could barely afford to operate; as he put it, "the first gunshot [act of war] will drive the state to bankruptcy." Despite this warning, the king decided to support the American Revolution, delaying financial collapse by borrowing enormous sums and disguising the growing debt in misleading fiscal accounts. By the end of the war, more than half of France's national budget was required to pay the interest on its debt.

In 1787, the desperate king called an Assembly of Notables to approve a radical and comprehensive reform of economic and fiscal policy. Despite the fact that the king's advisers selected this assembly from the high nobility, the judiciary, and the clergy, these representatives of privilege proved unwilling to support the proposed reforms and new taxes.

Protest Turns to Revolution, 1789–1792   In frustration, the king dismissed the Notables and attempted to implement reforms on his own, but his effort was met by an increasingly hostile judiciary and by popular demonstrations. The refusal of the elite to grant needed tax concessions forced the king to call the **Estates General**, a customary consultative body representing the three estates that had not met since 1614. The narrow self-interest and greed of the rich—who would not tolerate an increase in their own taxes—rather than the grinding poverty of the common people had created the conditions for revolution.

In late 1788 and early 1789 members of the three estates came together throughout the nation to discuss grievances and elect representatives to meet at Versailles (vuhr-SIGH). The Third Estate's representatives were mostly men of substantial property, but some were angry with the king's ministers and inclined to move France toward constitutional monarchy with an elected legislature. Many nobles and members of the clergy sympathized with the reform agenda of the Third Estate, but deep internal divisions over procedural and policy issues limited the power of the First and the Second Estates. Nevertheless, some clergy, and eventually nobles, joined the debates of the Third Estate, beginning a transition toward an assembly that could claim to represent the nation.

After six weeks of deadlock, the Third Estate, with allies from the other estates, signaled its ambitions by calling itself the National Assembly. Fearful of the growing assertiveness of these representatives, the king locked them out of their meeting place. They then moved to an indoor tennis court and pledged to write a constitution. The ascendant ideas of the era, that the people are sovereign and the legitimacy of rulers depends on their fulfilling the people's will, now swept away the king's narrow desire to solve the nation's fiscal crisis. Louis prepared for a confrontation with the National Assembly by moving military forces to Versailles. Before he could act, the people of Paris intervened.

A succession of bad harvests beginning in 1785 had propelled bread prices upward throughout France and provoked an economic depression as demand for nonessential goods collapsed. By the time the Estates General met, nearly a third of the Parisian workforce was unemployed. Hunger and anger marched hand in hand through working-class neighborhoods.

When the people of Paris heard that the king was massing troops in Versailles to arrest the representatives, crowds of common people began to seize arms and mobilize. On July 14, 1789, a crowd attacked the Bastille (bass-TEEL), a medieval fortress used as a prison. The futile defense of the Bastille cost ninety-eight lives before its garrison surrendered. Enraged, the attackers hacked the commander to death and then paraded through the city with his head and that of Paris's chief magistrate stuck on pikes.

These events coincided with uprisings by peasants in the country. Peasants sacked manor houses and destroyed documents that recorded their traditional labor and tax obligations. They then refused to pay taxes and dues to landowners and seized common lands. Forced to recognize the fury raging through rural areas, the National Assembly voted to end traditional obligations and the privileges of the nobility and church, essentially ending the feudal system. Having won this victory, peasants ceased their revolt.

These popular uprisings strengthened the hand of the National Assembly in its dealings with the king and led to passage of the **Declaration of the Rights of Man and the Citizen,** which stated the principles for a future constitution. Similarities between the language of this declaration and the U.S. Declaration of Independence resulted in part from the limited participation of Thomas Jefferson, author of the American document, who was U.S. ambassador to Paris. The French declaration, however, was more sweeping in its language. Among the enumerated natural rights were "liberty, property, security, and resistance to oppression." The Declaration of the Rights of Man and the Citizen also guaranteed free expression of ideas, equality before the law, and representative government.

While delegates debated political issues in Versailles, the economic crisis worsened in Paris. Women employed in the garment industry and small shopkeepers were particularly hard hit. Because the working women of Paris faced high food prices every day as they struggled to feed their families, their anger had a hard edge. Public markets became political arenas where the urban poor met daily in angry assembly. Here the revolutionary link between the material deprivation of the French poor and the political aspirations of the French bourgeoisie was forged.

On October 5, thousands of market women marched the 12 miles (19 kilometers) to Versailles and forced their way into the National Assembly, shouting "the point is that we want bread." The crowd then entered the royal apartments, killed some of the king's guards, and searched for Queen Marie Antoinette (ann-twah-NET), whom they hated as a symbol of extravagance. They then forced the royal family to relocate to Paris.

With the king's ability to resist democratic change overcome by the Paris crowd, the National Assembly achieved a radically restructured French society in the next two years. A new constitution dramatically limited monarchial power and abolished the nobility as a hereditary class. Economic reforms swept away monopolies and trade barriers within France. Renamed the Legislative Assembly, legislators took on the church, seizing its lands to use as collateral for a new paper currency; they also mandated the election of priests and placed them on the public payroll. When the Assembly forced priests to take a loyalty oath, however, many Catholics joined a growing counterrevolutionary movement.

At first, many European monarchs welcomed the weakening of the French king, but by 1791 Austria and Prussia threatened to intervene in support of the monarchy. The Legislative Assembly responded by declaring war. Although the war went badly at first for French forces, people across France responded patriotically to foreign invasions, forming huge new volunteer armies and mobilizing national resources to meet the challenge.

**The Terror,
1793–1794**
In this period of national crisis and foreign threat, the French Revolution entered its most radical phase. A failed effort by the king and queen to escape from Paris cost the king his remaining popular support. On August 10, 1792, a crowd invaded his palace in Paris, forcing the king to seek protection in the Legislative Assembly, which suspended his authority and ordered his imprisonment. These actions helped lead to the formation of a new legislative and executive body, the National Convention. They also created a political environment where competing political factions used rumors of plots and conspiracies to justify the use of violence against their enemies.

Rumors of counterrevolutionary plots also kept working-class neighborhoods in an uproar, and in September a mob surged through the city's prisons, killing nearly half the prisoners. Swept along by popular passion and fear of conspiracy, the newly elected National Convention convicted Louis XVI of treason, sentenced him to death, and proclaimed France a republic. The guillotine ended the king's life in January 1793 (see Environment and Technology: The Guillotine). These events precipitated a wider war with nearly all of Europe's powers allied against France.

The National Convention—the new legislature of the French Republic—convened in September. Almost all its members were from the middle class, and nearly all were **Jacobins** (JAK-uh-bin)—the most uncompromising democrats. Deep political differences, however, separated moderate Jacobins—called "Girondists (juh-RON-dist)," after a region in southern France—and radicals known as "the Mountain." Members of the Mountain—so named because their seats were on the highest level in the assembly hall—were more sympathetic than the Girondists to the demands of the Parisian working class and less patient with parliamentary procedure. **Maximilien Robespierre** (ROBES-pee-air), a young, little-known lawyer influenced by Rousseau's ideas, dominated the Mountain.

With the French economy in crisis and Paris suffering from inflation, high unemployment, and scarcity, Robespierre used the popular press and political clubs to forge an alliance with the volatile Parisian working class. His growing strength in the streets allowed him to purge and execute many of his enemies in the National Convention and to restructure the government. He placed executive power in the hands of the newly formed Committee of Public Safety, which created special courts to seek out and punish enemies of the Revolution.

Among the groups that lost influence were the active feminists of the Parisian middle class and the working-class women who had sought the right to bear arms in defense of the Revolution. These women had provided decisive leadership at crucial times, helping propel the Revolution toward widened suffrage and a more democratic structure. Armed women had actively participated in every confrontation with conservative forces. It is ironic that the National Convention—the revolutionary era's most radical legislative body—chose to repress the militant feminist forces that had prepared the ground for its creation.

Faced with rebellion in the provinces and foreign invasion, Robespierre and his allies unleashed a period of repression called the Reign of Terror (1793–1794). During the Terror, executions and deaths in prison claimed 40,000 lives while another 300,000 suffered imprisonment. In the Vendée region as many as 170,000 died as the government in Paris asserted control. One general stated, "I crushed the children under the feet of the horses, massacred the women who, at least for these,

The Guillotine

No machine more powerfully symbolizes the revolutionary era than the guillotine. The machine immortalizes Joseph Ignace Guillotin (1738–1814), a physician and member of the French Constituent Assembly. In 1789, Guillotin recommended that executions be made more humane by use of a beheading device. He sought to replace hangings, used for commoners, and beheadings by axe, used for the nobility. Both forms of execution were often conducted with little skill, leading to gruesome and painful deaths. Guillotin believed that a properly designed machine would produce predictable, nearly painless deaths and remove the social distinction between commoners and nobles, seen as embarrassing in a more egalitarian age.

After 1791 execution by beheading became the common sentence for all capital crimes. Another physician, Antoine Louis, secretary of the College of Surgeons, designed the actual machine. Once directed to produce a suitable device, Louis, in many ways a typical technician of his time, systematically examined devices used elsewhere and experimented until satisfied with his results. Praised by contemporaries because it seemed to remove human agency, and therefore revenge, from the death penalty, the guillotine became the physical symbol of the Terror.

The Guillotine *The guillotine, introduced as a more humane and democratic alternative to traditional executions, came to symbolize the arbitrary violence of the French Revolution. In this contemporary cartoon Robespierre, the architect of the Terror, serves as executioner while surrounded by guillotines.*

The Art Archive

will not give birth to any more brigands. I do not have a prisoner to reproach me. I have exterminated all."[2]

The revolutionary government also took new actions against the clergy as well, including the provocative measure of forcing priests to marry. Even time was subject to revolutionary change. A new republican calendar created twelve 30-day months divided into 10-day weeks. Sunday, with its Christian meanings, was removed from this revolutionary calendar.

By spring 1794 the Revolution was secure from foreign and domestic enemies, but repression continued. Among the victims were some of Robespierre's closest political collaborators during the Terror. The execution of these former allies prepared the way for Robespierre's own fall by undermining the sense of invulnerability that had secured the loyalty of his remaining partisans. After French victories eliminated the immediate foreign threat in 1794, conservatives in the Convention voted to arrest Robespierre and then ordered his execution along with that of nearly a hundred of his allies in July.

Reaction and the Rise of Napoleon, 1795–1815 Purged of Robespierre's collaborators, the Convention began to undo the radical reforms. It removed emergency economic controls that held down prices and protected the working class. Gone also was toleration for violent popular demonstrations. When the Paris working class rose in protest in 1795, the Convention reacted with overwhelming military force. It allowed the Catholic Church to regain much of its former influence, but it did not return the church's confiscated wealth. It also put in place a more conservative constitution that protected property, established a voting process that reduced the power of the masses, and created a new executive authority, the Directory.

After losing the election of 1797, the Directory refused to give up power, effectively ending the republican phase of the Revolution. Political authority now depended on coercive force rather than elections. Two years later, a brilliant young general in the French army, **Napoleon Bonaparte** (1769–1821), seized power. Just as the American and French Revolutions had been the start of the modern democratic tradition, the military intervention that brought Napoleon to power in 1799 marked the advent of another modern form of government: popular authoritarianism.

The American and French Revolutions resulted in part from conflicts over representation. If the people were sovereign, what institutions best expressed popular will? In the United States the answer was the expansion of the right to vote and creation of representative institutions. The French Revolution took a different direction with the Reign of Terror. Interventions on the floor of the National Convention by market women and soldiers, the presence of common people at revolutionary tribunals and at public executions, and the expansion of military service were all forms of political communication that temporarily satisfied the French people's desire to influence their government. Napoleon tamed these forms of political expression to organize Europe's

---

[2] Quoted in David A. Bell, *The First Total War: Napoleon's Europe and the Birth of Warfare as We Know It* (Boston: Houghton Mifflin, 2007), 173.

Playing Cards from the French Revolution *Even playing cards could be used to attack the aristocracy and Catholic Church. In this pack of cards, "Equality" and "Liberty" replaced kings and queens.*

first popular dictatorship. He succeeded because his military reputation promised order to a society exhausted by a decade of crisis, turmoil, and bloodshed.

Napoleon sought to realize France's dream of dominating Europe while providing effective protection for persons and property at home. Negotiations with the Catholic Church led to the Concordat of 1801. This agreement gave French Catholics the right to freely practice their religion, but it also recognized the French government's authority to nominate bishops and retain priests on the state payroll. In his comprehensive rewriting of French law, the Civil Code of 1804, Napoleon won the support of the peasantry and the middle class by asserting two basic principles inherited from the moderate first stage of the French Revolution: equality in law and protection of property. Some members of the nobility were won over when Napoleon declared himself emperor and France an empire in 1804. Despite his willingness to make dramatic changes, however, Napoleon continued the denial of political rights for women begun during the Terror. The Civil Code denied women basic political rights and only allowed them to participate in the economy with the guidance and supervision of fathers and husbands.

While it re-established order, the Napoleonic system denied or restricted many individual rights. Free speech was limited. Criticism of the government, viewed as subversive, was proscribed, and most opposition newspapers disappeared. Spies and informers directed by the minister of police enforced these draconian policies.

Ultimately, the Napoleonic system depended on the success of French arms. From Napoleon's assumption of power until his fall, no single European state could defeat the French military. Austria and Prussia suffered humiliating defeats and became allies of France. Only Britain, protected by its powerful navy, remained able to thwart Napoleon's plans to dominate Europe.

Desiring to again extend French power to the Americas, Napoleon invaded Portugal in 1807 and Spain in 1808. Despite early French victories, Spanish and

Portuguese patriots supported by Great Britain eventually tied French armies down in a costly conflict. Frustrated by events on the Iberian Peninsula and faced with a faltering economy, Napoleon made the fateful decision to invade Russia. In June 1812, he began his campaign with the largest army ever assembled in Europe, approximately 600,000 men. His army took Moscow but after five weeks abandoned the city. During the retreat, the brutal Russian winter and attacks by Russian forces destroyed Napoleon's army. A broken and battered remnant of 30,000 men made it back to France.

After the debacle in Russia, Austria and Prussia deserted Napoleon and entered an alliance with England and Russia against France. Unable to defend Paris, Napoleon abdicated the throne in April 1814 and was exiled to the island of Elba off the coast of Italy. The victorious allies then restored the French monarchy. The following year Napoleon escaped from Elba and returned to France, but an allied army defeated his forces in 1815 at Waterloo, in Belgium. His final exile was on the distant island of St. Helena in the South Atlantic, where he died in 1821.

Revolution Spreads, Conservatives Respond, 1789–1850

Even as the dictatorship of Napoleon tamed the democratic legacy of the French Revolution, revolutionary ideology was spreading and taking hold in Europe and the Americas. In Europe the French Revolution promoted nationalism and republicanism. In the Americas the legacies of the American and French Revolutions led to a new round of struggles for independence. News of revolutionary events in France destabilized the colonial regime in Saint Domingue (present-day Haiti), a small French colony on the western half of the island of Hispaniola, and helped initiate the first successful slave rebellion. In Europe, however, the spread of revolutionary fervor was met by the concerted reaction of an alliance of conservative monarchs committed to extinguishing further revolutionary outbreaks.

The Haitian Revolution, 1789–1804   In 1789, the French colony of Saint Domingue was among the richest colonies in the Americas. Its production of sugar, cotton, indigo, and coffee accounted for two-thirds of France's tropical imports and generated nearly one-third of all French foreign trade. This wealth depended on a brutal slave regime. The harsh punishments and poor living conditions experienced by Saint Domingue's slaves were notorious throughout the Caribbean. The resulting high mortality and low fertility rates created an insatiable demand for African slaves. As a result, in 1790 the majority of the colony's 500,000 slaves were African-born.

When news of the meeting of the Estates General arrived on the island in 1789, wealthy planters sent a delegation to Paris to seek more home rule and greater economic freedom for Saint Domingue. The free mixed-race population, the **gens de couleur** (zhahn deh koo-LUHR), also sent representatives. Representing a large class of free black planters and urban merchants who owned slaves, they sought political rights and a limit to race discrimination, not an end to slavery. As the French Revolution became more radical, the gens de couleur forged an alliance with sympathetic French radicals, who saw the colony's wealthy planters as royalists and aristocrats.

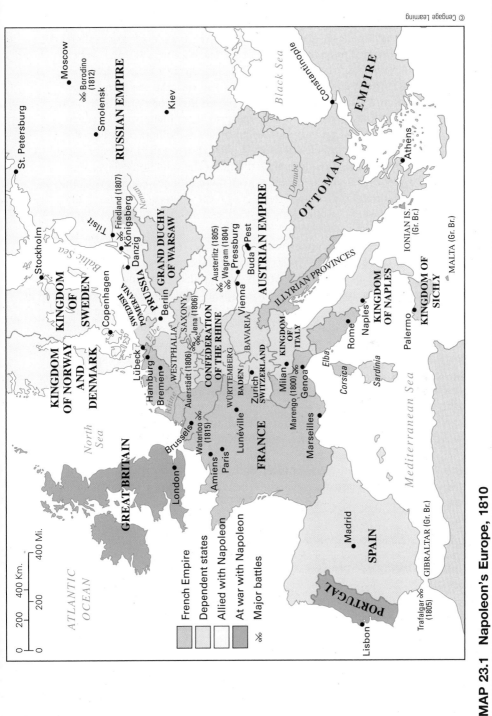

© Cengage Learning

MAP 23.1 Napoleon's Europe, 1810

By 1810, Great Britain was the only remaining European power at war with Napoleon. Because of the loss of the French fleet at the Battle of Trafalgar in 1805, Napoleon was unable to threaten Britain with invasion, and Britain was able to actively assist the resistance movements in Spain and Portugal, thereby helping weaken French power.

The political turmoil in France weakened the authority of colonial administrators in Saint Domingue. In the vacuum that resulted, rich planters, poor whites, and the gens de couleur all pursued their narrow interests, engendering an increasingly bitter and confrontational struggle. Given the slaves' hatred of the brutal regime that oppressed them and the accumulated grievances of the free people of color, there was no way to limit the violence once the control of the slave owners slipped. When Vincent Ogé (oh-ZHAY), a leader of the gens de couleur mission to France, returned to Saint Domingue in 1790, the planters captured him and ordered his torture and execution. The free black and slave populations soon repaid this cruelty in kind.

By 1791 whites, led by the planter elite, and the gens de couleur were engaged in open warfare. This conflict was transformed when a slave rebellion began on the plantations of the north. Rebelling slaves destroyed plantations, killed masters and overseers, and burned crops. A leadership emerged among the rebellious slaves that relied on elements of African political practice and revolutionary ideology from France to mobilize and direct their supporters. With the colony in flames, the French Assembly finally granted political rights to the gens de couleur in April 1792.

The rebellious slaves gained the upper hand under the command of **François Dominique Toussaint L'Ouverture**, a former domestic slave, who created a disciplined military force. While some French radicals had attacked the institution of slavery from the early days of the Revolution, the radical National Convention in Paris only abolished slavery in all French possessions in 1794. This was not narrowly the triumph of idealism over greed. With France at war with Britain and other European powers and Saint Domingue threatened by a British military force, the French government realized that its control of its colony could only be salvaged by acknowledging Toussaint's political and military dominance. Legitimized by the French government's decision, Toussaint swept aside his local rivals, defeated the British expeditionary force in 1798, and then led an invasion of the neighboring Spanish colony of Santo Domingo, freeing slaves there. While Toussaint asserted his loyalty to France, he gave the French government no effective role in local affairs.

As reaction overtook revolution in France, both the abolition of slavery and Toussaint's political position were threatened. When the Directory contemplated the re-establishment of slavery, Toussaint protested:

> Do they think that men who have been able to enjoy the blessing of liberty will calmly see it snatched away? They supported their chains only so long as they did not know any condition of life more happy than slavery. But today when they have left it, if they had a thousand lives they would sacrifice them all rather than be forced into slavery again.[3]

In 1802, Napoleon sent a large military force to re-establish both French colonial authority and slavery in Saint Domingue, as well as in Guadeloupe. At first French forces were successful, capturing Toussaint and sending him to France, where he died in prison. Eventually, however, the loss of thousands of lives to yellow fever and the resistance of the revolutionaries turned the tide. In 1804

---

[3] Quoted in C. L. R. James, *The Black Jacobins*, 2d ed. (New York: Vintage Books, 1963), 196.

Toussaint's successors declared independence, and the free republic of Haiti joined the United States as the second independent nation in the Western Hemisphere.

The Congress of Vienna and Conservative Retrenchment, 1815–1820
In 1814–1815 representatives of Britain, Russia, Austria, Prussia, and other European nations met as the **Congress of Vienna** to re-establish political order in Europe. The French Revolution and Napoleon's imperial ambitions had threatened the survival of Europe's old order. The very existence of the nobility and church had seemed at risk at the height of the revolutionary era. Ancient monarchies had been overturned and dynasties had been replaced with interlopers, often relatives of Napoleon. International borders were redrawn or ignored, while long-established political institutions were threatened or overturned. Responding to more than two decades of revolution and war, the Austrian foreign minister, Prince Klemens von Metternich (MET-uhr-nik) (1773–1859), provided key leadership as the victorious allies sought to create a comprehensive peace settlement that would safeguard the conservative order.

The central objective of the Congress of Vienna was to create a strong and stable France as the best guarantee of future peace. To this end it re-established the French monarchy and recognized France's 1792 borders, although most of the allies received some territorial gains. Metternich believed that a strong and stable France had to be offset by a balance of power. Austria, Russia, and Prussia therefore formed a separate alliance to repress revolutionary and nationalist movements that sought to imitate the French Revolution. In 1820 this "Holy Alliance" used military force to defeat liberal revolutions in Spain and Italy. The Holy Alliance also attempted to blunt the force of revolutionary ideas by repressing republican and nationalist ideas in universities and the press.

Nationalism, Reform, and Revolution, 1821–1850
While Metternich's program of conservative retrenchment succeeded in the short term, the powerful ideas associated with liberalism and nationalism remained a vital part of European political life throughout the nineteenth century. Despite the power of the conservative monarchs, popular support for national self-determination and democratic reform grew throughout Europe.

Greece had been under Ottoman control since the fifteenth century. In 1821 Greek patriots launched an independence movement. While Metternich and other conservatives opposed Greek independence, European artists and writers enamored with the cultural legacy of ancient Greece rallied political support for intervention. After years of struggle, Russia, France, and Great Britain forced the Ottoman Empire to recognize Greek independence in 1830.

In 1814 the victorious allies placed Louis XVIII, brother of the executed Louis XVI, on the throne of France. Unlike his ancestors, he ruled as a constitutional monarch until his death in 1824, when his brother, the conservative Charles X, inherited the throne. In 1830 Charles decided to repudiate the constitution, provoking a mass uprising in Paris that forced him to abdicate. The crown then went to the king's cousin, Louis Philippe (loo-EE fee-LEEP) (r. 1830–1848), who agreed to accept the constitution and extended voting privileges.

Revolutionary violence in France made the British aristocracy and the conservative Tory Party fearful of democracy and mass movements of any kind. In 1815 the British government passed the Corn Laws, which limited the importation of foreign grains. The laws favored the profits of wealthy landowners who produced grain, rather than the poor who would now be forced to pay more for their bread. When poor consumers organized to overturn these laws, the government outlawed public meetings and used troops to crush protest in Manchester. Reacting against these policies, English reformers increased the power of the House of Commons, redistributed votes from agricultural to industrial districts, and increased the number of voters by nearly 50 percent. Although the most radical demands of reformers, called Chartists, were defeated, new labor and economic reforms addressing the grievances of workers were put in place (see Chapter 22).

Despite the achievement of Greek independence and limited political reform in France and Great Britain, conservatives continued to hold the upper hand. In 1848, the desire for democratic reform and national self-determination led to upheavals across Europe. The **Revolutions of 1848** began in Paris, where members of the middle class and workers united to overthrow the regime of Louis Philippe and create the Second French Republic. Reformers gave adult men voting rights, abolished slavery in French colonies, ended the death penalty, and legislated the ten-hour workday. But Parisian workers' demands for programs to reduce unemployment and prices provoked conflicts with the middle class, which wanted to protect property rights. When workers rose up against the government, French troops crushed them. Desiring the re-establishment of order, the French elected Louis Napoleon, nephew of the former emperor, president in December 1848. Three years later, he overturned the constitution and, after ruling briefly as dictator, proclaimed himself Emperor Napoleon III.

In 1848, reformers in Hungary, Italy, Bohemia, and elsewhere pressed for greater national self-determination from the Austro-Hungarian Empire. When the monarchy did not meet their demands, students and workers in Vienna took to the streets to force political reforms similar to those sought in Paris. With revolution spreading throughout the empire, Metternich, the symbol of reaction, fled Vienna in disguise. Little lasting change occurred, however, because the new Austrian emperor, Franz Joseph (r. 1848–1916), used Russian military assistance and loyal Austrian troops to re-establish his authority.

Similarly, middle-class reformers and workers in Berlin joined forces to force the Prussian king to accept a liberal constitution and seek German unification. But the Constituent Assembly called to write a constitution and negotiate national integration was diverted to deal with diplomatic conflicts with Austria and Denmark. As a result, Frederick William IV (r. 1840–1861) reasserted his authority and thwarted constitutional reform and unification.

Despite their heroism on the barricades of Paris, Vienna, Rome, and Berlin, the revolutionaries of 1848 failed to gain their nationalist and republican objectives. Monarchs retained the support not only of aristocrats but also of professional militaries, largely recruited from among peasants who had little sympathy for urban workers. Revolutionary coalitions, in contrast, proved fragile, as when workers' demands for higher wages and labor reform drove their middle-class allies into the arms of the reactionaries.

CONCLUSION

The last decades of the eighteenth century began a long period of revolutionary upheaval in the Atlantic world. Costly wars in Europe and along Europe's colonial frontiers in the Americas and Asia helped to provoke change, forcing European monarchs to impose new and unpopular taxes. The American Revolution initiated these transformations. Having defeated Britain, the citizens of this new American republic created the most democratic government of the time. While full rights were limited and slavery persisted, many Europeans saw this experiment as demonstrating the efficacy of the Enlightenment's most revolutionary political ideas. In the end, however, the compromises over slavery that had made a new Constitution possible in 1787 failed, and, as discussed in Chapter 25, the new nation nearly disintegrated after 1860.

The French Revolution led temporarily to a more radical formulation of representative democracy, but it also led to the Terror, which cost tens of thousands of lives, the militarization of western Europe, and a destructive cycle of wars. Yet, despite these terrible costs, the French Revolution propelled the idea of democracy and the ideal of equality far beyond the boundaries established by the American Revolution. The Haitian Revolution, set in motion by events in France, not only created the second independent nation of the Western Hemisphere but also delivered a powerful blow to the institution of slavery. In Europe, the excesses of the French Revolution and the wars that followed in its wake promoted the political ascent of Napoleon Bonaparte and democracy's modern nemesis, popular authoritarianism.

Each revolution had its own character. The revolutions in France and Haiti proved to be more violent and destructive than the American Revolution. American revolutionaries defeated Great Britain and established independence without overturning a colonial social and political order that depended on slavery in most of the southern colonies. Revolutionaries in France and Haiti faced more strongly entrenched and more powerful oppositions as well as greater social inequalities than American revolutionaries. The resistance of entrenched and privileged elites led inexorably to greater violence. Both French and Haitian revolutionaries also faced powerful foreign interventions that intensified the bloodshed and destructiveness of these revolutions.

The conservative retrenchment that followed the defeat of Napoleon succeeded in the short term. Monarchy, multinational empires, and the established church retained the loyalty of millions of Europeans and could count on the support of many of Europe's wealthiest and most powerful individuals. But liberalism and nationalism continued to stir revolutionary sentiment. The contest between adherents of the old order and partisans of change was to continue well into the nineteenth century. In the end, the nation-state, the Enlightenment legacy of rational inquiry, broadened political participation, and secular intellectual culture prevailed. This outcome was determined in large measure by the old order's inability to satisfy the demands of new social classes tied to an emerging industrial economy. The narrow confines of a hereditary social system could not contain the material transformations generated by industrial capitalism, and the doctrines of traditional religion could not contain the rapid expansion of scientific learning.

These revolutions began the transformation of Western society, but they did not complete it. Only a minority gained full political rights. Women did not achieve full political rights until the twentieth century. Democratic institutions, as in revolutionary France, often failed. Moreover, as Chapter 25 discusses, slavery endured in the Americas past the mid-1800s, despite the revolutionary era's enthusiasm for individual liberty.

IMPORTANT EVENTS 1750–1850

1754–1763	French and Indian War
1756–1763	Seven Years War
1770	Boston Massacre
1776	American Declaration of Independence
1778	United States alliance with France
1778	Death of Voltaire and Rousseau
1781	British surrender at Yorktown
1783	Treaty of Paris ends American Revolution
1789	Storming of Bastille begins French Revolution; Declaration of Rights of Man and Citizen in France
1791	Slaves revolt in Saint Domingue (Haiti)
1793–1794	Reign of Terror in France
1795–1799	The Directory rules France
1798	Toussaint L'Ouverture defeats British in Haiti
1799	Napoleon overthrows the Directory
1804	Haitians defeat French invasion and declare independence
1804	Napoleon crowns himself emperor
1814	Napoleon abdicates; Congress of Vienna opens
1815	Napoleon defeated at Waterloo
1830	Greece gains independence; revolution in France overthrows Charles X
1848	Revolutions in France, Austria, Germany, Hungary, and Italy

24

LAND EMPIRES IN THE AGE OF IMPERIALISM, 1800–1870

During the late 1860s, a little-known warlord named Yaqub Beg unified several Muslim uprisings in Central Asia against a foreign occupier, the Qing Empire. Only a hundred years earlier, in 1759, Qing armies had successfully conquered a vast region of Central Asia and called it Xinjiang, meaning "new territory." Despite attempts to work with local leaders, tensions between locals and Chinese never eased, and the natives rebelled.

Yaqub took full diplomatic advantage of the empires surrounding him. To his south lay India, under control of an expanding British Empire. To his north was the Russian Empire, Britain's rival in the quest to gain territory in Central Asia. Yaqub sent emissaries to both empires in 1868 and signed commercial treaties in 1872 in exchange for their recognition of his rule over Xinjiang. He even received military support from the distant Ottoman Empire, whose ruler bestowed upon him the title *Commander of the Faithful*. For a time it seemed that the Qing might not try to retake Xinjiang. It would be an expensive venture for a government that was looking to spend money modernizing its army and navy. But fears that Russia might take over neighboring Mongolia drove the Chinese back into Xinjiang, and Yaqub's regime collapsed in 1877.

Yaqub's story illustrates the challenges facing Eurasian empires as they overextended themselves. The largest problem, common to all the land-based empires of Eurasia, was the old and inefficient ways of governing that put states at risk. While the international climate was increasingly dominated by industrializing European economies drawing on the wealth of their overseas colonies, during the early 1800s rapid population growth and slow agricultural growth affected much of Eurasia. In addition, earlier military expansion had stretched the resources of imperial treasuries (see Chapter 21), leaving the land-based empires vulnerable to European military pressure. Responses to this pressure varied, with reform and adaptation gaining headway in some lands and tradition being reasserted in others. In the long run, attempts to meet western Europe's economic and political demands produced financial indebtedness to France, Britain, and other Western powers.

This chapter contrasts the experiences of the Qing Empire with those of the Russian and Ottoman Empires. Whereas the Qing opted for resistance, the others made varying attempts to adapt and reform. Russia eventually became part of Europe and shared in many aspects of European culture, while the Ottomans and the Qing became subject to ever-greater imperialist pressure. These different responses raise the question of the role of culture in shaping western Europe's relations with the rest of the world in the nineteenth century.

THE OTTOMAN EMPIRE

During the eighteenth century the central government of the Ottoman Empire lost much of its power to provincial governors, military commanders, ethnic leaders, and bandit chiefs. In several parts of the empire local officials and large landholders tried to increase their independence and divert imperial funds into their own coffers.

A kingdom in Arabia led by the Saud family, following the puritanical and fundamentalist religious views of an eighteenth-century leader named Muhammad ibn Abd al-Wahhab (moo-HAH-muhd ib-uhn ab-dahl-wa-HAHB), took control of the holy cities of Mecca and Medina and deprived the sultan of the honor of organizing the annual pilgrimage. Meanwhile, in Egypt factions of mamluk slave-soldiers purchased as boys in Georgia and nearby parts of the Caucasus and educated for war reasserted their influence. Such soldiers had ruled Egypt between 1260 and 1517, when they were defeated by the Ottomans. Now Ottoman weakness allowed mamluk factions based on a revival of the slave-soldier tradition to re-emerge as local military forces.

For the sultans, the outlook was bleak. At the end of the eighteenth century, the inefficient Janissary corps used the political power it enjoyed in Istanbul to force Sultan Selim III to abandon efforts to train a modern, European-style army. This situation unexpectedly changed when France invaded Egypt.

Egypt and the Napoleonic Example   Napoleon Bonaparte and an invasion force of 36,000 men and four hundred ships invaded Egypt in May 1798. The French quickly defeated the mamluk forces that for several decades had dominated the country under the loose jurisdiction of the Ottoman sultan in Istanbul. Fifteen months later, after being stopped by Ottoman land and British naval forces in an attempted invasion of Syria, Napoleon secretly left Cairo and returned to France. Three months later he seized power and made himself emperor.

Back in Egypt, his generals tried to administer a country that they only poorly understood. Cut off from France by British ships in the Mediterranean, they had little hope of remaining in power and agreed to withdraw in 1801. For the second time in three years, a collapse of military power produced a power vacuum in Egypt. The winner of the ensuing contest was **Muhammad Ali** (moo-HAM-mad AH-lee), the commander of a contingent of Albanian soldiers sent by the sultan to restore imperial control. By 1805 he had taken the place of the official Ottoman governor, and by 1811 he had dispossessed the mamluks of their lands and privileges.

Muhammad Ali's rise to power coincided with the meteoric career of Emperor Napoleon I. It is not surprising, therefore, that he adopted many French practices in rebuilding the Egyptian state. Militarily, he established special schools for training artillery and cavalry officers, army surgeons, military bandmasters, and others. The curricula of these schools featured European skills and sciences, and Muhammad Ali began to send promising officer trainees to France for education. In 1824 he started a gazette devoted to official affairs, the first newspaper in the Islamic world.

As discussed in Chapter 22, Muhammad Ali built all sorts of factories to outfit his new army. These did not prove efficient enough to survive, but they showed a determination to achieve independence and parity with the European powers.

In the 1830s Muhammad Ali's son Ibrahim invaded Syria and instituted some of the changes already under way in Egypt. The improved quality of the new Egyptian army had been proven during the Greek war of independence (see below), when Ibrahim had commanded an expeditionary force to help the sultan. In response, the sultan embarked on building his own new army in 1826. The two armies met when Ibrahim attacked northward into Anatolia in 1839 and defeated the army of his suzerain, the Ottoman sultan. The road to Istanbul seemed open until the European powers intervened and forced a withdrawal to the present-day border between Egypt and Israel.

Muhammad Ali remained Egypt's ruler, under the suzerainty of the sultan, until his death in 1849; and his family continued to rule the country until 1952. But his dream of making Egypt a mighty country capable of standing up to Europe faded. What survived was the example he had set for the sultans in Istanbul.

Ottoman Reform and the European Model, 1807–1853   At the end of the eighteenth century Sultan Selim (seh-LEEM) III (r. 1789–1807), a forward-looking ruler who stayed abreast of events in Europe, introduced reforms to create European-style military units, bring provincial governors under central government control, and standardize taxation. The rise in government expenditures to implement the reforms was supposed to be offset by taxes on selected items, primarily tobacco and coffee.

The reforms failed for political more than economic reasons. The most violent and persistent opposition came from the **Janissary** (JAN-nih-say-ree) military corps (see Chapter 20). In the eighteenth century the Janissaries became a significant political force in Istanbul and in provincial capitals like Damascus and Aleppo. Their interest in preserving special economic privileges made them resist the creation of new military units.

At times, Janissary power produced military uprisings. In the Ottoman territory of **Serbia**, local residents intensely resented the control exercised by Janissary governors. The Orthodox Christians claimed that the Janissaries abused them. In response, Selim threatened to reassign the Janissaries to Istanbul. Suspecting that the sultan wanted to curb their political power, in 1805 the Janissaries revolted and massacred Christians in Serbia. Unable to re-establish central Ottoman rule over Serbia, the sultan had to rely on the ruler of Bosnia, another Balkan province, who joined his troops with the peasants of Serbia to suppress the Janissary uprising. The threat of Russian intervention prevented the Ottomans from disarming the victorious Serbians, so Serbia became effectively independent.

Other opponents of reform included ulama, or Muslim religious scholars, who distrusted the secularization of law and taxation that Selim proposed. In the face of widespread rejection of his reforms, Selim suspended his program in 1806. Nevertheless, a massive military uprising occurred at Istanbul, and the sultan was deposed and imprisoned. Reform forces recaptured the capital, but not before Selim had been executed.

Selim's cousin, Sultan Mahmud (mah-MOOD) II (r. 1808–1839), cautiously revived Selim's program, but he realized that reforms needed to be more systematic and imposed more forcefully. The effectiveness of radical reform in Muhammad Ali's Egypt drove this lesson home, as did the insurrection in Greece, during which the Egyptian military performed much better than the main Ottoman army.

Greek independence in 1830 had dramatic international significance. A combination of Greek nationalist organizations and interlopers from Albania formed the independence movement. Europe's interest in the classical age of Greece and Rome led many Europeans to consider the Greeks' struggle for independence a campaign to recapture their classical glory from Muslim oppression. Some—including the "mad, bad and dangerous to know" English poet Lord Byron, who lost his life in the war—went to Greece to fight as volunteers. When the combined squadrons of the British, French, and Russian fleets, under orders to observe but not intervene in the war, made an unauthorized attack that sank the Ottoman fleet at the Battle of Navarino, Greek victory was assured.

Mahmud II concurred with the pro-Greek Europeans in viewing Ottoman military reversals in Greece as a sign of profound weakness. With popular outrage over the military setbacks strong, the sultan made his move in 1826. First he announced the creation of a new artillery unit, which he had secretly been training. When the Janissaries rose in revolt, he ordered the new unit to bombard the Janissary barracks. The Janissary corps was officially dissolved.

Like Muhammad Ali, Mahmud felt he could not implement major changes without reducing the political power of the religious elite. He visualized restructuring the bureaucracy and the educational and legal systems, where ulama power was strongest. Before such strong measures could be undertaken, however, Ibrahim attacked from Syria in 1839. Battlefield defeat, the decision of the rebuilt Ottoman navy to switch sides and support Egypt, and the death of Mahmud, all in the same year, left the empire completely dependent on the European powers for survival.

Mahmud's reforming ideas received their widest expression in the **Tanzimat** (TAHNZ-ee-MAT) ("reorganization"), a series of reforms announced by his sixteen-year-old son and successor, Abdul Mejid (ab-dul meh-JEED), in 1839 and strongly endorsed by the European ambassadors. One proclamation called for public trials and equal protection under the law for all, whether Muslim, Christian, or Jew. It also guaranteed some rights of privacy, equalized the eligibility of men for conscription into the army (a practice copied from Egypt), and provided for a new, formalized method of tax collection that legally ended tax farming in the Ottoman Empire. It took many years and strenuous efforts by reforming bureaucrats, known as the "men of the Tanzimat," to give substance to these reforms.

Over time, one legal code after another—commercial, criminal, civil procedure—was introduced to take the place of the corresponding areas of religious legal jurisdiction. All the codes were modeled closely on those of Europe. The Shari'a, or Islamic law, gradually became restricted to matters of family law such as marriage and inheritance. As the Shari'a was displaced, job opportunities for the ulama shrank.

European observers praised the reforms for their noble principles and rejection of religious influence. Ottoman citizens were more divided; the Christians and Jews, for whom the Europeans showed the greatest concern, were generally more enthusiastic than the Muslims. Many historians see the Tanzimat as the dawn of modern

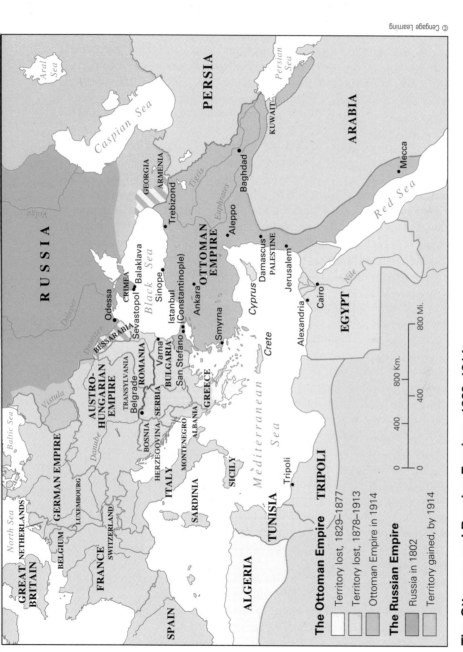

MAP 24.1 The Ottoman and Russian Empires, 1829–1914

At its height the Ottoman Empire controlled most of the perimeter of the Mediterranean Sea. But in the 1800s Ottoman territory shrank as many countries gained their independence. The Black Sea, where the Turkish coast was vulnerable to assault, became a weak spot as Russian naval power grew. Russian challenges to the Ottomans at the eastern end of the Black Sea and to the Persians east and west of the Caspian aroused fears in Europe that Russia was trying to reach the Indian Ocean.

thought and enlightened government in the Middle East. Others point out that removing the religious elite from influence in government also removed the one remaining check on authoritarian rule.

Like Muhammad Ali, Sultan Mahmud sent military cadets to France and the German states for training. In the 1830s an Ottoman imperial school of military sciences, later to become Istanbul University, was established in which instructors from western Europe taught chemistry, engineering, mathematics, and physics in addition to military history. Military education became the model for more general educational reforms. In 1838 the first medical school was established to train army doctors and surgeons. Later, a national system of preparatory schools was created to feed graduates into the military schools. The subjects that were taught and many of the teachers were foreign, raising the issue of whether Turkish should be a language of instruction. Because it was easier to import and use foreign textbooks than to write new ones in Turkish, French became the preferred language in all advanced professional and scientific training. In numerical terms, however, the great majority of students still learned to read and write in Quran schools down to the twentieth century.

In the capital city of Istanbul, the reforms stimulated the growth of a small but cosmopolitan milieu embracing European language and culture. The first Turkish newspaper, a government gazette modeled on that of Muhammad Ali, appeared in 1831. Other newspapers followed, many written in French. Travel to Europe— particularly to England and France—became popular among wealthy Turks. Interest in importing European military, industrial, and communications technology remained strong through the 1800s.

Changes in military practice had unforeseen cultural and social effects. Accepting the European notion that modern weapons and drill required modern military dress, beards were deemed unhygienic and, in artillery units, a fire hazard. Military headgear also became controversial. European military caps, which had leather bills on the front to protect against the glare of the sun, were not acceptable because they interfered with Muslim soldiers' touching their foreheads to the ground in prayer. The compromise was the brimless cap now called the *fez*, which was adopted by the military and then by Ottoman civil officials in the early years of Mahmud II's reign.

The empire's new orientation spread beyond the military. Government ministries that normally recruited from traditional bureaucratic families and relied on on-the-job training were gradually transformed into formal civil services hiring men educated in the new schools. Among self-consciously progressive men, particularly those in government service, European dress became the fashion in the Ottoman cities of the later 1800s, while traditional dress became a symbol of the religious, the rural, and the parochial.

Secularization of the legal code particularly affected non-Muslim Ottoman subjects. Islamic law had required non-Muslims to pay a special head tax that was sometimes explained as a substitute for military service. Under the Tanzimat, the tax was abolished and non-Muslims became liable for military service—unless they bought their way out by paying a new military exemption tax. The new law codes gave all male subjects equal access to the civil courts, while the operations of the Islamic law courts shrank. What enhanced the status of non-Muslims most, however, was the strong concern for their welfare consistently expressed by the European powers. The Ottoman Empire became a rich field of operation for

Christian missionaries and European supporters of Jewish community life in the Muslim world.

The public rights and political participation granted during the Tanzimat applied specifically to men. Private life, including everything connected to marriage and divorce, remained within the sphere of religious law, and at no time was there a question of political participation or reformed education for women. Indeed, the reforms may have decreased the influence of women. The political changes ran parallel to economic changes that also narrowed women's opportunities.

After silver from the Americas began to flood the empire in the 1600s, workers were increasingly paid in cash rather than in goods, and businesses associated with banking and finance developed. But women were barred from the early industrial labor and the professions, and traditional "woman's work" such as weaving was increasingly mechanized and done by men.

Nevertheless, in the early 1800s women retained considerable power in the management and disposal of their own property, gained mostly through fixed shares of inheritance. After marriage a woman was often pressured to convert her landholdings to cash in order to transfer her personal wealth to her husband's family, with whom she and her husband would reside. However, this was not a requirement, since men were legally obligated to support their families single-handedly. Until the 1820s many wealthy women retained their say in the distribution of property through the creation of charitable trusts for their offspring. Because these trusts were set up in the religious courts, they could be designed to conform to the wishes

From Ignatius Mouradgea d'Ohsson, *Tableau General de l'Empire Ottoman*, large folio edition, Paris, 1787–1820, pl. 178, following p. 340

Interior of the Ottoman Financial Bureau *This engraving from the eighteenth century depicts the governing style of the Ottoman Empire before the era of westernizing reforms. By the end of the Tanzimat period in 1876, government offices and the costumes of officials looked much more like those in contemporary European capitals.*

Street Scene in Cairo *This engraving from Edward William Lane's influential travel book,* Account of the Manners and Customs of the Modern Egyptians Written in Egypt During the Years 1833–1835 *conveys the image of narrow lanes and small stores that became stock features of European thinking about Middle Eastern cities.*

From Edward William Lane, *The Manners and Customs of the Modern Egyptians* (London: J. M. D & Co. 1860)

of family members. Then, in the 1820s and 1830s the secularizing reforms of Mahmud II, which did not always produce happy results, transferred jurisdiction over the charitable trusts from religious courts to the state and ended women's control over this form of property.

The Crimean War and Its Aftermath

Since the reign of Peter the Great (r. 1689–1725), the Russian Empire had been attempting to expand southward at the Ottomans' expense (see the section on Russia and Asia). His successor, Catherine the Great (r. 1762–1796), had captured control of the north shore of the Black Sea by 1783, and by 1815 Russia had pried the Georgian region of the Caucasus away from the Ottomans. Moreover, the threat of Russian intervention had prevented the Ottomans from crushing Serbian independence. When Muhammad Ali's Egyptian army invaded Syria in 1833, Russia signed a treaty in support of the Ottomans. In return, the sultan recognized Russia's claim to being the protector of all of the empire's Orthodox subjects. This set the stage for an obscure dispute that resulted in war.

Bowing to British and French pressure, the sultan named France Protector of the Holy Sepulchre in Jerusalem in 1852. Russia protested, but the sultan held firm. So Russia invaded Ottoman territories in what is today Romania, and Britain and France went to war as allies of the sultan. The real causes of the war went beyond church quarrels in Jerusalem and involved diplomatic maneuvering among European powers over whether the Ottoman Empire should continue to exist and, if not, who should take over its territory. The *Eastern Question* was the simple name given to this complex issue. Though the powers, including Russia, had agreed to save the empire in 1839, Britain subsequently became suspicious of Russian ambitions. Prominent anti-Russian politicians in Britain feared that Russia would threaten the British hold on India.

Between 1853 and 1856 the **Crimean** (cry-ME-uhn) **War** raged in Romania, on the Black Sea, and on the Crimean peninsula. Britain, France, and the Italian kingdom of Sardinia-Piedmont sided with the Ottomans. Britain and France trapped the Russian fleet in the Black Sea, where its commanders decided to sink the ships to protect the approaches to Sevastopol, their main base in Crimea. However, an army largely made up of British and French troops landed and laid siege to the city. Official corruption and lack of railways hampered the Russians' attempts to supply their forces. On the Romanian front, the Ottomans resisted effectively. At Sevastopol, the Russians were outmatched militarily and suffered badly from disease. Tsar Nicholas died as defeat loomed, leaving his successor, Alexander II (r. 1855–1881), to sue for peace when Sevastopol finally fell three months later.

The Crimean War brought significant changes to all the combatants. The tsar and his government, already beset by demands for the reform of serfdom, education, and the military (discussed later), were further discredited. In Britain and France, the conflict was accompanied by massive propaganda campaigns. For the first time newspapers effectively mobilized public support for a war. British press accounts so glamorized British participation that the false impression has lingered that Ottoman troops played a negligible role in the conflict. At the time, however, British and French commanders noted the massive losses among Turkish troops in particular. The French press, dominant in Istanbul, promoted a sense of unity between Turkish and French society that continued to influence many aspects of Turkish urban culture.

The larger significance of the Crimean War was that it marked the transition from traditional to modern warfare. All the combatants had previously prided themselves on the use of highly trained cavalry to smash through the front lines of infantry. Cavalry coexisted with firearms until the early 1800s, primarily because early rifles were awkward to load and not very accurate. Cavalry could attack during the intervals between volleys. Then in the 1830s and 1840s, percussion caps that did away with pouring gunpowder into the barrel of a musket came into use. In Crimean War battles many cavalry units were destroyed by the rapid fire of rifles that loaded at the breech rather than down the barrel. That was the fate of the famed British Light Brigade, which was sent to relieve an Ottoman unit surrounded by Russian troops.

After the Crimean War, the Ottoman Empire increased its involvement with European commerce. The Ottoman imperial bank was founded in 1840, and a few years later currency reform pegged the value of Ottoman gold coins to the British pound. Sweeping changes in the 1850s expedited the creation of banks, insurance companies, and legal firms throughout the empire. Bustling trade also encouraged a migration from country to city between about 1850 and 1880. Many of the major cities of the empire—Istanbul, Damascus, Beirut, Alexandria,

Cairo—expanded. A small but influential urban professional class emerged, as did a considerable class of wage laborers. Other demographic shifts involved refugees from Poland and Hungary, where rivalry between the European powers and the Russian Empire caused political tension and sporadic warfare, and from Georgia and other parts of the Caucasus, where Russian expansion forced many Muslims to emigrate (discussed later).

However, commercial vigor and urbanization could not make up for declining revenues and the chronic insolvency and corruption of the imperial government. From the conclusion of the Crimean War in 1856 on, the Ottoman government became heavily dependent on foreign loans. In return it lowered tariffs to favor European imports and allowed European banks to open in Ottoman cities. Europeans living in Istanbul and other commercial centers enjoyed **extraterritoriality**, the right to be subject to their own laws and exempt from Ottoman jurisdiction.

As the result of these measures, imported goods multiplied, but—apart from tobacco and the Turkish opium that American traders took to China to compete against British opium from India—Anatolia produced few exports. As foreign debt grew, so did inflationary trends that left urban populations in a precarious position. By contrast, Egyptian cotton exports soared during the American Civil War, when American cotton exports plummeted; but the profits benefited Muhammad Ali's descendants, who had become the hereditary governors of Egypt, rather than the Ottoman government. The Suez Canal, which was partly financed by cotton profits, opened in 1869, and Cairo was redesigned and beautified. Eventually overexpenditure on such projects plunged Egypt into the same debt crisis that plagued the empire as a whole.

The decline of Ottoman power and prosperity had a strong impact on a group of well-educated young urban men who aspired to wealth and influence. They doubted that the empire's rulers and the Tanzimat officials who worked for them would ever stand up to European domination. Though lacking a sophisticated organization, these Young Ottomans (sometimes called Young Turks, though that term properly applies to a later movement) promoted a mixture of liberal ideas derived from Europe, national pride in Ottoman independence, and modernist views of Islam. Prominent Young Ottomans helped draft a constitution that was promulgated in 1876 by a new and as yet untried sultan, Abdul Hamid II. This apparent triumph of liberal reform was short-lived. With war against Russia again threatening in the Balkans in 1877, Abdul Hamid suspended the constitution and the parliament that had been elected that year. Though he ruthlessly opposed further political reforms, the Tanzimat programs of extending modern schooling, utilizing European military practices and advisers, and making the government bureaucracy more orderly continued during his reign.

THE RUSSIAN EMPIRE

In 1812, when Napoleon's march on Moscow ended in a disastrous retreat brought on more by what a later tsar called "Generals January and February" than by Russian military action, the European image of Russia changed. Just as Napoleon's withdrawal from Egypt led to Muhammad Ali briefly becoming a political power, so his withdrawal from Russia conferred status on Tsar Alexander I (r. 1801–1825). Conservative Europeans still saw Russia as alien, backward, and oppressive, but they acknowledged its immensity and potential and included the tsar in efforts to suppress revolutionary tendencies throughout Europe.

In several important respects Russia resembled the Ottoman Empire more than the conservative kingdoms of Europe whose autocratic practices it so staunchly supported. Socially dominated by nobles whose country estates were worked by unfree serfs, Russia had almost no middle class. Industry was still at the threshold of development by the standards of the rapidly industrializing European powers, though it was somewhat more dynamic than Ottoman industry. Like Egypt and the Ottoman Empire, Russia engaged in reforms from the top down under Alexander I, but when his conservative brother Nicholas I (r. 1825–1855) succeeded to the throne, iron discipline and suspicion of modern ideas took priority over reform.

Russia and Europe   In 1700 only three Russians out of a hundred lived in cities, two-thirds of them in Moscow alone. By the mid-1800s the town population had grown tenfold, though it still accounted for only 6 percent of the total because the territories of the tsars had grown greatly through wars and colonization (see Chapter 21). These figures demonstrate that, like the Ottoman Empire, Russia was an overwhelmingly agricultural land. However, it had poorer transportation than the Ottoman Empire, since many Ottoman cities were seaports. Both empires encompassed peoples speaking many different languages.

Well-engineered roads did not begin to appear until 1817, and steam navigation commenced on the Volga in 1843. Tsar Nicholas I built the first railroad from St. Petersburg, the Russian capital, to his summer palace in 1837. A few years later his commitment to strict discipline led him to insist that the trunk line from St. Petersburg to Moscow run in a perfectly straight line. American engineers, among them the father of the painter James McNeill Whistler, who learned to paint in St. Petersburg, oversaw the laying of track and built locomotive workshops. Industrialization projects depended heavily on foreign expertise. British engineers set up the textile mills that gave woolens and cottons a prominent place among Russia's industries.

Until the late nineteenth century the Russian government's interest in industry was limited. An industrial revolution required educated and independent-minded artisans and entrepreneurs, but Nicholas feared the spread of literacy and modern education—especially anything smacking of liberalism, socialism, or revolution—beyond the minimum needed to train the officer corps and the bureaucracy. He preferred serfs to factory workers, and he paid for imported industrial goods with exports of grain and timber.

Like Egypt and the Ottoman Empire, Russia aspired to Western-style economic development. But when France and Britain entered the Crimean War, they faced a Russian army equipped with obsolete weapons and bogged down by lack of transportation. At a time when European engineers were making major breakthroughs in loading cannon through an opening at the breech end, muzzle-loading artillery remained the Russian standard.

Yet in some ways Russia bore a closer resemblance to other European countries than the Ottoman Empire did. From the point of view of the French and the British, the Cyrillic alphabet and the Russian Orthodox form of Christianity seemed foreign, but they were not nearly as foreign as the Arabic alphabet and the Muslim faith. Britain and France feared Russia as a rival for power in the east, but they increasingly accepted Tsar Nicholas's view of the Ottoman Empire as "the sick man of Europe," capable of surviving only so long as the European powers permitted.

From the Russian point of view, kinship with western Europe was of questionable value. Westernizers, like the men of the Tanzimat in the Ottoman Empire, put their trust in technical advances and governmental reform. Opposing them were intellectuals known as **Slavophiles**, who considered the Orthodox faith, the solidity of peasant life, and the tsar's absolute rule to be the proper bases of Russian civilization. After Russia's humiliation in the Crimea, the Slavophile tendency gave rise to **Pan-Slavism**, a militant political doctrine advocating unity of all the Slavic peoples, including those living under Austrian and Ottoman rule.

On the diplomatic front, the tsar's inclusion as a major European ruler contrasted sharply with the sultan's exclusion. However, this did not prevent a powerful sense of Russophobia from developing in the West. Britain in particular saw Russia as a threat to India and despised the subjection of the serfs, who gained their freedom from Tsar Alexander II only in 1861, twenty-seven years after the British had abolished slavery. In addition, the passions generated by the Crimean War and its outcome affected the relations of Russia, Europe, and the Ottoman Empire for the remainder of the nineteenth century.

Russia and Asia   The Russian drive to the east in the eighteenth century brought the tsar's empire to the Pacific Ocean and the frontiers of China by century's end. In the nineteenth century Russian expansionism focused on the south. There the backwardness of the Russian military did not matter since the peoples they faced were even less industrialized and technologically advanced. In 1860, Russia established a military outpost on the Pacific coast that would eventually grow into the great naval port of Vladivostok, today Russia's most southerly city. In Central Asia the steppe lands of the Kazakh nomads came under Russian control early in the century, setting the stage for a confrontation with three Uzbek states farther south. They succumbed one by one, beginning in 1865, giving rise to the new province of Turkestan, with its capital at Tashkent in present-day Uzbekistan.

In the region of the Caucasus Mountains, the third area of southward expansion, Russia first took over Christian Georgia (1786), Muslim Azerbaijan (ah-zer-by-JAHN) (1801), and Christian Armenia (1813) before gobbling up the many small principalities in the heart of the mountains. Between 1829 and 1864 Dagestan, Chechnya (CHECH-nee-yah), Abkhazia (ab-KAH-zee-yah), and other regions that would one day gain political prominence after the breakup of the Soviet Union became parts of the Russian Empire.

The drive to the south intensified political friction with Russia's new neighbors: Qing China and Japan in the east, Iran on the Central Asian and Caucasus frontiers, and the Ottoman Empire at the eastern end of the Black Sea. In the latter two instances, Muslim refugees from the territories newly absorbed by Russia spread anti-Russian feelings, though some of them brought with them modern skills and ideas gained from exposure to Russian administration and education.

The Russian drive to the south added a new element to the Eastern Question. Many British statesmen and strategists reckoned that a warlike Russia would press on until it had conquered all the lands separating it from British India, a prospect that made them shudder, given India's enormous contribution to Britain's prosperity. The competition that ensued over which power would control southern Central Asia resulted in a standoff in Afghanistan, which became a buffer zone under the control of neither. In Iran, the standoff between the powers helped preserve the weak Qajar dynasty of shahs.

Cultural Trends   Unlike Egypt and the Ottoman Empire, which began to send students to Europe for training only in the nineteenth century, Russia had been in cultural contact with western Europe since the time of Peter the Great (r. 1689–1725). Members of the Russian court knew Western languages, and the tsars employed officials and advisers from Western countries. Peter had also enlisted the well-educated Ukrainian clerics who headed the Russian Orthodox Church to help spread a Western spirit of education. As a result, Alexander I's reforms met a more positive reception than those of Muhammad Ali and Mahmud II. However, his reforms promised more on paper than they brought about in practice. It took many years to develop a sufficient pool of trained bureaucrats to make the reforms effective.

Ironically, much of the opposition to Alexander's reforms came from well-established families that were not at all unfriendly to Western ideas. Their fear was that the new government bureaucrats, who often came from humbler social origins, would act as agents of imperial tyranny. This fear was realized during the conservative reign of Nicholas I in the same way that the Tanzimat-inspired bureaucracy of the Ottoman Empire served the despotic purposes of Sultan Abdul Hamid II after 1877. Individuals favoring more liberal reforms, including military officers who had served in western Europe, intellectuals who read Western political tracts,

Visual Connection Archive

Raising of the Alexander Monument in St. Petersburg *The death of Alexander I in 1825 brought to power his conservative brother Nicholas I. Yet Alexander remained a heroic figure for his resistance to Napoleon. This monument in Winter Palace Square was erected in 1829.*

and members of Masonic lodges who exchanged views with Freemasons in the West, formed secret societies of opposition. Some placed their highest priority on freeing the serfs; others advocated a constitution and a republican form of government. When Alexander I died in December 1825, confusion over who was to succeed him encouraged a group of reform-minded army officers to try to take over the government and provoke an uprising. This so-called **Decembrist revolt** failed, and many of the participants were severely punished. These events ensured that the new tsar, Nicholas I, would pay little heed to calls for reform over the next thirty years.

The great powers meeting in Paris to settle the Crimean War in 1856 forced Russia to return land to the Ottomans in both Europe and Asia. This humiliation spurred Nicholas's son and successor, Alexander II (r. 1855–1881), to institute major new reforms to reinvigorate the country. The greatest of his reforms was the emancipation of the serfs in 1861. He also authorized new joint-stock companies, projected a railroad network to tie the country together, and modernized the legal and administrative arms of government.

Earlier intellectual and cultural trends flourished under Alexander II. More and more people became involved in intellectual, artistic, and professional life. Most prominent intellectuals received some amount of instruction at Moscow University or some German university. Universities also appeared in provincial cities like Kharkov in Ukraine and Kazan on the Volga River. Student clubs, along with Masonic lodges, became places for discussing new ideas. As Russian scholars and scientists began to achieve recognition for their contributions to European thought, scholarly careers attracted young men from clerical families, who in turn helped stimulate reforms in religious education.

Just as the Tanzimat reforms of the Ottoman Empire preceded the emergence of the Young Ottomans as a new and assertive political and intellectual force in the second half of the nineteenth century, so the initially ineffective reforms of Alexander I set in motion cultural currents that would make Russia a dynamic center of intellectual, artistic, and political life under his nephew Alexander II. Thus Russia belonged to two different spheres of development. It entered the nineteenth century a recognized force in European politics, but in other ways it resembled the Ottoman Empire. Rulers in both empires instituted reforms, overcame opposition, and increased the power of their governments. These activities stimulated intellectual and political trends that would ultimately work against the absolute rule of tsar and sultan. Yet Russia would eventually develop much closer relations with western Europe and become an arena for every sort of European intellectual, artistic, and political tendency, while the Ottoman Empire would ultimately succumb to European imperialism.

THE QING EMPIRE

In 1800 the Qing Empire faced many problems, but no reform movement of the kind initiated by Sultan Selim III emerged in China. The reasons are not difficult to understand. The Qing emperors had skillfully countered Russian strategic and diplomatic moves in the 1600s. Instead of having a Napoleon threatening them with invasion, they enjoyed the admiration of Jesuit priests, who likened them to enlightened philosopher-kings. In 1793, however, a British attempt to establish diplomatic and trade relations—the Macartney mission—turned European opinion against China (see Chapter 21).

China's most serious crises were domestic, not foreign: rebellions by displaced indigenous peoples and the poor, and protests against the injustice of the local magistrates. The Qing dealt with these problems by suppressing rebels and dismissing incompetent or untrustworthy officials. They also brushed aside the complaints from European merchants who chafed against the restrictions of the "Canton system" by which the Qing limited and controlled foreign trade.

Economic and Social Disorder
Early Qing successes and territorial expansion sowed the seeds of the domestic and political chaos of the later period. The early emperors encouraged the recovery of farmland, the opening of previously uncultivated areas, and the restoration and expansion of the road and canal systems. These measures expanded the agricultural base and supported a doubling of the population between about 1650 and 1800. Enormous numbers of farmers, merchants, and day laborers migrated in search of less crowded conditions, and a permanent floating population of the unemployed and homeless emerged. By 1800, population strain had caused serious environmental damage in some parts of central and western China.

While farmers tried to cope with agricultural deterioration, other groups vented grievances against the government: minority peoples in central and southwestern China complained about being driven off their lands during the boom of the 1700s; Mongols resented appropriation of their grazing lands and the displacement of their traditional elites. In some regions, village vigilante organizations took over policing and governing functions from Qing officials who had lost control. Growing numbers of people mistrusted the government, suspecting that all officials were corrupt. The increasing presence of foreign merchants and missionaries in Canton and in the Portuguese colony of Macao aggravated discontent in neighboring districts.

In some parts of China the Qing were hated as foreign conquerors and were suspected of sympathy with the Europeans. In 1794 the White Lotus Rebellion— partly inspired by a messianic ideology that predicted the restoration of the Chinese Ming dynasty and the coming of the Buddha—raged across central China and was not suppressed until 1804. It initiated a series of internal conflicts that continued through the 1800s (see discussion of Yaqub Beg's revolt at the beginning of this chapter). Ignited by deepening social instabilities, these movements were sometimes intensified by local ethnic conflicts and by unapproved religions. The ability of some village militias to defend themselves and attack others intensified the conflicts, though the same techniques proved useful to southern coastal populations attempting to fend off British invasion.

The Opium War and Its Aftermath, 1839–1850
Unlike the Ottomans, the Qing knew little about the enormous fortunes being made in the early 1800s by European and American merchants smuggling opium into China. They did not know that silver gained in this illegal trade was helping finance the industrial transformation of England and the United States. Only slowly did Qing officials become aware of British colonies in

India that grew and exported opium, and of the major naval base at Singapore through which British opium reached East Asia.

In 1729, the first Qing law banning opium imports was promulgated. By 1800, however, opium smuggling had swelled the annual import level to as many as four thousand chests. Though British merchants had pioneered this profitable trade, Chinese merchants likewise profited from distributing the drugs. A price war in the early 1820s stemming from competition between British and American importers raised demand so sharply that as many as thirty thousand chests were being imported by the 1830s. Addiction spread to people at all levels of Qing society, including high-ranking officials. The Qing emperor and his officials debated whether to legalize and tax opium or to enforce the existing ban more strictly. Having decided to root out the use and importation of opium, in 1839 they sent a high official to Canton to deal with the matter.

Britain considered the ban on opium importation an intolerable limitation on trade, a direct threat to Britain's economic health, and a cause for war. British naval and marine forces arrived on the south China coast in late 1839. The **Opium War** (1839–1842) broke out when negotiations between the Qing official and British representatives reached a stalemate. The war exposed the fact that the traditional, hereditary soldiers of the Qing Empire—the **Bannermen**—were, like the Janissaries of the Ottoman Empire, hopelessly obsolete. As in the Crimean War, the British excelled at sea, where they deployed superior technology. British ships landed marines who pillaged coastal cities and then sailed to new destinations. The Qing lacked a navy powerful enough to deal with the British. Thus until they were able to engage the British in prolonged fighting on land, they were unable to defend themselves against British attacks. Even in the land engagements, Qing resources proved woefully inadequate. The British could quickly transport their forces by sea along the coast, whereas Qing troops moved primarily on foot. Moving Qing reinforcements from central to eastern China took more than three months; and when the defense forces arrived, they were exhausted and basically without weapons.

The Bannermen used the few muskets the Qing had imported during the 1700s. The weapons were matchlocks, which required the soldiers to ignite the load of gunpowder in them by hand. Firing the weapons was dangerous, and the canisters of gunpowder that each musketeer carried on his belt were likely to explode if a fire broke out nearby—a frequent occurrence in encounters with British artillery. Most of the Bannermen, however, had no guns at all and fought with swords, knives, spears, and clubs. They were greatly outmatched by the soldiers under British command—many of them Indians—who carried percussion-cap rifles, which were far quicker, safer, and more accurate than the matchlocks. In addition, the long-range British artillery could be moved from place to place and proved deadly in the cities and villages of eastern China.

Qing commanders thought that British gunboats rode so low in the water that they could not sail up the Chinese rivers. So they evacuated the coastal areas to counter the British threat. But the British deployed new gunboats for shallow waters and moved without difficulty up the Yangzi River (see Chapter 22).

When the invaders approached Nanjing, the former Ming capital, the Qing decided to negotiate. In 1842 the terms of the **Treaty of Nanking** (the British name for Nanjing) dismantled the old Canton system. The number of **treaty ports**—cities opened to foreign residents—increased from one (Canton) to five (Canton, Xiamen, Fuzhou, Ningbo, and Shanghai [shahng-hie]). The island of Hong Kong became a British colony, and British residents in China gained extraterritorial rights. The Qing government agreed to set a low tariff of 5 percent on imports and to pay Britain an indemnity of 21 million ounces of silver as a penalty for having started the war. A supplementary treaty the following year guaranteed **most-favored-nation status** to Britain: any privileges that China granted to another country would be automatically extended to Britain as well. This provision effectively prevented the colonization of China, because giving land to one country would have necessitated giving it to all.

With each round of treaties came a new round of privileges for foreigners. In 1860 a new treaty legalized their right to import opium. Later, French treaties established the rights of foreign missionaries to travel in the Chinese countryside and preach their religion. The number of treaty ports grew, too; by 1900 they numbered more than ninety.

The treaty system and the principle of extraterritoriality resulted in the colonization of small pockets of Qing territory, where foreign merchants lived at ease. Greater territorial losses resulted when outlying regions gained independence or were ceded to neighboring countries. Districts north and south of the Amur River in the northeast fell to Russia by treaty in 1858 and 1860; parts of modern Kazakhstan and Kyrgyzstan in the northwest met the same fate in 1864. From 1865 onward the British gradually gained control of territories on China's Indian frontier. In the late 1800s France forced the court of Vietnam to end its tribute relationship to the Qing, while Britain encouraged Tibetan independence.

In Canton, Shanghai, and other coastal cities, Europeans and Americans maintained offices and factories that employed local Chinese as menial laborers. The foreigners built comfortable housing in zones where Chinese were not permitted to live, and they entertained themselves in exclusive restaurants and bars. Around the foreign establishments, gambling and prostitution offered employment to part of the local urban population.

Whether in town or in the countryside, Christian missionaries whose congregations sponsored hospitals, shelters, and soup kitchens or gave stipends to Chinese who attended church enjoyed a good reputation. But just as often the missionaries themselves were regarded as another evil. They seemed to subvert Confucian beliefs by condemning ancestor worship, pressuring poor families to put their children into orphanages, or fulminating against footbinding. The growing numbers of foreigners, and their growing privileges, became targets of resentment for a deeply dissatisfied, daily more impoverished, and increasingly militarized society.

The Taiping Rebellion, 1850–1864

The inflammatory mixture of social unhappiness and foreign intrusion exploded in the great civil war usually called the **Taiping** (tie-PING) **Rebellion**. In Guangxi, where the Taiping movement originated, entrenched social problems had been generating disorders for half a century. Agriculture in the region was unstable, and many people made their living from arduous and despised trades such as disposing of human waste, making charcoal, and mining. Ethnic divisions complicated economic distress. The lowliest trades frequently involved a minority group, the Hakkas, and tensions between them and the majority were rising. Problems may have been intensified by sharp fluctuations in the opium trade and reactions to the cultural and economic impact of the Europeans and Americans in Canton.

Hong Xiuquan (hoong shee-OH-chew-an), the founder of the Taiping movement, experienced all of these influences. Hong came from a humble Hakka background. After years of study, he competed in the provincial Confucian examinations, hoping for a post in government. He failed the examinations repeatedly, and it appears that he suffered a nervous breakdown in his late thirties. Afterward he spent some time in Canton, where he met both Chinese and American Protestant missionaries, who inspired him with their teachings. Hong had his own interpretation of the Christian message. He saw himself as the younger brother of Jesus, commissioned by God to found a new kingdom on earth and drive the Manchu conquerors, the Qing, out of China. The result would be universal peace. Hong called his new religious movement the "Heavenly Kingdom of Great Peace."

Hong quickly attracted a community of believers, primarily Hakkas like himself. They believed in the prophecy of dreams and claimed they could walk on air. Hong and his rivals for leadership in the movement went in and out of ecstatic trances. They denounced the Manchus as creatures of Satan. News of the sect reached the government, and Qing troops arrived to arrest the Taiping leaders. But the Taipings soundly repelled the imperial troops. Local loyalty to the Taipings spread quickly; their numbers multiplied; and they began to enlarge their domain.

The Taipings relied at first on Hakka sympathy and the charismatic appeal of their religious doctrine to attract followers. But as their numbers and power grew, they altered their methods of preaching and governing, replacing the anti-Chinese appeals used to enlist Hakkas with anti-Manchu rhetoric designed to enlist Chinese. They forced captured villages to join their movement. Once people were absorbed, the Taipings strictly monitored their activities. They also segregated men and women and organized them into work and military teams. Women were forbidden to bind their feet (the Hakkas had never practiced footbinding) and participated fully in farming and labor. Brigades of women soldiers took to the field against Qing forces.

As the movement grew, it began to move toward eastern and northern China. Panic preceded the Taipings. Villagers feared being forced into Taiping units, and Confucian elites recoiled in horror from the bizarre ideology of foreign gods, totalitarian rule, and walking, working, warring women. But the huge numbers the Taipings were able to muster overwhelmed attempts at local defense. The tremendous growth in the number of Taiping followers required the movement to establish a permanent base. When the rebel army conquered Nanjing in 1853, the Taiping leaders decided to settle there and make it the capital of the new "Heavenly Kingdom of Great Peace."

Qing forces attempting to defend north China became more successful as problems of organization and growing numbers slowed Taiping momentum. Increasing Qing military success resulted mainly from the flexibility of the imperial military commanders in the face of an unprecedented challenge. In addition, the military commanders received strong backing from a group of civilian provincial governors who had studied the techniques developed by local militia forces for self-defense.

Certain provincial governors combined their knowledge of civilian self-defense and local terrain with more efficient organization and the use of modern weaponry. The result was the formation of new military units, in which many of the Bannermen voluntarily served under civilian governors. The Qing court agreed to special taxes to fund the new armies and acknowledged the new combined leadership.

When the Taipings settled into Nanjing, the new Qing armies surrounded the city, hoping to starve out the rebels. The Taipings, however, had provisioned and fortified themselves well. They also had the services of several brilliant young military commanders, who mobilized enormous campaigns in nearby parts of eastern China, scavenging supplies and attempting to break the encirclement of Nanjing. For more than a decade the Taiping leadership remained ensconced at Nanjing, and the "Heavenly Kingdom" endured.

In 1856 Britain and France, freed from their preoccupation with the Crimean War, turned their attention to China. European and American missionaries had visited Nanjing, curious to see what their fellow Christians were up to. Their reports were discouraging. Hong Xiuquan and the other leaders appeared to lead lives of indulgence and abandon, and more than one missionary accused them of homosexual practices. Relieved of the possible accusation of quashing a pious Christian movement, the British and French surveyed the situation. Though the Taipings were not going to topple the Qing, rebellious Nian ("Bands") in northern China added a new threat in the 1850s. A series of simultaneous large insurrections might indeed destroy the empire. Moreover, since the Qing had not observed all the provisions of the treaties signed after the Opium War, Britain and France were now considering renewing war on the Qing themselves.

In 1856 the British and French launched a series of swift, brutal coastal attacks—a second opium war, called the Arrow War (1856–1860)—that culminated in a British and French invasion of Beijing and the sacking of the Summer Palace in 1860. A new round of treaties punished the Qing for not enacting all the provisions of the Treaty of Nanking. Having secured their principal objective, the British and French forces then joined the Qing campaign against the Taipings. Attempts to coordinate the international forces were sometimes riotous and sometimes tragic, but the injection of European weaponry and money helped quell both the Taiping and the Nian rebellions during the 1860s.

The Taiping Rebellion ranks as the world's bloodiest civil war and the greatest armed conflict before the twentieth century. Estimates of deaths range from 20 million to 30 million. The loss of life came primarily from starvation and disease, for most engagements consisted of surrounding fortified cities and waiting until the enemy forces died, surrendered, or were so weakened that they could be easily defeated. Many sieges continued for months. Reports of people eating grass, leather, hemp, and human flesh were widespread. The dead were rarely buried properly, and epidemic disease was common.

The area of early Taiping fighting was close to the regions of southwest China in which bubonic plague had been lingering for centuries. When the rebellion was suppressed, many Taiping followers sought safety in the highlands of Laos and Vietnam, which soon showed infestation by plague. Within a few years the disease reached Hong Kong. From there it spread to Singapore, San Francisco, Calcutta, and London. In the late 1800s there was intense apprehension over the possibility of a worldwide outbreak, and Chinese immigrants were regarded as likely carriers. This fear became a contributing factor in the passage of discriminatory immigration bans on Chinese in the United States in 1882.

The Taiping Rebellion devastated the agricultural centers of China. Many of the most intensely cultivated regions of central and eastern China were depopulated. Some were still uninhabited decades later, and major portions of the country did not recover until the twentieth century.

Cities, too, were hard hit. Shanghai, a treaty port of modest size before the rebellion, saw its population multiplied many times by the arrival of refugees from war-blasted neighboring provinces. The city then endured months of siege by the Taipings. Major cultural centers in eastern China lost masterpieces of art and architecture; imperial libraries were burned or their collections exposed to the weather; and the printing blocks used to make books were destroyed. While the empire faced the mountainous challenge of dealing with the material and cultural destruction of the war, it also was burdened by a major ecological disaster in the north.

Tz'u Hsi (1835–1908) Empress Dowager of China, 1903 (b/w photo), French Photographer, (20th century)/Private Collection/The Bridgeman Art Library

Cixi's Allies *In the 1860s and 1870s, Cixi was a supporter of reform. In later years she was widely regarded as corrupt and self-centered and as an obstacle to reform. Her greatest allies were the court eunuchs. Introduced to palace life in early China as managers of the imperial harems, eunuchs became powerful political parties at court. The first Qing emperors refused to allow the eunuchs any political influence, but by Cixi's time the eunuchs once again were a political factor.*

The Yellow River changed course in 1855, destroying the southern part of impoverished Shandong province with flood and initiating decades of drought along the former riverbed in northern Shandong.

Decentralization at the End of the Qing Empire, 1864–1875   The Qing government emerged from the 1850s with no hope of achieving solvency. The corruption of the 1700s, attempts in the very early 1800s to restore waterworks and roads, and declining yields from land taxes had bankrupted the treasury. By 1850, before the Taiping Rebellion, Qing government expenditures were ten times revenues. The indemnities demanded by Europeans after the Opium and Arrow Wars compounded the problem. Vast stretches of formerly productive rice land were devastated, and the population was dispersed. Refugees pleaded for relief, and the imperial, volunteer, foreign, and mercenary troops that had suppressed the Taipings demanded unpaid wages.

Britain and France became active participants in the period of recovery that followed the rebellion (see Diversity and Dominance: Chinese Responses to Imperialism). To ensure repayment of the debt to Britain, Robert Hart was installed as inspector-general of a newly created Imperial Maritime Customs Service. Britain and the Qing split the revenues he collected. Britons and Americans worked for the Qing government as advisers and ambassadors, attempting to smooth communications between the Qing, Europe, and the United States.

The real work of the recovery, however, was managed by provincial governors who had come to the forefront in the struggle against the Taipings. To prosecute the war, they had won the right to levy their own taxes, raise their own troops, and run their own bureaucracies. These special powers were not entirely canceled when the war ended. Chief among these governors was Zeng Guofan (zung gwoh-FAN), who oversaw programs to restore agriculture, communications, education, and publishing, as well as efforts to reform the military and industrialize armaments manufacture.

Like many provincial governors, Zeng preferred to look to the United States rather than to Britain for models and aid. He therefore hired American advisers to run his weapons factories, shipyards, and military academies. He also sponsored a daring program in which promising Chinese boys were sent to Hartford, Connecticut, a center of missionary activity, to learn English, science, mathematics, engineering, and history. They returned to China to assume some of the positions previously held by foreign advisers. Though Zeng was never an advocate of participation in public life by women, his Confucian convictions taught him that educated mothers were more than ever a necessity. He not only encouraged but also partly oversaw the advanced classical education of his own daughters. Zeng's death in 1872 deprived the empire of a major force for reform.

The period of recovery marked a fundamental structural change in the Qing Empire. Although the emperors after 1850 were ineffective rulers, a coalition of aristocrats supported the reform and recovery programs. Without their legitimization of the new powers of provincial governors like Zeng Guofan, the empire might have evaporated within a generation. A crucial member of this alliance was Cixi (TSUH-shee), who was known as the "Empress Dowager" after the 1880s.

Chinese Responses to Imperialism

The Opium War, followed by the Taiping Rebellion, revealed China's weakness for all to see, but there was no agreement on what should be done to restore its strength. A few provincial officials were able to take effective action, but the competing ideas that were heard at the imperial court tended to cancel each other out.

Feng Guifen, an official and a scholar, came into contact with Westerners defending Shanghai when he took refuge there from the Taipings. The following is from a book of essays he published in 1861.

According to a general geography compiled by an Englishman, the territory of China is eight times that of Russia, ten times that of the United States, one hundred times that of France, and two hundred times that of Great Britain.... Yet we are shamefully humiliated by the four nations, not because our climate, soil, or resources are inferior to theirs, but because our people are inferior.... Now, our inferiority is not due to our allotment from Heaven [i.e., our inherent nature], but is rather due to ourselves....

Why are the Western nations small and yet strong? Why are we large and yet weak? We must search for the means to become their equal, and that depends solely upon human effort....

We have only one thing to learn from the barbarians, and that is strong ships and effective guns.... Funds should be allotted to establish a shipyard and arsenal in each trading port. A few barbarians should be employed, and Chinese who are good in using their minds should be selected to receive instruction so that in turn they may teach many craftsmen. When a piece of work is finished and is as good as that made by the barbarians, the makers should be rewarded with an official *juren* degree and be permitted to participate in the metropolitan examinations on the same basis as other scholars. Those whose products are of superior quality should be rewarded with the *jinshi* degree [ordinarily conferred in the metropolitan examinations] and be permitted to participate in the palace examinations like others. The workers should be paid double so that they will not quit their jobs.

Our nation's emphasis on civil service examinations has sunk deep into people's minds for a long time. Intelligent and brilliant scholars have exhausted their time and energy in such useless things as the stereotyped examination essays, examination papers, and formal calligraphy.... We should now order one-half of them to apply themselves to the manufacturing of instruments and weapons and to the promotion of physical studies.... The intelligence and ingenuity of the Chinese are certainly superior to those of the various barbarians; it is only that hitherto we have not made use of them. When the government above takes delight in something, the people below will pursue it further: their response will be like an echo carried by the wind. There ought to be some people of extraordinary intelligence who can have new ideas and improve on Western methods. At first they may take the foreigners as their teachers and models; then they may come to the same level and be their equals; finally they may move ahead and surpass them. Herein lies the way to self-strengthening.

In 1867 the debate over how to resist foreign military pressure surged through the imperial court. Woren, a Mongol who held the rank of grand secretary, spoke for the conservatives.

Mathematics, one of the six arts, should indeed be learned by scholars as indicated in the imperial decree, and it should not be considered an unworthy subject. But according to the viewpoint of your servant, astronomy and mathematics are of very little use. If these subjects are going to be taught by Westerners as regular studies, the damage will be great. . . . Your servant has learned that the way to establish a nation is to lay emphasis on rites and rightness, not on power and plotting. The fundamental effort lies in the minds of people, not in techniques. Now, if we seek trifling arts and respect barbarians as teachers .... all that can be accomplished is the training of mathematicians. From ancient down to modern times, your servant has never heard of anyone who could use mathematics to raise the nation from a state of decline or to strengthen it in time of weakness....

Since the conclusion of the peace, Christianity has been prevalent, and half of our ignorant people have been fooled by it. The only thing we can rely on is that our scholars should clearly explain to the people the Confucian tenets, which may be able to sustain the minds of the ignorant populace. Now if these brilliant and talented scholars, who have been trained by the nation and reserved for great future usefulness, have to change from their regular course of study to follow the barbarians, then the correct spirit will not be developed, and accordingly the evil spirit will become stronger. After several years it will end in nothing less than driving the multitudes of the Chinese people into allegiance to the barbarians.

The opposing group of ministers who backed the idea of "self-strengthening" responded.

Your ministers have examined the memorial of Woren: the principles he presents are very lofty and the opinion he maintains is very orthodox. Your ministers' point of view was also like that before they began to manage foreign affairs; and yet today they do not presume to insist on such ideas, because of actual difficulties that they cannot help....

From the beginning of foreign relations to the present there have been twenty or thirty years. At first the officials inside and outside the capital did not grasp the crux of the matter, and whether they negotiated peace or discussed war, generally these were empty words without effect.... Therefore your ministers have pondered a long-term policy and discussed the situation thoroughly with all the provincial officials. Proposals to learn the written and spoken languages of foreign countries, the various methods of making machines, the training of troops with foreign guns, the dispatching of officials to travel in all countries, the investigation of their local customs and social conditions ... all these painstaking and special decisions represent nothing other than a struggle for self-strengthening....

We too are afraid that the people who are learning these things will have no power of discrimination and are likely to be led astray by foreigners, as Woren fears. Therefore we have deliberated and decided that those who participate in these examinations must be persons from regular scholastic channels. It is indeed those students who have read widely and who understand right principles and have their minds set upon upright and grand purposes—and the present situation is just what causes the scholars and officials to feel pain in heart and head—who would certainly be able to lie on faggots and taste gall [i.e., nurse vengeance] in order to encourage each other vigorously to seek the actual achievement of self-strengthening. They are different from those who have vague, easygoing, or indifferent ideas.

Questions for Analysis

1. How do the views of the writers reflect their own backgrounds as officials who achieved their offices through the traditional examination system?

2. In what ways do these passages indicate a deep or a shallow understanding of the West?

3. How do the ideas expressed here compare with the attitudes toward reform in the Ottoman and Russian Empires as discussed elsewhere in this chapter?

Source: Essays of Feng Tuifen published in 1861 in Jiaobinlu kangyi (Personal Protests from the Study of Jiaobin). English translations from Chester Tan, published in Wm. Theodore de Bary and Richard Lafrano, *Sources of Chinese Tradition*, vol. 2, 2d ed. pp. 235–236, 238–239. Copyright © 2000 Columbia University Press. Reprinted with permission of the publisher.

Later observers, both Chinese and foreign, reviled her as a monster of corruption and arrogance. But in the 1860s and 1870s Cixi supported the provincial governors, some of whom became so powerful that they were managing Qing foreign policy as well as domestic affairs.

No longer a conquest regime dominated by a Manchu military caste and its Chinese civilian appointees, the empire came under the control of a group of reformist aristocrats and military men, independently powerful civilian governors, and a small number of foreign advisers. The Qing lacked strong, central, unified leadership and could not recover their powers of taxation, legislation, and military command once these had been granted to the provincial governors. From the 1860s forward, the Qing Empire disintegrated into a number of large power zones in which provincial governors handed over leadership to their protégés in a pattern that the Qing court eventually could only ritually legitimate.

CONCLUSION

The Ottoman, Qing, and Russian Empires shared several characteristics both in their early successes and late-stage challenges. All three maintained a flexible approach when incorporating a diverse group of peoples and cultures into their growing empires. Around the mid-eighteenth century, however, the need to maintain order and increase tax revenues pushed rulers to differentiate groups of people and create stricter hierarchies within each empire, leading to conflict between the minority rulers and the ruled. In addition, population growth that began in the sixteenth century throughout Eurasia, which had been sustainable and beneficial in the expanding territories of Russia and the Qing, eventually became unsupportable. By the nineteenth century, even the Qing Empire, the largest and most advanced Eurasian empire in terms of commercial economy and efficient bureaucratic structures, could no longer effectively deal with the increasing demographic pressures, regional conflict, and political dysfunctions.

Most of the subjects of the Ottoman, Russian, and Qing rulers did not think of European pressure or competition as determining factors in their lives during the first half of the nineteenth century. They continued to live according to the social and economic institutions they inherited from previous generations. By the 1870s, however, the challenge of Europe had become widely realized. The Crimean War, where European allies achieved a hollow victory for the Ottomans and then pressured the sultan for more reforms, confirmed both Ottoman and Russian military weakness. The Opium War did the same for China. But China, unlike the other empires, was also stricken by rampaging civil war and regional uprisings.

In analyzing the crises of the three empires, historians today stress European economic pressures and observe that all three empires ultimately became insolvent and saw the overthrow of their ruling dynasties. However, at the time what most impressed the Ottomans, Russians, and Chinese was European military superiority, as demonstrated in the Greek war of independence, the Crimean War, and the Opium War. Thus for all three empires, dealing with military emergency took priority over deeper reforms throughout most of the time period of this chapter.

IMPORTANT EVENTS 1800–1908	
1794–1804	White Lotus Rebellion
1801–1825	Reign of Alexander I
1805–1849	Muhammad Ali governs Egypt
1808–1839	Rule of Mahmud II
1812	Napoleon's retreat from Moscow
1825	Decembrist revolt
1825–1855	Reign of Nicholas I
1826	Janissary corps dissolved
1829	Greek independence
1839	Abdul Mejid begins Tanzimat reforms
1839–1842	Opium War
1850–1864	Taiping Rebellion
1853–1856	Crimean War
1855–1881	Reign of Alexander II
1856–1860	Arrow War
1860	Sack of Beijing
1861	Emancipation of the serfs
1861–1873	Empress Dowager Cixi wields power during her son's minority
1875–1908	After her son's death, Empress Dowager Cixi resumes power behalf of minor successors
1876	First constitution by an Islamic government

25

NATION BUILDING AND ECONOMIC TRANSFORMATION IN THE AMERICAS, 1800–1890

D uring the nineteenth century the newly independent nations of the Western Hemisphere sought to emulate the rapid economic progress of Europe under the influence of the Industrial Revolution. No technology seemed to represent that progress better than railroads. Everywhere from Argentina to Canada, governments sponsored railroad development. By 1850 there were 9,000 miles (14,480 kilometers) of track in the United States, as much as in the rest of the world. Latin American nations committed to this technology later than the United States, but railroads there also soon proved important to exports, to new industries, and to political and cultural integration.

Mexico granted the first concession for railroad construction in 1837, but the first significant rail line was completed in 1873. Few new projects were begun until the presidency of Porfirio Díaz (1876–1880 and 1884–1911), who promoted railroad construction. By the time revolutionaries forced him from office, Mexico had 12,000 miles (19,300 kilometers) of track. Although railroads proved crucial to Mexican economic growth, there was a downside. Foreign investment helped pay for new railroads, but this dependence on foreign capital led to political protests and economic nationalism. Railroad development also had a powerful effect on native peoples, who still controlled large areas of rural Mexico. Because railroads made their lands more valuable, powerful landed families used their political influence to strip this land from indigenous subsistence farmers and use it to produce export crops. As Amerindian villagers lost their traditional lands, the number of rural uprisings increased.

In the nineteenth century the Western Hemisphere witnessed radical political and social changes in addition to technological innovations and economic expansion. Brazil and nearly all of Spain's American colonies achieved independence by 1825. As was true in the earlier American and French Revolutions (see Chapter 23), rising nationalism and the ideal of political freedom promoted these changes. Despite the achievement of independence, however, Mexico and other nations in the hemisphere faced foreign interventions and other threats to sovereignty, including regionalism and civil war.

The new nations of the Western Hemisphere faced difficult questions. If colonies could reject submission to imperial powers, could not regions with distinct cultures, social structures, and economies refuse to accept the political authority of newly formed national governments? How could nations born in revolution accept the political strictures of written constitutions—even those they wrote themselves? How could the ideals of liberty and freedom expressed in those constitutions be reconciled with the denial of rights to Amerindians, slaves, recent immigrants, and women?

While trying to resolve these political questions, the new nations also attempted to promote economic growth. They imported new technologies like railroads, opened new areas to settlement, and promoted immigration. But the legacy of colonial economic development, with its emphasis on agricultural and mining exports, inhibited efforts to promote diversification and industrialization, just as the legacy of class and racial division thwarted the realization of political ideals.

INDEPENDENCE IN LATIN AMERICA, 1800–1830

As the eighteenth century drew to a close, Spain and Portugal held vast colonial possessions in the Western Hemisphere, although their power had declined relative to that of their British and French rivals. Both Iberian empires had reformed their colonial administration and strengthened their military forces in the eighteenth century (see Chapter 18). Despite these efforts, the same economic and political forces that had undermined Britain's rule in its colonies were present in Spanish America and Brazil.

Roots of Revolution, to 1810

The great works of the Enlightenment as well as revolutionary documents like the American Declaration of Independence and the French Declaration of the Rights of Man and the Citizen circulated widely in Latin America, but few colonial residents wanted revolutionary change. While colonial elites and middle classes were frustrated by imperial policies, it was events in Europe that propelled the colonies toward independence. Napoleon's decision to invade Portugal (1807) and Spain (1808), not revolutionary ideas, created a crisis of legitimacy that undermined the authority of colonial officials and ignited Latin America's struggle for independence.

As a French army neared Lisbon in 1808, the Portuguese royal family fled to Brazil. Once arrived, King John VI would maintain his court there for over a decade. Soon Napoleon forced King Ferdinand VII of Spain to abdicate and placed his own brother, Joseph Bonaparte, on the throne. Spanish patriots fighting against the French created a new political body, the Junta (HUN-tah) Central, to administer the areas they controlled. The junta claimed authority over Spain's colonies, inviting the election of colonial deputies to help write the nation's first written constitution.

Most residents of colonial Spanish America favored obedience to the Junta Central and many colonies elected deputies, but a vocal minority, including some members of the elite, objected. These dissenters argued that they were subjects of the king, not dependents of the Spanish nation. They wanted to create local juntas and govern their own affairs until Ferdinand regained the throne. Spanish loyalists resisted this assertion of local autonomy, provoking armed uprisings. In late 1808 and 1809 popular movements overthrew Spanish colonial officials in Venezuela, Mexico, and Alto Peru (modern Bolivia) and created local juntas. In each case, Spanish officials quickly reasserted control and punished the leaders. This harsh repression, however, further polarized public opinion in the colonies and gave rise to a greater sense of a separate American nationality. By 1810 Spanish colonial authorities were facing a new round of revolutions now focused on independence.

Spanish South America, 1810–1825   In Caracas (the capital city of modern Venezuela) a revolutionary junta led by creoles (colonial-born whites) declared independence in 1811. Although this group espoused representative democracy, its leaders were landowners who defended slavery and opposed full citizenship for the black and mixed-race majority. Their aim was to expand their own privileges by eliminating Spaniards from the upper levels of government and the church. The junta's narrow agenda spurred Spanish loyalists to rally thousands of free blacks and slaves to defend the Spanish Empire. Faced with this determined resistance, the revolutionary movement placed overwhelming political authority in the hands of its military leader **Simón Bolívar** (see-MOAN bow-LEE-varh) (1783–1830), who would become the preeminent leader of the independence movement.

The son of wealthy Venezuelan planters, Bolívar had traveled in Europe and studied the works of the Enlightenment. He was a charismatic personality who effectively mobilized political support and held the loyalty of his troops. Defeated on many occasions, Bolívar successfully adapted his objectives and policies to attract new allies and build coalitions. Although initially opposed to the abolition of slavery, for example, he agreed to support emancipation in order to draw slaves and freemen to his cause and to gain military supplies from Haiti. Bolívar was also capable of using harsh methods to ensure victory, proclaiming in 1813 that "any Spaniard who does not ... work against tyranny in behalf of this just cause will be considered an enemy and punished; as a traitor to the nation, he will inevitably be shot by a firing squad."[1]

Military advantage shifted back and forth between the patriots and loyalists until Bolívar enlisted demobilized English and French veterans of the Napoleonic Wars. Spanish resolve was then fatally weakened by a military revolt in Spain in 1820. The European veterans, hardened by combat, improved the battlefield performance of Bolívar's army, while the revolt in Spain in 1820 forced Ferdinand VII—restored to power in 1814—to accept a constitution that limited the powers of both the monarch and the church. Colonial loyalists who for a decade had fought to maintain the authority of monarch and church viewed these reforms as unacceptably liberal.

---

[1] Quoted in Lyman L. Johnson, "Spanish American Independence and Its Consequences," in *Problems in Modern Latin American History: A Reader*, ed. John Charles Chasteen and Joseph S. Tulchin (Wilmington, DE: Scholarly Resources, 1994), 21.

With the king's supporters now divided, momentum swung to the patriots. After liberating present-day Venezuela, Colombia, and Ecuador, Bolívar's army entered Peru and Bolivia and defeated the last Spanish armies in 1824. Bolívar and his supporters then attempted to create a confederation of the former Spanish colonies. The first steps were the creation of Gran Colombia (now Venezuela, Colombia, and Ecuador) and the unification of Peru and Bolivia, but these initiatives had failed by 1830.

Buenos Aires (the capital city of modern Argentina) was the second important center of revolutionary activity in Spanish South America. In Buenos Aires news of French victories in Spain led to the creation of a junta organized by militia commanders, merchants, and ranchers, which overthrew the viceroy in 1810. To deflect the opposition of Spanish loyalists, the junta claimed loyalty to the imprisoned king. Two years after Ferdinand regained the Spanish throne in 1814, junta leaders declared independence as the United Provinces of the Río de la Plata.

Patriot leaders in Buenos Aires at first sought to retain control over the territory of the Viceroyalty of Río de la Plata, but Spanish loyalists in Uruguay and Bolivia and a separatist movement in Paraguay defeated these ambitions. Even within the territory of Argentina, the government in Buenos Aires was unable to control regional rivalries and political differences. As a result, the region rapidly descended into political chaos.

A weak succession of juntas, collective presidencies, and dictators lost control over much of the interior of Argentina. But the government in Buenos Aires did manage to support a mixed force of Chileans and Argentines led by José de San Martín (hoe-SAY deh san mar-TEEN) (1778–1850), who crossed the Andes Mountains to attack Spanish forces in Chile and Peru. During this campaign San Martín's most effective troops were former slaves, who had gained their freedom by enlisting in the army. After gaining victory in Chile, San Martín pushed on to Peru in 1820, but he failed to gain a clear victory there. Unable to make progress, San Martín surrendered command of patriot forces in Peru to Simón Bolívar, who overcame final Spanish resistance in 1824.

Mexico,
1810–1823

In 1810 Mexico was Spain's wealthiest and most populous colony. Its silver mines were the richest in the world, and the colony's capital, Mexico City, was larger than any city in Spain. Mexico also had the largest population of Spanish immigrants among the colonies. When news of Napoleon's invasion of Spain reached Mexico, conservative Spaniards in Mexico City overthrew the local viceroy, thinking him too sympathetic to the creoles. This action by Spanish loyalists underlined the new reality: with the king removed from his throne by the French, colonial authority now rested on brute force.

The first stage of the revolution against Spain occurred in central Mexico, where ranchers and farmers had aggressively forced Amerindian communities from their traditional agricultural lands. Crop failures and epidemics afflicted the region's rural poor, while miners and the urban poor faced higher food prices and rising unemployment as well. With the power of colonial authorities weakened by events in Spain, anger and fear spread through towns and villages in central Mexico.

MAP 25.1 Latin America by 1830

By 1830 patriot forces had overturned the Spanish and Portuguese Empires of the Western Hemisphere. Regional conflicts, local wars, and foreign interventions challenged the survival of many of these new nations following independence.

On September 16, 1810, the parish priest of the small town of Dolores, **Miguel Hidalgo y Costilla** (mee-GEHL ee-DAHL-go ee cos-TEA-ah), rang the church bells and attracted a crowd. In a fiery speech he urged the crowd to rise up against the oppression of Spanish officials. Tens of thousands of the rural and urban poor soon joined his movement. While they lacked military discipline and weapons, they knew who their oppressors were, the Spanish and colonial-born whites who owned the ranches and mines. Recognizing the threat posed by the angry masses following Hidalgo, most wealthy Mexicans supported the Spanish authorities. The military tide quickly turned, and Spanish forces captured and executed Hidalgo in 1811.

The revolution continued under the leadership of another priest, **José María Morelos** (hoe-SAY mah-REE-ah moh-RAY-los), a former student of Hidalgo's. A more adept military and political leader than his mentor, Morelos created a formidable fighting force and, in 1813, convened a congress that declared independence and drafted a constitution. Despite these achievements, loyalist forces defeated and executed Morelos in 1815. Although small numbers of insurgents continued to fight Spanish forces, colonial rule seemed secure in 1820, but news of the military revolt in Spain unsettled the conservative groups who had opposed Hidalgo and Morelos. In 1821, Colonel Agustín de Iturbide (ah-goos-TEEN deh ee-tur-BEE-deh) and other loyalist commanders forged an alliance with insurgents to declare Mexico's independence. The conservative origins of Mexico's independence were made clear by the decision to create a monarchial government and crown Iturbide emperor. In early 1823, however, the army overthrew Iturbide and Mexico became a republic. When Iturbide returned to Mexico from exile in 1824, he was captured and, like Hidalgo and Morelos, was executed by a firing squad.

Brazil, to 1831   The arrival of the Portuguese royal family in Brazil in 1808 helped maintain the loyalty of the colonial elite. With Napoleon's defeat, the Portuguese government called for King John VI to return to Portugal. At first he resisted, but a liberal revolt in Portugal forced the king to return to Portugal in 1821 to protect his throne. He left his son Pedro in Brazil as regent.

By this date the Spanish colonies along Brazil's borders had experienced ten years of revolution and civil war, and some, like Argentina and Paraguay, had gained independence. Unable to ignore these struggles, some Brazilians began to reevaluate Brazil's relationship with Portugal. Many resented their homeland's economic subordination to Portugal, while the arrogance of Portuguese soldiers and bureaucrats led others to talk openly of independence.

Unwilling to return to Portugal and committed to maintaining his family's hold on Brazil, Pedro aligned himself with rising separatist sentiment, and in 1822 declared Brazilian independence. Pedro's decision launched Brazil on a unique political trajectory. Unlike its neighbors, which became constitutional republics, Brazil gained independence as a constitutional monarchy with Pedro I, son of the king of Portugal, as emperor.

Pedro I was committed to both monarchy and to liberal principles. The constitution of 1824 provided for an elected assembly and granted rights to the

Padre Hidalgo *Padre Miguel Hidalgo y Costilla led the first stage of Mexico's revolution for independence by rallying the rural masses. His defeat, trial, and execution made him one of Mexico's most important political martyrs.*

Schaalkwijk/Art Resource, NY

political opposition, but Pedro made enemies by protecting the Portuguese who remained in Brazil from arrest and seizure of property. Pedro I also opposed slavery, even though the slave-owning class dominated Brazil. In 1823, he anonymously published an article that characterized slavery as a "cancer eating away at Brazil." His decision in 1831 to ratify a treaty with Great Britain ending Brazilian participation in the slave trade provoked opposition, as did his use of military force to control neighboring Uruguay. As military losses and costs rose, the Brazilian public grew impatient. A vocal minority that sought the creation of a democracy used these issues to rally public opinion against the emperor. Confronted by street demonstrations, Pedro I abdicated the throne in 1831 in favor of his five-year-old son Pedro II. After a nine-year regency, Pedro II assumed full powers as emperor of Brazil and reigned until overthrown by republicans in 1889.

THE PROBLEM OF ORDER, 1825–1890

All the newly independent nations of the Western Hemisphere encountered difficulties establishing stable political institutions. Popular sovereignty found broad support across the hemisphere as all the new nations sought to establish constitutions and elected assemblies. However, this widespread support for constitutional order and for representative government failed to prevent bitter factional conflict, regionalism, and the threats posed by charismatic political leaders and military uprisings.

Constitutional Experiments   In reaction to what they saw as arbitrary and tyrannical rule by colonial authorities, revolutionary leaders in the United States and Latin America espoused constitutionalism. They believed that the careful description of political powers in written constitutions offered the best protection for individual rights and liberties. In practice, however, many new constitutions proved unworkable. In the United States, George Washington, James Madison, and other leaders became dissatisfied with the first constitution, the Articles of Confederation, and helped write a new constitution. In Latin America few constitutions survived the rough-and-tumble of national politics. For example, Venezuela and Chile ratified and then rejected a combined total of nine constitutions between 1811 and 1833.

Important differences in colonial political experience influenced later political developments in the Americas. The ratification of a new constitution in the United States was the culmination of a long historical process that had begun with the development of English constitutional law and continued under colonial charters. The British colonies provided many opportunities for holding elective offices, and, by the time of independence, citizens had grown accustomed to elections, political parties, and factions. In contrast, neither Brazil nor Spanish America had significant experience with elections and representative institutions prior to independence.

Democratic passions and the desire for effective self-rule led to significant political reform in the Americas, even in regions that remained colonies. British Canada included a number of separate colonies and territories, each with a discrete government. A provincial governor and appointed advisory council drawn from the local elite dominated political life in each colony, while elected assemblies exercised limited power. The desire to make government responsive to the will of the assemblies led to armed rebellion in 1837. Britain responded by establishing limited self-rule in each of the Canadian provinces. By the 1860s regional political leaders realized that economic development required a government with a "national" character. Negotiations between Canadian leaders and the British government led to a union of Canadian provinces, the **Confederation of 1867**, and to the creation of the Dominion of Canada with a central government in Ottawa.

The path to effective constitutional government was rockier to the south. Because neither Spain nor Portugal had permitted anything like the elected legislatures and municipal governments of colonial British America, the drafters of Latin American constitutions were less constrained by practical political experience. As a result, many of the new Latin American nations experimented with untested political institutions.

Latin American nations found it particularly difficult to define the role of the Catholic Church after independence. In the colonial period the Catholic Church was a religious monopoly that controlled all levels of education and dominated intellectual life. Many early constitutions aimed to reduce this power by making education secular and by permitting other religions. The church reacted by organizing and financing conservative movements. Conflicts between liberals who sought the separation of church and state and conservatives who supported the church's traditional powers dominated political life in the nineteenth century.

Limiting the power of the military was another obstacle to the creation of constitutional governments in Latin America. The wars for independence elevated the prestige of military leaders, and, when the wars were over, military commanders seldom proved willing to subordinate themselves to civilian authorities. Frustrated by the chaotic workings of democracy, many citizens saw dictatorships led by the heroes of independence as better protection for their lives and property.

Personalist Leaders   Patriot leaders in both the United States and Latin America gained mass followings during the wars for independence, and some used these followings to gain political power. George Washington's ability to dominate early republican politics in the United States anticipated the later political ascendancy of revolutionary heroes such as Iturbide in Mexico and Bolívar in Gran Colombia. In each case, military reputation provided the foundation for personal political power. Washington was distinguished from most other military leaders by his willingness to surrender power at the end of a term determined by a constitution. More commonly, **personalist leaders** relied on their mass followings rather than on constitutions and laws to govern. In Latin America, a personalist leader who gained and held political power without constitutional sanction was called a *caudillo* (kouh-DEE-yoh).

Powerful personal followings allowed **Andrew Jackson** of the United States and **José Antonio Páez** (hoe-SAY an-TOE-nee-oh PAH-ays) of Venezuela to challenge constitutional limits to their authority. During the independence wars in Venezuela and Colombia, Páez (1790–1873) was one of Bolívar's most successful generals. Like most of his followers, Páez was uneducated and poor, but his physical strength, courage, and guile made him a natural guerrilla leader and helped him build a powerful political base. Páez described his authority in the following manner: "[The soldiers] resolved to confer on me the supreme command and blindly to obey my will, confident … that I was the only one who could save them."[2] Able to count on the personal loyalty of his followers, Páez was seldom willing to accept the constitutional authority of a distant president.

After defeating the Spanish, Bolívar pursued his dream of forging a union of former Spanish colonies modeled on the United States. But he underestimated the strength of nationalist sentiment unleashed by the independence wars. Páez and other Venezuelan leaders resisted the surrender of their hard-won power to Bolívar's Gran Colombian government in distant Bogotá. When political opponents challenged Bolívar in 1829, Páez declared Venezuela's independence. Merciless to his enemies and indulgent with his followers, Páez ruled the country as president or dictator for the next eighteen years. Despite implementing an economic program favorable to the elite, Páez remained popular with the masses. Even as his personal wealth grew, he took care to present himself as a common man.

Andrew Jackson (1767–1845) was the first U.S. president born in humble circumstances. A self-made man who eventually acquired substantial property and

---

[2] José Antonio Páez, *Autobiografía del General José Antonio Páez*, vol. 1 (New York: Hallety Breen, 1869), 83.

owned over a hundred slaves, Jackson was extremely popular among frontier residents, urban workers, and small farmers. Although he was notorious for his untidy personal life as well as for dueling, his courage, individualism, and willingness to challenge authority helped him attain political success as judge, general, congressman, senator, and president.

During his military career, Jackson proved to be impatient with civilian authorities. Widely known because of his victories over the Creek and Seminole peoples, he was elevated to the pinnacle of American politics by his celebrated defeat of the British at the Battle of New Orleans in 1815 and by his seizure of Florida from the Spanish in 1818. In 1824 he received a plurality of the popular votes for president but failed to win a majority of electoral votes. His followers were embittered when the House of Representatives chose John Quincy Adams as president.

Jackson's followers viewed his landslide election victory in 1828 and reelection in 1832 as the triumph of democracy over entrenched aristocracy. In office Jackson challenged constitutional limits on his authority, increasing presidential power at the expense of Congress and the Supreme Court. Like Páez, Jackson was able to dominate national politics by blending a populist political style that celebrated the virtues and cultural enthusiasms of common people with support for policies that promoted the economic interests of powerful propertied groups.

Personalist leaders were common in both Latin America and the United States, but Latin America's weaker constitutional tradition, more limited protection of property rights, lower literacy levels, and less-developed communications systems facilitated the ambitions of popular politicians. Latin America's personalist leaders often ignored constitutional restraints on their authority, and election results seldom determined access to presidential power. As a result, by 1900 every independent Latin American nation had experienced periods of dictatorship.

The Threat of Regionalism   After independence, national governments were generally weaker than the colonial governments they replaced. Debates over tariffs, tax and monetary policies, and, in many nations, slavery and the slave trade led regional elites to attempt secession. Some of the hemisphere's newly independent nations did not survive these struggles, while others lost territories to aggressive neighbors.

In Spanish America all efforts to forge large multistate federations after independence failed. The Viceroyalty of New Spain had included Central America and Mexico, but after independence this union failed when in 1823 local elites broke with Mexico to form the Republic of Central America. A new round of regional disputes and civil wars led to the creation of five separate nations during the 1820s and 1830s. In South America, Bolívar attempted to maintain the colonial unity of Venezuela, Colombia, and Ecuador by creating Gran Colombia with its capital in Bogotá. But even before his death in 1830, Venezuela and Ecuador had become independent states. In the colonial era Argentina, Uruguay, Paraguay, and Bolivia were organized as a single viceroyalty with its capital in Buenos Aires. After the defeat of Spain, the leaders in Paraguay, Uruguay, and Bolivia declared their independence from Argentina.

Regionalism threatened the United States as well. The defense of state and regional interests played an important role in the framing of the U.S. Constitution.

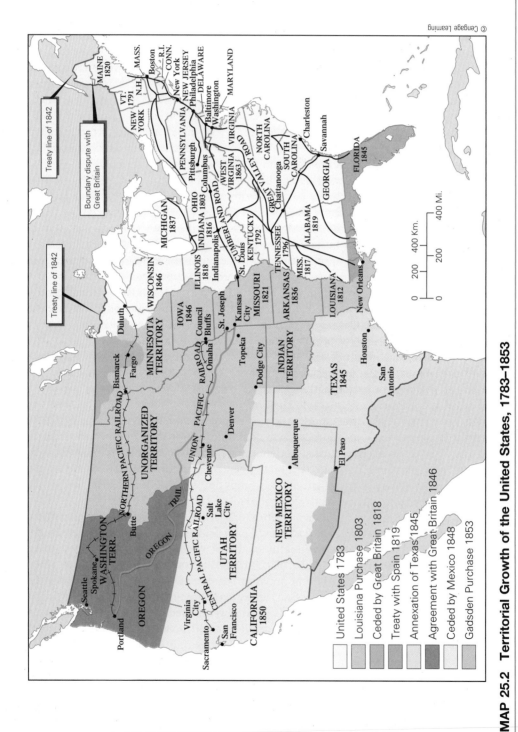

MAP 25.2 Territorial Growth of the United States, 1783–1853

The rapid western expansion of the United States resulted from aggressive diplomacy and warfare against Mexico and Amerindian peoples. Railroad development helped integrate the trans-Mississippi west and promote economic expansion.

© Cengage Learning

Many important constitutional provisions represented compromises forged among competing state and regional leaders. Yet, despite these constitutional compromises, regional rivalries still threatened the nation.

Slavery divided the nation into two separate and competitive societies. A rising tide of immigration to the northern states in the 1830s and 1840s began to move the center of political power away from the South. Southern leaders sought to protect slavery by expanding into new territories. They supported the Louisiana Purchase in 1803, which transferred to the United States a vast French territory extending from the Gulf of Mexico to Canada, and the Mexican-American War in 1846, which added nearly half of Mexico to the United States. However, this territorial expansion forced a national debate about slavery that contributed to the election of Abraham Lincoln as president in 1860.

Lincoln was committed to checking the spread of slavery, and his election provoked the southern planter elite to choose the dangerous course of secession from the Union. The seceding states formed a new government, the Confederate States of America, known as the Confederacy. Lincoln preserved the Union but at an enormous cost. The U.S. Civil War (1861–1865) was the most destructive conflict in the history of the Western Hemisphere. Up to 750,000 lives were lost before the Confederacy surrendered in 1865. The Union victory led to the abolition of slavery and also transferred national political power to a northern elite committed to industrial expansion and federal support for the construction of railroads and other internal improvements.

The Confederate States of America was better prepared politically and economically for independence than were the successful secessionist movements that broke up Gran Colombia and other Spanish American federations. Nevertheless, the Confederacy failed, in part because of poor timing. The new nations of the Western Hemisphere were most vulnerable to secessionist movements in the early years of their existence; indeed, all the successful secessions occurred shortly after independence. In the case of the United States, an experienced national government legitimated and strengthened by more than seven decades of relative stability and reinforced by dramatic economic and population growth defeated secession only with enormous effort.

Foreign Interventions and Regional Wars

Wars often determined national borders, access to natural resources, and control of markets in the Western Hemisphere. Even after the achievement of independence, Mexico and other Western Hemisphere nations were forced to defend themselves against Europe's great powers. Contested national borders and regional rivalries also led to wars between Western Hemisphere nations. By the end of the nineteenth century the United States, Brazil, Argentina, and Chile had all successfully waged wars against their neighbors and established themselves as regional powers.

Within thirty years of independence, the United States fought a second war with England—the War of 1812. The burning of the White House and Capitol by British troops in 1814 symbolized the weakness of the new republic. By the end of the nineteenth century, however, the United States was the hemisphere's greatest military power. Its war against Spain in 1898–1899 created an American empire that reached from the Philippines in the Pacific Ocean to Puerto Rico in the Caribbean (see Chapter 26).

European powers challenged the sovereignty of Latin American nations as well. Following independence Argentina faced British and French naval blockades, and British naval forces systematically violated Brazil's territorial waters to stop the importation of slaves. Mexico faced the most serious threats to sovereignty, defeating a weak Spanish invasion in 1829, a French assault on the city of Veracruz in 1838, and a large-scale French invasion in 1862.

Mexico also faced a grave threat from the United States. In the 1820s Mexico had encouraged Americans to immigrate to its northern province of Texas. By the early 1830s Americans outnumbered Mexican nationals in Texas and were aggressively challenging Mexican laws such as the prohibition of slavery. An alliance of Mexican liberals and American settlers rebelled in 1835 and gained independence for Texas in 1836. In 1845 the United States made Texas a state, provoking war with Mexico a year later. The surrender of Mexico City in 1848 to American forces compelled Mexico to accept a harsh treaty that forced it to cede vast territories to the United States, including present-day New Mexico, Arizona, and California.

Erich Lessing/Art Resource, NY

Execution of Emperor Maximilian of Mexico *This painting by Edouard Manet shows the 1867 execution by firing squad of Maximilian and two of his Mexican generals. The defeat of the French intervention was a great triumph for Mexican patriots led by Benito Juárez.*

In return Mexico received $15 million. When gold was discovered in California in 1848, the magnitude of Mexico's loss became clear.

With the very survival of the nation at stake, Mexico's liberals took power and imposed sweeping reforms, including a new constitution in 1857 that limited the power of the Catholic Church and military. This provoked a civil war with conservatives (1858–1861). **Benito Juárez** (beh-NEE-toh WAH-rez) assumed the presidency and defeated the conservatives, who then turned to Napoleon III of France for assistance. In 1862, French forces invaded Mexico, forced Juárez to flee Mexico City, and installed the Austrian Habsburg Maximilian as emperor of Mexico. After years of warfare, Juárez drove the French army out of Mexico in 1867, aided by U.S. diplomatic pressure. After capturing Maximilian, Juárez ordered his execution.

This victory over a powerful foreign enemy redeemed a nation humiliated two decades earlier by the United States. But the creation of democracy proved more elusive than the protection of Mexican sovereignty. Despite the Mexican constitution's prohibition of presidential reelection, Juárez would serve as president until his death in 1872.

As was clear in the Mexican-American War, wars between Western Hemisphere nations could lead to dramatic territorial changes. Chile established itself as the leading military and economic power on the west coast of South America when it fought two successful wars against an alliance of Peru and Bolivia (1836–1839 and 1879–1883). The second contest, the War of the Pacific, forced Bolivia to cede its only outlet to the sea and Peru to yield rich mining districts.

Argentina and Brazil fought for control of Uruguay in the 1820s, but a military stalemate eventually forced them to recognize Uruguayan independence. Then, in 1865, Argentina and Uruguay joined Brazil to wage war against Paraguay (War of the Triple Alliance). After five years of warfare, the Paraguayan dictator Francisco Solano López (fran-CEES-co so-LAN-oh LOH-pehz) and more than 20 percent of the nation's population had died. Paraguay then experienced military occupation, loss of territory, and economic penalties.

Native Peoples and the Nation-State   Both diplomacy and war shaped relations between the Western Hemisphere's new nation-states and indigenous peoples. During late colonial times, Spanish, Portuguese, and British colonial governments attempted to restrict the expansion of settlements into territories occupied by Amerindians. With independence, the colonial powers' role as mediator and protector ended.

Still-independent Amerindian peoples posed a significant military challenge to many Western Hemisphere republics. Weakened by civil wars and constitutional crises, new nations were less able to maintain frontier peace than the colonial governments they replaced. After independence Amerindian peoples in Argentina, the United States, Chile, and Mexico succeeded in pushing back frontier settlements. But despite early victories, native military resistance was overcome in most of the hemisphere by 1890.

After the American Revolution, tens of thousands of settlers entered territories previously guaranteed to Amerindians by treaties with Britain. Indigenous leaders responded by forging military alliances with British officials in Canada and with other native peoples. In the Ohio River Valley two Shawnee brothers, **Tecumseh** (teh-CUM-sah) and the Prophet (Tenskwatawa), created a broad, well-organized alliance among Amerindian peoples that gained British support. During the War of 1812, American military forces defeated the alliance. Tecumseh died in battle fighting alongside his British allies.

Throughout the 1820s native peoples lost lands to settlers across the Midwest and Southeast. The 1828 presidential election of Andrew Jackson, a veteran of earlier wars against native peoples, brought matters to a head. The Indian Removal Act of 1830 forced the resettlement of Cherokee, Creek, Choctaw, and other eastern peoples to land west of the Mississippi River. Nearly half these forced migrants died on this journey, known as the Trail of Tears.

The native peoples of the Great Plains offered formidable resistance to the expansion of white settlement. By the time substantial numbers of white buffalo hunters, cattlemen, and settlers reached the American west, indigenous peoples were skilled in the use of horses and firearms. These technologies allowed the Sioux, Comanche, Pawnee, Kiowa, and other plains peoples to hunt more efficiently and develop potent military capacities.

After the Civil War, however, a new wave of settlers pushed onto the plains. Buffalo herds were hunted to near extinction and native lands were appropriated by farmers and ranchers. Amerindian resistance to these assaults on their way of life led to four decades of armed conflict with the United States Army. The U.S. government forced the Comanche, who had long dominated the southern plains, to cede their traditional lands in Texas in 1865. The Sioux and their allies held

Navajo Leaders Gathered in Washington to Negotiate *As settlers pushed west in the nineteenth century, Amerindian peoples were forced to negotiate territorial concessions with the U.S. government. This photo shows Navajo leaders and their Anglo translators in Washington, D.C., in 1874.*

out longer, overwhelming General George Armstrong Custer and the Seventh Cavalry in the Battle of Little Bighorn in 1876, but they were also soon forced to accept reservation life. Military campaigns in the 1870s and 1880s then broke the resistance of the Apache.

The indigenous peoples of Argentina and Chile experienced a similar trajectory of adaptation, resistance, and defeat. Herds of wild cattle provided these peoples with a limitless food supply, and their mastery of the horse increased their military capacities. For a while the natives of Argentina and Chile were able to check the southern expansion of agriculture and ranching. Unable to defeat these resourceful enemies, the governments of Argentina and Chile relied on an elaborate system of gift giving and prisoner exchanges to maintain peace on the frontier.

By the 1860s, however, population increase, political stability, and military modernization allowed Argentina and Chile to take the offensive. In the 1870s the government of Argentina used a large military force armed with modern weapons to crush native resistance on the pampas. In the 1850s, civil war and an economic depression weakened the Chilean government, and the Mapuches (mah-POO-chez) (also called "Araucanians") pushed back frontier settlements, but by the 1870s Chilean forces had overwhelmed Amerindian resistance.

In Chile, Argentina, and the United States, national governments justified military campaigns by demonizing native peoples. Newspaper editorials and the speeches of politicians portrayed Amerindians as brutal and cruel and as obstacles to progress. In April 1859 a Chilean newspaper commented:

> The necessity, not only to punish the Araucanian [Mapuche] race, but also to make it impotent to harm us, is well recognized ... as the only way to rid the country of a million evils. It is well understood that they are odious and prejudicial guests in Chile ... conciliatory measures have accomplished nothing with this stupid race—the infamy and disgrace of the Chilean nation.[3]

The author of this racist pronouncement apparently felt no obligation to explain how his nation's original inhabitants had become "guests."

Political divisions and civil wars within the new nations also provided opportunities for some long-pacified native peoples to rebel. In the Yucatán region of Mexico, large landowners forced many Maya (MY-ah) communities from traditional agricultural lands, reducing thousands to peonage. Weakened by internal rebellions and by the American invasion, the Mexican government faced a mass rebellion by the Maya in 1847. This well-organized and popular uprising, known as the **Caste War**, nearly returned the Yucatán to native control. Grievances accumulated over more than three hundred years led to great violence and property destruction. The end of the war with the United States allowed the government of Mexico to regain control of major towns. Even then, some Maya rebels retreated to unoccupied territories and created an independent state, which they called the "Empire of the Cross." Organized around a mix of traditional beliefs and Christian symbols, this indigenous state resisted Mexican forces until 1870. A few Maya strongholds survived until 1901.

---

[3] Quoted in Brian Loveman, *Chile: The Legacy of Hispanic Capitalism* (New York: Oxford University Press, 1979), 170.

THE CHALLENGE OF SOCIAL AND ECONOMIC CHANGE

During the nineteenth century the newly independent nations of the Western Hemisphere struggled to realize the Enlightenment ideals of freedom and individual liberty that had helped ignite the revolutions for independence. The persistence of slavery and other oppressive colonial-era institutions slowed this process. Nevertheless, by century's end reform movements had ended the slave trade, abolished slavery, expanded voting rights, and assimilated immigrants from Asia and Europe.

Industrialization and integration in the world economy sometimes challenged political stability and social arrangements. While a small number of Western Hemisphere nations embraced industrialization, most were dependent on the export of agricultural and mining production. By the end of the century it was clear that the industrializing nations had grown richer than the nations that remained exporters of raw materials. All the region's economies, regardless of development path, had become more vulnerable and volatile as a result of greater dependence on foreign markets. Like contemporary movements for social reform, efforts to assert economic sovereignty produced powerful new political forces.

The Abolition of Slavery Leaders of the independence movements of the United States and Latin America asserted ideals of universal freedom and citizenship that contrasted sharply with the reality of slavery. Those who sought to end the institution were called **abolitionists**. Despite their efforts, slavery survived in most of the hemisphere until the 1850s. It proved especially difficult to eradicate in regions where the export of plantation products was most important—such as the United States, Brazil, and Cuba.

Slavery in the United States was weakened first by the abolition of slavery in some northern states and by the end of the African slave trade in 1808. But the profitable expansion of cotton agriculture after the War of 1812 stalled further progress. In Spanish America tens of thousands of slaves gained freedom by joining revolutionary armies during the wars for independence (see Chapter 23). After independence, most Spanish American republics prohibited the slave trade, but growing international demand for sugar and coffee slowed the achievement of abolition. As prices rose for plantation products, Brazil and Cuba increased their imports of slaves.

During the long struggle to end slavery in the United States, American abolitionists argued that slavery offended Christian morality and the universal rights asserted in the Declaration of Independence. Abolitionist Theodore Weld articulated the religious objection to slavery in 1834:

> No condition of birth, no shade of color, no mere misfortune of circumstance, can annul the birth-right charter, which God has bequeathed to every being upon whom he has stamped his own image, by making him a free moral agent [emphasis in original], and that he who robs his fellow man of this tramples upon right, subverts justice, outrages humanity ... and sacrilegiously assumes the prerogative of God.[4]

---

[4] Quoted in Bernard Bailyn, David Brion Davis, David Herbert Donald, John L. Thomas, Robert H. Wiebe, and Gordon S. Wood, *The Great Republic: A History of the American People* (Lexington, MA: D. C. Heath, 1981), 398.

Two groups denied full rights under the Constitution, women and free African Americans, played important roles in the abolition of slavery. Women were among the leaders of the American Anti-Slavery Society and produced effective propaganda against slavery. Eventually, thousands of women joined the abolitionist cause. Social conservatives attacked their highly visible public role, leading many women to become public advocates of female suffrage as well. Frederick Douglass, a former slave, was one of the most visible and effective leaders of the abolitionist movement. Some black leaders, believing that peaceful means would fail, pushed the abolitionist movement to accept the inevitability of violence. In 1843 Henry Highland Garnet stirred the National Colored Convention when he demanded, "Brethren, arise, arise, arise! ... Let every slave in the land do this and the days of slavery are numbered."[5]

In the 1850s the electoral strength of the newly formed Republican Party forced a confrontation between slave and free states. Following the election of Abraham Lincoln in 1860, eleven southern states seceded from the Union. During the Civil War pressure for emancipation rose as tens of thousands of black freemen and escaped slaves joined the Union army. In 1863, in the midst of the Civil War and two years after the abolition of serfdom in Russia (see Chapter 27), Lincoln issued the Emancipation Proclamation, ending slavery in rebel states not occupied by the Union army. In 1865 the Thirteenth Amendment to the Constitution abolished slavery completely, but most African Americans continued to live in harsh conditions. By the end of the century southern states had instituted "Jim Crow" laws that segregated blacks in public transportation, jobs, and schools. The implementation of these laws coincided with increased racial violence that saw an average of fifty African Americans lynched each year.

In Brazil slavery survived for more than two decades after abolition in the United States. Britain, Brazil's major trading partner, pressed for an end to the slave trade after prohibiting this trade to its own colonies. Despite agreeing to end the trade in 1830, Brazil imported another half-million African slaves before the British navy forced compliance in the 1850s. The Brazilian emperor, Pedro II, and many liberals worked to abolish slavery, but their effort to find a form of gradual emancipation acceptable to slave owners failed.

During Brazil's war with Paraguay (1865–1870), large numbers of slaves joined the Brazilian army in exchange for freedom. Their patriotism and heroism convinced many Brazilians of the injustice of slavery. Educated Brazilians had also come to view slavery as an obstacle to economic development and as an impediment to democratic reform. As political support for slavery weakened in the 1880s, growing numbers of slaves fled their masters and army officers resisted demands to capture and return the runaways. Brazil finally abolished slavery in 1888. A year later a rebellion ended the Brazilian monarchy.

The Caribbean received almost 40 percent of all African slaves shipped to the New World. Throughout the region, tiny white minorities lived surrounded by slave and free colored majorities. In the eighteenth century the slave rebellion in Saint Domingue (see Chapter 23) spread terror among slave owners across the

---

[5] Quoted in Mary Beth Norton et al., *A People and a Nation: A History of the United States*, 6th ed. (Boston: Houghton Mifflin, 2001), 284.

Caribbean, convincing slave owners that any effort to overthrow colonial rule would unleash new insurrections. As a result, there was little local support for abolition in the Caribbean. In these colonies abolition would result from decisions made in Europe by imperial governments.

In the Caribbean, as in Brazil and other plantation economies, slaves helped to force abolition by rebelling, running away, and resisting in more subtle ways. Although slave rebellions in Jamaica and Cuba and other Caribbean colonies failed to achieve the success of the Haitian Revolution (1791–1804), they made clear that slaves would never accept their condition.

After 1800, when the profitability of sugar plantations in the British West Indian colonies declined, a coalition of British labor unions, Protestant ministers, and free traders pushed for the abolition of slavery. Britain, the major participant in the eighteenth-century expansion of slavery in the Americas, ended its participation in the slave trade in 1807. It then negotiated treaties with Spain, Brazil, and other importers of slaves to eliminate the slave trade and used its naval forces to force compliance.

Abolition in British colonies occurred in 1834, but "freed" slaves were compelled to remain with former masters as "apprentices." Abuses by planters and resistance to apprenticeship by former slaves led to complete abolition in 1838. A decade later, France abolished slavery in its Caribbean colonies. The decision to abolish slavery in the Dutch Empire in 1863 freed 33,000 slaves in Surinam and 12,000 in the Antilles.

In the Caribbean, slavery lasted longest in Spain's remaining colonies of Cuba and Puerto Rico. Britain used diplomatic pressure and naval force to undermine the slave trade after 1820, but local support for abolition appeared as well. Both Cuba and Puerto Rico had larger white and free colored populations than did the Caribbean colonies of Britain and France, and there was little fear that abolition would lead to the political ascendancy of former slaves. In Puerto Rico, where slaves numbered approximately 30,000, local reformers secured the abolition of slavery in 1873. In Cuba, where slavery was much more important because of a booming sugar industry, forces supporting independence helped propel the Spanish colonial government toward abolition (see Environment and Technology: Industrializing Sugar Agriculture in Cuba). Beginning in the 1870s, Spain passed a series of laws promoting gradual abolition but requiring long periods of service to former masters. Spain finally abolished slavery in 1886.

Immigration   During the colonial period free Europeans were a minority among immigrants to the Western Hemisphere. From 1500 to 1760 imported African slaves outnumbered European immigrants in the Western Hemisphere by nearly two to one. Another 4 million African slaves were then imported before the end of the slave trade in the 1850s. After the African slave trade came to an end, millions of Europeans and Asians arrived in the Western Hemisphere as immigrants. This new flood of immigrants in the nineteenth century helped foster the rapid economic growth and territorial occupation of frontier regions in the United States, Canada, Argentina, Chile, and Brazil. By century's end nearly all of the hemisphere's fastest-growing cities (Buenos Aires, Chicago, New York, and São Paulo, for example) had large immigrant populations.

In general, European immigrants avoided regions that had depended on slavery with their traditions of oppressive labor conditions and low wages. At the same time, tens of thousands of immigrants from China and India arrived with indenture contracts that directed them to plantation zones in the Caribbean region.

Europe provided the majority of immigrants to the Western Hemisphere in the nineteenth century. Initially, most came from western Europe, but after 1870 most immigrants were southern or eastern Europeans. The United States received approximately 600,000 European immigrants in the 1830s, 1.5 million in the 1840s, and then 2.5 million per decade until 1880. In the 1890s an astonishing total of 5.2 million immigrants arrived. Immigration helped push the national population from 39 million in 1871 to 63 million in 1891. Most of these immigrants settled in cities. Chicago, for example, grew from 444,000 in 1870 to 1.7 million in 1900.

European immigration to Latin America also increased dramatically. Combined immigration to Argentina and Brazil rose from under 130,000 in the 1860s to 1.7 million in the 1890s. By 1910, 30 percent of the Argentine population was foreign-born, more than twice the proportion in the U.S. population. Argentina was an extremely attractive destination for European immigrants, receiving more than twice as many immigrants as Canada between 1870 and 1930. Even so, immigration to Canada increased tenfold during this period.

Asian immigration to the Western Hemisphere also increased after 1850. Between 1849 and 1875, approximately 100,000 Chinese immigrants arrived in Peru and another 120,000 entered Cuba. Canada attracted about 50,000 Chinese immigrants in the second half of the century, and the United States received 300,000 Chinese immigrants between 1854 and 1882. India also contributed to the social transformation of the Western Hemisphere, sending more than a half-million immigrants to the Caribbean region. British Guiana alone received 238,000 immigrants, mostly indentured laborers, from the Asian subcontinent.

Despite the obvious economic benefits that accompanied this inflow of people, hostility to immigration mounted in many nations. Nativist political movements argued that it was impossible to integrate large numbers of foreigners into national political cultures. By the end of the century, fear and prejudice led many governments in the Western Hemisphere to limit immigration or to distinguish between "desirable" and "undesirable" immigrants, commonly favoring Europeans over Asians.

Asians faced more obstacles than did Europeans and were more often victims of violence and discrimination. In the 1870s and 1880s anti-Chinese riots erupted in many western cities in the United States. Congress responded to this wave of racism by passing the Chinese Exclusion Act in 1882, which eliminated most Chinese immigration. In 1886, popular fears that "inferior races" threatened Canada led that government to impose a head tax, making immigration more difficult for Chinese families. During this same period strong anti-Chinese prejudice surfaced in Peru, Mexico, and Cuba. Japanese immigrants in Brazil and East Indians in the English-speaking Caribbean faced similar prejudice.

European immigrants faced prejudice and discrimination as well. Popular opinion portrayed Italians as criminals or anarchists. In Argentina and the United States, some social scientists argued that Italian immigrants were more violent and less honest than the native-born population. Immigrants from Spain were widely stereotyped in Argentina as miserly and dishonest. Eastern European Jews seeking to

Archivo General de la Nación, Buenos Aires

Arrest of Labor Activist in Buenos Aires *The labor movement in Buenos Aires grew in numbers and became more radical with the arrival of tens of thousands of Italian and Spanish immigrants. Fearful of socialist and anarchist unions, the government of Argentina used an expanded police force to break strikes.*

escape pogroms and discrimination at home found themselves barred from many educational institutions and professional careers in both the United States and Latin America. Irish, German, Swedish, Polish, and Middle Eastern immigrants were branded with negative stereotypes as well. The justifications for these prejudices were remarkably similar from Canada to Argentina. Immigrants, critics claimed, threatened the well-being of native-born workers by accepting low wages and threatened national culture by resisting assimilation.

Many intellectuals and political leaders wondered if the evolving mix of culturally diverse populations could sustain a common citizenship. This concern led to efforts to compel immigrants to assimilate. Schools became cultural battlegrounds where language, cultural values, and patriotic attitudes were transmitted to the children of immigrants. Ignoring Canada's large French-speaking population, an English-speaking Canadian reformer commented on recent immigration: "If Canada is to become in a real sense a nation, if our people are to become one people, we must have one language."[6] These fears and prejudices promoted the singing of patriotic songs, the veneration of national flags and other symbols, and the writing of national histories that emphasized patriotism and civic virtue.

---

[6] J. S. Woodsworth in 1909, quoted in R. Douglas Francis, Richard Jones, and Donald B. Smith, *Destinies: Canadian History Since Confederation*, 2d ed. (Toronto: Holt, Rinehart and Winston, 1992), 141.

American Cultures   Despite discrimination, immigrants continued to stream into the Western Hemisphere, where they introduced new languages, living arrangements, technologies, and customs. Immigrants also altered politics in many of the hemisphere's nations as they sought to influence government policies and gain access to power. To compensate for their isolation from home, language, and culture, most immigrant groups created ethnically based mutual aid societies, sports and leisure clubs, and neighborhoods. These organizations provided valuable social and economic support for recent arrivals while sometimes worsening the fears of the native-born that immigration posed a threat to national culture. At the same time, shared experiences in their adopted nations as workers, neighbors, or soldiers changed immigrants individually and collectively. The modification of language, customs, values, and behaviors as a result of contact with people from another culture is called **acculturation**.

Immigrants and their children, in turn, made their mark on the cultures of their adopted nations. They learned the language spoken in their adopted countries as fast as possible in order to improve their earning capacity, while words and phrases from their languages entered the vocabularies of their adoptive nations. Languages as diverse as Yiddish and Italian strongly influenced American English, Argentine Spanish, and Brazilian Portuguese. Dietary practices introduced from Europe and Asia altered the cuisine of nearly every American nation. In popular music, the Argentine tango, based on African rhythms, was transformed by new instrumentation and orchestral arrangements brought by Italian immigrants. Mexican ballads blended with English folk music in the U.S. Southwest, and Italian operas played to packed houses in Buenos Aires.

Union movements and electoral politics in the hemisphere also felt the influence of new arrivals who aggressively sought to influence politics and improve working conditions. The anarchist and socialist beliefs of European immigrants influenced the labor movements of Mexico, Argentina, and the United States. Immigrants also helped form new political movements. Their mutual benevolent societies and less formal ethnic associations pooled resources to help immigrants open businesses, aid the immigration of relatives, or bury family members.

Women's Rights and the Struggle for Social Justice   In 1848, a group of women angered by their exclusion from an international antislavery meeting issued a call for a conference to discuss women's rights. The resulting **Women's Rights Convention** at Seneca Falls, New York, issued a statement that said, in part, "We hold these truths to be self-evident: that all men and women are equal." While moderates focused on the issues of economic independence and legal rights, increasing numbers of women demanded the right to vote. Others lobbied to provide better conditions for women working outside the home, especially in textile factories. Sarah Grimké responded to criticism of women's activism:

> This has been the language of man since he laid aside the whip as a means to keep woman in subjection. He spares her body, but the war he has waged against her mind, her heart, and her soul, has been no less destructive to her as a moral being. How monstrous is the doctrine that woman is to be dependent on man![7]

---

[7] Sarah Grimké, "Reply to the Massachusetts Clergy," in *Early American Women: A Documentary History*, 1600–1900, ed. Nancy Woloch (Belmont, CA: Wadsworth, 1992), 343.

Progress toward equality between men and women was equally slow in Canada and in Latin America. Canada's first women doctors received their training in the United States because women could not receive medical degrees until 1895. Argentina and Uruguay were among the first Latin American nations to provide public education for women, introducing coeducation in the 1870s. Chilean women gained access to some careers in medicine and law in the 1870s, while in Brazil the first women graduated in medicine in 1882. In Argentina the first woman doctor graduated from medical school in 1899.

Throughout the hemisphere more rapid progress occurred in lower-status careers that threatened male economic power less directly, and, by the end of the century, women dominated elementary school teaching. From Canada to Argentina and Chile, the majority of working-class women, although having no direct involvement in reform movements, succeeded in transforming gender relations in their daily lives. By the end of the nineteenth century, large numbers of poor women worked outside the home on farms, in markets, and, increasingly, in factories. Many bore full responsibility for providing for their children. Whether men thought women should remain in the home or not, by the end of the century women were unambiguously present in the economy (see also Chapter 27).

There was little progress toward eliminating racial discrimination in the nineteenth century. Blacks were denied the vote throughout the southern United States and were subjected to the indignity of segregation—consigned to separate schools, hotels, restaurants, seats in public transportation, and even water fountains. Racial discrimination against men and women of African descent was also common in Latin America. Unlike the southern states of the United States, however, Latin American nations did not insist on formal racial segregation or permit lynching. Nor did they enforce a strict color line. Many men and women of mixed background were able to enter the skilled working class or middle class, and some rose to political prominence. Latin Americans tended to view racial identity across a continuum of physical characteristics rather than in the narrow terms of black and white that defined race relations in the United States.

The abolition of slavery in Latin America did not end discrimination. Some leaders of the abolition struggles later organized to promote racial integration. They demanded access to education, the right to vote, and greater economic opportunity, pointing out the economic and political costs of denying full rights to all citizens. Their success depended on effective political organization and on forging alliances with sympathetic white politicians. Black intellectuals also struggled to overturn racist stereotypes. In Brazil, Argentina, and Cuba, as in the United States, political and literary magazines celebrating black cultural achievement became powerful weapons in the struggle against racial discrimination. While men and women of African descent continued to experience prejudice and discrimination everywhere in the Americas, successful men and women of mixed descent in Latin America confronted fewer obstacles to advancement than did similar groups in the United States.

Development and Underdevelopment   While the Atlantic economy experienced three periods of severe economic contraction during the nineteenth century, nearly all the nations of the Western Hemisphere were richer in 1900 than in 1800. The effects of the Industrial Revolution, worldwide population growth, and an increasingly integrated world market combined to stimulate economic expansion (see Environment and Technology: Industrializing Sugar Agriculture in Cuba). Wheat, corn, wool, meats, and nonprecious minerals joined the region's earlier exports of silver, sugar, dyes, coffee, and cotton. The United States was the only Western Hemisphere nation to industrialize, but nearly every government promoted new industries and technologies. Governments invested in roads, railroads, canals, and telegraph systems to better serve distant markets, while adopting tariff and monetary policies to foster economic diversification and growth. Despite these efforts, by 1900 only three Western Hemisphere nations—the United States, Canada, and Argentina—achieved individual income levels similar to those of western Europe. All three nations had open land, temperate climates, diverse resources, and large inflows of immigrants.

New demands for copper, zinc, lead, coal, and tin unleashed by the Industrial Revolution led to mining booms in the western United States, Mexico, and Chile. The mining companies of the late nineteenth century were heavily capitalized international corporations that could bully governments and buy political favors. By 1900 European and North American corporations owned nearly all the largest mining enterprises in Latin America. Petroleum development, which occurred at the end of the century in Mexico and elsewhere, followed this pattern as well (see the discussion of the Mexican economy during the Díaz dictatorship in Chapter 26).

New technology accelerated economic integration, but the high cost of this technology often increased dependence on foreign capital. Many governments promoted railroads by granting tax benefits, free land, and monopoly rights to both domestic and foreign investors. As a result, by 1890 vast areas of the Great Plains in the United States, the Canadian prairie, the Argentine pampas, and parts of northern Mexico were producing grain and livestock for foreign markets opened by the development of railroads. Steamships also lowered the cost of transportation to distant markets, and the telegraph stimulated expansion by speeding information about the demand for and availability of products.

The simultaneous acquisition of several new technologies could have a dramatic effect on a nation's economy. In Argentina, for example, the railroad, the telegraph, barbed wire, and refrigeration were all introduced in the 1870s and 1880s. Although Argentina had had abundant livestock herds since the colonial period, the distance from Europe's markets prevented Argentine cattle raisers from exporting fresh meat or live animals. Technology overcame these obstacles. The combination of railroads and the telegraph lowered freight costs and improved information about markets, steamships shortened the time needed for transatlantic crossings, and refrigerated ships made it possible to sell meat in distant markets. As land values rose and livestock breeding improved, ranchers protected new investments with barbed wire, the first inexpensive fencing available on the nearly treeless plains.

Growing interdependence and increased competition produced deep structural differences among Western Hemisphere economies by 1900. Two distinct economic tracks became visible. One led to industrialization and prosperity: **development**. The other continued colonial dependence on exporting raw materials and on low-wage industries: **underdevelopment**. By 1900 prosperity was greater and economic development more diversified in English-speaking North America than in the nations of Latin America. With a temperate climate, vast fertile prairies, and an influx of European immigrants, Argentina was the only Latin American nation to approach the prosperity of the United States and Canada in 1900.

ENVIRONMENT + TECHNOLOGY

Industrializing Sugar Agriculture in Cuba

Sugar played a key role in the development of the Western Hemisphere, with the profits of sugar plantations rivaling the vast wealth in silver and gold extracted from Spain's colonial empire. The expansion of sugar agriculture from Brazil to the Caribbean was the major driving force in the African slave trade until its effective end in the 1850s. The fact that 70 percent of all African slaves brought to the Americas were distributed to sugar-producing regions is one measure

Cuban Sugar Refinery Showing Mix of Traditional and Modern Technologies *Sugar cane was delivered to the crushing mill by both ox carts and railroad lines. In the background, steam-driven machinery moves cane to a crusher.*

Changes in the performance of international markets helped determine the trajectory of Western Hemisphere economies as new nations promoted economic development. When the United States gained independence, the world economy enjoyed rapid growth. With a large merchant fleet, a diversified economy that included some manufacturing, and adequate banking and insurance services, the United States benefited from this expansion. Rapid population growth due in large measure to immigration, high levels of individual wealth, widespread landownership, and of sugar's influence in the hemisphere. When most of Haiti's sugar plantations were destroyed by revolutionary violence, world sugar prices shot upward in the early nineteenth century. Cuban planters jumped into the vacuum, importing tens of thousands of slaves and opening new lands to sugar production. Within two decades, Cuba had become the world's largest sugar producer.

Cuba's sugar industry soon confronted two challenges to its ascendency. Having already ended the slave trade to its own sugar islands in 1807, Great Britain pushed Spain to end the slave trade to Cuba, ultimately using its navy to reduce imports to a trickle. Almost simultaneously, new technologies were introduced in Europe that permitted the profitable extraction of sugar from beets. As a result, labor became more expensive for Cuban planters at the same time that sugar prices fell internationally. To remain profitable, the Cuban sugar industry embraced technological innovations that had earlier revolutionized manufacturing.

Planters with the largest estates and the largest numbers of slaves had always enjoyed a competitive advantage over smaller producers because they could afford the most efficient crushing and refining technologies, benefiting from what economists call economies of scale (see Chapter 19). With beet sugar production driving prices lower, Cuba's large-scale producers displaced their less efficient competitors while at the same opening virgin land to sugar production.

Between 1878 and 1900 alone, more than 1.4 million acres of forest were lost to the expanding sugar plantations. As lower prices increased competition and as the volume of sugar production soared in Cuba, the number of sugar producers steadily decreased, a pattern that neither political violence nor the abolition of slavery (1886) could alter.

Concentration was also promoted by the high cost of mechanization. The most heavily capitalized producers imported steam engines to replace the animal traction and water power previously used to crush cane and then introduced new, more efficient refining technologies. As crushing and refining capacities expanded in the modern mills, called *centrales* in Spanish, small-scale producers closed their expensive and inefficient mills to concentrate on growing sugar cane. Railroad construction multiplied the effects of these innovations, tying distant sugar growers to the mechanized refiners, many of them foreign owned. As had happened in English textile manufacturing during the Industrial Revolution (see Chapter 22), technological innovation in Cuba's sugar industry had concentrated the control of production and wealth in the hands of a new elite. The centrales were truly factories in the fields. As Cuba neared independence in the 1890s, the island's modernized sugar sector consisted of a relatively small number of industrialized refiners and a mass of increasingly vulnerable and dependent cane farmers.

relatively high literacy rates also fostered rapid economic development. By 1865 the United States had already established the world's largest railroad network, but by 1915 railroad mileage had multiplied elevenfold. Steel production grew rapidly as well, with the United States overtaking world leaders Britain and Germany in the 1890s.

Canada's achievement of greater political autonomy, the Confederation of 1867, coincided with a second period of global economic expansion. Canada also benefited from a special trading relationship with Britain, the world's preeminent industrial nation, and from a rising tide of immigrants after 1850. Nevertheless, some regions within each of these prosperous North American nations—Canada's Maritime Provinces and the southern part of the United States—demonstrated the same patterns of underdevelopment found in Latin America.

Most Latin American nations gained independence in the 1820s when the global economy contracted. In the colonial period, Spain and Portugal had promoted the production of agricultural and mining exports in their colonies. After independence these exports faced increased competition. Although these sectors experienced periods of great prosperity in the nineteenth century, they also faced stiff competition and falling prices as new regions began production or competing products captured markets.

The history of the Latin American economies, subject to periodic problems of oversupply and low prices, was one of boom and bust. Many Latin American governments sought to promote exports in the face of increased competition and falling prices by resisting union activity and demands for higher wages and by opening domestic markets to foreign manufactures. The resulting low wages and an abundance of foreign manufactured goods, in turn, undermined efforts to promote industrialization in Latin America.

Weak governments, political instability, and, in some cases, civil war also slowed Latin American economic development. Because Latin America was also dependent on importing foreign capital and technology, Great Britain and, by the end of the century, the United States often imposed unfavorable trade conditions or even intervened militarily to protect their investments. The combined impact of these domestic and international impediments to development became clear when Mexico, Chile, and Argentina failed to achieve high levels of domestic investment in manufacturing late in the nineteenth century, despite a rapid accumulation of wealth derived from traditional exports.

Altered Environments

Population growth, economic expansion, new technologies, and the introduction of foreign plants and animals dramatically altered American environments in the nineteenth century. Cuba's planters cut down the island's forests in the early nineteenth century to expand sugar production. Growing demand for meat led ranchers to expand livestock-raising into fragile environments in Argentina, Uruguay, southern Brazil, and the southwestern United States. Other forms of commercial agriculture also threatened the environment. Farmers in South Carolina and Georgia gained a short-term increase in cotton production by abandoning crop rotation after 1870, but this practice quickly led to soil exhaustion and erosion. Similarly, coffee planters in Brazil exhausted fertility with a destructive cycle of overplanting followed by expansion onto forest reserves cleared by cutting and burning. The transfers of land from public to private ownership in order to promote livestock-raising and agriculture also altered landscapes. Finally, new technologies had environmental effects. For example, the use of steel plows on North American prairies and Argentine pampas eliminated many native grasses and increased the threat of soil erosion.

Rapid urbanization also imposed environmental costs. New York, Chicago, Rio de Janeiro, Buenos Aires, and Mexico City were among the world's fastest-growing cities in the nineteenth century, and governments strained to provide sewers, clean water, and garbage disposal. Timber companies clear-cut large areas of Michigan, Wisconsin, and the Appalachian Mountains in the United States to provide lumber for railroad ties and housing, pulp for paper, and fuel for locomotives and foundries. At the same time, the forest industries of British Honduras (now Belize), Nicaragua, and Guatemala grew rapidly in response to demand in Europe and North America for tropical hardwoods like mahogany. As forests throughout the hemisphere were cleared, animal habitats and native plant species disappeared.

The scale of mining in Nevada, Montana, and California accelerated erosion and pollution. Similar results occurred in other mining areas as well. Nitrate mining and open-pit copper mining in Chile scarred and polluted the environment. The state of Minas Gerais (ME-nas JER-aize) in Brazil experienced a series of mining booms that began with gold in the late seventeenth century and continued with iron ore in the nineteenth. By the end of the nineteenth century, its red soil had been ripped open, its forests were depleted, and erosion was uncontrolled. Similar devastation afflicted parts of Bolivia and Mexico.

By the end of the nineteenth century, small-scale conservation efforts were under way in many nations, and the first national parks and nature reserves were created. In the United States large areas remained undeveloped. In 1872 Yellowstone in Wyoming became the first national park. President Theodore Roosevelt (1901–1909) and the naturalist John Muir played major roles in preserving large areas of the western states. Canada created its first national park in Banff in 1885 and expanded it from 10 to 260 square miles (26 to 673 square kilometers) two years later. When confronted with a choice between economic growth and environmental protection, however, the hemisphere's nations embraced growth.

Conclusion

While the new nations of the Western Hemisphere faced similar challenges in the nineteenth century, they had developed from different colonial traditions. The effort to establish stable constitutional systems proved difficult nearly everywhere. While the constitution of the United States endured, conflict over slavery led to a civil war that threatened the nation's survival. Elsewhere most new constitutions failed within a generation. In Argentina, for example, fifty years passed before a stable national government was in place. Personalist political leaders with large followings, like José Antonio Páez and Andrew Jackson, resisted the constraints of constitutions. Regionalism, ideological confrontations, racial divisions, and conflict with native peoples all threatened stability as well.

New nations also faced foreign interventions and local wars with regional powers. By 1850, Mexico had lost 50 percent of its territory to the United States and then faced a French invasion in 1862. Bolivia and Peru lost territory to an expansive Chile, while Paraguay lost a disastrous war to an alliance of Argentina, Brazil, and Uruguay. American nations also fought numerous wars with indigenous peoples, crushing resistance by the 1890s.

The nations of the hemisphere also experienced a series of dramatic social and economic changes in this period. The slave trade and slavery persisted long after independence (see Chapter 19), but after a century of protest and political mobilization, the hemisphere's last slave state, Brazil, freed its slaves in 1888. Slavery left a legacy of racism and discrimination across the Americas. In places where the institution was most important—the plantation regions of Brazil, the Caribbean, and the American South—racial prejudice, discrimination, and persistent low levels of investment in education and internal improvements slowed economic growth and weakened democracy. By 1890 many of the hemisphere's poorest nations or poorest regions within nations were those that had depended on slavery.

Amerindian populations experienced centuries of exploitation, forced integration in market economies, and compulsory removal to marginal lands. In most of Latin America, Amerindians had been subjected to exploitation for centuries when the Spanish and Portuguese empires finally fell. Once in place, forced labor and other abuses persisted into the twentieth century in nations like Guatemala and Bolivia. With independence, new national governments undertook the pacification of the hemisphere's remaining independent native peoples. By the 1890s nearly all were reduced to reservations or forced onto marginal lands. As a result, Amerindians were among the poorest peoples in the hemisphere, suffering oppression, poverty, and disenfranchisement.

Immigration transformed many Western Hemisphere nations. As a general rule, the millions of European immigrants that entered the Western Hemisphere in the nineteenth century avoided regions where slavery dominated or where indigenous populations were compelled to labor. Argentina, Brazil, Canada, and the United States were the most popular destinations, and immigrants to Brazil and the United States avoided the former plantation zones. Instead, hundreds of thousands of Chinese and East Indians, migrating as indentured laborers, were directed to plantation regions, especially in the Caribbean, where they faced racism and discrimination.

Industrialization had a transforming effect on the hemisphere. Wealth, political power, and population were increasingly concentrated in urban areas, and bankers and manufacturers, rather than farmers and plantation owners, increasingly directed national destinies. Industrialization altered the natural environment in dramatic ways. Modern factories consumed huge amounts of raw materials and energy. Copper mines in Chile and Mexico, Cuban sugar plantations, Brazilian coffee plantations, and Canadian lumber companies all left their mark on the natural environment, and all had ties to markets in the United States.

In 1900 nearly every American nation was wealthier, better educated, more democratic, and more populous than at independence. But most of these new nations were also more vulnerable to distant economic forces and more profoundly split between haves and have-nots. The hemisphere was also more clearly divided into a rich north and a poorer south. A small number of nations located in the temperate regions—Canada, the United States, Argentina, and Chile—had become prosperous regional powers relative to their neighbors. While most of the hemisphere's growth continued to depend on the export of agricultural goods and raw materials—sugar, cotton, grains, minerals, and livestock products—the United States had become one of the world's richest industrial nations by 1890.

IMPORTANT EVENTS 1800–1890

1789	U.S. Constitution ratified
1803	Louisiana Purchase
1808	Portuguese royal family arrives in Brazil
1808–1809	Revolutions for independence begin in Spanish South America
1810–1821	Mexican movement for independence
1812–1815	War of 1812
1822	Brazil gains independence
1831	Brazil signs treaty with Great Britain to end slave trade. Illegal trade continues.
1836	Texas gains independence from Mexico
1845	Texas admitted as a state
1846–1848	War between Mexico and the United States
1847–1870	Caste War
1848	Women's Rights Convention in Seneca Falls, New York
1850	Brazilian illegal slave trade suppressed
1857	Mexico's new constitution limits power of Catholic Church and military
1861–1865	Civil War
1862–1867	French invade Mexico
1865–1870	Argentina, Uruguay, and Brazil wage war against Paraguay
1867	Creation of Dominion of Canada
1867	Emperor Maximilian executed
1870s	Governments of Argentina and Chile begin final campaigns against indigenous peoples
1876	Sioux and allies defeat U.S. Army in Battle of Little Bighorn
1879–1881	Chile wages war against Peru and Bolivia; telegraph, refrigeration, and barbed wire introduced in Argentina
1888	Abolition of slavery in Brazil
1890	"Jim Crow" laws enforce segregation in South
1890s	United States becomes world's leading steel producer

State Power, the Census, and the Question of Identity

Between the American Revolution and the last decades of the nineteenth century, Europe and the Americas were transformed. The ancient power of kings and the authority of religion were eclipsed by muscular new ways of organizing political, economic, and intellectual life. The Western world was vastly different in 1870 than it had been a century earlier. One of the less heralded but enduringly significant changes was the huge expansion of government statistical services.

The rise of the nation-state was associated with the development of modern bureaucratic departments that depended on reliable statistics to measure the nation's achievements and discover its failures. The nation-state, whether democratic or not, mobilized resources on a previously unimaginable scale. Modern states were more powerful and wealthier, and they were also more ambitious and more intrusive. The growth of their power can be seen in the modernization of militaries, the commitment to internal improvements such as railroads, and the growth in state revenues. In recent years historians have begun to examine a less visible but equally important manifestation of growing state power: census taking.

Governments and religious authorities have counted people since early times. Our best estimates of the Amerindian population of the Western Hemisphere in 1500 rest almost entirely on what were little more than missionaries' guesses about the numbers of people they baptized. Spanish and Portuguese kings were eager to count native populations, since "indios" (adult male Amerindians) were subject to special labor obligations and tribute payments. So, from the mid-sixteenth century onward, imperial officials conducted regular censuses of Amerindians, adapting practices already in place in Europe.

The effort to measure and categorize populations was transformed in the last decades of the eighteenth century when the nature of European governments began to change. The Enlightenment belief that the scientific method could be applied to human society proved to be attractive both to political radicals, like the French revolutionaries, and to reforming monarchs like Maria Theresa of Austria. Enlightenment philosophers had argued that a science of government could remove the inefficiencies and irrationalities that had long subverted the human potential for prosperity and happiness. The French intellectual Condorcet wrote in 1782:

Those sciences, created almost in our own days, the object of which is man himself, the direct goal of which is the happiness of man, will enjoy a progress no less sure than that of the physical sciences. . . . In meditating on the nature of the moral sciences [what we now call the social sciences], one cannot help seeing that, as they are based like the physical sciences on the observation of fact, they must follow the method, acquire a language equally exact and precise, attaining the same degree of certainty.[1]

As confidence in this new "science" grew, the term previously used to describe the collection of numbers about society, *political arithmetic*, was abandoned by governments and practitioners in favor of *statistics*, a term that clearly suggests its close ties to the "state." In the nineteenth century the new objectives set out by Condorcet and others led to both the formal university training of statisticians and the creation of government statistical services.

The ambitions of governments in this new era were great. Nation-states self-consciously sought to transform society, sponsoring economic development, education, and improvements in health and welfare. They depended on statistics to measure the effectiveness of their policies and, as a result, were interested in nearly everything. They counted taverns, urban buildings, births and deaths, and arrests and convictions. They also counted their populations with a thoroughness never before seen. As statistical reporting became more uniform across Europe and the Americas, governments could measure not only their own progress but also that of their neighbors and rivals.

The revolutionary governments of France modernized the census practices of the overthrown monarchy. They spent much more money, hired many more census takers, and devoted much more energy to training the staff that designed censuses and analyzed results. Great Britain set up an official census in 1801, but it established a special administrative structure only in the 1830s. In the Western Hemisphere nearly every independent nation provided for "scientific" censuses. In the United States the federal constitution required that a census be taken every ten years. Latin American nations, often torn by civil war in the nineteenth century, took censuses less regularly, but even the poorest nations took censuses when they could. It was as if the census itself confirmed the existence of the government, demonstrating its modernity and seriousness.

Until recently, historians who relied on these documents in their research on economic performance, issues of race and ethnicity, family life, and fertility and mortality asked few questions about the politics of census design. What could be more objective than rows of numbers? But the advocates of statistics who managed census taking were uninhibited in advertising the usefulness of reliable numbers to the governments that employed them. At the 1860 International Statistical Congress held in London, one speaker said, "I think the true meaning to be attached to 'statistics' is not every collection of figures, but figures collected with the sole purpose of applying the principles deduced from them to questions of importance to the state."[2] The desire to be useful meant that statistics could not be fully objective.

Subjectivity was an unavoidable problem with censuses. Censuses identified citizens and foreign residents by place of residence, sex, age, and family relationships within households as well as profession and literacy. These determinations were sometimes subjective. Modern scholars have demonstrated that census takers also routinely undercounted the poor and those living in rural areas.

Because census takers, as agents of nation-states, were determined to be useful, they were necessarily concerned with issues of nationality and, in the Americas, with race because these characteristics commonly determined political rights and citizenship. The assessment and recording of nationality and race would prove to be among the most politically dubious objectives of the new social sciences.

Nationality had not been a central question for traditional monarchies. For the emerging nation-state, however, nationality was central. A nation's strength was assumed to depend in large measure on the growth of its population, a standard that, once articulated, suggested that the growth of minority populations was dangerous. Who was French? Who was Austrian or Hungarian? European statisticians relied on both *language of use* and *mother tongue* as proxies for *nationality*, the first term being flexible enough to recognize the assimilation of minorities, the second suggesting a more permanent identity based on a person's original language. Both terms forced bilingual populations to simplify their more complex identities. Ethnic minorities, once identified, were sometimes subject to discrimination such as exclusion from military careers or from universities. In parts of Spanish America, *language* was used as a proxy for *race*. Those who spoke Spanish were citizens in the full sense, even if they were indistinguishable from Amerindians in appearance. Those who spoke indigenous languages were "indios" and therefore subject to special taxes and labor obligations and effectively denied the right to vote.

Beyond providing a justification for continuing discrimination, census categories compressed and distorted the complexity and variety of human society to fit the preconceptions of bureaucrats and politicians. Large percentages of the residents of Mexico, Peru, and Bolivia, among other parts of the Americas, were descended from both Europeans and Amerindians and, in the Caribbean region, from Europeans and Africans. Census categories never adequately captured the complexities of these biological and cultural mixtures. We now know that the poor were often identified as "indios" or "blacks" and the better-off were often called something else—"Americanos," "criollos" (creoles), or even whites. Since this process flattened and streamlined the complexities of identity, censuses on their own are not reliable guides to the distribution of ethnicity and race in a population.

In Europe, the issue of nationality proved similarly perplexing for census takers and similarly dangerous to those identified as minorities. Linguistic and ethnic minorities had always lived among the politically dominant majorities: Jewish and Polish minorities in areas controlled by German speakers, German speakers among the French, and Serbo-Croatian speakers among Hungarians, for example. The frontiers between these minority populations and their neighbors were always porous. Sexual unions and marriages were common, and two or more generations of a family often lived together in the same household, with the elder members speaking one language and the younger members another. Who was what? In a very real sense, nationality, like race in the Americas, was ultimately fixed by the census process, as the nation-state forced a limited array of politically utilitarian categories onto the rich diversity of ethnicity and culture.

[1]Quoted in James C. Scott, *Seeing like a State. How Certain Schemes to Improve the Human Condition Have Failed* (New Haven: Yale University Press, 1998), 91.

[2]This discussion relies heavily on Eliza Johnson (now Ablovatski), "Counting and Categorizing: The Hungarian Gypsy Census of 1893" (M.A. Thesis, Columbia University, 1996), especially Chapter III. She quotes from the *Proceedings of the Sixth International Statistical Congress Held in London, 1860*, 379.

PART SEVEN

GLOBAL DIVERSITY AND DOMINANCE, 1750–1945

During the century that preceded 1830, European imperialism gained new footholds, sometimes against intense resistance, in parts of Africa and Asia. Most expansion continued earlier patterns in which European trading companies rather than governments took the initiative.

From roughly 1830 onward, formal colonies governed by state-appointed administrators and supported by European armies came to the fore in a scramble for territory in Africa and the Pacific region. By World War I Europe, the United States, and Japan collectively dominated much of the world and tried to convert other peoples to their own cultures and ways of life.

In Europe, mounting tensions led to the Great War of 1914–1918. Russia and China erupted in revolution. Soon after, the heartland of the Ottoman Empire became modern Turkey, while its Arab provinces were taken over by France and Britain.

Amidst a worldwide transformation of lifestyles brought on by new technologies, the political and economic system the European powers crafted after the war fell apart in the 1930s. While the capitalist nations fell into a depression, the Soviet Union industrialized at breakneck speed. In Germany and Japan, extremists sought to solve their countries' grievances by military conquest.

As World War II loomed, nationalists in India yearned for independence while nationalists in Latin America sought an end to foreign military interventions, increasing global economic and political tensions.

The war caused the death of millions of people and the destruction of countless cities. It also weakened Europe's overseas empires. India gained its independence in 1947. Two years later, Mao Zedong led the Chinese communists to victory. Latin American leaders embraced nationalist economic and social policies that challenged the traditional role of foreign investors. Of all the once great powers, only the United States and the Soviet Union remained to compete for global dominance.

26

VARIETIES OF IMPERIALISM IN AFRICA, INDIA, SOUTHEAST ASIA, AND LATIN AMERICA, 1750–1914

L ike many regions that looked to be coherent countries on the maps drawn by imperialism, Algeria was not a unified realm in 1830 when France landed 35,000 troops outside of Algiers. Five days later, at a cost of 6,000 dead and wounded Frenchmen, the *dey* (ruler) of Algiers, an autonomous governor ruling under Ottoman suzerainty, surrendered the city. French nationalists called the invasion a defense of French honor because three years earlier the dey had struck a French diplomat with a fly whisk during an argument over debts lingering from the Napoleonic wars, which had ended more than a decade earlier. Actually the invasion plan had been drawn up by Napoleon himself in 1808 in response to commercial interests in southern France that sought to acquire new land in North Africa.

Control of Algiers, however, did not prevent the king of Morocco from pressing a claim to rule Algeria's western region, nor did it fit the political interests of the country's five major Sufi brotherhoods, which had earlier staged revolts against Ottoman imperialism. The brotherhood that would prove the hardest for the French to defeat was the Qadiriya, which waged a sixteen-year *jihad* (holy war) that only ended in 1847 with the surrender of its leader Abd al-Qadir.

Abd al-Qadir (AHB-dahl-KAH-deer) was only twenty-five when he took over from his father as head of the brotherhood, but he had spent three years traveling in the Middle East, making the pilgrimage to Mecca, getting to know other Qadiriya leaders, and studying at famous institutions of learning in Tunis and Cairo. He had also observed the efforts of Muhammad Ali in Egypt to build a modern army and state.

The key to Abd al-Qadir's success was a network of religious centers (*zawiyas*) that trained judges and administrators and disseminated his vision of an egalitarian society that would observe Islamic law and be dominated by neither Ottoman officials nor French generals. Other Sufi brotherhoods fought separately against the French, but not as successfully.

Though Abd al-Qadir was allowed to settle in Damascus after his defeat and there pursued an eminent career as a leader of the Muslim community, his historical image is primarily one of resistance to imperialism. Like most movements elsewhere opposing imperialist aggression, Abd al-Qadir's Sufi followers could not prevail against European firepower. In the long run, however, such histories of resistance laid the ideological, if sometimes semilegendary, groundwork for anticolonial movements that would gain momentum after World War II.

Defenders of imperialism often cite the benefits of European rule in terms of railroad construction, orderly governance, integration of local production with currents of international trade, and similar economic and administrative factors. But the reputations or legends of leaders like Abd al-Qadir would eventually eclipse the memory of some of the generals and administrators who oversaw a massive increase in European imperialism starting in the late eighteenth century.

CHANGES AND EXCHANGES IN AFRICA

In the century before 1870, Africa underwent dynamic political changes and a great expansion of foreign trade. While a few indigenous African leaders held out against European imperialism, maps of Africa became increasingly tinted with pink and green, the conventional colors of British and French colonies, respectively. On the economic plane, however, as the slave trade died under British pressure, trade in other goods grew sharply. Africans consumed large quantities of machine-made textiles, and those rulers who retained a measure of independence purchased European firearms.

Southern Africa   For many centuries the Nguni (ng-GOO-nee) peoples had farmed and raised cattle in the fertile coast-lands of southeastern Africa. When drought hit the region at the beginning of the nineteenth century, an upstart military leader named Shaka (r. 1818–1828) created the **Zulu** kingdom. Strict military drill and close-combat tactics featuring ox-hide shields and lethal stabbing spears made the Zulu the most powerful and most feared fighters in southern Africa.

Shaka expanded his kingdom by raiding his African neighbors, seizing their cattle, and capturing their women and children. Breakaway military bands spread this system of warfare and state building inland to the high plateau country as far north as Lake Victoria. As the power and population of these new kingdoms increased, so too did the number of displaced and demoralized refugees around them.

To protect themselves from the Zulu, some neighboring Africans created their own states. The Swazi kingdom consolidated north of the Zulu, and the kingdom of Lesotho (luh-SOO-too) grew by attracting refugees to strongholds in southern Africa's highest mountains. Both Lesotho and Swaziland survive as independent states to this day.

Although Shaka ruled for little more than a decade, he left behind a mythic identity as well as a new kingdom. These were destined to conflict, however, with southern Africa's attractiveness to European settlers. The Cape Colony, first a Dutch possession but definitively under British rule after 1806, flourished because of Cape Town's strategic importance as a supply station for ships making the long voyages between Europe and India. With the port city came some twenty thousand descendants of Dutch and French settlers who occupied farms and ranches in its hinterland. Despite their European origins, these people thought of themselves as permanent residents of Africa and were beginning to refer to themselves as **Afrikaners** (af-rih-KAHN-uhr). British governors prohibited any expansion of the white settler frontier because such expansion invariably led to wars with indigenous Africans. This decision, along with the

Zulu in Battle Dress, 1838 *Elaborate costumes helped impress opponents with the Zulus' strength. Shown here are long-handled spears and thick leather shields.*

imposition of laws protecting African rights within Cape Colony (including the emancipation of slaves in 1834), alienated many Afrikaners.

Between 1836 and 1839 parties of Afrikaners embarked on a "Great Trek," leaving British-ruled Cape Colony for the fertile high *veld* (plateau) to the north that two decades of Zulu wars had depopulated. The Great Trek laid the foundation of three new settler colonies in southern Africa: the Afrikaners' Orange Free State and Transvaal on the high veld and the British colony of Natal on the Indian Ocean coast. Although firearms enabled the settlers to win some important battles against the Zulu and other Africans, they were still a tiny minority surrounded by the populous and powerful independent African kingdoms.

Phenomenal deposits of diamonds, gold, and copper, as well as coal and iron ore, soon added to the appeal of good pasture and farmland. The discovery of diamonds at Kimberley in 1868 lured thousands of European prospectors as well as Africans looking for work. Great Britain annexed the diamond area in 1871, angering the Afrikaners. Once in the interior, the British defeated the Xhosa (KOH-sah) people in 1877 and 1878. Then in 1879 they confronted the Zulu, militarily the most powerful of the African peoples in the region.

The Zulu, led by their king Cetshwayo (set-SHWAH-yo), resented their encirclement by Afrikaners and British, and their proud military tradition led them into a war with the British in 1879. They defeated the British at Isandhlwana (ee-sawn-dull-WAH-nuh), but a few months later they were in turn defeated. Cetshwayo was captured and sent into exile, and the Zulu lands were given to white ranchers.

Relations between the British and the Afrikaners, already tense as a result of British encroachment, took a turn for the worse when gold was discovered in the Afrikaner republic of Transvaal (trans-VAHL) in 1886. In the gold rush that ensued, the British soon outnumbered the Afrikaners.

Britain's invasion of southern Africa was driven in part by the ambition of **Cecil Rhodes** (1853–1902), who once declared that he would "annex the stars" if he could. Rhodes made his fortune in the Kimberley diamond fields, founding De Beers Consolidated, a company that has dominated the world's diamond trade ever since. He then turned to politics. He encouraged a concession company, the British South Africa Company, to push north into Central Africa, where he named two new colonies after himself: Southern Rhodesia (now Zimbabwe) and Northern Rhodesia (now Zambia). The Ndebele (en-duh-BELL-ay) and Shona peoples, who inhabited the region, resisted this invasion, but the machine guns of the British finally defeated them (see Diversity and Dominance: Two Africans Recall the Arrival of the Europeans).

The inflow of English-speaking whites into the gold- and diamond-mining areas and British attempts to annex the two Afrikaner, also called Boer, republics, Transvaal and Orange Free State, led to the South African or Boer War, which lasted from 1899 to 1902. At first the Afrikaners had the upper hand, for they were highly motivated, possessed modern rifles, and knew the land. In 1901, however, Great Britain brought in 450,000 troops and crushed the Afrikaner armies. Ironically, the Afrikaners' defeat in 1902 led to their ultimate victory. Wary of costly commitments overseas, the British government expected European settlers in Africa to manage their own affairs, as they were doing in Canada, Australia, and New Zealand. Thus, in 1910 the European settlers created the Union of South Africa, in which the Afrikaners eventually emerged as the ruling element.

Unlike Canada, Australia, and New Zealand, South Africa had a majority of indigenous inhabitants and substantial numbers of Indians and "Cape Coloureds" (people of mixed ancestry). Yet the Europeans were both numerous enough to demand self-rule and powerful enough to deny the vote and other civil rights to the majority. In 1913 the South African parliament passed the Natives Land Act, assigning Africans to reservations and forbidding them to own land elsewhere. This and other racial policies turned South Africa into a land of segregation and oppression.

West and Equatorial Africa   Simultaneous with the formation of Shaka's Zulu kingdom, Islamic reform movements were creating another cluster of powerful states in the savannas of West Africa. Islam had long been a force in the politics and cities of this region, but most Muslim rulers had found it prudent to tolerate the older religious practices of their subjects. In the 1770s, however, Muslim scholars began preaching the need to reform Islamic practices. They condemned the accommodations Muslim rulers had made with older traditions and called for a forcible conquest of rural "pagans." Their jihad added new lands where governments enforced Islamic laws and promoted the religion's spread.

The largest of the new Muslim reform movements occurred in the Hausa (HOW-suh) states (in northern Nigeria) under the leadership of Usuman dan Fodio (OO-soo-mahn dahn FOH-dee-oh) (1745–1817). He charged that the Hausa kings, despite their official profession of Islam, were "undoubtedly unbelievers ... because they practice polytheistic rituals and turn people away from the path of God." Muslims unhappy with their social or religious position spread the movement to other Hausa states. The successful armies united the conquered Hausa states and neighboring areas under a caliph who ruled from the city of Sokoto.

These new Muslim states became centers of Islamic learning and reform. Schools for training boys in Quranic subjects spread rapidly, and the great library at Sokoto attracted many scholars. Officials permitted non-Muslims within the empire to follow their religions in exchange for paying a special tax, but they suppressed dances and ceremonies associated with traditional religions. The **Sokoto Caliphate** (1809–1906) was the largest state in West Africa since the sixteenth century.

In coastal West Africa, however, the French, who had maintained a foothold in Senegal for centuries, envisioned building a railroad from the upper Senegal River to the upper Niger in order to open the interior to French merchants. This in turn led the French military to undertake the conquest of the interior. Sokoto remained independent, but after 1890 it was embattled both by neighboring rulers and European encroachment. In 1906 the empire came to an end with France, Britain, and Germany gobbling up various portions.

Farther south, **King Leopold II** of Belgium, following the advice of an American journalist and explorer, **Henry Morton Stanley**, invested his personal fortune in "opening up"—that is, occupying—the Congo Basin, an enormous forested region in the heart of equatorial Africa. With Leopold's money, Stanley returned to Africa from 1879 to 1884 to establish trading posts along the southern bank of the Congo River. At the same time, **Savorgnan de Brazza**, an Italian officer serving in the French army, obtained from an African ruler living on the opposite bank a treaty that placed the area under the "protection" of France.

The Berlin Conference   These events sparked a flurry of diplomatic activity. German chancellor Bismarck called the **Berlin Conference** on Africa of 1884 and 1885. There the major powers agreed that henceforth "effective occupation" would replace the former trading relations between Africans and Europeans. Every country with colonial ambitions had to send troops into Africa and participate in the division of the spoils. As a reward for triggering the "scramble" for Africa, Leopold II acquired a personal domain under the name *Congo Free State*, while France and Portugal took most of the rest of equatorial Africa. In this manner, the European powers and King Leopold managed to divide Africa among themselves, at least on paper.

Except in Kenya, Northern Rhodesia, and South Africa, where Europeans found the land and climate to their liking and forced Africans to become squatters, sharecroppers, or ranch hands on land they had farmed for generations, the colonial rulers declared any land that was not farmed to be "vacant" and gave it to

Two Africans Recall the Arrival of the Europeans

We know a great deal about the arrival of the Europeans into the interior of Africa from the perspective of the conquerors, but very little about how the events were experienced by Africans. Here are two accounts by African women, one from northern Nigeria whose land was occupied by the British, the other from the Congo Free State, a colony of King Leopold II of Belgium. They show not only how Africans experienced European colonial dominance but also how diverse these African experiences were.

Baba of Karo, a Nigerian Woman, Remembers Her Childhood

When I was a maiden the Europeans first arrived. Ever since we were quite small the *malams* had been saying that the Europeans would come with a thing called a train, they would come with a thing called a motor-car, in them you would go and come back in a trice. They would stop wars, they would repair the world, they would stop oppression and lawlessness, we should live at peace with them. We used to go and sit quietly and listen to the prophecies.

I remember when a European came to Karo on a horse, and some of his foot soldiers went into the town. Everyone came out to look at them, but in Zerewa they didn't see the European. Everyone at Karo ran away—"There's a European, there's a European!"

At that time Yusufu was the king of Karo. He did not like the Europeans, he did not wish them, he would not sign their treaty. Then he say that perforce he would have to agree, so he did. We Habe wanted them to come, it was the Fulani who did not like it. When the Europeans came the Habe saw that if you worked for them

they paid you for it, they didn't say, like the Fulani, "Commoner, give me this! Commoner, bring me that!" Yes, the Habe wanted them; they saw no harm in them.

The Europeans said that there were to be no more slaves; if someone said "Slave!" you could complain to the *alkali* who would punish the master who said it, the judge said, "That is what the Europeans have decreed." The first order said that any slave, if he was younger than you, was your younger brother, if he was older than you was your elder brother—they were all brothers of their master's family. No one used the word "slave" any more. When slavery was stopped, nothing much happened at our *rinji* except that some slaves whom we had bought in the market ran away. Our own father went to his farm and worked, he and his son took up their large hoes; they loaned out their spare farms. Tsoho our father and Kadiri my brother with whom I live now and Babambo worked, they farmed guineacorn and millet and groundnuts and everything; before this they had supervised the slaves' work— now they did their own.

In the old days if the chief liked the look of your daughter he would take her and put her in his house; you could do nothing about it. Now they don't do that.

Ilanga, a Congolese Woman, Recounts Her Capture by Agents of the Congo Free State

… we were all busy in the fields hoeing our plantations, for it was the rainy season, and the weeds sprang quickly up, when a runner came to the village saying that a large band of men was coming, that they all wore red caps and blue cloth, and carried guns and long knives, and that many white men were with them, the chief of whom was *Kibalanga* (Michaux). Niendo at once called all the chief men to his house, while the drums were beaten to summon the people to the village. A long consultation was held, and finally we were all told to go quietly to the fields and bring in ground-nuts, plantains, and cassava for the warriors who were coming, and goats and fowl for the white men. The women all went with baskets and filled them, and put them in the road, which was blocked up, so many were there. Niendo then commanded everyone to go and sit quietly in the houses until he gave other orders. This we did, everyone remaining quietly seated while Niendo went up the road with the head men to meet the white chief. We did not know what to think, for most of us feared that so many armed men coming boded evil; but Niendo thought that, by giving presents of much food, he would induce the strangers to pass on without harming us. And so it proved, for the soldiers took the baskets, and were then ordered by the white men to move off through the village. Many of the soldiers looked into the houses and shouted at us words we did not understand. We were glad when they were all gone, for we were much in fear of the white men and the strange warriors, who are known to all the people as being great fighters, bringing war wherever they go....

When the white men and their warriors had gone, we went again to our work, and were hoping that they would not return; but this they did in a very short time. As before, we brought in great heaps of food; but this time *Kibalanga* did not move away directly, but camped near our village, and his soldiers came and stole all our fowl and goats and

tore up our cassava; but we did not mind as long as they did not harm us. The next morning it was reported that the white men were going away; but soon after the sun rose over the hill, a large band of soldiers came into the village, and we all went into the houses and sat down. We were not long seated when the soldiers came rushing in shouting, and threatening Niendo with their guns. They rushed into the houses and dragged the people out. Three or four came to our house and caught hold of me, also my husband Oleka and my sister Katinga. We were dragged into the road, and were tied together with cords about our necks, so that we could not escape. We were all crying, for now we knew that we were to be taken away to be slaves. The soldiers beat us with the iron sticks from their guns, and compelled us to march to the camp of *Kibalanga*, who ordered the women to be tied up separately, ten to each cord, and the men in the same way. When we were all collected—and there were many from other villages whom we now saw, and many from Waniendo—the soldiers brought baskets of food for us to carry, in some of which was smoked human flesh (*niama na nitu*).

We then set off marching very quickly. My sister Katinga had her baby in her arms, and was not compelled to carry a basket; but my husband Oleka was made to carry a goat. We marched until the afternoon, when we camped near a stream, where we were glad to drink, for we were much athirst. We had nothing to eat, for the soldiers would give us nothing, so we lay upon the ground, and at night went to sleep. The next day we continued the march, and when we camped at noon were given some maize and plantains, which were gathered near a village from which the people had run away. So it continued each day until the fifth day, when the soldiers took my sister's baby and threw it in the grass, leaving it to die, and made her carry some cooking pots which they found in the deserted village. On the sixth day we became very weak from lack of food and from constant marching and sleeping in the damp grass, and my husband, who marched behind us with the goat, could not stand up longer, and so he sat down beside the path and refused to walk more. The soldiers beat him, but still he refused to move. Then one of them struck him on the head with the end of his gun, and he fell upon the ground. One of the soldiers caught the goat, while two or three others stuck the long knives they put on the ends of their guns into my husband. I saw the blood spurt out, and then saw him no more, for we passed over the brow of a hill and he was out of sight. Many of the young men were killed the same way, and many babies thrown into the grass to die. A few escaped; but we were so well guarded that it was almost impossible.

Questions for Analysis

1. How do Baba and Ilanga recall their existence before the Europeans came?
2. What did they expect when they first heard of the arrival of Europeans? Instead, what happened to them, their relatives, and their towns?
3. How do you explain the difference between these two accounts?

Sources: From M. F. Smith, ed., *Baba of Karo: A Woman of the Muslim Hausa* (New York: Philosophical Library, 1955), 66–68. Edgar Canisius, *A Campaign Amongst Cannibals* (London: R. A. Everett & Co., 1903), 250–256.

private concession companies. In the Gold Coast (now Ghana), British trading companies bought the cocoa grown by African farmers at low prices and resold it for large profits. The interior of French West Africa lagged behind. Although the region could produce cotton, peanuts, and other crops, the difficulties of transportation limited its development before 1914.

Compared to West Africa, equatorial Africa had few inhabitants and little trade. Rather than try to govern these vast territories directly, authorities in the Congo Free State, the French Congo, and the Portuguese colonies of Angola and Mozambique farmed out huge pieces of land to private concession companies, offering them monopolies on the natural resources and trade of their territories and the right to employ soldiers and tax the inhabitants. Freed from outside supervision, the companies forced the African inhabitants at gunpoint to produce cash crops and carry them, on their heads or backs, to the nearest railroad or navigable river. The worst abuses took place in the Congo Free State, where a rubber boom made it profitable for private companies to brutalize Africans collecting latex from vines that grew in the forests. After 1906 the British press began publicizing the horrors. The public outcry that followed, coinciding with the end of the rubber boom, convinced the Belgian government to take over Leopold's private empire in 1908.

Modernization in Egypt and Ethiopia

While colonial states were arising elsewhere, in northeastern Africa Egypt and Ethiopia retained their independence and experimented with **modernization**. Muhammad Ali, who ruled Egypt from 1805 to 1849, began a series of reforms aimed at creating a modern Egypt (see Chapter 24). European pressure sharply curtailed these efforts after 1839, but by the end of his reign Egypt's population had nearly doubled; trade with Europe had expanded by almost 600 percent; and a new class of educated Egyptians was beginning to wield some influence.

Muhammad Ali's grandson Ismail (is-mah-EEL) (r. 1863–1879) focused on westernizing Egypt rather than confronting Europe militarily. "My country is no longer in Africa," Ismail declared, "it is in Europe."[1] His efforts increased the number of European advisers in Egypt, as well as Egypt's debts to French and British banks. In the first decade of his reign, revenues increased thirtyfold and exports doubled (largely because of a huge increase in cotton exports during the American Civil War). By 1870 Egypt had a network of new irrigation canals, 800 miles (1,300 kilometers) of railroads, a postal service, and a few dazzling modernization projects in the capital city of Cairo. It also had the **Suez Canal**, which opened in 1969 and immediately affected communications between Europe and Asia.

Ambitions like the canal and Ismail's dream of an Egyptian empire extending south into Sudan and Ethiopia cost vast sums of money, which the khedives borrowed from European creditors at high interest rates. When the market for Egyptian cotton collapsed after the American Civil War, these debts became a problem. By 1876 foreign debt had risen to £100 million sterling, and the interest payments alone consumed one-third of Egypt's foreign export earnings. To avoid bankruptcy the Egyptian government sold its shares in the Suez Canal to Great Britain and accepted four foreign "commissioners of the debt" to oversee its finances. French and British bankers, still not satisfied, lobbied their governments to secure the loans by stronger measures. In 1878 the two governments obliged Ismail to appoint a Frenchman as minister of public works and a Briton as minister of finance. When high taxes caused hardship and popular discontent, the French and British persuaded the Ottoman sultan to depose Ismail. This foreign intervention provoked a military uprising under Egyptian army colonel Arabi Pasha, which threatened the Suez Canal.

Fearing for their investments, the British sent an army into Egypt in 1882. So important was the Suez Canal to Britain's maritime supremacy that they stayed for seventy years. During those years the British ruled Egypt "indirectly"—that is, they maintained the Egyptian government and the fiction of Egyptian sovereignty but retained real power in their own hands.

Eager to develop Egyptian cotton production, the British brought in engineers and contractors to build the first dam across the Nile, at Aswan in Upper Egypt. When completed in 1902, it captured the annual Nile flood and released its waters throughout the year, allowing farmers to grow two, sometimes three, crops a year. The economic development of Egypt by the British enriched a small elite of landowners and merchants, many of them foreigners. Egyptian peasants got little relief from the heavy taxes collected to pay for their country's crushing foreign debt and the expenses of the British army of occupation. Most Egyptians found British rule more onerous than that of the Ottomans. By the 1890s Egyptian politicians and intellectuals were demanding that the British leave.

State building and reform were also under way in Christian Ethiopia. Beginning in the 1840s, Ethiopian rulers purchased modern weapons from European sources and

---

[1]Quoted in P. J. Vatikiotis, *The History of Modern Egypt: From Muhammad Ali to Mubarak*, 4th ed. (Baltimore: Johns Hopkins University Press, 1991), 74.

created strong armies loyal to the ruler. Emperor Téwodros (tay-WOH-druhs) II (r. 1833–1868) also encouraged the manufacture of weapons locally. However, his efforts to coerce more technical aid by holding some British officials captive backfired when the British invaded instead. As the British forces advanced, Téwodros committed suicide to avoid being taken prisoner. Satisfied that their honor was avenged, the British withdrew. Téwodros's successor Yohannes (yoh-HAHN-nehs) IV (r. 1872–1889) continued to bring most highland regions under imperial rule. The only large part of ancient Ethiopia that remained outside Emperor Yohannes's rule was the independent Shoa kingdom, ruled by **Menelik II** (MEN-uh-lik) from 1865.

In 1889 Menelik II became emperor of Ethiopia, at a time when his country was threatened by Sudanese Muslims to the west and by France and Italy, which controlled the coast of the Red Sea to the east. As already stated, Ethiopia had been purchasing European and American weapons for many years. When Italians attempted to establish a protectorate over Ethiopia, they found the Ethiopians armed with thousands of rifles and even machine guns and artillery pieces. Although Italy sent twenty thousand troops to attack Ethiopia, in 1896 they were defeated at Adowa (AH-do-ah) by a larger and better-trained Ethiopian army.

Transition from the Slave Trade   The successful slave revolt in Saint Domingue in the 1790s (see Chapter 23) ended slavery in the largest plantation colony in the West Indies. Elsewhere in the Americas, however, slave revolts were brutally repressed. As news of the slave revolts and their repression spread, humanitarians and religious reformers called for an end to the trade. Support for abolition of the trade was found even among Americans wanting to preserve slavery. In 1807 both Great Britain and the United States made importing slaves from Africa illegal for their citizens. Most other Western countries followed suit by 1850, but few enforced abolition with the vigor of the British.

Once the world's greatest slave traders, the British became the most aggressive abolitionists. Britain sent a naval patrol to enforce the ban along the African coast and negotiated treaties allowing the patrol to search other nations' vessels suspected of carrying slaves. Although British patrols captured 1,635 slave ships and liberated over 160,000 enslaved Africans, the trade proved difficult to stop. Cuba and Brazil continued to import huge numbers of slaves, which drove prices up and persuaded some African rulers and merchants to continue to sell slaves and to help foreign slavers evade the British patrols. Because the slave trade moved to other parts of Africa, the transatlantic slave trade did not end until 1867.

In exchange for slaves, Africans purchased cloth, metals, and other goods. To continue those imports, Africans expanded their **"legitimate" trade** (exports other than slaves). As the Atlantic slave trade was shut down, they revived old exports or developed new ones. The most successful of the new exports from West Africa was palm oil, used by British manufacturers for soap, candles, and lubricants. Though still a major source of slaves until the mid-1830s, the trading states of the Niger Delta emerged as the premier exporters of palm oil. Coastal African traders bought the palm oil at inland markets and delivered it to European ships at the coast.

The dramatic increase in palm-oil exports—from a few hundred tons at the beginning of the century to tens of thousands of tons by midcentury—altered the social structure of the coastal trading communities. Coastal traders used their

King Jaja of Opobo *This talented man rose from slavery in the Niger Delta port of Bonny to head one of the town's major palm-oil trading firms, the Anna Pepple House, in 1863. Six years later, Jaja founded and ruled his own trading port of Opobo.*

wealth to buy slaves to paddle the giant dugout canoes that transported palm oil from inland markets along the narrow delta creeks to the trading ports. Niger Delta slavery could be as harsh and brutal as slavery on New World plantations, but it offered some slaves a chance to gain wealth and power. Male slaves who supervised canoe fleets were well compensated, and a few even became wealthy enough to take over the leadership of coastal "canoe houses" (companies). The most famous, known as "Jaja" (ca. 1821–1891), rose from canoe slave to become the head of a major canoe house. In 1869, to escape discrimination by free-born Africans, he founded the new port of Opobo, which he ruled as king. In the 1870s Jaja of Opobo was the greatest palm-oil trader in the Niger Delta.

Another effect of the suppression of the slave trade was the spread of Western cultural influences in West Africa. To serve as a base for their anti-slave-trade naval squadron, the British had taken over the small colony of Sierra Leone (see-AIR-uh lee-OWN) in 1808. Over the next several years, 130,000 men, women, and children taken from "captured" vessels were liberated in Sierra Leone. Christian missionaries helped settle these **recaptives** in and around Freetown, the capital. Mission churches and schools made many converts among such men and women.

Sierra Leone's schools also produced a number of distinguished graduates. Samuel Adjai Crowther (1808–1891), freed from a slave ship in 1821, became the first Anglican bishop in West Africa in 1864, administering a pioneering diocese along the lower Niger River. James Africanus Horton (1835–1882), the son of slaves liberated in Sierra Leone, became a doctor and the author of many studies of West Africa.

Other Western cultural influences came from people of African birth or descent returning to their ancestral homeland. In 1821, free black Americans founded a settlement that grew into the Republic of Liberia, a place of liberty at a time when slavery was legal and flourishing in the United States. After their emancipation in 1865 other African Americans moved to Liberia. Emma White, a literate black woman from Kentucky, moved from Liberia to Opobo in 1875, where King Jaja employed her to write his commercial correspondence and run a school for his children. Edward Wilmot Blyden (1832–1912), born in the West Indies and proud of his West African parentage, emigrated to Liberia in 1851 and became a professor of Greek, Latin, and Arabic at the fledgling Liberia College.

Secondary Empire in Eastern Africa

When British patrols hampered the slave trade in West Africa, slavers moved to eastern Africa. There the Atlantic slave trade joined an existing trade in slaves to the Islamic world that also was expanding. Two-thirds of the 1.2 million slaves exported from eastern Africa in the nineteenth century went to markets in North Africa and the Middle East; the other third went to plantations in the Americas and to European-controlled Indian Ocean islands.

Slavery also became more prominent within eastern Africa itself. Between 1800 and 1873 Arab and Swahili (swah-HEE-lee) owners of clove plantations along the coast purchased some 700,000 slaves to do the hard work of harvesting this spice. The plantations were on Zanzibar Island and in neighboring territories belonging to the Sultanate of Oman, an Arabian kingdom on the Persian Gulf that had been expanding its control over the East African coast since 1698. The sultan had even moved his court to Zanzibar in 1840 to take advantage of the burgeoning trade in cloves. Zanzibar also was an important center of ivory and slaves until British pressure induced the sultan to ban the export of slaves in 1857 and their import in 1873.

INDIA UNDER BRITISH RULE

The might of the Mughal Empire did not long outlast the reign of Aurangzeb, who died in 1707 (see Chapter 20). In 1739 Iranian invaders sacked Delhi and carried off vast amounts of booty. Indian states also took advantage of Mughal weakness to assert their independence. By midcentury, the Maratha (muh-RAH-tuh) Confederation, a coalition of states in central India, controlled more land than the Mughals did. Several **nawabs** (NAH-wab), a term used for Muslim princes who were nominally deputies of the Mughal emperor, carved out powerful states of their own.

Ambitious young "company men" employed by British, French, and Dutch trading companies used hard bargaining, and hard fighting when necessary, to persuade Indian rulers to allow them to establish coastal trading posts protected by Indian troops known as **sepoys** (SEE-poy). In divided India these private armies came to hold the balance of power.

East India Company

In 1691, Great Britain's East India Company (EIC) had persuaded the nawab of Bengal in northeast India to allow a company trading post at the fishing port of Calcutta. In 1756, a new nawab overran the post and imprisoned a group of EIC men in a cell so small that many died of suffocation. To avenge their deaths in this "Black Hole of Calcutta," a large EIC force from Madras, led by Robert Clive, overthrew the nawab. The weak Mughal emperor was persuaded to acknowledge the East India Company's right to rule Bengal in 1765. By 1788, Calcutta had grown into a city of 250,000.

Bombay was the third major center of British power in India. There, in 1818, the East India Company annexed large territories to form the core of what was called the "Bombay Presidency." This gave the East India Company an empire more populous than western Europe and with fifty times the population of the colonies the British had lost in North America. One goal of the **British raj** (regime) was to remake India on a British model through administrative and social reform, economic development, and the introduction of new technology. Yet the company men—like the Mughals before them—had to temper their interference with Indian social and religious customs lest they provoke rebellion or lose the support of their Indian princely allies.

Another British policy was to substitute private property for India's complex and overlapping patterns of landholding. In Bengal this reform worked to the advantage of large landowners, but in Mysore the peasantry gained. Private ownership made it easier for the state to collect the taxes that were needed to pay for administration, the army, and economic reform.

Such policies of "westernization, Anglicization, and modernization," as they have been called, were only one side of British rule. The other side was the bolstering of "traditions"—both real and newly invented. In the name of tradition the Indian princes who ruled nearly half of British India were frequently endowed by their British overlords with greater power and splendor and longer tenure than their predecessors had ever had. Likewise, Hindu and Muslim holy men were able to expand their "traditional" power over property and people far beyond what had been the case in earlier times. At the same time, princes, holy men, and other Indians frequently used claims of tradition to resist British rule as well as to turn it to their advantage. The British rulers themselves invented many "traditions"—including elaborate parades and displays—half borrowed from European royal pomp, half from Mughal ceremonies.

The British and Indian elites worked sometimes in close partnership, sometimes in opposition, but always at the expense of the ordinary people of India. Women of every status, members of subordinate Hindu castes, the "untouchables" and "tribals" outside the caste system, and the poor experienced few benefits from the British reforms and much new oppression from the taxes and "traditions" that exalted their superiors' status.

The transformation of British India's economy was also doubled-edged. On the one hand, the raj created many new jobs as a result of the growth of trade and expanded crop production, such as opium in Bengal, largely for export to

China (see Chapter 24); coffee in Ceylon; and tea in Assam in northeastern India. On the other hand, competition from cheap cotton goods produced in Britain's industrial mills drove many Indians out of the handicraft textile industry. In the eighteenth century India had been the world's greatest exporter of cotton textiles; in the nineteenth century India increasingly shipped raw cotton fiber to Britain.

During the first half of the nineteenth century, British rulers readily handled these isolated local rebellions, but they were more concerned about the loyalty of their Indian sepoys. The EIC employed 200,000 sepoys in 1857, along with 38,000 British troops. Armed with modern rifles and disciplined in fighting methods, the sepoys had a potential for successful rebellion that other groups lacked.

In the early decades of EIC rule, most sepoys came from Bengal. The Bengali sepoys resented the active recruitment of other ethnic groups into the army after 1848, such as Sikhs (sick) from Punjab and Gurkhas from Nepal. In addition, many high-caste Hindus objected to a new law in 1856 requiring new recruits to be available for service overseas in the growing British empire, for their religion prohibited ocean travel. Finally, the replacement of the standard military musket by the more accurate Enfield rifle in 1857 required soldiers to use their teeth to tear open the ammunition cartridges, which were greased with animal fat. Hindus were offended by this order if the fat came from cattle, which they considered sacred. Muslims were offended if the fat came from pigs, which they considered unclean.

Although the cartridge-opening procedure was quickly changed, the initial discontent grew into rebellion by Hindu sepoys in May 1857. British troubles mushroomed when Muslim sepoys, peasants, and discontented elites joined in. The rebellion was put down ten months later, but it shook this empire to its core.

Historians have attached different names and meanings to the events of 1857 and 1858. Nineteenth-century British historians labeled it the "**Sepoy Rebellion**" or "Mutiny." Seeing in these events the beginnings of the later movement for independence, some modern Indian historians have termed it the "Revolution of 1857."

Political Reform and Industrial Impact   Regardless of label, the events of 1857–1858 marked a turning point in the history of modern India. In their wake Indians gained a new centralized government, entered a period of rapid economic growth, and began to develop a new national consciousness.

In 1858, Britain eliminated the last traces of Mughal and Company rule. In their place, a new secretary of state for India in London oversaw Indian policy, and a new governor-general in Delhi acted as the British monarch's viceroy. In November 1858, Queen Victoria guaranteed all Indians equal protection of the law and the freedom to practice their religions and social customs; she also assured Indian princes that so long as they were loyal to the queen British India would respect their control of territories and "their rights, dignity and honour."[2]

---

[2]Quoted by Bernard S. Cohn, "Representing Authority in Victorian India," in *The Invention of Tradition*, ed. Eric Hobsbawm and Terence Ranger (Cambridge, England: Cambridge University Press, 1983), 165.

MAP 26.1   India, 1707–1805

As Mughal power weakened during the eighteenth century, other Indian states and the East India Company expanded their territories.

British rule continued to emphasize both tradition and reform after 1857. At the top, the British viceroys lived in enormous palaces amid hundreds of servants and gaudy displays of luxury meant to convince Indians that the British viceroys were legitimate successors to the Mughal emperors. They treated the quasi-independent Indian princes with elaborate ceremonial courtesy and maintained them in splendor. When Queen Victoria was proclaimed "Empress of India" in 1877 and periodically thereafter, the viceroys put on great pageants known as **durbars**. At the durbar in Delhi in 1902–1903 to celebrate the coronation of King Edward VII, Viceroy Lord

Curzon honored himself with a 101-gun salute and a parade of 34,000 troops in front of 50 princes and 173,000 visitors.

Meanwhile, a powerful and efficient bureaucracy controlled India. Members of the elite **Indian Civil Service** (ICS) held the senior administrative and judicial posts. Numbering only a thousand at the end of the nineteenth century, these men visited the villages in their districts, heard lawsuits and complaints, and passed judgments.

Recruitment into the ICS was by open examinations. In theory any British subject could take these exams; since they were given in England, however, in practice the system worked to exclude Indians. In 1870 only one Indian was a member of the ICS. Subsequent reforms led to fifty-seven Indian appointments by 1887, but there the process stalled. Working under the ICS were thousands of lesser Indian officials.

The reason qualified Indians were denied entry into the upper administration of their country was the racist contempt most British officials felt for the people they ruled. When he became commander-in-chief of the Indian army in 1892, Lord Kitchener declared:

> It is this consciousness of the inherent superiority of the European which had won for us India. However well educated and clever a native may be, and however brave he may have proved himself, I believe that no rank we can bestow on him would cause him to be considered an equal of the British officer.[3]

After 1857 the government invested millions of pounds sterling in harbors, cities, irrigation canals, and other public works. Forests were felled to make way for tea plantations. Indian farmers were persuaded to grow cotton and jute for export. Engineers built great irrigation systems to alleviate the famines that periodically decimated whole provinces. As a result, India's trade expanded rapidly.

Most of the exports were agricultural commodities: cotton fiber, opium, tea, silk, and sugar. In return India imported manufactured goods from Britain, including machine-made cotton textiles that undercut Indian hand-loom weavers. Some women found jobs at very low pay on plantations or in the growing cities, where prostitution flourished. Everywhere in India poverty remained the norm.

The Indian government also promoted the introduction of new technologies into India. Earlier in the century there were steamboats on the rivers and a massive program of canal building for irrigation. Beginning in the 1840s a railroad boom gave India its first national transportation network, followed by telegraph lines, and by 1870 India had the fifth largest rail network in the world. Originally designed to serve British commerce, the railroads were owned by British companies, constructed with British rails and equipment, and paid dividends to British investors. Ninety-nine percent of the railroad employees were Indians, but Europeans occupied all the top positions—"like a thin film of oil on top of a glass of water, resting upon but hardly mixing with [those] below," as one official report put it.

Although some Indians opposed the railroads at first because the trains mixed people of different castes, faiths, and sexes, the Indian people took to rail travel with great enthusiasm. Indians rode trains on business, on pilgrimage, and in search of work. In 1870 over 18 million passengers traveled along the network's

---

[3]James Truslow, *Empire of the Seven Seas: The British Empire 1784–1939* (New York: Charles Scribners Sons, 2007), 268.

4,775 miles (7,685 kilometers) of track, and more than half a million messages were sent up and down the 14,000 miles (22,500 kilometers) of telegraph wires.

But the freer movement of Indian pilgrims and the flood of poor Indians into the cities also promoted the spread of cholera (KAHL-uhr-uh), a disease transmitted through water contaminated by human feces. Cholera deaths rose rapidly during the nineteenth century, and eventually the disease spread to Europe. In many Indian minds *kala mari* ("the black death") was a divine punishment for failing to prevent the British takeover. This chastisement also fell heavily on British residents, who died in large numbers. In 1867, officials demonstrated the close connection between cholera and pilgrims who bathed in and drank from sacred pools and rivers. The installation of a new sewerage system and a filtered water supply (1869) in Calcutta dramatically reduced cholera deaths there. Similar measures in Bombay and Madras also led to great reductions, but most Indians lived in small villages where famine and lack of sanitation kept cholera deaths high.

Indian Nationalism   After the failure of the rebellion of 1857 to overthrow British rule, some Indians argued that the only way for Indians to regain control of their destiny was to reduce their country's social and ethnic divisions and promote Pan-Indian nationalism.

Individuals such as Rammohun Roy (1772–1833) had promoted development along these lines a generation earlier. A Western-educated Bengali from a Brahmin family, Roy was a successful administrator for the East India Company and a student of comparative religion. His Brahmo Samaj (BRAH-moh suh-MAHJ) (Divine Society), founded in 1828, attracted Indians who sought to reconcile the values of the West with the religious traditions of India. They advocated reforming some Hindu customs, such as the caste system and child marriage, and urged a return to the founding principles of the *Upanishads*, ancient sacred writings of Hinduism. They also backed British efforts to ban practices they found repugnant. Widow burning (*sati* [suh-TEE]) was outlawed in 1829 and slavery in 1843. Reformers sought to correct other abuses of women: prohibitions against widows remarrying were revoked in 1856, and female infanticide was made a crime in 1870.

Although Brahmo Samaj remained influential after the rebellion of 1857, many Indian intellectuals turned to Western secular values and nationalism as the way to reclaim India. In this process the spread of Western education played an important role, a process aided by European and American missionaries. Roy had studied both Indian and Western subjects and helped found the Hindu College in Calcutta in 1816. Other Western-curriculum schools quickly followed, including Bethune College in Calcutta, the first secular school for Indian women, in 1849. India's three universities were established in 1857. In 1870 there were over 24,000 elementary and secondary schools, whose graduates articulated a new Pan-Indian nationalism that transcended regional and religious differences.

Many of the new nationalists came from the Indian middle class, which had prospered from the increase of trade and manufacturing. Educated people were angered by the obstacles that British rules and prejudices put in the way of their advancement. Hoping to increase their influence and improve their employment opportunities in the Indian government, they convened the first **Indian National Congress** in 1885. The members sought a larger role for Indians in the Civil Service.

They also called for reductions in military expenditures, which consumed 40 percent of the government's budget, so that more could be spent on alleviating the poverty of the Indian masses. But although the Indian National Congress promoted unity among the country's many religions and social groups, most early members were upper-caste Western-educated Hindus and Parsis. Until it attracted the support of the masses, it could not hope to challenge British rule.

SOUTHEAST ASIA AND THE PACIFIC

Different parts of Southeast Asia and the Pacific region had differing histories, yet all came under intense imperialist pressure during the nineteenth century. Thomas Stamford Raffles had governed Java from 1811 to 1814, when the politics of Napoleon's wars in Europe allowed the English to displace the Dutch. After a peace treaty in Europe dictated Java's return to the Dutch, Raffles helped establish, in 1824, a new free port at Singapore on the site of a small Malay fishing village with a superb harbor. British merchants and Chinese businessmen and laborers soon made Singapore the paramount center of trade and shipping between the Indian Ocean and China. Along with Malacca and other possessions on the strait, Singapore formed the "Straits Settlements," which British India administered until 1867.

British expansion came more quickly in neighboring Burma, which had emerged as a powerful kingdom by 1750. In 1785 Burma tried to annex neighboring territories of Siam (now Thailand) to the east, but a coalition of Thai leaders thwarted Burmese advances by 1802. Burma next attacked Assam to the west, but this provoked a war with British India. After a two-year war, India annexed Assam in 1826 and occupied two coastal provinces of northern Burma. As the rice and timber trade from these provinces grew important, the occupation became permanent, and in 1852 British India annexed the rest of coastal Burma. The last piece of the country was annexed in 1885, but Thailand remained an independent kingdom.

Indochina fell under French control piece by piece until it was finally subdued in 1895. Similarly, Malaya (now Malaysia) came under British rule in stages during the 1870s and 1880s. In northern Sumatra, however, a region that supplied half the world's production of black pepper, the Dutch fought a ferocious war between 1873 and 1913 against the rulers of Acheh. The Achehnese warriors were inspired, in part, by the mystique of an Islamic jihad, thus creating a tradition of resistance that would continue to resonate throughout the twentieth century.

Australia   In the once-remote South Pacific, British settlers displaced the indigenous populations of Australia and New Zealand, just as they had done in North America. Portuguese mariners had sighted Australia in the early seventeenth century, but it was too remote to be of much interest to Europeans. However, after the English captain James Cook explored New Zealand and the eastern coast of Australia between 1769 and 1778, expanding shipping networks brought in growing numbers of visitors and settlers.

At the time of Cook's visits, Australia was the home of about 650,000 hunting-and-gathering people, whose Melanesian (mel-uh-NEE-zhuhn) ancestors had settled there some forty thousand years earlier. New Zealand was inhabited by about 250,000 Maori (MOW-ree [ow as in cow]), who practiced hunting, fishing, and simple forms of agriculture, which their Polynesian ancestors had introduced around 1200. Because of their long isolation from the rest of humanity, the populations of Australia and New Zealand were as vulnerable as the Amerindians had been to unfamiliar diseases introduced by new overseas contacts. By the 1890s, only 93,000 aboriginal Australians and 42,000 Maori survived, and British settler populations outnumbered and dominated the indigenous peoples.

The first permanent British settlers in Australia were 736 convicts, of whom 188 were women, sent into exile in 1788. Over the next few decades, Australian penal colonies grew slowly and had only slight contact with the indigenous population, whom the British called "Aborigines." However, the discovery of gold in 1851 brought a flood of free European settlers (and some Chinese) and hastened the end of the penal colonies. When the gold rush subsided, government subsidies enabled tens of thousands of British settlers to settle "down under." Though it still took more than three months to reach Australia from Britain, by 1860 Australia had a million immigrants, and the settler population doubled during the next fifteen years.

New Zealand   British settlers were drawn more slowly to New Zealand. Some of the first were temporary residents along the coast who slaughtered seals and exported pelts to Western countries to be made into men's felt hats. A single ship in 1806 took away sixty thousand sealskins. By the early 1820s overhunting had nearly exterminated the seal population. Special ships also hunted sperm whales extensively near New Zealand for their oil, used for lubrication, soap,

Bettmann/CORBIS

Emilio Aguinaldo *In 1896, a revolt led by Emilio Aguinaldo attempted to expel Spaniards from the Philippines. When the United States purchased the Philippines from Spain two years later, the Filipino people were not consulted. Aguinaldo continued his campaign, this time against the American occupation forces, until his capture in 1901. In this picture, he appears on horseback, surrounded by some of his troops.*

and lamps; ambergris (AM-ber-grees), an ingredient in perfume; and whalebone (actually baleen, feeding bristles made like fingernails of keratin), used as stays in women's corsets. A brief gold rush and faster ships and subsidized passages attracted more British immigrants after 1860. The colony especially courted women immigrants to offset the preponderance of single men. By the early 1880s this most distant frontier of the British Empire had a settler population of 500,000. Britain encouraged the settlers in Australia and New Zealand to become self-governing, following the 1867 model that had formed the Dominion of Canada out of the diverse and thinly settled colonies of British North America. By gradually turning over governing power to the colonies' inhabitants, Britain satisfied the settlers' desire for greater control over their own territories, muted demands for independence, and made the colonial governments responsible for most of their own expenses.

North American patterns also shaped the indigenous peoples' fate. Aborigines lacked the rights of Australian citizens. The requirement that voters had to be able to read and write English kept Maori from voting in early New Zealand elections, but four seats in the lower house of the legislature were reserved for Maori from 1867 on.

Hawaii and the Philippines, 1878–1902   The United States was a latecomer in the race for colonial territories. However, by the 1890s it had a fast-growing population and industries that produced more manufactured goods than they could sell at home. This growth contributed to economic depressions in 1893 and 1896 and led merchants and bankers to look to China as a new export market. Guam, Hawaii, and the Philippines being naval stations on the route to China, the new expansionism looked in that direction. China was in the minds of those who agreed with the naval strategist Alfred T. Mahan (mah-HAHN): "Whether they will or no, Americans must now begin to look outward. The growing production of the country requires it."

This was not the beginning of American interest in the Pacific. In 1878 the United States obtained the harbor of Pago Pago in Samoa as a coaling and naval station, and in 1887 it secured the use of Pearl Harbor in Hawaii for the same purpose. By 1898, the United States under President William McKinley (1897–1901) had become openly imperialistic and annexed Hawaii as a steppingstone to Asia. As the United States became ever more involved in Asian affairs, Hawaii's strategic location brought an inflow of U.S. military personnel, and its fertile land caused planters to import laborers from Japan, China, and the Philippines. These immigrants soon outnumbered the native Hawaiians.

While large parts of Asia were falling under colonial domination, the people of the Philippines were chafing under their Spanish rulers. **Emilio Aguinaldo**, leader of a secret society, rose in revolt and proclaimed a republic in 1899. The revolutionaries had a good chance of winning independence, for Spain had its hands full with a revolution in Cuba. Unfortunately for Aguinaldo and his followers, the United States declared war against Spain in April 1898 and quickly overcame Spanish forces in the Philippines and Cuba. After the Spanish defeat, President McKinley realized that a weakened Spain might lose the islands to another imperialist power. Japan, having recently defeated China in the Sino-Japanese War (1894–1895) and annexed Taiwan (see Chapter 27), was eager to expand its empire. So was Germany, which had taken over parts of New Guinea and Samoa and several

Pacific archipelagoes during the 1880s. To forestall them, McKinley purchased the Philippines from Spain for $20 million.

The Filipinos were not eager to trade one master for another. For a while, Aguinaldo cooperated with the Americans in the hope of achieving full independence. When his plan was rejected, he rose up again in 1899 and proclaimed the independence of his country. In spite of protests by anti-imperialists in the United States, the U.S. government decided that its global interests outweighed the interests of the Filipino people. In rebel areas, a U.S. army of occupation tortured prisoners, burned villages and crops, and forced the inhabitants into "reconcentration camps." By the end of the insurrection in 1902, the war had cost the lives of 5,000 Americans and 200,000 Filipinos.

After the insurrection ended, the United States attempted to soften its rule with public works and economic development projects. New buildings went up in the city of Manila; roads, harbors, and railroads were built; and the Philippine economy was tied ever more closely to that of the United States. In 1907 Filipinos were allowed to elect representatives to a legislative assembly, but ultimate authority remained in the hands of a governor appointed by the president of the United States. In 1916 the Philippines were the first U.S. colony to be promised independence, a promise fulfilled only thirty years later.

IMPERIALISM IN LATIN AMERICA

The United States played a lesser role than Britain and other European countries in the economic dominance that characterized imperialism in Latin America, and business played a more important role than military intervention. But America's clash with Spain over control of the Philippines carried over into Spanish possessions closer to home.

American Expansionism and the Spanish-American War, 1898   The United States had long had interests in Cuba, the closest and richest of the Caribbean islands and a Spanish colony. American businesses had invested great sums of money in Cuba's sugar and tobacco industries, and thousands of Cubans had migrated to the United States. In 1895, the Cuban nationalist José Martí started a revolution against Spanish rule. American newspapers thrilled readers with lurid stories of Spanish atrocities; businessmen worried about their investments; and politicians demanded that the U.S. government help liberate Cuba.

On February 15, 1898, the U.S. battleship *Maine* accidentally blew up in Havana harbor, killing 266 American sailors. The U.S. government immediately blamed Spain and issued an ultimatum that the Spanish evacuate Cuba. Spain agreed to the ultimatum, but the American press and Congress were eager for war, and President McKinley did not restrain them.

The **Spanish-American War** was over quickly. On May 1, 1898, U.S. warships destroyed the Spanish fleet at Manila in the Philippines. Two months later the United States Navy sank the Spanish Atlantic fleet off Santiago, Cuba. By mid-August Spain was suing for peace. U.S. Secretary of State John Hay called it "a splendid little war." The United States purchased the Philippines from Spain but took over Puerto Rico and Guam as war booty. The two islands remain American possessions to this day. Cuba became an independent republic, subject to interference by the United States.

Economic Imperialism

Latin America achieved independence from Spain and Portugal in the nineteenth century but did not industrialize.

Most Latin American republics, suffering from ideological divisions, unstable governments, and violent upheavals, traded their commodities for foreign manufactured goods and investments and became economically dependent on Great Britain or other foreign countries. A traumatic social revolution and civil war shook Mexico, but even there the region-wide deep split between wealthy landowners and desperately poor peasants persisted.

Yet Latin America's economic potential was huge, for the region could produce many agricultural and mineral products in demand in the industrial countries. What was needed was a means of opening the interior to development. Railroads seemed the perfect answer.

Foreign merchants and bankers and Latin American landowners and politicians embraced the new technology. Starting in the 1870s, almost every country in Latin America acquired railroads, usually connecting mines or agricultural regions with the nearest port rather than linking up the different parts of the interior. All the equipment and building material came from Britain or the United States. So did the money to build the networks, the engineers who designed and maintained them, and the managers who ran them.

Argentina, a land of rich soil that produced wheat, beef, and hides, gained the longest and best-developed rail network south of the United States. By 1914, 86 percent of the railroads in Argentina were owned by British firms; 40 percent of the employees were British; and the official language of the railroads was not Spanish but English. The same was true of mining and industrial enterprises and public utilities throughout Latin America.

In many ways, the situation resembled those of India and Ireland, which also obtained rail networks in exchange for raw materials and agricultural products. The difference was that the Indians and Irish had little say in the matter because they were under British rule. But in Latin America the political elites encouraged foreign companies with generous concessions as the most rapid way to modernize their countries and enrich the property owners. The majority were neither consulted nor allowed to benefit from the railroad boom.

Revolution and Civil War in Mexico

At the beginning of the twentieth century Mexican society was divided into rich and poor and into populations of Spanish, Indian, and mixed ancestry. A few very wealthy families of Spanish origin, less than 1 percent of the population, owned 85 percent of Mexico's land, mostly in huge *haciendas* (estates). A handful of American and British companies controlled most of Mexico's railroads, silver mines, plantations, and other productive enterprises. At the other end of the social scale were Indians, many of whom did not speak Spanish. *Mestizos* (mess-TEE-so), people of mixed Indian and European ancestry, were only slightly better off; most of them were peasants who worked on the haciendas or farmed small communal plots near their ancestral villages.

After independence in 1821 wealthy Mexican families and American companies used bribery and force to acquire millions of acres of good agricultural land from villages in southern Mexico. Peasants lost not only their fields but also their access to firewood and pasture and had little choice but to work on haciendas. To survive, they had to buy food and other necessities on credit from the landowner's store; eventually, they fell permanently into debt.

For thirty-four years General Porfirio Díaz (DEE-as) (1830–1915) had ruled Mexico under the motto "Liberty, Order, Progress." To Díaz "liberty" meant freedom for rich hacienda owners and foreign investors to acquire more land. The government imposed "order" through rigged elections, bribes to Díaz's supporters, and summary justice for those who opposed him. "Progress" meant mainly the importing of foreign capital, machinery, and technicians to take advantage of Mexico's labor, soil, and natural resources.

During the Díaz years (1876–1910) Mexico City became a showplace with paved streets, streetcar lines, electric street lighting, and public parks. New telegraph and railroad lines connected cities and towns throughout Mexico. But this material progress benefited only a handful of well-connected businessmen and lowered the average Mexican's standard of living.

Though a mestizo himself, Díaz discriminated against the nonwhite majority of Mexicans. He and his supporters tried to eradicate what they saw as Mexico's rustic traditions. On many middle- and upper-class tables French cuisine replaced traditional Mexican dishes, and the wealthy traded sombreros and ponchos for European garments. To the educated middle class—the only group with a strong sense of Mexican nationhood—this devaluation of Mexican culture became a symbol of the Díaz regime's failure to defend national interests against foreign influences.

The **Mexican Revolution** was a social revolution that developed haphazardly under ambitious but limited leaders, each representing a different segment of Mexican society. The first was American-educated Francisco I. Madero (1873–1913), the son of a wealthy landowning and mining family. Strongly opposed to Díaz, he called on his fellow citizens to oppose electing him for a sixth term. This sparked a revolution in 1910 and the election of Madero as Díaz's successor. While the Madero presidency was welcomed in some quarters, it was opposed in others. The American ambassador Henry Lane Wilson helped General Victoriano Huerta, one of Madero's former supporters, engineer a coup d'état in 1913, and Madero was assassinated after only two years in the presidency. President Woodrow Wilson then disavowed American support of Huerta, recalled Ambassador Wilson, and, as a token of American concern with Mexican unrest, sent United States Marines to seize the port city of Veracruz, which they occupied for six months.

The inequities of Mexican society and foreign intervention angered Mexico's middle class and industrial workers. They found leaders in Venustiano Carranza, a landowner, and in Alvaro Obregón (oh-bray-GAWN), a schoolteacher. Calling themselves Constitutionalists, Carranza and Obregón organized private armies and overthrew Huerta in 1914. By then, the revolution had spread to the countryside.

Madero's key "popular" ally in 1910–1911 had been **Emiliano Zapata** (sah-PAH-tah) (1879–1919), but the two parted ways on the issue of land reform. Himself an Indian farmer, Zapata had led a revolt against the haciendas in the mountains of Morelos, south of Mexico City. His soldiers were peasants mounted on horseback and armed with pistols and rifles. For several years they periodically came down from the mountains, burned hacienda buildings, and returned land to the Indian villages to which it had once belonged.

Another leader appeared in Chihuahua, a northern state where seventeen individuals owned two-fifths of the land and 95 percent of the people had no land at all. Starting in 1913, **Francisco "Pancho" Villa** (1877–1923), a former ranch hand, mule driver, and bandit, organized an army of three thousand men, most of them cowboys, and divided large haciendas into family ranches. After a failed and unexplained attack on the town of Columbus, New Mexico, the U.S. Army sent General John Pershing on a nine-month mission to hunt Villa down. The mission was cut short by American entry into World War I, but, like the occupation of Veracruz, it demonstrated increasing American concern for protecting land and business interests in Mexico.

Zapata and Villa enjoyed tremendous popular support but could never rise above their regional and peasant origins and lead a national revolution. The Constitutionalists had fewer soldiers than Zapata and Villa, but they held the major cities and used the proceeds of oil sales to buy modern weapons. Gradually the Constitutionalists took over most of Mexico. In 1919 they defeated and killed Zapata; Villa was given a large estate to retire to but was assassinated in 1923 after resuming political activity. An estimated 2 million people lost their lives in the civil war, and much of Mexico lay in ruins.

During their struggle to win support against Zapata and Villa, the Constitutionalists adopted many of their rivals' agrarian reforms, such as restoring communal lands to the Indians of Morelos. They also proposed social programs designed to appeal to workers and the middle class. The Constitution of 1917 set out first principles: a one-term limit on presidential power; economic nationalism (recapturing subsoil rights from foreigners, land reform, and the right of labor to organize); and severe constraints on the church. However, powerful Mexican forces and the United States sought to prevent full implementation of the constitution. By 1928 the Mexican government had made more progress against the church than in the implementation of either political or economic reform.

By the early 1920s a decade of violence had drained the country without resolving the question of who would rule. Carranza, elected president in 1917, did not wish Obregón to succeed him. In response, Obregón allied with two other ambitious leaders and marched on Mexico City. Carranza was killed as he fled. Following the constitution, Obregón served one four-year term as president. He then managed the election of Plutarco Elías Calles (KAH-yace), his colleague in the anti-Carranza plot, who served one term with the understanding that Obregón would return to the presidency in 1928. A Catholic militant put a stop to this arrangement by assassinating Obregón before he could take office.

American Intervention in the Caribbean and Central America, 1901–1914

American intervention in the Western Hemisphere was not limited to Mexico. The nations of the Caribbean and Central America were small and poor, and their governments were corrupt, unstable, and often bankrupt. They seemed to offer an open invitation to foreign interference. A government would borrow money to pay for railroads, harbors, electric power, and other symbols of modernity. When it could not repay the loan, the lending banks in Europe or the United States would ask for assistance from their home governments, which sometimes threatened to intervene. To ward off European intervention, the United States sent in the marines on more than one occasion.

Presidents Theodore Roosevelt (1901–1909), William Taft (1909–1913), and Woodrow Wilson (1913–1921) felt impelled to intervene in the region, though they differed sharply on the proper policy the United States should follow toward the small nations to the south. Roosevelt encouraged regimes friendly to the United States; Taft sought to influence them through loans from American banks; and the moralist Wilson tried to impose clean governments by military means.

Having "liberated" Cuba from Spain, in 1901 the United States forced the Cuban government to accept the Platt Amendment, which gave the United States the "right to intervene" to maintain order on the island. The United States used this excuse to occupy Cuba militarily from 1906 to 1909, in 1912, and again from 1917 to 1922. In all but name Cuba became an American protectorate. U.S. troops also occupied the Dominican Republic from 1904 to 1907 and again in 1916, Nicaragua and Honduras in 1912, and Haiti in 1915. They brought sanitation and material progress but no political improvements.

The United States was especially forceful in Panama, which was a province of Colombia. Here the issue was not corruption or debts but a more vital interest. When the United States acquired Hawaii and the Philippines, it recognized the need for a canal that would allow warships to move quickly between the Atlantic and Pacific Oceans. The main obstacle was Colombia, which refused to give the United States a piece of its territory. In 1903 the U.S. government supported a Panamanian rebellion against Colombia and quickly recognized the independence of Panama. In exchange, it obtained the right to build a canal and to occupy a zone 5 miles (8 kilometers) wide on either side of it. Work began in 1904, and the **Panama Canal** opened on August 15, 1914.

THE WORLD ECONOMY AND THE GLOBAL ENVIRONMENT

The nineteenth-century imperialists were not traditional conquerors or empire builders like the Spanish conquistadors. They expressed their belief in progress and their good intentions in the clichés of the time: "the conquest of nature," "the annihilation of time and space," "the taming of the wilderness," and "our civilizing mission."

Expansion of the World Economy
For centuries Europe had been a ready market for spices, sugar, silk, and other imported products. The Industrial Revolution expanded this demand, especially for stimulants such as tea, coffee, and chocolate. The trade in industrial raw materials grew even faster, as well as trade in agricultural products like cotton, jute for bags, palm oil for soap and lubricants, and minerals like diamonds, gold, and copper. Some wild forest products eventually came to be cultivated: timber for buildings and railroad ties, cinchona bark, rubber for rainwear and tires, and gutta-percha (guttah-PER-cha) (the sap of a Southeast Asian tree) to insulate electric cables.

Economic botany and agricultural science were applied to every promising plant species. European botanists had long collected and classified exotic plants

A Rubber Plantation

As bicycles and automobiles proliferated in the early twentieth century, the demand for rubber outstripped the supply available from wild rubber trees in the Amazon forest. Rubber grown on plantations in Southeast Asia came on the market from 1910 on. The rubber trees had to be tapped very carefully and on a regular schedule to obtain the latex or sap from which rubber was extracted. In this picture a woman and a boy perform this operation on a plantation in British Malaya.

Mary Evans Picture Library/The Image Works

from around the world. In the nineteenth century they founded botanical gardens in Java, India, Mauritius (maw-REE-shuss), Ceylon, Jamaica, and other tropical colonies. These gardens not only collected local plants but also transferred commercially valuable plant species from one tropical region to another. Cinchona (sin-CHO-nah) (the source of the antimalarial drug quinine), tobacco, sugar, coffee, tea, and other crops were introduced, improved, and vastly expanded in the colonies of Southeast Asia and Indonesia. Cacao and coffee growing spread over large areas of Brazil and Africa; oil-palm plantations were established in Nigeria and the Congo Basin. After 1910, rubber, used to make waterproof garments and bicycle tires, came from plantations in Southeast Asia.

Throughout the tropics, land once covered with forests or devoted to slash-and-burn agriculture was transformed into permanent farms and plantations. In Java and India farmers felled trees to obtain arable land and firewood, terraced hillsides, drained swamps, and dug wells. Colonial rule also fostered population growth. Even in areas not developed to export crops, growing populations put pressure on the land. For example, the population of Java, an island the size of Pennsylvania, doubled from 16 million in 1870 to over 30 million in 1914.

Free Trade By 1870, Britain had added several dozen colonies to the twenty-six colonies it had in 1792. The underlying goal of most British imperial expansion during these decades was trade rather than territory. Most of the new colonies were meant to serve as ports in the growing network of shipping that encircled the globe or as centers of production and distribution for those networks.

This new commercial expansion was closely tied to the needs of Britain's growing industrial economy and reflected a new philosophy of overseas trade. Rather than rebuilding the closed mercantilist network of trade with its colonies, Britain sought to trade freely with all parts of the world. Free trade was also a wise policy in light of the independence of so many former colonies in the Americas (see Chapter 23).

Whether colonized or not, more and more lands were being drawn into the commercial networks created by British expansion and industrialization. Uncolonized parts of West Africa became major exporters to Britain of vegetable oils and forest products, while areas of eastern Africa free of European control exported ivory that ended up as piano keys and decorations in the homes of the middle and upper classes.

In return for the foodstuffs and industrial raw materials that flowed toward Europe and the United States, the factories of the industrialized nations supplied manufactured goods at very attractive prices. By the mid-nineteenth century a major part of their textile production was destined for overseas markets. Sales of cotton cloth to Africa increased 950 percent from the 1820s to the 1860s. British trade to India grew 350 percent between 1841 and 1870, while India's exports increased 400 percent. Trade with other regions also expanded rapidly. In most cases such trade benefited both sides, but there is no question that the industrial nations were the dominant partners.

New Labor Between 1834 and 1870 many thousands of Indians, Chinese, **Migrations** and Africans went overseas to work, especially on sugar plantations. In the half century after 1870, tens of thousands of Asians and Pacific islanders made similar voyages.

In part these migrations were linked to the end of slavery. After their emancipation in British colonies in 1834, many slaves left the plantations. To compete with sugar plantations in Cuba, Brazil, and the French Caribbean that were still using slave labor, British colonies had to recruit new laborers.

India's impoverished people seemed one obvious alternative. After planters on Mauritius successfully introduced Indian laborers, the Indian labor trade moved to the British Caribbean in 1838. In 1841, the British government also allowed Caribbean planters to recruit Africans whom British patrols had rescued from slave ships and liberated in Sierra Leone and elsewhere. By 1870 nearly 40,000 Africans had settled in British colonies, along with over a half-million Indians and over 18,000 Chinese. After the French and Dutch abolished slavery in 1848, their colonies also recruited new laborers from Asia and Africa.

Slavery was not abolished in Cuba until 1886, but the rising cost of slaves led the burgeoning sugar plantations to recruit 138,000 new laborers from China between 1847 and 1873. Indentured labor recruits also became the mainstay of new sugar plantations in places that had never known slave labor. After 1850 American planters in Hawaii recruited labor from China and Japan; British planters in Natal (in South Africa) recruited from India; and those in Queensland (in northeastern Australia) relied on laborers from neighboring South Pacific islands.

Larger, faster ships (see Chapter 27) made transporting laborers halfway around the world affordable, though voyages from Asia to the Caribbean still took an average of three months. Despite close regulation and supervision of shipboard conditions, the crowded accommodations encouraged the spread of cholera and other contagious diseases that took many migrants' lives.

All of these laborers served under **contracts of indenture**, which bound them to work for a specified period (usually from five to seven years) in return for free passage to their overseas destination. They were paid a small salary and were provided with housing, clothing, and medical care. Indian indentured laborers also received the right to a free passage home if they worked a second five-year contract. British Caribbean colonies required forty women to be recruited for every hundred men as a way to promote family life. So many Indians chose to stay in Mauritius, Trinidad, British Guiana, and Fiji that they constituted a third or more of the total population of these colonies by the early twentieth century.

The indentured labor trade reflected the unequal commercial and industrial power of the West, but it was not an entirely one-sided creation. The men and women who signed indentured contracts were trying to improve their lives by emigrating, and many succeeded. Whether for good or ill, more and more of the world's peoples saw their lives being influenced by the existence of Western colonies, Western ships, and Western markets.

CONCLUSION

What is the global significance of these complex political and economic changes in southern Asia, Africa, the South Pacific, and Latin America? One perspective stresses the continuing and growing imperialist exploitation of non-Europeans. From another perspective what was most important about this period was not the political and military strength of the Europeans but their growing domination of the world's commerce, especially investment in plantations, railroads, mines, and long-distance ocean shipping. Motives differed somewhat from region to region. Imperialists were drawn to Africa and Southeast Asia by a desire for tropical foodstuffs and industrial raw materials. Land for settlement was the attraction in Australia, New Zealand, and South Africa, as it earlier had been for European settlers in the New World. India and Latin America, having more prosperous middle classes, provided markets for European and American manufactures.

The growing exchanges could be mutually beneficial. As in Europe itself, overseas consumers found industrially produced goods far cheaper and sometimes better than the handicrafts they replaced. Industrialization also created new markets for African and Asian goods, as in the case of palm oil from West Africa or rubber from Malaya. There were also negative impacts, as in the case of weavers thrown out of work in India and the beginnings of deforestation in Southeast Asia.

Imperialist military and commercial strength did not reduce Africa, Asia, Latin America, and the Pacific to mere appendages of Europe. While the balance of power shifted in the Europeans' favor between 1750 and 1914, other cultures were still vibrant and local initiatives often dominant. Islamic reform movements, the rise of the Zulu nation, and the Mexican revolution had greater significance for their respective regions than did Western forces. Despite European power, Latin Americans and Southeast Asians were still largely in control of their own destinies. Even in India, most people's lives and beliefs maintained continuity with the past.

IMPORTANT EVENTS 1750–1914	
1756	Black Hole of Calcutta
1765	East India Company (EIC) rule of Bengal begins
1807	Britain outlaws slave trade
1808	Britain takes over Sierra Leone
1809	Sokoto Caliphate founded
1818	Shaka founds Zulu kingdom
1818	EIC creates Bombay Presidency
1821	Foundation of Republic of Liberia
1826	EIC annexes Assam and northern Burma
1828	Brahmo Samaj founded
1831–1847	Algerians resist French takeover
1834	Indentured labor migrations begin
1834	Britain frees slaves in its colonies
1836–1839	Afrikaners' Great Trek
1840	Omani sultan moves capital to Zanzibar
1848	France abolishes slaves in its colonies
1857–1858	Sepoy Rebellion leads to end of EIC rule and Mughal rule
1867	End of Atlantic slave trade
1869	Jaja founds Opobo
1876–1910	Porfirio Díaz, dictator of Mexico
1877	Queen Victoria becomes Empress of India
1885	First Indian National Congress formed
1898	Spanish-American War. U.S. takes over Cuba and Philippines
1899–1902	Boer War
1900s	Railroads connect ports to the interior of Africa
1910	Mexican Revolution begins
1917	New constitution proclaimed in Mexico

27

THE NEW POWER BALANCE, 1850–1900

On July 8, 1853, four American warships, two of them steam-powered, appeared in Edo Bay, close to the capital of Japan. The commander of the fleet, **Commodore Matthew Perry**, delivered a letter from the president of the United States, demanding that Japan open its ports to foreign trade. Japan had had contact with Europe since the sixteenth century, when Portuguese mariners and Jesuit missionaries arrived. The Dutch followed in the seventeenth century. Worried by the disruptive effects of this Western presence, Japan suppressed Christian conversion efforts and then "excluded" European merchants in 1639, although limited contact was permitted at the port of Nagasaki.

While Japan had rejected a similar request delivered by a smaller U.S. naval force in 1845, Perry's modern, well-armed fleet and a series of threatening military maneuvers made clear the dangers associated with refusing his demand to open Japanese markets. When he returned the following year, the Japanese agreed to end the exclusion policies that had kept the nation isolated for two and a half centuries. If his display of military force had compelled change, Perry's visit also served to introduce a compelling array of the Industrial Revolution's technological and scientific triumphs to Japan, including a miniature railroad, a short telegraph line, and other marvels. For the next twenty years, Japanese society was torn between those who wanted to retreat into isolation and those who wished to embrace the foreign ways and acquire modern machines. For it was now clear that only by industrializing could Japan escape the fate of weaker nations then being taken over by Europe and the United States.

In the late nineteenth century a very small number of states, known as "great powers," dominated the world. Great Britain and France had been recognized as great powers long before the industrial age. Russia achieved that status as an ally against Napoleon and began industrializing in the late nineteenth century, as did Germany, the United States, and Japan. At the dawn of the twentieth century the economic and military capacities of these rapidly industrializing powers had dramatically altered long-standing political and cultural arrangements globally. Each had extended its territorial reach by establishing new colonies and also by creating informal empires where weak local authorities were compelled to grant preferable trade concessions. While rivalries among these powers could lead to conflict and competition, they collectively exercised a world-wide ascendancy never previously witnessed.

New Technologies and the World Economy

The Industrial Revolution marked the beginning of a massive transformation of the world. In the nineteenth century the technologies discussed in Chapter 22—textile mills, railroads, steamships, the telegraph, and others—spread from Britain to other parts of the world. By 1890, Germany and the United States had surpassed Great Britain as the world's leading industrial powers. Industrialization also introduced entirely new technologies, notably electricity and the steel and chemical industries, which revolutionized everyday life and transformed the world economy. The motive force behind this second phase of industrialization consisted of potent combinations of business, engineering, and science. By the mid-nineteenth century this combination was institutionalized in engineering schools and research laboratories, first in Germany and then in the United States.

Railroads
By the mid-nineteenth century, steam engines had become the prime mover of industry and commerce. Nowhere was this more evident than in the spread of **railroads**. By 1850 the first railroads had proved so successful that every industrializing country, and many that aspired to become industrial, began to build lines. The next fifty years saw a tremendous expansion of the world's rail networks. After a rapid spurt of building new lines, British railroad mileage leveled off in the 1870s at around 20,000 miles (over 32,000 kilometers). France and Germany ultimately built networks larger than Britain's, as did Canada and Russia. The nation with the largest railroad network in 1865, the United States, then increased its mileage eleven times by 1917.

Railroads were not confined to the industrialized nations; they could be constructed almost anywhere they would be of value to business or government. That included regions with abundant raw materials or agricultural products, like South Africa, Mexico, and Argentina, or densely populated countries like Egypt. Great Britain built the fourth largest rail network in the world in its largest colony, India, to reinforce political control and develop new trade opportunities.

With the exception of Japan, European or American engineers built the railroads of Africa, Asia, and Latin America with equipment imported from the West. In 1855, barely a year after Commodore Perry's visit, the Japanese instrument maker Tanaka Hisashige built a model steam train that he demonstrated to an admiring audience. In the 1870s, the Japanese government hired British engineers to build the first line from Tokyo to Yokohama and then sent them home in the 1880s once they had trained Japanese engineers. Within a few years, Japan began manufacturing its own railroad equipment.

Railroads consumed huge amounts of land. Many old cities doubled in size to accommodate railroad stations, sidings, tracks, warehouses, and repair shops. In the countryside, railroads required bridges, tunnels, and embankments. They also consumed vast quantities of timber, initially for fuel and then for ties to support the rails and for bridges. As railroads pushed across the landscape, they often left miles of deforested land on either side of their tracks. At the same time, railroads opened new land to agriculture, mining, and other human exploitation of natural resources wherever they were built, becoming major engines of global economic development.

Steamships and Telegraph Cables

In the mid-nineteenth century, a series of developments radically transformed ocean shipping. First iron, then steel, replaced the wood that had been used for hulls since shipbuilding began. Paddle wheels replaced sails and then were replaced by propellers as engineers built more powerful and fuel-efficient engines. The average size of freighters also increased, growing from an average of 200 tons in 1850 to 7,500 tons in 1900. As both the size of ships and the number of ships grew, coaling stations and ports able to handle large ships were built around the world. For example, the Suez Canal, constructed in 1869, shortened the distance between Europe and Asia and triggered a massive switch from sail power to steam (see Chapter 26).

These modern shipping lines offered fast, punctual, and reliable service on a fixed schedule for passengers, mail, and perishable freight as the world's fleet of merchant ships grew from 9 million tons in 1850 to 35 million tons in 1910. The result was falling freight costs and greater commercial integration, changes that benefited not only the exporters of industrial products in Europe and North America but also the Asian, African, and Latin American exporters of agricultural and mining products.

At the same time, shipping companies and commercial firms were able to use a new medium of communication, **submarine telegraph cables**, to respond to changing conditions in distant markets. The early development of this technology depended on the financial support of the French and British governments, which sought to improve communication with distant colonies. European businesses were more interested in laying a cable across the Atlantic to further develop commercial linkages. The initial efforts of the 1850s failed, but an improved transatlantic cable was successfully laid in 1866. By the turn of the century, cables connected every country and almost every inhabited island. As they became the indispensable tools of modern shipping and business, the public and the press extolled this "annihilation of time and space."

The Steel and Chemical Industries

Until the nineteenth century **steel** could be made only by skilled blacksmiths in very small quantities and was reserved for swords, knives, axes, and watch springs. Then came a series of inventions that made it the cheapest and most versatile metal ever known. In the 1850s, the American William Kelly and the Englishman Henry Bessemer discovered that air forced through molten pig iron by powerful pumps turned it into steel without additional fuel. Other new processes permitted steel to be made from scrap iron, an increasingly important raw material, and from the phosphoric iron ores common in western Europe. Following these discoveries, steel became cheap and abundant enough to make rails, bridges, ships, and even "tin" cans meant to be used once and thrown away.

The chemical industry followed a similar pattern of innovation. In 1856 the Englishman William Perkin created the first synthetic dye, aniline purple, from coal tar; the next few years were known in Europe as the "mauve decade" from the color of fashionable women's clothes. Industry began mass-producing other organic chemicals—compounds containing carbon atoms. Toward the end of the century German chemists synthesized red, violet, blue, brown, and black dyes as well. These bright, long-lasting colors were cheaper to manufacture and could be produced in much greater quantities and at much lower prices than natural dyes. They delighted consumers but ruined the indigo plantations of India and Latin America. Chemistry also made important advances in the manufacture of explosives. The first of these, nitroglycerin, was so dangerous that it exploded when shaken. In 1866, the Swedish scientist Alfred Nobel found a way to turn nitroglycerin into a stable solid—dynamite. This and other new explosives were useful in mining and were critical in the construction of railroads and canals. They also enabled the armies and navies of the great powers to arm themselves with increasingly accurate and powerful rifles and cannon.

The growing complexity of industrial chemistry made it one of the first fields where science and technology interacted on a daily basis. This development gave a great advantage to Germany, which had the most advanced engineering schools and scientific institutes of the time and whose government funded research and encouraged cooperation between universities and industries. By the end of the nineteenth century, Germany was the world's leading producer of dyes, drugs, synthetic fertilizers, ammonia, and nitrates used in making explosives.

Environmental Problems   Industrialization and rapid urbanization powerfully affected entire regions such as the English Midlands, the German Ruhr, parts of Pennsylvania in the United States, and the regions around Tokyo and Osaka in Japan. The new steel mills took up as much space as whole towns, belched smoke and particulates, and left behind huge hills of slag and other waste products. Coal-burning steam engines powered the new machine age and, along with mounting domestic coal consumption for cooking and heating, also filled the skies of Manchester, England, and the world's other manufacturing centers with dense smog.

Rapidly growing urban populations in industrializing European and American cities overwhelmed primitive sanitation systems until the last decades of the nineteenth century. When a drought lowered water levels in Britain's Thames River in 1858, Londoners experienced what they called the Big Stink caused by the vast quantities of untreated human and industrial waste long dumped into the river. More threatening still were pollution-related diseases like typhoid and cholera.

The coal smoke of railroad locomotives and other steam engines contributed to air pollution as well. The chemical industries also produced tons of toxic effluents that were dumped into rivers. Thus while industrialization brought vast amounts of wealth, without environmental regulations it also caused considerable damage to nature and to the health of nearby human populations.

Electricity   No innovation of the late nineteenth century changed people's lives as radically as **electricity**. As an energy source, electricity was more flexible and much easier to use than water power or stationary steam engines. At first, producing electric current was so costly that it was used only for electroplating and telegraphy. Then in 1831, the Englishman Michael Faraday showed that the motion of a copper wire through a magnetic field induced an electric current in the wire. Based on this discovery, inventors in the 1870s devised generators that turned mechanical energy into electric current.

Electricity now had a host of new applications. Initially, arc lamps lit up public squares, theaters, and stores, while homes continued to rely on gas lamps, which produced a softer light. Then in 1879, in the United States, **Thomas Edison** developed an incandescent lamp well suited to lighting small rooms. In 1882, Edison created the world's first electrical distribution network in New York City. By the turn of the century electric lighting was rapidly replacing gas lamps in the cities of Europe and North America.

Other uses of electricity quickly appeared. Electric streetcars and subways transported people throughout the cities of Europe and North America. Electric motors replaced steam engines and power belts, increasing productivity and improving workers' safety. Commonly dependent on coal-fired generators, electric energy production contributed to air pollution as well. As demand for electricity grew, engineers built hydroelectric plants. The plant at Niagara Falls, on the border between Ontario, Canada, and New York State, produced an incredible 11,000 horsepower when it opened in 1895. At the newly created Imperial College of

akg-images/Newscom

Paris Lit Up by Electricity, 1900 *The electric light bulb was invented in the United States and Britain, but Paris made such extensive use of the new technology that it was nicknamed "city of lights." To mark the Paris Exposition of 1900, the Eiffel Tower and all the surrounding buildings were illuminated with strings of light bulbs while powerful spotlights swept the sky.*

Engineering in Japan, an Englishman, William Ayrton, became the first professor of electrical engineering anywhere in the world; his students later went on to found major corporations and government research institutes.

World Trade and Finance Improvements in transportation and communication, along with rising world population, led to a tenfold increase in international trade between 1850 and 1913. Europe imported wheat from Canada, the United States, and India, wool from Australia, and beef from Argentina, while it exported coal, railroad equipment, textiles, and machinery to Asia, Africa, and the Americas. Because steamships were much more efficient and faster than sailing ships, the cost of freight dropped dramatically, intensifying long-distance commercial links.

The growth of world trade transformed different parts of the world in different ways. The economies of western Europe and North America, the first to industrialize and the prime beneficiaries, grew more diversified and prosperous. Industries mass-produced consumer goods for a growing number of middle-class and even working-class customers: soap, canned and packaged foods, ready-made clothes, household items, and small luxuries like cosmetics and engravings. This revolution in consumption occurred at a much slower pace in the developing world and the benefits were more narrowly limited to elites and the middleclass. These privileged sectors often paid for imported novelties by imposing harsh conditions on the masses who labored in plantations and mines.

Even growing capitalist economies were prey to sudden swings in the business cycle—booms followed by deep depressions, or busts, in which workers lost their jobs and investors their fortunes. Because of the close connections among the industrial economies, the collapse of a bank in Austria in 1873 triggered a depression that spread to the United States, causing mass unemployment. Destabilizing worldwide recessions also occurred in the mid-1880s and mid-1890s. Many contemporaries feared that industrial production was growing faster than the capacity of traditional markets to consume goods, leading to falling prices and recession. The perceived solution, to expand markets and gain protected access to raw materials, helped propel the United States and the European powers to undertake a new wave of imperialist adventures in Asia, Africa, and Latin America (see Chapter 26). Tariffs could not insulate countries from the business cycle, for money continued to flow almost unhindered around the world. One of the main causes of the growing interdependence of the global economy was the financial power of Great Britain, which dominated the flow of trade, finance, and information. In 1900, two-thirds of the world's submarine cables were British owned or passed through Britain, and over half of the world's shipping was British owned. Britain invested one-fourth of its national wealth overseas, much of it in India, the United States, and Argentina. British money financed many of the railroads, harbors, mines, and other big projects outside Europe. While other currencies fluctuated, the pound sterling was as good as gold, and nine-tenths of international transactions used sterling.

Nonindustrial areas also were tied to the world economy as never before. Because many of them produced raw materials that could be replaced by synthetic substitutes (like dyestuffs) or alternative sources of supply, they were more vulnerable to changes in price and demand than were the industrialized nations. Developing regions that produced sugar, cotton, and dyes all experienced these upsets in the nineteenth century. Nevertheless, until 1913 the value of exports from the tropical countries generally kept up with the growth of their populations.

Social Changes

As fast-growing populations swelled Europe's cities to unprecedented size, millions of other Europeans emigrated to the Americas. At the same time, strained relations between industrial employers and workers spawned labor movements and new forms of radical politics. Women as well found their lives dramatically altered by economic and technological change, both in the home and in the public sphere.

Population and Migrations   The population of Europe grew faster from 1850 to 1914 than ever before or since, almost doubling from 265 million to 468 million. In non-European countries with predominantly white populations—the United States, Canada, Australia, New Zealand, and Argentina—the increase was even greater because of the inflow of European immigrants. There were many reasons for the mass migrations of this period: the Irish famine of 1847–1848; the persecution of Jews in Russia; poverty and population growth in Italy, Spain, Poland, and Scandinavia; and the cultural ties between Great Britain and English-speaking countries overseas. Equally important was the attraction of enhanced opportunities in places like Argentina, Australia, Canada, and the United States. The availability to travelers of cheap and rapid steamship and railroad transportation at both ends of immigration pathways also contributed to the scale of this massive population transfer (see Environment and Technology: Railroads and Immigration).

Between 1850 and 1900, on average, over 1 million Europeans migrated overseas every year; then, between 1900 and 1914, the flood rose to over 3 million a year. Over this same fifty-year period the population of the United States and Canada rose from 25 million to 98 million, and the proportion of people of European ancestry in the world's population rose from one-fifth to one-third. Great Britain was the most important source of immigrants by far, but very large numbers of Germans, Italians, and Spaniards joined the swelling ranks.

Why did the number of Europeans and their descendants overseas jump so dramatically? Much of the increase came from a drop in mortality, as epidemics and starvation became less common. The Irish famine of the 1840s was the last peacetime famine in European history. As farmers plowed up the plains of North America and planted wheat, much of which was shipped to Europe, food supplies increased faster than population. New technologies like canning and refrigeration also made food more abundant year-round, facilitating the export of Argentine beef and mutton to Europe. The diet of Europeans and North Americans also improved as meat, fruit, vegetables, and oils became part of the daily fare of city dwellers in winter as well as in summer.

During this period Asians also migrated in large numbers as indentured laborers who were recruited to work on distant plantations, in mines, and on railroads (see Chapter 26). Indians went to Africa, Southeast Asia, and other tropical colonies of Great Britain. Along with Chinese, Indians also emigrated to the East

Railroads and Immigration

Why did so many Europeans emigrate to North America in the late nineteenth and early twentieth centuries? The quick answer is that millions of people longed to escape the poverty or tyranny of their home countries and start new lives in a land of freedom and opportunity. Personal desire alone, however, does not account for the migrations. After all, poverty and tyranny existed long before the late nineteenth century. Two other factors helped determine when and where people migrated: whether they were allowed to migrate, and whether they were able to.

In the nineteenth century Asians were recruited to build railroads and work on farms. But from the 1890s on, the United States and Canada closed their doors to non-Europeans, so regardless of what they wanted, they could not move to North America. In contrast, emigrants from Europe were admitted almost without restriction until after the First World War.

The ability to travel was a result of improvements in transportation. Until the 1890s most immigrants came from Ireland, England, or Germany—countries with good rail transportation to their own harbors and low steamship fares to North America. As rail lines were extended into eastern and southern Europe, more and more immigrants came from Italy, Austria-Hungary, and Russia.

Similarly, until the 1870s most European immigrants to North America settled on the east coast. Then, as the railroads pushed west, more of them settled on farms in the central and western parts of the continent. The power of railroads moved people as much as their desires did.

Library of Congress

Emigrant Waiting Room *The opening of the western region of the United States attracted settlers from the east coast and from Europe. These migrants are waiting for a train to take them to the Black Hills of Dakota during one of the gold rushes of the late nineteenth century.*

Indies and the Caribbean to work on sugar plantations. At the same time, Japanese migrated in large numbers to Brazil and other parts of Latin America. Many Japanese, as well as Chinese and Filipinos, also went to work in agriculture and menial trade in Hawaii and California, where they encountered growing hostility from European–Americans.

Urbanization and Urban Environments   In 1851, Britain became the first nation with a majority of its population living in towns and cities. By 1914, 80 percent of Britain's population was urban, as were 60 percent of the German population and 45 percent of the French. Cities grew to unprecedented size. London grew from 2.7 million in 1850 to 6.6 million in 1900. New York, a small town of 64,000 people in 1800, reached 3.4 million by 1900, more than a fiftyfold increase. In 1800 New York had covered only the southernmost quarter of Manhattan Island, some 3 square miles (nearly 8 square kilometers); by 1900 it covered 150 square miles (390 square kilometers). In the English Midlands, in the German Ruhr, and around Tokyo Bay, fast-growing towns fused into one another, filling in the fields and woods that had once separated them.

As cities grew, they changed in character. Newly built railroads not only brought goods into the cities on a predictable schedule but also allowed people to live farther apart. At first, only the well-to-do could afford to commute by train; by the end of the century, electric streetcars and subways allowed working-class people to live miles from their workplaces.

In preindustrial and early industrial cities, the poor crowded together in tenements; sanitation was bad; water was often contaminated with sewage; and darkness made life dangerous. New urban technologies and the growing powers and responsibilities of governments transformed city life for all but the poorest residents. The most important change was the installation of pipes to bring in clean water and to carry away sewage. At the same time, gas lighting and then electric lighting made cities safer at night. By the turn of the twentieth century municipal governments in Europe and North America provided police and fire protection, sanitation and garbage removal, building and health inspection, schools, parks, and other amenities unheard of a century earlier.

As sanitation improved, epidemics became rare. For the first time, urban death rates fell below birthrates. The decline in infant mortality was an especially significant indicator of improved hygiene and medical care. Confident that their children would survive infancy, couples began to limit the number of children they had, and ancient scourges like infanticide and child abandonment became less frequent.

To accommodate the growing population, builders created new neighborhoods, from crowded tenements for the poor to opulent mansions for the newly rich. In the United States urban planners laid out new cities, such as Chicago, on rectangular grids, and middle-class families moved to new developments on the edges of cities, the suburbs. In Paris older neighborhoods with narrow crooked streets and rickety tenements were torn down to make room for broad boulevards and modern apartment buildings. Brilliantly lit by gas and electricity, Paris became the "city of lights," a model for city planners from New Delhi to Buenos Aires. The rich continued to live in inner cities that contained the monuments, churches, and palaces of preindustrial times, while workers often moved to the outskirts.

Lower population densities and better transportation divided cities into industrial, commercial, and residential zones occupied · by different social classes. Improvements such as water and sewerage, electricity, and streetcars always benefited the wealthy first, then the middle class, and finally the working class. In the complex of urban life, businesses of all kinds arose, and the professions—engineering, accounting, research, journalism, and the law, among others—took on increased importance. The new middle class exhibited its wealth in fine houses with servants and in elegant entertainment.

While urban environments improved in many ways, air quality worsened. Coal, burned to power steam engines and heat buildings, polluted the air, creating unpleasant and sometimes dangerous "pea-soup" fog and coating everything with a film of grimy dust. The thousands of horses that pulled carts and carriages covered the streets with their wastes, causing a terrible stench. The introduction of electricity helped alleviate some of these environmental problems. Electric motors and lamps did not pollute the air, and coal-burning power plants were built at a distance from cities. As electric trains and streetcars began replacing horse-drawn trolleys and coal-burning locomotives, cities became cleaner and healthier. However, most of the environmental benefits of electricity were to come in the twentieth century.

Middle-Class Women's "Separate Sphere"   In English-speaking countries the period from about 1850 to 1901 is known as the **Victorian Age**. The expression refers not only to the reign of Queen Victoria of England (r. 1837–1901) but also to rules of behavior and to an ideology surrounding the family and the relations between men and women. The Victorians contrasted the masculine ideals of strength and courage with the feminine virtues of beauty and kindness, and they idealized the home as a peaceful and loving refuge from the dog-eat-dog world of competitive capitalism.

Victorian morality claimed to be universal, yet it best fit upper- and middle-class European families. Men and women were thought to belong in **"separate spheres."** Successful businessmen spent their time at work or relaxing in men's clubs. They put their wives in charge of rearing the children, running the household, and spending the family money to enhance the family's social status. The majority of women from the less privileged classes, however, lived constantly with financial pressures. Many worked outside the home for wages. Others took in laundry or did low-wage piecework, like sewing for garment companies to supplement household income.

Before electric appliances, maintaining a middle-class home involved enormous amounts of work. Not only were families larger, but middle-class couples entertained often and lavishly. Carrying out these tasks required servants. A family's status and the activities and lifestyle of the "mistress of the house" depended on the availability of servants to help with household tasks. Only families that employed at least one full-time servant were considered middle class.

Toward the turn of the century modern technology began to transform middle-class homes. Plumbing eliminated the pump and the outhouse. Central heating replaced fireplaces, stoves, trips to the basement for coal, and endless dusting. Gas and electricity lit houses and cooked food without soot, smoke, and ashes. In the early twentieth century wealthy families acquired the first vacuum cleaners and washing machines. However, these technological advances did not mean less housework for women. As families acquired new household appliances, they raised their standards of cleanliness, thus demanding just as much labor as before.

The most important duty of middle-class women was raising children. Victorian mothers nursed their own babies and showered their children with love and attention. Even those who could afford governesses remained personally involved in their children's education. Girls' education was very different from that of boys. While boys were being prepared for the business world or the professions, girls were taught embroidery, drawing, and music, skills that enhanced their social graces and marriage prospects.

Young middle-class women could work until they got married, but only in genteel places like stores and offices, never in factories. When the typewriter and telephone were introduced into the business world in the 1880s, businessmen found that they could get better work at lower wages from educated young women than from men, and operating these machines was stereotyped as women's work.

Most professional careers were closed to women, and few universities granted women degrees. In the United States, higher education was available to women only at elite colleges in the East and teachers' colleges in the Midwest. European women had fewer opportunities. Before 1914 very few women became doctors, lawyers, or professional musicians. Instead, women were considered well suited to teaching young children and girls—an extension of the duties of Victorian mothers—but only until marriage. A married woman was expected to become pregnant right away and to stay home taking care of her own children rather than other people's.

A home life, no matter how busy, did not satisfy all middle-class women. Some became volunteer nurses or social workers, receiving little or no pay. Others organized to fight prostitution, alcohol, and child labor. By the turn of the century a few challenged male domination of politics and the law. Suffragists, led in Britain by Emmeline Pankhurst and in the United States by Elizabeth Cady Stanton and Susan B. Anthony, demanded the right to vote. By 1914 U.S. women had won the right to vote in twelve states. British women did not gain the right to vote until 1918.

Working-Class Women   In the new industrial cities, men and women no longer worked together at home or in the fields, a separation of work and home that affected women even more than men. While working-class women formed a majority of the workers in the textile industries and in domestic service, they also needed to keep homes and raise children. As a result, they led lives of toil and pain. Parents expected girls as young as ten to contribute to the household. In Japan, as in Ireland and New England, tenant farmers, squeezed by rising taxes and rents, were forced to send their daughters to work in textile mills. Others became domestic servants, commonly working sixteen or more hours a day, six and a half days a week, for little more than room and board, usually in attics or basements. Without appliances, much of their work was physically hard: hauling coal and water up stairs, washing laundry by hand.

Young women often preferred factory work to domestic service. Men worked in construction, iron and steel, heavy machinery, or on railroads; women worked

Jimmy Sime/Hulton Archive/Getty Images

Emmeline Pankhurst Under Arrest *The leader of the British women's suffrage movement frequently called attention to her cause by breaking the law to protest discrimination against women. Here she is being arrested and carried off to jail by the police.*

in textiles and the clothing trades, extensions of traditional women's household work. Appalled by the abuses of women and children in the early years of industrialization, most industrial countries eventually passed protective legislation limiting hours worked or forbidding the employment of women in the hardest and most dangerous occupations, such as mining and foundry work. While the stated intention was to protect women, such legislation reinforced gender divisions in industry, keeping women in low-paid, subordinate positions. Even where women worked alongside men, in factories, for example, they earned between one-third and two-thirds of the wages paid men.

Married women with children were expected to stay home, even if their husbands did not make enough to support the family. Yet they had to contribute to the family's income. Families who had room to spare, even a bed or a corner in the kitchen, took in boarders. Many women did piecework such as sewing dresses, making hats or gloves, or weaving baskets at home. The hardest and worst-paid work was washing other people's clothes. Overall, many poor women worked at home ten to twelve hours a day and enlisted the help of their small children, perpetuating practices long outlawed in factories. Without electric lighting and indoor plumbing, even ordinary household duties like cooking and washing remained heavy burdens.

SOCIALISM AND LABOR MOVEMENTS

The experience of industrialization combined with the revolutionary ideas of the late eighteenth century to produce two kinds of movements that demanded economic and political reforms: socialism and labor unions. **Socialism** was an ideology developed by radical thinkers who questioned the sanctity of private property and argued in support of industrial workers against their employers. **Labor unions** were organizations formed by industrial workers to defend their interests in negotiations with employers. The socialist and labor movements were never identical. Most of the time they were allies; occasionally they competed for the support of workers.

Revolutionary Alternatives   The growing wealth and power of new industrial elites and the harsh living and working conditions experienced by industrial workers led to the formation of labor unions, the creation of the first social welfare policies, demands for voting rights, and, for some, the dream of revolutionary transformation. Those seeking a revolution were divided among numerous parties and factions. Within the diverse and contentious world of left-leaning politics (see Chapter 22), **Karl Marx** was a formidable theorist of revolution as well as a major contestant for power. Marx shared the Enlightenment's enthusiasm for reason and logic and identified his revolutionary ideal as "scientific socialism." His adherents generally referred to themselves as communists or Marxists. Marx believed that the relentless competition inherent in industrial capitalism would lead ultimately to a social order divided between a wealthy powerful few and a mass of exploited and impoverished workers. This division, once in place, would inevitably lead in Marx's view to revolutions that would end capitalism and create a dictatorship of the proletariat (industrial workers). Once accomplished, this revolution by workers would distribute the material benefits and scientific progress achieved by the Industrial Revolution to society in general. With private property abolished, Marx asserted, the resources of government and industry could be harnessed to end poverty and injustice.

Many of those committed to revolutionary change rejected Marx's insistence that revolutionary action, violent resistance to the status quo, wait for the full development of industrial capitalism and the appearance of the proletariat. Although in broad agreement with Marx's critique of capitalism, they believed that the levels of injustice and inequality already present in society justified revolutionary violence immediately. Some of the revolutionaries rejected Marx's belief that his proposed dictatorship of the proletariat, or, indeed, any form of government, could avoid recreating the inequality and injustice that already oppressed the poor. The Russian intellectual Mikhail Bakunin (1814–1876) argued forcibly that peasants, displaced and unemployed artisans, and other exploited groups also had revolutionary potential and, consequently, that many unindustrialized regions of Europe were ready for revolution. He also dismissed Marx's faith in a future worker's government as naive.

Bakunin exercised a powerful influence over the development of anarchism, the chief revolutionary alternative to communism. Anarchists believed that revolution could be achieved through direct action by individuals and small groups, what they called "propaganda of the deed." The result of this movement's development was a series of assassinations and bombings that shook the political structures of Europe and the Americas. These attacks included the bombings of the opera (1893) and Corpus

Christi celebration (1896) in Spain and the Haymarket bombing in Chicago (1896). They also included the assassinations of President Carnot of France (1894), Prime Minister Cánovas del Castillo of Spain (1897), Empress Elizabeth of Austria (1898), King Umberto of Italy (1900), and President McKinley of the United States (1901).

The conflict between Marx and Bakunin culminated in 1872 when Bakunin and his adherents were expelled from the revolutionary umbrella organization, the International Workingman's Association. While the followers of Marx forced Bakunin from the center of revolutionary activity, his followers remained a potent source of political violence and working-class mobilization in Italy, Spain, and Argentina well into the twentieth century.

Labor Unions and Movements Since the beginning of the nineteenth century, workers had united to create "friendly societies" for mutual assistance in times of illness, unemployment, or disability. Laws that forbade workers to strike were abolished in Britain in the 1850s and in the rest of Europe soon thereafter. Labor unions sought not only better wages but also improved working conditions and insurance against illness, accidents, disability, and old age. They grew slowly because they required a permanent staff as well as a great deal of money to sustain their members during strikes. Nevertheless, by the end of the century, British labor unions counted 2 million members, and German and American unions had 1 million members each. Once organized, unions became a political force in all democratic countries, advocating for improved wages and working conditions.

Just as labor unions strove to share in the benefits of a capitalist economy, so did electoral politics persuade workers to become part of the existing political system. The nineteenth century saw a gradual extension of the right to vote throughout Europe and North America. Universal male suffrage became law in the United States in 1870, in France and Germany in 1871, in Britain in 1885, and in the rest of Europe soon thereafter. With so many newly enfranchised workers, many socialist politicians hoped to capture seats in their nations' parliaments. Rather than seize power through revolution, these democratic socialists expected to obtain concessions from government and eventually even to form a government.

Working-class women, burdened with both job and family responsibilities, found little time for politics and were not welcome in the male-dominated trade unions or radical political parties. A few radicals such as the German socialist Rosa Luxemburg and the American **anarchist** Emma Goldman became famous but did not have a large following. It was never easy to reconcile the demands of male workers with those of women. In 1889 the German socialist Clara Zetkin wrote: "Just as the male worker is subjected by the capitalist, so is the woman by the man, and she will always remain in subjugation until she is economically independent. Work is the indispensable condition for economic independence." Six years later, she recognized that the liberation of women would have to await a change in the position of the working class as a whole: "The proletarian woman cannot attain her highest ideal through a movement for the equality of the female sex, she attains salvation only through the fight for the emancipation of labor."[1]

---

[1]Quoted in Bonnie S. Anderson and Judith P. Zinsser, *A History of Their Own: Women in Europe from Prehistory to the Present*, vol. 2 (New York: Harper & Row, 1988), 372, 387.

NATIONALISM AND THE RISE OF ITALY, GERMANY, AND JAPAN

The most influential idea of the nineteenth century was **nationalism**. Whereas people had previously been considered the subjects of a sovereign, French revolutionaries defined people as the citizens of a *nation*—a concept identified with a territory, the state that ruled it, and the culture of its people.

Language and National Identity in Europe before 1871
Language was usually the crucial element in creating a feeling of national unity. It was important both as a way to unite the people of a nation and as the means of persuasion by which political leaders could inspire their followers. Language was the tool of the new generation of political activists, most of them lawyers, teachers, students, and journalists. Yet language and citizenship seldom coincided perfectly.

The fit between France and the French language was closer than in most large countries, though some French-speakers lived outside of France and some French people spoke other languages. Italian- and German-speaking people, however, were divided among many small states. Living in the Austrian Empire were peoples who spoke German, Czech, Slovak, Hungarian, Polish, and other languages. Even where people spoke a common language, they could be divided by religion or institutions. The Irish, though English-speaking, were mostly Catholic, whereas the English were primarily Protestant.

The idea of redrawing the boundaries of states to accommodate linguistic, religious, or cultural differences was revolutionary. In Italy and Germany, it led to the forging of large new states out of many small ones in 1871. In central and eastern Europe, nationalism threatened to break up large states into smaller ones.

Until the 1860s nationalism was associated with **liberalism**, the revolutionary middle-class ideology that emerged from the French Revolution, asserted the sovereignty of the people, and demanded constitutional government, a national parliament, and freedom of expression (see Chapter 23). The most famous nationalist of the early nineteenth century was the Italian liberal Giuseppe Mazzini (jew-SEP-pay mots-EE-nee) (1805–1872), the leader of the failed revolution of 1848 in Italy. Mazzini sought to unify the Italian peninsula into one nation and associated with revolutionaries elsewhere to bring nationhood and liberty to all peoples oppressed by tyrants and foreigners. The governments of Russia, Prussia, and Austria censored the new ideas but could not quash them.

The revolutions of 1848 convinced conservatives that governments could not forever keep their citizens out of politics and that mass politics, if properly managed, could strengthen rather than weaken the state (see Chapter 23). A new generation of conservative political leaders learned how to preserve the status quo through public education, universal military service, and colonial conquests, all of which built a sense of national unity.

The Unification of Italy, 1860–1870
By midcentury, popular sentiment was building throughout Italy for unification. Opposing it were Pope Pius IX, who abhorred everything modern, and Austria, which controlled two Italian provinces, Lombardy and Venetia. The prime minister of

Piedmont-Sardinia, Count Camillo Benso di Cavour, saw the rivalry between France and Austria as an opportunity to unify Italy. He secretly formed an alliance with France and then instigated a war with Austria in 1858. The war was followed by uprisings throughout northern and central Italy in favor of joining Piedmont-Sardinia, a moderate constitutional monarchy under King Victor Emmanuel.

MAP 27.1 Unification of Italy, 1859–1870

The unification of Italy was achieved by the expansion of the kingdom of Piedmont-Sardinia, with the help of France.

If Cavour's conservative, top-down approach to unification prevailed in the north, a more radical approach was still possible in the south. In 1860 the fiery revolutionary **Giuseppe Garibaldi** (jew-SEP-pay gary-BAHL-dee) and a small band of followers landed in Sicily and then in southern Italy, overthrew the Kingdom of the Two Sicilies, and prepared to found a democratic republic. The royalist Cavour, however, took advantage of the unsettled situation to sideline Garibaldi and transform Piedmont-Sardinia into a new Kingdom of Italy. Unification was completed with the addition of Venetia in 1866 and the Papal States in 1870.

The process of Italian unification illustrates the shift of nationalism from a radical democratic idea to a conservative method of building popular support for a strong centralized government, even an aristocratic and monarchical one.

The Unification of Germany, 1866–1871
The unification of most German-speaking people into a single state in 1871 had momentous consequences for the world. Until the 1860s the region of central Europe where people spoke German consisted of Prussia, the western half of the Austrian Empire, and numerous smaller states. Some German nationalists wanted to unite all Germans under the Austrian throne. Others wanted to exclude Austria with its many non-Germanic peoples and unite all other German-speaking areas under Prussia. The divisions were also religious: Austria and southwestern Germany were Catholic; Prussia and the northeast were Lutheran. The Prussian state had two advantages: (1) the newly developed industries of the Rhineland, and (2) the first European army to make use of railroads, telegraphs, breechloading rifles, steel artillery, and other products of modern industry.

During the reign of King Wilhelm I (r. 1861–1888), Prussia was ruled by a brilliant and authoritarian aristocrat, Chancellor **Otto von Bismarck** (UTT-oh von BIS-mark) (1815–1898). Bismarck was determined to use Prussian industry and German nationalism to make his state the dominant power in Germany. In 1866, Prussia attacked and defeated Austria. To everyone's surprise, Prussia took no Austrian territory. Instead, Prussia and some smaller states formed the North German Confederation, the nucleus of a future Germany. Then in 1870 Bismarck attacked France. Prussian armies, joined by troops from other German states, used their superior firepower and tactics to achieve a quick victory. "Blood and iron" were the foundation of the new German Empire.

The spoils of victory included a large indemnity and two provinces of France bordering on Germany: Alsace and Lorraine. The French paid the indemnity easily enough but resented the loss of their provinces. To the Germans, this region was German because a majority of its inhabitants spoke German. To the French, it was French because most of its inhabitants considered themselves French. These two conflicting definitions of nationalism kept enmity between France and Germany smoldering for decades. In this case, nationalism turned out to be a divisive rather than a unifying force.

The West Challenges Japan
In Japan the emperor was revered but had no power. Instead, Japan was governed by the Tokugawa Shogunate—a secular government under a military leader, or *shogun*, that had come to power in 1600 (see Chapter 21). Local lords, called

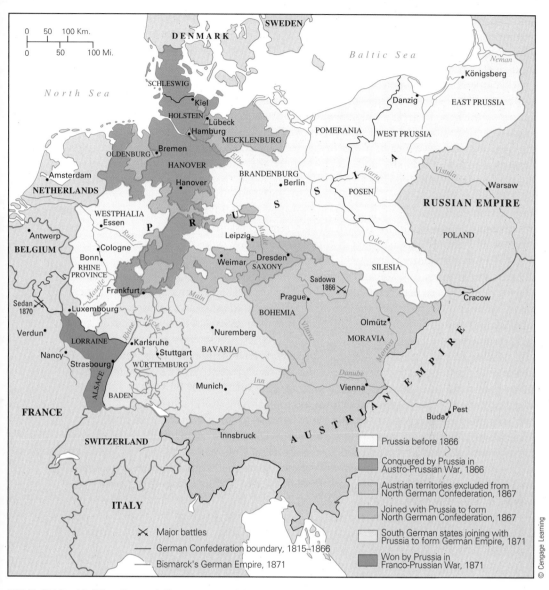

MAP 27.2 Unification of Germany, 1866–1871

Germany was united after a series of short, successful wars by the kingdom of Prussia against Austria in 1866 and against France in 1871.

daimyos, were permitted to control their lands and populations with very little interference from the shogunate.

When threatened from outside, this system showed many weaknesses. For one thing, it did not permit the coordination of resources necessary to resist major political or military challenges. Attempting to minimize exposure to Christianity and other threats to traditional culture, the shoguns prohibited foreigners from entering Japan and Japanese from going abroad in the early 1600s. They did permit the Dutch to retain a small commercial outpost at Nagasaki. While the penalty for breaking these laws was death, many Japanese ignored them. The most flagrant violators were powerful lords in southern Japan who ran large and very successful pirate or black-market operations and benefited from the decentralization of the shogunal political system in their entrepreneurial activities. But when a genuine foreign threat was suggested—as when, in 1792, Russian and British ships were spotted off the Japanese coast—the local lords realized that Japan was too weak and decentralized to resist a foreign invasion. As a result, a few of the regional lords began to develop their own reformed armies, arsenals, and shipyards. At the same time a small number of Japanese intellectuals engaged European culture, what they called Dutch learning.

By the 1800s Satsuma (SAT-soo-mah) and Choshu (CHOE-shoo), two large domains in southern Japan, had become wealthy and ambitious, enjoying high rates of revenue and population growth. Their remoteness from the capital Edo (now Tokyo) and their economic vigor also fostered a strong sense of local self-reliance.

When Commodore Matthew C. Perry, backed by a powerful fleet, demanded that Japan open its ports to trade and allow American ships to refuel and take on supplies during their voyages between China and California in 1853, he precipitated a political crisis. After consultation with the provincial daimyos, the shogun's advisers advocated capitulation to Perry, pointing to China's humiliating defeats in the Opium and Arrow Wars. As a result, when Perry returned in 1854, representatives of the shogun indicated their willingness to sign the Treaty of Kanagawa (KAH-nah-GAH-wah), modeled on the unequal treaties between China and the Western powers. Angry and disappointed, some provincial governors began to encourage an underground movement calling for the destruction of the Tokugawa regime and the banning of foreigners from Japan.

Tensions between the shogunate and some provincial leaders, particularly in Choshu and Satsuma, increased in the early 1860s. Young, ambitious, educated men who faced mediocre prospects under the rigid Tokugawa class system emerged as provincial leaders. When British and French ships shelled the southwestern coasts in 1864 to protest the treatment of foreigners, the action enraged the provincial samurai who rejected the Treaty of Kanagawa and resented the shogunate's inability to protect the country. In 1867, the Choshu leaders Yamagata Aritomo and Ito Hirobumi finally realized that they should stop warring with their rival province, Satsuma, and join forces to lead a rebellion against the shogunate.

The Meiji Restoration and the Modernization of Japan, 1868–1894

The civil war was intense but brief. In 1868, provincial rebels overthrew the Tokugawa Shogunate and declared young emperor Mutsuhito (moo-tsoo-HEE-toe) (r. 1868–1912) "restored." The new leaders called their regime the "**Meiji** (MAY-gee) **Restoration**" after Mutsuhito's reign name (*Meiji* means "enlightened rule"). The "Meiji oligarchs," as the new rulers were known, were extraordinarily talented and far-sighted. Determined to protect their country from Western imperialism, they encouraged its transformation into "a rich country with a strong army" with world-class industries. Though imposed from above, the Meiji Restoration marked as profound a change as the French Revolution.

The oligarchs were under no illusion that they could fend off the Westerners without changing their institutions and their society. In the Charter Oath issued in

1868, the young emperor included a prophetic phrase: "Knowledge shall be sought throughout the world and thus shall be strengthened the foundation of the imperial polity." It was to be the motto of a new Japan, which embraced all foreign ideas, institutions, and techniques that could strengthen the nation. The literacy rate in Japan was the highest in Asia at the time, and the oligarchs shrewdly exploited it in their introduction of new educational systems, a conscript army, and new communications. The government was able to establish heavy industry, thanks to decades of industrial development and financing in the provinces in the earlier

MAP 27.3 Expansion and Modernization of Japan, 1868–1918

As Japan acquired modern industry, it followed the example of the European powers in seeking overseas colonies. Its colonial empire grew at the expense of its neighbors: Taiwan was taken from China in 1895; Karafutu (Sakhalin) from Russia in 1905; and all of Korea became a colony in 1910.

1800s. With a conscript army and a revamped educational system, the oligarchs attempted to create a new citizenry that was literate and competent but also loyal and obedient.

The Meiji leaders copied the government structure of imperial Germany and modeled the new Japanese navy on the British and the army on the Prussian. They also introduced Western-style postal and telegraph services, railroads and harbors, banking, clocks, and calendars. To learn the secrets of Western strength, they sent hundreds of students to Britain, Germany, and the United States. Western-style clothing and hairstyles and garden parties as well as formal dances became popular.

The government was especially interested in Western technology. It opened vocational, technical, and agricultural schools, founded four imperial universities, and brought in foreign experts to advise on medicine, science, and engineering. To encourage industrialization, the government set up state-owned enterprises to manufacture cloth and inexpensive consumer goods for sale abroad. The first Japanese industries exploited their workers ruthlessly, just as the first industries in Europe and America had done. In 1881 the government sold these enterprises to private investors, mainly large *zaibatsu* (zye-BOT-soo), or conglomerates, and also encouraged individual technological innovation. Thus the carpenter Toyoda Sakichi founded the Toyoda Loom Works (now Toyota Motor Company) in 1906; ten years later he patented the world's most advanced automatic loom.

Nationalism and Social Darwinism   The Franco-Prussian War of 1870–1871 changed the political climate of Europe, making France more liberal. Germany, Austria-Hungary (as the Austrian Empire had renamed itself in 1867), and Russia remained conservative and used nationalism to maintain the status quo. The kingdom of Italy completed the unification of the peninsula begun decades earlier.

Nationalism and parliamentary elections made politicians of all parties appeal to public opinion. They were greatly aided by the press, especially cheap daily newspapers that sought to increase circulation by publishing sensational articles about overseas conquests and foreign threats. As governments increasingly came to recognize the advantages of an educated population in the competition between states, they opened public schools in every town and admitted women into public-service jobs for the first time. Politicians and journalists appealed to the emotions of the poor, diverting their anger from their employers to foreigners and their votes from socialist to nationalist parties.

In many countries the dominant group used nationalism to impose its language, religion, or customs on minority populations. The Russian Empire attempted to "Russify" its diverse ethnic populations. The Spanish government made Spanish compulsory in the schools, newspapers, and courts of its Basque- and Catalan-speaking provinces. Similarly, immigrants to the United States were expected to learn English.

Western culture in the late nineteenth century exalted the powerful over the weak, men over women, rich over poor, Europeans over other races, and humans over nature. Some people attempted to use science to justify the harsh inequalities of gender, ethnicity, and class that were common across Europe and the Americas.

One of the most influential scientists of the century, and the one whose ideas were most widely appropriated and misinterpreted, was the English biologist Charles Darwin (1809–1882).

In his 1859 book *On the Origin of the Species*, Darwin challenged common assumptions derived from religious beliefs by arguing that the earth was much older than previously believed. Based on years of research of the fossil record and careful observation of nature, he proposed that all forms of life had either evolved in the struggle for survival or become extinct over the course of hundreds of thousands of years. While controversial initially, Darwin's discoveries led to a revolution in the life sciences.

The philosopher Herbert Spencer (1820–1903) and others took up Darwin's ideas of "natural selection" and "survival of the fittest" and applied them to human society. These Social Darwinists developed elaborate pseudo-scientific theories of racial and ethnic differences, claiming that they were the result not of history but of biology. They saw social and racial differences as resulting from natural processes and opposed state intervention to alleviate inequities. Although not based on any research, these ideas gave a scientific-sounding justification for the power of the privileged and for imperialism.

THE GREAT POWERS OF EUROPE, 1871–1900

After the middle of the century, politicians and journalists discovered that minor incidents involving foreigners could be used to stir up popular indignation against neighboring countries. Military officers, impressed by the awesome power of the weapons that modern industry provided, began to think that the weapons were invincible. As a result, rivalries over colonial territories, ideological differences, and even minor border incidents or trade disagreements contributed to growing international tensions and, ultimately, to war.

Germany at the Center of Europe International relations revolved around Germany because it was located in the center of Europe and had the most powerful army on the European continent. After creating a unified Germany in 1871, Bismarck declared that his country had no further territorial ambitions, and he put his efforts into maintaining the peace in Europe. To isolate France, he forged a loose coalition with Austria-Hungary and Russia, the other two conservative monarchical powers. Despite their competing ambitions in the Balkans, he was able to keep his coalition together for twenty years.

Bismarck proved equally adept at strengthening German unity at home. To weaken the influence of middle-class liberals, he extended the vote to all adult men, thereby allowing Socialists to win seats in the *Reichstag* or parliament. By imposing high tariffs on manufactured goods and wheat, he gained the support of both the wealthy industrialists of the Rhineland and the great landowners of eastern Germany, traditional rivals for power. His government supported public and technical education as a means to stimulate industrial expansion. Bismarck also introduced path-breaking social legislation—medical, unemployment, and disability insurance as well as old age pensions—long before other industrial countries.

Under his leadership, the German people developed a strong sense of national unity and pride in their industrial and military power.

In 1888 Wilhelm I was succeeded by his grandson Wilhelm II (r. 1888–1918), an insecure and arrogant man who tried to gain respect by making belligerent speeches. Within two years he had dismissed Chancellor Bismarck and surrounded himself with yes men. He talked about his "global policy" and demanded the creation of a colonial empire. Ruler of the nation with the mightiest army and the largest industrial economy in Europe, he felt that Germany deserved "a place in the sun."

The Liberal Powers: France and Great Britain   France, once the dominant nation in Europe, had difficulty reconciling itself to being in second place. Though a prosperous country with flourishing agriculture and a large colonial empire, the French republic had some serious weaknesses. France trailed Great Britain and Germany in the development of modern heavy industry. Also troubling was the fact that France's population was scarcely growing; in 1911 France had only 39 million people compared to Germany's 64 million. In an age when the power of nations was roughly proportional to the size of their armies, France could field an army only two-thirds the size of Germany's.

The French people were also deeply divided over the very nature of the state: some were monarchists and Catholic, but a growing number held republican and anticlerical views. Yet if French political life seemed fragile and frequently in crisis, a long tradition of popular participation in politics and a strong sense of nationhood, reinforced by a fine system of public education, gave the French people a deeper cohesion than appeared on the surface.

Great Britain had a long experience with parliamentary elections and competing parties. The British government alternated smoothly between the Liberal and Conservative Parties, and the income gap between rich and poor gradually narrowed. Nevertheless, Britain had problems that grew more apparent as time went on. One was Irish resentment of English rule. Nationalism had strengthened the allegiance of the English, Scots, and Welsh to the British state. But the Irish, excluded from meaningful participation in government because they were Catholic and predominantly poor, saw the British as a foreign occupying force.

Another problem was the British economy. By the last decades of the nineteenth century, Great Britain had fallen behind the United States and Germany in such important industries as steel, chemicals, electricity, and textiles. Even in shipbuilding and shipping, Britain's traditional specialty, Germany was catching up.

Britain was also preoccupied with its enormous and fast-growing empire. A source of wealth for investors and the envy of other imperialist nations, the empire was a constant drain on Britain's finances, for it required Britain to maintain costly fleets of warships throughout the world.

For most of the nineteenth century Britain pursued a policy of "splendid isolation." Britain's preoccupation with India led British statesmen to exaggerate the Russian threat to the Ottoman Empire and to the Central Asian approaches to India. Periodic "Russian scares" and Britain's age-old rivalry with France for overseas colonies diverted the attention of British politicians from the potent threat posed by the rise of Germany.

The Conserva-
tive Powers:
Russia and
Austria-Hungary

The forces of nationalism weakened rather than strengthened Russia and Austria-Hungary. Their populations were far more divided, socially and ethnically, than were the German, French, or British peoples.

Nationalism was most divisive in south-central Europe, where many different language groups lived in close proximity. In 1867, the Austrian Empire renamed itself the Austro-Hungarian Empire to appease its Hungarian critics. Although its attempts to promote the cultures of its Slavic-speaking minorities failed to gain their political allegiance, it still thought of itself as a great power and attempted to dominate the Balkans. This strategy irritated Russia, which thought of itself as the protector of Slavic peoples everywhere.

Ethnic diversity also contributed to the instability of imperial Russia. The Polish people rebelled in 1830 and again in 1863–1864. The tsarist empire also included Finland, Estonia, Latvia, Lithuania, and Ukraine; the Caucasus; and the Muslim population of Central Asia conquered between 1865 and 1881. Furthermore, Russia had the largest Jewish population in Europe, and the harshness of its anti-Semitic laws and periodic *pogroms* (massacres) prompted many Jews to flee to America. Given this ethnic complexity, the state's attempts to impose the Russian language on its subjects were divisive instead of unifying.

In 1861, the moderate conservative Tsar Alexander II (r. 1855–1881) emancipated the peasants from serfdom. He did so partly out of a genuine desire to strengthen the bonds between the monarchy and the Russian people, and partly to promote industrialization by enlarging the labor pool. That half-hearted measure, however, only turned serfs into farm workers with few skills and little capital. Though "emancipated," the great majority of Russians had little education, few legal rights, and no say in the government. After Alexander's assassination in 1881, his successors Alexander III (r. 1881–1894) and Nicholas II (r. 1894–1917) reluctantly permitted limited attempts at social change. The Russian commercial middle class was small and had little influence. Industrialization consisted largely of state-sponsored projects, such as railroads, iron foundries, and armament factories, and led to social unrest among urban workers. Wealthy landowning aristocrats continued to dominate the Russian court and administration and blocked most reforms.

The weaknesses in Russia's society and government became glaringly obvious during a war with the rapidly industrializing Japan in 1904 and 1905. The fighting took place in Manchuria, a province in northern China far from European Russia and both armies suffered large losses. Ultimately, the Russian army, which received all its supplies by means of the inefficient Trans-Siberian Railway, was defeated by the better-trained and better-equipped Japanese. When the Russian navy finally arrived in Asian waters in 1905 after its long voyage around Eurasia and Africa, it was destroyed by the Japanese fleet at Tsushima Strait, validating the Meiji commitment to military modernization.

The shock of defeat caused a revolution in 1905 that forced Tsar Nicholas II to grant a constitution and permit an elected Duma (parliament). But as soon as he was able to rebuild the army and the police, he reverted to the traditional despotism of his forefathers. In response, small groups of radical intellectuals, angered by the contrast between the wealth of the elite and the poverty of the common people, began plotting the violent overthrow of the tsarist autocracy.

CHINA, JAPAN, AND THE WESTERN POWERS

After 1850, China and Japan—the two largest countries in East Asia—felt the influence of the Western powers as never before, but their responses were completely opposite. China resisted Western influence and became weaker, while Japan transformed itself into a major industrial and military power. One reason for this difference was the Western powers' already deep involvement in China and the distance to Japan, the nation most remote from Europe by ship. More important was the difference between the Chinese and Japanese elites' attitudes toward foreign cultures.

China in Turmoil   China had been devastated by the Taiping (tie-PING) Rebellion that raged from 1850 to 1864 (see Chapter 24). The French and British took advantage of China's weakness to demand the establishment of treaty ports where they could trade at will. In addition, the British took over China's customs enforcement and allowed the free import of opium until 1917. In response a Chinese "self-strengthening movement" tried in vain to bring about significant reforms by

The Boxer Uprising
In 1900 a Chinese secret society, the Righteous Fists, rose up with the encouragement of the Empress Dowager Cixi and attacked foreigners and their establishments. In the Western press they were known as "Boxers." These men are putting up a poster that reads "Death to Foreigners!"

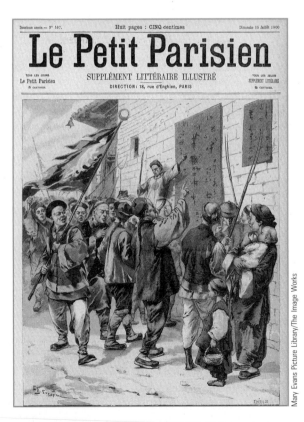

Mary Evans Picture Library/The Image Works

reducing government expenditures and eliminating corruption. While Meiji reformers in Japan sought foreign technologies to defend against imperialist aggressions, the **Empress Dowager Cixi** (TSUH-shee) (r. 1862–1908) of China opposed railways and other foreign technologies that could carry foreign influences to the interior. Government officials, who did not dare resist the Westerners outright, secretly encouraged crowds to attack and destroy the intrusive devices. They were thus able to slow the foreign intrusion, but in doing so, they denied themselves the best means of defense against foreign pressure.

Japan Confronts China   The late nineteenth century marked the high point of European power and arrogance, as the nations of Europe, in a frenzy known as the "New Imperialism," rushed to gobble up the last remaining unclaimed pieces of the world. Yet at that very moment two nations outside Europe were becoming great powers. One of them, the United States, was inhabited mainly by people of European origin. Its rise to great-power status had been predicted early in the nineteenth century by astute observers like the French statesman Alexis de Tocqueville. The other one, Japan, seemed so distant and exotic in 1850 that no European guessed that it would join the ranks of the great powers.

The motive for the transformation of Japan was to protect the nation from the Western powers, but the methods that strengthened Japan against the imperial ambitions of others could also be used to carry out its own conquests. Japan's path to imperialism was laid out by **Yamagata Aritomo**, a leader of the Meiji oligarchs. He believed that to be independent Japan had to define a "sphere of influence" that included Korea, Manchuria, and part of China. If other countries controlled this sphere, Japan would be at risk. To protect this sphere of influence, Yamagata insisted, Japan must sustain a vigorous program of military industrialization, culminating in the building of battleships.

As Japan grew stronger, China was growing weaker. In 1894 the two nations went to war over Korea. The Sino-Japanese War lasted less than six months, and it forced China to evacuate Korea, cede Taiwan and the Liaodong (li-AH-oh-dong) Peninsula, and pay a heavy indemnity. France, Germany, Britain, Russia, and the United States, upset at seeing a newcomer join the ranks of the imperialists, made Japan give up Liaodong in the name of the "territorial integrity" of China. In exchange for their "protection," the Western powers then made China grant them additional territorial and trade concessions, including ninety treaty ports.

In 1900, Chinese officials around the Empress Dowager Cixi encouraged a series of antiforeign riots known as the Boxer Uprising. Military forces from the European powers, Japan, and the United States put down the riots and occupied Beijing. Emboldened by China's obvious weakness, Japan and Russia competed for possession of the mineral-rich Chinese province of Manchuria.

Japan's participation in the suppression of the Boxer Uprising demonstrated its military power in East Asia. Then in 1905 Japan surprised the world by defeating Russia in the Russo-Japanese War. By the Treaty of Portsmouth that ended the war, Japan established a protectorate over Korea. In spite of Western attempts to restrict it to the role of junior partner, Japan continued to increase its influence. It gained control of southern Manchuria, with its industries and railroads, and in 1910 it finally annexed Korea, joining the ranks of the world's colonial powers.

CONCLUSION

After World War I broke out in 1914, many people, especially in Europe, looked back on the period from 1850 to 1914 as a golden age. For some, and in certain ways, it was. Industrialization was a powerful torrent changing Europe, North America, and East Asia. While shipping and railroads increased their global reach, new technologies—electricity, the steel and chemical industries, and the global telegraph network—contributed to the enrichment and empowerment of the industrial nations.

With these new technologies, memories of the great scourges—famines, wars, and epidemics—faded. Clean water, electric lights, and railways began to improve the lives of city dwellers, even the poor. Municipal services made city life less dangerous and chaotic. Goods from distant lands, even travel to other continents, came within the reach of millions. Middle-class women continued to focus on domestic pursuits and lived in a "separate sphere" from men, but access to education and professional careers initiated a long cycle of change. Many working-class women took jobs in the textile industry, yet their work outside the home paid less that similar jobs held by men and their traditional domestic and child-rearing responsibilities continued.

Though Karl Marx predicted a class struggle between workers and employers, socialism became more an intellectual current than a revolutionary movement. Workers achieved improvements in wages, job security, and workplace safety through labor unions, not revolutions. By the turn of the century, liberal political reforms had taken hold in western Europe. Universal male suffrage became law in the United States in 1870 and in various parts of Europe by the 1880s. At the same time women mobilized in large numbers to demand political rights, an objective not attained in Europe or North America until the twentieth century.

The framework for all these changes was the nation-state. Until the 1860s nationalism was associated with liberalism, but later generations of conservatives used public education, military service, and colonial conquests to build a sense of national unity. By 1871 both Italy and Germany had become unified states. In Japan, the Meiji Restoration restored power to the emperor and ushered in a period of Western influences and rapid economic growth.

The world economy, international politics, and even cultural and social issues revolved around a handful of countries—the great powers—that believed they controlled the destiny of the world. These included the most powerful European nations of the previous century, as well as three newcomers—Germany, the United States, and Japan.

IMPORTANT EVENTS 1850–1910	
1851	Majority of British population living in cities
1853–1854	Commodore Matthew Perry visits Japan
1856	Bessemer converter; first synthetic dye
1859	Charles Darwin, *On the Origin of Species*
1860–1870	Unification of Italy
1861	Emancipation of serfs (Russia)

1861–1865	American Civil War
1862–1908	Rule of Empress Dowager Cixi (China)
1866	Alfred Nobel develops dynamite
1867	Karl Marx, *Das Kapital*
1868	Meiji Restoration begins modernization drive in Japan
1868–1894	Japan undergoes Western-style industrialization and societal changes
1870–1871	Franco-Prussian War
1871	Unification of Germany
1875	Social Democratic Party founded in Germany
1879	Thomas Edison develops incandescent lamp
1894	Sino-Japanese War
1894–1906	Dreyfus affair (France)
1900	Boxer Uprising (China)
1904–1905	Russo-Japanese War
1905	Revolution of 1905 (Russia)
1910	Japan annexes Korea

28

THE CRISIS OF THE IMPERIAL ORDER, 1900–1929

On June 28, 1914, Archduke Franz Ferdinand, heir to the throne of Austria-Hungary, was riding in an open carriage through Sarajevo, a city Austria had annexed six years earlier. When the carriage stopped momentarily, Gavrilo Princip, member of a pro-Serbian conspiracy, fired his pistol twice, killing the archduke and his wife.

Those shots ignited a global conflict. All previous wars had caused death and destruction, but they were also marked by heroism and glory. In this new war, four years of bitter fighting produced no victories, no gains, and no glory, only death for millions of soldiers. The war became global as the Ottoman Empire fought against Britain and Japan attacked German positions in China. France and Britain involved their empires in the war and brought Africans, Indians, Australians, and Canadians to Europe to fight and labor on the front lines. Finally, in 1917, the United States entered the fray.

In this chapter, we will look at the causes of war between the great powers, the consequences of that conflict in Europe, the Middle East, and Russia, and the upheavals in China and Japan. We will also look at the more indirect impact of the war on noncombatant states in Latin America.

ORIGINS OF THE CRISIS IN EUROPE AND THE MIDDLE EAST

When the twentieth century opened, the world seemed firmly under the control of the great powers (see Chapter 27). The first decade of the twentieth century was a period of relative peace and economic growth in most of the world. Several new technologies—airplanes, automobiles, radio, and cinema—aroused much excitement (see Chapter 29). The great powers consolidated their colonial conquests of the previous decades, and their alliances were evenly matched. The only international war of the period, the Russo-Japanese War (1904–1905), ended quickly with a decisive Japanese victory.

However, two major changes undermined the apparent stability. In Europe, tensions mounted as Germany, with its growing industrial and military might, challenged Britain at sea and France in Morocco. And the Ottoman Empire grew weaker, leaving a dangerous power vacuum. The resulting chaos in the Balkans gradually drew the European powers into a web of hostilities.

The Ottoman Empire and the Balkans   From the fifteenth to the nineteenth centuries the Ottoman Empire was one of the most powerful states. By the late nineteenth century, however, it had fallen behind economically, technologically, and militarily. Europeans referred to it as the "sick man of Europe."

As the Ottoman Empire weakened, it began losing European provinces: Macedonia in 1902–1903, Bosnia in 1908, Crete in 1909, Albania in 1910. In 1912 Italy conquered Libya, the Ottomans' last foothold in Africa. In 1912–1913 Serbia, Bulgaria, Romania, and Greece chased the Ottomans out of Europe, except for a small enclave around Constantinople.

In reaction, the Turks began to assert themselves against rebellious minorities and meddling foreigners. Many officers in the army, the most Europeanized segment of Turkish society, blamed Sultan Abdul Hamid II (r. 1876–1909) for the decline of the empire. A group known as "Young Turks" plotted to force the sultan to reinstate a stillborn constitution that he had suspended in 1876 before it could have an impact. They alienated other anti-Ottoman groups by advocating centralized rule and the Turkification of ethnic minorities.

In 1909 the parliament, dominated by Young Turks, overthrew Abdul Hamid. The new regime reinvigorated the Tanzimat reform movement (see Chapter 24) that had begun in the early nineteenth century. At the same time, it cracked down on Greek and Armenian minorities. Galvanized by their defeat in the Balkan Wars, the Turks hired a German general to modernize their armed forces. The dangerous mixture of modern armies and nationalism was not limited to the Ottoman Empire, however.

Nationalism, Alliances, and Military Strategy   The assassination of Franz Ferdinand triggered a chain of events over which military and political leaders lost control. The escalation from assassination to global war had causes that went back many years. One was nationalism, which bound citizens to their ethnic group and led them, when called upon, to kill people they viewed as enemies. Another was the system of alliances and military plans that the great powers had devised to protect themselves from their rivals. A third was Germany's yearning to dominate Europe.

Nationalism united the citizens of France, Britain, and Germany behind their respective governments and gave them tremendous cohesion and strength of purpose. Only the most powerful feelings could inspire millions of men to march into battle and sustain civilian populations through years of hardship.

Nationalism could also be a dividing force. The Russian, Austro-Hungarian, and Ottoman Empires, large but fragile, contained numerous ethnic and religious minorities. Having repressed some minorities for centuries, the governments could never count on their full support. The very existence of an independent Serbia threatened Austria-Hungary by stirring up the hopes and resentments of its Slavic populations.

Imbued with nationalism, most people viewed war as a crusade for liberty or as long-overdue revenge for past injustices. During the nineteenth century, as memories of the misery and carnage caused by the Napoleonic Wars faded, revulsion against war gradually weakened. The Crimean War of 1853–1856 and the Franco-Prussian War of 1871 had caused few casualties or long-term consequences. And in the imperialist wars in Africa and Asia (see Chapter 26), Europeans almost always had been victorious at a small cost in money and manpower.

What turned an incident in the Balkans into a conflict involving all the great powers was the system of alliances. At the center of Europe stood Germany, the most heavily industrialized country in Europe. Its army was the best trained and equipped, and it challenged Great Britain's naval supremacy by building "dreadnoughts"—heavily armed battleships. In 1882 it joined Austria-Hungary and Italy in the Triple Alliance, while France allied itself with Russia. In 1904 Britain and France reached an Entente (on-TONT) ("understanding"), joined by Russia in 1907. Europe was thus divided into two blocs of roughly equal power.

The alliance system was cursed by inflexible military planning. In 1914, western and central Europe had highly developed railroad networks but very few motor vehicles, and European armies had grown to include millions of soldiers and reservists. To mobilize these forces and transport them to battle would require thousands of trains running on precise schedules. Once under way, a country's mobilization could not be canceled or postponed without causing chaos.

In the years before World War I, military planners in France and Germany had worked out elaborate railroad timetables to mobilize their respective armies in a few days. Russia, a large country with an underdeveloped rail system, needed several weeks to mobilize its forces. Britain, with a tiny volunteer army, had no mobilization plans, and German planners believed that the British would stay out of a war on the European continent. So that Germany could avoid having to fight France and Russia at the same time, German war planners expected to defeat France in a matter of days, then transport the entire army across Germany to the Russian border by train before Russia could fully mobilize.

On July 28, Austria-Hungary declared war on Serbia. The declaration of war triggered the general mobilization plans of Russia, France, and Germany. On July 29 the Russian government ordered general mobilization to force Austria to back down. On August 1 France ordered general mobilization. Minutes later Germany did likewise. Because of the rigid railroad timetables, war was now automatic.

The German plan was to wheel around through neutral Belgium and into northwestern France. The German General Staff expected France to capitulate before the British could get involved. But on August 3, when German troops entered Belgium, Britain demanded their withdrawal. When Germany refused, Britain declared war on Germany.

THE "GREAT WAR" AND THE RUSSIAN REVOLUTIONS, 1914–1918

Throughout Europe, people greeted the outbreak of war with parades and flags, expecting a quick victory. German troops marched off to the front shouting "To Paris!" Spectators in France encouraged marching French troops with shouts of

"Send me the Kaiser's moustache!" The German sociologist Max Weber wrote: "This war, with all its ghastliness, is nevertheless grand and wonderful. It is worth experiencing."[1]

When the war began, very few imagined that their side might not win. No one foresaw that everyone would lose.

Stalemate,   The war that erupted in 1914 was known as the "Great
1914–1917   War" until the 1940s, when a far greater one overshadowed
    it. Its form came as a surprise to all belligerents, from the generals on down. In the classic battles that every officer studied, the advantage always went to the fastest-moving army led by the boldest general. In 1914 the generals' carefully drawn plans went awry from the start. Believing that a spirited attack would always prevail, French generals hurled their troops, dressed in bright blue-and-red uniforms, against the well-defended German border and suffered a crushing defeat. In battle after battle the much larger German armies defeated the French and the British. By early September the Germans held Belgium and northern France and were fast approaching Paris.

German victory seemed assured. But German troops, who had marched and fought for a month, were exhausted, and their generals wavered. A gap opened between two German armies along the Marne River, into which General Joseph Joffre moved France's last reserves. At the Battle of the Marne (September 5–12, 1914), the Germans were thrown back several miles.

During the next month, both sides spread out until they formed an unbroken line extending over 300 miles (some 500 kilometers) from the North Sea to the border of Switzerland. All along this **Western Front**, the opposing troops prepared their defenses. Their most potent weapons were machine guns, which provided an almost impenetrable defense against advancing infantry but were useless for the offensive because they were too heavy for one man to carry and took too much time to set up.

To escape the deadly streams of bullets, soldiers dug holes in the ground, connected the holes to form shallow trenches, then dug communications trenches to the rear. Within weeks, the battlefields were scarred by lines of trenches several feet deep, their tops protected by sandbags and their floors covered with planks. Trenches were nothing new. What was extraordinary was that the trenches along the entire Western Front were connected, leaving no gaps through which armies could advance. How, then, could either side ever hope to win?

For four years, generals on each side again and again ordered their troops to attack. In battle after battle, thousands of young men on one side climbed out of their trenches, raced across the open fields, and were mowed down by enemy machine-gun fire. Hoping to destroy the machine guns, the attacking force would saturate the entrenched enemy lines with artillery barrages. But this tactic alerted the defenders to an impending attack and allowed them to rush in reinforcements and set up new machine guns.

The year 1916 saw the bloodiest and most futile battles of the war. The Germans attacked French forts at Verdun, losing 281,000 men and causing 315,000 French

---

[1]Frank B. Tipton, *A History of Modern Germany since 1815* (Berkeley: University of California Press, 2003), 295.

casualties. In retaliation, the British attacked the Germans at the Somme River and suffered 420,000 casualties—60,000 on the first day alone—while the Germans lost 450,000 and the French 200,000.

Warfare had never been waged this way before. It was mass slaughter in a moonscape of mud, steel, and flesh. Both sides attacked and defended, but neither side could win, for the armies were stalemated by trenches and machine guns. During four years of the bloodiest fighting the world had ever seen, the Western Front moved no more than a few miles one way or another.

At sea, the war was just as inconclusive. As soon as war broke out, the British cut the German overseas telegraph cables, blockaded the coasts of Germany and Austria-Hungary, and set out to capture or sink all enemy ships still at sea. The German High Seas Fleet, built at enormous cost but mostly coal-fueled, seldom left port. Only once, in May 1916, did it confront the oil-fueled and thus more efficient British Grand Fleet. At the Battle of Jutland, off the coast of Denmark, the two fleets lost roughly equal numbers of ships, and the Germans escaped back to their harbors.

Women in World War I *Women played a more important role in World War I than in previous wars. As the armies drafted millions of men, employers hired women for essential war work. This poster extolls the importance of women workers in supplying munitions.*

Imperial War Museum/The Art Archive

In early 1915, in retaliation for the British naval blockade, Germany announced a blockade of Britain by submarines. German submarines attacked every vessel they could. One of their victims was the British ocean liner *Lusitania*. The death toll from that attack was 1,198 people, 139 of them Americans. When the United States protested, Germany ceased its submarine campaign, hoping to keep America neutral.

Airplanes were used for reconnaissance and engaged in spectacular but inconsequential dogfights above the trenches. Poison gas, introduced on the Western Front in 1915, killed and wounded attacking soldiers as well as their intended victims, adding to the horror of battle. Primitive tanks aided, but did not cause, the collapse of the German army in the last weeks of the war. Although these weapons were of limited effectiveness in World War I, they offered an insight into the future of warfare.

The Home Front and the War Economy   Trench-bound armies demanded ever more weapons, ammunition, and food, so civilians had to work harder, eat less, and pay higher taxes. Textiles, coal, meat, fats, and imported products such as tea and sugar were strictly rationed. Governments gradually imposed stringent controls over all aspects of their economies.

The war economy transformed civilian life. In France and Britain food rations were allocated according to need, improving nutrition among the poor. Unemployment vanished. Thousands of Africans, Indians, and Chinese were recruited for heavy labor in Europe. Employers hired women to fill jobs vacated by men off to war. Some women became streetcar drivers, mail carriers, and police officers. Others found work in the burgeoning government bureaucracies. Many joined auxiliary military services as doctors, nurses, mechanics, and ambulance drivers; after 1917, as the war took its toll of young men, the British government established women's auxiliary units for the army, navy, and air force. These positions gave thousands of women a sense of participation in the war effort and a taste of personal and financial independence.

German civilians paid an especially high price for the war, for the British naval blockade severed their overseas trade. Wheat flour disappeared, replaced first by rye, then by potatoes and turnips, then by acorns and chestnuts, and finally by sawdust. After the failure of the potato crop in 1916 came the "turnip winter," when people had to survive on 1,000 calories per day, half the normal amount that an active adult needed. Women, children, and the elderly were especially hard hit. Soldiers at the front raided enemy lines to scavenge food.

The war also brought hardships to Europe's African colonies. When the war began, the British and French overran German Togo on the West African coast. The much larger German colonies of Southwest Africa and German Cameroon were conquered in 1915. In German East Africa, the Germans remained undefeated until the end of the war. The Europeans requisitioned foodstuffs, imposed heavy taxes, and forced Africans to grow export crops and sell them at low prices. As Europeans stationed in Africa joined the war, the combination of increased demands on Africans and fewer European officials led to uprisings that lasted for several years. Over a million Africans served in the various armies, and perhaps three times that number were drafted as porters to carry army equipment. Faced with a shortage of young Frenchmen, France drafted Africans into its army, where many fought side by side with Europeans.

One country grew rich during the war: the United States. For two and a half years the United States stayed technically neutral but did a roaring business supplying France and Britain. When the United States entered the war in 1917, businesses engaging in war production made spectacular profits. Civilians were exhorted to help the war effort by investing their savings in war bonds and growing food in backyard "victory gardens." Employment opportunities created by the war played a major role in the migration of African Americans from the rural South to the cities of the North.

The Ottoman Empire at War   On August 2, 1914, the Turks signed a secret alliance with Germany. In November they joined the fighting, hoping to gain land at Russia's expense. During the campaign in the Caucasus the Turks expelled the Armenians, whom they suspected of being pro-Russian, from their homelands in eastern Anatolia. Hunger and exposure killed hundreds of thousands during the forced march to Syria across the mountains in the winter. Many others were killed by regular and irregular Ottoman military forces.

The Turks also closed the Dardanelles, the strait between the Mediterranean and Black Seas. Seeing little hope of victory on the Western Front, Britain tried to open the Dardanelles by landing troops on the nearby Gallipoli Peninsula in 1915. Turkish troops pushed the invaders back into the sea. The British then promised the emir (hereditary governor) of Mecca, Hussein ibn Ali, a kingdom of his own if he would lead an Arab revolt against the Turks. In 1916 Hussein rose up and was proclaimed king of Hejaz (heh-JAHZ) (western Arabia). His son **Faisal** (FIE-sahl) then led an Arab army in support of the British advance from Egypt into Palestine and Syria. The Arab Revolt of 1916 did not affect the struggle in Europe, but it did contribute to the defeat of the Ottoman Empire.

The British made promises to Jews as well as Arabs. For centuries, Jewish minorities in eastern and central Europe had developed a thriving culture despite frequent persecutions. By the early twentieth century a nationalist movement called Zionism, led by **Theodore Herzl**, arose among those who wanted to return to their ancestral homeland in Palestine. The concept of a Jewish homeland appealed to many Europeans as a humanitarian solution to the problem of anti-Semitism.

By 1917 Chaim Weizmann (hi-um VITES-mun), leader of the British Zionists, had persuaded several British politicians that a Jewish homeland in Palestine should be carved out of the Ottoman Empire and placed under British protection, thereby strengthening the Allied cause. In November, as British armies were advancing on Jerusalem, Foreign Secretary Sir Arthur Balfour wrote:

His Majesty's Government view with favor the establishment in Palestine of a national home for the Jewish people and will use their best endeavours to facilitate the achievement of that object, it being clearly understood that nothing shall be done which may prejudice the civil and religious rights of existing non-Jewish communities in Palestine.[2]

---

[2]Walter Z. Laqueur and Barry Rubin, eds., *The Arab-Israeli Reader: A Documentary History of the Middle East Conflict*, 4th ed. (New York: Penguin Books, 1984), 18.

The British did not foresee that this statement, known as the **Balfour Declaration**, would lead to conflicts between Arabs living in Palestine and Jewish settlers.

Double Revolution in Russia	At the beginning of the war Russia had the largest army in the world, but its generals were incompetent, supplies were lacking, and soldiers were poorly trained and equipped. In August 1914 two Russian armies invaded eastern Germany

but were thrown back.

In 1916, after a string of defeats, the Russian army ran out of ammunition and other essential supplies. Soldiers were ordered into battle unarmed and told to pick up the rifles of fallen comrades. Railroads broke down for lack of fuel and parts, and crops rotted in the fields. Civilians faced shortages and widespread hunger, and food and fuel became scarce in the cities. During the bitterly cold winter of 1916–1917, factory workers and housewives had to line up in front of grocery stores before dawn to get food. The court of Tsar Nicholas II, however, remained as extravagant and corrupt as ever.

In early March 1917 (February by the old Russian calendar), food ran out in Petrograd (St. Petersburg), the capital. Women staged mass demonstrations, and soldiers mutinied and joined striking workers to form soviets (councils) to take over factories and barracks. A few days later the tsar abdicated, and leaders of the parliamentary parties, led by Alexander Kerensky, formed a Provisional Government. Thus began what Russians called the "February Revolution."

Revolutionaries formerly hunted by the tsar's police came out of hiding. Most numerous were the Social Revolutionaries, who advocated the redistribution of land to the peasants. The Mensheviks advocated electoral politics and reform in the tradition of European socialists and had a large following among intellectuals and factory workers. The **Bolsheviks**, their rivals, were a small but tightly disciplined group of radicals obedient to the will of their leader, **Vladimir Lenin** (1870–1924).

Lenin, the son of a government official, became a revolutionary in his teens when his older brother was executed for plotting to kill the tsar. He spent years in exile, first in Siberia and later in Switzerland, where he devoted his full attention to organizing his followers. His goal was to create a party that would lead the revolution rather than wait for it. He explained: "The will of a class is sometimes fulfilled by a dictator.... Soviet socialist democracy is not in the least incompatible with individual rule and dictatorship."[3]

In early April 1917 the German government, hoping to destabilize Russia, allowed Lenin to travel from Switzerland to Russia in a sealed railway car. As soon as he arrived in Petrograd, he announced his program: immediate peace, all power to the soviets, and transfers of land to the peasants and factories to the workers. This plan proved immensely popular among soldiers and workers exhausted by the war.

The next few months witnessed a tug-of-war between the Provisional Government and the various revolutionary factions in Petrograd. When Kerensky ordered another offensive against the Germans, Russian soldiers began to desert by the

---

[3]David Shub, *Lenin: A Biography* (Garden City, NY: Doubleday, 1948), 257.

hundreds of thousands, throwing away their rifles and walking back to their villages. As the Germans advanced, the government lost the little support it had.

Meanwhile, the Bolsheviks were gaining support among the workers of Petrograd and the soldiers and sailors stationed there. On November 6, 1917 (October 24 in the Russian calendar), they rose up and took over the city, calling their action the "October Revolution." Their sudden move surprised rival revolutionary groups that believed that a "socialist" revolution could happen only after many years of "bourgeois" rule. Lenin, more interested in power than in the fine points of Marxist doctrine, overthrew the Provisional Government and arrested Mensheviks, Social Revolutionaries, and other rivals.

Seizing Petrograd was only the first step, for the rest of Russia was in chaos. The Bolsheviks nationalized all private land and ordered the peasants to hand over their crops without compensation. The peasants, having seized their landlords' estates, resisted. In the cities the Bolsheviks took over the factories and drafted the workers into compulsory labor brigades. To enforce his rule Lenin created the Cheka, a secret police force with powers to arrest and execute opponents.

The Bolsheviks also sued for peace with Germany and Austria-Hungary. By the Treaty of Brest-Litovsk, signed on March 3, 1918, Russia lost territories containing a third of its population and wealth. Poland, Finland, and the Baltic states (Estonia, Latvia, and Lithuania) became independent republics. Russian colonies in Central Asia and the Caucasus broke away temporarily.

The End of the War in Western Europe, 1917–1918   Like many Americans, President **Woodrow Wilson** wanted to stay out of the European conflict. For nearly three years he kept the United States neutral and tried to persuade the belligerents to compromise. But in late 1916, German leaders decided to starve the British into submission by using submarines to sink ships carrying food supplies to Great Britain. The Germans knew that unrestricted submarine warfare was likely to bring the United States into the war, but they were willing to gamble that Britain and France would collapse before the United States could send enough troops to help them.

The submarine campaign resumed on February 1, 1917, and the German gamble failed. The British organized their merchant ships into convoys protected by destroyers, and on April 6 President Wilson asked the United States Congress to declare war on Germany.

In January 1918, President Wilson presented his **Fourteen Points**, a peace plan that called for the German evacuation of occupied lands, the settling of territorial disputes by the decisions of the local populations, and the formation of an association of nations to guarantee the independence and territorial integrity of all states. In response, General Erich von Ludendorff launched a series of surprise attacks that pushed to within 40 miles (64 kilometers) of Paris, but victory eluded him. Meanwhile, every month brought another 250,000 American troops to the front. In August the Allies counterattacked, and the Germans began a retreat that could not be halted.

In late October Ludendorff resigned, and sailors in the German fleet mutinied. Two weeks later, a new German government signed an armistice. At 11 A.M. on November 11, the guns on the Western Front went silent.

PEACE AND DISLOCATION IN EUROPE, 1919–1929

The Great War lasted four years. Millions of people had died or been disabled; political tensions and resentments lingered; and national economies remained depressed until the mid-1920s. In the late 1920s peace and prosperity finally seemed assured, but this hope proved to be illusory.

The Impact of the War   Between 9 million and 10 million soldiers died in the war, almost all of them young men. Among the dead were about 2 million Germans, 1.7 million Russians, and 1.7 million Frenchmen. Austria-Hungary lost 1.5 million, the British Empire a million, the Ottoman Empire half a million, Italy 460,000, and the United States 115,000. Perhaps twice that many returned home wounded, gassed, or shell-shocked, many of them injured for life.

War and revolution forced almost 2 million Russians, 750,000 Germans, and 400,000 Hungarians to flee their homes. Postwar conflicts also led to the expulsion of hundreds of thousands of Greeks from Anatolia and Muslims from Greece. Many refugees found shelter in France, which welcomed 1.5 million people to bolster its declining population. About 800,000 immigrants reached the United States before immigration laws passed in 1921 and 1924 closed the door to eastern and southern Europeans. Canada, Australia, and New Zealand adopted similar restrictions on immigration. The Latin American republics welcomed European refugees, but their poverty discouraged potential immigrants.

One unexpected byproduct of the war was the great influenza epidemic of 1918–1919, which started among soldiers heading for the Western Front. This virulent strain infected almost everyone on earth and killed one person in every forty. Half a million Americans perished in the epidemic—five times as many as died in the war. Worldwide, some 20 million people died.

The war also caused serious damage to the environment. No place was ever so completely devastated as the scar across France and Belgium known as the Western Front. The fighting ravaged forests and demolished towns. The earth was gouged by trenches, pitted with craters, and littered with ammunition, broken weapons, chunks of concrete, and the bones of countless soldiers. After the war, it took a decade to clear away the debris, rebuild the towns, and create dozens of military cemeteries with neat rows of crosses stretching for miles.

The Peace Treaties   In early 1919 delegates of the victorious powers met in Paris. The defeated powers were kept out until the treaties were ready for signing. Russia was not invited.

From the start, three men dominated the Paris Peace Conference: U.S. president Wilson, British prime minister David Lloyd George, and French premier Georges Clemenceau (zhorzh cluh-mon-SO). They ignored the Italians, who had joined the Allies in 1915, and paid even less attention to the delegates of smaller European nations. They rejected the Japanese proposal that all races be treated equally. They ignored the Pan-African Congress organized by the African American W. E. B. Du Bois to call attention to the concerns of African peoples around the world. They also ignored the ten thousand other delegates of various nationalities that did not

MAP 28.1 Territorial Changes in Europe After World War I

Although the heaviest fighting took place in western Europe, the territorial changes there were relatively minor. In eastern Europe, in contrast, the changes were enormous. The disintegration of the Austro-Hungary Empire and the defeat of Russia allowed a belt of new countries to arise, stretching from Finland in the north to Yugoslavia in the south.

represent sovereign states—the Arab leader Faisal, the Zionist Chaim Weizmann, and several Armenian delegations—but came to Paris to lobby for their causes. They were, in the words of Britain's Foreign Secretary Balfour, "three all-powerful, all-ignorant men, sitting there and carving up continents"[4]

Wilson, a high-minded idealist, wanted to apply the principle of self-determination to European affairs, by which he meant creating nations that reflected

---

[4]David Vital, *A People Apart: The Jews of Europe, 1789–1939* (Oxford: Oxford University Press, 1999), 756.

ethnic or linguistic divisions. He proposed a **League of Nations,** a world organization to safeguard the peace and foster international cooperation. His idealism clashed with the more hardheaded and self-serving nationalism of the Europeans. Lloyd George insisted that Germany pay a heavy indemnity, while Clemenceau wanted Germany to return Alsace and Lorraine, provinces France had lost in the Franco-Prussian War of 1870–1871.

The result was a series of compromises that satisfied no one. The European powers formed a League of Nations, but the U.S. Congress refused to let the United States join. France recovered Alsace and Lorraine but had to content itself with vague promises of British and American protection if Germany ever rebuilt its army. Britain acquired new territories in Africa and the Middle East but was greatly weakened by human losses and the disruption of its trade.

On June 28, 1919, the German delegates reluctantly signed the **Treaty of Versailles** (vuhr-SIGH). Germany was forbidden to have an air force and was permitted only a token army and navy. It also gave up large parts of its eastern territory to a newly reconstituted Poland. The Allies made Germany promise to pay reparations to compensate the victors for their losses, but they did not set a figure or a period of time for payment. A "guilt clause," which was to rankle for years to come, obliged the Germans to accept "responsibility for causing all the loss and damage" of the war. The treaty left Germany humiliated but largely intact. Establishing a peace neither of punishment nor of reconciliation, it was one of the great failures in history.

Meanwhile, the Austro-Hungarian Empire fell apart. New countries appeared in the lands lost by Russia, Germany, and Austria-Hungary: Poland, resurrected after over a century; Czechoslovakia, created from the northern third of Austria-Hungary; and Yugoslavia, combining Serbia and the former south Slav provinces of Austria-Hungary. The new boundaries coincided with the major linguistic groups of eastern Europe, but they all contained disaffected minorities. These small nations were safe only as long as Germany and Russia lay defeated and prostrate.

Russian Civil War and the New Economic Policy   In December 1918, civil war broke out in Russia. The Communists—as the Bolsheviks called themselves after March 1918—held central Russia, but all the surrounding provinces rose up against them. Counter-revolutionary armies led by former tsarist officers obtained weapons and supplies from the Allies. For three years the two sides burned farms and confiscated crops, causing a famine that claimed 3 million victims, more than had died in Russia in seven years of fighting. By 1921 the Communists had defeated most of their enemies.

Finland, the Baltic states, and Poland remained independent, but the Red Army reconquered other parts of the tsar's empire one by one. In 1922, Ukraine merged with Russia to create the Union of Soviet Socialist Republics (USSR), or Soviet Union. In 1920–1921 the Red Army reconquered the Caucasus and replaced the indigenous leaders with Russians. In 1922 the new Soviet republics of Georgia, Armenia, and Azerbaijan joined the USSR. In this way the Bolsheviks retained control over lands and peoples that had been part of the tsar's empire.

Years of warfare, revolution, and mismanagement had ruined the Russian economy. Factories and railroads had shut down for lack of fuel, raw materials, and parts. Farmland had been devastated and livestock killed, causing hunger in the cities. Finding himself master of a country in ruin, Lenin announced the **New Economic Policy** (NEP) in 1923. It allowed peasants to own land and sell their crops, private merchants to trade, and private workshops to produce goods and sell them on the free market. Only the biggest businesses, such as banks, railroads, and factories, remained under government ownership.

The relaxation of controls had an immediate effect. Production began to climb, and food and other goods became available. But the NEP reflected no change in the ultimate goals of the Communist Party. It merely provided breathing space, what Lenin called "two steps back to advance one step forward." The Communists had every intention of creating a modern industrial economy without private property. This meant investing in heavy industry and electrification and moving farmers to the cities to work in the new industries. It also meant providing food for the urban workers without spending scarce resources to purchase it from the peasants. In other words, it meant making the peasants, the great majority of the Soviet people, pay for the industrialization of Russia. This policy turned them into bitter enemies of the Communists.

When Lenin died in January 1924, his associates jockeyed for power. The leading contenders were Leon Trotsky, commander of the Red Army, and Joseph Stalin, general secretary of the Communist Party. Trotsky had the support of many "Old Bolsheviks" who had joined the party before the revolution. Having spent years in exile, he saw the revolution as a spark that would ignite a world revolution of the working class. Stalin, the only leading Communist who had never lived abroad, insisted that socialism could survive "in one country."

Stalin filled the party bureaucracy with individuals loyal to himself. In 1926–1927 he had Trotsky expelled for "deviation from the party line," and in January 1929 he forced Trotsky to flee the country. Then, as absolute master of the party, he prepared to industrialize the Soviet Union at breakneck speed.

An Ephemeral Peace   After the enormous sacrifices made during the war, the survivors developed hugely unrealistic expectations and were soon disillusioned. Conservatives in Britain and France longed for a return to the stability of the prewar era—the hierarchy of social classes, prosperous world trade, and European dominance over the rest of the world. All over the rest of the world, people's hopes had been raised by the rhetoric of the war, then dashed by its outcome. In Europe, Germans felt cheated out of a victory that had seemed within their grasp, and Italians were disappointed that their sacrifices had not been rewarded with large territorial gains. Arabs and Indians longed for independence; the Chinese looked for social justice and a lessening of foreign intrusion; and the Japanese hoped to expand their influence in China. In Russia, the Communists were eager to consolidate their power and export their revolution to the rest of the world.

In 1923 Germany suspended reparations payments. In retaliation for the French occupation of the Ruhr, the German government began printing money recklessly, causing the most severe inflation the world had ever seen. Soon German money was worth so little that it took a wheel-barrow full of it to buy a loaf of bread. As Germany teetered on the brink of civil war, radical nationalists tried to overthrow the government. Finally, the German government issued a new currency and promised to resume reparations payments, and the French agreed to withdraw their troops from the Ruhr.

Beginning in 1924 the world enjoyed a few years of calm and prosperity. After the end of the German crisis of 1923, the western European nations became less confrontational, and Germany joined the League of Nations. The vexed issue of reparations also seemed to vanish, as Germany borrowed money from New York banks to make its payments to France and Britain, which used the money to repay their wartime loans from the United States. This triangular flow of money, based on credit, stimulated the rapid recovery of the European economies. France began rebuilding its war-torn northern zone; Germany recovered from its hyperinflation; and a boom began in the United States that was to last for five years.

While their economies flourished, governments grew more cautious and businesslike. Even the Communists, after Lenin's death, seemed to give up their attempts to spread revolution abroad. Yet neither Germany nor the Soviet Union accepted its borders with the small nations that had arisen between them. In 1922, they signed a secret pact allowing the German army to conduct maneuvers in Russia (in violation of the Versailles treaty) in exchange for German help in building up Russian industry and military potential.

The League of Nations proved adept at resolving numerous technical issues pertaining to health, labor relations, and postal and telegraph communications. Without U.S. participation, however, sanctions against states that violated League rules carried little weight.

CHINA AND JAPAN: CONTRASTING DESTINIES

China and Japan were both subject to Western pressures, but their modern histories have been strikingly opposite. China clung much longer than Japan to a traditional social structure and economy, then collapsed into chaos and revolution. Japan experienced reform from above (see Chapter 27), acquiring industry and a powerful military, which it used to take advantage of China's weakness. Their different reactions to the pressures of the West put these two great nations on a collision course.

Social and Economic Change   China's population—about 400 million in 1900—was the largest of any country in the world and growing fast. In 1900 peasant plots averaged between 1 and 4 acres (less than 2 hectares) apiece, half as large as they had been two generations earlier. Farming methods had not changed in centuries, and landlords and tax collectors took more than half of the harvest. Most Chinese worked incessantly, survived on a diet of grain and vegetables, and spent their lives in fear of floods, bandits, and tax collectors.

Above the peasantry, Chinese society was divided into many groups and strata. Landowners lived off the rents of their tenants. Officials, chosen through an elaborate examination system, enriched themselves from taxes and the

Bettmann/Corbis

The Bund in Shanghai *On the Bund, the most important street in Shanghai, banks, corporate headquarters, and luxury hotels faced the waterfront where ships from around the world docked. Although Shanghai was China's industrial and commercial center, many of its workers loaded and unloaded ships by hand or pulled wealthy customers in rickshaws.*

government's monopolies on salt, iron, and other products. Shanghai, China's financial and commercial center, was famous for its wealthy foreigners and its opium addicts, prostitutes, and gangsters.

Although foreign trade represented only a small part of China's economy, contact with the outside world had a tremendous impact on Chinese politics. Young men living in the treaty ports saw no chance for advancement in the old system of examinations and official positions. Some learned foreign ideas in Christian mission schools or abroad. The contrast between the squalor in which most urban residents lived and the luxury of the foreigners' enclaves in the treaty ports sharpened the resentment of educated Chinese.

Japan had few natural resources and very little arable land on which to grow food for its rising population. Typhoons regularly hit its southern regions, and earthquakes periodically shook the country, which lies on the great ring of tectonic fault lines that surround the Pacific Ocean. The Kanto earthquake of 1923 destroyed all of Yokohama and half of Tokyo and killed some 200,000 people.

Japan's population reached 60 million in 1925 and was increasing by a million a year. The crash program of industrialization begun in 1868 by the Meiji oligarchs (see Chapter 27) accelerated during the First World War, when Japan's economy grew four times as fast as western Europe's and eight times faster than China's.

Economic growth aggravated social tensions. The *narikin* ("new rich") affected Western ways and lifestyles that clashed with the austerity of earlier times. In the big cities *mobos* (modern boys) and *mogas* (modern girls) shocked traditionalists with their foreign ways: dancing together, wearing short skirts and tight pants, and behaving like Americans. Students who flirted with dangerous thoughts were called "Marx boys."

The main beneficiaries of prosperity were the *zaibatsu* (zie-BOT-soo), or conglomerates, four of which—Mitsubishi, Sumitomo, Yasuda, and Mitsui—controlled most of Japan's industry and commerce. Farmers, who constituted half of the population, remained poor; in desperation some sold their daughters to textile mills or into domestic service. Labor unions were weak and repressed by the police.

Japanese prosperity depended on foreign trade. The country exported silk and light manufactures and imported almost all its fuel, raw materials, and machine tools, and even some of its food. Though less at the mercy of the weather than China, Japan was much more vulnerable to swings in the world economy.

Revolution and War, 1900–1918 In 1900 China's Empress Dowager Cixi (TSUH-shee), who had seized power in a palace coup two years earlier, encouraged a secret society, the Righteous Fists, or Boxers, to rise up and expel all the foreigners from China. When the Boxers threatened the foreign legation in Beijing, an international force from the Western powers and Japan captured the city and forced China to pay a huge indemnity. Shocked by these events, many Chinese students became convinced that China needed a revolution to get rid of the Qing dynasty and modernize their country.

When Cixi died in 1908, the Revolutionary Alliance led by **Sun Yat-sen** (soon yot-SEN) (1866–1925) prepared to take over. Sun had spent much of his life in Japan, England, and the United States, plotting the overthrow of the Qing dynasty. His ideas were a mixture of nationalism, socialism, and Confucian philosophy. His patriotism, his powerful ambition, and his tenacious spirit attracted a large following.

The military thwarted Sun's plans. After China's defeat in the war with Japan in 1895, the government had agreed to equip the army with modern rifles and machine guns. This, combined with the fact that local armies were beholden to warlords rather than to the central government, created a threatening situation for the Qing. When a regional army mutinied in October 1911, **Yuan Shikai** (you-AHN she-KIE), the most powerful of the regional generals, refused to defend the Qing. A revolutionary assembly at Nanjing elected Sun Yat-sen president of China in December 1911, but he had no military forces at his command. To avoid a clash with the army, he resigned after a few weeks, and a new national assembly elected Yuan president of the new Chinese republic.

Yuan was an able military leader, but he had no political program. When Sun reorganized his followers into a political party called the **Guomindang** (gwo-min-dong) (National People's Party), Yuan quashed every attempt at creating a Western-style government and harassed Sun's followers. Victory in the first round of the struggle to create a new China went to the military.

Meanwhile, the Japanese were quick to join the Allied side in World War I, since they saw the war as an opportunity to advance their interests while the Europeans were occupied elsewhere. They quickly conquered the German colonies in the northern Pacific and on the coast of China, then turned their attention to the rest of China. In 1915 Japan presented China with Twenty-One Demands, which would have turned it into a virtual protectorate. Britain and the United States persuaded Japan to soften the demands but could not prevent it from keeping the German coastal enclaves and extracting railroad and mining concessions at China's expense. In protest, anti-Japanese riots and boycotts broke out throughout China. Thus began a bitter struggle between the two countries that was to last for thirty years.

Chinese Warlords and the Guomindang, 1919–1929

At the Paris Peace Conference, the great powers accepted Japan's seizure of the German enclaves in China. To many Chinese, this decision was a cruel insult. On May 4, 1919, students demonstrated in front of the Forbidden City of Beijing. Despite a government ban, the May Fourth Movement spread to other parts of China. A new generation was growing up to challenge the old officials, the regional generals, and the foreigners.

Sun Yat-sen tried to make a comeback in Guangzhou (Canton) in the early 1920s. Though not a Communist, he was impressed with the efficiency of Lenin's revolutionary tactics and let a Soviet adviser reorganize the Guomindang along Leninist lines. He also welcomed members of the newly created Chinese Communist Party into the Guomindang.

When Sun died in 1925, the leadership of his party passed to Jiang Jieshi, known in the West as **Chiang Kai-shek** (chang kie-shek) (1887–1975). An officer and director of the military academy, Chiang trained several hundred young officers who remained loyal to him thereafter. In 1927 he determined to defeat the regional warlords. As his army moved north from its base in Canton, he briefly formed an alliance with the Communists. Once his troops occupied Shanghai, however, he crushed the labor unions and decimated the Communists, whom he considered a threat. He then defeated or co-opted most of the other warlords and established a dictatorship.

Chiang's government issued ambitious plans to build railroads, develop agriculture and industry, and modernize China from the top down. However, his followers were neither competent administrators nor ruthless modernizers. Instead, his government attracted thousands of opportunists whose goals were to "become officials and get rich" by taxing and plundering businesses. In the countryside tax collectors and landowners squeezed the peasants ever harder, even in times of natural disasters. What little money reached the government's coffers went to the military. Thus for twenty years after the fall of the Qing, China remained mired in poverty, subject to corrupt officials and the whims of nature.

THE NEW MIDDLE EAST

After the war, the Arab peoples expected to have a say in the outcome of the Great War. But the victorious French and British planned to treat the Middle East like a territory open to colonial rule. The result was a legacy of instability that has persisted to this day.

The Mandate System   At the Paris Peace Conference, France, Britain, Italy, and Japan proposed to divide the former German colonies and the territories of the Ottoman Empire among themselves, but their ambitions clashed with President Wilson's ideal of national self-determination. Eventually, the victors arrived at a compromise solution called the **mandate system**: colonial rulers would administer the territories but would be accountable to the League of Nations for "the material and moral well-being and the social progress of the inhabitants."

Class C Mandates—those with the smallest populations—were treated as colonies by their conquerors. South Africa replaced Germany in Southwest Africa (now Namibia); Britain, Australia, New Zealand, and Japan took over the German islands in the Pacific. Class B Mandates, larger than Class C but still underdeveloped, were to be ruled for the benefit of their inhabitants under League of Nations supervision. Most of Germany's African colonies, including Tanganyika, Cameroon, and Togo, fell into this category.

The Arab-speaking territories of the old Ottoman Empire were Class A Mandates. The League of Nations declared that they had "reached a state of development where their existence as independent nations can be provisionally recognized subject to the rendering of administrative advice and assistance by a Mandatory, until such time as they are able to stand alone." While Arabs interpreted this ambiguous wording as a promise of independence, Britain and France sent troops into the region "for the benefit of its inhabitants." Palestine (divided now into Israel in the west, Jordan in the east, and the Occupied West Bank in between) and Iraq (formerly Mesopotamia) became British mandates; France claimed Syria and Lebanon. (See Diversity and Dominance: The Middle East After World War I.)

The Rise of Modern Turkey   At the end of the war, as the Ottoman Empire teetered on the brink of collapse, France, Britain, and Italy saw an opportunity to expand their empires, and Greece eyed those parts of Anatolia inhabited by Greeks. In 1919 French, British, Italian, and Greek forces occupied Constantinople and parts of Anatolia. By the Treaty of Sèvres (1920) the Allies made the sultan give up most of his lands.

In 1919, Mustafa Kemal had formed a nationalist government in central Anatolia with the backing of fellow army officers. In 1922, after a short but fierce war against invading Greeks, his armies reconquered Anatolia and the area around Constantinople. The victorious Turks forced hundreds of thousands of Greeks from their ancestral homes in Anatolia. In response the Greek government expelled all Muslims from Greece. A Turkish Republic was proclaimed in 1923.

As a war hero and proclaimed savior of his country, Mustafa Kemal was able to impose wrenching changes on his people. An outspoken modernizer, he was

The Middle East After World War I

During the First World War, Entente forces invaded and occupied Palestine, Mesopotamia, and Syria. This raised the question of what to do with these territories after the war. Would they be returned to the Ottoman Empire? Would they simply be added to the colonial empires of Britain and France? Or would they become independent Arab states?

The following documents illustrate the diversity of opinions among various groups planning the postwar settlement: Great Britain, concerned with defeating Germany and maintaining its empire; the United States, basing its policies on lofty principles; and Arab delegates from the Middle East, seeking self-determination.

In the early twentieth century, in response to the rise of anti-Semitism in Europe, a movement called Zionism had arisen among European Jews. Zionists, led by Theodore Herzl, hoped for a return to Israel, the ancestral homeland of the Jewish people. For two thousand years this land had been a province of various empires—the Roman, Byzantine, Arab, and Ottoman—and was inhabited by Arabic-speaking people, most of whom practiced the Islamic religion.

During the war the British government was receptive to the idea of establishing a Jewish homeland in Palestine. It was motivated by the need to win the war, but it also considered the more distant future. The result was a policy statement, sent by Foreign Secretary Arthur James Balfour to Baron Rothschild, a prominent supporter of the Zionist movement in England. This statement, called the "Balfour Declaration," has haunted the Middle East ever since.

The Balfour Declaration of 1917

Foreign Office
November 2nd, 1917

Dear Lord Rothschild:

I have much pleasure in conveying to you, on behalf of His Majesty's Government, the following declaration of sympathy with Jewish Zionist aspirations which have been submitted to, and approved by, the Cabinet:

> His Majesty's Government view with favor the establishment in Palestine of a national home for the Jewish people, and will use their best endeavors to facilitate the achievement of this object, it being clearly understood that nothing shall be done which may prejudice the civil and religious rights of existing non-Jewish communities in Palestine, or the rights and political status enjoyed by Jews in any other country.

I should be grateful if you would bring this declaration to the knowledge of the Zionist Federation.

Yours,
Arthur James Balfour

On January 8, 1918, the American president Woodrow Wilson issued his famous Fourteen Points proposal to end the war. Much of his speech was devoted to European affairs or to international relations in general, but two of his fourteen points referred to the Arab world.

Woodrow Wilson's Fourteen Points

What we demand in this war ... is that the world be made fit and safe to live in; and particularly that it be made safe for every peace-loving nation which, like our own, wishes to live its own life, determine its own institutions, be assured of justice and fair dealing by the other peoples of the world as against force and selfish aggression. All the peoples of the world are in effect partners in this interest, and for our own part we see very clearly that unless justice be done to others it will not be done to us. The programme of the world's peace, therefore, is our programme; and that programme, the only possible programme, as we see it, is this:

XII. The Turkish portions of the present Ottoman Empire should be assured a secure sovereignty, but the other nationalities which are now under Turkish rule should be assured an undoubted security of life and an absolutely unmolested opportunity of autonomous development....

When the war ended, the victorious Allies assembled in Paris to determine, among other things, the fate of the former Arab provinces of the Ottoman Empire. Arab leaders had reason to doubt the intentions of the great powers, especially Britain and France. When the Allies decided to create mandates in the Arab territories on the grounds that the Arab peoples were not ready for independence, Arab leaders expressed their misgivings, as in the following statement:

Memorandum of the General Syrian Congress, July 2, 1919

We the undersigned members of the General Syrian Congress, meeting in Damascus on Wednesday, July 2nd, 1919, made up of representatives from the three Zones, viz., The Southern, Eastern, and Western, provided with credentials and authorizations by the inhabitants of our various districts, Moslems, Christians, and Jews, have agreed upon the following statement of the desires of the people of the country who have elected us....

1. We ask absolutely complete political independence for Syria....

3. Considering the fact that the Arabs inhabiting the Syrian area are not naturally less gifted than other more advanced races and that they are by no means less developed than the Bulgarians, Serbians, Greeks, and Roumanians at the beginning of their independence, we protest against Article 22 of the Covenant of the League of Nations, placing us among the nations in their middle stage of development which stand in need of a mandatory power.

4. ... relying on the declarations of President Wilson that his object in waging war was to put an end to the ambition of conquest and colonization, ... and believing that the American Nation is furthest from any thought of colonization and has no political ambition in our country, we will seek the technical and economic assistance from the United States of America, provided that such assistance does not exceed 20 years.

5. In the event of America not finding herself in a position to accept our desire for assistance, we will seek this assistance from Great Britain, also provided that such does not prejudice our complete independence and unity of our country and that the duration of such assistance does not exceed that mentioned in the previous article.

6. We do not acknowledge any right claimed by the French Government in any part whatever of our Syrian country and refuse that she should assist us or have a hand in our country under any circumstances and in any place.

7. We opposed the pretensions of the Zionists to create a Jewish

commonwealth in the southern part of Syria, known as Palestine, and oppose Zionist migration to any part of our country; for we do not acknowledge their title but consider them a grave peril to our people from the national, economical, and political points of view. Our Jewish compatriots shall enjoy our common rights and assume our common responsibilities.

Questions for Analysis

1. Was there a contradiction between Balfour's proposal to establish "a national home for the Jewish people" and the promise "that nothing shall be done which may prejudice the civil and religious rights of existing non-Jewish communities in Palestine"? If so, why did he make two contradictory promises?

2. How would Woodrow Wilson's statements about "an absolutely unmolested opportunity of autonomous development" apply to Palestine?

3. Why did the delegates to the General Syrian Congress object to the plan to create mandates in the former Ottoman provinces? What alternatives did they offer?

4. Why did the delegates object to the creation of a Jewish commonwealth?

Sources: The Balfour Declaration, *The Times* (London), November 9, 1917. Memorandum of the General Syrian Congress, *Foreign Relations of the United States: Paris Peace Conference*, vol. 12 (Washington, DC: Government Printing Office, 1919), 780–781.

eager to bring Turkey closer to Europe as quickly as possible. He abolished the sultanate, declared Turkey a secular republic, and introduced European laws. In a radical break with Islamic tradition, he suppressed Muslim courts, schools, and religious orders and replaced the Arabic alphabet with the Latin alphabet.

He also attempted to westernize the traditional Turkish family. Women received civil equality, including the right to vote and to be elected to the national assembly. Kemal forbade polygamy and instituted civil marriage and divorce. He even changed people's clothing, strongly discouraging women from veiling their faces, and replacing the fez, a men's hat adopted as a symbol of reform in the nineteenth century, with the European brimmed hat. He ordered everyone to take a family name, choosing the name **Atatürk** ("father of the Turks") for himself. His reforms spread quickly in the cities; but in rural areas, where Islamic traditions remained strong, resistance continued.

Arab Lands and the Question of Palestine
Among the Arab people, the thinly disguised colonialism of the mandate system set off protests and rebellions. Arabs viewed the European presence not as liberation from Ottoman oppression, but as foreign occupation, such as fellow Arabs in Algeria, Tunisia, and Morocco were experiencing under French rule.

After World War I, which had left enormous numbers dead from violence and famine, Middle Eastern society underwent dramatic changes. Trucks replaced camel caravans, and landless peasants migrated to the swelling cities. The population of the region is estimated to have bounced back by 50 percent between 1914 and 1939, while that of large cities such as Constantinople, Baghdad, and Cairo doubled.

The urban and mercantile middle class, encouraged by the transformation of Turkey, adopted Western ideas, customs, and styles of housing and clothing. To prepare their sons for jobs in government and business, some families sent them to European secular or mission schools, then to Western colleges in Istanbul, Cairo, or Beirut or to universities abroad. A few women became schoolteachers or nurses. Secular educational opportunities varied widely from Lebanon, where French influence was strong; to Iran, whose first university was established in 1933; to Saudi Arabia, which strongly resisted Western influences.

The region in closest contact with Europe was the Maghrib—Algeria, Tunisia, and Morocco—which the French army considered its private domain. Alongside the old native quarters, the French built modern neighborhoods inhabited mainly by Europeans. France had occupied Algeria since 1830 and had encouraged European immigration. The settlers owned the best lands and monopolized government jobs and businesses, while Arabs and Berbers remained poor and suffered intense discrimination.

The British attempted to control the Middle East with a mixture of bribery and intimidation. They made Faisal, leader of the Arab Revolt, king of Iraq and used aerial bombing of rebellious nomads to enforce their will. In 1931 they reached an agreement with King Faisal's government: official independence for Iraq in exchange for the right to keep two air bases, a military alliance, and an assured flow of petroleum. France, meanwhile, sent thousands of troops to Syria and Lebanon to crush nationalist uprisings.

In Egypt, as in Iraq, the British substituted a phony independence for official colonialism. They declared Egypt independent in 1922 but reserved the right to station troops along the Suez Canal to secure their link with India in the event of war. Most galling to the Wafd (Nationalist) Party was the British attempt to remove Egyptian troops from Sudan, a land many Egyptians considered a colony of Egypt. Britain was successful in keeping Egypt in limbo—neither independent nor a colony—thanks to an alliance with King Fuad and conservative Egyptian politicians who feared both secular and religious radicalism.

Before the war, a Jewish minority lived in Palestine, as in other Arab countries. Small numbers of Jews had immigrated to Palestine following their expulsion from Spain in 1492, and a trickle continued into the nineteenth century. As soon as Palestine became a British mandate in 1920, however, many more came from Europe, encouraged by the Balfour Declaration of 1917. Those supporting a socialist version of Zionism established *kibbutzim*, or communal farms, while nonsocialists belonging to the Revisionist wing of the Zionist movement preferred to settle in the cities. But purchases of land by Jewish agencies angered the indigenous Arabs, especially tenant farmers who were evicted to make room for settlers, and in 1920–1921 riots erupted between Jews and Arabs. When far more Jewish immigrants arrived than they had anticipated, the British tried to limit immigration, thereby alienating the Jews without mollifying the Arabs. Increasingly, Jews arrived without papers, smuggled in by militant Zionist organizations. In the 1930s the country was torn by strikes and guerrilla warfare that the British could not control. In the process, Britain earned the hatred of both sides.

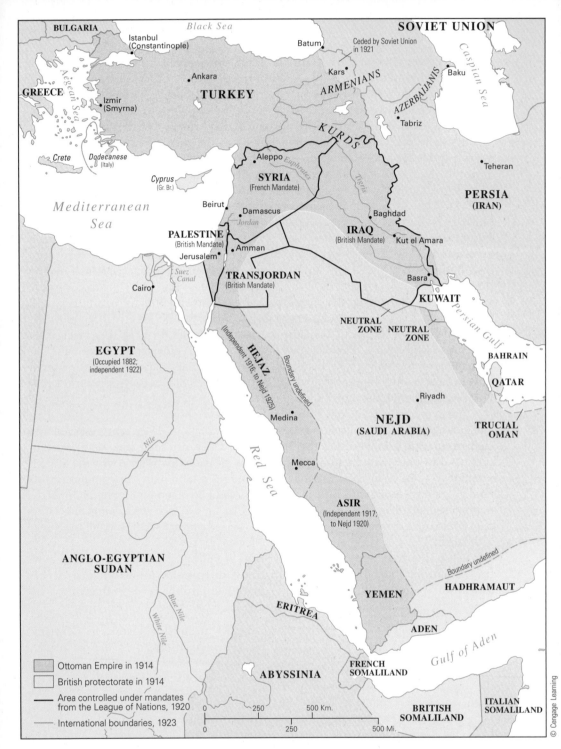

MAP 28.2 Territorial Changes in the Middle East After World War I

The defeat and dismemberment of the Ottoman Empire at the end of World War I resulted in an entirely new political map of the region. The Turkish Republic inherited Anatolia and a small piece of the Balkans, while the Ottoman Empire's Arab provinces were divided between France and Great Britain. Only Iran and Egypt did not change.

The Jewish Settlement of Palestine *Thousands of Jews fleeing persecution and discrimination in Europe settled on the land and founded kibbutzim, or collective farms. In this picture taken in 1912, an eighty-four-year-old immigrant from Russia learns to plow the land.*

CONCLUSION

In the late 1920s it seemed as though the victors in the Great War might reestablish the prewar prosperity and European dominance of the globe. But the spirit of the 1920s was not real peace; instead it was the eye of a hurricane. The Great Depression and World War II were in the offing.

The Great War caused a major realignment among the nations of the world. France and Britain, the two leading colonial powers, emerged economically weakened despite their victory. The war brought defeat and humiliation to Germany but did not reduce its military or industrial potential. It destroyed the old regime of Russia, leading to civil war and revolution from which the victorious powers sought to isolate themselves. Two other old empires—the Austro-Hungarian and the Ottoman—were divided into many smaller and weaker nations.

Japan took advantage of the European conflict to develop its industries and press its demands on a China weakened by domestic turmoil and social unrest. The United States emerged as the most prosperous and potentially most powerful nation, restrained only by the isolationist sentiments of many Americans.

In the Middle East, the fall of the Ottoman Empire awakened aspirations of nationhood among the Turkish, Arab, Armenian, and Kurdish inhabitants and

Jewish immigrants. These aspirations were thwarted when France and Great Britain succeeded in imposing their rule upon the former Ottoman lands, giving rise to conflicts and bitter enmities.

IMPORTANT EVENTS 1900–1929	
1900	Boxer uprising in China
1904	British-French Entente
1904–1905	Russo-Japanese War
1907	British-Russian Entente
1909	Young Turks overthrow Sultan Abdul Hamid
1911	Chinese revolutionaries led by Sun Yat-sen overthrow Qing dynasty
1912	Italy conquers Libya, last Ottoman territory in Africa
1912–1913	Balkan Wars
1914	Assassination of Archduke Franz Ferdinand sparks World War I
1915	British defeat at Gallipoli
1915	Japan presents Twenty-One Demands to China
1916	Battles of Verdun and the Somme
1916	Arab Revolt in Arabia
1917	Russian Revolutions; United States enters the war
1917	Balfour Declaration
1918	Armistice ends World War I
1918–1921	Civil war in Russia
1919	Treaty of Versailles
1919	May Fourth Movement in China
1919–1922	War between Turkey and Greece
1922	Egypt nominally independent
1923	Mustafa Kemal proclaims Turkey a republic
1923–1928	New Economic Policy in Russia
1927	Guomindang forces occupy Shanghai and expel Communists

29

REVOLUTIONS IN LIVING, 1900–1950

In 1869 three Japanese businessmen—an entrepreneurial former cook, a greengrocer, and a wagon builder—responded to government concerns about urban congestion and applied for a license to build a *jinriksha* ("man-power-vehicle"). They described it as "a little seat in the Western style, mounted on wheels so that it can be pulled about. It does not shake as much as the usual cart, and it is easy to turn round. It will not hinder other traffic, and since it can be pulled by one person, it is very cheap."[1] Their first vehicles, which quickly came to be called rickshaws, appeared a year later. A year after that, in 1871, Japan enacted its first patent law, and the three applied for exclusive manufacturing rights. However, so many workshops were by then turning out rickshaws that their application was denied.

An alternative claim of invention arose when an irascible American Baptist missionary named Jonathan Goble petitioned the Tokyo Metropolitan Government to grant him a share of the tax levied on the thirty thousand rickshaws then officially registered. He claimed to be the inventor, and a number of Westerners living in Japan supported him, some stating that Goble had built the first rickshaw for his ailing wife, and others that he had designed it at the request of a Japanese officer for use in the "imperial pleasure gardens."

The Japanese version of the story, which was reinforced in 1900 by government cash awards to the three businessmen, is highly credible since two-wheeled carts with a similar arrangement of shafts for pulling were in use on Japanese farms and for transporting loads well before European carriages came to be known through the "opening of Japan" in the 1850s (see Chapter 27). Moreover, Japan became the export source for rickshaws throughout Asia and the Indian Ocean region. The Goble story, however, made better sense to Westerners, who had a hard time crediting non-Europeans with inventiveness.

People today often look back and marvel at the incredible material changes their parents and grandparents lived through in the twentieth century. Movies, radio, television, telephones, automobiles, and airplanes all developed during the

---

[1] F. Calvin Parker, *Jonathan Goble of Japan: Marine, Missionary, Maverick* (Lanham, MD: University Press of America, 1990), 222.

first half of the century. Norms of daily life rooted in the nineteenth century gave way to new assumptions about many aspects of human life.

Yet many of these assumptions applied more to the industrialized countries of Europe and North America than to those parts of the world that before World War II consisted mostly of imperial possessions or, in the case of Latin America, politically independent countries whose economies were dominated by European or American businesses and investors. Automobiles may have changed dating habits in the United States, but not in China or India, where few private individuals owned cars. Telephones may have put people in easy contact with family and friends in Europe, but not in Africa, where imperialist economic interests saw no profit in stringing copper wire throughout the land.

Changes in the way people lived in the West between 1900 and 1950 will be discussed later in this chapter. First we will consider how other parts of the world experienced change in more limited ways, often incorporating local cultural traditions that took their societies in distinctive directions.

New Technology Outside the Industrialized World

Urbanization According to one estimate, Constantinople, the capital of the Byzantine Empire, had a population of 200,000 in 1000 C.E. and was the only European city to be ranked among the world's ten largest cities. By 1500 Paris had joined Constantinople on the list, and by 1800 so had London. Beijing, the most populous city, then had over 1 million inhabitants, about twice as many as the largest city in 1000.

Industrialization deeply affected population distribution in the course of the nineteenth century. By 1900 all of the world's top ten cities were European or American except for Tokyo. The largest, London, had 6.4 million inhabitants. European dominance waned in the first half of the twentieth century. In 1950 Shanghai, Buenos Aires, Tokyo, and Calcutta (now Kolkata) were on the list, and 12.4 million people resided in the largest city, New York. Today, two European cities, Moscow and Istanbul (formerly Constantinople), make the top ten. Of the rest, four are in China and two in South Asia. Tehran (Iran) and Sao Paulo (Brazil) round out the list. New York is nineteenth. The largest city, Shanghai, has a population of 17.8 million.

In Asia and the Indian Ocean basin, the rickshaw (see chapter opening) contributed to this transformation of urban life just as streetcars had earlier done in Europe and America. Before 1850, Japanese civilians either walked or were carried in plain (*kago*) or fancy (*norimono*) palanquins, small seats or cabins suspended from poles carried on the shoulders of bearers. A palanquin required a minimum of two men, or more if the trip was long or the rider wanted to display his or her wealth. The rickshaw cut the expense of personal transport in half and doubled its speed because a rickshaw puller, unlike palanquin bearers, usually ran rather than walked. Rickshaw transport effectively enlarged the area of cities that had previously been scaled for pedestrian access, just as public transport made it possible for Bostonians and Londoners to live away from the city center. Rickshaws also avoided the plague of Western cities: horse manure.

The technical specifications of the first rickshaws have not survived, but the claim that "it does not shake as much as the usual cart" suggests that what made the vehicle a sensational success from the very start was the provision of leaf springs (arced steel strips bound at the ends to form an ellipse). The first leaf spring design had been patented in England in 1804 and was probably in use on carriages imported into Japan in the 1850s. Early drawings and photographs of rickshaws consistently show them with leaf springs.

Japanese-made rickshaws stimulated the growth of big Asian cities like Shanghai, Beijing, Singapore, Calcutta, and Bombay and reached across the Indian Ocean to Madagascar and South Africa. Tens of thousands of unskilled workers flocked to these cities to become rickshaw pullers in the way that European villagers entered the urban economy by way of unskilled manufacturing jobs. Like European mill-hands, rickshaw pullers endured miserable living conditions and occasionally banded together in strikes, particularly in opposition to streetcar companies that threatened their livelihoods. However, streetcars could not deliver passengers directly to their homes or take children safely to school, so the rickshaws survived and evolved into the pedicabs and auto-rickshaws that are still common today.

The rickshaw provides a rare example of an Asian invention transforming urban life in ways unfamiliar to Europeans and Americans. The more frequently told stories focus on Western inventions like railroads and automobiles transforming the non-Western world. Yet even there, the innovations of the Industrial Revolution (see Chapter 22) that imperialist governments and businesses exported to their colonies affected the non-Western world differently than later innovations that spread worldwide in the first half of the twentieth century. Whereas railroads and automobiles required steel mills and factories, other new inventions were comparatively inexpensive and adaptable to local customs.

Electricity

Electricity, produced in industrial quantities since the 1890s (see Chapter 27), transformed home life in Europe and North America by attracting private customers. Middle-class homeowners wanted to replace their gas lamps with tungsten filament incandescent bulbs, which improved greatly in brightness and durability between 1904 and World War I. Household items like electric irons, fans, washing machines, and hot plates followed.

Outside of Europe and North America, however, the small size of the middle class made private subscription a poor business model. Electrical generators might be acquired to run factories or light a ruler's palace, but an appliance-oriented lifestyle was slow to develop. Consequently the foot-operated sewing machine, which had undergone a long development in America and Europe in the nineteenth century, had a wider global spread before World War II than any other appliance. The enormous Japanese electronics company Brother Industries, Ltd. began in 1908 as the Yasui Sewing Machine Company.

New Media

Auguste and Louis Lumière projected the first motion pictures in Paris in 1895. The following year the brothers held demonstrations in Bombay, London, Montreal, New York, and Buenos Aires. Other exhibitors soon showed off the new medium in Johannesburg, Alexandria, and Tokyo. Unlike expensive innovations like automobiles and airplanes, motion pictures could be made cheaply using fairly inexpensive equipment. The idea of moving images appealed just as much to non-European audiences as it did to Europeans.

The first experiments with film in India appeared two years after the Lumières' visit. The first full-length feature, screening in 1912, told the story of a legendary Indian king from the classical Sanskrit epics. Movies also caught on quickly in

Japan, which had a tradition of magic lantern displays. Local theatrical traditions like *kabuki* and *bunraku* influenced the style and content of the earliest films just as early European film makers concentrated on reproducing stage plays. Japanese films of the silent era were usually accompanied by spoken narration, as were the films the Japanese exported to Formosa (now Taiwan), a Chinese-speaking island that came under Japanese control in 1895.

American and European silent films found ready markets around the world, but non-Western film making flourished in some countries. Moreover, the impact of film was not limited to entertainment. Documentary films and especially newsreels became major sources of information. Filmed news coverage of key political figures like Mahatma Gandhi in India played a major role in their success, especially after the advent of sound in the late 1920s.

Practical photography began in Europe in 1839, and forty years later an efficient way was developed for printing photographs in newspapers. Photographic images soon became common throughout the world, often as picture postcards. European photographers, however, tended to look upon Asians and Africans, particularly seminude women, as exotic subjects and thereby catered to common European assumptions about racial superiority.

Non-European photographers rarely became known outside their home countries. Nevertheless, they produced thousands of images that are now used to reconstruct history. Chinese newspapers and magazines usually published images without naming the photographers. A dozen early photographers became famous in Japan, however, possibly because popular woodblock prints had created an audience for artistic images of everyday scenes. In Iran, the most avid photographer was the ruler Naser al-Din Shah (r. 1848–1896). Despite Muslim clerical disapproval of making images of human beings, the shah shot some forty-eight thousand pictures, including members of his own family and even nudes and prisoners.

Photography enabled newspapers, magazines, and advertisements to inform even illiterate people about what their country and their fellow citizens looked like, who was ruling them, and how traditional elites and prosperous Europeanized families lived. Thus photography contributed to feelings of national identity and common experience even in lands that were internally divided by language and ethnicity.

Radio had served ships and the military during the Great War as a means of point-to-point telecommunication. After the war, amateurs used surplus radio equipment to talk to one another. The first commercial station began broadcasting in Pittsburgh in 1920. By 1924 six hundred stations were broadcasting news, sports, soap operas, and advertising to homes throughout North America. By 1930, 12 million families owned radio receivers. In Europe radio spread more slowly because governments reserved the airwaves for cultural and official programs and taxed radio owners to pay for the service.

Japan followed the North American model of commercial radio. The first AM station began broadcasting in 1925, and by 1941 there were almost fifty stations organized in two networks covering both the home islands and imperial possessions in Formosa (Taiwan), Korea, and Manchuria. Programming increasingly reflected the militarist tendencies of the government, but it also included Japanese and classical Western music, English lessons, exercise programs, and tips for urban gardeners.

Radio development in Shanghai was also robust, with 100,000 receivers in use by 1936. Most were imported, but small local manufacturers contributed to the new fad. British authorities in India and Africa, on the other hand, established central control of radio transmissions and programming. French colonial administrations did likewise.

New Ways of Living in the Industrialized World

World War I left a deep imprint on European society and culture. After the war, class and gender distinctions began to fade. Many European aristocrats had died on the battlefields, and with them went their class's long domination of the army, the diplomatic corps, and other elite sectors of society. The United States and Canada had never had as rigidly defined a class structure as European societies or as elaborate a set of traditions and manners. On both sides of the Atlantic, engineers, businessmen, lawyers, and other professionals rose to prominence while department stores, banks, insurance companies, and other businesses increased their white-collar workforce. At the same time government administrative jobs expanded in the areas of housing, transportation, schools, public health, and other services. The ambitions and tastes of the rapidly expanding middle class became increasingly evident in the postwar period, while the role of the working class remained about the same.

Identity   As the centuries-old European distinction between aristocrats and commoners faded in significance, standardized forms of identity became more common. An American passport issued in 1905 was a single 12- by 17-inch piece of paper bearing the seal of the State Department, the secretary of state's signature in facsimile, and in lieu of a photograph, one- or two-word descriptions of the holder's forehead, eyes, nose, mouth, chin, complexion, and facial shape. A Chinese passport of the same period was entirely in Chinese. Crossing international borders became a more complicated process during World War I, and in 1920 the League of Nations held the first of several conferences that standardized the now familiar photograph-and-booklet design.

Prussia in 1910 was the first country to require every automobile operator to have a driver's license, and the practice spread rapidly. In 1913 New Jersey was the first American state to institute such a requirement. These documents eventually became standard proofs of identity in countries that did not issue identity cards to their citizens. Social Security cards began to be issued in the United States in the 1930s, and they too acquired some of the functions of identity cards. In other countries, such as Germany, Great Britain, and Japan, national health system documents took on similar roles.

Hereditary titles and listings of noble lineages in reference books like *Burke's Peerage* continued in use among the nobility. However, the idea increasingly spread that a person's identity was tied to his or her name (without title), a photograph, and one or more official numbers issued by government agencies. This idea spread much more slowly outside of Europe and North America.

An additional form of personal identification came forth in 1897 when the world's first fingerprint bureau opened under British auspices in Calcutta (Kolkata). Two Indians, Azizul Haque and Hem Chandra Bose, devised the system of determining every human being's unique identity, but it became known as the Henry System from the name of their British supervisor. Scotland Yard adopted the system in 1901, and the New York Police Department did so in 1906.

Women's Lives   Women's lives changed more rapidly in the 1920s than ever before. Although the end of the war saw the end of wartime job opportunities, some women remained in the workforce. The young and wealthy enjoyed more personal freedoms than their mothers had before the war; they drove cars, played sports, traveled alone, and smoked in public. For others, the upheavals of war brought more suffering than liberation. Millions of women had lost their male kin in the war or in the great influenza epidemic. After the war many single women led lives of loneliness and destitution.

In Europe and North America advocates of women's rights had been demanding the vote for women since the 1890s. New Zealand was the only nation to grant women the vote before the twentieth century. Women in Norway were the first to obtain it in Europe, in 1915. Russian women followed in 1917, and Canadians and Germans in 1918. Britain gave women over age thirty the vote in 1918 and later extended it to younger women. The Nineteenth Amendment to the U.S. Constitution granted suffrage to American women in 1920. Women in Turkey began voting in 1934. Everywhere, their influence on politics was less radical than feminists had hoped and conservatives had feared. Even when it did not transform politics and government, however, the right to vote was a potent symbol.

Women were active in many other areas besides the suffrage movement. On both sides of the Atlantic women participated in social reform movements to prevent mistreatment of women and children and of industrial workers. In the United States such reforms were championed by Progressives like Jane Addams (1860–1935), who founded a settlement house in a poor neighborhood and received the Nobel Peace Prize in 1931. In Europe reformers were generally aligned with Socialist or Labour Parties.

Among the most controversial, and eventually most effective, of the reformers were those who advocated contraception, such as the American **Margaret Sanger** (1883–1966). Her campaign brought her into conflict with many authorities, who equated birth control with pornography. Finally, in 1923 she was able to found a birth control clinic in New York. In France, the government prohibited contraception and abortion in 1920 in an effort to increase the birthrate and make up for the loss of so many young men in the war.

Revolution in the Sciences: The New Physics   The word *progress*, as much associated with extending "modern civilization" to the non-Western world as with technological developments such as railroads and undersea cables, had been a hallmark of most nineteenth-century Euro–American ideologies. After 1900 the word *science* increasingly took its place as a signifier of Western self-esteem. At the end of the nineteenth century, a revolution in physics undermined the old certainties about nature that had already been shaken by Darwinism. Physicists discovered that atoms, the building blocks of matter, are not indivisible, but consist of far smaller subatomic particles. In 1900, the German physicist **Max Planck** (1858–1947) found that atoms emit or absorb energy in discrete amounts called *quanta*.

Few people understood these findings at the time, much less **Albert Einstein's** (1879–1955) pronouncement in 1916 that time, space, energy, and mass are not fixed but are relative to one another. But scientific discovery, punctuated by prestigious Nobel prizes that began to be awarded in 1901, excited pride and wonder in nations that contributed to such advances.

The New Social Sciences   The new social sciences were more understandable, and thus more unsettling, than the new physics, for they challenged Victorian morality and middle-class values. **Sigmund Freud** (1856–1939), a Viennese physician, developed the technique of psychoanalysis to probe the minds of his patients. His technique uncovered hidden layers of emotion and desire repressed by social restraints. "It is during this [childhood] period of . . . latency that the psychic forces develop which later act as inhibitions on the sexual life, and narrow its direction like dams. These psychic forces are loathing, shame, and moral and esthetic ideal demands,"[2] he declared. Meanwhile, sociologists and anthropologists had begun the empirical study of societies, both Western and non-Western. Before the war the French sociologist Emile Durkheim (1858–1917) had come to the then shocking conclusion that "there are no religions that are false. All are true after their own fashion."[3]

If the words *primitive* and *savage* applied to Europeans as well as to other peoples, and if religions were all equally "true," then what remained of the superiority of Western civilization? Cultural relativism, as the new approach to human societies was called, could be as unnerving as relativity in physics; but for many it stimulated a tenacious desire to cling to the old truths.

The arts became a battlefield for confronting traditional values with new images and rhythms. Cubism, an approach to painting and sculpture that sought to go beyond realism and depict many aspects of an image simultaneously, aroused lively debates in the 1910s. A painter like the Spaniard **Pablo Picasso** (1881–1973) changed his nonrealistic style of painting time and again over his long career. Paralleling his audacity in the field of music, the Russian composer **Igor Stravinsky** (1882–1971) incorporated so-called primitive rhythms in his ballet *The Rite of Spring*, which debuted in 1913.

The incredible human losses experienced during the Great War shook many artists' and intellectuals' faith in reason and progress. Some poets and artists joined the **Dada** movement, which abandoned rationality and relied instead on intuition, randomness, and nonsense—*dada* stood for the use of meaningless syllables in poetry. Others became Surrealists and produced dreamlike images incorporating what they considered to be symbols of the unconscious mind. Some people accepted the new ideas with enthusiasm. Others condemned and rejected them, particularly in the United States, and clung to the sense of order and faith in progress that had energized Western culture before the war.

New Technologies and Activities   Some people viewed the sciences with mixed feelings, but new technologies aroused almost universal excitement. In North America even working-class people could afford some of the new products of inventors' ingenuity (see Environment and Technology: New Materials). Mass consumption in Europe lagged behind the United States, but science and technology were just as advanced, and public fascination with the latest inventions—the cult of the modern—was just as strong.

---

[2]Sigmund Freud, *Three Contributions to the Theory of Sex*, tr. A. A. Brill, 2 ed. (Washington: Nervous and Mental Health Disease Publishing Company, 1920), 40.

[3]Emile Durkheim, *The Elementary Forms of Religious Life*, trans. by Karen Elise Fields (New York: Free Press, 1995), 2.

Museum of Flight/Corbis

First Aluminum Airplane *From the Wright Brothers' first aircraft in 1903 down to the air battles of World War I, wood, cloth, and wire made up the wings and bodies of airplanes. Metals were too heavy for anything but engines and weapons until the German manufacturer Hugo Junkers designed the first aluminum flying machine, shown here, in 1917.*

Of all the innovations of the time, none attracted public interest more than airplanes. In 1903 two young American mechanics, **Wilbur and Orville Wright,** built the first aircraft that was heavier than air and could be maneuvered in flight. From that moment on, airplanes fascinated people. In 1911 a French pilot flew 6,500 letters from one city in British India to another 8.1 miles (13 kilometers) away, thus inaugurating the first important use of air transport. Military observation and aerial warfare came second. During the Great War the exploits of air aces relieved the tedium of news from the front.

The first flight of **KLM Royal Dutch Airlines,** the oldest continuously operating airline, took off in 1920. That year it carried 440 passengers and 22 tons of cargo. Scheduled service to a number of northern European cities soon followed. Its most important service, as an air link to the Dutch East Indies (now Indonesia), began in 1929. Every country with imperial possessions saw international air service as a political necessity. Two of the oldest airlines, however, Qantas in Australia and the German-owned precursor of Avianca in Colombia, functioned entirely outside of Europe.

Health and hygiene were part of the cult of modernity. Advances in medicine—some learned on the battlefield—saved many lives. Wounds were regularly disinfected, and **Marie Curie** (1867–1934), the French discoverer of x-rays, organized radiology vans to help army doctors diagnose fractures during the Great War. Cities built costly water supply and sewage treatment systems. By the 1920s indoor plumbing and flush toilets were becoming common even in working-class neighborhoods.

Interest in cleanliness entered private life. Doctors and home economists bombarded women with warnings and advice on how to banish germs. Soap and appliance manufacturers filled women's magazines with advertisements for products to help keep homes and clothing spotless and meals fresh and wholesome. The decline in infant mortality and improvements in general health and life expectancy in this period owe as much to the cult of cleanliness as to advances in medicine.

Organized baseball leagues arose in America after the Civil War. Football found favor as a college sport around the same time, while basketball originated in 1891 as a YMCA activity. In Britain soccer (football) and rugby leagues formed in the 1880s. All of these sports flourished as spectator activities in the early twentieth century and gave rise to lively press coverage in newspapers. Soccer and rugby, along with the much older sport of cricket, spread readily into Europe's colonies, while baseball found limited favor overseas, primarily in Japan, Cuba, and the Dominican Republic.

Internationally, the upsurge in the role of sports and spectating was closely tied to the revival of the Olympic Games. The ancient Greek games had been discontinued in 393 C.E. The inspiration to create a modern form came from **Baron Pierre de Coubertin** (1863–1937), a French educator who was impressed by the sports played at English private schools like Eton and Rugby. He concluded that "organised sport can create moral and social strength."

Coubertin's aristocratic vision of purely amateur international competition came to fruition in Athens in 1896 when fourteen countries, all of them European except Australia and Chile, sent athletes to compete in nonteam sports like tennis, fencing, shooting, cycling, and gymnastics. Women were not included, nor did Coubertin realize his idea that medals should also be given for sports-themed art and architecture. The male-only rule was dropped starting with the Paris Olympics of 1900, where women competed in tennis and golf. The role of women increased steadily after that, though the arts medals were only given seven times between Stockholm in 1912 and London in 1948.

Individual excellence was the touchstone of Olympic competition, but nationalistic pride increasingly marked the quadrennial events. The Berlin Olympics of 1936 thus became a showcase for Nazi ideology and spectacle.

Technology and the Environment

Two new technologies—the skyscraper and the automobile—transformed the urban environment even more radically than the railroad had done. At the end of the nineteenth century architects had begun to design ever-higher buildings using load-bearing steel frames and elevators. Major corporations in Chicago and New York competed to build the most daring buildings in the world, such as New York's fifty-five-story Woolworth Building (1912). A building boom in the late

ENVIRONMENT + TECHNOLOGY

New Materials

Nineteenth-century commerce brought many raw materials from European colonies and other faraway places into industrial use. Examples include rubber, a Southeast Asian tree sap called gutta-percha used for electrical insulation, Central Asian camel's hair used for transmission belts, and whale oil for lighting. These exotic materials were valuable, but they did not change the age-old pattern of almost every useful item being manufactured from natural substances.

The first half of the twentieth century saw a revolutionary change in this

Bakelite Jewelry *This pioneering plastic was so attractive that it was made into jewelry. However, its ease of manufacture, hardness, and resistance to electricity, heat, and chemicals suited it to thousands of other uses from clarinets to wire insulation to kitchenware. During World War II it was even considered as a replacement for the copper penny.*

1920s produced dozens of skyscrapers, culminating with the eighty-six-story Empire State Building in New York in 1932.

European cities restricted the height of buildings to protect their architectural heritage; Paris forbade buildings over 56 feet (17 meters) high. In the 1920s the Swiss architect Charles Edouard Jeanneret (1887–1965), known as **Le Corbusier** (luh cor-booz-YEH), outlined a new approach to architecture that featured pattern. Metallurgists and chemists led the way in creating new materials that wrought permanent changes in the look and feel of everyday life. Materials science would go on to become one of the most important areas of technical innovation in later decades.

Though aluminum follows oxygen and silicon as the third most abundant element, it combines so readily with other elements that it was not discovered until 1827. Initially as precious as silver, a 2.4-kilogram piece was installed as the capstone of the Washington Monument in 1884. Four years later, however, almost simultaneously in the United States and France, an inexpensive electrolytic method of extracting the metal from bauxite ore was discovered. The lightweight, noncorrosive metal now became available for all manner of uses, from airplanes, beginning with a design by the German Hugo Junkers in 1917, to aluminum foil, which was invented in 1910.

Stainless steel, made by combining noncorrosive chromium with steel, was invented in 1912, and its many uses accustomed people to thinking of metal products as shiny. Electroplating with chromium came into use in 1924 in Germany and two years later in the United States. The shiny, rust-free metal, which could be deposited as a thin film on either a metallic or plastic base, found numerous uses from musical instruments to automobiles.

Plastics were invented at about the same time. Alexander Parkes invented celluloid, a stable form of explosive guncotton—itself made by soaking fine cotton in sulfuric and nitric acids—and exhibited it at London's Great Exhibition in 1862. The first thermoplastic, it could be molded above a certain temperature but became solid when it cooled. It was used for detachable men's shirt collars, ping-pong balls, and photographic film, but it was both fragile and flammable.

Belgian-born Leo Hendrik Baekeland invented Bakelite, a more durable plastic that was also attractive enough to be used for jewelry in 1907. Five years later the Swiss chemist Jacques E. Brandenberger, trying to discover a way of waterproofing cloth, experimented with a cellulose-based coating that failed to stick to the cloth and instead peeled off in a clear sheet. Thus was cellophane invented. In the 1930s an American, Richard Drew, coated cellophane with adhesive and Scotch tape was born.

And there were others. Silklike rayon, 1904; isoprene synthetic rubber, 1909; vinyl, 1926; neoprene synthetic rubber, 1931; plexiglass, 1933; nylon, 1935; Lucite, 1936; fiberglass, 1938—the list goes on, with even more new materials being developed in the later decades of the century.

Questions for Analysis

1. Why do we take for granted a material environment constructed from manufactured substances that did not even exist before 1900?

2. What are the objects we use every day made of?

3. Why did new materials find such broad acceptance?

---

simplicity of form, absence of surface ornamentation, easy manufacture, and inexpensive materials such as concrete and glass. Other architects—including the Finn Eero Saarinen, the Germans Ludwig Mies van der Rohe (LOOD-vig MEES fon der ROW-uh) and Walter Gropius, and the American Frank Lloyd Wright—also contributed to what became known as the International Style.

Meanwhile, outlying areas were spreading far into the countryside, thanks to the automobile. The assembly line pioneered by Henry Ford mass-produced vehicles in ever-greater volume and at falling prices. By 1929 the United States had one car for every five people, five-sixths of the world's automobiles. Automobiles were praised as the solution to urban pollution; as they replaced carts and carriages, horses disappeared from city streets, as did tons of manure.

The most important environmental effect of automobiles was suburban sprawl. Middle-class families could now live in single-family homes too far apart to be served by public transportation. As middle- and working-class families bought cars, cities acquired rings of automobile suburbs. Los Angeles, the first true automobile city, consisted of suburbs spread over hundreds of square miles and linked together by broad avenues. Many Americans saw Los Angeles as the portent of a glorious future in which everyone would have a car.

European cities that had inherited narrow streets from the premodern past adapted less easily to passenger automobiles. In the countryside, however, high-speed, limited-access expressways, called *autostrada* in Italy and *autobahn* in Germany, became sources of national pride for the regimes of Benito Mussolini and Adolf Hitler. Yet compared with the United States, private automobile ownership remained uncommon.

Technological advances also transformed rural economies. In 1915 Ford introduced a gasoline-powered tractor, and by the mid-1920s these versatile machines began replacing horses. Larger farms profited most from this innovation, while small farmers sold their land and moved to the cities. Tractors and other expensive equipment hastened the transformation of agriculture from family enterprises to larger businesses, or in the USSR to collective farms with state-owned tractor stations (see Chapter 30).

In India, Australia, and the western United States, engineers built dams and canals to irrigate dry lands. Dams offered the added advantage of producing electricity, for which there was a booming demand. The immediate benefits of water control—irrigated land, prevention of floods, and generation of electricity—far outweighed such distant negative consequences as salt deposits on irrigated fields and harm to wildlife.

A New India, 1905–1947

Some parts of the world, such as India, became much more involved in the emerging technologically oriented culture than others, such as sub-Saharan Africa (see below). The consequences of this inequality of access to "modern" developments are still felt today.

Under British rule India acquired railroads, harbors, modern cities, and cotton and steel mills, as well as an active and worldly middle class. The economic transformation of the region awakened in this educated middle class a sense of national dignity that demanded political fulfillment. In response, the British gradually granted India a limited amount of political autonomy while maintaining overall control. Religious and communal tensions among the Indian peoples were carefully papered over, and when the British, exhausted by World War II (see Chapter 30), withdrew in 1947, violent conflicts tore India apart.

The Land and the People   Much of India is fertile land, but it is vulnerable to droughts caused by the periodic failure of the monsoons. When the rains failed from 1896 to 1900, 2 million people died of starvation.

Despite periodic famines, the Indian population grew from 250 million in 1900 to 319 million in 1921 and 389 million in 1941. This growth created pressures in many areas. Landless young men converged on the cities, exceeding the number of jobs available in the slowly expanding industries. Many of them entered the urban economy as rickshaw pullers. To produce timber for construction and railroad ties and to clear land for tea and rubber plantations, foresters cut down most of the tropical hardwood forests that had covered the subcontinent in the nineteenth century. But in spite of deforestation and extensive irrigation, the amount of land available to peasant families shrank with each successive generation. Economic development hardly touched the average Indian.

Indians were divided into many classes. Peasants, always the great majority, paid rents to landowners, interest to village moneylenders, and taxes to the government and had little left to improve their land or raise their standard of living. The government protected property owners, from village moneylenders all the way up to the maharajahs (mah-huh-RAH-juh) or ruling princes, who owned huge tracts of land. The cities were crowded with craftsmen, traders, and workers of all sorts, most very poor. Although the British had banned the burning of widows on their husbands' funeral pyres, in other respects women's lives changed little under British rule.

Indians also spoke many different languages. As a result of British rule, increasing trade and travel, and newspapers like *The Times of India*, established under that name in 1861, English became the common medium of communication for the Western-educated middle class. This new class of English-speaking bureaucrats, professionals, and merchants was to play a leading role in the independence movement.

The majority of Indians who practiced Hinduism were subdivided into hundreds of castes (*jati*), each affiliated with a particular occupation or kinship group. Hinduism discouraged intermarriage and other social interactions among the castes and with non-Hindus. Until displaced by the British in the eighteenth century, Muslim rulers had dominated northern and central India, and Muslims now constituted one-quarter of the Indian population while forming a majority in the northwest and in eastern Bengal. They felt discriminated against by both British and Hindus.

British Rule and Indian Nationalism   Colonial India was ruled by a viceroy appointed by the British government and administered by a few thousand members of the Indian Civil Service. These men, drawn mostly from the English gentry, believed it was their duty to protect the Indian people from the dangers of industrialization and to defend their own positions from Indian nationalists.

As Europeans they admired modern technology. They encouraged railroads, harbors, telegraphs, and other communications technologies, as well as irrigation and plantations, because these increased India's foreign trade and strengthened British control. Yet, they discouraged the cotton and steel industries and limited the training of Indian engineers, to spare India the social upheavals that had accompanied the Industrial Revolution in Europe while protecting British industry from Indian competition.

At the turn of the century most Indians—especially peasants, landowners, and princes—accepted British rule. But the Europeans' racist attitude toward dark-skinned people increasingly offended Indians who had learned English and absorbed English ideas of freedom and representative government, only to discover that racial quotas excluded them from the Indian Civil Service, the officer corps, and prestigious sporting clubs.

In 1885, a small group of English-speaking Hindu professionals founded a political organization called the **Indian National Congress**. For twenty years its members respectfully petitioned the government for access to higher administrative positions and for a voice in official decisions, but they had little influence. Then, in 1905, Viceroy Lord Curzon divided the province of **Bengal** in two to improve the efficiency of its administration. This decision, made without consulting anyone, angered not only educated Indians, who saw it as a way to lessen their influence, but also millions of uneducated Hindu Bengalis, who found themselves outnumbered by Muslims in East Bengal. Soon Bengal was the scene of demonstrations, boycotts of British goods, and even incidents of violence against the British.

In 1906, while the Hindus of Bengal were protesting the partition of their province, Muslims, fearful of Hindu dominance elsewhere in India, founded the **All-India Muslim League**. (Note the English names of these political groups.) The government responded by granting Indians a limited franchise based on wealth. Muslims, however, were on average poorer than Hindus, possibly because many poor and low-caste Hindus had converted to Islam to escape caste discrimination. Taking advantage of these religious divisions, the British instituted separate representation and different voting qualifications for Hindus and Muslims. Then, in 1911, the British transferred the capital of India from Calcutta (Kolkata) to Delhi (DEL-ee), the former capital of the Mughal (MOO-guhl) emperors. These changes disturbed Indians of all classes and religions and raised their political consciousness. Politics, once primarily the concern of westernized intellectuals, turned into two mass movements: one by Hindus and one by Muslims.

British geologists looked for minerals like coal and manganese that British industry required. However, when the only Indian member of the Indian Geological Service, Pramatha Nath Bose, wanted to prospect for iron ore, he had to resign because the government wanted no part of an Indian steel industry that might compete with that of Britain. Bose joined forces with Jamsetji Tata, a Bombay textile magnate who decided to produce steel in spite of British opposition. With the help of German and American engineers and equipment, Tata's son Dorabji opened the first steel mill in India in 1911, in a town called Jamshedpur in honor of his father.

Although it produced only a fraction of the steel that India required, Jamshedpur became a powerful symbol of Indian national pride. It also prompted Indian nationalists to ask why a country that could produce its own steel needed foreigners to run its government.

During World War I Indians supported Britain enthusiastically; 1.2 million men volunteered for the army, and millions more voluntarily contributed money to the government. Many expected the British to reward their loyalty with political concessions. Others organized to demand a voice in the government. In 1917, in response to the agitation, the British government announced "the gradual development of self-governing institutions with a view to the progressive realization of responsible government in India as an integral part of the British Empire." This sounded like a promise of self-government, but the timetable was so vague that nationalists denounced it as a devious maneuver to postpone India's independence.

On April 13, 1919, in the city of Amritsar, General Reginald Dyer ordered his troops to fire into a peaceful crowd of some 10,000 demonstrators, killing at least 379 and wounding 1,200. While waves of angry demonstrations swept over India, the British House of Lords voted to approve Dyer's actions, and a fund was raised in appreciation of his services. Indians interpreted these gestures as showing British contempt for their colonial subjects. In the charged atmosphere of the time, the period of gradual accommodation between the British and the Indians came to a close.

Mahatma Gandhi and Militant Nonviolence

For the next twenty years India teetered on the edge of violent uprisings and harsh repression. That it did not succumb was due to **Mohandas K. Gandhi** (GAHN-dee) (1869–1948), a man known to his followers as "Mahatma," the "great soul."

Gandhi began life with every advantage. His family was wealthy enough to send him to England for his education. After his studies he lived in South Africa and practiced law for the small Indian community there. During World War I he returned to India and was one of many Western-educated Hindu intellectuals who joined the Indian National Congress.

Unlike many radical political thinkers of his time, Gandhi denounced the popular ideals of power, struggle, and combat. Instead, inspired by both Hindu and Christian ideals, he preached the saintly virtues of *ahimsa* (uh-HIM-sah) (nonviolence) and *satyagraha* (suh-TYAH-gruh-huh) (the search for truth). He refused to countenance violence among his followers and called off several demonstrations when they turned violent.

In 1921, Gandhi gave up the Western-style suits worn by lawyers and the fine raiment of wealthy Indians and henceforth wore simple peasant garb: a length of homespun cloth below his waist (*dhoti*) and a shawl to cover his torso. He spoke for the farmers and the outcasts, whom he called *harijan* (HAH-ree-jahn), "children of God." He attracted ever-larger numbers of followers among the poor and the illiterate, who soon began to revere him; and he transformed the cause of Indian independence from an elite movement of the educated into a mass movement with a quasi-religious aura.

Gandhi was a brilliant political tactician and a master of public relations gestures. In 1929, for instance, he led a few followers on an 80-mile (129-kilometer) walk, camped on a beach, and gathered salt from the sea in a blatant and well-publicized act of civil disregard for the government's monopoly on salt. But he discovered that unleashing the power of popular participation was one thing and controlling its direction was quite another. Within days of his "Walk to the Sea," demonstrations of support broke out all over India, in which the police killed a hundred demonstrators and arrested over sixty thousand.

Many times during the 1930s Gandhi threatened to fast "unto death," and several times he came close to death, to protest the violence of both the police and his followers and to demand independence. He was repeatedly arrested and spent a total of six years in jail. But every arrest made him more popular. He became a figure of adulation not only in his own country but also in the Western media. In the words of historian Percival Spear, he made the British "uncomfortable in their cherished field of moral rectitude," and he gave Indians the feeling that theirs was the ethically superior cause.

Gandhi's Salt March to the Sea *Mohandas Gandhi, bareheaded and more simply dressed than his followers, led a march of 80 miles to collect sea salt in an act of civil disobedience. News photographs like this played a key role in popularizing his cause and displaying his saintly habits. To his left one man carries a sitar and another has a drum hanging from his shoulder.*

**India Moves
Toward
Independence**

In the 1920s, slowly and reluctantly, the British handed over control of "national" areas such as education, the economy, and public works to Indians. They also gradually admitted more Indians into the Civil Service and the officer corps.

In the years before the Second World War, Indian politicians obtained the right to erect high tariff barriers against imports to protect India's infant industries from foreign competition. Behind these barriers, Indian entrepreneurs built plants to manufacture iron and steel, cement, paper, textiles, sugar, and other products. This early industrialization did not provide enough jobs to improve the lives of the Indian peasants or urban poor, but it created a class of wealthy Indian businessmen who supported the Indian National Congress and its demands for independence. Though paying homage to Gandhi, they preferred his designated successor as leader of the Indian National Congress, **Jawaharlal Nehru** (NAY-roo) (1889–1964). Unlike Gandhi, Nehru looked forward to creating a modern industrial India.

Congress politicians won regional elections but continued to be excluded from the viceroy's cabinet, the true center of power. When World War II began (see Chapter 30), Viceroy Lord Linlithgow declared war without consulting a single Indian. The Congress-dominated provincial governments resigned in protest and found that boycotting government office increased their popular support. When the British offered to give India its independence once the war ended, Gandhi demanded full independence immediately. His "Quit India" campaign aroused popular demonstrations against the British and provoked a wave of arrests, including his own. The Second World War divided the Indian people. Most Indian soldiers felt they were fighting to defend their country rather than to support the British Empire. As in World War I, Indians contributed heavily to the Allied war effort, supplying 2 million soldiers and enormous amounts of resources, especially the timber needed for emergency construction. A small number of Indians were so anti-British that they joined the Japanese side.

**Partition and
Independence**

When the war ended, Britain's new Labour Party government prepared for Indian independence, but deep suspicions between Hindus and Muslims complicated the process. The break between the two communities had started in 1937, when the Indian National Congress won provincial elections and refused to share power with the Muslim League. In 1940 the leader of the League, **Muhammad Ali Jinnah** (JIH-nah) (1876–1948), demanded what many Muslims had been dreaming of for years: a country of their own, to be called Pakistan.

As independence approached, talks between Jinnah and Nehru broke down and battle lines were drawn. Violent rioting between Hindus and Muslims broke out. Gandhi's appeals for tolerance and cooperation fell on deaf ears. The British made frantic proposals to keep India united, but their authority was waning fast.

In early 1947 the Indian National Congress accepted the partition of India into two states, one secular but dominated by Hindus, the other Muslim. On August 15

British India gave way to a new India and Pakistan. The Indian National Congress, led by Nehru, formed the first government of India; Jinnah and the Muslim League established a government for the provinces that made up Pakistan.

The rejoicing over independence was marred by violent outbreaks between Muslims and Hindus. In protest against the mounting chaos, Gandhi refused to attend the independence day celebration. Throughout the land, Muslim and Hindu neighbors turned on one another, and armed members of one faith hunted down people of the other faith. Leaving most of their possessions behind, Hindus fled from predominantly Muslim areas, and Muslims fled from Hindu areas. Trainloads of desperate refugees of one faith were attacked and massacred by members of the other or were left stranded in the middle of deserts. Within a few months some 12 million people had abandoned their ancestral homes and a half-million lay dead. In January 1948 Gandhi died too, gunned down by an angry Hindu refugee.

After the sectarian massacres and flights of refugees, Muslims were a minority in all but one state of India. That state was Kashmir, a strategically important region in the foothills of the Himalayas. India annexed Kashmir because the local maharajah was Hindu and because the state held the headwaters of the rivers that irrigated millions of acres of farmland. Most inhabitants would have joined Pakistan if they had been allowed to vote on the matter. The annexation of Kashmir turned India and Pakistan into bitter enemies that fought several wars over the next half century.

MEXICO, ARGENTINA, AND BRAZIL, 1917–1949

Though some parts of the world, notably Latin America, were untouched by the Great War, they still experienced the disruptions and new ways of life of the postwar period. In the early 1920s, after a decade of violence that exhausted all classes (see Chapter 26), the Mexican Revolution lost momentum. President Obregón and his closest associates made all the important decisions, and his successor, Plutarco Elías Calles (KAH-yace), founded the National Revolutionary Party, or PNR (the abbreviation of its name in Spanish). The PNR was a forum where all the pressure groups and vested interests—labor, peasants, businessmen, landowners, the military, and others—worked out compromises. The establishment of the PNR gave the Mexican Revolution a second wind.

The Cárdenas Reforms   **Lázaro Cárdenas** (LAH-sah-roe KAHR-dih-nahs), chosen by Calles to be president in 1934, brought peasants' and workers' organizations into the party, removed generals from government positions, and implemented the reforms promised in the Constitution of 1917.

In 1938 Cárdenas seized the foreign-owned oil industry, which had gained importance with the wartime recognition that modern navies needed petroleum. The American and British oil companies expected their governments to come to their rescue, perhaps with military force. But Mexico and the United States chose to resolve the issue through negotiation, and Mexico retained control of its oil.

The Transformation of Argentina

Most of Argentina consists of *pampas* (POM-pus), flat, fertile land that is easy to till, much like the prairies of the midwestern United States and Canada. At the end of the nineteenth century railroads and refrigerator ships changed Argentina's exports and land use. In the 1920s, European consumers, freed from wartime rationing, savored fresh meat. To safeguard valuable herds, the pampas were divided, cultivated, and fenced with barbed wire. Wheat- and grain-fed beef and mutton replaced the lean free-range cattle of earlier generations. Soon the pampas became one of the world's great centers of wheat and meat production.

Argentina's government represented the interests of the *oligarquía* (oh-lee-gar-KEE-ah), a small group of wealthy landowners and exporters. They owned fine homes in Buenos Aires (BWAY-nos EYE-res), a city that was built to resemble Paris, traveled frequently to Europe, and spent lavishly. However, they were content to let British companies build Argentina's railroads, processing plants, and public utilities. Argentina imported almost all its manufactured goods from Europe and the United States. So important were British interests in the Argentinean economy that English, not Spanish, was used on the railroads.

Brazil and Argentina, to 1929

Before the First World War, Brazil produced most of the world's coffee and cacao, grown on vast estates. Natural rubber came from rubber trees growing wild in the Amazon rain forest but had not yet been recognized as a key strategic commodity. Like their Argentinean counterparts, Brazil's elite built palaces in Rio de Janeiro (REE-oh day zhuh-NAIR-oh) and even an opera house deep in the Amazon. British companies build railroads, harbors, and other infrastructure and imported most manufactured goods.

Both Argentina and Brazil had small but outspoken middle classes that demanded a share in government and looked to European models. The poor, at the bottom of the social pyramid, were mainly Spanish and Italian immigrants turned landless laborers and meat processors in Argentina or sharecroppers and plantation workers, many descended from slaves, in Brazil.

Rubber exports collapsed after 1912, replaced by cheaper plantation rubber from Southeast Asia. Two years later the outbreak of war put an end to imports from Europe as Britain and France focused all their industries on war production and Germany was cut off entirely. The disruption of the old trade patterns weakened the landowning class. In Argentina the urban middle class obtained the secret ballot and universal male suffrage in 1916 and elected a liberal politician, **Hipólito Irigoyen** (ee-POH-lee-toe ee-ree-GO-yen), as president. To a certain extent, the United States replaced the European countries as suppliers of machinery and consumers of coffee. European immigrants built factories to manufacture textiles and household goods.

The postwar years were a period of prosperity in South America. Trade with Europe resumed; prices for agricultural exports remained high; and both Argentina and Brazil used profits accumulated during the war to industrialize and improve their transportation systems and public utilities. Yet it was also a time of social turmoil, as workers and middle-class professionals demanded the same social reforms and enhanced voice in politics as their European counterparts. In Argentina students' and workers' demonstrations were brutally crushed. In Brazil junior officers faced off several times against the government. Though they accomplished little, these demonstrations laid the groundwork for later reformist movements.

Yet as Argentina and Brazil prospered, new technologies again left them dependent on the advanced industrial countries. Aviation reached Latin America after World War I, when European and American companies such as Aéropostale and Pan American Airways introduced airmail service between cities and linked Latin America with the United States and Europe.

Before and during World War I, radio was used only for point-to-point communications. Transmitters powerful enough to send messages across oceans or continents were complex and expensive, with antennas covering many acres. They used as much electricity as a small town. Right after the war, no Latin American country possessed the knowledge or funds to build its own transmitters. Four powerful radio companies—one British, one French, one German, and one American—formed a cartel to control all radio communications in Latin America. Thus, even as Brazil and Argentina were asserting state control over their railroads and older industries, as Mexico had done with its oil industry, the major industrial countries controlled the diffusion of the newer aviation and radio technologies.

The Depression and the Vargas Regime in Brazil   The Great Depression (see Chapter 30) hit Latin America as hard as it hit Europe and the United States and proved a more important turning point for the region than either world war. As long-term customers cut back orders, the value of agricultural and mineral exports fell by two-thirds between 1929 and 1932. Argentina and Brazil could no longer afford imported manufactured goods. An imploding economy also undermined their shaky political systems. Like European countries, Argentina and Brazil veered toward authoritarian regimes that promised to solve their economic problems.

In 1930 **Getulio Vargas** (jay-TOO-lee-oh VAR-gus) (1883–1954), a state governor, staged a coup and proclaimed himself president of Brazil. He proved to be a masterful politician. He wrote a new constitution that broadened the franchise and limited the president to one term. He also raised import duties and promoted national firms and state-owned enterprises. By 1936 industrial production had doubled, especially in textiles and small manufactures. Under his guidance, Brazil was on its way to becoming an industrial country, as well as a model for other Latin American countries attempting to break away from neocolonial dependency.

The industrialization of Brazil brought the familiar environmental consequences. Powerful new machines allowed the reopening of old mines and the digging of new ones. Cities grew as poor peasants looking for work arrived from the countryside. In Rio de Janeiro and São Paulo (sow PAL-oh), the poor turned steep hillsides and vacant lands into immense *favelas* (feh-VEL-luhs) (slums) of makeshift shacks.

The countryside also was transformed. Scrubland was turned into pasture or planted in wheat, corn, and sugar cane. Even the Amazon rain forest—half of the

Juan and Eva Perón

Juan Perón's presidency of Argentina (1946–1955) relied on his, and especially on his wife Eva's, popularity with the working class. To sustain their popularity, they often organized parades and demonstrations in imitation of the fascist dictators of Europe. This picture shows them riding in a procession in Buenos Aires in 1952.

Brown Brothers

land area of Brazil—was affected. In 1930, American industrialist Henry Ford invested $8 million to clear land along the Tapajós River and prepare it to become the site of the world's largest rubber plantation. Ford encountered opposition from Brazilian workers and politicians; the rubber trees proved vulnerable to diseases; and he had to abandon the project—but not before leaving 3 million acres (1.2 million hectares) denuded of trees.

Although Vargas instituted many reforms favorable to urban workers, he refused to help the millions of landless peasants or challenge the great landowners. In 1938, prohibited by his own constitution from being reelected, Vargas staged another coup, abolished the constitution, and instituted the Estado Novo (esh-TAH-doe NO-vo), or "New State," with himself as supreme leader. He abolished political parties, jailed opposition leaders, and turned Brazil into a fascist state, though one that contributed troops and ships to the Allied war effort once the Second World War broke out.

Argentina After 1930   Economically, the depression hurt Argentina almost as badly as it hurt Brazil. Politically, however, the consequences were delayed. In 1930 General José Uriburu (hoe-SAY oo-ree-BOO-roo) overthrew the popularly elected President Irigoyen. For thirteen years the generals and the oligarchy ruled, doing nothing to lessen the poverty of the workers or the frustrations of the middle class. When World War II broke out, Argentina remained officially neutral.

In 1943 another military revolt flared, this one among junior officers led by Colonel **Juan Perón** (hoo-AHN pair-OWN) (1895–1974). The intentions of the rebels were clear:

> Civilians will never understand the greatness of our ideal; we shall therefore have to eliminate them from the government and give them the only mission which corresponds to them: work and obedience.[4]

Once in power the officers took over the highest positions in government and business and began to lavish money on military equipment and their own salaries. Their goal, inspired by Nazi victories (see Chapter 30), was nothing less than the conquest of South America.

As the war turned against the Nazis, the officers saw their popularity collapse. Perón, however, had other plans. Inspired by his charismatic wife **Eva Duarte Perón** (AY-vuy doo-AR-tay pair-OWN) (1919–1952), he appealed to the urban workers. Eva Perón became the champion of the *descamisados* (des-cah-mee-SAH-dohs), or "shirtless ones," and campaigned tirelessly for social benefits and for the cause of women and children. With his wife's help, Perón won the presidency in 1946 and created a populist dictatorship in imitation of the Vargas regime in Brazil. When Eva died in 1952, however, he lost his political skills (or perhaps they were hers), and soon thereafter was overthrown in yet another military coup.

SUB-SAHARAN AFRICA, 1900–1945

In contrast with India and Latin America, sub-Saharan Africa experienced very few of the transformations that marked the first half of the twentieth century. Africa was the last continent to come under European rule (see Chapter 26), and it was still being subjected to the economic and political organizational forces of imperialism when territories that had been colonized longer were already in the beginning stages of political awakening. After World War I Britain, France, Belgium, and South Africa divided Germany's African colonies among themselves. Then in the 1930s Italy invaded Ethiopia. The colonial empires reached their peak shortly before World War II.

Yet it would be a mistake to conclude that developments in Africa would have resembled those elsewhere if imperialism had started sooner. European attitudes toward sub-Saharan African peoples were affected by a long history of racism. One economic theory, for example, "the backward bending supply curve of labor," maintained that people who were accustomed to living at a bare subsistence level would work fewer hours if their pay was raised above what little was needed to maintain that level. They would prefer to idle their lives away sitting around the village rather than striving to better their standard of living the way European workers theoretically would. This theory was used to stigmatize African workers and justify paying them very low wages.

---

[4]George Blankstein, *Perón's Argentina* (Chicago: University of Chicago Press, 1953), 37.

Colonial Africa: Economic and Social Changes   Outside of Algeria, Kenya, and South Africa, few Europeans lived in Africa, and they variously spoke Portuguese, Spanish, German, French, English, or Afrikaans. In 1930 Nigeria, with a population of 20 million, was ruled by 386 British officials and by 8,000 policemen and military personnel, of whom 150 were European. Yet even such a small presence stimulated deep social and economic changes.

The colonial powers had built railroads from coastal cities to mines and plantations in the interior to transport raw materials to the industrial world, but few Africans benefited from these changes. Colonial governments took lands from Africans and sold or leased them to European companies or to white settlers. Large European companies dominated wholesale commerce, while Indians, Greeks, and Syrians handled much of the retail trade.

Where land was divided into small farms, some Africans benefited from the boom. Farmers in the Gold Coast (now Ghana [GAH-nuh]) profited from the high price of cacao, as did palm oil producers in Nigeria and coffee growers in East Africa. In most of Africa women played a major role in the retail trades, selling cloth, food, pots and pans, and other items in the markets. Many maintained their economic independence and kept their household finances separate from those of their husbands, following a custom that predated the colonial period.

For many Africans, however, economic development meant working in European-owned mines and plantations, often under compulsion. Colonial governments were eager to develop the resources of the territories under their control but would not pay wages high enough to attract workers. Instead, they used their police powers to force Africans to work under harsh conditions for little or no pay. In the 1920s, when the government of French Equatorial Africa decided to build a railroad from Brazzaville to the Atlantic coast, a distance of 312 miles (502 kilometers), it drafted 127,000 men to carve a roadbed across mountains and through rain forests. For lack of food, clothing, and medical care, 20,000 of them died, an average of 64 deaths per mile of track.

Europeans prided themselves on bringing modern health care to Africa; yet before the 1930s other aspects of colonialism actually worsened public health. Migrants and soldiers spread syphilis, gonorrhea, tuberculosis, and malaria. Sleeping sickness and smallpox epidemics raged throughout Central Africa. In recruiting men to work, colonial governments also depleted rural areas of farmers needed to plant and harvest crops. Forced requisitions of food to feed the workers left the remaining populations undernourished and vulnerable to diseases. Not until the 1930s did colonial governments realize the negative consequences of their labor policies and begin to invest in agricultural development and health care for Africans.

In 1900 Ibadan (ee-BAH-dahn) in Nigeria was the only city in sub-Saharan Africa with more than 100,000 inhabitants; fifty years later, dozens of cities had reached that size. Africans migrated to cities because they offered hope of jobs and excitement and, for a few, the chance to become wealthy.

However, migrations damaged the family life of those involved, for almost all the migrants were men leaving women in the countryside to farm and raise children. Reflecting the colonialists' attitudes, cities built during the colonial period had racially segregated housing, clubs, restaurants, hospitals, and other institutions.

Patterns of racial discrimination were most rigid in the white-settler colonies of eastern and southern Africa.

Religious and Political Changes   Traditional religious belief could not explain the dislocations that foreign rule, migrations, and sudden economic changes brought to the lives of Africans. Many therefore turned to Christianity or Islam.

Christianity was introduced into Africa by Western missionaries, except in Ethiopia, where it was indigenous. It was most successful in West and South Africa, where the European influence was strongest. A major attraction of the Christian denominations was their mission schools, which taught both craft skills and basic literacy, providing access to employment as minor functionaries, teachers, and shopkeepers. These schools educated a new elite, many of whom learned not only skills and literacy but Western political ideas as well. Yet very few students continued their education to the university level. Many Africans accepted Christianity enthusiastically, reading the suffering of their own peoples into the biblical stories of Moses and the parables of Jesus. The churches trained some pupils to become catechists, teachers, and clergymen. Independent Christian churches associated Christian beliefs with radical ideas of racial equality and participation in politics.

A Quranic School *In Muslim countries, religious education is centered on learning to read, write, and recite the Quran, the sacred book of the Islamic religion, in the original Arabic. This picture shows boys in a Libyan madrasa (Quranic school) studying writing and religion.*

Islam spread inland from the East African coast and southward from the Sahel (SAH-hel) through the influence and example of Arab and African merchants. Islam also emphasized literacy—in Arabic rather than a European language—and was less disruptive of traditional African customs such as polygamy. In some areas, such as Somalia, Sudan, and Mali, certain Muslim Sufi brotherhoods became associated with resistance to European imperialism.

In Dakar in Senegal and Cape Town in South Africa, small numbers of Africans could obtain secondary education. Even smaller numbers went on to college in Europe or America. Though few in number, they became the leaders of political movements. The contrast between the liberal ideas imparted by Western education and the realities of racial discrimination under colonial rule contributed to the rise of nationalism among educated Africans. In Senegal **Blaise Diagne** (dee-AHN-yuh) agitated for African participation in politics and fair treatment in the French army during World War I, and in the 1920s J. E. Casely Hayford began organizing a movement for greater autonomy in British West Africa. These nationalist movements were inspired by the ideas of Pan-Africanists from America such as W. E. B. Du Bois and Marcus Garvey, who advocated the unity of African peoples around the world, as well as by European ideas of liberty and nationhood. To defend the interests of Africans, Western-educated lawyers and journalists in South Africa founded the **African National Congress** in 1912. Before World War II, however, these nationalist movements were small and had little influence.

The Second World War had a profound effect on the peoples of Africa, even those far removed from the theaters of war. The war brought hardships, such as increased forced labor, inflation, and requisitions of raw materials. Yet it also brought hope. During the campaign to oust the Italians from Ethiopia, Emperor **Haile Selassie** (HI-lee seh-LASS-ee) (r. 1930–1974) led his own troops into Addis Ababa, his capital, and reclaimed his title. A million Africans served as soldiers and carriers in Burma, North Africa, and Europe, where many became aware of Africa's role in helping the Allied war effort. They listened to Allied propaganda in favor of European liberation movements and against Nazi racism and returned to their countries with new and radical ideas.

Africa and the New Media   South Africa saw the first tries at radio broadcasting in 1924, but these enjoyed very little success until the South African Broadcasting Corporation was established with monopolistic control over the medium in 1936. Down to World War II it broadcast only in English and Afrikaans. Most efforts in other colonies, such as Mozambique and Kenya, likewise targeted European listeners. The exception was British West Africa—Sierra Leone, Ghana, and Nigeria—where African languages were used. Rather than wireless service, subscribers had loudspeakers in their homes that were connected by wire to the radio station. After 1936 the British authorities generally began to see radio as a medium for reaching Africans who did not understand English.

Africa had almost no cinematic presence prior to World War II, apart from fourteen stereotype-filled Tarzan films made in Hollywood between 1918 and 1949. A few films were made for British and Afrikaner audiences in South Africa, but the French issued a decree in 1934 prohibiting the shooting of movies.

Conclusion

The First and Second World Wars and the intervening period of economic depression, fascism, and militarism constituted the great dramas of the first half of the twentieth century. But not all parts of the world experienced these convulsions to the same degree. Moreover, these narratives of world war, global depression, and varying regional development do not incorporate the profound changes in ways of living that affected most parts of the world between 1900 and 1950.

While participating in many of these changes, the nonindustrialized nations also had their own technological breakthroughs, such as the rickshaw, and did not use some inventions, such as electricity, in the same way as the West. New media such as cinema and radio were used in different ways as well and sometimes perpetuated themes and images from local cultural sources. At the same time, traditional patterns of village life began to erode as cities grew and urban life, at least for the privileged classes, took on the demeanor and attitudes of Europe. But becoming like Europe did not mean coming to like Europe.

To a much greater degree, the industrialized world experienced a flood of new inventions—automobiles, electric lights, radios, movies, airplanes—that stimulated not only a broader respect for science, but also an expectation that science would continue indefinitely to improve human lives. This was the cult of the modern. Technology even affected the arts, providing new materials for architecture and furniture design, new electronic means of amplifying and distributing music, and an ever-expanding array of tools for making and reproducing images, both still and moving. Yet the devastating human tragedies of war and depression also encouraged currents of nihilism, despair, and questioning of faith.

Imperialism being focused, as always, on benefits for the home country and disdain for native peoples with darker skins, colonial administrators in different parts of the world tried to control the flow of global technological and ideological changes. Having a larger and better-educated middle class than many other non-European lands, India entered more fully into the new ways of living than did sub-Saharan Africa. Latin America, with many European immigrants, was closer economically and ideologically to Europe. Political and cultural independence became a realizable goal in India, where Mahatma Gandhi's nonviolent movement pioneered an entirely new form of political activism. In sub-Saharan Africa, however, European racism and the unwavering favoritism shown to European settlers stifled almost all attempts at change.

IMPORTANT EVENTS 1900–1950	
1903	Wright brothers fly first airplane
1905	Viceroy Curzon splits Bengal; mass demonstrations
1906	Muslims found All-India Muslim League
1911	British transfer capital from Calcutta to Delhi
1912	African National Congress founded

1912	First feature-length movie in India
1913	Henry Ford introduces assembly-line production
1915–1920	Women gain vote in Norway, Russia, Canada, Germany, Britain, and the United States
1919	Amritsar Massacre
1920	Commercial radio begins in United States
1920s	J. E. Casely Hayford organizes political movement in British West Africa
1923	Margaret Sanger opens first birth control clinic
1925	Commercial radio begins in Japan
1928	Plutarco Elías Calles founds Mexico's National Revolutionary Party
1929	Gandhi leads March to the Sea
1930s	Gandhi calls for independence; he is repeatedly arrested
1930–1945	Getulio Vargas, dictator of Brazil
1932	Empire State Building opens
1934–1940	Lázaro Cárdenas, president of Mexico
1936	Olympic games in Berlin
1938	Cárdenas nationalizes Mexican oil industry; Vargas proclaims Estado Novo in Brazil
1939	British bring India into World War II
1939–1945	A million Africans serve in World War II
1940	Muhammad Ali Jinnah demands a separate nation for Muslims
1943	Juan Perón leads military coup in Argentina
1946	Perón elected president of Argentina
1947	Partition and independence of India and Pakistan

30

THE COLLAPSE OF THE OLD ORDER, 1929–1949

Before the First World War the Italian poet Filippo Marinetti exalted violence as noble and manly: "We want to glorify war, the world's only hygiene— militarism, deed, destroyer of anarchisms, the beautiful ideas that are death-bringing, and the subordination of women."[1] His friend Gabriele d'Annunzio added: "If it is a crime to incite citizens to violence, I shall boast of this crime."[2] Poets are sometimes more prescient than they imagine.

In the nineteenth century the governments of the great powers were manipulated by politicians through appeals to popular nationalism. Internationally, the world order relied on the maintenance of empires by military or economic means. And the global economy was based on free-market capitalism in which the industrial countries exchanged manufactured goods for the agricultural and mineral products of the nonindustrial world.

After the trauma of World War I the world seemed to return to what U.S. president Warren Harding called "normalcy": prosperity in Europe and America, European colonialism in Asia and Africa, American domination of Latin America, and peace almost everywhere. But in 1929 normalcy vanished. As the Great Depression spread around the world, governments turned against one another in desperate attempts to protect their people's livelihood.

Most survivors of the war had learned to abhor violence. For a few, however, war and domination became a creed, a goal, and a solution to their problems. The Japanese military tried to save their country from the depression by conquering China, which erupted in revolution. In Germany many blamed their troubles on communists and Jews and turned to the Nazis, who promised to save German society by crushing others. In the Soviet Union, Stalin used energetic and murderous means to force his country into a communist version of the Industrial Revolution.

As the old order collapsed, the world was engulfed by a second Great War, one far more global and destructive than the first. Unlike World War I, this was a war

---

[1]Apollonio Umbro, ed., *Documents of Twentieth Century Art: Futurist Manifestos* (New York: Viking Press, 1973), 23.

[2]Richard F. Hamilton and Holger H. Herwig, *Decisions for War, 1914–1917* (Cambridge: Cambridge University Press, 2004), 199.

of movement in which entire countries were conquered in a matter of weeks. It was also a war of machines: fighter planes and bombers that targeted civilians, tanks, aircraft carriers, and, finally, atomic bombs that obliterated entire cities.

At the end of World War II much of Europe and East Asia lay in ruins, and millions of destitute refugees sought safety in other lands. The colonial powers were either defeated or so weakened that they could no longer prevent their Asian and African subjects from demanding independence.

THE STALIN REVOLUTION

During the 1920s the Soviet Union recovered from the Revolutions of 1917 and the civil war that followed (see Chapter 28). After Stalin achieved total mastery over this huge nation in 1929, he led it through an economic and social transformation that turned it into a great industrial and military power and intensified both admiration for and fear of communism throughout the world.

Five-Year Plans   **Joseph Stalin** (1879–1953) was the son of a poor shoemaker. Before becoming a revolutionary, he studied for the priesthood. Under the name *Stalin* (Russian for "man of steel"), he played a small part in the Revolutions of 1917. He was a hard-working and skillful administrator who rose within the party bureaucracy and filled its upper ranks with men loyal to himself. He then proceeded to make himself absolute dictator and transform Soviet society.

Stalin's ambition was to turn the USSR into an industrial nation. However, industrialization was to serve a different purpose than in other countries. It was not expected to produce consumer goods for a mass market or to enrich individuals. Instead, its aim was to increase the power of the Communist Party domestically and that of the Soviet Union in relation to other countries.

Stalin was determined to prevent a repetition of the humiliating defeat Russia had suffered at the hands of Germany in 1917. His goal was to quintuple the output of electricity and double that of heavy industry—iron, steel, coal, and machinery—in five years. To do so, he devised the first of a series of **Five-Year Plans**. Beginning in October 1928, the Communist Party and government created whole industries and cities from scratch, then trained millions of peasants to work in the new factories, mines, and offices. In every way except actual fighting, Stalin's Russia resembled a nation at war.

Rapid industrialization hastened environmental changes. Hydroelectric dams turned rivers into strings of reservoirs. Roads, canals, and railroad tracks cut the landscape. Forests and grassland were turned into farmland. From an environmental perspective, the Five-Year Plans resembled the transformation that had occurred in the United States and Canada a few decades earlier.

Collectivization   Since the Soviet Union was still a predominantly agrarian
of Agriculture   country, the only way to pay for these massive investments, provide the labor, and feed the millions of new industrial workers was to squeeze the peasantry. Stalin therefore proceeded with the most radical social experiment conceived up to that time: the collectivization of agriculture.

Collectivization meant consolidating small private farms into vast collectives and making the farmers work together in commonly owned fields. Each collective was expected to supply the government with a fixed amount of food and distribute what was left among its members. Collectives were to become outdoor factories where food was manufactured through the techniques of mass production and the application of machinery. The purpose of this collectivization was to bring the peasants under government control so they never again could withhold food supplies, as they had done during the Russian civil war of 1918–1921.

When collectivization was announced, the government mounted a massive propaganda campaign and sent party members into the countryside to enlist the farmers' support. At first all seemed to go well, but soon *kulaks* (COO-lock) ("fists"), the better-off peasants, began to resist giving up all their property. When soldiers came to force them into collectives at gunpoint, they burned their crops, smashed their equipment, and slaughtered their livestock. Within a few months they slaughtered half of the Soviet Union's horses and cattle and two-thirds of the sheep and goats. In retaliation, Stalin ruthlessly ordered the "liquidation of kulaks as a class" and incited the poor peasants to attack their wealthier neighbors. Over 8 million kulaks were arrested. Many were executed, and the rest were sent to slave labor camps, where most starved to death.

The peasants who were left had been the least successful before collectivization and proved to be the least competent after. Many were sent to work in factories. The rest were forbidden to leave their farms. With half of their draft animals gone, they could not plant or harvest enough to meet the swelling demands of the cities. Yet government agents took whatever they could find, leaving little or nothing for the farmers themselves. After bad harvests in 1933 and 1934, a famine swept through the countryside, killing some 5 million people, about one in every twenty farmers.

Stalin's second Five-Year Plan, designed to run from 1933 to 1937, was originally intended to produce consumer goods. But when the Nazis took over Germany in 1933 (see below), Stalin changed the plan to emphasize heavy industries that could produce armaments. Between 1927 and 1937 the Soviet output of metals and machines increased fourteen-fold while consumer goods became scarce and food was rationed. After a decade of Stalinism, the Soviet people were more poorly clothed, fed, and housed than they had been before the war.

Terror and Opportunities   The 1930s brought both terror and opportunities to the Soviet people. The forced pace of industrialization, the collectivization of agriculture, and the uprooting of millions of people could be accomplished only under duress. To prevent any possible resistance or rebellion, the NKVD, Stalin's secret police force, created a climate of suspicion and fear.

As early as 1930 Stalin had hundreds of engineers and technicians arrested on trumped-up charges of counterrevolutionary ideas and sabotage. Three years later, he expelled a million members of the Communist Party—one-third of the membership—on similar charges. He then turned on his most trusted associates.

In December 1934 Sergei Kirov, the party boss of Leningrad (now St. Petersburg), was assassinated, perhaps on Stalin's orders. Stalin made a public display of mourning Kirov while blaming others for the crime. He then ordered a series of spectacular purge trials in which he accused most of Lenin's associates of treason. In 1937 he had his eight top generals and many lower officers executed, leaving the Red Army dangerously weakened. Under torture or psychological pressure, almost all the accused confessed to the "crimes" they were charged with.

While "Old Bolsheviks" and high officials were being put on trial, terror spread steadily downward. The government regularly made demands that people could not meet, so everyone was guilty of breaking some regulation or other. People from all walks of life were arrested, some on mere suspicion or because of a false accusation by a jealous coworker or neighbor, some for expressing a doubt or working too hard or not hard enough, some for being related to someone previously arrested, some for no reason at all. Millions of people were sentenced without trials. At the height of the terror, some 8 million were sent to *gulags* (GOO-log) (labor camps), where perhaps a million died each year of exposure or malnutrition. To its victims the terror seemed capricious and random. Yet it turned a sullen and resentful people into docile hard-working subjects of the party.

In spite of the fear and hardships, many Soviet citizens supported Stalin's regime. Suddenly, with so many people gone and new industries and cities being built everywhere, there were opportunities for those who remained, especially the poor and the young. Women entered careers and jobs previously closed to them, becoming steelworkers, physicians, and office managers; but they retained their household and child-rearing duties, receiving little help from men (see Diversity and Dominance: Women, Family Values, and the Russian Revolution). People who moved to the cities, worked enthusiastically, and asked no questions could hope to rise into the upper ranks of the Communist Party, the military, the government, or the professions—where the privileges and rewards were many.

Stalin's brutal methods helped the Soviet Union industrialize faster than any country had ever done. By the late 1930s the USSR was the world's third largest industrial power, after the United States and Germany. To foreign observers it seemed to be booming with construction projects and labor shortages. Even anti-Communist observers admitted that government planning worked. To millions of Soviet citizens who took pride in the new strength of their country and to many foreigners who contrasted conditions in the Soviet Union with the unemployment and despair in the West, Stalin's achievement seemed worth any price.

THE DEPRESSION

On October 24, 1929—"Black Thursday"—the New York stock market went into a dive. Within days stocks had lost half their value. The fall continued for three years, ruining millions of investors. People with bank accounts rushed to make withdrawals, causing thousands of banks to collapse.

Economic Crisis   What began as a stock market crash soon turned into the deepest depression in history. As consumers reduced their purchases, businesses cut production, laying off thousands of workers. Female employees were the first laid off on the grounds that men had to support families while women worked only for "pin money." Jobless men deserted their families. Small farmers went bankrupt and lost their land. By mid-1932 the American economy had shrunk by half, and unemployment had risen to an unprecedented 25 percent of the workforce. Many observers thought that free-enterprise capitalism was doomed.

In 1930 the U.S. government, hoping to protect American industries from foreign competition, imposed the Smoot-Hawley tariff, the highest in American history. In retaliation, other countries raised their tariffs in a wave of "beggar thy neighbor" protectionism. The result was crippled export industries and shrinking world trade. While global industrial production declined by 36 percent between 1929 and 1932, world trade dropped by a breathtaking 62 percent.

Depression in Industrial Nations   By 1931 the depression had spread to Europe. Governments canceled reparations payments and war loans, but it was too late to save the world economy. Though their economies stagnated, France and Britain weathered the depression by making their colonial empires purchase their products rather than the products of other countries. Nations that relied on exports to pay for imported food and fuel suffered much more. In Germany unemployment reached 6 million by 1932, twice as high as in Britain. Half the German population lived in poverty, while those who kept their jobs saw their salaries cut and their living standards fall. In Japan the burden of the depression fell hardest on the farmers and fishermen.

This massive economic upheaval had profound political repercussions. Nationalists everywhere called for autarchy, or independence from the world economy. In the United States Franklin D. Roosevelt was elected president in 1932 on a "New Deal" platform of government programs to stimulate and revitalize the economy. Although the American, British, and French governments intervened in their economies, they remained democratic. In Germany and Japan, as economic grievances worsened long-festering political resentments, radical leaders came to power and turned their nations into military machines, hoping to acquire, by war if necessary, empires large enough to support self-sufficient economies and at the same time provide employment in arms factories.

Depression in Nonindustrial Regions   The depression also spread to Asia, Africa, and Latin America, but very unevenly. In 1930 India erected a wall of import duties to protect its infant industries from foreign competition; its living standards stagnated but did not drop. China was little affected by trade with other countries; its problems were more political than economic.

Two Views of the American Way *In this classic photograph,* Life *magazine photographer Margaret Bourke-White captured the contrast between advertisers' view of the ideal American family and the reality of bread lines for the poor.*

Countries that depended on exports were hard hit by the depression. Malaya, Indochina, and the Dutch East Indies produced most of the world's natural rubber; when automobile production in the United States and Europe dropped by half, so did imports of rubber, devastating their economies. Egypt, dependent on cotton exports, was also affected, and in the resulting political strife, the government became autocratic and unpopular.

Throughout Latin America unemployment and homelessness increased markedly. The industrialization of Argentina and Brazil was set back a decade or more. Disenchanted with liberal politics, military officers seized power in several Latin American countries (see Chapter 29). Consciously imitating dictatorships emerging in Europe, they imposed authoritarian control over their economies, hoping to stimulate local industries and curb imports.

Other than the USSR, only southern Africa boomed during the 1930s. As other prices dropped, gold became relatively more valuable. Copper deposits, found in Northern Rhodesia (now Zambia) and the Belgian Congo (now Democratic Republic of the Congo), proved to be cheaper to mine than Chilean copper. But this mining boom benefited only a small number of European and white South African mine owners. For Africans it was a mixed blessing; mining provided jobs and cash wages to men while women stayed behind in the villages, farming, herding, and raising children without their husbands' help.

Women, Family Values, and the Russian Revolution

The Bolsheviks were of two minds on the subject of women. They were opposed to bourgeois morality and to the oppression of women, especially working-class women, under capitalism. But what to put in its place?

Alexandra Kollontai was the most outspoken of the Bolsheviks on the subject of women's rights. She advocated the liberation of women, the replacement of housework by communal kitchens and laundries, and divorce on demand. Under socialism, love, sex, and marriage would be entirely equal, reciprocal, and free of economic obligations. Childbearing would be encouraged, but children would be raised communally: "The worker mother ... must remember that there are henceforth only our children, those of the communist state, the common possession of all workers."

In a lecture she gave at Sverdlov University in 1921, Kollontai declared:

... it is important to preserve not only the interests of the woman but also the life of the child, and this is to be done by giving the woman the opportunity to combine labour and maternity. Soviet power tries to create a situation where a woman does not have to cling to a man she has learned to loathe only because she has nowhere else to go with her children, and where a woman alone does not have to fear for her life and the life of her child. In the labour republic it is not the philanthropists with their humiliating charity but the workers and peasants, fellow-creators of the new society, who hasten to help the working woman and strive to lighten the burden of motherhood....
I would like to say a few words about ... the question of abortion, and Soviet Russia's attitude toward it. On 20 November 1920 the labour republic issued a law abolishing the penalties that had been attached to abortion. What is the reason behind this new attitude? Russia after all suffers not from an overproduction of living labour but rather from a lack of it. Russia is thinly, not densely populated. Every unit of labour power is precious. Why then have we declared abortion to be no longer a criminal offence? ...

Abortion exists and flourishes everywhere, and no laws or punitive measures have succeeded in rooting it out. A way round the law is always found. But "secret help" only cripples women; they become a burden on the labour government, and the size of the labour force is reduced. Abortion, when carried out under proper medical conditions, is less harmful and dangerous, and the woman can get back to work quicker. Soviet power realizes that the need for abortion will only disappear on the one hand when Russia has a broad and developed network of institutions protecting motherhood and providing social education, and on the other hand when women understand that *childbirth is a social obligation*; Soviet power has therefore allowed abortion to be performed openly and in clinical conditions.

Besides the large-scale development of motherhood protection, the task of labour Russia is to strengthen in women the healthy instinct of motherhood, to make motherhood and labour for the collective compatible and thus do away with the need for abortion. This is the approach of the labour republic to the question of abortion, which still faces women in the bourgeois countries in all its magnitude. In these countries women are exhausted by the dual burden of hired labour for capital and motherhood. In Soviet Russia the working woman and peasant woman are helping the Communist Party to build a new society and to undermine the old way of life that has enslaved women. As soon as woman is viewed as being essentially a labour unit, the key to the solution of the complex question of maternity can be found.

Fifteen years later Joseph Stalin reversed the Soviet policy on abortion.

The published draft of the law prohibiting abortion and providing material assistance to mothers has provoked a lively reaction throughout the country. It is being heatedly discussed by tens of millions of people and there is no doubt that it will serve as a further strengthening of the Soviet family....

When we speak of strengthening the Soviet family, we are speaking precisely of the struggle against the survivals of a bourgeois attitude towards marriage, women, and children. So-called "free love" and all disorderly sex life are bourgeois through and through, and have nothing to do with either socialist principles or the ethics and standards of conduct of the Soviet citizens. Socialist doctrine shows this, and it is proved by life itself.

The elite of our country, the best of the Soviet youth, are as a rule also excellent family men who dearly love their children. And vice versa: the man who does not take marriage seriously, and abandons his children to the whims of fate, is usually also a bad worker and a poor member of society....

It is impossible even to compare the present state of the family with that which obtained before the Soviet regime—so great has been the improvement towards greater stability and, above all, greater humanity and goodness. The single fact that millions of women have become economically independent and are no longer at the mercy of men's whims, speaks volumes. Compare, for instance, the modern woman collective farmer who sometimes earns more than her husband, with the pre-revolutionary peasant woman who completely depended on her husband and was a slave in the household. Has not this fundamentally changed family relations, has it not rationalized and strengthened the family? The very motives for setting up a family, for getting married, have changed for the better, have been cleansed of atavistic and barbaric elements. Marriage has ceased to be a matter of sell-and-buy. Nowadays a girl from a collective farm is not given away (or should we say "sold away"?) by her father, for now she is her own mistress, and no one can give her away. She will marry the man she loves....

We alone have all the conditions under which a working woman can fulfill her duties as a citizen and as a mother responsible for the birth and early upbringing of her children.

A woman without children merits our pity, for she does not know the full joy of life. Our Soviet women, full-blooded citizens of the freest country in the world, have been given the bliss of motherhood. We must safeguard the family and raise and rear healthy Soviet heroes!

Questions for Analysis

1. How does Kollontai expect women to be both workers and mothers without depending on a man? How would Soviet society make this possible?

2. Why does Alexandra Kollontai advocate the legalization of abortion in Soviet Russia? Does she view abortion as a permanent right or as a temporary necessity?

3. Why does Stalin characterize a "light-hearted, negligent attitude toward marriage" and "all disorderly sex life" as "bourgeois through and through"?

4. How does Stalin's image of the Soviet family differ from Kollontai's? Are his views a variation of her views, or the opposite?

Sources: First selection from Alexandra Kollontai, "The Labour of Women in the Revolution of the Economy," in *Selected Writings of Alexandra Kollontai,* translated by Alix Holt (Lawrence Hill & Company, 1978), pp. 148–149. Second selection from Discussion of the Law on Abolition of Legal Abortion, Pravda, Editorials of May 28 and June 9, 1936 (English translation in Rudolf Schlesinger, ed., Changing Attitudes in Soviet Russia: The Family in the USSR, London, Routledge & Kegan Paul, 1949, pp. 251–54, 268–69.

THE RISE OF FASCISM

The Russian Revolution and its Stalinist aftermath frightened property owners in Europe and North America. In western Europe and North America, middle- and upper-income voters took refuge in conservative politics. In southern and central Europe, the war had turned people's hopes of victory to bitter disappointment. Many blamed ethnic minorities, especially Jews, for their troubles. In their yearning for a mythical past of family farms and small shops, increasing numbers rejected representative government and sought more dramatic solutions.

Radical politicians applied wartime propaganda techniques to appeal to a confused citizenry. They promised to use any means necessary to bring back full employment, stop the spread of communism, and achieve the territorial conquests that World War I had denied them. While defending private property from communism, they borrowed the communist model of politics: a single party and a secret police that ruled by terror and intimidation.

Mussolini's Italy   The first country to seek radical answers was Italy. World War I, which had never been popular, left thousands of veterans who found neither pride in their victory nor jobs in the postwar economy. Unemployed veterans and violent youths banded together into *fasci di combattimento* (fighting units) to demand action and intimidate politicians. When workers threatened to strike, factory and property owners hired gangs of these *fascisti* to defend them.

Benito Mussolini (1883–1945) had supported Italy's entry into the war. A spellbinding orator, he quickly became the leader of the **Fascist Party**, which glorified warfare and the Italian nation. By 1921 the party had 300,000 members, many of whom used violent methods to repress strikes, intimidate voters, and seize municipal governments. A year later Mussolini threatened to march on Rome if he was not appointed prime minister. The government, composed of timid parliamentarians, gave in.

Mussolini proceeded to install Fascist Party members in all government jobs, crush all opposition parties, and jail anyone who criticized him. The party took over the press, public education, and youth activities and gave employers control over their workers. The Fascists lowered living standards but reduced unemployment and provided social security and public services. They proved to be neither ruthless radicals nor competent administrators.

What Mussolini and the Fascist movement really excelled at was bombastic speeches, spectacular parades, and signs everywhere proclaiming "Il Duce (eel DOO-chay) [the Leader] is always right!" Mussolini's genius was to apply the techniques of modern mass communications and advertisement to political life. Movie footage and radio news bulletins galvanized the masses in ways never before done in peacetime. His techniques of whipping up public enthusiasm were not lost on other radicals. By the 1930s fascist movements had appeared in most European countries, as well as in Latin America, China, and Japan. Fascism appealed to many people who were frightened by rapid changes and placed their hopes in charismatic leaders. Of all of Mussolini's imitators, none was as sinister as Adolf Hitler.

Hitler's
Germany

Germany had lost the First World War after coming very close to winning. The hyperinflation of 1923 wiped out the savings of middle-class families. Less than ten years later the depression caused more unemployment and misery than in any other country. Millions of Germans blamed Socialists, Jews, and foreigners for their troubles.

Adolf Hitler (1889–1945) joined the German army in 1914 and was wounded at the front. He later looked back fondly on the clear lines of authority and the camaraderie he had experienced in battle. After the war he used his gifts as an orator to lead a political splinter group called the National Socialist German Workers' Party—**Nazis** for short. While serving a brief jail sentence he wrote *Mein Kampf* (mine compf) (*My Struggle*), in which he outlined his goals and beliefs.

When it was published in 1925, *Mein Kampf* attracted little notice. Its ideas seemed so insane that almost no one took it, or its author, seriously. Hitler's ideas went far beyond ordinary nationalism. He believed that Germany should incorporate all German-speaking areas, even those in neighboring countries. He distinguished among a "master race" of Aryans (he meant Germans, Scandinavians, and Britons), a degenerate "Alpine" race of French and Italians, and an inferior race of Russian and eastern European Slavs, fit only to be slaves of the master race. He reserved his most intense hatred for Jews, on whom he blamed every disaster that had befallen Germany, especially the defeat of 1918. He glorified violence and looked forward to a future war in which the "master race" would defeat and subjugate all others.

Hitler's first goal was to reverse the humiliation and repeal the military restrictions of the Treaty of Versailles. Next he planned to annex all German-speaking territories to a greater Germany, then gain *Lebensraum* (LAY-bens-rowm) (room to live) at the expense of Poland and the USSR. Finally, he planned to eliminate all Jews from Europe.

From 1924 to 1930 Hitler's followers remained a tiny minority, for most Germans found his ideas too extreme. But when the depression hit, the Nazis gained supporters among the unemployed, who believed their promises of jobs for all, and among property owners frightened by the growing popularity of communists.

In March 1933 Hitler became chancellor of Germany. Once in office, he quickly assumed dictatorial powers. He put Nazis in charge of all government agencies, educational institutions, and professional organizations; banned all other political parties; and threw their leaders into concentration camps. The Nazis deprived Jews of their citizenship and civil rights, prohibited them from marrying "Aryans," ousted them from the professions, and confiscated their property. In August 1934 Hitler proclaimed himself *Führer* (FEW-rer) ("leader") and called Germany the "Third Reich," the third German empire after the Holy Roman Empire of medieval times and the German Empire of 1871 to 1918.

The Nazis' economic and social policies were spectacularly effective. The government undertook massive public works projects. Businesses got contracts to manufacture weapons. Women who had entered the workforce were urged to release their jobs to men. By 1936 business was booming; unemployment was at its lowest level since the 1920s; and living standards were rising. Most Germans believed that their economic well-being outweighed the loss of liberty.

The Road to War, 1933–1939 However, Hitler's goal was not prosperity or popularity, but conquest. As soon as he came to office, he began to build up the armed forces. Meanwhile, he tested the reactions of the other powers through a series of surprise moves followed by protestations of peace.

In 1933 Hitler withdrew Germany from the League of Nations. Two years later he announced that Germany was going to introduce conscription, build up its army, and create an air force—in violation of the Versailles treaty. Neither Britain nor France was willing to risk war by standing up to Germany.

In 1935, emboldened by the weakness of the democracies, Italy invaded Ethiopia, the last independent state in Africa and a member of the League of Nations. The League and the democracies protested but refused to close the Suez Canal to Italian ships or impose an oil embargo. The following year, when Hitler sent troops into the Rhineland on the borders of France and Belgium, the other powers merely protested.

By 1938 Hitler decided that his rearmament plans were far enough advanced that he could afford to escalate his demands. In March Germany invaded Austria. Most Austrians were German-speakers and accepted the annexation of their country without protest. Then came Czechoslovakia, where a German-speaking minority lived along the German border. Hitler first demanded their autonomy from Czech rule, then their annexation to Germany. Throughout the summer he threatened to

A Nazi Rally *Hitler organized mass rallies at Nuremberg to whip up popular support for his regime and to indoctrinate young Germans with a martial spirit. Thousands of men in uniform marched in torch-lit parades before Hitler and his top officials.*

AP/Wide World Photos

go to war. At the Munich Conference of September 1938, the leaders of France, Britain, and Italy gave him everything he wanted without consulting Czechoslovakia. Once again, Hitler learned that aggression paid off.

The weakness of the democracies—now called "appeasement"—had three causes. The first was the deep-seated fear of war among people who had lived through World War I. Unlike the dictators, politicians in the democracies could not ignore their constituents' yearnings for peace. Most people believed that the threat of war might go away if they wished for peace fervently enough. The second cause of appeasement was fear of communism among conservatives, who feared Stalin more than Hitler because Hitler claimed to respect Christianity and private property. The third cause was the very novelty of fascist tactics. Britain's prime minister Neville Chamberlain assumed that political leaders (other than the Bolsheviks) were honorable men and that an agreement was as valid as a business contract. Thus, when Hitler promised to incorporate only German-speaking people into Germany and said he had "no further territorial demands," Chamberlain believed him.

After Munich it was too late to stop Hitler, short of war. Germany and Italy signed an alliance called the Axis, and in March 1939 Germany invaded what was left of Czechoslovakia. Belatedly realizing that Hitler could not be trusted, France and Britain sought Soviet help. Stalin, however, distrusted the "capitalists" as much as they distrusted him. When Hitler offered to divide Poland between Germany and the Soviet Union, Stalin accepted. The Nazi-Soviet Pact of August 23, 1939, freed Hitler from the fear of a two-front war and gave Stalin time to build up his armies. One week later, on September 1, German forces swept into Poland, and the war was on.

EAST ASIA, 1931–1945

When the depression hit, the collapse of demand for silk and rice ruined thousands of Japanese farmers; to survive, some even sold their daughters into prostitution, while many poor young men flocked to the military. Ultranationalists resented their country's dependence on foreign trade and what they believed was unnecessary party politics that sullied the righteousness of the divine imperial will. If only Japan had a colonial empire, they thought, it would not be beholden to the rest of the world. But Europeans and Americans had already taken most potential colonies in Asia. Japanese nationalists saw the conquest of China, with its vast population and resources, as the solution to their country's problems.

The Manchurian Incident of 1931   Meanwhile, in China the Guomindang (gwo-min-dong) (see Chapter 28) was becoming stronger and preparing to challenge the Japanese presence in Manchuria, a province rich in coal and iron ore. Junior officers in the Japanese army, frustrated by the caution of their superiors, took action. In September 1931 they blew up part of a railroad track as a pretext for invading the entire province. This invasion was promoted as achieving the "independence" of Manchuria under the name *Manchukuo* (man-CHEW-coo-oh), but in reality, Manchukuo remained under Japanese control. Many civilian officials and military leaders back in Tokyo had not approved of the attack, but they soon joined the overwhelming positive reaction to the incident expressed by the public, press, and even leftist critics.

The U.S. government condemned the Japanese conquest, and the League of Nations refused to recognize Manchukuo and urged the Japanese to remove their troops from China. Persuaded that the Western powers would not fight, Japan resigned from the League.

During the next few years the Japanese built railways and heavy industries in Manchuria and northeastern China and sped up their rearmament. At home, production was diverted to the military, especially to building warships. The government grew more authoritarian, jailing thousands of dissidents. On several occasions, ultranationalists, many of them junior officers, mutinied or assassinated leading political figures. The mutineers received mild punishments, and generals and admirals sympathetic to their views replaced more moderate civilian politicians.

The Long March   Until the Japanese seized Manchuria, the Chinese government seemed to be creating conditions for a national recovery. The main challenge to the government of **Chiang Kai-shek** (chang kie-shek) came from the Communists. The Chinese Communist Party had been founded in 1921 by a handful of intellectuals, and for several years it lived in the shadow of the Guomindang. Its efforts to recruit members among industrial workers came to naught in 1927, when Chiang Kai-shek arrested and executed Communists and labor leaders alike. The few Communists who escaped the mass arrests fled to the remote mountains of Jiangxi (jang-she), in southeastern China.

Among them was **Mao Zedong** (ma-oh zay-dong) (1893–1976), a farmer's son who had left home to study philosophy. Mao was a man of action whose first impulse was to call for violent effort: "To be able to leap on horseback and to shoot at the same time; to go from battle to battle; to shake the mountains by one's cries, and the colors of the sky by one's roars of anger." In the early 1920s Mao discovered the works of Karl Marx, joined the Communist Party, and soon became one of its leaders.

In Jiangxi Mao began studying conditions among the peasants, in whom Communists had previously shown no interest. He planned to redistribute land from the wealthier to the poorer peasants, thereby gaining adherents for the coming struggle with the Guomindang army. His goal was a complete social revolution from the bottom up. Mao's reliance on the peasantry was a radical departure from Marxist-Leninist ideology, which stressed the backwardness of the peasants and pinned its hopes on industrial workers. Mao therefore had to be careful to cloak his pragmatic tactics in communist rhetoric to allay the suspicions of Stalin and his agents.

Mao was an advocate of women's equality. Before 1927 the Communists had organized the women who worked in Shanghai's textile mills, the most exploited of all Chinese workers. Later, in their mountain stronghold in Jiangxi, they organized women farmers, allowed divorce, and banned arranged marriages and footbinding. But the party was still run by men whose primary task was warfare.

The Guomindang army pursued the Communists into the mountains, building small forts throughout the countryside. Rather than risk direct confrontations, Mao responded with guerrilla warfare. He harassed the army at its weak points with hit-and-run tactics, relying on the terrain and the support of the peasantry. Whereas government troops often mistreated civilians, Mao insisted that his soldiers help the peasants, pay a fair price for food and supplies, and treat women with respect.

In spite of their good relations with the peasants of Jiangxi, the Communists gradually found themselves encircled by government forces. In 1934 Mao and his followers decided to break out of the southern mountains and trek to Shaanxi (SHAWN-she), an even more remote province in northwestern China. The so-called **Long March** took them 6,000 miles (nearly 9,700 kilometers) in one year over desolate mountains and through swamps and deserts, pursued by the army and bombed by Chiang's aircraft. Of the 100,000 Communists who left Jiangxi in October 1934, only 4,000 reached Shaanxi a year later. Chiang's government thought it was finally rid of the Communists.

The Sino-Japanese War, 1937–1945   In Japan politicians, senior officers, and business leaders disagreed on how to solve their country's economic problems. Some proposed a quick conquest of China; others advocated war with the Soviet Union. While their superiors hesitated, junior officers decided to take matters into their own hands.

On July 7, 1937, Japanese troops attacked Chinese forces near Beijing. The junior officers who ordered the attack quickly obtained the support of their commanders and then, reluctantly, of the government. Within weeks Japanese troops seized Beijing, Tianjin, Shanghai, and other coastal cities, and the Japanese navy blockaded the entire coast of China.

Once again, the United States and the League of Nations denounced the Japanese aggression. Yet the Western powers were too preoccupied with events in Europe and with their own economic problems to risk a military confrontation in Asia. When the Japanese sank a U.S. gunboat and shelled a British ship on the Yangzi River, the U.S. and British governments responded only with righteous indignation and pious resolutions.

The Chinese armies were large and fought bravely, but they were poorly led and armed and lost every battle. Japanese planes bombed cities while soldiers broke dikes and burned villages, killing thousands of civilians. Within a year Japan controlled the coastal provinces of China and the lower Yangzi and Yellow River Valleys, China's richest and most populated regions.

In spite of Japanese organizational and fighting skills, the attack on China did not bring the victory Japan had hoped for. The Chinese people continued to resist, either in the army or with the Communist guerrilla forces. As Japan sank deeper into the Chinese quagmire, life became harsher and more repressive for the Japanese people, as taxes rose, food and fuel became scarce, and more and more young men were drafted.

Warfare between the Chinese and Japanese was incredibly violent. In the winter of 1937–1938 Japanese troops took Nanjing, raped 20,000 women, killed roughly 200,000 prisoners and civilians, and looted and burned the city. To slow them down, Chiang ordered the Yellow River dikes blasted open, causing a flood that destroyed four thousand villages, killed 890,000 people, and made millions homeless. Two years later, when the Communists ordered a massive offensive, the

Japanese retaliated with a "kill all, burn all, loot all" campaign, destroying hundreds of villages down to the last person, building, and farm animal.

The Chinese government, led by Chiang Kai-shek, escaped to the mountains of Sichuan in the center of the country. There Chiang built up a huge army, not to fight Japan but to prepare for a future confrontation with the Communists. The army drafted over 3 million men, even though it had only a million rifles and could not provide food or clothing for all its soldiers. The Guomindang raised farmers' taxes, even when famine forced farmers to eat the bark of trees. Such taxes were not enough to support both a large army and the thousands of government officials and hangers-on who had fled to Sichuan. To avoid taxing its wealthy supporters the government printed money, causing inflation, hoarding, and corruption.

From his capital of Yan'an in Shaanxi province, Mao also built up his army and formed a government. Unlike the Guomindang, the Communists listened to the grievances of the peasants, especially the poor, to whom they distributed land confiscated from wealthy landowners. They imposed rigid discipline on their officials and soldiers and tolerated no dissent or criticism from intellectuals. Though they had few weapons, the Communists obtained support and intelligence from farmers in Japanese-occupied territory. They turned military reversals into propaganda victories, presenting themselves as the only group in China that was serious about fighting the Japanese.

THE SECOND WORLD WAR

Many people feared that the Second World War would be a repetition of the First. Instead, it was much bigger in every way. It was fought around the world, from Norway to New Guinea and from Hawaii to Egypt, and on every ocean. It killed far more people than World War I, involved all civilians and productive forces, and showed how effectively industry, science, and nationalism could be channeled into mass destruction.

The War of Movement   In World War II motorized weapons gave back the advantage to the offensive. Opposing forces moved fast, their victories hinging as much on the aggressive spirit of their commanders and the military intelligence they obtained as on numbers of troops and firepower.

The Wehrmacht (VAIR-mokt), or German army, was the first to learn this lesson. It not only had tanks, trucks, and fighter planes but had also perfected their combined use in a tactic called *Blitzkrieg* (BLITS-creeg) (lightning war): fighter planes scattered enemy troops and disrupted communications, tanks punctured the enemy's defenses, and then, with the help of the infantry, they encircled and captured enemy troops. At sea, both Japan and the United States had developed aircraft carriers that could launch planes against targets hundreds of miles away.

Armies ranged over vast theaters of operation, and countries were conquered in days or weeks. The belligerents mobilized the economies of entire continents, squeezing them for every possible resource. They tried not only to defeat their enemies' armed forces but—by blockades, submarine attacks, and bombing raids—to damage the economies that supported those armed forces. They thought of civilians as legitimate targets and, later, as vermin to be exterminated.

War in Europe and North Africa   It took less than a month for the Wehrmacht to conquer Poland. Britain and France declared war on Germany but took no military action. Meanwhile, the Soviet Union invaded eastern Poland and the Baltic republics. Although the Poles fought bravely, their infantry and cavalry were no match for German and Russian tanks. During the winter of 1939–1940 Germany and the Western democracies faced each other in what soldiers called a "phony war."

In March 1940 Hitler went on the offensive again, conquering Denmark, Norway, the Netherlands, and Belgium in less than two months. In May he attacked France. Although the French army had as many soldiers, tanks, and aircraft as the Wehrmacht, its morale was low and it quickly collapsed. By the end of June Hitler was master of all of Europe between Russia and Spain.

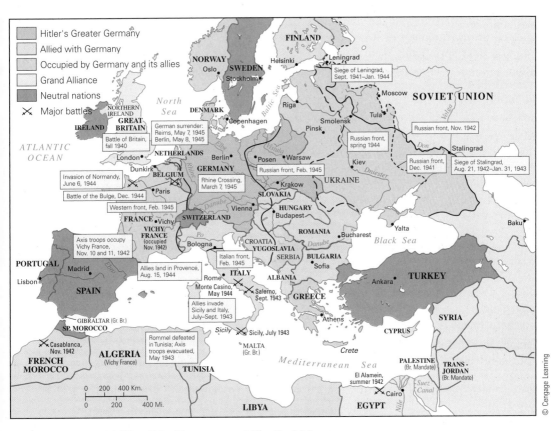

MAP 30.1   World War II in Europe and North Africa

In a series of quick and decisive campaigns from September 1939 to December 1941, German forces overran much of Europe and North Africa. There followed three years of bitter fighting as the Allies slowly pushed the Germans back.

Germany still had to face Britain. The British had no army to speak of, but they had other assets: the English Channel, the Royal Navy and Air Force, and a tough new prime minister, Winston Churchill. The Germans knew they could invade Britain only by gaining control of the airspace over the Channel, so they launched a massive air attack—the Battle of Britain—lasting from June through September. The attack failed because the Royal Air Force used radar and code-breaking to detect approaching German planes.

Frustrated in the west, Hitler turned his attention eastward, even though it meant fighting a two-front war. So far he had gotten the utmost cooperation from Stalin, who supplied Germany with grain, oil, and strategic raw materials. Yet he had always wanted to conquer Lebensraum in the east and enslave the Slavic peoples who lived there, and he feared that if he waited, Stalin would build a dangerously strong army. In June 1941 Hitler launched the largest attack in history, with 3 million soldiers and thousands of planes and tanks. Within five months the Wehrmacht conquered the Baltic states, Ukraine, and half of European Russia, captured a million prisoners of war, and reached the very gates of Moscow and Leningrad. The USSR seemed on the verge of collapse. Then the weather turned cold, machines froze, and the fighting came to a halt. Like Napoleon, Hitler had ignored the environment of Russia to his peril.

The next spring the Wehrmacht renewed its offensive. It surrounded Leningrad in a siege that was to cost a million lives. Leaving Moscow aside, it turned toward the Caucasus and its oil wells. In August the Germans attacked **Stalingrad** (now Volgograd), the key to the Volga River and the supply of oil. For months German and Soviet soldiers fought over every street and every house. When winter came, the Red Army counterattacked and encircled the city. In February 1943 the remnants of the German army in Stalingrad surrendered. Hitler had lost an army of 200,000 men and his last chance of defeating the Soviet Union and of winning the war.

From Europe the war spread to Africa. When France fell in 1940, Mussolini decided that the time had come to realize his imperial ambitions. Italian forces quickly overran British Somaliland, then invaded Egypt. Their victories were ephemeral, however, for when the British counterattacked, Italian resistance crumbled. During 1941 British forces conquered Italian East Africa and invaded Libya as well. The Italian rout in North Africa brought the Germans to their rescue, and during 1942 the German army and the forces of the British Commonwealth seesawed back and forth across the deserts of Libya and Egypt. At **El Alamein** in northern Egypt the British prevailed because they had more weapons and supplies and were better informed about their enemies' plans. The Germans were finally expelled from Africa in May 1943.

War in Asia and the Pacific   The fall of France and the involvement of Britain and the USSR against Germany presented Japan with the opportunity it had been looking for. Suddenly the European colonies in Southeast Asia, with their abundant oil, rubber, and other strategic materials, seemed ripe for the taking. In July 1941, when the French government, then under German control, allowed Japanese forces to occupy Indochina, the United States stopped shipments of steel, scrap iron, oil, and other products that

Japan desperately needed. This left Japan with three alternatives: giving up its conquests, as the Americans insisted; facing economic ruin; or widening the war. Japan chose war.

Admiral Isoroku Yamamoto, commander of the Japanese fleet, told Prime Minister Fumimaro Konoye: "If I am told to fight regardless of the consequences, I shall run wild for the first six months or a year, but I have utterly no confidence for the second or third year... . I hope that you will endeavor to avoid a Japanese-American war." Ignoring his advice, the war cabinet made plans for a surprise

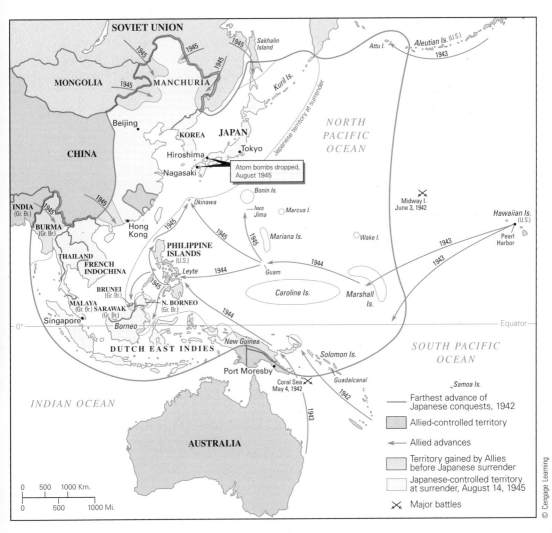

MAP 30.2 World War II in Asia and the Pacific

Having conquered much of China between 1937 and 1941, Japanese forces launched a sudden attack on Southeast Asia and the Pacific in late 1941 and early 1942. American forces slowly reconquered the Pacific islands and the Philippines. In August 1945, the atomic bombing of Hiroshima and Nagasaki forced Japan's surrender.

attack on the United States Navy, followed by an invasion of Southeast Asia. They knew they could not hope to defeat the United States, but they calculated that the shock of the attack would be so great that isolationist Americans would accept the Japanese conquest of Southeast Asia as readily as they had acquiesced to Hitler's conquests in Europe.

On December 7, 1941, Japanese planes bombed the U.S. naval base at **Pearl Harbor**, sinking or damaging scores of warships but missing the aircraft carriers, which were at sea. Then, in early 1942, the Japanese conquered all of Southeast Asia and the Dutch East Indies. They soon began to confiscate food and raw materials and demand heavy labor from the inhabitants.

Japan's dream of an East Asian empire seemed within reach, for its victories surpassed even Hitler's in Europe. The United States, however, quickly began preparing for war. In April 1942 American planes bombed Tokyo. In May the United States Navy defeated a Japanese fleet in the Coral Sea, ending Japanese plans to conquer Australia. A month later, at the **Battle of Midway**, Japan lost four of its six largest aircraft carriers. Without them, Japan faced a long and hopeless war.

The End of War   After the Battle of Stalingrad the advantage on the Eastern Front shifted to the Soviet Union. By 1943 the Red Army was receiving a growing stream of supplies from factories in Russia and the United States. Slowly at first and then with increasing vigor, it pushed the Wehrmacht back toward Germany.

The Western powers, meanwhile, staged two invasions of Europe. Beginning in July 1943 they captured Sicily and invaded Italy. Italy signed an armistice, but German troops held off the Allied advance for two years. On June 6, 1944—forever after known as D-day—156,000 British, American, and Canadian troops landed on the coast of Normandy in western France—the largest shipborne assault ever staged. Within a week the Allies had more troops in France than Germany did, and by September Germany faced an Allied army of over 2 million men and half a million vehicles.

Although the Red Army was on the eastern border of Germany, ready for the final push, Hitler transferred part of the Wehrmacht westward. Despite overwhelming odds, Germany held out for almost a year, a result of the fighting qualities of its soldiers and the terror inspired by the Nazi regime, which commanded obedience to the end. On May 7, 1945, a week after Hitler committed suicide, German military leaders surrendered.

Japan fought on a while longer because the United States had aimed most of its war effort at Germany. Pacific islands had to be captured by amphibious landings, with high casualty rates on both sides. In June 1944, U.S. bombers began attacking Japan and American submarines sank many Japanese merchant ships, cutting Japan off from its sources of oil and other raw materials. After May 1945, with Japanese fighters grounded for lack of fuel, U.S. planes began destroying Japanese shipping, industries, and cities at will.

Even as their homeland was being pounded, the Japanese still held strong positions in Asia. Despite its name, "Greater East Asian Co-Prosperity Sphere," the Japanese occupation was harsh and brutal. By 1945 Asians were eager to see the Japanese leave, but not to welcome back the Europeans. Instead, they looked forward to independence (see Chapters 29 and 32).

Bettmann/CORBIS

Hiroshima After the Atomic Bomb *On August 6, 1945, an atomic bomb destroyed the city, killing some eighty thousand people. This fire truck, stationed at the Hiroshima Fire Department, is one of the few identifiable objects in the photo. It was located 4,000 feet from ground zero.*

On August 6, 1945, the United States dropped an atomic bomb on **Hiroshima**, killing some 80,000 people in a flash and leaving about 120,000 more to die in agony from burns and radiation. Three days later another atomic bomb destroyed Nagasaki. On August 14 Emperor Hirohito gave the order to lay down arms. Two weeks later Japanese leaders signed the terms of surrender. The war was officially over.

Were these atomic weapons necessary? At the time, Americans believed that the conquest of the Japanese homeland would take more than a year and cost the lives of hundreds of thousands of American soldiers. Although some believed the Japanese were determined to fight to the bitter end, others thought they would surrender if they could retain their emperor. Winston Churchill wrote: "It would be a mistake to suppose that the fate of Japan was settled by the atomic bomb. Her defeat was certain before the first bomb fell."[3]

Collapse of the Guomindang and Communist Victory   The formal Japanese surrender in September 1945 surprised the Guomindang. The United States gave millions of dollars of aid and weapons to the Guomindang, all the while urging "national unity" and a "coalition government" with the Communists. But Chiang used all means available to prepare for a civil war. By late 1945 he had U.S. support, control of China's cities, and an

---

[3]Gar Alperowitz, *Atomic Diplomacy: Hiroshima and Potsdam* (New York: Simon & Schuster, 1965), 176–181 and 236–242.

Henri Cartier-Bresson/Magnum Photos

Sale of Gold in the Last Days of the Guomindang *This picture was taken by famed French photojournalist Henri Cartier-Bresson in Shanghai just before the arrival of the Communist-led People's Liberation Army in 1949. It shows people desperate to buy gold before their Guomindang currency becomes worthless.*

army of 2.7 million, more than twice the size of the Communist forces. But the Guomindang's behavior eroded whatever popular support they had. As they moved into formerly Japanese-held territory, they acted like an occupation force. They taxed the people they "liberated" more heavily than the Japanese had, confiscated supplies, and enriched themselves at the expense of the population. Chiang's government printed money so fast that it soon lost all its value. In the countryside the Guomindang's brutality alienated the peasants.

Meanwhile, the Communists obtained Japanese equipment seized by the Soviets in the last weeks of the war and American weapons brought over by deserting Guomindang soldiers. In Manchuria, where they were strongest, they pushed through a radical land reform program, distributing the properties of wealthy landowners among the poorest peasants. In battles against government forces, the higher morale and popular support they enjoyed outweighed the heavy equipment of the Guomindang, whose soldiers began deserting by the thousands.

By 1949 the Guomindang armies were collapsing everywhere, defeated more by their own greed and ineptness than by the Communists. As the Communists advanced, high-ranking members of the Guomindang fled to Taiwan, protected from the mainland by the U.S. Navy. On October 1, 1949, Mao Zedong announced the founding of the People's Republic of China.

THE CHARACTER OF WARFARE

The war left an enormous death toll. Recent estimates place the figure at close to 60 million deaths, six to eight times more than in World War I. Over half of the dead were civilian victims of massacres, famines, and bombs. The Soviet Union lost between 20 million and 25 million people, more than any other country. China suffered 15 million deaths; Poland lost some 6 million, of whom half were Jewish; the Jewish people lost another 3 million outside Poland. Over 4 million Germans and over 2 million Japanese died. Great Britain lost 400,000 people, and the United States 300,000. In much of the world, families mourned one or more of their members.

Many parts of the world were flooded with refugees. Some 90 million Chinese fled the Japanese advance. In Europe millions fled from the Nazis or the Red Army or were herded back and forth on government orders. Many refugees never returned to their homes.

Belligerents identified not just soldiers but entire peoples as enemies. Some even labeled their own ethnic minorities as "enemies." Another reason for the devastation was the appearance of new technologies that carried destruction deep into enemy territory, far beyond the traditional battlefields. New technologies of warfare and changes in morality formed a lethal combination.

The Science and Technology of War   As fighting spread around the world, the mobilization of manpower and economies and the mobility of the armed forces grew increasingly crucial, while new aspects of war took on a growing importance. Chemists found ways to make synthetic rubber from coal or oil. Physicists perfected radar, which warned of approaching enemy aircraft and submarines. Cryptanalysts broke enemy codes and were able to penetrate secret military communications. Pharmacologists developed antibiotics that saved the lives of wounded soldiers, who in any earlier war would have died of infections. The war also brought new inventions in media technology.

Aircraft development was especially striking. As war approached, German, British, and Japanese aircraft manufacturers developed fast, maneuverable fighter planes. U.S. industry was especially noted for heavy bombers designed to fly in huge formations and drop tons of bombs on enemy cities. Germany responded with radically new designs, including the first jet fighters, low-flying unmanned buzz bombs, and, finally, V-2 missiles against which there was no warning or defense.

Military planners expected scientists to furnish secret weapons that could doom the enemy. In October 1939 President Roosevelt received a letter from physicist Albert Einstein, a Jewish refugee from Nazism, warning of the dangers of nuclear power: "There is no doubt that sub-atomic energy is available all around us, and that one day man will release and control its almost infinite power. We cannot prevent him from doing so and can only hope that he will not use it exclusively in blowing up his next door neighbor." Roosevelt placed the vast resources of the U.S. government at the disposal of physicists and engineers. By 1945 they had built two atomic bombs, each one powerful enough to annihilate an entire city.

U.S. Army Medics and Holocaust Victims *When Allied troops entered the Nazi concentration camps, they found the bodies of thousands of victims of the Holocaust. In Dachau in southern Germany, two U.S. Army medics are overseeing a truckload of corpses to be taken to a burial site.*

Hulton Deutsch Collection/Corbis

Bombing Raids   Since it was very hard to pinpoint individual buildings, especially at night, British air chief marshal Arthur "Bomber" Harris decided that "operations should now be focused on the morale of the enemy civilian population and in particular the industrial workers."

In May 1942, 1,000 British planes dropped incendiary bombs on Cologne, setting fire to the old city. Between July 24 and August 2, 1943, 3,330 British and American planes fire-bombed Hamburg, killing 50,000 people, mostly women and children. Later raids destroyed Berlin, Dresden, and other German cities. The bombing raids against Germany killed 600,000 people—more than half of them women and children—and injured 800,000, but they failed to break the morale of the German people. German armament production continued to increase until late 1944, and the population remained obedient and hard-working. However, bombing raids against oil depots and synthetic fuel plants almost brought the German war effort to a standstill by early 1945.

Japanese cities were also the targets of American bombing raids. As early as April 1942 sixteen planes launched from an aircraft carrier bombed Tokyo. Later, as American forces captured islands close to Japan, the raids intensified. Their effect was even more devastating than the fire-bombing of German cities, for Japanese cities were made mostly of wood. In March 1945 bombs set Tokyo ablaze, killing 80,000 people and leaving a million homeless.

The Holocaust   In World War II, for the first time, more civilians than soldiers were deliberately put to death. The champions in the art of killing defenseless civilians were the Nazis. Their murders were not the accidental byproducts of some military goal but a calculated policy of exterminating whole races of people.

Their first targets were Jews. Soon after Hitler came to power, he deprived German Jews of their citizenship and legal rights. When eastern Europe fell under Nazi rule, the Nazis herded its large Jewish population into ghettos in the major cities, where many died of starvation and disease. Then, in early 1942, the Nazis decided to carry out Hitler's "final solution to the Jewish problem" by applying modern industrial methods to the slaughter of human beings. Thousands of ordinary German citizens supported and aided the genocide. Every day trainloads of cattle cars arrived at the extermination camps in eastern Europe and disgorged thousands of captives and the corpses of those who had died along the way. The strongest survivors were put to work and fed almost nothing until they died. Women, children, the elderly, and the sick were shoved into gas chambers and asphyxiated with poison gas. **Auschwitz**, the biggest camp, was a giant industrial complex designed to kill up to twelve thousand people a day. This mass extermination, now called the **Holocaust** ("burning"), claimed some 6 million Jewish lives.

Besides the Jews, the Nazis also killed 3 million Polish Catholics—especially professionals, army officers, and the educated—in an effort to reduce the Polish people to slavery. They also exterminated homosexuals, Jehovah's Witnesses, Gypsies, the disabled, and the mentally ill—all in the interests of "racial purity." Whenever a German was killed in an occupied country, the Nazis retaliated by burning a village and all its inhabitants. After the invasion of Russia the Wehrmacht was given orders to execute all captured communists, government employees, and officers. They also worked millions of prisoners of war to death or let them die of starvation.

The Home Front in Europe and Asia   In the First World War there had been a clear distinction between the "front" and the "home front." Not so in World War II, where rapid military movements and air power carried the war into people's homes. For the civilian populations of China, Japan, Southeast Asia, and Europe, the war was far more terrifying than their worst nightmares. Armies swept through the land, confiscating food, fuel, and anything else of value. Bombers and heavy artillery pounded cities into rubble, leaving only the skeletons of buildings, while survivors cowered in cellars. Even when a city was not targeted, air-raid sirens awakened people throughout the night. In countries occupied by the Germans, the police arrested civilians, deporting many to die in concentration camps or to work as slave laborers in armaments factories. Millions fled their homes in terror, losing their families and friends. Even in Britain, children and the elderly were sent to live in the countryside.

The war demanded an enormous and sustained effort from all civilians, but more so in some countries than in others. In 1941, the Soviets dismantled over fifteen hundred factories and rebuilt them in the Ural Mountains and Siberia, where they soon turned out more tanks and artillery than the Axis.

Half of the ships afloat in 1939 were sunk during the war, but the Allied losses were more than made up for by American shipyards, while Axis shipping was reduced to nothing by 1945. The production of aircraft, trucks, tanks, and other materiel showed a similar imbalance. Although the Axis powers made strenuous efforts to increase their production, they could not compete with the vast outpouring of Soviet tanks and American materiel.

The Red Army eventually mobilized 22 million men; Soviet women took over half of all industrial and three-quarters of all agricultural jobs. In the other Allied countries, women also played major roles in the war effort, replacing men in fields, factories, and offices. The Nazis, in contrast, believed that German women should stay home and bear children, and they imported 7 million "guest workers"—a euphemism for captured foreigners.

The Home Front in the United States   The United States flourished during the war. Safe behind their oceans, Americans felt no bombs, saw no enemy soldiers, had almost no civilian casualties, and suffered fewer military casualties than other countries. The economy went into a prolonged boom after 1940. By 1944 the United States was producing twice as much as all the Axis powers combined. Thanks to huge military orders, jobs were plentiful, bread lines disappeared, and nutrition and health improved. Most Americans saved part of their paychecks, laying the basis for a phenomenal postwar consumer boom. Many Americans later looked back on the conflict as the "good war."

World War II also did much to weaken the hold of traditional ideas, as employers recruited women and members of racial minorities to work in jobs once reserved for white men. Six million women entered the labor force during the war, 2.5 million of them in manufacturing jobs previously considered "men's work." In a book entitled *Shipyard Diary of a Woman Welder* (1944), Augusta Clawson recalled her experiences in a shipyard in Oregon:

> *The job confirmed my strong conviction—I have stated it before—what exhausts the woman welder is not the work, not the heat, nor the demands upon physical strength. It is the apprehension that arises from inadequate skill and consequent lack of confidence; and this can be overcome by the right kind of training. . . . And so, in spite of the discomforts of climbing, heavy equipment, and heat, I enjoyed the work today because I could do it.[4]*

Many men opposed women doing work that would take them away from their families. As the labor shortage got worse, however, employers and politicians grudgingly admitted that the government ought to help provide day care for the children of working mothers. The entry of women into the labor force proved to be one of the most significant consequences of the war.

---

[4]Rosalyn Fraad Baxandall, Linda Gordon, and Susan Reverby, eds., *America's Working Women* (New York: Random House, 1976), 253.

The war loosened racial bonds as well. Seeking work in war industries, 1.2 million African Americans migrated to the north and west. In the southwest Mexican immigrants took jobs in agriculture and war industries. But no new housing was built to accommodate the influx of migrants to the industrial cities, and many suffered from overcrowding and discrimination. In addition, 112,000 Japanese Americans living on the west coast of the United States were arrested and herded into remote interior internment camps until the war was over, ostensibly for fear of spying and sabotage, but actually because of their race.

War and the Environment   During the depression, construction and industry had slowed to a crawl, reducing environmental stress. The war reversed this trend, sharply accelerating pressures on the environment.

One reason for the change was the fighting itself. Battles scarred the landscape, leaving behind spent ammunition and damaged equipment. Retreating armies flooded large areas of China and the Netherlands. The bombing of cities left ruins that remained visible for a generation or more.

The main cause of environmental stress, however, was not the fighting but the economic development that sustained it. The war's half-million aircraft required thousands of air bases, many of them in the Pacific, China, Africa, and other parts of the world that had seldom seen an airplane before. Barracks, shipyards, docks, warehouses, and other military construction sprouted on every continent.

As war industries boomed, so did the demand for raw materials. Mining companies opened new mines and towns in Africa to supply strategic minerals. Latin American countries deprived of manufactured imports began building their own steel mills, factories, and shipyards. In India, China, and Europe, timber felling accelerated far beyond the reproduction rate of trees, replacing forests with denuded land. In a few instances, however, the war was good for the environment. For example, submarine warfare made fishing and whaling so dangerous that fish and whale populations had a few years in which to increase.

CONCLUSION

After the Great War ended, the world seemed to return to its prewar state, but it was an illusion. In the Soviet Union, Joseph Stalin was determined to turn his country into a modern industrial state at breakneck speed, regardless of the human cost. Several million people—most of them peasants—died, and millions more were enslaved during the Five-Year Plans and the collectivization of agriculture. By 1941 the USSR was much better prepared for a war with Germany than Russia had been in 1914–1917.

In 1929, after a few years of prosperity, the New York stock market collapsed. Within a few months, the world economy fell into the Great Depression, throwing millions out of work throughout the world. France and Britain survived the depression by making their colonial empires purchase their products. Countries that were dependent on exports, such as Germany and Japan, suffered more until they turned their economies toward arms production. Only the USSR and southern Africa boomed during the 1930s.

In Italy, Mussolini installed Fascist Party members in all government jobs and jailed anyone who criticized him. In Germany, economic collapse led people to entrust their government to Adolf Hitler and his Nazi followers, who quickly set to work establishing a totalitarian government. Nazi Germany's rebuilding of its military and its invasion of Austria and Czechoslovakia were greeted with a policy of appeasement by Western democracies, until finally they could no longer overlook Germany's intentions.

Hard hit by the depression, Japan saw China as a potential colony with resources to help solve its economic problems. In 1931, Japan conquered Manchuria. The United States and the League of Nations protested but did little else. Starting in 1937, a long and brutal war with China became a drain on the Japanese economy and resources. Meanwhile, the Communists, led by Mao Zedong, were slowly gaining support in the Chinese countryside.

The war spread to Europe in 1939 when Germany conquered Poland, then Denmark, Norway, the low countries, and France in 1940. The war turned global in 1941 when Germany invaded the Soviet Union and Japan attacked the United States. In 1943, the Red Army began to push the Germans back. Beginning in June 1944, Anglo-American forces, backed by the overwhelming industrial resources of the United States, drove German forces back from the west. U.S. naval victories in the Pacific and atomic weapons defeated Japan and ended the war in 1945.

The Second World War was by far the deadliest in history. Modern mechanized forces swept across entire nations and oceans. Their targets were not only each other's armed forces, but their civilian populations as well. Though Germany had considerable scientific and technical talent, the war favored the nations with the most heavy industries, namely, the United States and the Soviet Union. The Allies destroyed German and Japanese cities with fire-bombs, and the United States dropped atomic bombs on Hiroshima and Nagasaki. Of the roughly 60 million people who died in the war, most were civilians.

IMPORTANT EVENTS 1920s–1949

1928	Stalin introduces Five Year Plans and the collectivization of agriculture
1929	Great Depression begins in United States
1931	Great Depression reaches Europe
1931	Japanese forces occupy Manchuria
1933	Hitler comes to power in Germany
1934–1935	Mao leads Communists on Long March
1936	Hitler invades the Rhineland
1937	Japanese troops invade China, conquer coastal provinces; Chiang Kai-shek flees to Sichuan
1937–1938	Japanese troops take Nanjing
1939 (Sept. 1)	German forces invade Poland

1940 (March–April)	German forces conquer Denmark, Norway, the Netherlands, and Belgium
1940 (May–June)	German forces conquer France
1940 (June–Sept.)	Battle of Britain
1941 (June 21)	German forces invade USSR
1941 (Dec. 7)	Japanese aircraft bomb Pearl Harbor
1942 (Jan.–March)	Japanese conquer Thailand, Philippines, and Malaya
1942 (June)	United States Navy defeats Japan at Battle of Midway
1942–1943	Allies and Germany battle for control of North Africa
1943	Soviet victory in Battle of Stalingrad
1943–1944	Red Army slowly pushes Wehrmacht back to Germany
1944 (June 6)	D-day: U.S., British, and Canadian troops land in Normandy
1945 (May 7)	Germany surrenders
1945 (Aug. 6)	United States drops atomic bomb on Hiroshima
1945 (Aug. 14)	Japan surrenders
1945–1949	Civil war in China
1949 (Oct. 1)	Communist defeat Guomindang; Mao proclaims People's Republic

ISSUES IN WORLD HISTORY

Famines and Politics

Human history is filled with tales of famines—times when crops failed, food supplies ran out, and people starved.

Natural Famines

India, dependent on the monsoon rains, has been particularly prone to such calamities, with famines striking two to four times a century, whenever the rains fail for several years in succession. Three times in the eighteenth century famines killed several million people. The nineteenth century was worse, with famines in 1803–1804, 1837–1838, 1868–1870, and 1876–1878. The famine of 1876–1878 also afflicted northern China, causing between 9 and 13 million deaths from hunger and from the diseases of malnutrition. There were even incidents of cannibalism, as starving adults ate starving children.

When drought hit a region, it decimated not only the human population but also the animals they relied on to transport crops or plow the land. When water levels dropped in rivers and canals, food could not be transported by boat to areas where people were starving.

Commercial Famines

That all changed in the nineteenth century. Railroads and steamships could transport foodstuffs quickly across great distances, regardless of the weather. Great Britain, for example, became dependent on imports of wheat and beef. Yet the global death toll from starvation has been far higher since the mid-nineteenth century than ever before. Why?

Consider Ireland. By the early nineteenth century the potato had become the main source of nutrition for the Irish people. Potatoes grew abundantly and produced more calories per acre than any other crop, allowing the population to increase dramatically.

In 1845 a blight turned the potatoes in the fields black, mushy, and inedible. The harvest was ruined the following year as well. It recovered slightly in 1847 but was bad again in 1848. Tens of thousands died of starvation, while hundreds of thousands died from dysentery, typhus, or cholera. Travelers saw corpses rotting in their hovels or on the sides of roads. Altogether, a million or more people died, while another million emigrated, reducing the population of Ireland by half.

Throughout those years, Ireland exported wheat to England, where people had money to pay for it. Food cost money, and the Irish, poor even before the famines, were destitute and could not afford to buy wheat or bread. The British government was convinced that interfering with the free market would only make things worse. Relief efforts were half-hearted at best; the official responsible for Irish affairs preferred to leave the situation to "the operation of natural causes."

The same held true in India, like Ireland a colony of Great Britain. The drought of 1876–1878 killed over 5 million Indians in the Deccan region, while British officials stood by helpless or indifferent. Part of the problem was transportation. In the 1870s most goods were still transported in bullock carts, but the bullocks starved during the drought. Another obstacle was political. The idea that a government should be responsible for feeding the population was unthinkable at the time. And so, while millions were starving in the Deccan, the Punjab was exporting wheat to Britain.

Over the next twenty years, so-called famine railways were built in the regions historically most affected by the failures of the monsoon. When drought struck again at the end of the century, the railways were ready to transport food to areas that had previously been accessible only by bullock carts. However, the inhabitants of the affected regions had no money with which to buy what little food there was, and the government was still reluctant to interfere with free enterprise. Grain merchants bought all the stocks, hoarded them until the price rose, then used the railways to transport them out of the famine regions to regions where the harvests were better and people had more money.

In the twentieth century, commercial famines became rare as governments realized that they had a responsibility to provide food not only for their own people but also for people in other countries. Yet commercial famines have not entirely disappeared. In 1974, when a catastrophic flood covered half of Bangladesh, the government was too disorganized to distribute its stocks of rice, while merchants bought what they could and exported it to India. Thousands died, and thousands more survived only because of belated shipments of food from donor countries.

Political Famines

To say that governments are responsible for food supplies does not mean that they exercise that responsibility for the good of the people. Some do, but in many instances food is used as a weapon. In the twentieth century, global food supplies were always adequate for the population of the world, and transportation was seldom a problem. Yet the century witnessed the most murderous famines ever recorded.

As commercial famines declined, war famines became common. The destruction or requisitioning of crops caused famines in the Russian civil war of 1921–1922, the Japanese occupation of Indochina in 1942–1945, and the Biafran war in Nigeria in 1967–1969.

In 1942 the Japanese army had conquered Burma, a rich rice-producing colony. Food supplies in Bengal, which imported rice from Burma, dropped by 5 percent. As prices began to rise, merchants bought stocks of rice and held them in the hope that prices would continue to increase. Sharecroppers sold their stocks to pay off their debts to landlords and village moneylenders. Meanwhile, the railroads that in peacetime would have carried food from other parts of India were fully occupied with military traffic. By the time Viceroy Lord Wavell ordered the army to transport food to Bengal in October 1943, between 1.5 and 2 million Bengalis had died.

Worst of all were the famines caused by deliberate government policies. The most famous was the famine of 1932–1933 caused by Stalin's collectivization of agriculture. The Communists tried to force the peasants to give up their land and livestock and join collectives, where they could be made to work harder and provide food for the growing cities and industries. When the peasants resisted, their crops were seized. Millions were sent to prison camps, and millions of others died of starvation.

An even worse famine took place in China from 1958 to 1961 during the "Great Leap Forward" (see Chapter 32). Communist Party Chairman Mao Zedong decided to hasten the transformation of China into a communist state by relying not on the expertise of economists and technocrats but on the enthusiasm of the masses. Farms were consolidated into huge communes. Peasants were told to make steel out of household utensils in backyard furnaces. The harvest of 1959 was poor, and later ones were even worse. The amount of grain per person declined from 452 pounds (205 kilograms) in 1957 to 340 pounds (154 kilograms) in 1961. Since the Central Statistical Bureau had been shut down, the central government was unaware of the shortages and demanded ever higher requisitions of food to feed the army and urban and industrial workers and to export to the Soviet Union to pay off China's debts. The amount of food left to the farmers was between one-fifth and one-half of their usual subsistence diet. From 1958 to 1961 between 20 and 30 million Chinese are estimated to have starved or died of the diseases of malnutrition. It was the worst famine in the history of the world. Mao denied its existence.

Nothing quite as horrible has happened since the Great Leap Forward. During the droughts in Africa in the 1970s and 1980s, most people in the affected regions received international food aid. However, to crush rebellions, the governments of Ethiopia and Sudan denied that their people were hungry and prevented food shipments from reaching drought victims.

In the world today, natural disasters are as frequent as ever, and many countries are vulnerable to food shortages. No one now claims that governments have no business providing food to the starving. Though food is not equitably distributed, there is enough for all human beings now, and there will be enough for the foreseeable future. However, humanitarian feelings compete with other political agendas, and the specter of politically motivated famines still stalks the world.

PART EIGHT

PERILS AND PROMISES OF A GLOBAL COMMUNITY, 1945 TO THE PRESENT

After World War II an increasingly interconnected world faced new hopes and fears. The United Nations promoted peace, international cooperation, and human rights. Colonized peoples gained independence, and global trade expanded. At the same time the United States and the Soviet Union, victorious former Allies in the war against the Axis, mobilized every resource in a global contest for economic and political influence. This "Cold War" led to nuclear stalemate as well as a new round of warfare, dispelling dreams of world peace. Wars in Korea and Vietnam, as well as proxy conflicts from Nicaragua to Afghanistan, pitted the United States against communist regimes. Following the Cold War, nuclear proliferation and terrorism became top concerns. The 9/11 attacks by Muslim extremists on the World Trade Center and the Pentagon triggered an American-led "global war on terrorism." The ensuing invasions of Afghanistan and Iraq made the Middle East a top danger spot.

The industrialized nations, including Germany and Japan, recovered quickly from World War II. Elsewhere economic development came slowly, except in a handful of countries: South Korea, Taiwan, Brazil, Argentina, and, after 2000, China and India. In Africa and other poor regions, population growth usually offset economic gains.

Although the Green Revolution of the 1960s and the fruits of genetic engineering thirty years later alleviated much world hunger, industrial growth and automobile use increased pollution and competition for petroleum supplies. Global warming became an international concern, along with overfishing, deforestation, and endangerment of wild species.

Globalization affected culture as well. Transnational corporations selling uniform products threatened localized economic enterprises, and Western popular culture aroused fears of cultural imperialism, fear offset in part by the rise of Asian economic powers. The Internet and the emergence of English as the global language improved international communication but also stimulated fears that cultural diversity could be lost.

31

THE COLD WAR AND DECOLONIZATION, 1945–1975

O n January 1, 1959, the thirty-two-year-old Fidel Castro entered Havana, Cuba, after having successfully defeated the dictatorship of Fulgencio Batista (ful-HEHN-see-oh bah-TEES-tah). Castro had initiated his revolution in 1953 with an attack on a military barracks, but the attack failed. At his trial, Castro put on a spirited defense that he later published as *History Will Absolve Me*. He proclaimed his objectives as the restoration of Cuban democracy and an ambitious program of social and economic reforms designed to ameliorate the effects of underdevelopment.

On September 26, 1960, Castro addressed the United Nations General Assembly. Relations between the Castro government and the United States were already heading toward confrontation as a result of Castro's policies. In his speech, Castro offered a broad internationalist and anti-imperialist criticism of the world's developed nations and of the United Nations. He criticized the role of the United Nations in the Congo, suggesting that it had supported Colonel Mobutu Sese Seko, a client of imperialism, rather than Patrice Lumumba, identified by the United States as a dangerous radical. He also strongly supported the independence struggle of the Algerians against the French.

In this speech, Castro outlined an ambitious program of new revolutionary reforms in Cuba, claiming that the United States had supported the Batista dictatorship to protect American investors. Once back in Cuba, Castro pressed ahead with economic reforms that included concentrating power in the hands of his closest allies and nationalizing most American investments. Cuba became a flash point in the Cold War when the United States tried and failed to overthrow Castro in 1961. Castro declared himself to be a socialist and forged an economic and military alliance with the Soviet Union that led in 1962 to the Cuban missile crisis.

The intensity of the Cold War, with its accompanying threat of nuclear destruction, obscured a postwar phenomenon of more enduring importance. The colonial empires were overthrown, and Western power and influence declined in Asia, Africa, and Latin America. The leaders who headed these new nations were sometimes able to use Cold War antagonisms to their own advantage when they sought economic or military assistance. Some, like Castro, became frontline participants in this struggle, but most focused on nation building.

Each former colony had its own history and followed its own route to independence. Thus these new nations had difficulty finding a collective voice in a world increasingly oriented toward two superpowers, the United States and the Soviet Union. Some former colonies sided openly with one or the other, while others banded together in a posture of neutrality. All spoke with one voice about their need for economic and technical assistance and the obligation of the wealthy nations to satisfy those needs.

The Cold War military rivalry led to extraordinary advances in weaponry and associated technologies, but many new nations faced basic problems of educating their citizens, nurturing industry, and escaping the economic constraints imposed by their former imperialist masters. The environment suffered severe pressures from oil exploration and transport to support the growing economies of the wealthy nations and from deforestation and urbanization in poor regions. Neither rich nor poor nations fully anticipated the ultimate costs that would be associated with these environmental changes.

THE COLD WAR

For more than a century, political and economic leaders in the industrialized West had viewed socialism as a threat to free markets and private property. The Russian Revolution as well as the destabilizing economic effects of the Great Depression heightened these fears. The wartime alliance between the United States, Great Britain, and the Soviet Union had therefore succeeded despite these antagonisms and fears. With the defeat of Germany, however, growing Soviet assertiveness in Europe and communist insurgencies in China and elsewhere confirmed to Western leaders the threat of worldwide revolution.

Western leaders identified the Soviet Union as the sponsor of world revolution and as a military power capable of launching a war as destructive and terrible as the one recently ended. As early as 1946 Great Britain's wartime leader, Winston Churchill, said in a speech in Missouri, "From Stettin in the Baltic to Trieste in the Adriatic, an iron curtain has descended across the Continent.... I am convinced there is nothing they [the communists] so much admire as strength, and there is nothing for which they have less respect than weakness, especially military weakness." The phrase "**iron curtain**" became a watchword of the **Cold War**, the state of political tension and military rivalry then beginning between the United States and its allies and the Soviet Union and its allies.

Each side viewed every action by its rival a direct threat. Fearful of growing Soviet power, the United States and the nations of western Europe established a military alliance in 1949, the **North Atlantic Treaty Organization (NATO)**. Soviet leaders, struggling to recover from the terrible losses sustained in the war against the Axis, responded by creating their own military alliance, the **Warsaw Pact**, in 1955. The distrust and suspicion of the two alliances would now play out on a worldwide stage.

The United Nations

In 1944 representatives from the United States, Great Britain, the Soviet Union, and China drafted proposals that led to a treaty called the United Nations Charter, ratified on October 24, 1945.

Like the earlier League of Nations, the **United Nations** had two main bodies: the General Assembly, with representatives from all member states; and the Security Council, with five permanent members—China (the anticommunist Chinese government based in Taiwan until 1971), France, Great Britain, the United States, and the Soviet Union—and seven rotating members. A full-time bureaucracy headed by a Secretary General carried out the organization's day-to-day business and directed agencies focused on specialized international problems—for example, UNICEF (United Nations Children's Emergency Fund), FAO (Food and Agriculture Organization), and UNESCO (United Nations Educational, Scientific and Cultural Organization) (see Environment and Technology: The Green Revolution). Unlike the League of Nations, which required unanimous agreement in both deliberative bodies, the United Nations operated by majority vote, except that the five permanent members of the Security Council had veto power in that chamber.

All signatories to the United Nations Charter renounced war and territorial conquest. Nevertheless, peacekeeping, the sole preserve of the Security Council, became a vexing problem as permanent members exercised their vetoes to protect their allies and interests. Throughout the Cold War the United Nations was seldom able to forestall or quell international conflicts, though from time to time it sent observers or peacekeeping forces to monitor truces or other international agreements.

The decolonization of Africa and Asia greatly swelled the size of the General Assembly but not the Security Council. Many newly independent countries looked to the United Nations for material assistance and access to a wider political world. While the rivalry of the Security Council's permanent members stymied actions that even indirectly touched on Cold War concerns, the General Assembly became an arena for debates over issues like decolonization and development.

In the early years of the United Nations, General Assembly resolutions carried great weight. An example is a 1947 resolution that sought to divide Palestine into sovereign Jewish and Arab states. Gradually, though, the flood of new members produced a voting majority concerned more with poverty, racial discrimination, and the struggle against imperialism than with the Cold War. As a result, Western powers increasingly disregarded the General Assembly, allowing new countries to have their say but effectively preventing any collective action contrary to their interests.

Capitalism and Communism   In July 1944, with Allied victory inevitable, economic specialists representing over forty countries met at Bretton Woods, a New Hampshire resort, to devise a new international monetary system. The signatories eventually agreed to fix exchange rates and to create the International Monetary Fund (IMF) and World Bank. The IMF used currency reserves from member nations to finance temporary trade deficits, while the **World Bank** provided funds for reconstructing Europe and helping needy countries after the war.

The Soviet Union attended the Bretton Woods Conference and signed the agreements that went into effect in 1946. But growing hostility between the Soviet Union and the United States and Britain undermined cooperation. While the United States held reserves of gold and the rest of the world held reserves of dollars to maintain the stability of the monetary system, the Soviet Union established a closed monetary system for itself and for allied communist regimes in eastern Europe. In Western countries, supply and demand determined production priorities and prices; in the Soviet command economy, government agencies allocated resources, labor, and goods and even set prices according to governmental priorities, irrespective of market forces.

Many leaders of newly independent states, having won their nation's independence from European colonial powers, preferred the Soviet Union's socialist example to the capitalism of their former masters. Thus, the relative success of economies patterned on Eastern or Western models became part of the Cold War argument. Each side trumpeted economic successes measured by industrial output, changes in per capita income, and productivity gains.

During World War II the U.S. economy escaped the lingering effects of the Great Depression (see Chapter 30) as increased military spending and the military draft raised employment and wages. During the war, U.S. factories were converted from the production of consumer goods to weapons. With peace, the pent-up demand for consumer goods led to a period of rapid economic growth and prosperity. Europe, still rebuilding from the destruction of the war, at first lagged behind.

World War II had heavily damaged the economy of western Europe. Bombs had flattened cities and destroyed railroads, port facilities, and communication networks. Populations had lost their savings and struggled to find employment. Seeking to forestall the radicalization of European politics and the potential expansion of Soviet influence, the United States decided to financially support the reconstruction of Europe. The **Marshall Plan** and other aid programs provided more than $20 billion to Europe by 1961 (about $155 billion in 2013). European determination backed by American aid spurred recovery, and by 1963 the resurgent European economies had doubled their total 1940 output.

Given that public funds played a significant role in this process, recovering western European governments sought a greater role in economic management than was common in the United States. In Great Britain, for example, the Labour Party government of the early 1950s nationalized coal, steel, railroads, and health care. Similarly, the French government nationalized public utilities; the auto, banking, and insurance industries; and parts of the mining industry. These steps provided large infusions of capital for rebuilding and acquiring new technologies and enhanced economic planning.

In 1948 European nations initiated a process of economic cooperation and integration with the creation of the Organisation for European Economic Co-operation (OEEC). They began by cooperating on coal and steel production. Located in disputed border areas, these industries had previously been flash points that led to war. With success in these areas, some OEEC countries lowered tariffs to encourage trade. Then in 1957 France, West Germany, Italy, the Netherlands, Belgium, and Luxembourg signed a treaty creating the **European Economic Community**, also known as the **Common Market**. By the 1970s this economic alliance had nearly overtaken the United States in industrial production. Then between 1973 and 1995, Great Britain, Denmark, Greece, Ireland, Spain, Portugal, Finland, Sweden, and Austria joined the alliance, renamed the European Union (EU) in 1993 to reflect growing political integration.

The Green Revolution

Concern about world food supplies appeared with the serious shortages caused by the devastation and trade disruptions of World War II. Feeding the world's fast-growing population also provided an immediate challenge to long-established agricultural practices. The Food and Agriculture Organization of the United Nations, the Rockefeller Foundation, and the Ford Foundation took leading roles in fostering crop research and agricultural education. In 1966 the International Rice Research Institute (established in 1960–1962) began distributing seeds for an improved rice variety known as IR-8. Crop yields from this and other new varieties, along with improved farming techniques, were initially so impressive, especially in Asia, that a hoped-for new era in agriculture was called the Green Revolution.

After the successful introduction of new rice strains, scientists developed new varieties of corn and wheat. Building on twenty years of Rockefeller-funded research in Mexico, the Centro Internacional de Mejoramiento de Maiz y Trigo (International Center for the Improvement of Maize and Wheat) was established in 1966. This organization distributed new varieties of wheat that were resistant to disease and responsive to fertilizer. By 1970 other centers for research on tropical agriculture were established.

Despite these advances, experts believed that the success of the Green Revolution required a more comprehensive effort that would mobilize government, foundation, and private-sector resources. The Consultative Group on International Agricultural Research brought together World Bank expertise, private foundations, international organizations, and national foreign aid agencies to undertake worldwide support of efforts to increase food productivity and improve natural resource management. Soon 25 percent of U.S. development assistance and 30 percent of World Bank lending went to agriculture. The combination of innovation and investment led to approximately 2 percent per year in increased productivity in the 1970s.

Early optimism about these innovations is now muted. Although crop yields often improved as a result of new seeds, improved fertilizers, and irrigation, these improvements were too expensive for poor farmers to employ. While both Asian and Latin American agriculture became much more productive, small farmers were often sacrificed. Africa was little affected by these changes, and only today, as Africa faces deepening cycles of famine, is an

The resulting prosperity brought dramatic changes to the societies of western Europe. Wages increased and social welfare benefits expanded. Governments increased spending on health care, unemployment benefits, old-age pensions, public housing, and grants to poor families, with richer nations like Germany subsidizing the mounting prosperity of poorer nations like Ireland, Spain, Portugal, and Greece. The combination of economic growth and income redistribution raised living standards and fueled demand for consumer goods, leading to the development of a mass consumer society. These benefits would be threatened by the growing health-care and retirement needs of Europe's rapidly aging populations after 2000 (see Chapter 32).

international effort under way to introduce reforms. Where the Green Revolution's innovations have been the most successful, dependence on patented, costly seed varieties, chemical fertilizers, and irrigation has promoted agricultural consolidation and rewarded large investors. This has meant in practice that, as agricultural production has risen, land has been increasingly concentrated in the hands of the rich and the rural poor have been forced to become laborers or migrate to cities.

Miracle Rice *New strains of so-called miracle rice made many nations in South and Southeast Asia self-sufficient in food production. Genetically altered rice is now planted in the Ivory Coast and other African nations.*

The Soviet experience was dramatically different. The rapid growth of the Soviet state after 1917 had challenged traditional Western assumptions about economic development and social policy. From the 1920s the Soviet state relied on bureaucratic agencies and political processes to determine the production, distribution, and price of goods. The government regulated and administered nearly every area of the society, including housing, medical services, retail shops, factories, and the land. Despite many problems, the Soviet state achieved a dramatic expansion in basic industrial production.

As in western Europe, the economies of the Soviet Union and its eastern European allies were devastated at the end of the Second World War, but they took a different path to reconstruction. The Soviet command economy had enormous natural resources, a large population, and abundant energy at its disposal. It also benefited from the state's large investments in technical and scientific education and heavy industries during the 1930s and war years.

As a result, recovery was rapid at first, creating the structural basis for modernization and growth. However, as industrial production throughout the world refocused on consumer goods such as television sets and automobiles rather than coal and steel, the inefficiencies of bureaucratic control became obvious. By the 1970s the economic gap with the West had widened. Soviet industry failed to meet domestic demand for clothing, housing, food, automobiles, and consumer electronics, while Soviet agricultural production failed to meet even domestic needs. More significant still, the Soviet Union fell behind the West in civilian sector technological innovation.

West Versus East in Europe and Korea   In Germany, Austria, and Japan, the end of the war meant foreign military occupation and governments controlled by the victors. The Soviet Union initially seemed willing to accept governments in neighboring states that included a mix of parties as long as they were not hostile to local communist groups or to the Soviets. In the nations of central and eastern Europe, many remembered the Soviets as enemies of the fascists and were eager to support local communist parties. As relations between the Soviets and the West worsened in the late 1940s, communists gained a series of political victories across eastern Europe. Western leaders saw the emergence of communist regimes in Poland, Czechoslovakia, Hungary, Bulgaria, Romania, Yugoslavia, and Albania as a sign of growing Soviet aggressiveness.

By 1948 the United States viewed the Soviet Union as an adversary and threat. While the United States had seemed amenable to the Soviet desire for access to the Mediterranean through the Bosporus and Dardanelles straits at war's end, by 1947 it acted to strengthen Turkey and Greece to resist Soviet military pressure and local communist subversion. This decision to hold the line against further Soviet expansion led to the admission of Turkey and Greece to NATO and to the decision to allow West Germany to rearm. The Soviets created the Warsaw Pact in 1955 as a strategic counterweight to NATO.

Increased hostility did not lead to a direct military confrontation between the two powerful alliances. But the Soviet Union did test Western resolve, first by blockading the British, French, and American zones of Berlin (located in Soviet-controlled East Germany) in 1947–1948 and then in 1961 by building the Berlin Wall to prevent East Germans from fleeing to West Berlin.

In turn, the West tested the East by encouraging divisions within the Warsaw Pact. This policy contributed to an armed anti-Soviet revolt in Hungary that Soviet troops crushed in 1956. Then, in 1968, Soviet troops repressed a peaceful democratic reform effort in Czechoslovakia, making clear that, like the West, it would defend its sphere of influence. By failing to support either of these challenges to Soviet control, the West effectively accepted the political and ideological boundaries established by the Cold War. In 1968 Leonid Brezhnev, general secretary of the Soviet Union (1964–1982), asserted that all communist countries would be defended if they "fell to 'bourgeois forces,'" meaning, in effect, that any country in

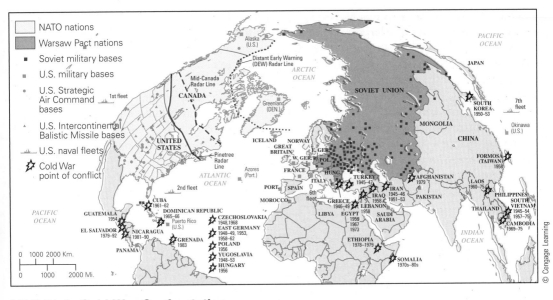

MAP 31.1 Cold War Confrontation

A polar projection is shown on this map because Soviet and U.S. strategists planned to attack one another by missile in the polar region; hence the Canadian-American radar lines.

communist eastern Europe would be invaded if it decided to embrace western-style democracy and capitalism.

By the end of the Second World War, Soviet troops controlled the Korean peninsula north of the thirty-eighth parallel, while American troops controlled the south. When these two powers could not reach an agreement to hold countrywide elections, a communist North Korea and a noncommunist South Korea emerged as independent states in 1948. Two years later North Korea invaded South Korea. The United Nations Security Council, in the absence of the Soviet delegation, condemned the invasion and called on its members to come to the defense of South Korea. In the ensuing **Korean War**, which lasted until 1953, the United States was the primary military ally of South Korea. Victories by American and South Korean forces forced North Korean forces north until the People's Republic of China entered the war in support of North Korea's communist regime.

Because the United States feared that launching attacks into China might prompt China's ally, the Soviet Union, to retaliate, the conflict remained limited to the Korean peninsula. When the contending armies eventually reached a stalemate along the thirty-eighth parallel, the two sides agreed to a truce but could not agree to a formal peace treaty. As a result, fear of renewed warfare between the two Koreas has lingered until the present.

The United States and Vietnam

The most important postwar communist movement arose in French Indochina in Southeast Asia. The Vietnamese leader Ho Chi Minh (hoe chee min) (1890–1969) had spent several years in France during World War I and helped form the French Communist Party. In 1930, after training in Moscow, he returned to Vietnam to found the Indochina Communist Party. Forced to take refuge in China during World War II, Ho cooperated with the United States while Japan controlled Vietnam.

At war's end the French government was determined to keep its colonial possessions. Ho Chi Minh's nationalist coalition, called the Viet Minh, fought the French with help from the People's Republic of China. After a brutal struggle, the French stronghold of Dienbienphu (dee-yen-bee-yen-FOO) fell in 1954, marking the end of France's colonial enterprise. Ho's Viet Minh government took over in the north, and a noncommunist nationalist government ruled in the south.

Under President Dwight D. Eisenhower (1953–1961), the United States provided limited support to the French but ultimately decided not to prop up French

The Vietnamese People at War

American and South Vietnamese troops burned many villages to deprive the enemy of civilian refuges. This policy undermined support for the South Vietnamese government in the countryside.

Dana Stone/Black Star

colonial rule in Vietnam, perceiving that the European colonial empires were doomed (see Chapter 32). After winning independence, communist North Vietnam supported a communist guerrilla movement—the Viet Cong—against the noncommunist government of South Vietnam. At issue was the ideological and economic orientation of an independent Vietnam.

As President John F. Kennedy (served 1961–1963) changed American policy to support the South Vietnamese government of President Ngo Dinh Diem (dee-YEM), North Vietnam committed its military forces more directly to the war with support from the Soviet Union and the Republic of China. Although he knew that the Diem government was corrupt and unpopular, Kennedy feared that a communist victory would encourage communist movements throughout Southeast Asia and alter the Cold War balance of power. He therefore significantly increased the number of American military advisers and also encouraged South Vietnamese military officers to overthrow their government. After Diem was overthrown and assassinated in early November 1963, American military involvement grew. On November 22, 1963, the unrelated assassination of President Kennedy in Dallas, Texas, elevated Lyndon B. Johnson (served 1963–1969) to the American presidency. He gained congressional support for an unlimited U.S. military deployment that eventually reached 500,000 troops. Because South Vietnam's new rulers proved to be as corrupt and unpopular as the earlier Diem government, many South Vietnamese supported the Viet Cong and Hanoi's drive for national reunification. Despite battlefield success in the **Vietnam War**, the United States failed to achieve a comprehensive victory. In the massive 1968 Tet Offensive, the Viet Cong guerrillas and their North Vietnamese allies gained significant military credibility while suffering significant losses. With a clear victory now unlikely, the antiwar movement in the United States grew in strength (see below).

In 1973 a treaty between North Vietnam and the United States ended U.S. involvement in the war and promised future elections. Two years later, in violation of the treaty, Viet Cong and North Vietnamese troops overran the South Vietnamese army and captured the southern capital of Saigon, renaming it Ho Chi Minh City. They then united the two Vietnams in a single state ruled from the north. Over a million Vietnamese and 58,000 Americans had died during the war. As the victors imposed a new economic and political order, hundreds of thousands of refugees from South Vietnam left for the United States and other Western nations.

While the United States had rationalized its military involvement in South Vietnam as part of its global confrontation with communism, the communist-led government of a newly reunited Vietnam soon found itself at war with its communist neighbors, rather than with U.S. allies in the region. In 1975 communist revolutionaries (the Khmer Rouge) gained power in Cambodia, Vietnam's western neighbor. Not only did this brutal regime led by Pol Pot execute more than 1 million of their fellow citizens, but they also provoked a war with the communist government of Vietnam in 1978. A Vietnamese force of more than 150,000 defeated the Khmer Rouge and set up an occupation government that lasted a decade. During this occupation, the Vietnamese found themselves facing a resilient guerrilla force that eventually compelled them to withdraw. The Vietnamese invasion of Cambodia also led the Vietnamese into a two-month-long war with the Republic of China, which favored the Cambodians.

President Johnson began his administration committed to a broad program of social reforms and civil rights initiatives, called the Great Society, and was instrumental in passing major civil rights legislation that responded to the heroic campaign for voting rights and integration led by Martin Luther King, Jr. As the commitment of U.S. troops in Vietnam grew, a massive antiwar movement applied the tactics of the civil rights movement to end the war. Growing economic problems and a rising tide of antiwar rallies, soon international in character, undermined support for Johnson, who declined to seek reelection.

The Race for Nuclear Supremacy   The terrible devastation of Hiroshima and Nagasaki by atomic weapons (see Chapter 30) framed the strategic decisions in the Korean and Vietnamese Wars. The Soviet Union had exploded its first nuclear device in 1949. The United States claimed a new advantage when it exploded a more powerful hydrogen bomb in 1952, but the Soviet Union followed suit less than a year later. As a result, the United States took care not to directly challenge the Soviet Union or China (a nuclear power from 1964) during the Korean or Vietnamese conflicts. But while the Cold War rivals avoided a direct confrontation, the use of threats and the proliferation of small conflicts frightened a world deeply scarred by two world wars.

In 1954 President Eisenhower warned Soviet leaders against attacking western Europe. In response to such an attack, he said, the United States would reduce the Soviet Union to "a smoking, radiating ruin at the end of two hours." A few years later the Soviet leader Nikita Khrushchev (KROOSH-chef) made an equally stark promise: "We will bury you." He was referring to economic competition, but Americans interpreted the statement to mean literal burial. Rhetoric aside, both men—and their successors—had the capacity to deliver on their threats, and everyone in the world knew that all-out war with nuclear weapons would produce the greatest global devastation in human history.

The Soviet Union's deployment of nuclear missiles to Cuba in 1962 pushed the two sides to the brink of war. Reacting to U.S. efforts to overthrow the Cuban government, Khrushchev and Fidel Castro decided that the deployment of nuclear weapons in Cuba would force the United States to accept the island's status quo. When the missiles were discovered, the United States declared a naval blockade and prepared to invade Cuba, forcing Khrushchev to remove the missiles. As frightening as the **Cuban missile crisis** was, the fact that the superpowers chose diplomacy over war gave reason to hope that nuclear weapons might be contained.

Fear of a nuclear holocaust produced an international effort to limit proliferation. In 1963 Great Britain, the United States, and the Soviet Union agreed to ban the testing of nuclear weapons in the atmosphere, in space, and under water, thus reducing the danger of radioactive fallout. In 1968 the United States and the Soviet Union together proposed a world treaty against further proliferation, leading ultimately to the Nuclear Non-Proliferation Treaty (NPT) signed by 137 countries. Not until 1972, however, did the two superpowers begin the arduous and extremely slow process of negotiating weapons limits.

The atomic powers France and Britain were economically unable to keep up with the Soviet–American arms race. Instead, they led the European states in an effort to relax tensions. Between 1972 and 1975 the Conference on Security and Cooperation in Europe (CSCE) brought delegates from thirty-seven European states, the United States, and Canada to Helsinki. The Soviet Union's chief objective was European acceptance of the political boundaries of the Warsaw Pact nations as a condition for broad cooperation. In the end, the **Helsinki Accords** affirmed these boundaries and also called for economic, social, and governmental contacts and for cooperation in humanitarian fields between the rival alliances.

Space exploration was another offshoot of the nuclear arms race. The contest to build larger and more accurate missiles prompted the superpowers to prove their skills in rocketry by launching space satellites. The Soviet Union placed a small *Sputnik* satellite into orbit around the earth in October 1957, and the United States responded with its own satellite three months later. The space race was on, a contest in which accomplishments in space were understood to signify equivalent achievements in the military sphere. In 1969, when Neil A. Armstrong and Edwin E. ("Buzz") Aldrin became the first humans to walk on the moon, America had demonstrated its technological superiority.

DECOLONIZATION AND NATION BUILDING

After World War I Germany, Austria-Hungary, and the Ottoman Empire lost their empires, and many colonies and dependencies were transferred to the victors, especially to Great Britain and France. In the two decades following World War II, nearly all remaining colonies gained independence. Circumstances differed profoundly from place to place. In some Asian countries, where colonial rule was of long standing, new states possessed viable industries, communications networks, and education systems. In other countries, notably in Africa, decolonized nations faced dire economic problems and disunity resulting from language and ethnic differences.

Most Latin American nations had achieved political independence in the nineteenth century (see Chapter 25). Following World War II, mass political movements in this region focused on the related issue of economic sovereignty—freedom from growing American economic domination. Great Britain and other European nations still retained colonies in the Caribbean after World War II. In the 1960s Barbados, Guyana, Jamaica, and Trinidad Tobago gained independence from Britain, and the smaller British colonies followed in the 1970s and 1980s, as did Surinam, which gained independence from the Netherlands.

Despite their differences, a sense of kinship arose among the nations of Latin America, Africa, and Asia. All shared feelings of excitement and rebirth. As North Americans, Europeans, and the Chinese settled into the exhausting deadlock of the Cold War, visions of independence and national development captivated the rest of the world.

New Nations in South and Southeast Asia   After partition in 1947 the independent states of India and Pakistan were strikingly dissimilar. Muslim Pakistan defined itself according to religion and quickly fell under the control of military leaders. India, a secular republic led by Prime

Minister Jawaharlal Nehru, was much larger and inherited the considerable industrial and educational resources developed by the British, along with a large share of trained civil servants and military officers. Ninety percent of its population was Hindu and most of the rest Muslim.

Adding to the tensions of independence (see Chapter 29) was the decision by the Hindu ruler of the northwestern state Jammu and Kashmir, now commonly called Kashmir, to join India without consulting his overwhelmingly Muslim subjects. As a result, war between India and Pakistan over Kashmir broke out in 1947 and ended with an uneasy truce. In 1965 war broke out again, this time involving large military forces and the use of air power by both sides. Kashmir has remained a flash point, with new clashes in 1999 and 2000.

Despite early predictions that multilingual India might break up into a number of linguistically homogeneous states, most Indians recognized that unity benefited everyone; and the country pursued a generally democratic and socialist line of development. Pakistan, in contrast, did break up. In 1971 the Bengali-speaking eastern section seceded to become the independent country of Bangladesh. During the fighting Indian military forces again struck against Pakistan. Despite their shared political heritage, India, Pakistan, and Bangladesh have found cooperation difficult and have pursued markedly different economic, political, religious, and social paths.

During the war the Japanese supported anti-British Indian nationalists as a way to weaken their enemy; they also encouraged the aspirations of nationalists in the countries they occupied in Southeast Asia. Many Asian nationalists saw Japanese victories over British, French, and Dutch colonial armies as a demonstration of the political and military capacities of Asian peoples. In the Dutch East Indies, Achmad Sukarno (1901–1970) cooperated with the Japanese in the hope that the Dutch, who had dominated the region economically since the seventeenth century, could be expelled. The Dutch finally negotiated withdrawal in 1949, and Sukarno became dictator of the resource-rich but underdeveloped nation of Indonesia. He ruled until 1965, when a military coup ousted him and brutally eliminated the nation's once-powerful Communist Party. The nation's large Chinese ethnic community was the target of violence during this period, and the new Indonesian government attempted to compel its assimilation, leading to decades of ethnic tension and discrimination.

In 1946 the United States kept its promise of postwar independence for the Philippine Islands but retained close economic ties and leases on military bases, later renegotiated. Britain granted independence to Burma (now Myanmar [my-ahn-MAR]) in 1948 and established the Malay Federation the same year. Singapore, once a member of the federation, became an independent city-state in 1965.

The Struggle for Independence in Africa Between 1952 and 1956 France granted independence to Tunisia and Morocco, but it sought to retain Algeria. France had controlled this colony for nearly 150 years and had encouraged settlement; in 1950, 10 percent of the Algerian population was of French or other European origin. France also granted political rights to the settler population and asserted the fiction of Algeria's political and economic integration in the French nation. In reality few Algerians benefited from this arrangement, and most resented their continued colonial status.

The Vietnamese military victory over France in 1954 helped provoke a nationalist uprising in Algeria, during which both sides acted brutally. The Algerian revolutionary organization, the Front de Libération National (FLN), was supported by Egypt and other Arab countries who sought the emancipation of all Arab peoples. French colonists considered the country theirs and fought to the bitter end. When Algeria finally won independence in 1962, a flood of angry colonists returned to France. Since few Arabs had received technical training, this departure undermined the economy. Despite harsh feelings left by the war, Algeria retained close and seemingly indissoluble economic ties to France, and Algerians in large numbers emigrated to France in the decades that followed.

Independence was achieved in most of sub-Saharan Africa through negotiation, not revolution. In colonies with significant white settler minorities, however, the path to independence followed the violent experience of Algeria. African nationalists were forced to overcome many obstacles, but they were also able to take advantage of many consequential changes put in place during colonial rule. In the 1950s and 1960s world economic expansion and growing popular support for liberation overcame African worries about potential economic and political problems that

Bettmann/CORBIS

Jomo Kenyatta *Kenya's newly elected premier, Jomo Kenyatta, cheered by crowds in Nairobi in 1963. Kenyatta (waving ceremonial "wisk") had led the struggle to end British colonial rule in Kenya.*

might follow independence. Moreover, improvements in medical care and public health had led to rapid population growth in Africa, and the continent's young population embraced the idea of independence.

Western nationalist and egalitarian ideals also helped fuel resistance to colonialism. Most of the leaders of African independence movements were among the most westernized members of these societies. African veterans of Allied armies during World War II had exposure to Allied propaganda that emphasized ideas of popular sovereignty and self-determination. In addition, many leaders were recent graduates of educational institutions created by colonial governments, and a minority had obtained advanced education in Europe and the United States.

African nationalists were able to take advantage of other legacies of colonial rule as well. Schools, labor associations, and the colonial bureaucracy itself proved to be fertile nationalist recruiting centers. Languages introduced by colonial governments were useful in building multiethnic coalitions, while networks of roads and railroads built to promote colonial exports forged new national identities and a new political consciousness.

The young politicians who led the nationalist movements devoted their lives to ridding their homelands of foreign occupation. An example is Kwame Nkrumah (KWAH-mee nn-KROO-muh) (1909–1972), who in 1957 became prime minister of Ghana (formerly the Gold Coast), the first British colony in West Africa to achieve independence. After graduating from a Catholic mission school and a government teacher-training college, Nkrumah spent a decade studying philosophy and theology in the United States, where he absorbed ideas about black pride and independence propounded by W. E. B. Du Bois and Marcus Garvey.

During a brief stay in Britain, Nkrumah joined Kenyan nationalist Jomo Kenyatta, a Ph.D. in anthropology, to found an organization devoted to African freedom. In 1947 Nkrumah returned to the Gold Coast to work for independence. The time was right. There was no longer strong public support in Britain for colonialism, and Britain's political leadership was not enthusiastic about investing resources to hold restive colonies. When Nkrumah's party won a decisive election victory in 1951, the British Gold Coast governor appointed him prime minister. Full independence came in 1957. Although Nkrumah remained an effective international spokesman for colonized peoples, he was overthrown in 1966 by a disaffected group of army officers.

Britain soon granted independence to its other West African colonies, including large, populous, and resource-rich Nigeria in 1960. In some British colonies in eastern and southern Africa, however, long-established white settler populations resisted independence. In Kenya a small but influential group of wealthy coffee planters claimed that a protest movement among the Kikuyu (kih-KOO-you) people was proof that Africans were not ready for self-government. The settlers called the movement "Mau Mau," a made-up name meant to evoke an image of primitive savagery. When violence between settlers and anticolonial fighters escalated after 1952, British troops hunted down movement leaders and resettled the Kikuyu in fortified villages. They also declared a state of emergency, banned all African political protest, and imprisoned Kenyatta and other nationalists. Released in 1961, Kenyatta negotiated with the British to write a constitution for an independent Kenya, and in 1964 he was elected the nation's first president. Kenyatta proved to be an effective, though autocratic, ruler, and Kenya benefited from greater stability and prosperity than Ghana and many other former colonies.

African leaders in the sub-Saharan French colonies were more reluctant than their counterparts in British colonies to call for full independence. Promises made during World War II by the Free French movement of General Charles de Gaulle at a conference in Brazzaville, in French Equatorial Africa, seemed to offer dramatic changes without independence. Dependent on the troops and supplies of French African colonies, de Gaulle had promised Africans a more democratic government, broader suffrage, and greater access to employment in the colonial government. He had also promised better education and health services and an end to many abuses in the colonial system. He had not promised independence, but the politics of post-war colonial self-government ultimately proved irresistible.

Most Africans elected to office following the reforms were trained civil servants. Because of the French policy of job rotation, they had typically served in a number of different colonies and thus had a broad regional outlook. They realized that some colonies—such as Ivory Coast, with coffee and cacao exports, fishing, and hardwood forests—had good economic prospects, while others, such as landlocked, desert Niger, did not. Furthermore, they recognized the importance of French public investment in the region—a billion dollars between 1947 and 1956—and their own dependence on colonial civil service salaries. As a result, they generally looked to achieve greater self-government incrementally.

When Charles de Gaulle returned to power in France in 1958, at the height of the Algerian war, he warned that a rush to independence would have costs, saying, "One cannot conceive of both an independent territory and a France which continues to aid it." Ultimately, however, African patriotism prevailed in all of France's West African and Equatorial African colonies. Guinea, under the dynamic leadership of Sékou Touré (SAY-koo too-RAY), gained full independence in 1958 and the others in 1960.

Independence in the Belgian Congo was chaotic and violent. Contending political and ethnic groups found external allies; some were supported by Cuba and the Soviet Union, while others were supported by the West or by business groups tied to the rich mines. Civil war, the introduction of foreign mercenaries, and the rhetoric of Cold War confrontation roiled the waters and led to a heavy loss of life and great property destruction. In 1965 Mobuto Sese Seko seized power in a military coup that included the assassination of Patrice Lumumba, the nation's first prime minister. Once in power, Mobuto maintained one of the region's most corrupt governments until driven from power in 1997.

The opposition of European settler communities delayed decolonization in southern Africa. While the settler minority tried to defend white supremacy, African-led liberation movements were committed to the creation of nonracial societies and majority rule. In the 1960s African guerrilla movements successfully fought to end Portuguese rule in Angola and Mozambique. Their efforts led to both the overthrow of the antidemocratic government of Portugal in 1974 and independence the following year. After a ten-year fight, European settlers in the British colony of Southern Rhodesia accepted African majority rule in 1980. The new government changed the country's name to Zimbabwe, the name of a great stone city built by Africans long before the arrival of European settlers.

South Africa and neighboring Namibia remained in the hands of European minorities much longer. The large white settler population of South Africa achieved effective independence from Britain in 1961 but kept the black and mixed-race majority in colonial-era subjection, separating the races in a system they called *apartheid* (a-PART-hite). Descendents of Dutch and English settlers made up 13 percent of the population but controlled the productive land, the industrial, mining, and commercial enterprises, and the government. Meanwhile, discrimination and segregation in housing, education, and employment confined the lives of people of mixed parentage (10 percent of the population) and South Asians (less than 3 percent).

Indigenous Africans, 74 percent of the population, were subjected to even stricter limitations on housing, freedom of movement, and access to jobs and public facilities. The government created fictional African "homelands" as a way of denying the African majority citizenship and political rights. Not unlike Amerindian reservations, these "homelands" were located in poor regions far from the more dynamic and prosperous urban and industrial areas. Overcrowded and lacking investment, they were impoverished and lacking in services and opportunities.

The African National Congress (ANC), formed in 1912, led opposition to apartheid. After police fired on demonstrators in the African town of Sharpeville in 1960 and banned all peaceful political protest by Africans, a lawyer named Nelson Mandela 1918–2013 organized guerrilla resistance by the ANC. The government sentenced Mandela to life in prison in 1964 and persecuted the ANC, but it was unable to defeat the movement. Facing growing opposition internationally, South Africa freed Mandela from prison in 1990 and began the transition to majority rule (see Chapters 32 and 33).

The Quest for Economic Freedom in Latin America   Although Latin America had achieved independence from colonial rule more than a hundred years earlier, European and American economic domination of the region created a semicolonial order (see Chapters 26 and 29). Foreigners controlled Chile's copper, Cuba's sugar, Colombia's coffee, and Guatemala's bananas, leading by the 1930s to growing support for economic nationalism. During the 1930s and 1940s populist political leaders experimented with programs that would constrain foreign investors or, alternatively, promote local efforts to industrialize (see discussion of Getulio Vargas and Juan Perón in Chapter 29).

In Mexico the revolutionary constitution of 1917 began an era of economic nationalism that culminated in the expropriation of foreign oil interests, mostly American, in 1938. The Institutional Revolutionary Party, or PRI (the abbreviation of its name in Spanish), controlled Mexico until the 1990s and had overseen a period of economic expansion during World War II. But a yawning gulf between rich and poor persisted. Although the government dominated important industries like petroleum and restricted foreign investment, rapid population growth, uncontrolled migration to Mexico City and other urban areas, and political corruption undermined efforts to lift the nation's poor. Economic power was concentrated at the top of society, with two thousand elite families controlling much of the nation's wealth. At the other end of the economic scale were the millions of poor Mexicans struggling to survive. Thwarted by limited opportunities at home, millions of Mexicans migrated to the United States.

Guatemala's situation was more representative of Latin America in 1950. An American corporation, the United Fruit Company, was Guatemala's largest landowner; it also controlled much of the nation's infrastructure, including port facilities and railroads. To limit banana production and keep international prices high, United Fruit kept much of its Guatemalan lands fallow. Jacobo Arbenz Guzmán, elected in 1951, advocated positions broadly similar to those of leaders like Perón of Argentina and Vargas of Brazil (see Chapter 29), who confronted powerful foreign interests. He advocated land reform, which would have transferred these fallow lands to the nation's rural poor. The threatened expropriation angered the United Fruit Company. Simultaneously, Arbenz tried to reduce U.S. political influence, raising fears in Washington that he sought closer ties to the Soviet Union. Reacting to the land reform efforts and to reports that Arbenz was becoming friendly to communism, the U.S. Central Intelligence Agency (CIA), in one of its first major overseas operations, sponsored a takeover by the Guatemalan military in 1954. CIA intervention removed Arbenz, but it also condemned Guatemala to decades of governmental instability and violence.

By the 1950s American companies dominated the Cuban economy. They controlled sugar production, the nation's most important industry, as well as banking, transportation, tourism, and public utilities. The United States was also the most important market for Cuba's exports and the most important source of Cuba's imports. Thus the performance of the U.S. economy largely determined the ebb and flow of Cuban foreign trade. By 1956 sugar accounted for 80 percent of Cuba's exports and 25 percent of Cuba's national income. But demand in the United States dictated keeping only 39 percent of the land owned by the sugar companies in production, while Cuba experienced chronic underemployment. Similarly, immense deposits of nickel in Cuba went untapped because the U.S. government, which owned them, considered them to be a strategic reserve.

While high unemployment and slow growth afflicted the nation, profits went north to the United States or to a small class of wealthy Cubans. Cuba's government was also notoriously corrupt and subservient to the wishes of American interests. As reform-minded young Cubans organized for a national election, Fulgencio Batista, a former military leader and president, illegally seized power in a coup in 1953. Hostility to Batista and anger with the corruption, repression, and foreign economic domination of his government gave rise to the revolution led by Fidel Castro.

Fidel Castro (b. 1927), a young lawyer who had played a prominent role in left-wing politics while at university, led a failed uprising in 1953. Convicted, jailed, and then sent into exile, Castro returned to Cuba in 1956 to establish a successful revolutionary movement in the countryside. His supporters included student groups, labor unions, and adherents of Cuba's traditional parties. When he and his youthful followers took power in 1959, they vowed not to suffer the fate of Arbenz and the Guatemalan reformers. Ernesto ("Che") Guevara (CHAY-guh-VAHR-uh), Castro's Argentine-born chief lieutenant who became the main theorist of communist revolution in Latin America, had witnessed the CIA coup in Guatemala firsthand. He and Castro believed that confrontation with the United

States was inevitable and moved quickly to remove the existing military leadership and begin revolutionary changes in the economy.

Within a year Castro's government seized and redistributed land, lowered urban rents, and raised wages, effectively transferring 15 percent of the national income from the rich to the poor. Within two years the Castro government had nationalized the property of almost all U.S. corporations in Cuba as well as the wealth of Cuba's elite. To achieve his revolutionary objectives, Castro sought economic support from the Soviet Union. He also consolidated his personal political power, putting aside promises of democratic reform made when fighting Batista.

The United States responded by seeking to destabilize the Cuban economy and undermine the Castro government. These punitive measures by the United States, the nationalization of so much of the economy, and the punishment of Batista supporters caused tens of thousands of Cubans to leave, including some who had opposed Batista. Initially, most emigrants were from wealthy families and the middle class, but when the economic failures of the regime became clear, many poor Cubans fled to the United States or to other Latin American nations.

There is little evidence that Castro was committed to communism before the revolution, but his commitment to break the economic and political power of the United States in Cuba and undertake dramatic social reforms led inevitably to conflict with the United States and to reliance on the Soviet Union. In April 1961, in an attempt to apply the strategy that had removed Arbenz from power in Guatemala, an army of Cuban exiles trained and armed by the CIA landed at the Bay of Pigs in an effort to overthrow Castro. The Cuban army defeated the attempted invasion in a matter of days. The Eisenhower administration had planned the invasion, but the newly elected U.S. president, John F. Kennedy, agreed to carry it out and lived with the embarrassment. This failure helped precipitate the Cuban missile crisis. Fearful of a new invasion, Castro and Khrushchev placed nuclear weapons as well as missiles and bombers in Cuba to forestall an anticipated second attack.

The failure of the Bay of Pigs tarnished the reputation of the United States and the CIA and gave heart to revolutionaries all over Latin America. But the armed revolutionary movements that imitated the tactics and objectives of Cuba's bearded revolutionaries experienced little success. Among the thousands to lose their lives was Che Guevara, captured and executed in 1967 by Bolivian troops trained by the United States. Nevertheless, Castro had demonstrated that revolutionaries could successfully challenge American power and put in place a radical program of economic and social reform in the Western Hemisphere.

BEYOND A BIPOLAR WORLD

Although no one doubted the dominating role of the East-West superpower rivalry in world affairs, newly independent nations had concerns that were primarily domestic and regional. Their challenge was to pursue their ends within the bipolar structure of the Cold War—and when possible to take advantage of the East–West rivalry. Where nationalist forces sought to assert political or economic independence, Cold War antagonists provided arms and political support even when the nationalist goals were quite different from those of the supporting superpower. For other nations, the ruinously expensive superpower arms race opened opportunities to expand industries and exports. In short, the superpowers dominated the world but did not control it.

The Third World   As a leader of the decolonization movement, Indonesia's president Sukarno was an appropriate figure to host a 1955 meeting of twenty-nine African and Asian countries at Bandung, Indonesia, that proclaimed solidarity among those fighting against colonial rule. This conference marked the beginning of an effort by the many new, poor, mostly non-European nations emerging from colonialism to gain more influence in world affairs. The terms *nonaligned nations* and *Third World*, which became commonplace in the following years, signaled these countries' collective stance toward the rival sides in the Cold War. If the West, led by the United States, and the East, led by the Soviet Union, represented two worlds locked in mortal struggle, the Third World consisted of everyone else.

Leaders of so-called Third World countries preferred the label *nonaligned*, which signaled their independence from Soviet or U.S. control. Leaders in the West noted that the Soviet Union supported many national liberation movements

Bandung Conference, 1955 *India's Jawaharlal Nehru (in white hat) was a central figure at the conference held in Indonesia to promote solidarity among nonaligned developing nations.*

AP Photo/George Sweers

and that the nonaligned movement included communist countries such as China and Yugoslavia. As a result, they refused to take the term *nonaligned* seriously. In a polarized world, they saw Sukarno, Nehru, Nkrumah, and Egypt's Gamal Abd al-Nasir (gah-MAHL AHB-d al–NAH-suhr) as stalking horses for an ambitious campaign to extend Soviet influence globally. This may have been the view of some Soviet leaders as well, since they were quick to offer military and financial aid to many nonaligned countries.

For the movement's leaders, however, nonalignment was primarily a way to extract money and support from one or both superpowers. By flirting with the Soviet Union or its ally, the People's Republic of China, a country could get weapons, training, and barter agreements that offered an alternative to selling agricultural or mineral products on Western-dominated world markets. The same flirtation might also prompt the United States and its allies to proffer grants and loans, cheap or free surplus grain, and investments in new industries or in infrastructure development.

Nonaligned countries could sometimes play the Cold War rivals against each other. Nasir, who had led a military coup against the Egyptian monarchy in 1952, and his successor Anwar al-Sadat (al-seh-DAT) played this game skillfully. The United States offered to build a dam at Aswan (AS-wahn), on the Nile River, to increase Egypt's electrical generating and irrigation capacity, but it withdrew the offer when Egypt turned to the Warsaw Pact for armaments in 1956. Worsened relations with the West then led Nasir to nationalize the Suez Canal and the Soviet Union to commit to building the dam. Later that same year Israel, Great Britain, and France allied to invade Egypt, aiming to overthrow Nasir, regain the Suez Canal, and secure Israel from any Egyptian threat. The invasion succeeded militarily, but the United States and the Soviet Union both pressured the invaders to withdraw, thus saving Nasir's government. In 1972 Sadat evicted Soviet military advisers, but a year later he used his Soviet weapons to attack Israel. After he lost that war, he disengaged from the Soviets; he then improved relations with, and sought increased aid from, the United States.

Other nations adopted similar balancing strategies. In each case, local leaders sought to develop their nations' economies and assert or preserve their nations' interests. Manipulating the superpowers was a means toward those ends and implied very little about true ideological orientation.

Japan and China   No countries took more effective advantage of opportunities presented by the superpowers' preoccupations than Japan and China. Japan signed a peace treaty with most of its former enemies in 1951 and regained independence from American occupation the following year. Renouncing militarism and its imperialist past (see Chapter 30), Japan remained on the sidelines throughout the Korean War. Its new constitution, written under American supervision in 1946, allowed only a limited self-defense force, banned the deployment of Japanese troops abroad, and gave the vote to women.

Like the Europeans, the Japanese had suffered high levels of population loss and property destruction in the war. With peace restored, they focused their resources on rebuilding industries and expanding trade. Peace treaties with countries in Southeast

Asia specified reparations payable in the form of goods and services, thus reintroducing Japan to that region as a force for economic development rather than as a military occupier. Beginning during the U.S. occupation, Japan had become closely tied to the West by trade and soon benefited from the postwar recovery. At the same time, controls placed on Japan by peace conditions kept its military expenditures low during the Cold War, providing an exceptional environment to invest in economic development and infrastructure.

Three industries that took advantage of government aid and new technologies were key to Japan's emergence as an economic superpower after 1975. Electricity was in short supply in 1950, and Tokyo suffered from chronic power outages. Japan responded by constructing a power grid between 1951 and 1970 that produced 60 million kilowatts of electricity. Most of this new capacity came from hydroelectric sources. At the same time steel production and shipbuilding developed rapidly, placing Japan among world leaders in both industries.

While Japan benefited from avoiding the heavy defense costs associated with the Cold War, China was at the center of Cold War politics. When Mao Zedong (maow dzuh-dong) and the communists defeated the nationalists in 1949 and established the People's Republic of China (PRC), their main ally and source of arms was the Soviet Union. By 1956, however, the PRC and the Soviet Union were beginning to diverge politically, partly in reaction to the Soviet rejection of Stalinism and partly because of China's reluctance to accept the role of subordinate. Mao had his own notions of communism that focused strongly on the peasantry, which the Soviets had ignored in favor of the industrial working class.

Mao's Great Leap Forward in 1958 was intended to propel China into the ranks of world industrial powers by maximizing the output of small-scale, village-level industries and by instituting mass collectivization in agriculture. These untested policies demonstrated Mao's willingness to carry out massive economic and social experiments of his own devising in the face of criticism by the Soviets as well as by traditional economists. By 1962 the revolutionary reforms had failed comprehensively, leading to an estimated 20 to 30 million deaths.

In 1966 Mao instituted another radical program, the **Cultural Revolution**, that ordered the mass mobilization of Chinese youth into Red Guard units. His goal was to kindle revolutionary fervor in a new generation to ward off the stagnation and bureaucratization he saw in the Soviet Union, as well as to increase his own power within the Communist Party. Red Guard units criticized and purged teachers, party officials, and intellectuals for "bourgeois values." Executions, beatings, and incarcerations were widespread, leading to a half-million deaths and 3 million purged by 1971. Finally, Mao admitted that attacks on individuals had gotten out of hand and intervened to reestablish order. Mao's wife Jiang Qing (jyahn ching) and radical allies dominated the last years of the Cultural Revolution, harshly restricting artistic and intellectual activity.

The rift between the PRC and the Soviet Union allowed U.S. president Richard Nixon (served 1969–1974) to revive relations with China. In 1971 the United States agreed to allow the PRC to join the United Nations and occupy China's permanent seat on the Security Council. This decision necessitated the expulsion of the Chinese nationalist government based on the island of Taiwan, which had previously claimed to be the only legal Chinese authority. The following year, Nixon visited

Beijing, initiating a new era of enhanced cooperation between the People's Republic of China and the United States.

The Middle East   Independence came gradually to the Arab countries of the Middle East. Britain granted Syria and Lebanon independence after World War II. Iraq, Egypt, and Jordan enjoyed nominal independence between the two world wars but remained under indirect British control until the 1950s. Military coups overthrew King Faruq (fuh-ROOK) of Egypt in 1952 and King Faisal (FIE-suhl) II of Iraq in 1958. King Husayn (hoo-SANE) of Jordan dismissed his British military commander in 1956 in response to the Suez crisis, but his poor desert country remained dependent on British and later American financial aid.

Overshadowing all Arab politics, however, was the struggle with Israel, a clear illustration that the superpowers could not control all dangerous international disputes. British policy on Palestine between the wars oscillated between favoring Zionist Jews—who emigrated to Palestine, encouraged by the Balfour Declaration—and support for the indigenous Palestinian Arabs, who suspected that the Zionists were aiming at an independent state. As more and more Jews sought a safe haven from persecution by the Nazis, Arabs felt more and more threatened. The Arabs unleashed a guerrilla uprising against the British in 1936, and Jewish groups turned to militant tactics a few years later. Occasionally, Arabs and Jews confronted each other in riots or killings, making it clear that peaceful coexistence in Palestine would be difficult or impossible to achieve.

After the war, under intense pressure to resettle European Jewish refugees, Britain turned the Palestine problem over to the United Nations. In November 1947 the General Assembly voted in favor of partitioning Palestine into two states, one Jewish and one Arab. The Jewish community made plans to declare independence, while the Palestinians, who felt that the proposed land division was unfair, took up arms. When Israel declared its independence in May 1948, neighboring Arab countries sent armies to help the Palestinians crush the newborn state.

Israel prevailed and some 700,000 Palestinians became refugees, finding shelter in United Nations refugee camps in Jordan, Syria, Lebanon, and the Gaza Strip (a bit of coastal land on the Egyptian-Israeli border). The right of these refugees to return home remains a focal point of Arab politics today. In 1967 Israel responded to threatening military moves by Egypt's Nasir by preemptively attacking Egyptian and Syrian air bases. In six days Israel won a smashing victory. When Jordan entered the war, Israel took control of Jerusalem, which it had previously split with Jordan, and the West Bank. Acquiring all of Jerusalem satisfied Jews' deep longing to return to their holiest city, but Palestinians continued to regard Jerusalem as their destined capital, and Muslims in many countries protested Israeli control of the Dome of the Rock, a revered Islamic shrine located in the city. Israel also occupied the Gaza Strip, the strategic Golan Heights in southern Syria, and the entire Sinai Peninsula. These acquisitions resulted in a new wave of Palestinian refugees.

The rival claims to Palestine continued to plague Middle Eastern politics. The Palestine Liberation Organization (PLO), headed by Yasir Arafat (AR-uh-fat), waged guerrilla war against Israel, frequently engaging in acts of terrorism. The

James Pozarik/Getty Images

Shortage at the Pumps *As prices rose in the late 1970s, consumers tried to hoard supplies by filling gas cans at neighborhood stations. For the first time gas prices exceeded $1 a gallon.*

Israelis were able to blunt or absorb these attacks and launch counterstrikes that likewise involved assassinations and bombings. Though the United States was a firm friend to Israel and the Soviet Union armed the Arab states, neither superpower saw the struggle between Zionism and Palestinian nationalism as a vital concern—until oil became a political issue.

The phenomenal concentration of oil wealth in the Middle East—Saudi Arabia, Iran, Iraq, Kuwait, Libya, Qatar, Bahrain, and the United Arab Emirates—was not fully realized until after World War II, when demand for oil rose sharply as civilian economies recovered. In 1960, as world demand rose, oil-producing states formed the **Organization of Petroleum Exporting Countries (OPEC)** to promote their collective interest in higher revenues.

Oil politics and the Arab-Israeli conflict intersected in October 1973 during the Yom Kippur War. Surprise attacks by Syria and Egypt threw the Israelis into temporary disarray, but Israel won a clear military victory in the end. Supported by military supplies from the United States, it drove back Syrian forces and trapped an Egyptian army at the Suez Canal's southern end. The United States then arranged a ceasefire and the disengagement of forces. But before that could happen, the Arab oil-producing countries voted to embargo oil shipments to the United States and the Netherlands as punishment for their support of Israel.

The implications of using oil as an economic weapon profoundly disturbed the worldwide oil industry. Prices rose—along with feelings of insecurity. In 1974 OPEC responded to the turmoil in the oil market by quadrupling prices, setting the stage for massive transfers of wealth to the producing countries and provoking a feeling of crisis throughout the consuming countries.

The Emergence of Environmental Concerns   The Cold War and the massive investments made in postwar economic recovery focused public and governmental attention on technological innovations and enormous projects such as hydroelectric dams and nuclear power stations. Only a few people warned that untested technologies and industrial expansion were degrading the environment. The superpowers were particularly negligent of the environmental impact of pesticide and herbicide use, automobile exhaust, industrial waste disposal, and radiation.

The wave of student unrest that swept many parts of the world in 1968 and the early 1970s created a new awareness of environmental issues and a new constituency for environmental action. As youth activism grew, governments in the West began to pass new environmental regulations. Among them was the Clean Air Act of 1970. Earth Day, a benchmark of the new awareness, was also first celebrated in 1970, the year in which the United States also established its Environmental Protection Agency.

When oil prices skyrocketed, the problem of finite natural resources became more broadly recognized. Making gasoline engines and home heating systems more efficient and lowering highway speed limits to conserve fuel became matters of national debate in the United States, while poorer countries struggled to find the money to import oil. A widely read 1972 study called *The Limits of Growth* forecast a need to cut back on consumption of natural resources in the twenty-first century. Ecological and environmental problems now vied for public attention with superpower rivalry and Third World nation building.

CONCLUSION

The alliance between the Soviet Union and the Western democracies led by the United States did not survive into the post–World War II era. Shortly after the war, both sides began to prepare for a new round of hostilities, establishing competing military alliances and attempting to influence the new governments of nations formerly occupied by the Axis. In the end this confrontation was projected into space, as each side sought to advertise its technological capacity through satellite launches and finally a moon landing.

Each side portrayed this tension as a struggle between irreconcilably different social and economic systems, and each side emphasized the corruption, injustice, and unfairness of its opponent. When Winston Churchill spoke in 1946 of Soviet control in eastern Europe as an iron curtain, he suggested that the Soviet system was, in effect, a prison.

Massive armies armed with increasingly sophisticated weapons, including nuclear weapons far more destructive than those dropped on Japan, defended the boundary that separated the United States and its allies and the Soviet Union and its allies. This Cold War quickly became global in character as distant civil wars, regional conflicts, and nationalist revolutions were transformed by support provided by these rivals for global ascendancy.

The desire of colonized peoples to throw off imperial controls and establish independent nations provided many of the era's flash points. The Western nations had defined World War II as a war for freedom and self-determination. The Free

French had promised greater autonomy to African colonies, the United States had used nationalist forces to fight against the Japanese in the Philippines and in Vietnam, and Britain also had used forces recruited throughout its empire to fight the war. Once organized and set in motion, these nationalist energies eventually overwhelmed colonial rule. The most powerful force in the postwar era was nationalism, the desire of peoples to control their own destinies.

In Africa, the Middle East, South Asia, and Latin America, this desire to throw off foreign controls led to the creation of scores of new nations by the 1970s. Each nation's struggle had its own character. While in India these passions led to independence, similar sentiments led in China to the overthrow of a government seen as weak and subordinate to foreign powers and to the creation of a communist dictatorship. In much of Africa, the Middle East, and the Caribbean, nationalism overturned colonial rule. In the Middle East the desire for self-government was complicated by the creation of the state of Israel. In Latin America, where most nations had been independent for well over a century, nationalist passions focused on a desire for economic independence and an end to foreign military interventions.

The end of Japanese control in Korea and Vietnam led to territorial partitions that separated Soviet-leaning and Western-allied polities. Civil war and foreign interventions soon followed. In both cases the Soviet Union and China supported communist forces. The United States committed large military forces to protect the anticommunist governments, gaining a stalemate in Korea and eventually failing in Vietnam. While these outcomes were mixed for the superpowers, the wars were contained and managed so as to prevent direct engagement and nuclear conflict.

This period also witnessed the beginning of the international environmental movement. Public attention increasingly focused on resource management, pollution, and the preservation of endangered species. In response, the United States and governments in western Europe put in place the first generation of environmental laws. The Clean Air Act in the United States and other measures had an immediate impact, but both policymakers and the public grew aware of ever more serious challenges. The gas crisis of the 1970s gave these efforts a sense of urgency.

IMPORTANT EVENTS 1945–1975

1947	Partition of India
1949	NATO formed
1949	Dutch withdraw from Indonesia
1950–1953	Korean War
1952	United States detonates first hydrogen bomb
1954	CIA intervention in Guatemala; defeat at Dienbienphu ends French hold on Vietnam
1954	Jacobo Arbenz overthrown in Guatemala, supported by CIA
1955	Warsaw Pact created
1955	Bandung Conference

1956	Soviet Union suppresses Hungarian revolt
1957	Soviet Union launches first artificial satellite into earth orbit
1957	Ghana becomes first British colony in Africa to gain independence
1959	Triumph of Fidel Castro's revolution Cuba
1960	Shootings in Sharpeville intensify South African struggle against apartheid; Nigeria becomes independent
1961	East Germany builds Berlin Wall
1961	Bay of Pigs (Cuba)
1962	Cuban missile crisis
1962	Algeria wins independence
1968	Nuclear Non-Proliferation Treaty
1971	Bangladesh secedes from Pakistan
1975	Helsinki Accords; end of Vietnam War

32

The End of the Cold War and the Challenge of Economic Development and Immigration, 1975–2000

At the end of the 1970s China began an ambitious program of economic reforms. Until then China, with the world's largest population, was a very poor nation with a gross domestic product (GDP) per capita of approximately $110.00 per year (total goods and services produced divided by population). It lagged far behind the mature industrialized nations of Europe and North America in economic performance, as well as behind more dynamic neighboring nations like Japan and South Korea. Since the reforms, China has experienced rapid economic growth and has become one of the few socialist nations to successfully make the transition to a market economy, reaching a GDP per capita of $5,413.57 in 2010. Despite this remarkable expansion, millions of Chinese still live in poverty. As is indicated in the opening illustration, ancient technology and poverty can exist in close proximity with modernity and affluence in China. These same problems of poverty and inequality exist across the globe. In an era of astounding technological change and, until the recession of 2008, spreading prosperity, more than a billion of the world's population still live on less than $1.25 a day.

At the end of the twentieth century, population growth continued to outstrip economic resources in many of the nations of the developing world. Since the deep recession that began in 2008, politicians as well as social reformers in the wealthy industrialized nations have criticized the effects of high levels of unemployment, family breakdown, substance abuse, and homelessness. At the start of the twenty-first century, as in the Industrial Revolution (see Chapter 22), an era of relative affluence, increased global economic integration, and rapid technological progress coincided with problems of social dislocation and inequality. Among the most important events of the period were the emergence of new industrial powers in Asia, the precipitous demise of the Soviet Union and its socialist allies, and the migration of tens of millions of people from poor to rich nations.

POSTCOLONIAL CRISES AND ASIAN ECONOMIC EXPANSION

Between 1975 and the end of the century, wars and revolutions spread death and destruction through many of the world's least-developed regions. In most cases the origins of conflict were found in the experience of colonialism and foreign intervention, but each conflict also had a unique historical character. Throughout these decades of conflict the two superpowers sought to avoid direct military confrontation while working to gain strategic advantages. The United States and the Soviet Union each supplied arms and financial assistance to nations or insurgent forces hostile to the other. Once linked to superpower rivalries, local conflicts became deadlier. Conflicts where the rival superpowers financed and armed competing factions or parties are called **proxy wars**.

In Latin America superpower rivalry transformed limited conflicts over political rights, social justice, and economic policies into a violent cycle of revolution, military dictatorship, and foreign meddling. In Iran and Afghanistan resentment against foreign intrusion and a growing religious hostility to secular culture led to revolutionary transformations. Here again, superpower ambitions and regional political instability helped provoke war and economic decline. These experiences were not universal, however. During this period some Asian nations experienced rapid economic transformation. Japan emerged as one of the world's leading industrial powers, and a small number of other Asian economies entered the ranks of industrial and commercial powers. Socialist China joined this group of fast-developing Asian nations after initiating market-based economic reforms.

At the end of the 1980s the Cold War ended with the collapse of the Soviet system in eastern Europe, but the transition to democracy and market economy proved difficult. As both developing and former socialist nations opened their markets to foreign investment and competition, they experienced wrenching social change. Increased globalization coincided with increased inequality in many nations, but some developing nations also attained substantial benefits from rapid technological change and world economic integration.

This period also witnessed a great increase in world population and international immigration. Population growth and increased levels of industrialization had a dramatic impact on the global environment, with every continent feeling the destructive effects of forest depletion, soil erosion, and pollution. Wealthy nations with slow population growth found it easier to respond to these environmental challenges than did poor nations experiencing rapid population growth.

Revolutions, Repression, and Democratic Reform in Latin America   In the 1970s Latin America entered a dark era of political violence. When revolutionary movements challenged the established order, militaries in many countries overturned constitutional governments and instituted repressive measures. A region of weak democracies in 1960 became a region dominated by military dictatorships with little patience for civil liberties and human rights fifteen years later.

The ongoing confrontation between Fidel Castro and the government of the United States (see Chapter 31) helped propel the region toward crisis. The fact that the Cuban communist government survived efforts by the United States to overthrow it energized the revolutionary left throughout Latin America. Fearful that revolution would spread across Latin America, the United States increased support for its political and military allies in that region, training many of the military leaders who led coups during this period.

Brazil was the first nation to experience the region-wide conservative reaction to the Cuban Revolution. Claiming that Brazil's civilian political leaders could not protect the nation from communist subversion, the army overthrew the constitutional government of President João Goulart (ju-wow go-LARHT) in 1964. Once in power, the military suspended the constitution, outlawed all existing political parties, and exiled former presidents and opposition leaders. Death squads—illegal paramilitary organizations sanctioned by the government—detained, tortured, and executed thousands of citizens. The dictatorship also undertook an ambitious economic program that promoted industrialization through import substitution, using tax and tariff policies to successfully compel foreign-owned companies to increase investment in manufacturing, especially the auto industry.

This combination of dictatorship, violent repression, and government promotion of industrialization came to be called the "Brazilian Solution." Elements of this "solution" were later imposed across much of the region. In 1970 Chile's newly elected president, **Salvador Allende** (sal-VAH-dor ah-YEHN-day), undertook an ambitious program of socialist reforms and nationalized Chile's heavy industry and mines, including the American-owned copper companies that dominated the economy. From the beginning of Allende's presidency the administration of President Richard Nixon (served 1969–1973) sought to undermine the Chilean government. Afflicted by inflation, mass consumer protests, and declining foreign trade, a military uprising led by General Augusto Pinochet (ah-GOOS-toh pin-oh-CHET) and supported by the United States overthrew Allende in 1973. President Allende and thousands of Chileans died in the uprising, and thousands more were jailed, tortured, and imprisoned without trial. Once in power Pinochet rolled back Allende's socialist innovations, dramatically reducing state participation in the economy and encouraging foreign investment.

In 1976 Argentina followed Brazil and Chile into dictatorship. Juan Perón had been exiled in 1955 after a military uprising, but with Argentina torn by rising levels of political violence he was allowed to return and was then elected president in 1973 (see Chapter 29). Perón had insisted that his third wife, Isabel Martínez de Perón (EES-ah-bell mar-TEEN-ehz deh pair-OWN), be elected vice president, and she inherited the presidency after his death in 1974. Her weak administration faced a potent guerrilla insurgency, a wave of kidnappings, high inflation, and labor protests. Impatient with the policies of the president, the military seized power and suspended the constitution in 1976. During the next seven years it fought what it called the **Dirty War** against terrorism. More than nine thousand Argentines lost their lives, and thousands of others endured arrest and torture before democracy was restored.

While the left suffered these reverses in South America, a revolutionary movement came to power in Nicaragua in 1979, overthrowing the corrupt dictatorship of Anastasio Somoza. This broad alliance of revolutionaries and reformers called themselves **Sandinistas** (sahn-din-EES-tahs). They took their name from Augusto César Sandino, who had led Nicaraguan opposition to U.S. military intervention between 1927 and 1932. Once in power, the Sandinistas moved leftward, seeking to imitate the command economies of Cuba and the Soviet Union and nationalizing properties owned by members of the Nicaraguan elite and U.S. companies.

U.S. president Jimmy Carter (served 1977–1980) championed human rights in the hemisphere and stopped the flow of U.S. arms to military regimes with the worst records, like Argentina. Carter also agreed to the reestablishment of Panamanian sovereignty in the Canal Zone at the end of 1999, but his effort to find common ground with the Sandinistas failed due to their intransigence.

Carter was defeated in the next election by Ronald Reagan, who was committed to overturning the Nicaraguan Revolution and defeating a revolutionary movement in neighboring El Salvador. With the memory of the Vietnam War still strong (see Chapter 31), the U.S. Congress resisted any use of U.S. combat forces in Nicaragua and El Salvador and put strict limits on military aid. As a result, the Reagan administration tried to roll back the Nicaraguan Revolution through punitive economic measures and the recruitment and arming of a proxy force of anti-Sandinista Nicaraguans, called Contras (counter-revolutionaries).

Confident that they were supported by the majority of Nicaraguans and assured that the U.S. Congress was close to cutting off aid to the Contras, the Sandinistas called for free elections in 1990. But they had miscalculated politically. Exhausted by more than a decade of violence, a majority of Nicaraguan voters rejected the Sandinistas and elected a middle-of-the-road coalition led by Violeta Chamorro (vee-oh-LET-ah cha-MOR-roe).

In neighboring El Salvador another guerrilla movement, the Farabundo Martí (fah-rah-BOON-doh mar-TEE) National Liberation Front, or FMLN (acronym for Spanish name), seemed on the verge of taking power. The Reagan administration responded by providing hundreds of millions of dollars in military assistance and by training units of the El Salvadoran army. The assassination of Archbishop Oscar Romero and other members of the Catholic clergy by death squads tied to the Salvadoran government as well as the murder of thousands of noncombatants by military units trained by the United States undermined this effort. However, the electoral defeat of the Sandinistas in Nicaragua and the collapse of the Soviet Union (see below) finally forced the FMLN rebels to negotiate peace, transforming themselves into a civilian political party.

During this same period, the violent political confrontation of right and left abated in South America as well. The right-wing military dictatorships established in Brazil, Chile, and Argentina all came to an end between 1983 and 1990, brought down by their own excesses and by popular desires for a return to constitutional government. By 2000, with the Cold War ended, 95 percent of Latin America's population lived again under civilian rule.

At the same time, the influence of the United States grew substantially. The United States had thwarted the left in Nicaragua and El Salvador by funding military proxies. It used its own military in a 1983 invasion of the tiny Caribbean nation of Grenada and again in 1989 to overthrow and arrest dictator General Manuel Noriega (MAN-wel no-ree-EGG-ah) of Panama. These actions were powerful reminders to Latin Americans of prior interventions (see Chapter 26), but they also served as reminders of American power at a time when socialism was discredited by the collapse of the Soviet bloc.

From this position of strength the United States pushed Latin American nations to reform their economies by removing limitations on foreign investment, eliminating many social welfare programs, and reducing public-sector employment. Latin American governments responded by selling public-sector industries, like national airlines, manufacturing facilities, and public utilities, to foreign corporations. But popular support for these policies, what Latin Americans called neo-liberalism, eroded quickly due to political scandals and a slowing world economy. A catastrophic economic and political meltdown in Argentina between 2001 and 2002 contributed to the appearance of a reinvigorated nationalist left in Latin America that sought to roll back neo-liberal reforms (see Diversity and Dominance: The Struggle for Women's Rights in an Era of Global Political and Economic Change). Among the most vocal critic of neo-liberalism and American influence was Hugo Chávez (HUGH-go SHAH-vez), elected president of Venezuela in 1998 and serving as the region's chief critic of U.S. policy until his death in 2013. Left-of-center presidents were later elected in Brazil (Luiz Inácio Lula da Silva, 2002), Argentina (Néstor Kirchner, 2003), Bolivia (Evo Morales, 2005), and Ecuador (Rafael Correa, 2007).

Islamic Revolutions in Iran and Afghanistan	Although the Arab–Israel conflict and the oil crisis (see Chapter 31) concerned both superpowers, the prospect of direct military involvement remained remote. When unexpected crises developed in Iran and Afghanistan, however, significant strategic issues for the superpowers came to the

foreground. Both countries adjoined Soviet territory, making Soviet military intervention more likely. Exercising post–Vietnam War caution, the United States reacted with restraint in Iran. The Soviet Union chose a bolder and ultimately disastrous course in Afghanistan.

Muhammad Reza Pahlavi (REH-zah PAH-lah-vee) succeeded his father as shah of Iran in 1941. In 1953 covert intervention by the U.S. Central Intelligence Agency (CIA) helped the shah retain his throne in the face of a movement to overturn royal power. Even when he finally nationalized the foreign-owned oil industry, the shah continued to enjoy American support. As oil revenues increased following the price increases of the 1970s, the United States encouraged the shah to spend his nation's growing wealth on equipping the Iranian army with American weaponry. By the 1970s popular resentment against the ballooning wealth of the elite families that supported the shah and the brutality, inefficiency, malfeasance, and corruption of his government led to mass opposition.

Ayatollah Ruhollah Khomeini (A-yat-ol-LAH ROOH-ol-LAH ko-MAY-nee), a Shi'ite (SHE-ite) philosopher-cleric who had spent most of his eighty-plus years in religious and academic pursuits, became the leader of the opposition. Massive protests forced the shah to flee Iran and ended the monarchy in 1979. In the Islamic Republic of Iran, which replaced the monarchy, Ayatollah Khomeini was supreme arbiter of disputes and guarantor of the government's religious legitimacy. He oversaw a parliamentary regime based on European models but imposed religious control over legislation and public behavior. The electoral process was not open to monarchists, communists, and other opposition groups. Shi'ite clerics with little training for government service held many of the highest posts, and stringent

Mohsen Shandiz/Sygma/Corbis

Muslim Women Mourning the Death of Ayatollah Khomeini in 1989 *An Islamic revolution overthrew the shah of Iran in 1979. Ayatollah Khomeini sought to lead Iran away from the influences of Western culture and challenged the power of the United States in the Persian Gulf.*

measures were taken to combat Western styles and culture. Universities were temporarily closed, and their faculties were purged of secularists and monarchists. Women were compelled to wear modest Islamic garments outside the house, and semiofficial vigilante committees policed public morals and cast a pall over entertainment and social life. Many sectors of the Iranian economy were also placed under the direction of clerically controlled foundations, leading to massive capital flight. Clerical mismanagement and inflation have contributed to decades of economic stagnation in Iran.

President Carter had criticized the shah's repressive regime, but the overthrow of a long-standing ally and the creation of the Islamic Republic were blows to American prestige. The new Iranian regime was anti-Israeli and anti-American. Seeing the United States as a "Great Satan" opposed to Islam, Khomeini fostered Islamic revolutionary movements that threatened the United States and Israel. In November 1979 Iranian radicals seized the U.S. embassy in Tehran and held fifty-two diplomats hostage for 444 days. Americans felt humiliated by their inability to rescue the hostages or negotiate their release.

In the fall of 1980, shortly after negotiations for the release of the hostages began, **Saddam Hussein** (sah-DAHM hoo-SANE), the ruler of neighboring Iraq, invaded Iran to topple the Islamic Republic. His own dictatorial rule rested on a secular, Arab-nationalist philosophy and long-standing friendship with the Soviet

Union, which had provided him with advanced weaponry. He feared that the fervor of Iran's revolutionary Shi'ite leaders would infect his own country's Shi'ite majority and threaten his power. The war pitted American weapons in the hands of the Iranians against Soviet weapons in the hands of the Iraqis, but the superpowers avoided overt involvement during eight years of bloodshed. Covertly, however, the United States used Israel to transfer arms to Iran, hoping to gain the release of other American hostages held by radical Islamic groups in Lebanon and to help finance the Contra war against the Sandinista government of Nicaragua. When this deal came to light in 1986, the resulting political scandal intensified American hostility to Iran. Openly tilting toward Iraq, President Reagan sent the United States Navy to the Persian Gulf, ostensibly to protect nonbelligerent shipping. The move helped force Iran to accept a cease-fire in 1988.

While the United States dealt with Iran, the Soviet Union faced even more serious problems in neighboring Afghanistan. In 1978 a Marxist party with a secular agenda seized power. Offended by the new regime's efforts to reform education and grant rights to women, traditional Afghan ethnic and religious leaders led a successful rebellion. The Soviet Union responded by sending its army into Afghanistan to install a communist regime. With the United States, Saudi Arabia, and Pakistan paying, equipping, and training Afghan rebels, the Soviet Union found itself in an unwinnable war like the one the United States had stumbled into in Vietnam. Facing growing economic problems and widespread domestic discontent over the war, Soviet leaders withdrew their troops in 1989. Three years later rebel groups took control of the entire country and then began to fight among themselves over who should rule. In this chaotic situation a radical Islamic party with close ties to Pakistan, the Taliban, took power in 1996. They installed a harsh religious regime and soon faced armed opposition. The Taliban had received financial support from the Saudi Arabian Usama bin Laden during their rise to power and later provided him with protection as he organized the militant organization al-Qaeda that later attacked the United States (see Chapter 33).

Asian Transformation   Although Japan has few mineral resources and is dependent on oil imports, the Japanese economy weathered the oil price shocks of the 1970s much better than did the economies of Europe and the United States. In fact, Japan experienced a faster rate of economic growth in the 1970s and 1980s than did any other major developed economy, growing at about 10 percent a year and becoming the world's second largest economy. Average income also increased rapidly, overtaking that of the United States in 1986.

There were major differences between the Japanese and U.S. industrial models. During the American occupation, Japanese industrial conglomerates known as *zaibatsu* (see Chapter 27) were broken up. Although ownership of major industries became less concentrated, business leaders created new industrial alliances to control competition and facilitate the allocation of resources. During the period of dramatic growth there were six major **keiretsu** (kay-REHT-soo), each of which included a major bank as well as firms in industry, commerce, and construction tied together in an interlocking ownership structure. There were also minor keiretsu dominated by major industrial corporations, like Toyota.

The Struggle for Women's Rights in an Era of Global Political and Economic Change

The struggle for women's rights has been one of the most important social movements of the twentieth and twenty-first centuries. Although we can identify fundamental similarities in objectives across cultural and political boundaries, women in less developed nations are forced to recognize that their objectives and strategies must take into account international inequalities in power and wealth.

In this section Gladys Acosta, a militant Peruvian feminist, discusses the appropriate agenda for this struggle in the era after the fall of the Soviet Union and the rise of **neo-liberalism**, *the term used in Latin America to identify the free-market economic policies advocated by the United States. Among its chief characteristics are an end to the protection of local industries, a reduction in government social welfare policies, a reduction in public-sector employment, a commitment to paying debts to international creditors, and the removal of impediments to foreign investment. Many Latin Americans believe that neo-liberalism is a new form of imperialism. While written in the 1990s, this political manifesto deals directly with issues of great relevance today: international indebtedness, the social costs of austerity, and gender inequality.*

Neo-Liberalism in Action

When I talk of neo-liberalism, I mean austerity measures, foreign debts, and increased liberties for all those who have the power of money at their disposal and the power of repression over those who make demands. We have now reached a new form of capitalist accumulation. The world's economic system is in a state of change and capital has become more concentrated and centralised. I would not go as far as to say countries don't exist anymore but national identities do certainly play a different role now.... If we look at the bare face of neo-liberalism from a woman's point of view, we cannot fail to notice its murderous consequences.... At the moment we're experiencing capitalism's greatest ideological offensive. It's all business: everything is bought and sold and everything has its price.

The Consequences of Neo-Liberal Politics

[W]omen play an important role in this ever-more internationalized economy because we represent, as ever, a particularly exploitable workforce. A number of studies have revealed the existence of

Tariffs and import regulations inhibiting foreign competition were crucial to the early stages of development of Japan's major industries. These restrictions and Japanese success at exporting manufactured goods through the 1970s and 1980s produced huge trade surpluses with other nations. Although the United States and the European Community engaged in tough negotiations to try to force open the Japanese market, these efforts had only limited success, and by 1990 Japan's trade surplus with the rest of the world was double that of 1985.

subcontractor chains who work for transnational companies "informally" and mainly employ women. Basically we are dealing with a kind of integration into the world market which often uses our own homes as its outlet. Obviously, this work is badly paid and completely unprotected and has to be done without any of those social rights which were formerly achieved by trade union struggles.... As it advances worldwide, this capitalism also encourages the expansion of certain kinds of tourism. A visible increase in prostitution is part of this, whereby women from poor countries are smuggled into large, internationally operated rings which exploit them. The reports of Filipina women traded on the West German market send shivers down our spines....

How the Adoption of Austerity Measures Affects Women's Lives

It is obvious that foreign debt is one of the most inhuman forms of exploitation in our countries when one considers the ratio between work necessary for workers' needs and work producing profit for employers. The experts have already explained how the prevailing exchange and investment structures have created international finance systems which keep whole populations in inhuman conditions.... Women in every household are suffering every day as a result of impoverished economies and those who

are most exposed to the effects of foreign debt are women.

When it comes to shopping, caring for sick children or the impossibility of meeting their schooling costs, the illusion of "leaving poverty behind" evaporates. Yet the problem is not only of an economic nature because under such circumstances the constant tension leads to grave, often lasting exhaustion. The psychosocial damage is alarming. The adoption of austerity measures means a curtailment of the state's commitment to social services with a direct effect on women. Daily life becomes hell for them. The lack of even minimal state welfare presents women (and obviously children too) with crushing working days.

Questions for Analysis

1. What is neo-liberalism?
2. According to Acosta, how does global economic integration fostered by neo-liberalism affect the lives of women as workers?
3. Acosta claims that indebtedness to foreign lenders leads to austerity measures. How do these measures impact families in poor countries?

Source: From Gladys Acosta, "The View of a Peruvian Militant," in Compañeras. Voices from the Latin American Women's Movement, *edited by Gaby Küppers (London: Latin American Bureau, 1994). Reprinted with permission of the publisher.*

Many experts assumed that Japan's competitive advantages would propel it past the United States as the world's preeminent industrial economy, but during the 1990s Japan entered what would become a two-decade-long crisis that dramatically slowed the growth of both GDP (gross domestic product) and average income. In the thirty months between January 1990 and July 1992, Japanese stocks and real estate markets lost $2.5 trillion in market value, while the national growth rate fell from 3.1 percent a year to 0.2 percent.

Before the crisis, Japanese real estate and stock markets had become highly overvalued as the nation's huge trade imbalances with the United States and other trading partners flooded the economy with cash and fueled speculation. As the crisis deepened and prices collapsed, the close relationships between industry, government, and banks proved to be a liability, as these powerful institutions acted to prop up inefficient companies and support unsustainable market values. By the end of the 1990s Japan's GDP had suffered a loss greater than that suffered by the United States in the Great Depression, leaving the nation with a crushing debt burden. Despite government efforts to promote recovery with public works projects and low interest rates, Japan's economy has grown very slowly to the present.

Other Asian states imitated the Japanese model of development in the 1970s and 1980s. These nations protected new industries from foreign competition while encouraging close alliances among industries and banks. The largest and most successful of them, the Republic of Korea, commonly called South Korea, used a combination of inexpensive labor, strong technical education, and substantial domestic capital reserves to support a massive industrialization effort. Success in heavy industries such as steel and shipbuilding as well as in consumer industries such as automobiles and consumer electronics soon made it a global economic power.

The small nations of Taiwan and Singapore, along with Hong Kong, a British colony until 1997, also became industrial powerhouses. As a result of their rapid development, these three economies along with South Korea were called the **Asian Tigers**. While Taiwan suffered a number of political reverses, including the loss of its United Nations seat to the People's Republic of China in 1971 and the withdrawal of diplomatic recognition by the United States, it achieved remarkable economic progress, based in large part on investment in the economy of the People's Republic of China. Hong Kong and Singapore—long British colonies with extremely limited natural resources—also enjoyed rapid economic development. Both were historically important Asian ports and commercial centers that later developed successful manufacturing, banking, and commercial sectors.

These **newly industrialized economies (NIEs)** shared many characteristics that help explain their rapid industrialization. All had disciplined and hard-working labor forces, and all invested heavily in education. For example, as early as 1980 South Korea had as many engineering graduates as Germany, Britain, and Sweden combined. All had very high rates of personal saving, about 35 percent of GDP, that funded new technologies, and all emphasized outward-looking export strategies. And, like Japan, all benefited from government sponsorship and protection. Despite this momentum, the region was deeply shaken by a financial crisis that began in 1997. Like the recession that afflicted Japan in 1990, a combination of bad loans, weak banks, and the international effects of currency speculation led to a deep regional crisis that was stabilized only by the efforts of the United States, Japan, and international institutions like the International Monetary Fund.

China Rejoins the World Economy   After Mao Zedong's death in 1976, the Chinese communist leadership began economic reforms that relaxed state control, allowing more initiative and permitting individuals to accumulate wealth. The results were remarkable. Under China's leader **Deng Xiaoping** (dung shee-yao-ping) China permitted foreign investment for the first time since the communists came to power in 1949. Between 1979 and 2005 foreign direct investment in China grew to more than $600 billion as McDonald's, General Motors, Coca-Cola, Airbus, Toyota, and many other foreign companies began doing business. As a result, by 2010 China had become a major industrial power and the world's most important exporting nation. Despite these changes, state-owned enterprises still employed more than 100 million workers, and most foreign-owned companies were limited to special economic zones. The result was a dual industrial sector—one modern, efficient, and connected to international markets, the other directed by political decisions. While the Chinese have not yet privatized land, by 1990 over 90 percent of China's agricultural land was in the hands of farmers permitted to sell what they produced.

In 2010 China became the world's second largest economy, surpassing Japan. The scale of this achievement can be represented by the remarkable growth of China's GDP, the total value of all goods and services produced by the nation. In 1970 China, with a population of nearly 1 billion, had a GDP of $56 billion, smaller than the GDP of Italy ($111 billion), which had a population of 55 million people. By 2010 China's GDP had increased eighty-one times, surpassing $4,520 billion. Other developing countries grew substantially in this period as well. India's economy, for example, was larger than China's in 1970 ($66 billion) and increased nineteen times by 2010, to $1,251 billion.

Despite its enormous achievement, China, with a per capita GDP of $5,413.57, has remained substantially poorer than mature industrial economies, which have an average per capita GDP of $42,063. However, China is now richer than much of the developing world. Latin America has a per capita GDP of $4,299, the Middle East $2,329, and sub-Saharan Africa $940. While poverty levels in China have fallen swiftly during this period of rapid development, inequality, especially between rural and urban dwellers, has increased.

The combination of economic reforms, high levels of foreign investment, and technology transfers from developed industrial nations has helped make China one of the world's major industrial powers. As was true earlier with Japan and the Asian Tigers, China's expansion has depended heavily on exports, which accounted for over 40 percent of GPD in 2008. Success in foreign markets produced a large foreign trade surplus. As was the case with Japan three decades ago, these cash surpluses paid for the government's massive investments in infrastructure, promoted speculation in real estate and stocks, and propped up a weak banking sector. While the Chinese economy continued to grow at a healthy rate during the worldwide recession that began in 2008, some economists wonder if the speculative excesses can be overcome without a deep contraction similar to that experienced by Japan in the 1990s.

Deng Xiaoping's strategy of balancing change and continuity avoided some of the social and political costs experienced by Russia and other socialist countries that abruptly embraced capitalism and democracy (see next section), but he faced a major challenge in 1989. Responding to inflation and to worldwide mass movements in favor of democracy, Chinese students and intellectuals led a series of protests demanding more democracy and an end to corruption. This movement culminated in **Tiananmen** (tee-yehn-ahn-men) **Square**, in the heart of Beijing, where hundreds of thousands of protesters gathered and refused to leave. After weeks of standoff, tanks pushed into the square, killing hundreds and arresting thousands. The Communist Party has not faced another direct challenge to its power since then, but growing levels of labor unrest, protests in favor of political rights, corruption scandals, and ethnic confrontations continue to challenge this one-party dictatorship.

The End of the Bipolar World

After the end of World War II, competition between the alliances led by the United States and the Soviet Union created a bipolar world (see Chapter 31). Every conflict, no matter how local its origins, had the potential of engaging the attention of one or both of the superpowers. The Korean War, decolonization in Africa, the Vietnam War, the Cuban Revolution, and hostilities between Israel and its neighbors increased tension between the nuclear-armed superpowers. Given this succession of provocations, politics everywhere was dominated by arguments over the relative merits of the competing systems.

Few in 1980 predicted the startling collapse of the Soviet Union. Western observers tended to see communist nations as both more uniform in character and more subservient to the Soviet Union than was true. Long before the 1980s, deep divisions had appeared among communist states. Similarly, nationalism had reappeared as a powerful force among the once-independent nations and ethnic groups brought together within the Soviet Union. By the late 1980s these forces threatened the survival of this communist world power.

Crisis in the Soviet Union   Under U.S. president Ronald Reagan and the Soviet Union's general secretary Leonid Brezhnev (leh-oh-NEED BREZ-nef), Cold War rhetoric remained intense. Massive new U.S. investments in armaments placed heavy competitive burdens on a Soviet economy already suffering from shortages and mismanagement. Obsolete industrial plants and centralized planning stifled initiative in the Soviet Union and led to a declining standard of living relative to the West, while the arbitrariness of the bureaucracy, the manipulation of information, and material deprivations created a crisis in morale.

Despite the unpopularity of the war in Afghanistan and growing discontent, Brezhnev refused to modify his unsuccessful policies, but he could not escape criticism. Self-published underground writings (*samizdat* [sah-meez-DAHT]) by critics of the regime circulated widely despite government efforts to suppress them. In a series of powerful books, the writer Alexander Solzhenitzyn (sol-zhuh-NEET-sin) castigated the Soviet system. Although he won a Nobel Prize in literature, authorities charged him with treason and expelled him in 1974.

By the time **Mikhail Gorbachev** (GORE-beh-CHOF) came to power in 1985, weariness with war in Afghanistan, economic decay, and vocal protest had reached critical levels. Casting aside Brezhnev's hard line, Gorbachev authorized major reforms in an attempt to stave off total collapse. His policy of political openness (*glasnost*) permitted criticism of the government and the Communist Party. His policy of **perestroika** (per-ih-STROY-kuh) ("restructuring") was an attempt to address long-suppressed economic problems by moving away from central state planning. In 1989 he ended the unpopular war in Afghanistan.

The Collapse of the Socialist Bloc   In 1980 protests by Polish shipyard workers in the city of Gdansk led to the formation of **Solidarity**, a labor union that grew to 9 million members. The Roman Catholic Church in Poland, strengthened by the elevation of a Pole, Karol Wojtyla (KAH-rol voy-TIL-ah), to the papacy as John Paul II in 1978, gave strong moral support to the protest movement.

The Polish government imposed martial law in 1981 in response to the growing power of Solidarity and its allies, giving the army effective political control. Seeing Solidarity under tight controls and many of its leaders in prison, the Soviet Union decided not to intervene. But Solidarity remained a potent force with a strong institutional structure and nationally recognized leaders. As Gorbachev loosened political controls in the Soviet Union after 1985, communist leaders elsewhere lost confidence in Soviet resolve, and critics and reformers in Poland and throughout eastern Europe were emboldened.

Beleaguered Warsaw Pact governments vacillated between relaxation of control and suppression of dissent. Just as the Catholic clergy in Poland had supported Solidarity, Protestant and Orthodox religious leaders aided the rise of opposition groups elsewhere. This combination of nationalism and religion provided a powerful base for opponents of the communist regimes. Communist governments sought to quiet the opposition by turning to the West for trade and financial assistance. They also opened their nations to travelers, ideas, styles, and money from Western countries, all of which accelerated the demand for change.

By the end of 1989 communist governments across eastern Europe had fallen. The dismantling of the Berlin Wall vividly represented this transformation. While communist leaders in Poland, Hungary, Czechoslovakia, and Bulgaria decided that change was inevitable, the dictator Nicolae Ceausescu (nehk-oh-LIE chow-SHES-koo) of Romania refused to surrender power and was overthrown and executed. The comprehensiveness of these changes became clear in 1990, when the Polish people elected Solidarity leader Lech Walesa (leck wah-LEN-sah) as president and the people of Czechoslovakia elected dissident playwright Vaclav Havel (vah-SLAV hah-VEL) as president.

Following the fall of the Berlin Wall, a tidal wave of patriotic enthusiasm swept aside the once-formidable communist government of East Germany. In the chaotic months that followed, East Germans crossed to West Germany in large numbers, and government services in the eastern sector nearly disappeared. The collapse of the East German government led quickly in 1990 to reunification.

Soviet leaders knew that similarly powerful nationalist sentiments existed within the Soviet Union as well. The year 1990 brought declarations of independence by Lithuania, Estonia, and Latvia, three small states on the Baltic Sea that the Soviet Union had annexed in 1939. The end of the Soviet Union then came suddenly in 1991. After communist hardliners botched a coup against Gorbachev, disgust with communism boiled over. Boris Yeltsin, the president of the Russian Republic, emerged as the most powerful leader in the country. Russia, the largest republic in the Soviet Union, was effectively taking the place of the disintegrating

Bossu Regis/Corbis Sygma

The Fall of the Berlin Wall *The Berlin Wall was the most important symbol of the Cold War. Constructed to keep residents of East Germany from fleeing to the West and defended by armed guards and barbed wire, it was the public face of communism. As the Soviet system fell apart, the residents of East and West Berlin broke down sections of the wall.*

USSR. In September 1991 the Congress of People's Deputies—the central legislature of the USSR—voted to dissolve the union. Then in December a weak successor state with little central control, the Commonwealth of Independent States (CIS), was created and Gorbachev resigned.

The ethnic and religious passions that fueled the breakup of the Soviet Union also overwhelmed the Balkan nation of Yugoslavia. In 1991 it dissolved into a morass of separatism and warring ethnic and religious groups. Slovenia and Croatia, the most westerly provinces, both heavily Roman Catholic, became independent states in 1992. The population of Bosnia and Herzegovina was more mixed: 40 percent were Muslims, 30 percent Serbian Orthodox, and 18 percent Catholics. Following the declaration of Bosnian national independence in 1992, the nation's Orthodox Serbs attempted to rid the state of Muslims in a violent process called **ethnic cleansing**. After extensive television coverage of atrocities and wanton destruction, the United States intervened and eventually brokered a settlement in 1995 that effectively created two ethnically separate political entities.

In 1999 new fighting and a new round of ethnic cleansing occurred in the southernmost Yugoslavian province of Kosovo. Seen by Serbs as their homeland, Kosovo had a predominantly Muslim and Albanian population. When Serbia refused to stop military action, the United States, Britain, and France acted on behalf of NATO by launching an aerial war on Serbian targets in Kosovo and in Serbia itself that forced the withdrawal of Serbian forces from Kosovo. Serbia's president during this violent period, Slobodan Milosevic, was forced from power and turned over to a war crimes tribunal in The Hague, where he died in prison.

Africa in the Era of Global Political Change Sub-Saharan Africa has experienced political instability, military coups, civil wars, and conflicts over resources since independence. It has also remained among the poorest regions in the world. Southern Africa, however, has seen democratic progress and a steady decline in armed conflicts since 1991. A key change came in South Africa in 1994, when long-time political prisoner Nelson Mandela and his African National Congress (ANC) won the first national elections in which the African majority could participate equally. Also hopeful has been the return to democracy of Nigeria, Africa's most populous state, after decades of military rulers. In 1999, after a succession of military governments, Nigerians elected President Olusegun Obasanjo (oh-LOO-she-gun oh-BAH-san-jo) (a former coup leader), and a 2003 vote gave him a second term, despite serious voting irregularities. Similarly, in 2002 Kenyans voted out the Kenya African National Union Party that had held power for thirty-nine years.

Africa was also a scene of ethnic cleansing. In 1994 the political leaders of the Central African nation of Rwanda incited the Hutu people to massacre their Tutsi neighbors. Although the major powers had earlier promised to intervene in genocides, they sought to avoid military involvement in Rwanda by not using the word *genocide* to describe the slaughter. Without foreign intervention, the carnage claimed 750,000 lives, with millions more becoming refugees. Finally, the United States and other powers intervened and the United Nations set up a tribunal to try those responsible for the genocide. In 1998 violence spread from Rwanda to neighboring Congo, where growing opposition and ill health had forced President Joseph Mobutu from office after over three decades of dictatorial misrule. Various peacemaking attempts failed to restore order, and by mid-2003 more than 3 million Congolese had died from disease, malnutrition, and injuries related to the fighting.

The Persian Gulf War

The Persian Gulf War was the first significant military conflict to occur after the breakup of the Soviet Union and the end of the Cold War. Iraq's ruler, Saddam Hussein, had borrowed a great deal of money from neighboring Kuwait and failed to get Kuwait's royal family to reduce this debt. He was also eager to control Kuwait's oil fields. Hussein believed that the smaller and militarily weaker nation could be quickly defeated, and he suspected that the United States would not react. The invasion occurred in August 1990.

The United States decided to react. Saudi Arabia, an important ally of the United States and a major oil producer, also supported intervention. With his intention to use force endorsed by the United Nations and with many Islamic nations supporting military action, President George H. W. Bush ordered an attack in early 1991. Iraq's military defeat was comprehensive, but Hussein remained in power, crushing an uprising just months following his defeat. The United States imposed various conditions on Iraq that kept tensions high, helping create the conditions for a new, larger, war in 2003 (see Chapter 33).

MAP 32.1 The End of the Soviet Union

When communist hardliners failed to overthrow Gorbachev in 1991, popular anticommunist sentiment swept the Soviet Union. Following Boris Yeltsin's lead in Russia, the republics that constituted the Soviet Union declared their independence.

THE CHALLENGE OF POPULATION GROWTH

For most of human history, governments viewed population growth as beneficial, a source of national wealth and power. Since the late eighteenth century, however, many intellectuals and politicians have viewed population increases with alarm, fearing that the production of food and other essential resources could not keep up with population growth. Late in the nineteenth century some social critics expressed concern that growing populations would lead to class and ethnic struggle. By the second half of the twentieth century, fears of population growth were primarily attached to environmental concerns. Are urban sprawl, pollution, and soil erosion the inevitable results of population growth? The questions and debates continue today, but clearly population growth is both a cause and a result of increased global interdependency.

Demographic Transition   The population of Europe almost doubled between 1850 and 1914, putting enormous pressure on rural land and urban housing and overwhelming fragile public institutions that provided crisis assistance (see Chapter 27). This dramatic growth forced a large wave of immigration across the Atlantic, helping to develop the Western Hemisphere and invigorating the Atlantic economy (see Chapter 25). Population growth also contributed to Europe's Industrial Revolution by lowering labor costs and increasing consumer demand.

While some Europeans saw the rapid increase in human population as a blessing, others warned of disaster. The best-known pessimist was the English cleric **Thomas Malthus**, who in 1798 argued that unchecked population growth would outstrip food production. When Malthus looked at Europe's future, he used a prejudiced image of China to terrify his readers. A visitor to China, he claimed, "will not be surprised that mothers destroy or expose many of their children; that parents sell their daughters for a trifle; ... and that there should be such a number of robbers. The surprise is that nothing still more dreadful should happen."[1]

The generation that came of age in the years after World War II lived in a world where Malthus seemed to have little relevance. Industrial and agricultural productivity had multiplied supplies of food and other necessities. At the same time, cultural changes associated with expanded female employment, older age at marriage, and more effective family planning had slowed the rate of population increase. By the 1960s Europe and other industrial societies had made the **demographic transition** to lower fertility rates (average number of births per woman) and reduced mortality. This meant that populations would age quickly. In the world's most developed nations, for example, median age rose from twenty-nine years in 1950 and to thirty-seven years by 2000.

By the late 1970s, the developing world had still not experienced the demographic transition and the global discussion of population growth became politicized. Leaders in some developing nations actively promoted large families, arguing that larger populations increased national power. When industrialized

---

[1]Quoted in Antony Flew, "Introduction," in Thomas Robert Malthus, *An Essay on the Principle of Population and a Summary View of the Principle of Population* (New York: Penguin Books, 1970), 30.

实行计划生育　是我国的一项基本国策
FAMILY PLANNING—A BASIC NATIONAL POLICY OF CHINA

Sally and Richard Greenhill/Alamy

Chinese Family-Planning Campaign *To slow population growth, the Chinese government has sought to limit parents to a single child. Billboards and other forms of mass advertising have been an essential part of the campaign.*

nations, mostly white, raised concerns about rapid population growth in Asia, Africa, and Latin America, populist political leaders in these regions responded by asking whether these concerns were racist.

This question exposed the influence of racism in the population debate and temporarily disarmed Western advocates of birth control. However, once the economic shocks of the 1970s and 1980s had revealed the vulnerability of poor nations, governments in the developing world jettisoned policies that promoted population growth. Mexico is a good example. In the 1970s the government had encouraged high fertility, and population grew an average of 3 percent per year. In the 1980s Mexico rejected these policies and began to promote birth control, leading by the 1990s to an annual population growth of 1.7 percent.

World population exploded in the twentieth century, more than doubling between 1950 and 2000 (see Table 32.1). Although the rate of growth has slowed since the 1980s, world population still increases by a number equal to the total population of the United States roughly every three years. If fertility were to remain constant from today, with a world average of 2.5 children per woman, population would reach nearly 27 billion in 2100. This will not happen, however, because fertility is declining in most developing nations and is at less than replacement levels in most industrialized countries. As a result, most experts estimate a world population in 2100 of around 10 billion.

TABLE 32.1 | POPULATION FOR WORLD AND MAJOR AREAS, 1750–2050

Major Area	Population Size (Millions)						
	1750	1800	1850	1900	1950	1995	2050*
World	791	978	1,262	1,650	2,521	5,666	8,909
Africa	106	107	111	133	221	697	1,766
Asia	502	635	809	947	1,402	3,437	5,268
Europe	163	203	276	408	547	728	628
Latin America and the Caribbean	16	24	38	74	167	480	809
North America	2	7	26	82	172	297	398
Oceania	2	2	2	6	13	28	46

Major Area	Percentage Distribution						
	1750	1800	1850	1900	1950	1995	2050*
World	100	100	100	100	100	100	100
Africa	13.4	10.9	8.8	8.1	8.8	12	23.7
Asia	63.5	64.9	64.1	57.4	55.6	61	57.1
Europe	20.6	20.8	21.9	24.7	21.7	13	5.3
Latin America and the Caribbean	2.0	2.5	3.0	4.5	6.6	8	9.4
North America	0.3	0.7	2.1	5.0	6.8	5	4.1
Oceania	0.3	0.2	0.2	0.4	0.5	1	0.5

*Estimated

Source: J. D. Durand, "Historical Estimates of World Population: An Evaluation" (Philadelphia: University of Pennsylvania, Population Studies Center, 1974, mimeographed); United Nations, *The Determinants and Consequences of Population Trends*, vol. 1 (New York: United Nations, 1973); United Nations, *World Population Prospects as Assessed in 1963* (New York: United Nations, 1966); United Nations, *World Population Prospects: The 1998 Revision* (New York: United Nations, forthcoming); United Nations Population Division, Department of Economic and Social Affairs, World Population to 2300. (2004.), http://www.un.org/esa/population/publications/longrange2/World Pop2300final.pdf.

At the same time mortality rates have increased in some areas as immigration, commercial expansion, and improved transportation have facilitated the transmission of disease. The rapid spread of HIV/AIDS is an example of this phenomenon. Less developed regions with poorly funded public health institutions and with few resources to invest in prevention and treatment experience the highest rates of infection and the greatest mortality. Of the countries with the highest HIV/AIDS rates in 2010, thirty-seven are in Africa, three in Asia, and six in Latin America and the Caribbean. These countries are home to 87 percent of all HIV/AIDS infections. By 2007 approximately 25 million people had died of AIDS and another 33 million were infected worldwide. In recent years prevention programs and improved drug therapies have slowed both mortality and infection rates, with the greatest successes registered in rich countries with the greatest medical resources.

The Industrialized Nations   In the developed industrial nations of western Europe and in Japan, fertility levels are so low that population would fall without immigration. Japanese women have an average of 1.4 children, while Italian women have 1.2. Although Sweden tries to promote fertility with cash payments, tax incentives, and job leaves to families with children, the average number of births per woman is 1.4. By comparison, the average African woman now has 4.6 children. Higher levels of female education and employment, the material values of consumer culture, and access to contraception and abortion explain the low fertility of mature industrial nations. An Italian woman in Bologna, the city with the lowest fertility in the world, put it this way: "I'm an only child and if I could, I'd have more than one child. But most couples I know wait until their 30's to have children. People want to have their own life, they want to have a successful career. When you see life in these terms, children are an impediment."[2]

In industrialized nations life expectancy improved as fertility declined. The combination of abundant food, improved hygiene, and more effective medicines and medical care has lengthened human lives. In 2000 about 20 percent of the population in Europe was sixty-five or over. By 2050 this proportion will rise to over one-third. Italy soon will have more than twenty adults fifty years old or over for each five-year-old child. Because of higher fertility and greater levels of immigration, the United States is moving in this direction more slowly than western Europe; by 2050 the median age in Europe will be fifty-two, while it will be thirty-nine in the United States.

The combination of falling fertility and rising life expectancy in the industrialized nations presents a challenge very different from the one foreseen by Malthus. These nations generally offer a broad array of social services, including retirement income, medical services, and housing supplements for the elderly. As the number of retirees increases relative to the number of employed people, the cost of these programs may become unsustainable. Economists track this problem by using the PSR (potential support ratio): the ratio of persons fifteen to sixty-four years old (likely workers) to persons sixty-five or older (likely retirees). Between 1950 and 2000 the world's PSR fell from 12 to 9. In mature industrial countries the PSR fell from 8 to 5. By 2050 it will fall to 4 for the world's population and to an unsustainable 2 in mature industrial countries.

The Developing Nations   At current rates, 95 percent of all future population growth will be in developing nations (see Table 32.1). A comparison between Europe and Africa illustrates these changes. In 1950 Europe had more than twice the population of Africa. By 1985 Africa's population

---

[2]"Population Implosion Worries a Graying Europe," *New York Times*, July 10, 1998.

had drawn even with Europe, and, according to United Nations projections, its population will be three times larger than Europe's by 2050.

Rapid population growth continued after 2000 in the developing world even as birthrates fell. Among all developing nations, average birthrates fell from 44 births per thousand inhabitants in 1950 to 22 today. Birthrates fell most steeply in countries experiencing the most rapid economic development. In China the birthrate fell from 42 births per thousand in 1950 to a First World level of 13 today. In this same period birthrates declined from 43 per thousand to 23 in India, another fast-growing economy. Change occurred much more slowly in sub-Saharan Africa, where the birthrates fell from 47 per thousand to 38, and in Muslim countries like Pakistan and Afghanistan, where birthrates declined from 42 to 28 and 53 to 45 per thousand, respectively. The populations of Latin America were also expanding, but at rates much slower than in sub-Saharan Africa and the Muslim nations. In this same period, Latin America's birthrate declined from 43 per thousand in 1950 to 19 in 2010. Regardless of these changes, birthrates remain more than twice as high in the developing world as in the mature industrial nations, with the highest levels in the poorest countries.

Old and Young Populations   Population pyramids generated by demographers clearly illustrate the profound transformation in human reproductive patterns and life expectancy since World War II. Figure 32.1 shows the 2001 age distributions in Pakistan, South Korea, and Sweden—nations at three different stages of economic development. Sweden is a mature industrial nation. South Korea is rapidly industrializing and has surpassed many European nations in both industrial output and per capita wealth. Pakistan is a poor, traditional Muslim nation with rudimentary industrialization, low educational levels, and little effective family planning.

In 2001 nearly 50 percent of Pakistan's population was under age sixteen. The resulting pressures on the economy have been extraordinary. Every year

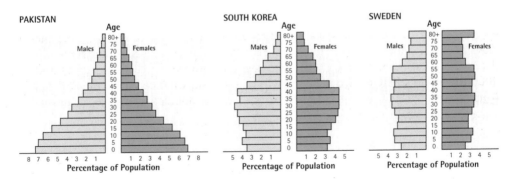

FIGURE 32.1 Age Structure Comparison

Islamic Nation (Pakistan), Non-Islamic Developing Nation (South Korea), and Developed Nation (Sweden), 2001.

Source: U.S. Bureau of the Census, *International Database*, 2001.

approximately 150,000 men reach age sixty-five—and another 1.2 million turn sixteen. Pakistan, therefore, has to create more than a million new jobs a year or face growing unemployment and declining wages. Sweden confronts a different problem. Sweden's aging population, growing demand for social welfare benefits, and declining labor pool means that its industries may become less competitive and living standards may decline. In South Korea, a decline in fertility dramatically altered the ratio of children to adults, creating an age distribution similar to that of western Europe.

Unequal Development and the Movement of Peoples

Two characteristics of the postwar world should now be clear. First, despite decades of experimentation with state-directed economic development, most nations that were poor in 1960 are still poor today. There are notable exceptions. In Asia, first Japan, then the Asian Tigers (Taiwan, Singapore, South Korea, and Hong Kong), and more recently China have generated high rates of growth and are now among the world's most competitive industrial powers. In recent years Brazil, Mexico, and India have also experienced significant growth. This industrial transformation has increased world demand for raw materials, which in turn has elevated the wealth of an equally small number of oil-exporting nations. Second, world population has increased to startlingly high levels, and much of the increase was, and will continue to be, in the poorest nations.

The combination of intractable poverty and growing population has generated a surge in international immigration. Few issues have stirred more controversy. Even moderate voices have sometimes framed this discussion of immigration as a competition among peoples. Large numbers of legal and illegal immigrants from poor nations with growing populations are entering the developed industrial nations, with the exception of Japan. Large-scale migrations within developing countries are a related phenomenon. The movement of impoverished rural residents to the cities of Asia, Africa, and Latin America (see Table 32.2) has increased steadily since the 1970s. This internal migration often serves as the first step toward migration abroad.

The Problem of Inequality
Since 1945 the global economy has expanded more rapidly than at any time in the past. Faster, cheaper communications and transportation have combined with improvements in industrial and agricultural technologies to create material abundance that would have amazed those who experienced the first Industrial Revolution (see Chapter 22). Despite this remarkable economic expansion, the differences between rich and poor nations remain stark.

The gap between rich and poor nations has grown wider since 1945, although the 2008 recession has had a powerful negative effect on many advanced industrial economies. China's spectacular rise as an industrial power since 1980 is a strong indicator that some once-poor countries can modernize and become competitive industrial nations. Nevertheless, the vast majority of the world's population continues to live in

TABLE 32.2	THE WORLD'S LARGEST CITIES (URBAN AGGLOMERATIONS OF 13 MILLION OR MORE)

City	1970	City	1990	City	2011	City	2025
1 Tokyo	23.3	1 Tokyo	32.5	1 Tokyo	37.2	1 Tokyo	38.7
2 New York	16.2	2 New York	16.1	2 Delhi	22.7	2 Delhi	32.9
		3 Mexico City	15.3	3 Mexico City	20.4	3 Shanghai	28.4
		4 São Paulo	14.8	4 New York	20.4	4 Mumbai	26.6
		5 Mumbai	12.4	5 Shanghai	20.2	5 Mexico City	24.6
		6 Osaka-Kobe	11.0	6 São Paulo	19.9	6 New York	23.6
		7 Calcutta	10.9	7 Mumbai	19.7	7 São Paulo	23.2
		8 Los Angeles	10.9	8 Beijing	15.6	8 Dhaka	22.9
		9 Seoul	10.5	9 Dhaka	15.4	9 Beijing	22.6
		10 Buenos Aires	10.5	10 Calcutta	14.4	10 Karachi	20.2
				11 Karachi	13.9	11 Lagos	18.9
				12 Buenos Aires	13.5	12 Calcutta	18.7
				13 Los Angeles	13.4	13 Manila	16.3
						14 Los Angeles	15.7
						15 Shenzhen	15.5
						16 Buenos Aires	15.5
						17 Guangzhou	15.5
						18 Istanbul	14.9
						19 Cairo	14.7
						20 Kinshasa	14.5
						21 Chongqing	13.6
						22 Rio de Janeiro	13.6
						23 Bangalore	13.2

Source: United Nations, Economic and Social Affairs, World Urbanization Prospects: The 2011 Revision Highlights, 6-7.

poverty. There are many measures of the relative wealth of nations; GDP (gross domestic product) per capita measured in U.S. dollars is among the most common.

In 2010 the per capita GDP of Luxembourg was the highest in the world, $104,512; the U.S. figure was $46,702, and the Japanese figure was $43,063. The countries of the European Union were generally rich, but some of the former Soviet satellites recently admitted to the European Union have the GDP per capita of developing nations. France and Germany have per capita GDPs of $39,170 and $39,852, respectively. The poorest countries in the European Union, Bulgaria and Romania, have per capita GDPs similar to Russia's ($6,335)—$7,539 and $10,481, respectively.

Many countries in the developing world now approach the poorest tier of European countries in per capita GDP. Per capita GDP for Mexico is $9,133, Brazil $10,993, Chile $12,640, South Africa $7,272, and Gabon $8,768. But many more countries, especially in Asia and Africa, remain very poor: the Philippines, $2,140; India, $1,375; Pakistan, $1,019; Nigeria, $1,242; and Sudan, $1,538. The poorest, like Haiti, Kenya, and Bangladesh, have per capita GDP levels under $1,000.

Internal Migration: The Growth of Cities   In developing nations migration from rural areas to urban centers increased threefold between 1925 and 1950; the pace of migration then accelerated (see Table 32.2). While slums around the major cities of developing nations are seen as signs of social breakdown and economic failure, life in these urban slums was generally better than life in the countryside. A World Bank study estimated that three out of four rural-to-urban migrants made economic gains. Residents of cities in sub-Saharan Africa, for example, were six times more likely than rural residents to have safe water. An unskilled migrant from the depressed northeast of Brazil could triple his or her income by moving to Rio de Janeiro.

Garbage Dump in Manila, Philippines *In Third World nations thousands of poor families live by sorting and selling bottles, aluminum cans, plastic, and newspapers in urban landfills.*

Eco Images/Universal Images Group/Getty Images

As the scale of rural-to-urban migration grew, these benefits became more elusive. In the cities of the developing world basic services have been crumbling under the pressure of rapid population growth. In cities like Mexico City and Manila, which are among the world's largest cities, tens of thousands live in garbage dumps, scavenging for food. In Rio de Janeiro alone an estimated 350,000 abandoned children live in the streets and parks, begging, selling drugs, stealing, and engaging in prostitution to survive. Some nations have tried to relocate migrants back to the countryside. Indonesia, for example, has relocated more than a half-million urban residents since 1969.

Global Migration   Each year hundreds of thousands of men and women leave developing nations to go to industrialized nations. Dramatically rising numbers after 1960 have led to increased ethnic and racial tensions. Political refugees and immigrants have faced murderous violence in Germany; growing anti-immigrant sentiment has strengthened right-wing political movements and led to riots in cities with large immigrant populations in France and Greece; and in the United States the government has dramatically expanded its effort to control its southern border.

Immigrants from developing nations have brought host nations many of the same benefits that the great migration of Europeans to the Americas provided a century earlier (see Chapter 25). The United States actively recruited Mexican workers during World War II, and many European nations promoted guest worker programs and other inducements to immigration in the 1960s, when an expanding European economy experienced labor shortages. However, attitudes toward immigrants have changed as the size of immigrant populations has grown, particularly during periods of economic contraction like the recession that began in 2008. Under intense pressure, native-born workers demanded an end to immigration, seeing immigrants as competitors willing to work for lower wages and less likely to support labor unions.

High fertility among immigrants contributes to these tensions. Most immigrants are young adults who retain the positive attitudes toward early marriage and large families of their native cultures in Latin America, Africa, and the Middle East and have higher fertility rates than do host populations. Spain provides a useful example. In 2000 Spain had one of the world's lowest fertility rates, 1.2 births per woman. A member of the European Union, its economy was growing and employment opportunities were available to immigrants from Latin America, North Africa, and elsewhere. As a result, Spain briefly became the major immigrant-receiving nation in the European Union, and the immigrant component of Spain's population rose from 2.1 to 14.1 percent between 1990 and 2010. Because the birthrate of the immigrant population is twice as high as that of the native-born population, the effect of this trend has been multiplied, with foreign-born mothers accounting for 20 percent of all births. Since the beginning of the recession in 2008, immigration to Spain has slowed and birthrates of both native-born and foreign-born have fallen. But even in this altered context, immigrant groups continue to grow much faster than the native-born population. Similarly, as immigrant populations have increased across Europe and in the

United States in the twenty-first century, the resulting cultural conflicts have tested definitions of citizenship and nationality.

TECHNOLOGICAL AND ENVIRONMENTAL CHANGE

Technological innovation powered the economic expansion that began after World War II. New technologies increased productivity and disseminated human creativity. They also altered the way people lived, worked, and played. Because most of the economic benefits were initially concentrated in the advanced industrialized nations, technology increased the power of those nations relative to the developing world. This has changed in the last decade with globalization and the rising industrial role of China. Even within developed nations, postwar technological innovations did not benefit all classes, industries, and regions equally. There were losers as well as winners.

Population growth and increased levels of migration and urbanization multiplied the numbers of acres farmed and factories, intensifying environmental threats. In the early twenty-first century, loss of rain forest, soil erosion, global warming, air and water pollution, and extinction of species threatened the quality of life and the survival of human societies. Environmental protection, like the acquisition of new technology, had progressed most in societies with the greatest economic resources.

New Technologies and the World Economy   Nuclear energy, jet engines, radar, and tape recording were among the many World War II developments that later had an impact on consumers' lives. New technology increased industrial productivity, reduced labor requirements, and improved the flow of information that made markets more efficient. The consumer electronics industry rapidly developed new products, changes seen in the music industry's movement from vinyl records to 8-track tapes, CDs, and then MP3 technologies. Computers became faster and less expensive, cell phones were transformed into smartphones, and the speed of news and data accelerated at an unanticipated rate, transforming business, education, and politics globally.

Improvements in existing technologies accounted for much of the developed world's productivity increases during the 1950s and 1960s, as faster, more efficient transportation and communication cut costs and expanded markets. But new technologies were important as well. Governments bore much of the cost of developing and constructing nuclear power plants and sponsored research into new technologies. None has proved more influential in the last four decades than the computer, which transformed both work and leisure. The first computers were expensive, large, and slow, and only corporations, governments, and universities could afford them. Each new generation of computer has been smaller, faster, and less expensive. As a result, the serial utilization of desktops, laptops, tablets, and smartphones transformed commerce, education, and government. Today the computational capacity of a 1970s university mainframe computer can be found in the affordable and portable laptops of individual university students. The modern smartphone continues this pattern, serving as a platform for basic computing, search functions, and gaming as well as a sophisticated means of communication.

Computers also altered manufacturing. Small dedicated computers now control and monitor machinery in most modern industries. In the developed world, as well as in China and other fast-growing developing economies, factories forced by global competition to improve efficiency and product quality increasingly depend on robots. Japan's early lead in robotics in the 1990s has been reduced as Europe, the United States, and China have all raced to introduce robotics across their economies.

The transnational corporation became the primary agent for these technological changes. By the twentieth century the growing economic power of corporations in industrialized nations allowed them to invest directly in the mines, plantations, and public utilities of less developed regions. In the post–World War II years many of these companies became truly transnational, having multinational ownership and management. International trade agreements and open markets furthered the process. Ford, Nissan, BMW, and other car companies not only produced and sold cars internationally, but their shareholders, workers, and managers also came from numerous nations.

The location of manufacturing plants overseas and the acquisition of corporate operations by foreign buyers rendered such global firms as transnational as the products they sold. In the 1970s and 1980s American brand names like Levi's, Coca-Cola, Marlboro, Gillette, McDonald's, and Kentucky Fried Chicken were global phenomena. But in time Asian names—Honda, Hitachi, Sony, Sanyo, and Mitsubishi—were blazoned in neon and on giant video screens on the sides of skyscrapers, along with European brands such as Nestlé, Mercedes, Pirelli, and Benetton. Since 1979, China's emergence as a global industrial power has accelerated this process of integration and diffusion.

As transnational manufacturers, agricultural conglomerates, and financial giants became wealthier and more powerful, they increasingly escaped the controls imposed by national governments. If labor costs were too high in Japan, antipollution measures too intrusive in the United States, or taxes too high in Great Britain, transnational companies relocated—or threatened to do so. In 1945, for example, the U.S. textile industry was located in low-wage southern states, dominating the American market and exporting to the world. As wages in the American South rose and global competition increased, producers began relocating plants to Puerto Rico in the 1980s and to Mexico after NAFTA went into effect in 1994 (see Chapter 33). Now China is the primary manufacturer of textiles.

Conserving and Sharing Resources   In the 1960s environmental activists and political leaders began warning about the devastating environmental consequences of population growth, industrialization, and the expansion of agriculture onto marginal lands. Assaults on rain forests, the disappearance of species, and the poisoning of streams and rivers raised public consciousness, as did the depletion and pollution of the world's oceans. Environmental damage occurred both in the advanced industrial economies and in developing nations. The former Soviet Union, where industrial and nuclear wastes were routinely dumped with little concern for environmental consequences, had the worst environmental record.

In the developed world, industrial activity increased much more rapidly than the population grew, and the consumption of energy (coal, electricity, and petroleum) rose proportionally. This pattern is now clear in India, China, and other industrializing nations as well. Indeed, the consumer-driven economic expansion of the post–World War II years became an obstacle to addressing environmental problems, since modern economies depend on a profligate consumption of goods and resources. When consumption slows, industrial nations enter a recession, as recently demonstrated in 2008. How could the United States, Germany, Japan, or China change consumption patterns to protect the environment without endangering corporate profits, wages, and employment levels?

Since 1945 population growth has been most dramatic in the developing countries, where environmental pressures have also been extreme. In Brazil, India, and China, for example, the need to expand food production led to rapid deforestation and the extension of farming and grazing onto marginal lands. The results were predictable: erosion and water pollution. These and many other poor nations sought to stimulate industrialization because they believed that the transition from agriculture to manufacturing was the only way to provide for their rapidly growing populations. The argument was compelling: Why should Indians or Brazilians remain poor while Americans, Europeans, and Japanese grew rich?

Responding to Environmental Threats   Despite the gravity of environmental threats, there were many successful efforts to preserve and protect the environment. The Clean Air Act, the Clean Water Act, and the Endangered Species Act were passed in the United States in the 1970s as part of an environmental effort that included the nations of the European Community and Japan. Grassroots political movements and the media encouraged environmental awareness, and most nations in the developed world enforced strict antipollution laws and sponsored massive recycling efforts. Many also encouraged resource conservation by rewarding energy-efficient factories and manufacturers of fuel-efficient cars and by promoting the use of alternative energy sources such as solar and wind power.

Environmental efforts produced significant results. In western Europe and the United States, air quality improved dramatically. Smog levels in the United States fell nearly a third from 1970 to 2000, even though the number of automobiles increased more than 80 percent. Emissions of lead and sulfur dioxide were down as well. The Great Lakes, Long Island Sound, and Chesapeake Bay were all much cleaner at the beginning of the new century than they had been in 1970.

New technologies made much of the improvement possible; for example, pollution controls on automobiles, planes, and factory smokestacks reduced harmful emissions. At the same time, the desire to preserve the natural environment was growing around the world. In developed nations continued political organization and enhanced awareness of environmental issues seemed likely to lead to step-by-step improvements in environmental policy. In the developing world and most of the former Soviet bloc, however, population pressures and weak governments were major obstacles to effective environmental policies. Since the 1990s the rapid expansion of China's industrial sector as well as industrial growth in other developing nations like India and Brazil has put additional pressure on the environment.

It now seems likely that industrialized nations will have to fund global improvements and that the cost will be high. Slow growth and fiscal crises in the mature industrial economies after the 2008 recession have politicized and slowed the progress of environmental reform. Nevertheless, growing evidence of environmental degradation and global warming have continued to propel popular reform efforts, as when the media drew attention to the precipitous shrinkage of Peru's Andean glaciers and to loss of rain forest in Brazil. Yet, without broad agreement among the rich nations, the economic and political power necessary for environmental protections on a global scale will be very difficult to institute. When representatives from around the world negotiated a far-reaching treaty to reduce greenhouse gases in Kyoto, Japan, in 1997, President George W. Bush refused American participation even though the treaty was affirmed by nearly all other industrial nations. Canada subsequently withdrew from the agreement, and China and other rapidly industrializing nations were largely exempted from the treaty's limits. This agreement, as a result, has had a limited effect on greenhouse gas emissions.

CONCLUSION

The world was profoundly altered between 1975 and the first decade of the twenty-first century. Both the United States and the Soviet Union feared that every conflict and every regime change represented a potential threat to their strategic interests, and every conflict threatened to provoke confrontation between them. As a result, the superpowers inserted themselves into a succession of civil wars and revolutions. The costs in lives and property were terrible, the gains small. As defense costs escalated, the Soviet system crumbled. By 1991 the Soviet Union and the socialist Warsaw Pact had disappeared, transforming the international stage.

The world was also altered by economic growth and globalization, by population growth and movement, and by technological and environmental change. Led by the postwar recovery of the industrial powers and the remarkable economic expansion of Japan, the Asian Tigers, and more recently China, the world economy grew dramatically until the global recession of 2008. The development and application of new technology contributed significantly to this process. International markets were more open and integrated than at any other time. However, not all the nations of the world benefited from the new wealth and exciting technologies of the postwar era. The capitalist West and a handful of Asian nations grew richer and more powerful, while most of the world's nations remained poor.

Population growth in the developing world was one reason for this divided experience. Despite falling birthrates in many poor countries, most of the world's population growth in recent decades is in developing nations with limited economic growth. Unable to find adequate employment or, in many cases, bare subsistence, people in developing nations have migrated across international borders, hoping to improve their lives. These movements have often provided valuable labor in the factories and farms of the developed world, but they have also provoked cultural, racial, and ethnic tension. Problems of inequality, population growth, and international migration will continue to challenge the global community in the coming decades.

Growing population and the development process have forced marginal lands into production and stimulated the exploitation of new resources. The need to feed a rapidly growing world population has also pressured ocean resources. As the world's population surpassed 6 billion and the largest cities reached 20 million, the need to produce and deliver raw materials and finished goods has put tremendous stress on the environment. In the 1990s the rapid development of the Chinese and Indian economies compounded these pressures.

At the same time, new technologies and the wealth produced by economic expansion have allowed the world's richest nations to implement ambitious programs of environmental protection. As a result, pollution produced by automobiles and factories has actually declined in the richest nations. The question that remains is whether rapidly developing nations, such as Brazil, China, and India, will move more quickly than the mature industrial nations did to introduce these new technologies.

IMPORTANT EVENTS 1970–2000

1970	Salvador Allende elected president of Chile
1973	Allende overthrown
1975	Vietnam War ends
1976	Military takeover in Argentina
1978	USSR sends troops to Afghanistan
1979	Sandinistas overthrow Anastasio Somoza in Nicaragua
1979	Shah of Iran overthrown in Islamic Revolution
1979	China begins economic reforms
1980–1988	Iran-Iraq War
1983–1990	Democracy returns in Argentina, Brazil, and Chile
1985	Mikhail Gorbachev becomes Soviet head of state
1986	Average Japanese income overtakes income in United States
1989	United States invades Panama
1989	USSR withdraws from Afghanistan
1989	Tiananmen Square confrontation
1989	Berlin Wall falls

1989–1991	Communism ends in eastern Europe
1990	Sandinistas defeated in elections in Nicaragua
1990	Iraq invades Kuwait
1990	Reunification of Germany
1990s	Japanese recession
1991	Persian Gulf War
1992	Yugoslavia disintegrates; Croatia and Slovenia become independent nations

33

NEW CHALLENGES
IN A NEW MILLENNIUM

The workday began normally at the World Trade Center in lower Manhattan on the morning of September 11, 2001. The 50,000 people who worked there were making their way to the two 110-story towers. Suddenly, at 8:46 A.M., an American Airlines Boeing 767 with 92 people on board, traveling at a speed of 470 miles per hour (756 kilometers per hour), crashed into floors 94 to 98 of the north tower, igniting the 10,000 gallons (38,000 liters) of fuel in its tanks. Just before 9:03 A.M. a United Airlines flight with 65 people on board and a similar fuel load hit floors 78 to 84 of the south tower.

As the burning jet fuel engulfed the collision areas, the buildings' occupants struggled through smoke-filled corridors and down dozens of flights of stairs. Many of those trapped above the crash sites used cell phones to say good-bye to loved ones. Rather than endure the flames and fumes, a few jumped to their deaths.

Just before 10 o'clock, temperatures that had risen to 2,3008 Fahrenheit (1,2608 Celsius) caused the steel girders in the impacted area of the south tower to give way. The collapsing upper floors crushed the floors underneath one by one, engulfing lower Manhattan in a dense cloud of dust. Twenty-eight minutes later the north tower pancaked in a similar manner. Miraculously, most of the buildings' occupants had escaped before the towers collapsed. Besides the people on the planes, nearly 2,600 lost their lives, including some 400 police officers and firefighters helping in the evacuation.

That same morning another American Airlines jet crashed into the Pentagon, killing all 64 people on board and 125 others inside the military complex near Washington, D.C. Passengers on a fourth plane managed to overpower their hijackers, and the plane crashed in rural Pennsylvania, killing all 45 on board.

The four planes had been hijacked by teams of Middle Eastern men who slit the throats of service and flight personnel and seized control. Of the nineteen hijackers, fifteen were from Saudi Arabia. All had links to an extremist Islamic organization, al-Qaeda (ahl-KAW-eh-duh) (the base or foundation), commanded by a rich Saudi named Usama bin Laden (oo-SAH-mah bin LAH-din), who was incensed with American political, military, and cultural influence in the Middle East. The men were educated and well traveled, had lived in the United States, and spoke English. Some had trained as pilots so that they could fly the hijacked aircraft.

The hijackers left few records of their motives, but the acts spoke for themselves. The World Trade Center was a focal point of international business, the Pentagon the headquarters of the American military. The fourth plane was probably meant to hit the Capitol or the White House, the legislative and executive centers of the world's only superpower.

The events of September 11, which became commonly referred to as 9/11, can be understood on many levels. The hijackers and those who sympathized with them saw themselves as engaged in a holy struggle against economic, political, and military institutions they believed to be evil. People directly affected, political leaders around the world, and most television watchers described the attacks as evil deeds against innocent victims.

To understand why the nineteen attackers were heroes to some and terrorists to others, one needs to explore the historical context of global changes at the turn of the millennium and the ideological tensions they have generated. The unique prominence of the United States in every major aspect of global integration, as well as its support for pro-American governments overseas, also elicits sharply divergent views.

GLOBALIZATION AND ECONOMIC CRISIS

The turn of the millennium saw the intensification of **globalization** trends that had been building since the 1970s. Growing trade and travel and new technologies were bringing all parts of the world into closer economic, political, and cultural integration and interaction. The collapse of the Soviet Union had completed the dissolution of territorial empires that had been under way throughout the twentieth century. Autonomous national states (numbering about two hundred) became an almost universal norm, and a growing number of them had embraced democratic institutions. However, increasing interdependency would also facilitate a global economic crisis that exploded in 2008 when the massive accumulation of debt in American financial institutions became unsustainable.

An Interconnected Economy   The expansion of trade, global interconnections, and privatization of government enterprises that gained momentum with the dismantling of Soviet-style socialist economies in the 1990s cooled abruptly in the wake of 9/11. The rate of growth in world trade fell from 13 percent in 2000 to only 1 percent in 2001.

Growth in China and India resumed quickly, however, and the large populations of these two countries marked them as future world economic powers. Their growth increased pressure on world energy supplies, though the United States continued to consume a quarter of the world's petroleum production and by

2013 had resumed its position of world's largest producer through the production of oil derived from shale deposits. OPEC's manipulation of world oil prices, combined with political instability in the Middle East, had caused crude oil prices to soar between 1973 and 1985. But aside from those years, the average price of oil remained consistently below $20 per barrel (adjusted for inflation) throughout the second half of the twentieth century. In the year 2000, however, oil prices began a new period of increase caused not by OPEC but by rising demand and confidence in the fevered pace of world economic expansion. By the middle of 2006, the price of a barrel of crude had crept past $70, and in 2008 it spiked to $145 a barrel. This increase fueled ambitious economic programs in producing countries like Russia, Venezuela, Iran, Saudi Arabia, and the small sheikhdoms of the Persian Gulf, as well as in the newer OPEC states Ecuador, Nigeria, and Angola. With the economic crisis of 2008, prices fell abruptly, but by 2013 the price per barrel was back in the $90–$100 range.

Regional trade associations came into being to promote growth, reduce the economic vulnerability of member states, and, less explicitly, balance American economic dominance. The twenty-seven-member European Union (EU) was the most successful. The euro, a common currency inaugurated in 2002 and used in twelve member states, competed with the U.S. dollar for investment and banking. However, unequal levels of development among members became a source of crisis in 2009 as the world economic downturn devastated stock markets and increased rates of unemployment. Countries like Greece that had taken on more debt than the revenues produced by their shrunken economies could cover sought assistance from the rest of the EU, but the wealthier countries, led by Germany, proved reluctant to rescue them. Instead they urged an austerity program of radical cutbacks in public expenditures, which increased unemployment and popular discontent. The idea of the euro, a common currency that symbolized Europe's progress toward unity, also came into question because countries belonging to the euro zone were not at liberty to devalue their currency and thereby reduce their debt burdens. In an increasingly globalized network of financial markets and institutions, Europe's recurrent debt crises generated economic anxiety from Japan to New York City.

Despite the EU's expansion, the North American Free Trade Agreement (NAFTA), which eliminated tariffs among the United States, Canada, and Mexico in 1994, governed the world's largest free-trade zone. Yet heated debate in the United States over illegal immigration across the Mexican border, as well anti-Hispanic prejudice, limited popular enthusiasm for the agreement. The third largest free-trade zone, Mercosur, created by Argentina, Brazil, Paraguay (now suspended), and Uruguay in 1991 and subsequently expanded to include Venezuela and Bolivia,, visualized a parliament consisting of eighteen representatives from each member state. Other free-trade associations operated in West Africa, southern Africa, Southeast Asia, Central America, the Pacific Basin, and the Caribbean.

The Shanghai Cooperation Organization (SCO), formed in 2001 with China, Russia, and four former Soviet Central Asian republics as members, originally pursued common security interests, such as combating separatist movements and terrorism. But the organization's five observer members—Iran, India, Pakistan,

Jorge Ferrari/epa/Corbis Sygma

Palm Island, Dubai *The seemingly unlimited wealth of the oil producing states of the Persian Gulf spurred ambitious development plans like this one in Dubai, one of the United Arab Emirates. Its publicists proclaimed that "Palm Island" would include 2,000 villas, up to 40 luxury hotels, shopping complexes, cinemas, and the Middle East's "first marine park" and would be "visible from the moon."*

Afghanistan, and Mongolia—the first a major oil exporter and the last two possessing huge unexploited mineral deposits, also lent credence to its twenty-year-plan for reducing barriers to trade and population movement. Iran's application for membership, formally made in 2008, has been held up by international pressure. U.S.-led international sanctions designed to curb Iran's nuclear program have encountered resistance from both Russia and China, but the SCO has a rule barring countries subjected to sanctions from membership.

In 1995 the world's major traders established the **World Trade Organization (WTO)**, dedicated to reducing barriers and enforcing international agreements. With the accession of Russia as its 157th member in 2012, the largest economy not to be included was Iran. The WTO had many critics and regularly encountered street protests during its ministerial meetings. Some protesters claimed that the organization's idea of free trade enabled low-cost foreign manufacturers to attract business and shrink the job opportunities in richer states; others demanded continuing tariff protection for local farmers.

Global Financial Crisis   The global financial crisis that began in 2008 had complicated roots. During an Asian financial crisis a decade earlier, vast amounts of European and American investment in Thailand, Indonesia, South Korea, and other East Asian countries had

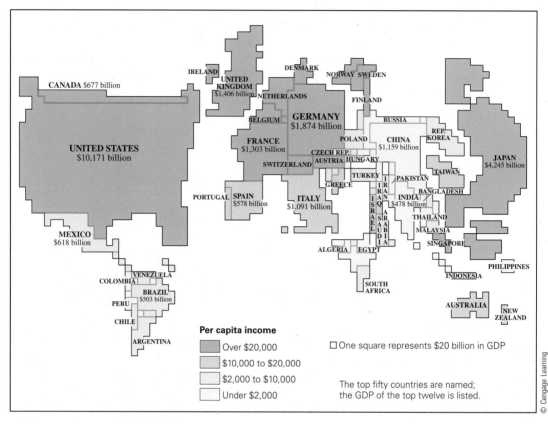

MAP 33.1 Global Distribution of Wealth

Early industrialization and efficient investment contributed to individual prosperity to the citizens of Japan and Western countries by the 1990s. However, economic dynamism in late-industrializing countries like China and India began to change the world balance of economic power in the early twenty-first century. In nearly all countries the distribution of wealth among individuals varies tremendously, with the gap between rich and poor generally increasing.

created an illusion of great economic dynamism. However, in 1997 the investment boom burst, leading to a severe economic downturn in the region. When economic stability returned, greater investor caution reversed the flow of money. The United States in particular became a favorite place to invest, helping spur a rapid increase in stock market and housing prices and massive growth in the purchase of imported goods. Seeing the value their houses increase at an unprecedented rate, Americans became wedded to borrowing money with their homes as collateral. Money from overseas invested in the U.S. treasury also made it possible for the United States to fight wars in Afghanistan and Iraq (see below) while lowering taxes. The American national debt climbed dramatically.

In 2008 the fevered boom in housing prices collapsed, leaving many homeowners so deeply in debt on their mortgages that they lost their homes. Their mortgage debts, however, were no longer being held by a local bank in the traditional fashion. New and risky lending techniques based on homeowners' assumptions that home prices would continue to rise indefinitely had caused the bad debts to be distributed throughout the banking system, not just in the United States but around the world. Similar housing speculation occurred in Spain and other countries. When Lehman Brothers, one of the country's foremost financial firms, declared bankruptcy in September, a recession turned into a catastrophic economic downturn. Stock prices fell, banks teetered on the brink of collapse, and unemployment climbed as employers laid off workers they could no longer afford or did not need as consumer demand plummeted. The effects spread worldwide. Knowledgeable political leaders and economists proclaimed it the worst economic crisis since the Great Depression of the 1930s.

The sense that Barack Obama had a firm understanding of the crisis and the ability to lead the country out of it contributed to his election as president. During the first weeks after he took office in January 2009, he proposed a series of steps, including massive increases in government spending, to jolt the economy back to health. Some of the plans yielded fruit, such as a rescue of

Unemployment Protest *Recovery from the job losses of the economic recession of 2008 proved particularly slow. In the United States, banks and businesses returned to profitability but found they did not need so many workers. In Spain, Greece, and other parts of Europe, the unemployment rate was triple that of the United States in 2013, sometimes fueling the growth of radical and anti-immigrant political movements.*

the American automobile industry. Others were stymied after 2010, however, when Republicans who felt national debt and government budget deficits were more important than unemployment took over the House of Representatives. The legislative deadlock that ensued curbed administration plans to address unemployment through increased government spending, but Republican sponsorship of tax and governmental budget cuts failed to attract enough voters to prevent Barack Obama from being reelected in 2012. Economic recovery remained slow and fragile. In both the United States and the European Union, the trade expansion that had signaled the promise of globalization at the beginning of the century faded from memory, and the interdependence that had bound the world's economies in a cycle of growth became a dead weight that dragged many countries down.

Globalization and Democracy   The last decades of the twentieth century saw expansions of democratic institutions and personal freedom. People in many countries recognized that elections offered a peaceful way to settle differences among a country's social classes, cultural groups, and regions. Although majority votes could swing from one part of the political spectrum to another, democracies tended to encourage political moderation. Moreover, wars between fully democratic states were extremely rare.

The nations of eastern Europe embraced democracy after the fall of the Soviet Union, though some newly democratic states became subject to great mood swings among the electorate. The shift to private ownership of businesses after decades of rigid state control brought riches to a select few, and the removal of trade barriers characteristic of Cold War rivalry opened up new markets and fostered investment from the West.

By 2008, however, rising unemployment and falling export levels and stock prices threatened these experiments in free elections and free markets. In Russia, the popular but somewhat authoritarian leader Vladimir Putin followed his country's constitution by stepping down in 2008 after two terms as president. However, he engineered the election of his protégé Dimitri Medvedev as his successor, took the office of prime minister for himself, and then was elected to a new presidential term in 2012. These moves led some political thinkers to fear a possible return to Soviet-era Russian domination.

Asian democracies proved somewhat more stable. Beginning with free parliamentary elections in 1999, the populous state of Indonesia moved from years of authoritarian and corrupt rule toward more open political institutions. The following years saw a violent independence movement of the Acheh (ah-CHEH) district of northern Sumatra, the secession in 2002 of East Timor after years of brutal Indonesian military occupation, terrorist bombings on the island of Bali in 2004, and a devastating earthquake and tsunami in the same year. But democratic elections were regularly held. The losing candidates left office peacefully, and the populace at large accepted the results.

Myanmar (formerly Burma), where stifling military governments had held sway since 1962, experienced a rapid move toward democracy after free elections were held in 2010. The following year the military junta was dissolved, and the formerly banned opposition party led by the female Nobel Peace Prize winner Aung San Suu Kyi (owng SAHN soo chi) gained a significant role in parliament.

In India a major political shift seemed to be at hand in 1998 when the Bharatiya Janata Party (BJP) secured an electoral victory that interrupted four decades of Congress Party rule. The BJP success came through blatant appeals to Hindu nationalism, the condoning of violence against India's Muslims, and opposition to the social and economic progress of the Untouchables (those traditionally confined to the dirtiest jobs). In 2004, however, the Congress Party returned to power and governmental stability proved strong even in the face of sensational terrorist attacks in Mumbai by Pakistani gunmen in 2008.

Democracy in Pakistan itself proved more uncertain. President and former military commander Pervez Musharraf's (pair-VEZ moo-SHAH-ref) abrupt firing of the country's chief justice, combined with his unpopular support of the Bush administration's war policies, sparked protests and calls for impeachment. He resigned the presidency in 2008. Asif Ali Zardari (AH-sef AH-lee zar-DAH-ree), who succeeded him, had inherited the leadership of the majority Pakistan People's Party after the assassination the year before of his charismatic wife Benazir Bhutto, the daughter of a popular earlier prime minister. Zardari faced difficulties forming a strong government because of the growing movement of the Pakistani Taliban to impose their own governance and a rigid Muslim behavioral code in outlying districts, as well as popular opposition to American antiterrorist attacks launched from Afghanistan. In 2013 he was succeeded by his long-time rival Nawaz Sharif.

In sub-Saharan Africa, democracy had mixed results. Nelson Mandela, the leader of the African National Congress (ANC) who had become the first post-apartheid president of South Africa in 1994 (see Chapters 31 and 32), left office in 1999 and was succeeded by the deputy president and ANC leader Thabo Mbeki (TAA-boh um-BEH-kee). Mbeki stepped down in 2008 amidst turmoil in the leadership of the ANC. But the democratic system did not seem threatened. Elsewhere some elected leaders, such as Robert Mugabe (moo-GAH-bay) in Zimbabwe, used violence and intimidation to hold on to power, and other states, such as Congo, were plagued with internal revolts and civil wars. Liberians emerged from fourteen years of civil war in 2003 and two years later chose Ellen Johnson-Sirleaf (SUHR-leef) to be Africa's first elected female head of state. In Sudan, the general who had led a military coup in 1989, Omar al-Bashir, became the first sitting head of state to be charged with genocide and crimes against humanity by the International Criminal Court in 2009. A festering conflict in Darfur in western Sudan, which had then cost hundreds of thousands of lives and displaced over 2 million people, was at the heart of the charges. However, a long rebellion in the south finally came to an end in 2011 with the creation of a new country with a democratic constitution, the Republic of South Sudan.

In the Arab world, a rash of popular demonstrations starting at the end of 2010 led to the "Arab Spring," an anti-authoritarian political current that toppled the rulers of Tunisia, Libya, Egypt, and Yemen and plunged Syria into a grinding civil war. Though not the instigators of the demonstrations, previously suppressed Muslim political parties like Egypt's Muslim Brotherhood emerged as the best-organized contenders as shaky democratic regimes struggled into being.

Regime Change in Iraq and Afghanistan   The most closely watched experiments in democratization took place in Iraq and Afghanistan, countries that the United States invaded after the terrorist attacks of 9/11. Afghanistan's provision of a safe haven for Usama bin Laden and his al-Qaeda organization gave clear justification for the overthrow in December 2001 of the militantly religious Taliban regime. However, the rationale for invading Iraq was less persuasive. Leading up to the war the American government contended that Iraq was a clear and present danger to the United States because it possessed **weapons of mass destruction** (WMDs): nuclear, chemical, and biological weapons that it might supply to terrorists like bin Laden.

When United Nations inspectors failed to find any banned weapons, a split widened between those nations wanting to continue inspections and those, led by the United States, wanting to intervene militarily. Deciding to go it alone, an American-led "coalition of the willing" opened the invasion of Iraq with a spectacular aerial bombardment of Baghdad on March 20, 2003. Twenty-five days later the United States declared that "major fighting" had ended, little realizing that guerrilla insurgency, sectarian violence, and economic devastation would continue for years.

AP Photos/Khalil Hamra

Arab Spring Demonstrators *Part of the enormous crowds that unseated the rulers of Egypt, Tunisia, Libya, and Yemen, these women in Cairo's Tahrir Square wear the colorful head scarves that are commonplace in Egypt, sometimes to demonstrate allegiance to Islam and sometimes because they are stylish.*

Though Iraq fell into a state of turmoil because the coalition army was too small or otherwise unprepared to prevent the looting and destruction of government facilities and other lawlessness, a thorough search was launched for WMDs. The search came up empty, and intelligence analyses failed to uncover any evidence that Saddam Hussein, Iraq's fallen dictator, had played a role in the 9/11 attacks. American troops finally withdrew from the country in 2010, leaving behind a government elected under a new constitution adopted in 2006 but nevertheless divided by strong animosity between a Shi'ite majority and separate Arab and Kurdish Sunni minorities.

American concern for WMDs was not confined to Iraq. North Korea had an open program to build nuclear weapons, and Iran was suspected of having a covert plan based in part on technological aid secretly given by the head of Pakistan's successful nuclear program. Iran's outspokenly anti-American and anti-Israeli president, Mahmoud Ahmedinejad, who served from 2005 to 2013, and North Korea's dictator Kim Jong-il (kim jong-ill) presented the United States with difficult challenges. But the military invasion option chosen for Iraq, though favored by some Bush advisers, was held in abeyance in favor of diplomatic initiatives that continued into Obama's second term in office.

Iran's challenge to America's hopes for a democratic reshaping of the Middle East took a step forward in 2005 when the Lebanese Shi'ite movement Hezbollah captured 23 out of 128 seats in the Lebanese parliament; then in 2006 the militantly anti-Israeli Hamas movement won an absolute majority of the vote in elections for the Palestine Governing Authority. Both groups were firmly allied with Iran. Attacks launched by Israel against both Hamas and Hezbollah in response to kidnappings of Israeli soldiers in 2006 suggested that Israeli fear of Islamic movements, and of Iran, might someday become more consequential than Arab world democratization, particularly if Iran should acquire a nuclear weapon.

In 2007 the elected Hamas government succeeded in driving its Palestinian rivals out of the Gaza Strip. During the following months, largely inaccurate rocket barrages launched from there against Israel became a major factor in Israeli politics. A security barrier built on the West Bank had almost eliminated attacks by Palestinian suicide bombers, but the rockets provoked public outrage even though the number of casualties was very small. During the final month of the manifestly pro-Israeli Bush administration, the Israel Defense Force undertook to deal once and for all with Hamas in the Gaza Strip. Aerial bombardments and ground force incursions left well over a thousand Palestinians dead, while Israeli casualties were negligible. However, there was no sign that Hamas had been seriously harmed as a political organization. Indeed, in 2012 a renewed exchange of Hamas rockets and Israeli air strikes showed the persistence of the stalemate in Gaza. Worldwide reactions to these events engendered sufficient criticism of Israel that a resolution in the United Nations General Assembly to grant the Palestinian Governing Authority enhanced observer status saw only one major nation, Canada, vote no along with the United States and Israel.

American hopes for democratization also were disappointed in Afghanistan. The Afghan government elected with enthusiastic American support in 2004 proved corrupt and uncooperative and did not extend over the entire country. By 2008 the Taliban were again a serious threat, and opium production, the key to the country's unrest, was higher than ever. Though the United States was able to enlist the participation of NATO forces in helping to police Afghanistan, the prospects for the country were so dim that President Barack Obama made intensification of efforts to bring peace and stability and suppress terrorism a key part of his foreign policy while at the same time promising to withdraw American troops by the end of 2014.

THE QUESTION OF VALUES

As people around the world first faced the opportunities of globalization and then the fear of global recession, they tried to make sense of these changes in terms of their own value systems. With 7 billion people, the world was big enough to include many different approaches, whether religious or secular, local or international, traditional or visionary. In some cases, however, conflicting visions fed violence.

Faith and Politics   Religious beliefs increasingly inspired political actions during the second half of the twentieth century, and the trend intensified in the new century. Though for Americans this change reversed two centuries of growing secularism, Western analysts did not agree on the cause of the religious revival.

Evangelical Protestants became a powerful conservative political force in the United States, particularly during the Bush presidency. Around the world, Catholic conservatives led by Pope John Paul II, Pope Benedict XVI, and Pope Francis who succeeded to the post in 2013 after Benedict's retirement, forcefully reiterated politically sensitive teachings: opposition to abortion, homosexuality, marriage of priests, and admission of women to the priesthood. In Israel, hyperorthodox Jews known as *haredim* played a leading role in settling the Palestinian territories captured by Israel in 1967 and vehemently resisted both Israel's unilateral withdrawal from Gaza in 2005 and subsequent plans for withdrawal from the West Bank. And in India, Hindu zealots made the BJP party a powerful political force.

Yet most discussions of faith and politics focused on Islam. The birth of the Islamic Republic of Iran in the revolution of 1979 made visible a current of Muslim political assertiveness that had been building there for twenty-five years. By the year 2000, however, non-Iranian Muslim groups claiming to be acting for religious reasons were capturing the headlines with acts of **terrorism**.

Terrorism is a political tactic by which comparatively weak militants use grotesquely inhumane and lethal acts to convince a frightened public that danger is everywhere and their government is incapable of protecting them. Although terrorism has a long history, the instantaneous media links made possible by satellite communications, and the tradition in the news business of publicizing violence, increased its effectiveness from the 1980s onward.

Bombings, kidnappings, and assassinations made political sense to all sorts of political groups: secular Palestinians confronting Israel; national separatists like the Tamils in Sri Lanka, Basques in Spain, and Chechens in Russia; and Catholic and Protestant extremists in Northern Ireland, to name a few. But Muslim groups gained the lion's share of attention when they targeted the United States and Europe, recruited from Muslim populations all over the world, and made effective use of news coverage and audiovisual communications.

Their media star and ideological spokesman was **Usama bin Laden**. Born into a wealthy Saudi family and educated as an engineer, bin Laden fought against the Soviet Union in Afghanistan and there recruited and trained a core group of fighters called al-Qaeda. Though his family disowned him and Saudi Arabia stripped him of his citizenship, his calls for holy war (*jihad*) and his portrayal of the United States as a puppet-master manipulating both non-Muslim (e.g., Israel, India, Russia) and Muslim (e.g., Egypt, Algeria, Saudi Arabia) governments to murder and oppress innocent Muslims made sense to millions of Muslims, even if only a very few committed themselves to follow him into battle.

Al-Qaeda blew up American embassies in Kenya and Tanzania in 1998, crippled the U.S. Navy destroyer *Cole* during a port call in Yemen in 2000, and then capped everything by attacking the World Trade Center and the Pentagon on 9/11. When the "global war on terrorism" declared by President Bush failed to eliminate bin Laden, his mystique grew. Further terrorist attacks—by Indonesians on tourists on the island of Bali in 2002, by North Africans on commuter trains servicing Madrid in 2004, by English-born Muslims on the London transit system in 2005, and by Pakistanis on luxury hotels in Mumbai, India, in 2008—made it clear that the current of violence unleashed by al-Qaeda had become decentralized and that recruits and cells might no longer be taking orders from bin Laden. Even after an American commando operation killed bin Laden in his hideout in Pakistan in 2011, groups affiliated with al-Qaeda continued to operate in Yemen, Libya, and Mali. In response, the United States expanded its use of pilotless drone aircraft to kill suspected terrorists from afar.

In trying to explain a current of violence that could strike anywhere in the world but seemed to be centered on Muslims, some analysts argued that Islam itself encouraged violence against non-Muslims. The counterargument pointed out that terrorists came from many backgrounds and that the vast majority of Muslims saw their religion as one of peace. Others maintained that rigidly conservative Muslims were blindly opposed to freedom and modernity. The counterargument pointed out that al-Qaeda used modern military and propaganda techniques and that many of its operatives, like bin Laden himself, graduated from modern technical programs. A third school of thought felt that the United States instigated al-Qaeda's wrath by supporting Israel and stationing troops in Saudi Arabia. The counterargument pointed out that the United

States had also championed the Muslim cause in Bosnia, driven the secular dictator Saddam Hussein out of Kuwait, and supported the popular uprisings of the Arab Spring.

Universal Rights and Values   Alongside the growing influence of religion on politics, efforts to promote adherence to universal human rights also expanded. The modern human rights movement grew out of secular statements like the French Declaration of the Rights of Man (1789) and the U.S. Constitution (1788) and Bill of Rights (1791). The **Universal Declaration of Human Rights**, passed by the United Nations General Assembly in 1948, culminated this movement by proclaiming itself "a common standard of achievement for all peoples and nations." Its thirty articles condemned slavery, torture, cruel and inhuman punishment, and arbitrary arrest, detention, and exile. The Declaration called for freedom of movement, assembly, and thought. It asserted rights to life, liberty, and security of person; to impartial public trials; and to education, employment, and leisure. The principle of equality was most fully articulated in Article 2:

> *Everyone is entitled to all the rights and freedoms set forth in this Declaration, without distinction of any kind, such as race, color, sex, language, religion, or political or other opinion, national or social origin, property, birth or other status.*[1]

This passage reflected an international consensus against racism and imperialism and a growing acceptance of the importance of social and economic equality. Most newly independent countries joining the United Nations willingly signed the Declaration because it implicitly condemned European colonial regimes.

Besides the official actions of the United Nations and various national governments, individual human rights activists, often working through philanthropic bodies known as **nongovernmental organizations (NGOs)**, have been important forces promoting human rights. Amnesty International, founded in 1961, concentrates on gaining the freedom of people who have been tortured or imprisoned without trial and campaigns against summary execution by government death squads or other gross violations of rights. Arguing that no right is more fundamental than the right to life, other NGOs have devoted themselves to famine relief, refugee assistance, and health care around the world. Médecins Sans Frontières (Doctors Without Borders), founded in 1971, was awarded the Nobel Peace Prize in 1999 for offering medical assistance in scores of crises.

While NGOs often worked in specific countries, other universal goals became enshrined in international agreements. Such agreements made genocide a crime

---

[1]"Universal Declaration of Human Rights," in *Twenty-five Human Rights Documents* (New York: Center for the Study of Human Rights, Columbia University, 1994), 6.

and promoted environmental protection of the seas, of Antarctica, and of the atmosphere (see Environment and Technology: Global Warming). The United States and a few other nations were greatly concerned that such treaties would limit their sovereignty or threaten their national interests. For this reason the U.S. Congress delayed ratifying the 1949 convention on genocide until 1986. More recently the United States drew widespread criticism for demanding exemption for Americans from the jurisdiction of the International Criminal Court, created in 2002 to try international criminals, and for declaring that "enemy combatants" taken prisoner during the "global war on terrorism" should not be treated in accordance with the Third Geneva Convention (1950) on humane treatment of prisoners of war.

Women's Rights   The women's rights movement, which began on both sides of the North Atlantic in the nineteenth century, became an important human rights issue in the twentieth century. Rights for women became accepted in Western countries and were enshrined in the constitutions of many nations newly freed from colonial rule. In 1979 the United Nations General Assembly adopted the Convention on the Elimination of All Forms of Discrimination Against Women, and in 1985 the first international conference on the status of women, sponsored by the United Nations Division for the Advancement of Women, was held in Nairobi, Kenya. A second conference in Beijing ten years later added momentum to the movement. By 2012, all but seven UN member countries—Iran, Palau, Somalia, Sudan, South Sudan, Tonga, and the United States—had ratified the convention, though the United States and Palau had signed it without ratification.

Besides highlighting the problems women face around the world, international conferences have also revealed great variety in the views and concerns of women. Feminists from the West, who had been accustomed to dictating the agenda and who had pushed for the liberation of women in other parts of the world, sometimes found themselves accused of having narrow concerns and condescending attitudes. Some non-Western women complained about Western feminists' endorsement of sexual liberation and about the deterioration of family life in the West. They found Western feminists' concern with matters such as comfortable clothing misplaced and trivial compared to the issues of poverty and disease.

Other cultures came in for their share of criticism. Western women and many secular leaders in Muslim countries protested Islam's requirement that a woman cover her head and wear loose-fitting garments to conceal the shape of her body, practices enforced by law in countries such as Iran and Saudi Arabia. Nevertheless, many outspoken Muslim women voluntarily donned concealing garments as expressions of personal belief, statements of resistance to secular dictatorship, or defense against coarse male behavior.

The conferences were more important for the attention they focused on women's issues than for the solutions they generated. Such efforts raised the

ENVIRONMENT + TECHNOLOGY

Global Warming

Until the 1980s environmental alarms focused mainly on localized episodes of air and water pollution, exposure to toxic substances, waste management, and the disappearance of wilderness. The development of increasingly powerful computers and complex models of ecological interactions in the 1990s, however, made people aware of the global scope of certain environmental problems.

Many scientists and policymakers came to perceive global warming, the slow increase of the temperature of the earth's lower atmosphere, as an environmental threat requiring preventive action on an international scale. The warming is caused by a layer of atmospheric gases (carbon dioxide, methane, nitrous oxide, and ozone) that allow solar radiation to reach earth and warm it but that keep infrared energy (heat) from radiating from earth's surface back into space. Called the *greenhouse effect*, this process normally keeps the earth's temperature at a level suitable for life. However, increases in greenhouse-gas emissions—particularly from the burning of fossil fuels in industry and transportation—have added to this insulating atmospheric layer.

Recent events have confirmed predictions of global temperature increases and

melting glaciers and icecaps. Greenland glaciers and Arctic Ocean sea ice are melting at record rates, and huge sections of the Antarctic ice shelf are breaking off and floating away. Andean glaciers are shrinking so fast they could disappear in a decade, imperiling water supplies for drinking, irrigation, and hydroelectric production. Drought has affected much of the United States in recent years, and Australia has experienced the "Big Dry," its worst drought in a century.

Despite this evidence, governments of the industrialized countries that produce the most greenhouse gasses have been slow to adopt measures stringent enough to reduce emissions. They cite the negative effects they believe this could have on their economies. Because of these fears, many nations hesitated to sign the 1997 Kyoto Protocol, the first international agreement to impose penalties on countries that failed to cut greenhouse-gas emissions. It was a major environmental victory when Japan added its signature in March 2001, but to the consternation of many world leaders President George W. Bush rejected the agreement.

Shortly after being elected in 2008, Barack Obama announced to an audience of scientists and citizens concerned

prominence of human rights as a global concern and put pressure on governments to consider human rights when making foreign policy decisions. Skeptics observed, however, that a Western country might successfully prod a non-Western country to improve its human rights performance—for example, by granting women better access to education and careers—but that reverse criticism of a Western country often fell on deaf ears—for example, condemnation of the death penalty in the United States. For such critics the human rights movement was seen not as an effort to make the world more humane but as another form of Western cultural imperialism.

with climate matters: "You can be sure that the United States will once again engage vigorously in these negotiations, and help lead the world toward a new era of global cooperation on climate change." Yet when he ran for reelection in 2012, the issue of global warming, which his Republican opponents denied was a real phenomenon, played no role in his campaign. Ironically, a tropical superstorm named Sandy that dealt a devastating blow to New York and New Jersey just before the election seemed to vindicate the prediction that the increased energy in the atmosphere caused by global warming would produce severe weather anomalies around the world.

David Greedy/Getty Images

Flooding in Bangladesh *Typhoon-driven floods submerge the low-lying farmlands of Bangladesh with tragic regularity. Any significant rise in the sea level will make parts of the country nearly uninhabitable.*

GLOBAL CULTURE

Because of changes in electronic technology, today political and economic events have almost instantaneous impact in all parts of the world. A global language, a global educational system, and global forms of artistic expression have all come into being. Trade, travel, and migration have made a common popular culture unavoidable. These changes have delighted and enriched some but angered others.

The Media and the Message   The fact that the most pervasive elements of global culture have their origins in the West raised concerns in many quarters about **cultural imperialism**. Critics complained that entertainment conglomerates were flooding the world's movie theaters and television screens with Western images and that goods catering to Western tastes but manufactured in countries with low labor costs, like China and Indonesia, were flooding world markets. In this view, global marketing was especially insidious in trying to shape a world with a single Western outlook based on capitalist ideology, and at the same time suppressing or devaluing traditional cultures and alternative ideologies. As the leader of the capitalist world, the United States was seen as the primary culprit.

The pace of cultural globalization began to quicken during the economic recovery after World War II. The Hollywood films and American jazz recordings that had become popular in Europe and parts of Asia before the war (see Chapter 29) continued to spread. But the birth of electronic technology opened contacts with large numbers of people who could never have afforded to go to a movie or buy a record.

The first step was the development of cheap transistor radios that could run on a couple of small batteries. Perfected by American scientists at Bell Telephone Laboratories in 1948, solid-state electronic transistors replaced power-hungry and less reliable glass tubes in radios and other devices. Tube radios, which in some countries required a license to own, had spread worldwide in the decades before the war, but small portable transistor radios reached parts of the world where homes lacked electricity.

Television, made possible by the electron-scanning gun invented in 1928, became widely available to Western consumers in the 1950s. In poorer parts of the world TVs were not common until the 1980s and 1990s, after mass production and cheap transistors made sets more affordable. Outside the United States, television broadcasting was usually a government monopoly at first, following the pattern of telegraph and postal service and radio broadcasting. Governments expected news reports and other programming to disseminate a unified national viewpoint.

However, government monopolies eroded as the high cost of television production opened up global markets for rebroadcasts of American, Indian, and Mexican soap operas and dramas. By the 1990s a global network of satellites brought privately owned television broadcasting to even remote areas of the world, and the VCR (videocassette recorder) provided an even greater variety of programs. In the following decade DVD players continued the trend. As a result of wider circulation of programming, people often became familiar with different dialects of English and other languages. People in Portugal who in the 1960s had found it difficult to understand Brazilian Portuguese became avid fans of Brazilian soap operas. And immigrants from Albania and North Africa often arrived in Italy with a command of Italian learned from Italian stations whose signals they could pick up at home.

CNN (Cable News Network) expanded its international market after becoming the most-viewed and informative news source during the 1991 Persian Gulf War, when it broadcast live from Baghdad. Other 24-hour news broadcasters followed this lead. Some, like CNN and the British Broadcasting Corporation (BBC), reflected the outlook of their home audiences. In response, Al-Jazeera, based in the Persian Gulf emirate of Qatar, broadcast statements by Usama bin Laden from 2001 onward and offered video footage and interpretation that differed greatly from American coverage of the war in Iraq in 2003. It gradually gained a reputation for vivid and generally reliable coverage of news events in the Muslim world.

The Internet, a linkage of academic, government, and business computers developed by the American Department of Defense in the 1960s, began to transform world culture in the early years of the twenty-first century. Personal computers proliferated in the 1980s, and with the establishment of the easy-to-use graphic interface of the World Wide Web in 1994, the number of Internet users skyrocketed. Myriad new companies formed to exploit "e-commerce," the commercial dimension of the Internet, and students were soon spending less time studying conventional books and more exploring the Web for information and entertainment. Blogs, or weblogs, offered a vehicle for anyone in the world to place his or her opinions, experiences, and creative efforts before anyone with access to a computer. Easy access to the Internet took a step forward with the establishment of "social media" sites like Facebook (2004) and Twitter (2006). Initially these were mainly means of keeping in touch with friends, but the Arab Spring of 2011 saw them develop as tools for communication among antiregime protesters.

As had happened so often throughout history, technological developments had unanticipated consequences. Although the new telecommunications and entertainment technologies derived disproportionately from American invention, industry, and cultural creativity, Japan and other East Asian nations took the lead in manufacturing and refining electronic devices. Cellular mobile phones became increasingly used for taking and transmitting pictures and connecting to the Internet. Non-Western countries that had adopted telephones late and had limited networks of copper wire benefited most from the improved communication. In 2012 the United States ranked 114th in per capita cellular phone use, sandwiched between the Congo Republic and the Dominican Republic. Qatar topped the list as the country with the highest per capita use.

The Spread of Pop Culture

For most of history, popular culture consisted of folk tales and highly localized styles of dress, cooking, music, and visual expression. Only the literate few had full access to the riches of a broader "great tradition," such as Confucianism, Islam, or Buddhism. In modern times, government school systems increased literacy rates but also promoted specifically national values and cultural tastes. Prescribed languages of

Eye Ubiquitous/Photoshot

Japanese Comic Books *After World War II comic magazines emerged as a major form of publication and a distinctive product of culture in Japan. Different series are directed to different age and gender groups. Issued weekly and running to some three hundred pages in black and white, the most popular magazines sell as many copies as do major newsmagazines in the United States.*

instruction eroded the use and memory of local languages and traditions. In their place there arose **global pop culture**.

Initially, the content was heavily American. Singer Michael Jackson was almost as well known to the youth of Dar-es-Salaam (Tanzania) and Bangkok (Thailand) as to American fans. Businesses sought out worldwide celebrities like basketball star Michael Jordan and championship golfer Tiger Woods to endorse their products. American television programs, following in the path of American movies, acquired immense followings and inspired local imitations.

But the United States had no monopoly on global pop culture. Rap music showed up in almost every language. Latin American soap operas, *telenovelas*, had a vast following in the Americas, eastern Europe, and elsewhere. Mumbai, India, long the world's largest producer of films, made or inspired more films for international audiences, like the 2009 Academy Award–winning *Slumdog Millionaire*. And the martial arts film makers of Hong Kong saw their style flourish in high-budget international spectaculars like director Ang Lee's *Crouching Tiger, Hidden Dragon* (2000) and the *Matrix* trilogy (1999–2003), which relied heavily on Hong Kong fight choreographers.

Emerging Global Elite Culture
While the globalization of popular culture has been criticized, cultural links across national and ethnic boundaries at a more elite level have generated little controversy. The end of the Cold War reopened intellectual and cultural contacts between former adversaries, making possible such things as Russian-American collaboration on space missions and extensive business contacts among former rivals. The English language, modern science, and higher education became the key elements of this **global elite culture**.

The emergence of English as the first global language began with the British Empire's introduction of the language to its far-flung colonies. After achieving independence in the wake of World War II, most former colonies chose to continue using English as an official language because it provided national unity and a link to the outside world that local languages could not. Countries that chose instead to make a local language official often found the decision counterproductive. Indian nationalists had pushed for Hindi to be India's official language, but they found that students taught in Hindi were unable to compete internationally because of poor knowledge of English. Sri Lanka, which had made Sinhala its official language in 1956, reversed itself after local reporters revealed in 1989 that prominent officials were sending their children to English-medium private schools.

While similar postcolonial language developments extended the reach of French, Spanish, and other European tongues, the use of English as a second language was greatly stimulated by the importance of the United States in postwar world affairs. After the collapse of Soviet domination, students in eastern Europe flocked to study English instead of Russian. Ninety percent of students in Cambodia (a former French colony) chose to study English, even though a Canadian agency offered a sizable cash bonus if they would study French. In the 1990s China made the study of English as a second language nearly universal from junior high school onwards.

English has become the language of choice for most international academic conferences, business meetings, and diplomatic gatherings. International organizations that provide equal status to many languages, such as the United Nations and the European Union, often conduct informal committee meetings in English. In cities throughout the world, signs and notices are commonly posted in the local language and in English. Writers from Africa and India have received high honors for novels written in English, as have Arab and Caribbean authors for works written in French. Nevertheless, world literature remains highly diverse in form and language.

By contrast, science and technology have become standardized components of global culture. Though imperialism helped spread the Western disciplines of biology, chemistry, and physics around the world, their importance expanded even further after decolonization as students from newly independent nations sought to compete at an international level. Standardization of scientific terms, weights and measures, and computer codes underlay the worldwide expansion of commerce.

The third pillar of global elite culture, along with science and globalized languages, is the university. The structure and curricula of modern universities are nearly indistinguishable around the world, making student experiences similar across national boundaries. Instruction in the pure sciences varies little from place to place. Some doctoral science programs in American universities now enroll mostly students from non-Western countries. Standardization is nearly as common in applied sciences such as engineering and medicine and only slightly less so in the social sciences. Although the humanities preserve greater diversity in subject matter and approach, professors and students around the world pay attention to the latest literary theories and topics of historical interest.

New universities, many of them privately funded, have mushroomed in many parts of the world as young people increasingly strive for learning that will improve their employment opportunities. Some American universities have contributed to this educational expansion by opening branches or research centers in foreign countries.

While university subjects are taught in many languages, instruction in English is spreading rapidly. Because discoveries are often first published in English, advanced students in science, business, and international relations need to know that language to keep up with the latest developments. Many courses in northern European countries have long been offered in English, and elsewhere in Europe courses taught in English have facilitated the EU's efforts to encourage students to study outside their home countries.

Enduring Cultural Diversity

Although protesters regularly denounce the "Americanization" of the world, a closer look suggests that cultural globalization is more complex. Just as English has spread widely as a second language, so global culture is primarily a second culture that dominates some contexts but does not displace other traditions. From this perspective, American music, fast food, and fashions are more likely to add to a society's options than to displace local culture.

Japan might appear to be the most "westernized" country in Asia. Japan was one of the first countries in Asia to adopt and adapt political, educational, military, and even corporate institutions from western Europe and the United States during the late nineteenth and early twentieth centuries. Those institutions promoted what many believed to be traditional Japanese cultural characteristics, such as respect for hierarchy, the importance of the group over the individual, and solid work ethic. Such traits, observers argued, contributed to Japan's rapid economic recovery and global eminence since the end of World War II. While culture may have played some role in Japan's economic success story, structural problems led to the bursting of the economic bubble during the 1990s. Those so-called traditional values were rejected by young people who could no longer find secure employment. Instead of touting business culture, then, the Japanese government promoted Japan's popular culture—graphic novels (manga), anime, and J-pop music—as its unique cultural contribution to the world.

As awareness of the economic impact of Japanese culture and society began to spread, it became apparent that Taiwan and South Korea, along with Singapore and Hong Kong (a British colony before being reunited with China in 1997), were developing dynamic industrial economies of their own. Today India, Brazil, Turkey, and the People's Republic of China are following the same path without forsaking their national tastes and heritages.

This does not mean that the world's cultural diversity is secure. Every decade a number of minority languages cease to be spoken. Televised national ceremonies or performances for tourists may prevent folk customs and costumes from dying out, but they also tend to devitalize rituals that once had many local variations. While a century ago it was possible to recognize the nationality of people from their clothing and grooming, today most urban men dress the same the world over, although women's clothing shows greater variety. As much as one may regret the disappearance or commercialization of some folkways, most anthropologists would agree that change is characteristic of all healthy cultures. What doesn't change risks extinction.

IMPORTANT EVENTS 2000–2012

2000	Al-Qaeda attacks American destroyer USS *Cole* in Yemen
2001	George W. Bush becomes president of the United States
2001	Terrorists destroy the World Trade Center and damage the Pentagon on September 11
2001–2003	Terrorist attacks trigger global recession
2001	Shanghai Cooperation Organization formed
2001	United States armed forces overthrow Taliban regime in Afghanistan
2002	Euro currency adopted in twelve European countries
2003	United States and Britain invade and occupy Iraq
2004	Terrorists bomb Spanish trains
2004	Facebook popularizes Internet social media
2004–2009	Genocidal conflict ongoing in Darfur region of Sudan
2005	Terrorists bomb London transport system
2005	Mahmoud Ahmedinejad elected president of Iran
2006	Iraqis elect a government under a new constitution
2006	Hamas movement defeats PLO in Palestinian election
2006	Israel attacks Hezbollah in Lebanon in response to its seizure of Israeli soldiers

2007	Assassination of Benazir Bhutto deepens political crisis in Pakistan
2008	Barack Obama elected president of the United States
2008	Collapse of mortgage debt bubble in United States triggers global recession
2010	American forces withdraw from Iraq
2011	Arab Spring demonstrators topple authoritarian governments
2011	American raiders kill Usama bin Laden in Pakistan
2011	Muslim Brotherhood emerges as a powerful force in Egypt
2012	Barack Obama reelected president of the United States
2012	Vladimir Putin returns to the presidency in Russia

Index